ALSO BY KATHERINE TURK

*Equality on Trial: Gender and Rights
in the Modern American Workplace*

THE WOMEN OF
NOW

THE WOMEN OF
NOW

HOW FEMINISTS BUILT

AN ORGANIZATION THAT

TRANSFORMED AMERICA

KATHERINE TURK

FARRAR, STRAUS AND GIROUX | NEW YORK

Farrar, Straus and Giroux
120 Broadway, New York 10271

Library of Congress Cataloging-in-Publication Data
Names: Turk, Katherine, author.
Title: The women of NOW : how feminists built an organization that transformed
America / Katherine Turk.
Description: First edition. | New York : Farrar, Straus and Giroux, 2023. | Includes
bibliographical references and index.
Identifiers: LCCN 2023003419 | ISBN 9780374601539 (hardcover)
Subjects: LCSH: National Organization for Women. | Feminism—United States—
History. | Women—Political activity—United States—History. | Women's rights—
United States—History.
Classification: LCC HQ1421 .T87 2023 | DDC 305.420973—dc23/eng/20230126
LC record available at https://lccn.loc.gov/2023003419

Designed by Gretchen Achilles

www.fsgbooks.com
www.twitter.com/fsgbooks • www.facebook.com/fsgbooks

1   3   5   7   9   10   8   6   4   2

Frontispiece photograph: Women join hands to display their unity at the four-day
National Women's Conference in Houston in November 1977
(Photograph by Bettmann / Getty Images)

For Vivian and Erik

CONTENTS

THE WOMEN OF
NOW

PROLOGUE:
YOU CAN'T STOP NOW

Here is a glimpse of a feminist movement, midstream.

Nineteen seventy-four was a rotten year for America. The economy was contracting, ending decades of postwar growth and shifting organized labor onto the defensive. The Watergate scandal had captivated the nation, and President Richard M. Nixon resigned in disgrace in August. The Vietnam War, part of a crusade to affirm America's global dominance, had spiraled into a humiliating defeat. The nonviolent interracial civil rights movement had yielded to the more militant Black Power movement, which had also lost its footing due to police repression and the increasingly hostile political climate. From the perspective of these—mostly male-led—movements and institutions, the possibilities for a more democratic society had narrowed.

But many women felt their fortunes moving along an upward trajectory in 1974. A clear majority of Americans favored adding to the U.S. Constitution the Equal Rights Amendment (ERA), which had recently sailed through both houses of Congress along with landmark federal laws affirming gender equality at work and in school. The previous year, the U.S. Supreme Court had framed the constitutional right to abortion in *Roe v. Wade*, ending decades of danger and secrecy. Ancient tropes about the sexes—that women belonged in the domestic sphere, unfit for equal participation in politics, at work, or as consumers, and thus should not control their bodies or their lives—had once been tacitly accepted as common sense. The burgeoning feminist movement had pried open these tropes, and they were beginning to crumble.

The National Organization for Women (NOW) had helped drive these changes and demanded more. In late May 1974, as many as three thousand women flooded the sidewalks and streamed into shops and restaurants in downtown Houston. Inside the Rice Hotel and three blocks down Texas Avenue at the new Albert Thomas Convention Center, women wedged into the lobbies, meeting rooms, and elevators. The air rang with their "scores of musical accents—'y'all from Boston?'" Ranging from "the barefoot to the silverblue-coiffed," these "working women, housewives, rich and poor, mostly somewhere in between," hailed from small towns, suburbs, and cities in all fifty states. They were "different races, old and young, stylishly pantsuited and hippy a la California." Many wore a button proudly resetting James Brown's hit from the previous decade: "It Was a Man's World."

The scene in Houston was NOW's seventh national conference. Gathered at the convention center, members reaffirmed their support for the rights of women of color, lesbians, and women in poverty and charted new advocacy for "older" women. They debated forty-nine resolutions before trimming their agenda to a final thirteen points. These included applying pressure on the nation's biggest corporations to treat workers more fairly, pushing for stronger laws against rape and protections for divorced women, pursuing a guaranteed income for homemakers, and seeking official nongovernmental organization consultative status with the United Nations as part of an expanded international program. Back home, approximately thirty-seven thousand additional members, organized into seven hundred local chapters in all fifty states and overseas, eagerly awaited news of their decisions. "You Can't Stop NOW," the theme of the Houston conference, captured members' momentum.

Their organization had developed a strength and scope that surprised even its ambitious founders. Only eight years earlier, when those twenty-eight women, all with relatively elite status, proposed forming a new group to "speak for women," they knew there was cause for skepticism. The priorities of individual women were not easily aligned. They had varied relationships to the law, to work, to men, to money, and to one another. Despite all of the problems they faced as women, they also lived as individuals and as members of families and communities. The very premise of a civil rights group for women was bold and uncertain.

———

I first encountered NOW as an undergraduate in search of a topic for my senior thesis in history. As I peered into folders of documents from NOW's past, what I found did not line up with what scholars had written about the organization. Since then, I have spent two decades traveling, from Massachusetts to California, from North Carolina to Wisconsin, to reach into the group's many archives and talk with its members, past and present. This work convinced me that NOW was singular in its foundational role, its flexible agenda and national reach, and the internal structures that have kept it running for half a century. The organization was the site, not simply the backdrop, of much of the feminist struggle in our recent past.

My research also pointed me beyond the founders who dominate most histories of NOW. While the original twenty-eight women, and the twenty-one women and men who soon joined them, set up the organization out of their belief that women were oppressed as a class and had to fight back together, their successors tested whether such an organization could work. Those newer members stretched NOW's core belief—a centrally organized feminism for all women and their male supporters—in different directions and as far as they could.

This book recounts the lives and activist careers of three such members who did the creative and challenging work of organizing other women. This trio represents the range of backgrounds and expansive feminist visions that members brought to NOW. Their biographies and their advocacy unfold together in these pages because the two aspects of their identities were interwoven. NOW members' experiences in their homes, schools, and workplaces brought them to feminist activism. That activism shifted their perspectives and recast their lives: their relationships, their careers, and their expectations of a democratic society.

Aileen Hernandez believed that feminism was central to every social justice effort. The Brooklyn-born daughter of Jamaican immigrants spent a decade organizing West Coast textile workers before President Lyndon Johnson tapped her in 1965 to serve on the new Equal Employment Opportunity Commission (EEOC), the federal agency created to act as a watchdog for workplace equality. Her four fellow commissioners—all men, three of them white—mostly treated women's rights as trivial. Hernandez shared their commitment to fighting racism, but one experience as an undergraduate at the historically Black Howard University stayed seared in her mind. If she was "not prepared to do all of the work," a political science professor mocked her without provocation in front of a classroom full of men, she should "leave now and sign up for home economics." That experience convinced Hernandez "that our society is replete with racism *and* sexism; they are very much intertwined." Hernandez would attempt to shape NOW to reflect her conviction that all social justice movements needed feminism. In her term as NOW's second president in the early 1970s and for several years that followed, Hernandez worked particularly to strengthen the group's appeal to women of color.

Patricia Hill Burnett focused on boosting NOW's political diversity and global reach. Burnett was the winner of the 1942 Miss Michigan pageant, the wife of a wealthy Detroit businessman, a mother of four, and a talented artist. She had once felt she was "everything little girls of the '40s and '50s dreamed about being when they grew up." But frustrations in her life persuaded her to make a transformation in middle age. At fifty years old, Burnett became a feminist activist and an active Republican at a time when the party was home to many moderates and even some liberals. Burnett defined feminism as personal freedom for women, which neatly aligned with the GOP's support for individual rights, and she worked to pull these two causes even closer together. Burnett also led NOW's international program after founding its Michigan chapter.

Mary Jean Collins, more than a decade younger than Hernandez and Burnett, was committed to a grassroots-driven and workplace-focused feminism. Collins grew up in a hardscrabble Wisconsin family grounded in Irish heritage, Catholic faith, and devotion to the Democratic Party. From her parents' viewpoint, "the Democrats were on your side and the Republicans were on the side of the rich," Collins said. At Alverno College, a Catholic women's school in Milwaukee, Collins enjoyed a feminist education from formidable sisters and soon discovered the city's robust civil rights movement. She lost her footing after college, when she met dead ends searching for decent work and contended with "lesbian feelings" that "weren't fully articulated." "Being out was a luxury" then, she said later; it was a time when lesbians faced more overt discrimination and cultural stigma. Collins moved to Chicago in 1968, then set up NOW chapters all over the Midwest, helped steer its largest anticorporate campaign, and became one of its two vice presidents in the early 1980s. She joined Hernandez, Burnett, and many other women who locked arms to work together in NOW.

————

I have taught women's history for more than a decade. Year after year, my students have been shocked to learn that in their grandparents' generation employers advertised separate jobs for men and women, colleges could limit the number of woman students to a tiny fraction or ban them outright, and abortion was illegal across the United States. They ask, who ended those injustices, and how did they accomplish it? If you consult opinion pieces in mainstream news outlets that are supposedly sympathetic to feminist history, you learn that feminism in the 1970s was plagued by "clique-iness and passive aggression disguised as politics," prone to "collapse," and "fatally privileged" by its white middle-class participants who were, according to some younger feminists, "oblivious to race and class." Though there is truth in those criticisms, they fail to capture the full scope of the movement that was "second-wave feminism," which hit its peak from the late 1960s to the early 1980s.

Key to this misunderstanding is a lack of knowledge about NOW, which was the largest and most expansive feminist organization of that time. Scholars have taken two different approaches to analyzing that group's history. Some pit NOW members against other feminists by freezing their image of the organization at its founding moment: a group of mostly liberal, white, middle-aged, professional women dedicated to incremental change. In stressing women's differences, this framing casts the feminist movement as local and atomized and dovetails with broader portrayals of the 1970s as a time of social breakdown. To trace NOW's longer arc, other scholars have sliced the enormous organization into pieces, spotlighting specific leaders, chapters, internal structures, or campaigns. NOW's own archive supports this segmented view. Its members have left millions of pieces of paper—letters, memos, journals, meeting minutes, newsletters, and photographs—piled across the country. Such scattered evidence doesn't lend itself easily to a coherent story.

Both of these approaches have led to misconceptions about NOW and what it sought to achieve. In our time, it is hard to imagine the organization, with its established prominence and decades-long endurance, as fledgling or controversial. But NOW's founding principle was an utterly radical idea: to organize and advocate for all women by channeling their efforts into one association that sought to end male supremacy. This book follows that radical idea into street protests, meeting rooms, courtrooms, homes, schools, and workplaces. It argues that while NOW's task was never easy, and it did not fully succeed, the organization transformed American life. The feminist movement of the 1970s, with NOW at the center, made gender equality a mainstream concept. NOW's flexible local chapters and strong national presence made that concept actionable.

Today, most Americans accept the idea of equal rights for women, but we continue to see ever-widening disparities in the rights among women. A handful of women have broken through the glass ceiling in traditionally masculine realms such as elected political leadership and the corporate C-Suite, but the floor keeps dropping for the many others who are left behind in our increasingly unequal society. Women's access to reproductive health care depends upon where they live and whether they can afford to travel. The presence of women in groups across the political spectrum disproves the notion that sex determines politics. Can any agenda unite them all? The notion is even more radical today than it was half a century ago. But how can our society, whose burdens women disproportionately bear, become more equitable without women coming together to demand changes? Women in the 1960s answered these questions with NOW, an ambitious feminist effort whose full story has never been told.

——

NOW was an experiment that aimed to ignite women's consciousnesses, harness their collective power, and wield it across the nation and abroad. The organization's history—its accomplishments as well as its shortcomings—offers lessons in how to challenge institutions, shift cultural norms, and foster solidarities. As NOW members attacked (and sometimes bested) male supremacy in American culture, law, and politics, they also struggled mightily, revealing blind spots and galvanizing a determined opposition that still shapes our politics and society today. Through Aileen Hernandez, Patricia Hill Burnett, and Mary Jean Collins, three women who were loyal yet critical members of NOW, this book tells the story of how organized feminism changed America: its aspirations, its triumphs, its failures, its unfinished business, the scars it left behind.

1.

WE RECOGNIZED
THE HONEST FIRE

At ten o'clock in the evening on June 29, 1966, about twenty women crowded into Betty Friedan's suite at the Washington Hilton hotel. The room's elegance matched the mandate of the conference that brought them to the capital—the third annual gathering of State Commissions on the Status of Women—as a place for ladies, not troublemakers. Returning to their hotel by chartered bus, after a boozy "reception and buffet" in the State Department's "beautiful" Thomas Jefferson Room, the women passed through the lobby, which was decked out with plush furniture, pink globe lights, and art nouveau stained-glass windows, and into one of six elevators. Once in Friedan's suite, they filled paper cups with liquor from Friedan's "little bar." Some lit cigarettes and kicked off their shoes, some folding their legs beneath their smart skirt suits or stretching them out. It was a relief to unwind after a "long, long" day packed with meetings.

Pauli Murray surveyed the swelling gathering she had helped to plan. Murray was a seasoned, fifty-five-year-old organizer and attorney with deep roots in the civil rights and workers' movements. The descendant of enslaved women and men, Murray was raised in segregated North Carolina. She understood how inequities of race, class, and gender interlocked in people's lives. In her view, the flourishing civil rights movement needed women's energies but gave priority to Black men's concerns. The labor movement privileged white women when it regarded their sex at all. Women's activism was segmented by race. Several decades earlier, white suffragists had marginalized Black women, then accepted narrowly framed voting rights that left Jim Crow limits intact.

Murray was on a mission to link the struggles for gender equality and racial justice by centering Black women in both. She and her co-author had recently coined the term "Jane Crow" in an article for *The George Washington Law Review*, where they wrote about an analogy between racism and sexism in the law. But Murray was not content to keep her ideas on the pages of an academic journal. She waited somewhat impatiently for everyone to settle in: she felt the moment's urgency.

After several minutes, Murray and Friedan told the group of their meeting's purpose: starting "an independent national civil rights organization for women," as Murray later described it, that would have "enough political power to compel government agencies to take seriously the problems of discrimination because of sex." Murray and most of the others had spent the past year debating how to end officials' foot-dragging, and they were ready for action. Those East Coast lawyers and government workers in the room had seen women's rights become a common joke among powerful men in Washington. Fearful that outspoken activism would jeopardize their own careers, they believed that Friedan—by then a minor celebrity for publishing *The Feminine Mystique* three years earlier—had the independence and notoriety to become the public face of a strong new organization. Such a group was needed, they explained, because the landscape of women's activism, while robust, was diffuse. There were women's groups dedicated to myriad causes; women were also active in political parties, labor unions, and civil rights, antiwar, and consumer groups. A new pressure group could unite them and focus their power.

Murray and her collaborators were surprised to be met with ambivalence. The Wisconsin labor leader Catherine Conroy was among those who listened with skepticism. At forty-seven, she was nearly a decade younger than Murray, but she, too, had spent many years inside male-led movements. Conroy was "built square," said a friend, "wore no makeup," and "dressed like a dowdy elementary school teacher," with "no pearls for sure." The daughter of a Milwaukee antiques dealer who was ruined in the Great Depression, Conroy found a job after high school as a telephone operator. It was hard work for low pay, and she saw how the bosses exploited women through stereotypes about their docility. She took a post in her union, the Communications Workers of America, where her "brothers" put their own needs first. But Conroy and the other members of Wisconsin's Commission on the Status of Women were working well with state lawmakers. Why should women jeopardize good relationships with government officials? Wouldn't another association simply stretch their efforts thinner?

Murray tried to keep order, explaining the plan she had outlined on her yellow legal pad. But the tensions escalated. The Wisconsinites became frustrated that the gathering they had believed was purely social seemed to have an unspoken agenda. Those from the East Coast in the room were treating their questions as though they were not "worth considering." As the Wisconsinites surmised, the meeting's planners, including Murray and Friedan, had already decided, after months of strategizing, that a new organization was desperately needed. After a few more minutes of debate, the room erupted into chaos. Eventually, Friedan, overcome with resentment, locked herself in the bathroom. The meeting was over, she claimed. Their proposed civil rights group for women seemed to collapse before they had finished drawing its blueprint.

———

These women had good reasons to gather that night and imagine their sex as a united class. Many Americans in the mid-1960s believed that their prospects were on the upswing. The previous two decades had been the longest era of economic expansion in world history. That strong postwar economy appeared capable of eternal growth, and President Lyndon Johnson's War on Poverty sought to help those it left behind. At that time, in the United States, any high school graduate, provided he was white and male, could expect his paycheck alone to support his family, secure his home and car, and bankroll his kids through college. Organized labor was still formidable, and the Black freedom movement was a powerful example of how collective action could change society. On the heels of the Civil Rights and Voting Rights Acts of 1964 and 1965, full citizenship was more available than ever before to any group that demanded inclusion. More radical advocates believed that the time was right to push for revolution.

Women often felt painted out of this optimistic portrait of America. Every aspect of their lives reinforced the message that men were, and should be, in charge. America was still firmly a patriarchy, still running a well-oiled, centuries-old system that funneled social, economic, and political power to white men. Across their differences, across the country, women started noticing the contrast between the nation's limitless potential and the limits they faced themselves. All of the major institutions in American life treated women as subordinate and unequal.

The nation's laws positioned women as second- and third-class citizens. Many states forced wives to take their husbands' surnames; if she refused, a wife could have her voter registration or driver's license withdrawn. Abortion was illegal, and rape was rarely prosecuted. State domestic violence laws were likewise weak and thin, with some requiring that a police officer personally witness abuse before charging the offender. Others applied a "stitch rule," punishing an abuser only when his spouse's wounds took more than a set number of stitches. States could exempt women from jury service; the U.S. Supreme Court reasoned that such a benign distinction did women a favor by preserving their time and energy for their families. For women of color, sexist injustices were compounded by explicitly racist provisions, such as sixteen states' bans on interracial marriage. Masculine women and those who desired women endured all of these harms and more. Some states prohibited women from wearing "men's" clothing, and every state criminalized sexual acts beyond heterosexual intercourse. In every way, the law kept women beholden to men's power and control.

Women's presumed inferiority shaped American culture as well. Paging through a magazine or an advice book in the early 1960s, a woman learned to prize marriage and protect her youthfulness above all else. One bestselling self-help manual in 1963 described a good wife as "the perfect follower" who only admonished her husband in ways that stroked his ego—by calling him a "big hairy beast," for example. Turning on her television, she would see only white male news anchors, for producers believed that such men were the only people credible enough to do the job. An anchor who read a feminine name might be referencing a film star or a First Lady, always covered for her fashion choices, or a hurricane, if one was coming. These major storms were always named for women: allegedly as volatile and destructive as foul weather.

If they ventured beyond home, women found their access to the public sphere restricted. In addition to the racial segregation that still plagued many areas of the country, some proprietors denied women access to bars and eateries in order to sell camaraderie to male customers. "It's men only at lunch," claimed the spokesman of a San Francisco hotel of its cocktail lounge, "with man-sized drinks and hearty sandwiches." Groups ranging from professional associations to Little League kept women and girls out. United Airlines offered an "executive flight" reserved for male travelers, although the flight attendants serving them were always young, attractive women. To test the policy and highlight its absurdity in the mid-1960s, the advertising executive Muriel Fox booked her young son on one such flight, unaccompanied, but she could not buy a ticket for herself. The Chicago "business woman" Nan Wood was able to make executive flight reservations for herself and her twelve-year-old grandson. When she arrived at the airport, the gate agents blocked her from boarding. They relented to Wood's pressure, but she had to ride to New York in the cockpit while her grandson sat with the men in the cabin. Political leadership, too, was a man's world, with women sidelined in civic groups and party auxiliaries. They folded pamphlets and rang doorbells but had no real power to shape platforms or hold office.

Despite these rigid rules and norms, women's lives were changing. The breadwinner-homemaker model had always been out of reach for some, but as the cost of living climbed, it became less possible for most families. Women's workforce participation rose in the 1950s, undermining the stereotype of the wife and homemaker, and it kept rising. Even before a female job seeker entered the labor force, she saw white male entitlement laid out in print. Classified ads in newspapers, the usual place to job hunt, were split into "Help Wanted—Men" and "Help Wanted—

Women." This separation previewed a divided labor force. Work assigned to women, especially women of color, was typically low paid and a dead end, reflecting the notions that their efforts were less valuable or that their pay merely topped off a husband's income. Sexual harassment, which was rampant, would not even be named for another decade. Activists coined the term in 1975, and the U.S. Supreme Court did not affirm it as discrimination until 1986.

Women's workplace experiences varied, but economic security and independence were almost always out of reach. Black women's pay was especially critical to their families' income because of discrimination against Black men, but some pundits accused them of eroding their husbands' rightful authority. For women who were not attached to male wage earners, welfare was stingy and paid out by biased bureaucrats with punitive aims. Even the most elite women huddled on the margins of the professions. "Hell yes, we have a quota" for women, said a medical school dean in 1961. It was as small as possible. "We do keep women out, when we can. We don't want them here," he bragged. Women were 7 percent of doctors in the United States, 3 percent of lawyers, and 1 percent of engineers, figures that had declined steadily since World War II, when they were not high. Ninety percent earned less than $5,000 annually, or just over $37,600 today. Even in the rare case where a wife outearned her husband, she could not legally control her money or qualify for a credit card. Unmarried women faced higher barriers to credit than their male counterparts.

This regime of white male supremacy was never uncontested, but those women demanding equality and respect were overlooked and even mocked. After the early twentieth-century push for voting rights further fractured in the 1920s, women remained active in all kinds of organizations and politics, but rarely fought on behalf of their entire sex. The concept of women's rights had atrophied and developed a negative connotation, with the label "feminist" deployed as a joke or an insult. Since the nineteenth century, women had built community and influence through reform movements, both domestic and international, but never before in the United States as part of a dedicated, expansive organization with the central mission to demand full equality.

Young women in the early 1960s, the first baby boomers to come of age, chafed against these limits. They sought out new concepts to describe their situation and tools for changing it. Meanwhile, an older generation of women approached the problem from their own perspective. Perhaps the way to dismantle these injustices, some suggested, was to start to act like the unified class they were so often treated as in the law, at work, and in the broader culture.

———

Many Americans in the 1960s were debating the nature of equality and identity-based rights, and this group included the women's advocates who worked inside the government and had for decades. Their most important official foothold was the U.S. Department of Labor's Women's Bureau, which opened in 1920. It was not a very powerful federal agency, but its leaders were respected reformers and intellectuals. The bureau's longtime priority was shoring up the patchwork of state laws designed to shield women from the abuses of industrial labor. These laws put a floor under many women's wages and a ceiling on their working hours, and they required employers to provide basic accommodations for woman workers like adequate restrooms and regular breaks. These protections granted some women valued benefits, but they also defined the sexes against each other; since women required accommodations, the better jobs—and pay—were saved for men.

The Women's Bureau adjusted its stance in the middle of the century as activists nationwide appealed to civil and human rights to attack broad social inequalities. The bureau struck a newly measured tone and balanced demands for gendered protections with calls for equality and opportunity. It also defined progress within the limits of Cold War liberalism. At the vanguard of this agenda was the human rights champion and former First Lady Eleanor Roosevelt. The first chairperson of the United Nations Commission on Human Rights, Roosevelt was instrumental in drafting the 1948 Universal Declaration of Human Rights, which affirmed equal "rights and freedoms" on account of sex. More than a decade later, President John F. Kennedy tapped Roosevelt to chair a new federal commission to study women's status in American life: the

President's Commission on the Status of Women (PCSW), which working women's advocates had pursued for more than a decade.

Brimming with bigwigs in white gloves and pearls from government, labor, and education, the twenty-six-member PCSW worked from the premise that women had enough in common to be studied as a group. Murray, who served on its Committee on Civil and Political Rights, called the PCSW "the most significant and exciting development affecting women in decades" because it opened up a national conversation on their status and how to improve it. The commission's final report in 1963, *American Women*, sought a balance between creating new opportunities and strengthening the older protections. Issued just weeks after the watershed March on Washington for Jobs and Freedom, where Martin Luther King Jr. gave his "I Have a Dream" speech to a crowd of two hundred thousand, *American Women* echoed that event's hopeful mood. Its authors encouraged employers to make their workplaces more equal and called for government services to help women live full, productive lives, whether they were wage earners or homemakers, and for women to have the freedom to choose either path, or both.

The reformers on the PCSW took a nuanced approach to gender equality, but other activist currents surged and reworked the terrain for women's rights campaigns. Kennedy was assassinated in November 1963, and Americans' grief helped to give new momentum to his civil rights agenda. Under pressure from a well-organized and grassroots-driven civil rights movement, legislators debated the Civil Rights Act, a bill designed to attack race discrimination in employment, public accommodations, voting, and education. Conservative members of Congress, including the Virginia segregationist Howard W. Smith, wanted to kill the bill. Smith believed that the gender issue could be his weapon. At the request of the National Woman's Party, which advocated for strict sex equality in the law, Smith proposed adding a ban on sex discrimination to Title VII—the portion of the act that addressed the workplace.

Simultaneous to Smith's maneuvering, feminist members of Congress promoted the sex amendment, and Murray saw Title VII's unique potential to help Black women. Born in Baltimore in 1910 and raised in Durham, North Carolina, Murray became an attorney and a labor and civil rights activist, as well as an architect of the legal strategy that persuaded the U.S. Supreme Court to outlaw school segregation in *Brown v. Board of Education*. Murray herself was denied admission to the University of North Carolina because of her race and Harvard Law School because of her sex. "The harsh reality," she noted, "was that I was a minority within a minority." Murray was also sexually attracted to women, and while she publicly identified as female, she knew herself to be male: she was, in her words, "one of nature's experiments: a girl who should have been a boy." While Congress debated Title VII, Murray sent a memo to federal officials arguing that without the sex amendment "the civil rights bill would be including only one half of the Negroes." Black women especially needed these protections. They had the harshest, lowest-paid jobs and were often breadwinners themselves.

Lawmakers signed the Civil Rights Act into law in 1964 with Title VII's sex amendment in place. A new lifeline for working women, it codified equality as the bedrock principle for women's rights. The leaders of the Women's Bureau, unlike Murray, took a cautious approach to Title VII. They feared that its sweeping guarantee of equality would uproot all of the state-level protections for working women, some of which put guardrails on the wages and working hours of women whose jobs were excluded from federal protections. But the officials charged with policing Title VII showed no interest in enforcing the law. Leaders of the Equal Employment Opportunity Commission disparaged the sex provision as a "fluke" that had been "conceived out of wedlock." Other D.C. power brokers derided Title VII as the "Bunny Law," feigning fear that in order to create the equality that the still-ambiguous law would require, men might have to don leotards and fluffy white tails as Playboy Club servers. Such wisecracks infuriated the women looking on.

But these reluctant officials could not contain the energy that Title VII unleashed. It transformed the legal landscape and inspired more women to demand equality outright. Among them were members of state commissions on the status of women that had sprouted alongside the PCSW and continued to meet after the federal body disbanded; women in government, who had firsthand knowledge of their male colleagues' sexist attitudes; union members frustrated with union men's lack of solidarity; and ordinary working women who claimed their rights as they understood them. Nearly one-third of complaints sent to the EEOC in its first year referred to sex discrimination. The concept of state-enforced sex equality had new momentum and a legal foundation.

Americans were beginning to challenge authority in other ways. Presidents Dwight D. Eisenhower and Kennedy, proponents of the Cold War foreign policy of containment, had edged into Vietnam's internal conflict to weaken the Communist cause. President Johnson sent a substantial military presence to the country in 1965. By the end of that year, a small but vocal core of antiwar activists was emerging on college campuses. Soon their cause rippled across the nation. In tandem with the civil rights movement, antiwar activists revealed that popular protest could reshape foreign and domestic policy.

By June 1966, when those twenty women were gathered in Betty Friedan's hotel room, Title VII was two years old. The law's watchdogs had done little about its ban on sex discrimination beyond making jokes. Many women no longer saw federal officials as powerful allies who could be trusted to act in the interest of their sex. Advocates' decades-old bargain—in which women received modest access to political power as long as their methods were polite and their demands incremental—seemed like a bad deal. Friedan and the fed-up participants who withdrew from the conference of state women's commissions with her would discuss a new feminism rooted in women's common need for equality. "How did we know each other?" she asked. "We recognized the honest fire."

———

That fire had been building for more than a decade. As a cohort of career women connected across boundaries of class, race, and region, a new feminism crystallized. Black women were at its core, for they had been central to the savvy activism of the National Association for the Advancement of Colored People (NAACP) since the World War II era as well as in newer upstart civil rights groups that had compelled government officials to promote racial equality. It had taken years of pressure from Black activists and white allies to pass the Civil Rights Act; now women would have to unite to make it work on their behalf, too. The Women's Bureau attorney Dollie Lowther Robinson, who was Black, told a meeting of women in the United Auto Workers (UAW) in Milwaukee in early 1966 that the EEOC was faltering. "What we need," she said, "is an NAACP for women."

Pauli Murray agreed. Frustrated by male civil rights movement leaders' "sex-based discrimination," she had been "incensed" when they excluded women from the delegation of civil rights leaders who met with President Kennedy on the morning of the March on Washington. Later that day, women were "accorded little more than token recognition on the March program," Murray fumed, and given none of the major speaker slots. Just before the event, the organizer A. Philip Randolph advertised it in a presentation at the National Press Club. That venue banned women from joining and from asking questions in its press conferences. Their sex could attend provided they sat in the balcony. Murray wrote Randolph an open letter: "It is as humiliating for a woman reporter assigned to cover Mr. Randolph's speech to be sent to the balcony as it would be for Mr. Randolph to be sent to the back of the bus."

Murray understood the power of social categories and the potential of solidarities that bridged them. Black women "can no longer postpone or subordinate the fight against discrimination because of sex to the civil rights struggle," she wrote in 1964, "but must carry on both fights simultaneously." Title VII's promise to women would never be realized, she determined, until women themselves applied united pressure. Murray outlined this idea in a speech to a conference of women's clubs in 1965. "It should not be necessary to have another March on Washington in order that there be equal job opportunities for all," she said. "But if this necessity should arise, I hope women will not flinch from the thought."

Murray joined a secretive network of Washington feminists who had firsthand evidence that officials were doing little to fight sex discrimination. Her closest tie was to Mary Eastwood, a white attorney at the Office of Legal Counsel at the Department of Justice. The two co-authored the landmark 1965 article "Jane Crow and the Law: Sex Discrimination and

Title VII." They also met Catherine East, a white researcher at the Department of Labor. East became adept at linking frustrated women with one another while remaining firmly in the background. Her fellow feminists later called her "Deep Throat," comparing her essential hidden efforts to those of the shadowy Watergate whistleblower Mark Felt. These and other white-collar women knew, from their own experience, that entry into male-typed jobs did not guarantee fair treatment there. They were well positioned to analyze gender bias at work and then take action in their off-hours.

This handful of professionals started plotting a new kind of women's association. They decided that Betty Friedan had the influence to lead it, and they knew her already. Friedan had contacted Murray after seeing coverage of her speech calling for a women's march on Washington, and Murray introduced Friedan around. Right away, the others noted Friedan's striking presence. She was not conventionally beautiful, recalled a colleague, yet she exerted "a powerful, haunting attractiveness." The author had dark, intense eyes, a high forehead, and graying hair that was "often askew" despite faithful trips to the beauty parlor. Friedan balked at the suggestion that she should be involved in a women's civil rights group. "I don't even *like* organizations," she protested. Traumatized by the Cold War persecutions of left-wing activists, writers, and actors, Friedan had long obscured her own history as a radical labor journalist and author of profiles of political women for women's magazines. From this experience, she was well aware of the impact that an outspoken *organization of women* could make.

Friedan warmed to the idea as she worked on a kind of sequel to *The Feminine Mystique*. Her first book had raised women's expectations, but she realized that they needed better access to the education and child care that would allow them to establish the "new life patterns" that bestseller had prescribed. Meanwhile, East and Eastwood flattered the author over dinner, and others nudged her, too. After Friedan addressed the group American Women in Radio and Television, its leader, Muriel Fox, followed up with a note: "If you ever start an NAACP for women, count me in." Friedan signed up to attend the 1966 conference of state women's commissions as a "writer-observer." She was not yet sold on forming a new group, but Murray, Eastwood, and the rest of their "underground network" were already planning to use the conference to do just that.

———

The venue for that conference, the third annual meeting of state women's commissions, did not invite militant activism. The "lavish" Washington Hilton, built the previous year for $40 million, was "an international status-symbol," gushed *The Washington Post.* The hotel stood on a "choice site" in the leafy Dupont Circle neighborhood and had a "clean, noble and impressive" facade. Groups of visitors took in its many luxuries "with a hushed reverence appropriate to a spin through Versailles." To one conference goer, the Hilton's maze of escalators and hallways resembled a closer landmark: "I might as well have been in the Pentagon."

Hundreds of women traveled to the capital as representatives of forty-four state commissions, all of which were relatively new. When the PCSW began its work in 1962, the National Federation of Business and Professional Women's Clubs lobbied all fifty governors to create their own commissions modeled on Kennedy's. Washington's governor responded first, appointing a commission in early 1963 that paralleled the PCSW. Illinois and Indiana soon followed suit, along with seven other states that formed commissions before the PCSW issued its report in 1963. Within four more years, every state had formed its own women's commission.

The women who convened in the capital on behalf of their state commissions met in general sessions and twenty-eight workshops. As they learned, the states' bodies varied in their goals and accomplishments. All but one (Alaska's) were active, and each had forged important bonds among women within their state. Some of the participants had gone to Washington to mingle and discuss the research their commission had produced. Others wanted to vent about roadblocks to women's progress. In Iowa, for example, their commission included women in both political parties, community organizations, and labor, church, and professional groups. But they could not even persuade state lawmakers to pay to print their report, which they funded from their own pockets. "We weren't able to get any good ideas into those male legislative heads at that time," explained its secretary, Betty Talkington.

Pauli Murray and the others in the "underground network" stepped into this bustling scene by downplaying their plan to secede. They knew it would startle women like those from Wisconsin, who were proud of their commission's official achievements. Its chair, the political scientist Kathryn "Kay" Clarenbach, had spent the previous decade turning the University of Wisconsin's Extension School into a crucible for women's vocational and political education and its alumnae into a formidable statewide network. With Clarenbach at the helm, Wisconsin's commission addressed domestic violence, marital property, divorce, and pay equity, and the group convinced the state Industrial Commission to advocate strong new labor standards and minimum wage legislation, among other changes.

Wisconsin's women's commission was "very vigorous," "truly representative," and "one of the best in the country," said Clarenbach's fellow commissioner Catherine Conroy, the labor leader from the Communications Workers of America. Their group had succeeded by cooperating with state officials and letting them set the pace. Thus, she and Clarenbach were not troubled by the opening remarks at the D.C. conference by the U.S. secretary of labor, W. Willard Wirtz. He urged the women to discuss goals and strategies, but to hold off on any action "until education and understanding can keep up or catch up again with knowledge." Other federal officials struck the same unhurried tone. Chairing a session titled "Labor Standards and Equal Employment Opportunities for Women," the Women's Bureau director, Mary Dublin Keyserling, conveyed her agency's cautious stance. She never mentioned workplace equality and only briefly referenced Title VII. Other workshop themes conveyed this less-than-militant message: family planning, consumer education, and services for the elderly.

The officials' efforts to keep the tone upbeat began to show strain as the participants built new connections with one another. In a session on women's legal status, Pauli Murray accused EEOC officials of fighting racism while condoning sexism, highlighting the commission's recent approval of sex-segregated newspaper job ads. Clarenbach chaired a session with the benign title "Creating Positive Attitudes" in which she decried the sexism in American culture that taught women to devalue themselves. In an employment workshop, Conroy met Friedan—the first time she had ever encountered the author or her book. "That was really a shame," Conroy later mused, "because I should have heard of her."

To Friedan, the whole conference was an outrage. She despised "the ladylike rows . . . the timidity . . . the suspicion," and found the bus trip to a White House tea party especially insulting. President Lyndon Johnson "figuratively patted our heads and said how happy we must all be now that the job had been done—those reports on the status of women—and now we must all go back home." Johnson told them that federal officials had completed their own work on sex equality. Praising the recent Equal Pay Act, executive orders, and court rulings, he appealed to the states to finish the job by expanding access to day care and education. Not only did Johnson ignore the problem of "discrimination against women," Friedan fumed, he and others gave the impression of wanting to send them away "feeling guilty about ever concerning themselves about the status of women." As the sessions continued, Friedan was "just loaded with anger, frustration and some quantities of hostility, too," noted another attendee. The author's mood, it turned out, was contagious.

———

On the second day of the conference, Murray and the rest of the "underground network" launched their plan into action. Friedan ran into Murray and Dorothy Haener of the UAW Women's Department on the hotel escalator that morning. The author told them that she would host a late-night gathering of "anyone we met who seemed likely to be interested in organizing women for action." Haener and the historian Caroline Ware found Friedan for lunch so they could be sure that when the meeting came, Haener recalled, "we had pretty well put our concepts together." But Friedan improvised, lengthening the guest list without consulting the others. The author was so inspired by Clarenbach's "biting" address on "creating positive attitudes" that she introduced herself and invited her. The others were "horrified," Friedan remembered. Known as "the darling of the Women's Bureau," Clarenbach might derail their plan to form a new organization separate from the political establishment.

At first, Clarenbach justified those fears. She, in turn, invited three friends from the Wisconsin Commission: Conroy, Nancy Knaak, and Gene Boyer. Conroy and Knaak, the dean of women at the University of Wisconsin's River Falls campus, were hesitant to attend without an invitation, but Clarenbach assured them the meeting would be "an informal affair and the gathering a random one," Knaak said. Boyer, who owned several furniture stores in Beaver Dam, Wisconsin, never showed. She had founded one of only two municipal women's commissions in the nation after the men in her local chamber of commerce lobbied her to skip their meetings. But Washington was no Beaver Dam. She never found the gathered women that night, instead spending hours "going up the escalators, down the escalators, trying to find where this room was."

That meeting in Friedan's suite had just begun when Clarenbach, Conroy, and Knaak arrived. They found twenty-odd women "jammed" into the two-hundred-square-foot space: in chairs, on the beds, on the floor, and leaning against the walls. Those women sipped water or stronger stuff out of paper cups. Cigarette smoke swirled in the air. "Everybody was feeling rather good by this time," Conroy noted, because the earlier reception had been "very generous with the liquor." Looking around, Murray noted that many of the women "were strangers to one another." She herself knew only a handful. Hopeful that these strangers were all on the same page, Murray opened a discussion about the EEOC's lack of progress on Title VII.

When Murray dove into her pitch about forming a militant women's group, the room's energy shifted. Knaak snapped to attention. "This was no random group at all," she realized. The leaders seemed to already have an agenda outlined and the vision sketched. They proposed the NOW acronym with astonishing speed. When Murray began to speak from notes on her pad, Knaak interrupted. "Do you think we really need another women's organization?" she asked, pointing out that there were dozens of women's groups—forty-nine of them, in fact—represented at that very conference, in addition to the state commissions. Suddenly the room exploded into an "all-out shouting match." Haener had wanted to set up a group like NOW for months, and she bristled when Knaak "talked to us like we were a bunch of campus students." Mary Eastwood was more understanding. Knaak "came to this cold," she said, so "she was way behind the rest of us."

The group's tenuous bonds quickly frayed. The meeting turned "very unpleasant" and "kind of nasty," Eastwood remembered. Friedan turned to Knaak and demanded to know, "Who in the hell invited you?" Opening the door, Friedan told her, "You know, this is my room and my liquor and you're perfectly free to say anything you please, but you're not going to use my room and my liquor while you're doing it." Clarenbach declared that she had invited Knaak and that she had a right to be there. "Get out! Get out!" Friedan insisted, but Knaak felt "entitled to disagree" in what seemed like a "fluid situation." Friedan stormed into the bathroom, with her "flowing, brightly colored cape" the last thing anyone saw before she slammed the door and locked it. "Perhaps I really didn't belong in that room," Knaak said, but "I also considered Betty's demonstration to be childish, so I decided to wait her out."

While Friedan seethed, the tensions eased. Clarenbach echoed Knaak's suggestion that a new group might not be needed; perhaps this very gathering of state women's commissions could endorse an action agenda and pressure federal officials. This strategy had been so effective in Wisconsin, after all. The "underground network" agreed to this approach. In the morning, those who wanted to "just work within the establishment" would propose a motion before the entire conference in support of the EEOC commissioner Richard Graham's reappointment. Graham, the agency's most vocal commissioner on women's rights, was nearing the end of his one-year term. For close to a year, Haener had held "very strong convictions" that a new organization was needed; "nothing was going to happen" without "a pressure group that was going to be pressuring." The D.C.-based feminists and their allies in the room already knew that Johnson would not reappoint Graham, and they believed the others overlooked the "terrible time" they had already had in prodding officials to move on Title VII. "Well, let them try," they huffed.

When Friedan emerged after fifteen minutes, she learned of the plan to pursue their agenda from within the conference rather than breaking away. Friedan and her collaborators "just looked at one another and shrugged," she said, as if to say, "*Women*—what can you expect?" The meeting's organizers worried that this bland plan was effectively a surrender. Murray "was thoroughly discouraged," she said later. She believed they had "fumbled a major opportunity to begin mobilizing women nationally to press for their civil rights." But although their momentum slowed that night, it did not stall.

———

In the morning, Clarenbach asked Keyserling, the Women's Bureau director and her longtime friend, whether the entire conference could debate issuing a public statement on the EEOC and Title VII. Keyserling refused. The conference was purely advisory, she told Clarenbach, and it could not pass resolutions. She also said that as a government-sponsored body the conference could not critique another federal agency. Personally, Keyserling did not want to pressure President Johnson or undermine gendered state labor laws.

This rebuff was the turning point. Clarenbach "was absolutely outraged," noted Friedan, that "with all her politeness, her responsible request, her put-down of my rabble-rousing" the night before, the conference organizers told her that the gathering would take no action. Conroy knew the Women's Bureau was "a pretty conservative gang," but she saw their refusal even to let them debate as a move to undercut successful commissions like Wisconsin's. Conroy reconsidered the previous night's conflict in light of her own commitments. "My job requires me to try to organize women, and not just in labor," Conroy had testified two years earlier at Wisconsin's inaugural conference on the status of women. "We as women should get organized," she urged them, "because you don't accomplish anything unless you are. And men learned this long ago." The women who had sparred in Friedan's room hours earlier felt a shared urgency. They strutted into the closing luncheon with clear-eyed determination.

The Hilton's elegant International Ballroom, oval shaped and large enough to seat thirty-two hundred diners, featured red faux-leather walls in a "padded-dashboard motif," elaborate lighting, and a tiered "sculptured ceiling." Members of Congress and other dignitaries who were in attendance dined on the stage. Conroy noted that even their seating arrangement conveyed order and hierarchy. "They had the head table and the head head table and the head head head table," she grumbled. "You never saw so many people at the head table." The speakers stuck to moderate themes. Congresswoman Martha Griffiths proposed adjustments to Social Security laws. The former Women's Bureau director Esther Peterson spoke in her role as President Johnson's special assistant for consumer affairs. Describing consumer protections as "where the action is," she urged the women to work on that issue when they returned home.

The real action unfolded right under Peterson's nose as NOW's founders launched a lunchtime revolt. The women who had been in Friedan's suite sat at the two tables closest to the stage. Conroy began the discussion by telling those women that since they had been barred from introducing resolutions, it was time to form a new organization. Ignoring the speakers and their neighbors' attempts to shush them, the women whispered "agitatedly" and "pass[ed] around notes written on paper napkins," debating NOW's name and founding statement. Some thought NOW should be a temporary name because it "sound[ed] kind of blah," according to Eastwood. The statement, too, had to be revised; the first draft "left out the activist part," implying that "it could be just a study organization." Other women began to wonder about this side conversation. Gene Boyer sat nearby, straining to overhear the conspirators. These "brilliant women must have some fabulous plans," she figured. As lunch ended, the group clapped, cheered, and whistled. Clarenbach captured their feeling of forming a new team when she joked, "Shall we choose our colors?"

After lunch, the women met for an hour in someone's room to settle the details. Word spread to the rest of the conference about the formation of a new group named NOW. This time Boyer found the room. "I just knew I had to be there, even if I missed my plane," she said. These founders agreed on the broad primary objective to "bring women into full participation in the mainstream of American society and in truly equal partnership with men." NOW would be nonpartisan, and it would get right to work on three issues: boosting women's access to jury service, desegregating newspaper classified advertisements, and strengthening Title VII enforcement. Their first act was approving two telegrams to send out that night. One asked the EEOC to overturn its recent affirmation of sex-segregated help-wanted ads. The second urged President Johnson to reappoint Richard Graham as an EEOC commissioner. Both telegrams bore the names of all twenty-eight women who joined NOW on that afternoon of June 30, 1966.

This group nailed down a few more details before leaving. They sketched a plan for the organization and agreed to hold a conference in several months. In the interim, Clarenbach was selected as temporary chair because she had an office and a secretary in her university job. None of them wanted to shoulder the group's clerical work, a problem that would only deepen over time. Clarenbach agreed to appoint a steering committee and create a membership form that Friedan would send to "everybody who was on her huge Rolodex." Conroy the union leader understood that dues were essential, both to finance a group and to cement members' commitment. She "pulled out $5, plunked it down and said to us, in essence, 'Put your money where your mouth is,'" remembered Boyer. "I could not get my wallet out fast enough." Some put cash on the table; others wrote checks. NOW opened its treasury with $135 ($1,153 today).

The women who signed their names and paid $5 that day, determined by who was in attendance at the conference of state commissions, were mostly white and middle-aged. They had relative job security in the fields of law, labor, medicine, government, and education. Some had been hardened by their experiences working alongside men; others were galvanized by their time building women's institutions and other activist campaigns. Very few of them rose to NOW's leadership or even remained active in it a few years later. And the organization's size and agenda soon outgrew their vision for a nimble pressure group focused on legal change. Yet these founders shattered the tacit mid-century agreement that saw federal officials control women's agenda by brokering access to influence and building courteous consensus. From then on, women would draft their own blueprints for change, then work to make them real.

———

The NOW architects Murray, Friedan, and Conroy all left its leadership within four years. But each also mentored a lesser-known builder who advanced her aspirations through the organization over a longer period. Aileen Hernandez, a frustrated EEOC commissioner at the time of NOW's founding, would champion Murray's vision for fusing women's rights and racial justice in the organization. The Republican housewife and artist Patricia Hill Burnett, unhappily ensconced in Detroit affluence when the women met in Washington at the conference of state commissions, would come to idolize Friedan for her writings on the frustrations of middle- and upper-class wives. And the working-class organizer Mary Jean Collins, in 1966 a recent college graduate discovering Milwaukee's civil rights movement and punishing labor market, would later seek to marshal NOW members to pressure sexist corporations, inspired by her mentor Conroy.

These three, who shaped NOW in its vital first two decades, also represented different kinds of members and their approaches to organizing women. Hernandez was an expander who sought to stretch the group's agenda. Burnett was a universalizer who reasoned from her own perspective to make broad claims on behalf of her sex. And Collins was a concentrator who pushed to focus NOW's resources in battling its rivals. NOW needed each of these approaches, but each came with risks. Expanding their agenda too far chanced diluting its focus. Overly general claims about women as a group threatened to paper over their real differences. Too much internal discipline could stifle democracy.

The federal official, the beauty queen, and the scrappy Catholic had little in common. But as each pursued personal fulfillment and wider influence, she came to believe that she needed the others. Sexism was the problem and equality was its solution, each one held, but each also defined these in her own way. Soon women were organizing everywhere, building power as women, often through NOW. They would learn that the category of "woman" was magnetic, but also volatile.

2.

BE WHAT YOU ARE, A WOMAN

The Detroit painter and socialite Patricia Hill Burnett, born in Brooklyn in 1920, wrestled with her conflicting desires to achieve as a professional and, at the same time, be admired for her domesticity. Aileen Hernandez, born to Jamaican immigrant parents in Brooklyn six years after Patricia, spent decades working in institutions controlled by white men. Both the labor movement and the federal government defied her efforts to foreground and fuse the fights against racism and sexism. Mary Jean Collins, born in 1939 to a family on the precarious edge of the middle class, struggled to square her commitment to social justice as well as her budding sexuality with her Catholic faith in Milwaukee, a city divided by ethnic loyalties.

Each of these women aspired to influence, although she was not always sure what shape it should take. Each spent formative years surrounded and mentored by other women. And each charted a course for her life that diverged from her mother's. Despite these parallels, their race and class gave them distinct perspectives. Patricia enjoyed material comfort and elite social status, while Aileen's racial consciousness as a Black woman formed her worldview. Mary Jean's family's struggles forced her to be self-sufficient. One commonality helped to diminish their differences. Throughout early life, each received the clear-cut message, spelled out, for example, in Mary Jean's college student handbook, to "be what you are, a woman, to your fullest capacity." Each found this message to be a contradiction. As they pursued their goals from within the bounds that existed, they ran into constraints that were not only frustrating, but seemingly insurmountable.

AMBITIOUS DAUGHTERS

Patricia Hill Burnett was born to a brief marriage that united old and new money, elite status and grit. Her father was William Burr Hill, a descendant of the former vice president Aaron Burr and the scion of a wealthy New England family. After prep school in Europe, he matriculated at Yale University, where, according to his daughter, he "just shone" as rowing team captain, noted violinist, and member of the elite campus secret society Skull and Bones.

Patricia's mother, Myrtle, was the daughter of a once-penniless immigrant, Migiel Uline, who arrived in America from Holland at age sixteen and found work in a Cleveland stone quarry. Uline noticed the ice that covered the pit in the winter, and then he started a side business harvesting and selling it. By the time he turned twenty-one, Uline had saved enough money to open the Colonial Ice Company and buy nineteen horse-drawn wagons. Within two years, his company owned 135 horses and wagons, four coal yards, and two ice plants. After cornering Cleveland's ice market, Uline expanded into Toledo.

Uline's daughter Myrtle met William Hill when he had just finished his service as an officer in World War I. The young couple married in 1918 in New York, had their daughter two years later, and settled in Toledo, with the Ulines nearby. Located where the Maumee River meets Lake Erie, Toledo was powered by the glass, refining, shipbuilding, and automobile manufacturing industries. City leaders were building public schools and bridges and updating roads at a steady clip, and the Toledo Museum of Art, near Patricia and Myrtle's eventual home on Collingwood Boulevard, would open a major addition in 1926. And as national chain stores began moving in, the downtown had a building boom and the city hosted its first commercial radio station. When the

Great Depression hit in 1929, Toledo would fare better than most, in part because huge orders for beer bottles rolled in to the "glass capital of the world" at Prohibition's end in 1933.

The Hills' marriage faltered despite their promising surroundings. Myrtle expected her husband to establish a career as her father had and to create a comfortable life for her. But for the first time in William's life, he struggled to get by on his charm and connections. By contrast to his own moneyed upbringing, he flitted from job to job and did not create much stability for his wife and daughter. He also expected his wife to busy herself at home while living in a series of furnished rented apartments. The couple divorced when "Patty" was four, and William left town. Divorce remained relatively rare and stigmatized in the 1920s, especially for women, although rates had been steadily climbing for decades: 0.54 per 1,000 Americans were divorced in 1891, and 1.63 had that status in 1928. Myrtle's father blamed his daughter for allowing her marriage to fail and cut her off completely. Accepting this assessment, Myrtle later taught her daughter, "It's 80–90% your job to keep your marriage going," and "if it fails, it's your fault."

While Myrtle channeled her shame into raising a daughter who would not repeat her own mistakes, her chosen career also showed her mettle. Scratching out a living as a writer, Myrtle pitched national magazines and contributed to local newspapers. Patricia recalled her mother writing in her car, illuminated by the dome light over the seats, while waiting for her to finish an evening art lesson. After spending a few years in "genteel poverty," Myrtle began earning a more stable living. She persuaded a sixteen-year-old farm girl named Claudis to move in with them to care for Patty and tend to the household chores in exchange for college tuition.

With Claudis's arrival, Patricia "grew up in a sort of matriarchy," and Myrtle could write and focus on her real life's work: molding her daughter into the kind of cultured beauty a great man would never leave. Those efforts cut against her young daughter's own strengths and instincts. "I was something of a tomboy," Patricia said: "good in school, but not very pretty and certainly not the perfectly demure and feminine creature my mother might have wished." When Patricia was ten, Claudis gave her a slingshot, and she used it to break a few neighbors' windows and a street-light. In response, Myrtle applied a firmer hand, teaching her daughter that the route to a desirable life was to be desirable to a well-off man. A woman must "be charming, be agreeable, be modest and . . . [she] will be taken care of," Patricia recalled. She had to conceal her intelligence and ambition, qualities that repelled men, and she should never trust another woman: "your eternal rival."

Patricia slowly came to accept her mother's worldview and the strategies it demanded. She succeeded in school thanks to molding by Myrtle, who found her daughter "lessons in everything but tree-climbing." The two discovered her notable artistic talent when Myrtle hired an artist to give Patricia drawing lessons. At age twelve, she won a four-year scholarship for art classes at Toledo Museum; soon she was selling portraits for $25 apiece. Myrtle also worked on her daughter's appearance. "I learned to use make-up and truly was transformed into the world's idea of what a pretty girl should be," Patricia said. Women's use of makeup had expanded in the past two decades, driven by a new mass market for all kinds of consumer products. By the 1930s, even the "natural look" required "a box full of beauty devices: foundation or vanishing cream, powder, rouge, lipstick, and for some, eyebrow pencil, mascara and eye shadow." More than 85 percent of college women wore makeup, according to a 1931 study; high school girls also bought and wore cosmetics, albeit in smaller numbers.

Myrtle dressed her daughter in elegant custom-made clothes and arranged modeling jobs for her at a local department store chain. She also encouraged Patricia to downplay her considerable successes in school. "It was my pride," Patricia said, "that not one date knew I had skipped a grade or that I was a national honor scholar." With the money from Myrtle's publications and Patricia's portraits and modeling, the family had a comfortable life.

Patricia's teenage years coincided with the national crisis of the Great Depression. As the nation tried to claw its way out of economic despair in the mid-1930s, her own fortunes skyrocketed. Her estranged grandfather Migiel Uline, by then divorced from Myrtle's mother and remarried to a younger woman, reconnected with Myrtle just as Patricia was finishing high school at age sixteen. The patriarch moved them both to Washington, D.C., where he was then living. Uline had expanded his ice business to the city and a few years later built the Uline Arena, a concert and sports venue that still stands. For a time he owned the Washington Capitols, the National Basketball Association team that played at the arena. The women settled into the house he bought them in a verdant Northwest D.C. neighborhood near Rock Creek Park.

Uline's change of heart transformed Patricia's life and brought Myrtle's aspirations for her daughter closer to fruition. With her grandfather's connections, Patricia came out as a debutante in 1939 at the private Sulgrave Club, housed in an elegant mansion on Embassy Row, and was presented to President Franklin Delano Roosevelt and First Lady Eleanor Roosevelt at the White House. Patricia's recent moves accelerated her "intensive training," she would later say, for "my real role in life—that of a first-class, top-drawer geisha girl."

———

While Patricia was making her debut at the White House, fulfilling her mother's ambitions, a thirteen-year-old girl in Brooklyn was striving to live up to her immigrant parents' expectations to be self-sufficient and high-achieving. Aileen Hernandez had been born Aileen Clarke in 1926, to Ethel Louise Hall, a seamstress, and Charles Henry Clarke Sr., a craftsman who made artists' brushes. Ethel and Charles, both born in Jamaica, had met and married three years earlier and put down roots in Harlem.

Harlem was widely considered the "world's greatest Negro city" in the early twentieth century. Tens of thousands of African Americans and West Indian immigrants moved to New York in the 1910s and 1920s, and many gravitated to that neighborhood. Those newcomers were flooded with new ideas. Harlem "was filled with street preachers and flamboyant orators haranguing the people from morning till night upon racial rights and wrongs," noted the *New York Amsterdam News*. "The West Indian Negro in America is a political conundrum. Conservative at home, he becomes radical abroad." Chief among these radicals was the Jamaican Black nationalist leader Marcus Garvey, who had also settled in Harlem around this time.

Life in the neighborhood was exciting, but it was not easy. Harlem was packed with Black-owned businesses and tidy homes. Black doctors, lawyers, and barbers served with pride and skill. But this density also arose in response to white New Yorkers' racist attitudes. Black men and women clustered in Harlem because whites would not sell or rent to them elsewhere. Nor would they hire them. The newspaperman Bazil O. Parks, who visited Harlem from Jamaica in 1921, wrote, "An educated and refined black young man of character from Jamaica would find it almost hopeless to obtain employment of the kind that he would expect to get at home." Parks revealed his intention to deter his fellow Jamaicans from leaving the island for an idealized vision of America, noting that while in Harlem "the people on the streets were well dressed and appeared contented," his overall assessment was that "natives of Jamaica will find the British West Indies more pleasant and more just than the United States."

Stepping into this dynamic world, the Clarkes carved out a full life. They loved the neighborhood, their daughter recalled, because so many of their fellow West Indian immigrants were there. "The Jamaicans who moved to New York came together in Harlem, so they had all kinds of activities—theatrical events, music, and all the rest," Aileen said. Her father, Charles, earned enough at Grumbacher's, an art supply manufacturer with a sterling reputation for quality, so that Ethel could be primarily a homemaker. She sewed clothes for her kids and neighbors—"I was always beautifully dressed," her daughter recalled—and occasionally bartered cleaning services for the family's doctor's visits.

The Clarkes believed that American life held great possibilities for their family. They named their daughter after Aileen Pringle, Ethel's favorite silent-film actress. Pringle was an American who was known for her quick wit and her marriage to a wealthy British Jamaican landowner and politician. Aileen's parents nicknamed her "ABC": her initials. They taught her and her brothers, Charles Jr. and Norris, that self-reliance was the avenue to success. All three kids learned to cook and sew, and their parents instilled in each of them a sense of optimism and a belief in the importance of personal accomplishment. Both of her brothers would go on to become engineers. Along with them, Aileen was "always told when

I was growing up that I had choices, even when really I didn't have a whole lot of them at the time," she said later.

As Harlem started to feel too crowded for their growing family, the Clarkes looked south and across the river to Bay Ridge, Brooklyn. "A small town in a big city," Bay Ridge was three square miles, historically a Scandinavian enclave, that overlooked New York Harbor. The neighborhood's population density nearly tripled between 1910 and 1930, in the years when the Clarkes arrived, but still it remained among the most sparsely populated areas of Brooklyn. Bay Ridge was also home to far fewer Black residents than nearby neighborhoods. As Blacks had sought housing in Brooklyn in the early twentieth century, "white attitudes, which at best had rarely extended beyond philanthropy to genuine fellowship, hardened into alarmed and militant opposition," according to one historian. To help offset their exclusion from politics, housing, and employment, African Americans in Brooklyn built their own civic groups and churches. This was the world the Clarkes entered when they rented a house in Bay Ridge, where they were the only Black family on their street.

Even before their arrival, some white residents learned of the Clarkes' plan to become their neighbors. They circulated petitions urging the bank that owned the house not to rent to them, alleging, as Aileen recalled, that "the neighborhood would deteriorate if we moved in." With the help of an elementary school principal who informed a meeting of the Parent-Teacher Association that he would house the Clarkes himself if the neighbors continued to resist, they moved in. They became "kind of a novelty—the one black family in the neighborhood," said Aileen. Her family was "tolerated to a great degree, coddled to a great degree, and made to feel that we were somehow very special and very different, and sometimes very different and *not* so special."

As the Clarkes settled in, the neighbors' hostility grated on Ethel and Charles. "Having come from Jamaica, which was quite different from the United States, they could not adjust to the idea of all this segregation," their daughter observed. One day Ethel took her daughter's hand, and they paid an unannounced visit to a resident who had started a second petition to oust them from Bay Ridge. Aileen listened as her mother "gave him a lecture about our family" and then "simply turned and walked out." Ethel and Charles channeled their frustration at such episodes into activism in the Brooklyn NAACP. They brought their children to meetings and gave them books to read in chairs in the hallway outside. Their daughter was proud and grateful for her parents' activism. They would always give her "a lot of support in being stubborn about doing things I really cared about."

Aileen established herself as a grade school striver at P.S. 176 in Brooklyn. To cap off her stint in junior high, she, like the other girls, sewed her graduation dress by hand. Aileen's was a short-sleeved white organdy dress with buttons down its length and a "dainty little bolero" to match. Aileen was a favorite to win the Golden Thimble Award, but the principal called her in just before the ceremony. He told her that her dress was undoubtedly superior, but they wanted to "spread the prizes around." After all, Aileen was valedictorian and received several other awards.

At the public, all-girls Bay Ridge High School, Aileen continued to blossom. Her classmates were predominantly white, but she and her brothers "got along fine" with the other kids. "I loved Brooklyn," she reflected. "We were the black people," but otherwise their neighborhood was "really very diverse. We had everybody. We had Germans. We had Jewish people." Unlike Patricia, who spent her teenage years downplaying her academic prowess, Aileen explored the full range of her interests and talents. She gave boys little mind apart from her brothers. Bay Ridge High had a strong reputation for "educational excellence," she said, and young women did not face the "early patterning to make sex-stereotyped choices about courses and careers" that often limited them in a coed environment. All her life she kept a note card signed by the high school principal that described her as an "enthusiastic participant in every phase of school activity," "an inspiring and popular grade leader," and "gifted with an unusually fine mind and remarkable literary and dramatic talent."

Aileen's high school years coincided with America's entry into World War II, and the war taught her the responsibilities of citizenship and shared sacrifice. As the salutatorian of the Bay Ridge High class of 1943, Aileen in her graduation speech described how America's entry into the war during their sophomore year had accelerated their maturity. They had pushed aside youthful amusements and "became air raid wardens, first aiders, fire wardens, members of the junior AWS and even commandos," she said. Many had gone to work or looked after younger siblings to free their mothers for the labor force. Aileen's own mother had taken a job sewing military uniforms for sailors and soldiers at a garment factory.

Encouraged by her parents, Aileen continued to chart a path toward independence and distinction. She won a scholarship to Mount Holyoke, the prestigious women's college in western Massachusetts. It was "a logical choice to continue an excellent, if segregated—and somewhat isolated—education," she said, referencing that college's single-sex and mostly white student body. When Aileen went to tell the "great advisor" who had "counseled" her "over the years" of her decision, that counselor encouraged her to take Howard University's scholarship exam. The young woman had never heard of the elite historically Black university in Washington, D.C., but the idea caught her interest. She passed the exam and won a scholarship.

Aileen had thrived at Bay Ridge High. But she decided it was time to "learn what I was all about" by departing "such an inaccurate little section of the world that didn't even include any other Negroes." Attending Howard became "the detour," she said, that "substantially changed my entire life."

———

Aileen was just beginning at Bay Ridge High, and Patricia was meeting the Roosevelts at her society debut, when Mary Jean Collins was born in a small Wisconsin town in 1939. Unlike Patricia, whose mother was narrowly focused on her marriage prospects, and Aileen, whose parents encouraged her along a self-reliant upward trajectory, Mary Jean was shaped during her youth by devotion to heritage and respect for institutions. Hardship plagued her loving family. Her community was guided by religious strictures that offered comfort and belonging but demanded reverence in return.

Mary Jean's Irish American parents, Emmett and Lucille, both grew up in Superior, Wisconsin, a small town in the state's northwest corner. Her father's family, who ran a grocery store, were "lace-curtain middle-class," and her mother's father was the town fire chief. Mary Jean moved with her parents and older sister Pat to the smaller town of Washburn, Wisconsin, about seventy miles due west, when Mary Jean started grade school. Even then, she understood that her father was an alcoholic, although her mother preferred to attribute the family's struggles to the Great Depression. After five hard years in Washburn, Lucille believed her husband needed a new start, so they moved south to Milwaukee.

That city proved to be an ideal destination for the Collins family. Emmett got a good job working for the A. O. Smith Company, a manufacturer, where he calculated railroad commodity shipping rates. Milwaukee was a bustling "patchwork of tight-knit, white ethnic neighborhoods" anchored by churches, which dominated the "social, spiritual, economic, and even political" life. A heavily industrial city, Milwaukee ranked second among the nation's largest cities in its percentage of workers in manufacturing. It had a strong labor movement and a white progressive left. Ethnic loyalties mattered a great deal there, where "the Germans and the Poles ran the city government," Mary Jean said.

About half of Milwaukee residents were Catholic, and the Collins family fit right in. Emmett was a regular usher and Lucille took part in "bake sales and all the kinds of activities that women did in the church at that time." Their daughters attended sixteen years of Catholic education. Most Milwaukee Catholics learned the Baltimore Catechism, which required rote memorization and complete acceptance of specific biblical interpretations. Mary Jean bristled at the obedience to hierarchy demanded of a Catholic kid. Even as a girl, she "felt a fierce sense of justice about people," she said. Visiting her grandparents each summer in tiny Superior, she overheard conversations that unsettled her. "People would talk about the Polacks, and the Swedes." She "always hated it; I hated that kind of prejudice."

Bound up with Emmett and Lucille's Catholic heritage was their commitment to the Democratic Party. The Collinses revered the late Franklin D. Roosevelt, the former president and father of the New Deal programs that empowered many workers and pulled the nation out of the Great Depression. Stirred by his example, Emmett and Lucille dove into the local political scene. They had their grade-school-age daughters handing out electoral materials at the polls to promote their favorite candidates, and they were ecstatic when John F. Kennedy, an Irish Catholic like them, became the Democratic Party nominee for president in 1960. When Senator Kennedy came to Milwaukee two years earlier to address the city's Jefferson-Jackson Day Dinner, a major party fundraiser, Mary Jean, then seventeen years old, delighted in the dessert course: ice cream with a shamrock stamped into it. "It was a big deal that one of ours was maybe going to be president," she said. Her early loyalty to the Democrats would endure throughout her life.

As her daughter came of age, Lucille herself was a powerful example for her, albeit a negative one. "Growing up what I saw," Mary Jean said, was "not a life I wanted to have." Because of Emmett's alcoholism and rigid notions of family roles, Lucille had a "sense of lack of control of her own destiny, within the family." When Emmett's disease proved debilitating, his wife went out to work to keep the family afloat, and Mary Jean's babysitting money brought in a substantial part of the family budget. Lucille's struggles showed her daughter how women "could be trapped in a bad marriage, what was expected of them, how little support they got," and how the community blamed wives for their husbands' shortcomings. When Emmett's condition worsened, the family bottomed out, losing their home several times.

Like Aileen Hernandez, Mary Jean craved independence, but she did not count on going to college. Lucille had not pursued education— college was "not a valued thing" for her or her seven siblings—and she did not encourage her own daughters to continue their educations. After high school, Mary Jean's older sister entered a Catholic order, the School Sisters of St. Francis: "our grade school nuns." Mary Jean doubted the family could afford to send her to college. Her father had not had "much of an income" for the past decade. Secretarial work was respectable and easy to find for a woman with a high school education, so Mary Jean worked in an office for two years after graduating in 1957. "I was very good at it," she said, but Emmett "started to nag me about going to school." His mother, Delia, had been "very positive on higher education," and "it always bothered" Emmett that he had dropped out after two years at the University of St. Thomas, a Catholic university in Minnesota. Now his daughter could fulfill his mother's dream for him. Mary Jean applied to two local Catholic institutions—Marquette University and Alverno College—and she chose the latter, a women's college, matriculating in September 1959.

Just as Mary Jean entered this new chapter of her life, tragedy struck her family. Lucille suddenly entered the hospital that November. The doctors were tight-lipped, but she appeared to be doing well when Mary Jean visited on a Friday night. She died the next morning of an aortic aneurysm at age fifty-one. Lucille smoked three packs of cigarettes per day, and her family had a history of heart trouble, but still, the death was "pretty shocking," said Mary Jean. It also felt like a betrayal; she believed the doctors knew her mother's health was declining and denied her the chance to say goodbye. Mary Jean determined to plow ahead into her freshman year studies despite her overwhelming grief. Her dad "seemed fine," and she decided that she simply "wasn't going to not be in college."

College was not a foregone conclusion for Mary Jean, Aileen, or Patricia, but each saw education as a route to a life that diverged from her mother's. Each began to imagine herself in a new way in college, surrounded by other young women and mentors. They entered a liberal arts college filled with wealthy daughters of the Chesapeake, a historically Black university in the nation's capital, and a tiny women's enclave run by forward-thinking Catholic sisters. These institutions offered traditions that could comfort but also chafe, and moments for profound if quiet rebellion.

COLLEGE WOMEN

Patricia Hill Burnett's social status shaped her prospects for education. She had begun taking courses at Toledo University when she and her mother were still in Ohio, but she withdrew at once when her grandfather beckoned them to Washington. Suddenly the high-society future her mother wanted for them was within their grasp. They selected a nearby women's college known for its challenging curriculum and elite pedigree:

the prestigious Goucher College, in Baltimore. Patricia enrolled in 1937 at age sixteen.

Goucher propelled this daughter of a single mother into a rarefied environment that emphasized tradition and the bold pursuit of achievement. Most of Patricia's classmates were from the East Coast, with many hailing from Maryland and New York, although one of her two roommates was native Hawaiian. About one-third of students were Baltimoreans who commuted from home. Goucher had been established fifty years earlier by the Methodist Episcopal Church as the Women's College of Baltimore City. It was renamed for its cofounder and second president, John F. Goucher, in 1910. The college was the first institution of higher learning to educate women in the state of Maryland. Its founders intended to provide women with "equal advantages in the business of life."

Goucher's administrators set out to prove that women like Patricia could meet the challenges of an elite education. The school's curriculum was so difficult that of the fifty students in the first class only five graduated four years later. At the turn of the century, Goucher ranked among the nation's top fourteen colleges and universities. Administrators at male-dominated institutions clearly respected Goucher women's pedigree. The college's graduates enrolled in the first classes at Johns Hopkins Medical School, established in 1893—eight years after Goucher opened its doors.

As time went on, the university's leaders added still more rigor to the curriculum. The "Goucher Plan," which the college president, David Allan Robertson, announced over Baltimore's radio waves in 1935, offered a new answer "to the question 'what is college for.'" "The answer of Goucher College is not in terms of semester hours or required courses," Robertson claimed, "but in terms of the life activities of an educated American woman of today and tomorrow." The new plan required students like Patricia to demonstrate their mental and physical health, master a foreign language, and take course work in science, literature, history, the arts, and religion. In order to progress to the junior year, students took tests and presented evidence from their course work and extracurricular activities that they had "demonstrated qualities of character appropriate to meeting a variety of life situations." The college continued to expand. Administrators made physical education, religion, and fine arts—the latter of which was Patricia's course of study—full departments in 1931, six years before her arrival.

Physical education played a major part in Patricia's college life, reflecting many educators' belief that women needed strong bodies to withstand the stresses of college. According to turn-of-the-century medical experts, too much mental exertion sapped one's physical energy. Boys' bodies were built to withstand it, these experts held, but mental strain threatened girls' health and fertility. Goucher's leaders anticipated their critics. Physical education at Goucher was not intended "to make athletes of our young women," the college president, William Hersey Hopkins, explained in his 1889 College Day address, "but only to secure the symmetrical development of the body and the mental health and vigor depending upon such a condition." To promote it, administrators built what they boasted was the best gymnasium for women anywhere in the world. It included the first swimming pool at a women's college. They also recruited an entirely Swedish physical education staff, whose members imported thirty-seven cutting-edge Zander exercise machines, designed to target young women's muscles with "modern" precision.

Goucher administrators sought to keep students somewhat protected and separated from Greater Baltimore, reflecting the school's religious roots. Required to attend daily prayers at the college chapel, the first on-campus students were also prohibited from attending the opera or the theater, playing cards, or dancing, either on campus or in public anywhere else. The women's lives were closely supervised by older women who lived with them. Initially called "ladies in charge" but renamed "heads of halls" by the time Patricia lived there, these chaperones served as "guides and mentors of the domestic life of hall students." Administrators began relaxing these rules and enhancing campus social life by the time Patricia arrived in 1937. This was partially due to pressure from students. A group petitioned in 1932 for permission to have radios in their rooms. Officials responded that they would need to study the issue, but they soon relented. Some Goucher students also flouted the strict rules: in 1933, the college council debated "problems incidental to repeal of the

Eighteenth Amendment"—students drinking alcohol. Perhaps administrators intended to defuse that situation that year in addressing students' longtime complaint that they lacked an "adequate social center." A small gym was converted into a dance hall and "club room." To open the new space in April 1933, the college hosted a coed dance with an eight-piece orchestra.

College leaders also granted students like Patricia new "minor liberties" by creating dedicated rooms for smoking and permitting students to play cards, entertain male visitors, and venture off campus at night. Still, students should observe the policy of "signing out," cautioned an alum in 1938. "College authorities" worried about them, "especially in these days of automobiles." When Patricia arrived the previous year, she joined one of Goucher's eight sororities, Alpha Phi. College leaders controlled these groups tightly, declining to permit them to have houses on campus and banning students from joining if their grades were not "sufficiently high."

As they relaxed the rules on campus, Goucher administrators also saw the educational value in exposure to the wider world. The students took frequent trips to Washington by train, chaperoned by college staff, to visit museums and the Capitol. The college also began allowing students to study abroad. Back on campus, half of the articles in the student newspaper in the 1930s related to talks on campus, according to a history of the college; "chapel talks especially, but also guest lectures, club talks by faculty and others, presidential talks, [and] readings." The college newspaper printed the university president's weekly calendar of activities, and these events, which students could attend, included visits by celebrities and intellectuals. There were also more men on campus because they were newly permitted to perform alongside Goucher women in plays and concerts.

Patricia was present for many of these transitions, but as an adult she did not say or write much about the impact college made on her. "Colleges for women need to be encouraged in every way," she wrote to a classmate decades later, explaining why she had volunteered to help with Goucher's fundraising drive, "for they are almost the only learning institution where a young woman can realize her full potential—every position of leadership is open to her." And yet, evidence does not suggest that Patricia seized this opportunity for leadership when she was at

Goucher. In fact, she left school in her junior year for unclear reasons—even her children never knew—and did not graduate with her class of 1941, or later.

Patricia left behind scant and conflicting evidence about her experience at Goucher. Over her lifetime, she displayed pride in the credential, always listing the affiliation on her résumé. Patricia stayed close to her college friends, attended her reunions, and taught her children Goucher songs that they grew up singing with her. Thirty years after leaving school, she wrote to the college president to ask whether she could apply her credits from a local Detroit university or a visual arts school in Mexico or other "recognition for studies and work done after college" toward completing her Goucher degree. But Patricia trivialized her years as a fine arts student in her 1995 memoir, labeling Goucher a "finishing school."

Still, Patricia's next steps suggest that Goucher widened her outlook. She had spent her childhood stifling her intellect and cultivating her potential for a prosperous marriage, but she did not pursue a husband when she left college. Instead, she declared her independence and leveraged what she believed were her strongest assets: her charm and beauty.

——

Three years after Patricia withdrew from Goucher, Aileen Hernandez left Brooklyn to start college. She and her father had their first exposure to southern-style segregation on the train to Washington that fall of 1943. All of the sleeping car porters and dining car waiters were Black, and when Aileen explained the purpose of her travel, she was astonished to learn that many of these men had also attended Howard. The railway men told the pair to look for a black taxi when they arrived at Union Station. They scoured the taxi lot in vain but saw no black cars. Aileen's father approached the nearest taxi, whose driver was reading a newspaper. He looked up from its pages and told them, "You'll have to get the black taxi." Eventually, they grasped his message: "It had *nothing* to do with the color of the cab; it had *everything* to do with the color of the rider and the color of the driver." While there was entrenched racism across the nation, Aileen was surprised to see it expressed so openly in the nation's capital. "I could not believe that a country that really believed itself to be a democracy was that way," she said. Riding up to campus, she began to doubt her choice of college.

Aileen settled in at "America's Leading Negro University," where woman students were temporarily in the majority. There were men on campus, but Howard's male enrollment was the lowest in its history due to the war. The school, coeducational since its creation just after the Civil War, had always fostered a mostly African American student body and faculty. It offered a more comprehensive curriculum than any other historically Black university, and it emphasized graduate study and the liberal arts rather than vocational training. When Aileen entered Howard's liberal arts college, it had about a thousand students. There were students from twenty-four nations and forty-five states, but more than half of them, like Aileen, were from parts of the American North, West, and Midwest that did not have state-enforced segregation. Pauli Murray, then a student at Howard University Law School, wrote of the undergraduates she met there, "They were a generation who tended to think of themselves as Americans without a hyphen" who had been "thrown rudely into the nation's capital where Jim Crow rides the American Eagle."

In many ways Howard's campus resembled that of any other urban university in the mid-1940s. There was a bustling social scene, with thriving fraternities and sororities. Homecoming was a major affair, and in 1946 *Life* magazine ran a photo spread marking the occasion. A "bevy of Howard beauties" paraded upon mobile thrones, and when the "radiant" queen traversed the field, the student newspaper recounted, "pandemonium really broke loose in the stands." Aileen was somewhat dismayed by most of her female classmates' preoccupation with their social lives. "People sent their daughters to Howard University to look for husbands much more than they thought about, 'What is going to be my career?'" she noted. Aileen found Howard undergraduates generally contributed to its climate as "a very uninvolved campus." Devoting herself to campus activities, she served as editor of the college newspaper, the *Hilltop*.

Aileen sought out those students and faculty who were interested in activism. She joined Howard's chapter of the NAACP, where women had a strong presence and where she met Murray. The early 1940s were "the great days of Howard University as the leading school in civil rights" and "the training ground" for the movement's lawyers, Murray said. She headed the civil rights committee of the Howard NAACP chapter, which formed in 1942, expanded during the war, and was voted "outstanding student organization of the year" in 1944. "The fact that an accident of gender exempted me from military service," Murray later wrote, "made me feel an extra responsibility to carry on the integration battle"—a burden felt by "many other Howard University women." Those women included Aileen, whose own older brother was serving in a segregated unit in the Pacific.

Local businesses were segregated not by law, as in many southern states, but by custom. To combine "nonviolence in our racial struggle" with "American techniques of showmanship," Murray organized Howard students—mostly "attractively dressed coeds," including Aileen—in a campaign to desegregate restaurants, theaters, and drugstores. They started with the "little restaurant across the road" from campus, recalled Aileen, "where you could buy something" but "could not sit there and eat it." NAACP chapter members took a pledge declaring equal access to public accommodations to be "one of the most precious of all human rights." They claimed their devotion to the campaign and promised to "employ dignity, courtesy and restraint at all times." Through their protests, the students desegregated that restaurant and another one near campus. Murray was elated. They "proved that intelligent, imaginative action could bring positive results," she said, and "without an embarrassing incident."

Aileen's years at Howard changed her plans and her outlook. Because women predominated on campus, they "could do things that they hadn't done before," such as take on a broader range of leadership roles. Some, like Aileen, changed their majors. Her initial plan was to become a teacher, "as most girls did in those days. There was not much else you could do." But she found political science especially absorbing. She wanted to understand how to reconcile the deep admiration for American democracy she had gleaned from her high school textbooks, the racist climate in Washington, and the power of protest she learned through the NAACP and from Murray, who was sixteen years older but had become a close friend. Aileen also developed a strong new sense of her Black identity. "One of the values of segregation," she said, was that Howard was then "the absolute center for practically every major black scholar." Those scholars helped students understand that "we were living in a very difficult kind of society" and "that we had a responsibility to change it." Such inspiring professors were mostly male. Howard's history department, for example, had no woman faculty until 1942, when the department hired one white woman, the future NOW founder Caroline Ware, for a permanent position, and Merze Tate, who was Black, for a contingent teaching job.

The men came flooding back from the war in 1946, Aileen's senior year, and Howard's buildings were "bulging" with the school's largest-ever enrollment of more than fifty-two hundred students. Sixteen hundred of these were veterans: one of the largest cohorts of ex-GIs "at any Negro institution." Suddenly men outnumbered their female counterparts by nearly three to two, and classes were held "in every nook and cranny of the campus." The mostly male veterans energized but also came to dominate the activist scene, Aileen said. "The vets coming to Howard under the G.I. Bill were obviously not going to tolerate" the racist customs of the capital city. She protested alongside them. With two male schoolmates and another female Howard student on Halloween night 1946, Aileen sought to attend a play starring Ingrid Bergman at the Lisner Auditorium. The doorman barred them from entry, citing "community policy." The students asked to see the manager, who "proved to be the little man nobody could find," and the doorman refunded their tickets. "One more blow was struck for American fascism" in "the shadow of the Nation's Capitol," the student newspaper asserted.

At Howard, the high-achieving rule follower grew into a newly politicized Black woman. She had spent college "picket[ing] for four years," Aileen reflected with pride decades later. Earning her Howard degree in 1947, she set out to apply her new knowledge beyond the school's red brick and cast-iron gates.

———

For Mary Jean Collins, like Patricia and Aileen, college was a chance to explore her interests and imagine a different life. Of the three, she stayed the closest to home in Milwaukee, but college might have stretched her the furthest.

Mary Jean's chosen college, Alverno, had been founded in 1887 as a one-year school to train members of a Catholic order on a farm outside Milwaukee. It was renamed and made a four-year school in 1936, and the first lay students arrived twelve years later, when the school moved to a new campus in the city. Most Catholic women's colleges modeled themselves upon elite secular institutions, but Alverno took a more vocational approach by offering practical skills to working- and lower-middle-class Catholic women. Mary Jean's college handbook described Alverno as "concerned with full, mature Catholic minds" and offering "the Church and society Catholic college graduates—mothers, teachers, musicians, nurses, artists."

As a regional school, Alverno sought to meet young women where they were. In 1960, Mary Jean's sophomore year, the college included nearly 600 lay students and 250 religious order students, largely from Wisconsin and Illinois. When Mary Jean graduated in the spring of 1963, most of her fellow graduates earned bachelor of arts degrees, but others earned degrees in home economics, education, medical technology, and nursing. The lay students were primarily working class; a 1963 school newspaper article noted that most of them spent summer vacation "working to pay next year's tuition." The college offered some classes on the weekend for full-time workers and others between 10:00 and 2:00 to overlap with the elementary school day. Alverno also administered English proficiency tests, which suggests that some students were not native English speakers.

Mary Jean was amazed that the religious women who taught them also ran the school. "You just didn't see that anywhere else," she said. In her world, "almost no women had decent jobs outside the home." The sisters who led Catholic women's colleges like Alverno had striking independence and autonomy. "There were male professors, but women were in charge," said Sister Joel Read, Mary Jean's European history professor and a NOW founder, who was then in her late thirties. Alverno was "an organization we could push around," she said, so the sisters devised an experimental, competency-based approach. The new curriculum placed Alverno among a handful of "lesser-known liberal arts institutions" at the cutting edge of a growing movement to assess students based on "life-related outcomes" rather than academic knowledge.

Alverno leaders' reforms ran parallel to efforts by the Catholic Church to modernize from the top down through Vatican II, the early 1960s meetings that liberalized church policies and rituals. Still, Alverno's leaders pushed further. "The whole intent of women's studies is infused into every course offered on our campus," Read wrote in 1973. "A women's college *is* a feminist institution." Read "didn't overemphasize" women's history in her European history courses, she said, "but I made sure it was there."

The instructors' outlooks were progressive, but student life was convent-like. There were two Masses on campus each weekday morning, and students needed special permission to attend Sunday Mass anywhere else. Those students who lived on campus had to sign out every time they left the grounds and were expected to adhere to a strict evening curfew. The total ban on men entering students' rooms must have been presumed, because the resident student handbook did not even mention it. A student needed her parents' permission to go home during the week or to spend a weekend anywhere but their home. There were mixers with local Catholic college men, but the landmark social event was the annual father-daughter dinner dance. Its theme in 1963, Mary Jean's senior year, was "Me and My Gal."

The student handbook specified a conservative dress code: "blouses, sweaters, skirts, jumpers, or dresses, with bobby socks or nylons and flats. Skirts must be below the knee and must not be too tight." In a photo in the student newspaper from Mary Jean's college years, lay students like her wore long dark shorts and collared white shirts, playing volleyball against "student-postulants" in full habits.

From inside this bounded world, the religious women who ran Alverno took bold steps to widen students' horizons. "I was really concerned that students at Alverno didn't see the world in perspective," Read said. "They saw it from Milwaukee." As faculty adviser to the International Relations Club, Read helped bring students from overseas to study at the college and made sure the student newspaper profiled Alverno students who were studying abroad. The campus library boasted a "spacious reading room" where students could peruse any of the collection's forty-five thousand volumes and "over 500 current periodicals." College leaders like Read encouraged students to pursue careers, helped students apply to graduate school, and spotlighted alumnae who worked as teachers and nurses.

Four years in this woman-centered ecosystem transformed Mary Jean's life. She thrived, serving as president of the junior class and then president of the student body. She also developed a crush on a classmate, the first evidence of a lesbian identity she would come to embrace in her thirties. Her Alverno professors connected her to other powerful women like Kay Clarenbach and Catherine Conroy, who would become her mentor. "Conroy was the kind of person who spots for leaders," Mary Jean said later. "She put her eye on me."

Alverno also gave Mary Jean tools to integrate her sense of social justice with her Catholic identity. She noted that this freed her "from some of the religious traditional things I had learned in grade school and high school," which were more rigid and backward looking. The women who taught her college theology classes, she said, "led me not to become an atheist but to hold on to the underlying principles of what Christianity should be." Mary Jean graduated from Alverno in 1963 with a degree in history and minors in theology and education. A fiery young woman, only five feet tall, she had dark eyes, what she called "a naturally curly Irish haircut that I do myself," and a radiant energy.

Patricia, Aileen, and Mary Jean all lacked a clear plan for the future when they left school. In environments brimming with driven women, they had found new role models and recast their expectations. But as each woman sought to make her mark, she met structural roadblocks and personal aggravations that showed her new reasons to forge bonds with other women.

"WHAT ARE YOU DOING HERE?"

Patricia's first move after college was to Detroit, alongside her mother. The two women had switched places in a way. Myrtle, the longtime breadwinner, won back the status she thought she'd lost after her first marriage failed when she married the chief of surgery at Henry Ford Hospital in 1941. Patricia left the cloistered world of Goucher College to pursue fame and a paycheck, spurning all of the twenty-five marriage proposals she claimed to have received by her early twenties.

Her first job was a modeling gig at Hudson's, a Detroit department store chain. A radio producer in the store one day overheard her speaking in her cultured tone, which Patricia herself described as "combin[ing] Northern efficiency with Southern charm." He told her he was developing a radio series whose female lead was a D.C. debutante. She was the person for the job, she told him, and lied about having taken acting lessons. After a tryout, WXYZ made her the female lead in two nationally syndicated radio shows: *The Lone Ranger* and *The Green Hornet*.

Emboldened by her radio stardom, Patricia accepted her new step-brother's dare to sign up for the 1942 Miss Michigan pageant. She told him that taking the crown would be a cinch. "Any woman with any intelligence could win one," she claimed. She even promised to wear her "baggiest bathing suit." She was not surprised to win the pageant, but she had not fully considered the implications. Myrtle responded, horrified, *"Patricia, you have just ruined your life."* With this one act, she undermined their entire family's respected status; her stepfather might even lose his job. "Beauty pageants were seen a little like 'wet T-shirt' contests might be today," Patricia wrote in her 1995 memoir. Unfortunately, she had signed a contract that required her to compete for the Miss America crown. When she tried to drop out, officials threatened to sue her, so she went to Atlantic City. Her mother insisted on coming along to chaperone.

Atlantic City, the home of the Miss America competition, was a tourist town that boasted cheap amusements, Broadway-quality theater, and free-flowing liquor. The pageant started out in 1920 as a gimmick to boost tourism, and participants performed in racy swimwear in bars and nightclubs. Pageant officials tightened the rules in the late 1930s, requiring contestants to be childless, single, and never seen talking to men, even their fathers, in the months running up to the event. The new rules "tamped down the erotic implications of women vamping in swimwear" while highlighting participants' sexual availability. The pageant peddled in stereotypes, but it also offered contestants like Patricia the rare chance to turn their beauty into influence when their routes to economic and professional advancement were so few.

When Patricia arrived in Atlantic City in 1942, the war effort had transformed the place. Most hotels were temporary hospitals and barracks. Soldiers practiced attacks along the shoreline, the coast guard paced along the boardwalk, and snipers ran drills from the rooftops. Military officials were so concerned that Nazi submarines lurked offshore that they enforced a citywide blackout each night. Rather than cancel the pageant, organizers rebranded it. They linked patriotism with traditional femininity, combating fears that women's dramatic entry into industrial jobs, symbolized by the celebrated omnipresent images of Rosie the Riveter, had made women too masculine.

The pageant was its own education for Patricia. She placed as second runner-up, and she bonded with the other contestants. "I kind of adopted everybody," she said of the other women, and she was delighted when they voted her Miss Congeniality. Patricia's official prize, by contrast, was "absolutely ghastly": not scholarship money, but months of appearances in nightclubs, vaudeville shows, and "sleazy dance halls" where the contestants were "pawed and mistreated backstage." The comedians hit on her constantly, but she and her mother were determined that she abstain from sex. "My virginity was seen as a priceless asset to be employed in the course of marital negotiations," she said. But she was still not ready to surrender to that fate. Instead, Patricia briefly moved to New York, where she worked as a model for the prestigious John Robert Powers Agency. "I was ambitious," she said of her early twenties. "The only way to catapult my way into recognition was to use my face and figure," and "it worked."

Finally, at age twenty-four, Patricia acquiesced to the pressure from her mother and the rest of society to find a man to marry. World War II had pulled men overseas by the millions, but she met and began dating a recently divorced plastic surgeon. William Lange was an Army Medical Corps major, twelve years older than Patricia. Myrtle adored him and urged her daughter to accept his proposal. They married in 1945 in her mother's home in a small candlelight ceremony followed by a reception for three hundred guests. *The Washington Post* praised her "heavy satin gown with an off-shoulder neckline and long train" and elaborate veil, embroidered with roses and arranged in a tall "Russian tiara effect." *The New York Times* also announced the event. After the wedding, the couple moved to Shepherdstown, West Virginia, where Dr. Lange was stationed at a plastic surgery center.

Marriage did not grant Patricia new freedom or even much time away from her mother. The union was rocky from the start. "I barely knew him really," Patricia said, and "had a miserable, miserable time with him." She missed her busy life in Detroit, and Lange expected her complete obedience and had a violent temper. She hoped that a pregnancy would help fix their marriage, but her husband sent her to live with her mother until after the baby was born. Just one year after their marriage, they began divorce proceedings. Patricia felt it was "my first great failure in life," and she and her infant son remained in Detroit, where her life was not much better. Their contested divorce would drag out for three years. Since Patricia remained legally married during that time, Myrtle forbade her to date. Patricia spent a few hours each week on modeling and acting gigs: "my only escape, except for my baby, from what had become a dreadful life."

Three years later, just as her divorce was wrapping up, Patricia met her next husband. Harry Burnett, a bachelor in his late thirties, lived just across the golf course. Patricia later learned that he had had his eye on her since before her first marriage. He wooed her lavishly, sending flowers daily and flying her to Havana for their first date. Harry was a chemist and microbiologist who ran his successful family business. Difco Laboratories "had more or less cornered the market on supplying the stuff scientists use to grow bacteria in their little petri dishes," as Patricia understood it. She was not especially attracted to him, but the marriage would extricate her, "hopefully forever, from under my mother's very heavy wing." They married in late 1948 and had three children in six years.

The Burnetts kept up a well-to-do lifestyle in a posh corner of an industrial city that was changing around them. Detroit had the nation's highest-paid blue-collar workers and was one of the fastest-growing cities in the 1940s. The city was bursting with relative newcomers, especially African Americans who had left the Jim Crow South by the millions in pursuit of relative freedom and safety in northern cities. When Detroit's heavy industry started to decline after World War II, many middle-class whites decamped to the suburbs. But most whites remained: either they could not afford to move or, like the Burnetts, they held on to their piece of the city. Many white Detroiters demanded racially segregated schools and neighborhoods, sometimes through violent confrontations and attacks on African Americans. At the same time, the city was a budding node of Black Power culture and politics, and the site of Malcolm X's iconic "Message to the Grass Roots" call to revolution in 1963. The city grew increasingly politically fragmented. While there were white segregationists and political conservatives, there were just as many white social liberals like the Burnetts who supported civil rights.

But families like the Burnetts, tucked away in pockets of white affluence, were largely insulated from the city's turbulence. They lived in a nine-bedroom house built by Harry's family in 1927—a replica English manor that was "vibrating with color and good taste," a reporter noted. To Patricia, her Palmer Woods neighborhood was "an oasis of greenery" and "the most ideal place in Detroit to live." Herself an emblem of the Burnetts' status, Patricia was frequently profiled in the local society pages. One reporter praised her "wealth of raven hair, dancing gray eyes and calla lily complexion," declaring her "one of Detroit society's most beauteous and talented adornments."

With the help of domestic workers, Patricia ran a busy household and burnished the family's reputation. Their child-care provider, Inez, who was either Black or biracial, had moved to Detroit from the South decades earlier. Inez had been a live-in cook for Myrtle and her husband before moving across the golf course to work for the Burnetts. Having already raised her own dozen children, she worked for the Burnetts until she remarried. The family's cook, Frida, had grown up in Sarajevo and was married. Inez and Frida lived part-time in a corner of the Burnetts' home that had two bedrooms, a bathroom, and its own separate stairway, although both also had their own homes. The Burnetts also employed a cleaner and a handyman.

Patricia's wealth gave her freedoms that Aileen and Mary Jean did not have. But she also felt different and intense pressures. In particular, she found that power was elusive inside the marriage that grounded her social capital. Harry was "a fine Victorian gentleman," she said, but also a "rigid, paternalistic dinosaur." Her husband and the rest of society told her that being a good wife meant hiding her own ambitions and preferences, to the point that she chose to mirror her husband's selections in the voting booth rather than making her own. Motherhood demanded her "total dedication," she vented, and running their household wasted her talents on "meaningless chores." A psychiatrist advised her to be grateful and recommit to her family. Patricia started to see her dependency as a trap. She felt she existed "only as a background for my husband and children" and "just slid down to nothing. I hated myself," she said. "I hated my life."

Patricia yearned to achieve on her own terms. Beauty pageants, modeling, and acting were unthinkable pursuits for a well-to-do wife, but it was "considered appropriate for lady-like, gentlewomen to stay home and do their little water colors," she said. For a decade, she had kept her easel in an alcove next to her kitchen and sold oil portraits for $50 each. She called this "a perfect arrangement" in 1961. But painting at home was a struggle, she said later. "My career was piece-mealed around my hard and fast duties as a housewife—cemented by custom, family expectation and guilt." Her daughter Hillary recalled her mother's restlessness. "She was someone we were always sort of trying to hold on to, like a helium balloon. It was a question of who had the string at a particular time."

Patricia decided to set up a separate art studio as a declaration that her painting was her vocation, not a hobby. In 1962, she sought to rent a studio space at the Scarab Club, a sixty-year-old, vaunted private institution. When the members received her application, they wrote to male artists they knew, hoping that one of them would take the open studio. Only after none applied did the men grudgingly allow Patricia to be the second woman ever to rent a studio there. When she arrived, the five male members refused to install a lock on the door of the building's single bathroom.

By all accounts, Patricia was a talented artist, and her rising profile opened her eyes to aspects of sexism she had never noticed before. When painting male subjects, she endured their belittling and sexualized comments from behind the canvas. Sometimes they menaced her in ways that were physically threatening; she was "nearly assaulted" in her studio in 1969. Patricia bristled one day when a male client asked her to "please sign your name 'Burnett,' just 'Burnett,' on the painting, because we all know that paintings have more value if they're done by men." Most of her patrons were men, but Patricia preferred to paint women and children.

"A woman can paint another woman better than anyone else," she said, because "a woman knows how a woman wants to appear." Local critics commended her work. "Her love of people comes through in her portraits," one wrote, "and her delight in handling oil paint is the benchmark of a skilled and trained hand."

Patricia spent the 1950s souring on the trade-offs that prosperous white wives had to make. She began to seek more respect and freedom without descending from her pedestal.

———

Buying and consuming characterized the Burnetts' lifestyle, while Aileen spent the 1950s advocating for the kinds of workers who made it possible. During her first summer after college, she traveled to Norway, where she took classes in comparative government at the University of Oslo. Then she served as a research assistant in Howard University's Department of Government, assisting with a project that was studying the highest-ranking African Americans in the federal workforce. Returning home to Brooklyn in 1948, she completed New York University's graduate program in public administration. Studying in the library one evening, she noticed a magazine advertisement for a job that "doesn't pay a lot of money but gives lots of satisfaction," she said. The ad was for the International Ladies' Garment Workers' Union (ILGWU) training school. Aileen had heard of the union because her mother had been a member during World War II. The possibility was electrifying. "They're talking to me," she thought.

The ILGWU had a long history of defending woman workers in a crucial but often overlooked sector. It was formed in the early twentieth century to fight the abysmal working conditions in New York's garment industry. Most of the union's first members were immigrant women from eastern Europe who had little experience in trade unions, but many had grown up in families with socialist ideas. The ILGWU thus developed a robust program of member education to convey "the importance of the union label" as well as economics, history, and government. The garment trade flourished after World War II as Americans clamored to buy new clothes. The union expanded but started "falling behind,"

Aileen explained later. Its predominantly female membership "had dual responsibilities in the house and the workplace," with little time for "after-work activities, which is how you got to be a union officer." As the union struggled to replace its mostly male and Jewish leadership, it devised the training institute to bring recent college graduates into the labor movement.

At the institute, like at Howard, Aileen had to tolerate biased instructors, but she still absorbed all she could. The union leaders' presumptions about who was leadership material shaped their selections for the program. Aileen joined a class of thirty-two trainees, of whom just four were women and two were Black. "We knew right away that just because 'women' is in the [union's] title doesn't mean that women are really in power," she said later. The organizers had picked her at least in part due to her mother's connections as a former member.

Aileen reveled in the yearlong program. The "excellent people" who led it taught them about how a garment factory worked, about the history of the labor movement and its legal context. They also emphasized "the importance of politics." Aileen was "delighted" on her first day to meet Eleanor Roosevelt, who had come to greet her cohort. The activist and former First Lady also addressed their graduation. Aileen's parents supported her career path, though they were also "appalled" when their educated daughter was punched in the eye during a three-month picket at a pajama factory. After finishing the training, Aileen moved to Los Angeles to work as an organizer in the union's regional office.

Aileen enjoyed teaching ILGWU members about union membership and American citizenship, but sexism was rampant even within this socially conscious union. Women's status in the union was "very simple," she said later. "They did certain kinds of jobs and the men did the other jobs," and "the jobs that the women did got paid less and the ones that the men did got paid more." After Aileen had worked for years as the assistant director of education, the director left, and most others in the office assumed that he would be replaced by another man. Aileen fought hard for his job and got it. But the union never replaced her with another assistant, so she had to do both jobs. "I soon found myself so swamped by routine clerical tasks that I felt like a glorified, but not very efficient, secretary," she wrote. Still, Aileen threw herself into the work and dove into L.A.'s activist scene, helping to organize protests of Angelenos from "every racial group" to protest the 1955 Mississippi lynching of Emmett Till.

As she soon discovered, traditional domesticity did not suit her. Aileen married the garment cutter Alfonso Hernandez in 1957. "I've seen some marriages that are really good," she said, "but not mine. My husband came from the Latin tradition, which taught him to expect subservience from women. Well, it just didn't work." They divorced in 1961. Speaking in general terms a decade later, Aileen said that marriage "definitely represents an easy way for a man to be serviced—in terms of sex, heirs, laundry, meals, and whatever." She never remarried, but instead cultivated deep friendships and a wide social circle that sustained her for the rest of her life. By her mid-forties, she was sending more than one thousand Christmas cards each year.

Aileen resigned from the union after eleven years, in 1961, newly divorced and unsure of her next step. She completed a part-time master's program in government at California State University, Los Angeles. Then she worked on a statewide political campaign and served as assistant director of the California State Division of Fair Employment Practices. The agency was pressuring national leaders to pass a comprehensive workplace equality law, which finally happened with the Civil Rights Act of 1964. Even in that job fighting to make California workplaces more fair, Aileen had to advocate for herself. While her two male predecessors were automatically paid the top rate permitted for the position, "the state of California couldn't conceive of a woman getting the maximum pay." Only after she complained did officials raise her pay to match what men had earned in the job.

During her decade at the union, Aileen had been active in Democratic politics in the state and "had met a lot of people." But she was still surprised to be appointed to the Equal Employment Opportunity Commission. That federal agency, created to police Title VII of the Civil Rights Act, had not yet opened its doors. Aileen wanted to stay in San Francisco, but decided "it would be absolutely unthinkable for me not to take this opportunity, in a field in which I have a lifetime interest, to have a greater impact than simply on the state level." She packed up and moved back east. Her salary of $26,000, or nearly $213,000 today, made her the highest-paid Black woman in the government, and she was not yet forty. A dozen news outlets covered her 1965 appointment. Reporters described her as an "attractive and smartly dressed" woman who walked with a "queenly stride" and spoke with the "measured, careful tones of a politician." She was "tall, arrow-postured, terribly assured, terribly fluent, a cool and brisk black woman who is never at a loss for an easy answer."

Despite the salary and the prestige, Aileen's appointment to the EEOC proved troubling even before it started. The other four commissioners were men, three of them white, and she was bombarded with veiled accusations that hers was a token appointment. Aileen tired of fielding the question of how she had been selected, a question reporters never asked the guys. Finally she began to claim that she had been "appointed by a computer." She would explain that she was the last commissioner selected, and the White House did a computerized search for all of the characteristics the four others were missing: a Black woman with a Latino last name and labor movement experience from the West Coast. "So, they punched that in, and the bells went off and the whistles blew, and out came my card," and they said, "how can we not select her." Reporters "loved the story," she remembered. "They thought it was true." She faced varied forms of casual sexism. A photographer once called out to her at the White House: "Don't wear that kind of hat"—a straw hat, floppy and pink—"it's pretty, but we can't see your face."

These initial slights aside, Aileen felt hope that she could shape the EEOC from the ground up. She and the other commissioners, nominated in April and confirmed in June, were barely in place before the commission opened on July 2. With scarce staff to support them, they set to work interpreting the new workplace equality law, Title VII. Commissioners were tasked with reviewing and investigating complaints of workplace discrimination, then attempting conciliation and referring potential violators to the Department of Justice for possible punishment.

The commission was working hard to get up and running on behalf of American workers, as Aileen wrote in the NAACP's official publication five months into her tenure. "If you are in Washington at night in the neighborhood of 1800 'G' Street, N.W.," she invited readers to "look up at the 12th floor," where "the lights still burn" at the EEOC. She described its thorough process of investigating workers' claims through the story of an archetypical but fictional male "laborer" named "John Johnson," whose employer relegated him and other "Negro workers" to "dingy" and "overcrowded" facilities and denied them promotions while offering white workers "all the employment goodies." "In the vast majority of the cases" that the EEOC sought to settle, including "open and shut" cases like Johnson's, Aileen wrote, its "skilled conciliators work out agreements to the satisfaction of all parties."

As she trumpeted the EEOC as an ally for workers facing race discrimination, Aileen sought to carve out her own role at the commission. She wanted the agency to take sexism seriously, but she did not want to be treated like its token woman. "I would be pleased to let my personal experience be a guide" in cases of sex discrimination, she told a reporter, but the other commissioners should receive their share of those cases, too. As the commission began its work, she noticed that not only did the other commissioners seem to downplay allegations of gender discrimination (with the exception of her ally, Richard Graham); they and some of the staffers "aided and abetted" the employers the commission was tasked with investigating. Even favorable coverage of the EEOC in the Black press misconstrued Aileen's role. *Jet*'s March 1966 cover story featured an image of Franklin Delano Roosevelt Jr. seated and smiling up at Aileen, his fellow commissioner. "FDR, Jr. Fights Job Bias," the caption declared: "Late president's son checks with his aide in anti-bias crusade."

The EEOC was generally overwhelmed in its first few years, but its struggles to interpret Title VII's sex provision were especially obvious. The commission received many complaints from flight attendants, a job mostly limited to women, who were systematically fired when they gained weight, married, or turned thirty-two. Aileen told the other commissioners that there was "no valid reason to discriminate against men, women who were older, women who were married, women who were not beauty queens." Her comrade on the commission, Richard Graham, agreed. But the other three countered that choosing to employ only young, thin, and single women as flight attendants seemed like an acceptable business practice for the airlines. The men similarly defended sex-segregated job advertisements in newspapers as a convenience for readers; they "felt that a 'little' sex discrimination was O.K.," she said later.

Aileen's coworkers contributed to the problem. The one hundred staffers at EEOC headquarters in the fall of 1965 generally "were there to fight discrimination against African Americans" and "didn't want the Commission's limited staff and resources diverted," noticed the attorney Sonia Pressman Fuentes. Luther Holcomb, a white Baptist minister from Dallas, was the most "conservative" commissioner and a confidant of Lyndon Johnson's. Holcomb openly opposed strong enforcement of the sex provision, and he and Johnson back channeled about developments at the EEOC as they bonded over their shared Texas roots. Roosevelt "had no real interest in the Commission" at all, Fuentes observed. Instead, he was focused on following in his father's footsteps as governor of New York. Because he left in May 1966 to run for that office, "he wasn't there long enough for his views on women's rights, whatever they were, to matter." The commissioner Samuel Jackson was an attorney and former president of the Topeka NAACP. As "the most political person" on the commission, Jackson "would not hold firm" on gender issues with Graham and Hernandez. Aileen realized that the three men who constituted a majority "were dealing with the race issues that they were familiar with," while women's claims were "going down the drain." Their dismissal was "totally frustrating."

Aileen started to wonder whether it was time to move on. Commission meetings were "a sea of male faces nearly all of which reflected attitudes that ranged from boredom to virulent hostility whenever the issue of sex discrimination was raised." Aileen was also concerned that the agency lacked "any real teeth" because it did not have the legal authority to enforce its findings or recommendations. She began to suspect that she might be "more useful as an activist *outside* of government who could help the 'good people' *inside* the bureaucracy to enforce the law."

———

Like Aileen's, Mary Jean Collins's head-spinning college years set her on a quest to find her purpose. The sisters at Alverno had opened her eyes to a world of possibilities, but Mary Jean soon learned that coming of age as a woman in the early 1960s brought constraints regardless of one's talents. "If you wanted to be a professional, just an ordinary worker with a professional job, there was no path to that," she recalled later. Still, she had to find work to support herself. She decided to try teaching, mostly because it seemed like her best option as a woman. "I didn't really feel a calling," she said. It showed. After one year teaching history and geography to 175 students each day at a local Catholic junior high school, Mary Jean lost her job and its puny $3,000 salary (just over $25,000 today).

With teaching ruled out, Mary Jean's options for work seemed even more limited. She went to a job placement office that had separate doors for men and women. "I went through the 'men' door," she recalled, "and they were horrified, asking, 'What are you doing here?'" Mary Jean returned to Taylor Electric, the RCA affiliate where she had briefly worked before college. The job of parts buyer was "a little better" than teaching, she said, but "I was a secretary, basically." At least the pay was more ample. Mary Jean had discovered that public school teachers in the city earned twice her Catholic school salary, so she knew that there were some working women in Milwaukee earning much more than she was. She decided to negotiate her starting salary. "I went in there, and I said, 'I want $6,000,' and they gave it to me."

Mary Jean's job was deadening, but she found meaning in her city's civil rights movement. As in Detroit, Milwaukee's racial tensions were worsening, and middle-class whites increasingly fled the city for its suburbs. Their exodus created an "iron ring" of eighteen predominantly white communities encircling the city. Worse-off whites could not afford to move to the suburbs, and when businesses also fled, they further eroded the city's tax base at the same moment when city leaders needed resources to aid a lower-income population. Working-class whites reacted to their declining job prospects and property values with more assertive racism. Through their tight-knit ethnic communities, they enforced rigid racial segregation.

The young white priest Father James Groppi became a leader of the resistance. The second youngest of twelve children of Italian immigrants, he worked alongside his siblings in the family-owned grocery store. Groppi felt bigotry firsthand when his local Irish parish tried to push out Italian families. An Italian priest had to hold a separate Mass in the neighborhood shoemaker's shop. Groppi attended St. Francis Seminary, the same order as the Alverno College sisters. From his parish on the white south side of Milwaukee, Groppi became increasingly outspoken about racism in the city. He traveled to gain a personal view of the civil rights movement, attending the 1963 March on Washington and the march at Selma—which he called "a conversion experience"—and brought the tactics of civil disobedience back home. Groppi began advising Milwaukee's NAACP youth council, which protested housing and educational segregation.

Throughout 1967, Groppi and other civil rights activists, most of whom were Black, held nightly marches in an open housing campaign throughout white working-class Milwaukee neighborhoods. They met heavy and sometimes violent resistance from whites as they walked in dense formation, their arms linked. This open housing campaign included two hundred consecutive nights of marching. Police wearing helmets and carrying riot sticks hovered nearby. An estimated thirteen thousand belligerent whites confronted the five thousand protesters on the busiest nights, which included activists from more than a dozen states. A local newspaperman described the conflict as "the ugliest display of mass hatred that has ever been witnessed in our city."

Among the nightly marchers was Mary Jean, who had been primed by her activist Catholic teachers at Alverno. "I never went to the South, but I was reading about" the movement there, she said. "When it came to my town I had to be involved." She went to St. Boniface Church every night to talk, rally, and march, first around the Black neighborhood surrounding the church and then in white ethnic neighborhoods. Her father supported civil rights, but when letters from the NAACP started arriving at their house, he feared for his daughter's safety. "It was terrifying," Mary Jean recalled. Other whites "were mean and hollering, screaming and throwing things at us."

Mary Jean was forever changed by facing down white spectators throwing rocks and debris and police in riot gear dispensing tear gas at the peaceful marchers. She saw whites waving Confederate flags and holding signs that read, WHITE POWER, BRING BACK SLAVERY, and WORK DON'T MARCH. Projectiles flew: "bottles, eggs, rocks, wood, firecrackers," along with spit and urine. "I saw what systematic oppression was," she said, and she began to understand how "lack of education, or lack of opportunity, or lack of money"—"all the things that went into reinforcing race discrimination"—"were also there for sex discrimination."

Mary Jean was coming of age in other ways as well. Her sense of connection with other women deepened, even as she still saw marriage to a man as a rite of adulthood. She took in her best friend from Alverno, Mary-Ann Lupa, who was hiding her pregnancy from her conservative parents in suburban Chicago. Mary Jean helped Lupa through her delivery, and the women found a family to adopt the baby. Soon after, Mary Jean met Jim Robson, a Harrisburg, Pennsylvania, native who was enrolled at the Milwaukee School of Engineering, at one of the nightly marches. They married in June 1968 and moved to Chicago, where Robson had a job waiting. Mary Jean left her bounded hometown for the bigger city, where hard-nosed men gripped the levers of power.

VISIONS OF EQUALITY

By the late 1960s, Patricia, Aileen, and Mary Jean needed to resolve different tensions in their lives and work. Patricia was among the millions of women captivated by Betty Friedan's *The Feminine Mystique.* The bestseller prompted Patricia's circle of friends to begin talking about how dissatisfied they felt with their own lives. The book seemed to speak directly to women like them: educated and talented, but frustrated by living vicariously through their families. To Patricia, her psychologist's admonishment to "forget my aspirations to be an artist" and instead "devote myself, heart and soul to my husband and children" seemed to match Friedan's definition of "the problem that has no name." Reading Friedan's words convinced Patricia that the world was deeply unfair in ways she had never fully appreciated. Now she and her husband, Harry, both had careers, but he still treated her "like a child" and left the household responsibilities entirely to her. The more she reflected on her life, she later wrote, "I became mad at myself for *not* having been angry for so many years."

After reading a newspaper story about NOW in 1969, Patricia organized the group's first meeting in her state, then set out to find its president, Betty Friedan. She found the author's address and went to New York. "I knocked on the door of her townhouse, and someone answered and called upstairs." She said, "Betty, you won't believe this. Here's this woman down here in a chinchilla hat and muff, who says she's a lifelong Republican." The author, who was then locked in a battle with radical feminists for the New York City chapter, sought to preserve NOW as a haven for respectable suburbanites. Hearing this description of Patricia, Friedan "charged down the stairs," grabbed her, and "yanked" her inside.

By then, Aileen already knew Friedan and all about NOW. The author had interviewed the federal official and a few others at the EEOC for her new book. Aileen explained that "very little was happening on the sex discrimination cases because very few women were protesting any abuse decisions." Because they were so short-staffed, "it was very much the squeaky wheel [that] got the grease." Aileen had also attended the 1966 State Commissions on the Status of Women meeting when NOW was proposed. "The women who came to that conference came from every part of the United States," she observed. "It was amazing." She kept a low profile there, unlike her fellow commissioners Richard Graham, a panelist in Clarenbach's "Creating Positive Attitudes" session, and Luther Holcomb, who was listed in the program as an "official observer," but she was intrigued by the dissidents' impolite protest at the closing luncheon.

Aileen watched for the next few months as NOW took root. "I'm basically an organizer," she realized, and it was increasingly clear to her that people outside the government, especially women, needed to organize to make sure Title VII was better enforced. Pauli Murray lobbied her to join the new group, arguing that NOW could do that organizing and apply targeted pressure. Aileen left her post at the EEOC eighteen months into a five-year term and moved to San Francisco in late 1966. Inspired by this new chance to organize and protest alongside Murray, she joined NOW and reinvented her career for a third time.

When Mary Jean arrived in Chicago in 1968, she and her husband put their progressive politics to work. They moved to the racially mixed South Side neighborhood of Hyde Park, which was surrounded by largely

Black communities. There, Mary Jean said, they "tried to really live out our principles, in terms of what we believed should happen in the late sixties—the interracial nature of society that should come, and [the belief that] we should help it come." As a symbol of their equal partnership, they both took the surname Collins-Robson for the short duration of their marriage. "His parents thought it was whacky, as did everybody in my family," she said, but "it meant something to us." Mary Jean found mundane work that paid the bills. Catherine Conroy, who had moved to the city on a short-term assignment for her union, set up a Chicago chapter of NOW and pulled Mary Jean in.

As members of NOW, Patricia, Aileen, and Mary Jean would soon be working arm in arm. Like many women in the late 1960s, they believed that an organized feminism could allow them to pursue gender equality as they each understood it. Newly energized and determined to collaborate, they rolled up their sleeves to start building.

3.

WOMEN ARE GOING TO HAVE TO ORGANIZE

Aileen Hernandez was in a bind. She had asked the women who were planning NOW's inaugural conference in late October 1966 to leave her out of it. "Don't do anything about putting me anywhere in this operation," she told them. A sitting federal official like her should not hold any formal role in the nation's vanguard feminist organization. But Hernandez had the visibility NOW's founders wanted for the new group's leadership, as well as experience in government and the labor movement: the group's two largest constituencies. In her absence, NOW's first meeting disregarded her wishes and elected her the organization's second-in-command.

This "charitable, but unauthorized gesture" to draft Hernandez into NOW's leadership "sounded very impressive," she said, but it caused a major headache. They named Hernandez executive vice president on their letterhead and announced her position "pending my agreement." Eager to claim her prestige but too "penniless" to pay for two printings, they exposed her and her employer, the EEOC, to charges of bias from the industries NOW targeted. Hernandez recalled that NOW's leaders unwittingly "made my life miserable for quite a period of time" by forcing her to spend December 1966 "in depositions" with airline industry attorneys seeking to discredit her vote that flight attendants' restrictive treatment violated Title VII.

Hernandez was already planning to leave her government post, but she had wanted to make a gradual return to activism. NOW's leaders kept pushing her. She moved to San Francisco, where employers also sought her out as an expert in antidiscrimination law. They invited her to lunch again and again. "I decided I had enough background and information that I might as well charge them for it," she said, and she opened up shop as an "industrial consultant." Hernandez finally agreed to help create a few NOW chapters in California, and the other leaders changed her title to vice president–West.

Hernandez found that her initial reservations about NOW were confirmed. "There was no money and there was no staff," she said. These problems also plagued the office she had just quit, but at least the EEOC had the legitimacy and funding of a federal agency. Those seeking to woo Hernandez to NOW also saw these challenges. "All we had was this little one sentence statement of purpose and the title" of NOW, "nothing more than that," said the group's interim leader, the Wisconsin political scientist Kay Clarenbach. She and the other founders set out to establish the group through disciplined advocacy by notable people. "We're not building a mass organization," Pauli Murray had emphasized in her recruitment pitch, "but trying to get key women around the country who can move quickly."

But the founders' efforts to control NOW's scope proved difficult as the nation's mood turned against authority and decorum in the late 1960s. With rising impatience, Americans were confronting President Johnson for escalating the Vietnam War. The interracial civil rights movement, which emphasized strategic nonviolent protest, gave way to the more assertive politics of Black Power. A defiant women's liberation movement began to surge around and through NOW. These more extreme social currents made NOW's approach seem moderate by comparison. Though the press initially covered NOW as a curiosity, reporters began to frame it instead as the main vehicle for women's rights and to acknowledge women's rights as the nation's next step in the march to perfect its democracy. NOW faced no initial resistance beyond entrenched male supremacy, and as members discovered, with just a few of them they could make the patriarchy quake.

Hernandez revisited her initial skepticism as NOW expanded. "It was much harder to organize in the West than it was in New York," she said, even as she started several California chapters. Along with newcomers like Mary Jean Collins and Patricia Hill Burnett, she came to share the belief that, as Betty Friedan put it, "women are going to have to organize." But Burnett and Collins were not among the luminaries Friedan personally invited. Instead, they heard about the new group on their own, sent in their dues, and set up local chapters. These women built NOW in their own ways, pursuing their notions of feminism from within their communities.

Hernandez became convinced that NOW was a tool she could use to weld feminism to other social justice campaigns. She accepted the national presidency in 1970. Her efforts and those of hundreds of unsung members would eclipse the founders' vision and culminate, in August 1970, in a day of mass protest nationwide—the largest demonstration for women's rights that America had ever seen.

————

When NOW was founded in Washington, D.C., in June 1966, Burnett was squeezing her painting time around her domestic commitments in Detroit, hemmed in by her husband's patriarchal power. Collins was working a dead-end job in Milwaukee, butting up against sexist corporate power. And Hernandez was growing frustrated at the EEOC in her quest to make government power work for women. None of these three was a NOW founder. Most of the twenty-eight women who had signed up as such left the capital that weekend, turning their attention elsewhere. While the founders believed in the new group dedicated to women's equality, they also had demanding careers in business, government, journalism, education, and the labor movement. Just a few of them spent the late summer and early fall setting the new group into motion.

The tensions that had flared at the conference of women's commissions where NOW was first proposed continued to smolder. Although Betty Friedan acknowledged that she was "a loner," not "an organization woman," she still wanted a starring role. Perhaps they should give the celebrity author what she wanted, the D.C.-based attorney Mary Eastwood wrote to Pauli Murray as they and a few other founders debated their next steps later that summer. "If she says NOW is advocating something, it will get the necessary publicity. If you say it, it might get good publicity, but if anyone else does, it would carry no more weight than an announcement of any ordinary women's club."

As Friedan sought center stage, Kay Clarenbach, who had been named NOW's temporary chairman at the June 1966 conference, started to identify issues and frame bylaws to give the new group some shape. She also oversaw its essential clerical work in her office at the University of Wisconsin. Clarenbach appointed six women to a temporary steering committee, including Betty Talkington and Dorothy Haener—union women from Iowa and Michigan. Haener's office at the United Auto Workers in Detroit handled "much of the printing and phone calling." While the committee also included Murray and the former Howard University history professor Caroline Ware, its makeup fueled the fears of those from the East Coast that Clarenbach would shape NOW as a Midwest-centered group focused on the moderate agendas of the state women's commissions.

Friedan convinced a few East Coast allies that Clarenbach was pulling NOW away from the nation's real centers of influence. That "paranoid" bunch included Eastwood. Her "reading" of the midwesterners' position was "fait accompli—we've taken this over." They wanted to hold their first conference in the East to prevent union women from defending the gendered protective labor laws most others in NOW wanted to overturn. That position reflected the fact that their unions officially backed the provisions, but these female unionists also believed that equality understood as interchangeability with men would not benefit working-class women. The freedom to cross over into factory and office jobs previously reserved for men offered little to the women who stayed behind in female-dominated pink-collar jobs. Workplace rights laws, if narrowly interpreted, would not help them.

Clarenbach felt the tension. She believed Friedan saw her as a "slow-witted Midwesterner" or even a spy because of her productive relationships with government officials. But she in turn worried that the abrasive author would repel potential allies. Nonetheless, Clarenbach agreed that NOW needed publicity and an activist stance, and Friedan's notoriety would free her to work behind the scenes. The two decided that Clarenbach would run for board chair at NOW's upcoming first meeting, which would happen in Washington that October, and Friedan would pursue the presidency. Over time, they learned to work together, although Clarenbach's family would continue to screen Friedan's calls when she lacked the energy to deal with her.

These leaders set out to establish NOW as an "elite cadre" of prominent figures in the fields of education, labor, government, and business. Friedan traveled the country as NOW's evangelist and sent scores of letters that described the group as "a kind of NAACP for women, a Civil Rights for Women organization." NOW would not be "a big bureaucratic organization with lots of members," she wrote, but rather a select group that could work efficiently rather than "wast[ing] time arguing the nature of woman and other abstract questions." They set their sights on the best-known figures they could find, even asking the U.S. representative Martha Griffiths, a Michigan Democrat, to take an office. She declined.

The founders believed that a national feminist organization needed ideological unity and geographic diversity. A phalanx of like-minded elites from around the country would be an effective political force to embody their message. Early documents noted members' home states, and the steering committee extended the deadline for charter membership to try to boost representation from the South and the West. By September 1966, NOW had $650 in its treasury and 120 paid members from Illinois, Indiana, Michigan, Minnesota, and Wisconsin; 22 from New York and the Washington, D.C., area; and 10 from everywhere else.

NOW's organizing conference took place on October 29 and 30, 1966, in the "community room" inside the Washington Post Building. This was the gathering that elected Hernandez to the vice presidency in her absence. Those thirty people included labor organizers, activists, civil servants, and other professionals. "It was a relative handful of people," Collins said, who were "educated, accomplished," and "mad as hell."

While the group left most questions open, the gathered members adopted a statement of purpose that integrated clear-eyed criticism of women's treatment with arguments for how it should change. With an urgency that surpassed the report of the President's Commission on the Status of Women from three years earlier, NOW's statement vowed to move women into the "mainstream of American society now . . . in truly equal partnership with men." It also rejected "the token appointment of a few women to high-level positions" as a substitute for "a serious continuing effort" to free women to advance "according to their individual abilities." Women's limited workforce prospects and pressures for full-time domesticity were problems for society, not each woman alone, to solve—through a national child-care system, for example. Murray had revised Friedan's first draft to de-emphasize equal legal rights and highlight the links between women's problems and "many broader questions of social justice."

The group did not take a position on the Equal Rights Amendment, a newly revived feminist issue, as a compromise with the labor women whose unions feared the federal amendment would wipe out gendered state protections. Friedan proposed asserting their support for birth control and abortion rights, but the others voted these down as too controversial. The $5 annual membership dues ($40 today) might be too low to keep the organization running, they agreed, but they made no decisions about finances. They planned to set up a modest headquarters in Washington.

There was little controversy about who would lead them. All five of the candidates for national offices ran unopposed—including Hernandez, listed on the ballot against her wishes. The new board included professors, union leaders, government officials, business executives, members of religious orders, and a doctor, and they shifted NOW's balance east. To hold the vice presidency for Hernandez, Murray proposed, and the others agreed, that the Black activist and National Council of Churches leader Anna Arnold Hedgeman would assume the position on a temporary basis. This plan was not watertight. When the board of directors met one month later, they noted with concern that Hernandez had still not accepted the vice presidency, paid membership dues, or even applied to join the organization.

Murray herself did not pursue an office. In fact, she had just accepted a job at the EEOC, and she worried about the same conflict of interest that had concerned Hernandez. Regardless, NOW's white founders also hesitated to elevate her to a top role. They had debated asking Friedan to be president and Murray to be chairwoman. The NOW founder and public relations executive Muriel Fox recalled her contribution to the debate. She said to Friedan, "Well, you, this liberal from New York, and Pauli, as a Negro, the establishment might not be terribly moved by that." She backed the plan to have Clarenbach chair the board instead, pointing to the professor's prestige and her midwestern location. It does not seem to have occurred to Fox or the others to place one of their most brilliant strategists at the helm or to ensure that their leadership reflected the nation's racial diversity.

Departing the conference, the members pursued the government action and press that would bring attention and clout. Stepping back her efforts, Murray continued to shape the organization behind the scenes. She wrote to a White House contact to protest President Johnson's refusal to meet with their delegation and hear their demands. NOW would not endure condescending tea parties with Johnson in exchange for access to his Rose Garden, as they had before seceding from the conference of women's commissions several months earlier. Their new group would hold his administration's feet to the fire. "The male White House staff seriously underestimates the potential power of the new civil rights action organization," Murray warned.

Meanwhile, Fox organized a press conference in Friedan's Manhattan apartment to broadcast that potential power. As NOW's publicist, Fox contacted editors beforehand, penning the invitation on her corporate letterhead to convey the group's importance. "Through the years I've used a lot of adjectives to describe press conferences, but this is the first time I'd presume to use the word 'historic,'" she wrote. At the event, Friedan commanded the room in her "gravelly alto," noted a reporter, at one point "punching the air as if it were something palpable." The press was not sure how to frame this bold new group. *The New York Times* recapped the meeting beneath three "untraditional" recipes for Thanksgiving stuffing. This was not the placement NOW's leaders had in mind. "The one thing we want most," Fox told reporters as they left another NOW press conference, "is that people will take us seriously."

Government officials were beginning to take them seriously. In November 1966, NOW wrote to President Johnson, the acting attorney general, Ramsey Clark, and three EEOC commissioners requesting interviews to discuss how to "bring women into full participation in the mainstream of American society *now*." Within two weeks, Friedan met with top EEOC officials and pointed out that the attorney general's office had not taken up a single sex discrimination case. A NOW delegation also met with the Civil Service Commission chairman, John W. Macy, and acting attorney general Clark to echo that concern and frame others. "We are off to a pretty good start," Murray wrote, recapping the first few months. "But we shall have all of the problems of mothers of a lusty infant."

———

Mary Jean Collins discovered the new group's combustible energy the following year. Then twenty-seven years old, she attended NOW's second national conference, which took place at the Mayflower Hotel in Washington, D.C., in November 1967. NOW membership had grown to twelve hundred, a fourfold expansion in one year. Aileen Hernandez, who was reelected vice president–West at the gathering, this time with her consent, was there despite having to shoulder the high price of travel. NOW could not have reimbursed her for a round-trip cross-country fare, which cost about $230 in 1959 ($2,163 today); the organization had just $1,062 in the bank. Catherine Conroy's union covered her NOW travel expenses, and she paid for Collins's ticket from Milwaukee to the capital. All of it impressed Collins. "I had never been in a room with women like that," she said. These "fancy people" on all sides made "amazing argument[s]" in "a pure discussion of, who are we and what are we for?" It was a master class in how to frame an organization.

Collins looked on, "fascinated by the process," as the 105 members present adopted a Bill of Rights for Women that NOW could use to hold political candidates accountable. The group easily adopted six of the eight proposed planks, especially those related to workplace rights. They called for paid maternity leave and mothers' ability to return to their jobs, supported by child-care facilities "established by law on the same basis as parks, libraries and public schools." Women also needed adequate job training, housing, and welfare programs that protected recipients' "dignity, privacy and self-respect," echoing the broader conversation on economic empowerment for the poor of Johnson's War on Poverty. The National Welfare Rights Organization (NWRO), established the previous year, had highlighted single mothers' struggles to earn enough in low-wage jobs to support their children and protect enough of their time to care for them.

NOW's leaders knew that the issue of reproductive rights would spark controversy. Just before the meeting, Friedan asked the attorney Marguerite Rawalt for a quick primer on *Robert's Rules of Order*. Rawalt marveled that Friedan thought she could master the complex system in a few minutes. Instead, the attorney sat beside the author and "kept her in line as much as she could," a friend recalled. Friedan supported abortion rights, and at the time the procedure was illegal or highly regulated in all fifty states. Women suffering from botched abortions, often procedures they had self-administered, were a common presence in hospital emergency departments. Even in states where abortion was sometimes legal, women had to navigate doctors' prerogatives and parental and spousal consent requirements. A coalition of reformers including medical workers, lawyers, social workers, and liberal Jews and Protestants was challenging the state limits. Their efforts had gained steam two years earlier, when the U.S. Supreme Court struck down an 1879 Connecticut law that banned contraception's use or prescription in the 1965 case *Griswold v. Connecticut*.

Abortion rights advocates framed a range of claims that swayed public opinion their way in the late 1960s: the importance of doctors' authority, the depth of women's suffering, and the logic of economic rationales for smaller families. But NOW's 1967 meeting was debating whether to defend abortion rights as "the fundamental human right . . . to one's own physical person." Some members who were present, like Collins, had religion-based concerns about the issue. As a Catholic, she was "sweating and wondering, what am I doing here?" she said. But she found the abortion rights presenter convincing. Friedan made clear her support for a reproductive rights resolution, grimacing on the podium as opponents spoke. In a vote of 54–14, with 37 present members refraining from the vote, the group endorsed sex education, freely available birth control, and the repeal of every law that penalized abortion. A contingent of Ohio members, including the national membership coordinator, left in protest.

The Equal Rights Amendment caused even more friction, but not for the reason that Friedan had anticipated. The author almost refused to consider the ERA at all because she viewed the measure as "old hat" and "so boring," said a friend. Indeed, constitutional equality had been a goal of some feminists since the 1920s, and when attorneys in NOW insisted, Friedan endorsed adding it to the Bill of Rights. Prior to the conference, the group's committee on women's constitutional rights—a committee Murray had been tapped to lead but that she declined due to her EEOC job—debated several proposals, including "Human Rights Amendments" that would have linked gender equality with civil rights and reproductive freedom. Working against them were veterans of the early twentieth-century suffrage struggle, including the National Woman's Party leader and ERA author Alice Paul, then eighty-two years old, who had spent months pushing for the amendment's original language. NOW kept it.

Murray opposed NOW's endorsement of the ERA in any form. Instead, she argued that feminists should advocate for courts to extend the due process and equal protection clauses of the Fourteenth Amendment to gender equality, as they had recently done for racial equality. This would make the ERA unnecessary. It would also grant more flexible legal protections. In the world of work, for example, Murray's Fourteenth Amendment strategy stood to end destructive forms of discrimination such as women's exclusion from traditionally male occupations while preserving sex-specific provisions "designed to protect the maternal and family functions through compensatory measures," she explained. The ERA was blunt, whereas Murray's strategy was subtle and adaptable and promised to "unite civil rights and feminism under one constitutional banner." Murray was also concerned about the energy and focus an amendment ratification campaign would take: the Fourteenth Amendment was already in place.

Murray was also especially attentive to poverty as a women's issue. She believed that NOW's mention of welfare rights in its new Bill of Rights was necessary but not sufficient. The recently issued Moynihan Report, a study of "the Negro family" written by an assistant U.S. secretary of labor, portrayed Black single mothers as contributing to, rather than suffering from, the economic problems in their communities. This appeared to validate male civil rights leaders' and government officials' emphasis on boosting Black men without regard to Black women. Hedgeman and Murray brought this concern to NOW, but they found the leaders more interested in pursuing legal equality than their proposed broader human rights framework.

These smoldering disagreements caused tensions to flare at the 1967 conference, where the issue of legal equality divided the group. The ERA's addition to the Bill of Rights placed the labor women among them in a bind because their own unions opposed it. UAW women went to the conference "in force" to request a yearlong delay on the vote so that they could keep "working on" union leaders, who were "almost ready to approve." ERA advocates threatened to leave if the vote was tabled. Murray highlighted the union women's dilemma in declaring that backing the ERA would "alienate organizations who have given us support until now." She suggested postponing the vote for seven months to give members time to consider all possible legal strategies. The civil rights attorney Phineas Indritz pointed out that the ERA was unlikely to succeed in the current Congress, so Murray's court-based strategy was more pragmatic.

But the women held different views of pragmatism. As the attorney Mary Eastwood wrote to Murray, "I do not see how a civil rights for women organization such as we hoped NOW would be can be effective if it must compromise with protective labor forces." The voting body skewed heavily toward ERA enthusiasts, among them "a row of suffragists . . . in hats and white gloves." When the conference voted to endorse the ERA by 82–3, with 12 abstentions, the UAW women left in protest. Collins, who "had no idea why they were fighting about it," gaped at the scene. "They voted [the] ERA up and labor walked out. They voted abortion up and Ohio walked out. I wondered if there would be anybody left by the time we got done." Her mentor Conroy just shook her head. The veteran unionist taught Collins that to build and protect an organization, "you have to keep your eye on the ball; you have to keep moving."

Murray had intended to keep moving ahead with NOW. Her stint at the EEOC had ended after eight months, and she had agreed to join NOW's national board. This conference changed her mind. The majority wanted to emphasize women's commonalities as they understood them, an approach that weakened the ties to the civil rights and labor movements that Murray sought to strengthen. She meant for her strategy of comparing women's oppression to that of people of color to center Black women, but instead white feminists viewed racism and sexism as parallel yet distinct problems. Murray wrote to Clarenbach that the pro-ERA contingent had steamrolled "members who had other loyalties, other identifications, and were trying desperately not to be fragmented or torn apart." Murray withdrew from NOW. She would return as an active member of the Boston chapter three years later, but white leaders' early failures to balance focus and openness caused undeniable damage.

———

Her mentor had left, but Hernandez saw glimmers of potential in NOW and stayed on as a vice president. "I've always been distressed by the separation of the closely related movements for the abolition of slavery and the rights of women," a split she traced to the nineteenth century but that was "beginning to heal—NOW," she said. She adopted Murray's message that Black women needed to fight for gender equality with the same energy they applied to racial justice if they were to gain what she called "the real freedom that will allow all of us to use our full capacities to bring about a truly pluralistic society."

Over the next few months, Hernandez and the other officers sought to build NOW through improvisation and high-profile victories. They persuaded the EEOC to hold public hearings on sex-segregated help-wanted ads and convinced President Johnson to add a sex provision to Executive Order 11246, his 1965 ban on discrimination by employers holding government contracts and the federal government itself. NOW also publicly supported flight attendants, demanding that airlines stop treating them like sex objects and firing them for appearance-related reasons. At a national board meeting in New York City, someone mentioned that United Airlines was running flights from New York to Chicago that were explicitly reserved for male passengers. The members decided to send a letter of protest to the airline and the Federal Aviation Administration and to sue if needed. Someone else pointed out that the Biltmore, the midtown hotel where they were meeting, had a Men's Bar that banned women. The group voted to go there and demand service. "Can't serve you ladies," insisted the man behind the "virtually empty" bar. When the women returned that afternoon "en masse" for a sit-in, the door was padlocked.

By early 1968, NOW had real momentum. New chapters were sprouting up weekly all over the country, and Friedan played a key role. As she traveled the country to promote *The Feminine Mystique*, she seeded NOW chapters at her destinations. NOW's tiny national office in Washington, D.C., which consisted of one ten-by-fourteen-foot former hotel room that members filled with donated furniture, struggled to keep up. Staffed by volunteers and vacant during business hours, the office received dozens of diverse inquiries each week: from prospective members, government officials, businesses, and students. The D.C. chapter president resigned that fall, citing overwork. The officers also set up a mimeo machine in Friedan's apartment to assist with document duplication. It was "an excellent machine," Friedan admitted, but she objected to its resting permanently in her dining room, the space blanketed with "innumerable sheets of paper."

Hernandez knew they had to get better organized and lay the right foundation. The leadership "suffer[ed] from a great deal of duplication and a fuzziness about who has responsibility for what," she wrote to the national board. Membership applications went unprocessed; letters of interest were not answered. Some who wanted to join NOW simply forged ahead on their own. In several instances, two chapters took root in the same city, unaware of each other. Financial problems fed these administrative struggles. The $5 annual dues rate "hardly covered anything," Clarenbach noted. But rather than raise the dues, which might alienate working-class women, they set out to "finance our own 'revolution,'" as Hernandez wrote, by recruiting more members. But she also told the others that not just any members would do. "If we are not to become simply another group of professional women operating in a middle-class,

Anglo-Saxon, almost 100% white atmosphere, we need to find ways of getting more varied in our membership ranks," she wrote to Friedan and Clarenbach.

In order to raise the funds the group needed, NOW had to not only expand its ranks but remind current members to renew their dues, which entailed sending mail, printing newsletters, and making long-distance telephone calls. Only one-third of NOW's members had paid their annual dues in early 1968, when the organization was one membership mailing away from bankruptcy. The leaders debated fundraising by selling jewelry, holiday cards, and bumper stickers and asking well-heeled members to solicit their friends. They even urged members to withhold their income taxes and donate that sum to NOW until the ERA was passed, for why should women bear the full burdens of citizenship without enjoying equal rights? The lack of funds compounded the chaos. "I don't know how many members we have," Friedan told NOW's 1968 convention. "It is no secret how bad our national housekeeping is." The yoked problems of scant resources and loose governance at the top would only worsen.

———

As the national leaders struggled with administration, local members forged ahead without asking permission. Mary Jean Collins had discovered NOW when she was still in Milwaukee. When her former history professor, Sister Joel Read, returned from the 1967 national conference, she formed a Milwaukee chapter and became its president. Collins was the treasurer, and she was honored that her mentors, including Catherine Conroy, trusted her to play that role. "I was a kid and they were grownups," she said.

Collins and the other Milwaukeeans attacked sexism in the everyday places where women experienced it. One of their earliest actions marked Collins's first open challenge to her religion. A local Catholic church had expelled a woman for attending Mass without a hat; men faced no similar requirement to cover their heads. "It turned out she wasn't even a Catholic, so it was particularly un-ecumenical for them to have done that," Collins said. A group of them bought "big, ugly" hats at the Salvation Army and went to church on Easter Sunday. They arrived early so they could sit up front, and at Communion time the women rose and placed their hats on the rail in protest. "No, not there, on your head," she recalled the priest admonishing them, "as though we were completely stupid."

Collins moved to Chicago with her new husband in 1968. She was hired as a re-buyer at Allied Electronics Company, stocking and purchasing parts. The secretarial skills she had honed in Milwaukee got her in the door, and when the manager let Collins try her hand at buying, she became the company's first woman in that role. She had also kept up her Milwaukee feminist connections, especially to Conroy. Collins was there when Conroy hosted Chicago NOW's organizing meeting. Conroy made sure to host that founding meeting after work in the downtown Loop, helping to cement the chapter's emphasis on workplace issues—a focus that Collins shared.

Collins's new hometown Chicago was an epicenter of dramatic political shifts that reflected the nation's unrest. The Vietnam War and the antiwar movements were both heating up. Collins arrived in Chicago just in time to attend the leftist protests at the Democratic National Convention (DNC) in August 1968, when police teargassed, beat, and arrested throngs of protesters in the name of keeping order. This bloody showdown and the Democrats' nomination of the moderate Hubert Humphrey for president dismayed social justice activists: there was now no chance for an antiwar president to be elected that November.

Leftists' frustration stressed fractures between militants and moderates, Blacks and whites, and women and men. New Left women criticized movement men for being unwilling to see their own sexism, which appeared to parallel the Johnson administration's refusal to acknowledge its wrongdoing in Vietnam. Separating from their male counterparts, some women began applying New Left critiques to their own sex in what they called a women's liberation movement. These self-proclaimed radical feminists demanded personal and societal transformations to end male supremacy in every setting.

Although radical feminist groups were forming in Chicago when Collins arrived, she believed that her Milwaukee connections "probably made it inevitable that I would end up in NOW." Radical feminists drew sharp contrasts with NOW, which they framed as too moderate, even outdated in its goals and methods, but that was not how Collins saw the difference. "NOW was more pragmatist" and radical in a different way, she asserted. "I was a radical feminist by my definition." That meant creating "structural change" that valued all forms of labor and granted social rights to everyone.

To Collins, connecting women across their differences was more important than sharpening their critiques of society and writing manifestos, which preoccupied many on the left. "All of us come out of some political bag," she told a group of women in 1970. "If we're going to unify, we're going to have to leave some of our politics at the door. If we insist on a particular political or economic system—particularly a heavy rap economic revolution—our movement's going to lose." To sustain an organized feminism, she claimed, women had to take practical actions that made noticeable change and forged solidarity. Radical feminists began their movement with intimate discussions: consciousness-raising sessions where women bonded and developed new language and political awareness. Collins had no interest in sitting around talking or fielding reporters' inquiries about what she called "the underwear question": whether feminists burned bras, or wanted to. She feared that too much debate would stoke divisions among women that would slow their movement before it could change anything.

Collins believed that NOW, with its open-ended agenda and emphasis on action, could be the vehicle for a mass movement of women. She explained the group's premise in 1970, as she saw it. "Society has chosen to consider women as a group. Women are petty; women are emotional; women are bad drivers. We're classified as a group and we must work as a group to solve the problems that face us as a group." She cited the problems of unequal pay and retirement benefits, scarce maternity leave and unequal access to abortion. New laws could help, but the first step was women's collective action: "the will for us to demand an end to inequality."

This kind of collective action required a new group consciousness; Collins believed that working women could find it in their jobs. "They say women can't work well together," she told the *Chicago Tribune* in 1969. "But if anyone is condemned to an inferior position as a file clerk or typist and knows there is no place to rise, there's going to be frustration, and it's going to be taken out on others. Women may not even be conscious of this." Organizing together could channel that frustration against their employers.

Despite their mutual critiques, NOW benefited from the radicals' emergence, which renewed feminism as a multifaceted movement and drew a new rush of media attention. At many newspapers, young, college-educated women reporters who had faced discrimination themselves were eager to cover the movement. Radicals' eye-catching demonstrations and shocking demands brought new attention to NOW and shifted the tone of its coverage. Outflanked on the left, NOW and its concerns looked more reasonable. An overview of the movement in the *Chicago Tribune* described "women's lib" groups as "hav[ing] intruded upon the American consciousness like a rude guest at an already uncomfortable party"; NOW was "working quietly" but effectively by comparison. "The women who burn bras in protest represent a novelty fringe," scoffed the *Hartford Courant*. "But others are deadly serious," with NOW the most prominent.

Together, NOW and the radicals were challenging the cultural misogyny that had once treated women's rights as a joke. That sexist opposition was fledgling and disoriented. Papers printed the occasional letter from a woman who sneered at feminism, such as Mrs. Clayton C. Moore, who wrote to the *Chicago Tribune* that she had no time for NOW because she was too busy driving the Cadillac her husband had bought her, spending the cash he earned, and picnicking while he worked. A few male columnists expressed concerns about men's place in this new social landscape. "If the old dragon-slayer came clanking out in his armor" and tried "to rescue any of today's fair females," one protested, "he would only wind up making an ass of himself." Indeed, feminists mocked a proposed 1969 Massachusetts law that sought to require housewives to do laundry and cook for their husbands. "So the nuclear age has produced a medieval man?" one retorted. A NOW official was more serious when she suggested that if the bill passed, lawmakers should next mandate wives be paid for their "24-hour-a-day job. How would he like to have to pay her $3, $4, or $5 an hour?" (That would be the equivalent of $23, $31, or $39 today.)

NOW was not quite a twenty-four-hour-a-day job for Collins, but it took up most of her time when she became Chicago chapter president in 1968. The chapter had about a hundred members, most of them white working women—especially teachers, secretaries, and other clericals from working-class and lower-middle-class families who understood workplace discrimination. They shared Collins's belief "that economic issues for women are at the core of whether or not women have a say in all other aspects in their lives."

As chapter president, Collins took up the work of building the membership. "I was a kid with a college degree; I was not a superwoman," Collins said. But she saw her middling status as an asset. "To do the day-to-day work, you need people who don't have the kind of jobs" the founders had: full-time careers in government, business, and the labor movement. Collins, by contrast, had time and energy to spare. By the summer of 1969, the chapter had established a weekly picket of the *Chicago Tribune* over its sex-segregated job ads, a speakers' bureau, and a monthly newsletter, and its members had appointed a finance chairman to assist chapter and national fundraising efforts. In early 1970, they hosted a workplace rights conference featuring Congresswoman Shirley Chisholm. "We had 150 people at the conference even though we didn't have 150 members," Collins reported. A few months later, Chicago hosted NOW's national conference. National leaders helped, but the chapter did the legwork.

Although the Chicago chapter focused especially on women's common workplace problems, members could pursue any goal they chose. Some organized sit-ins at Loop restaurants, including Berghoff's, ending its seventy-one-year tradition of banning women from the bar. To a reporter with the industry publication *Hospitality World*, Collins pointed out that most men-only establishments still permitted female servers. "It's kind of like being seen but not heard, and we resent it." Other chapter members printed stickers that said, "This insults women." "We would slap them on everything—on offensive magazines, on offensive store windows," Collins said. On billboards around the city, a dairy industry advertising campaign pictured "big-breasted women" with the caption, "Everybody needs milk." Chapter members "went out with our spray cans . . . in the middle of the night" to deface them.

To Collins, being in NOW in the late 1960s was "like waking up from a dead sleep, like 'this is wrong. That's wrong; and everything is wrong.' And away we went."

———

Unlike Collins and the members of the Chicago chapter, who took a bare-knuckle and bottom-up approach to building NOW, Patricia Hill Burnett veered away from her city's budding feminist scene in founding the Michigan chapter. Reasoning carefully from her own experiences, Burnett began by emphasizing NOW's elite appeal rather than its democratic potential. But as her eyes opened, her perspective shifted.

Burnett and Marj Levin, her freelance writer friend, started the Michigan chapter in 1969 by writing to every woman lawyer, judge, doctor, and organizational leader they could think of, acquaintances and strangers alike. The point was to gather "all the power that resided in women within forty miles." Many in the group, including Burnett, did not have full-time careers, but they were married to prosperous men or held prominent volunteer positions. Levin considered this "a wide variety of women." She and Burnett invited this choice group to a weekday luncheon at the Scarab Club, the artists' community where Burnett had her studio. At Burnett's advice, they wore skirt suits or dresses because pantsuits might mark them as extremist.

As this "chic" gathering began, the women sipped wine and listened to Burnett's pitch to form a Michigan chapter. She introduced NOW as a moderate force for respectable women. "We're trying to reach the great, silent majority of women who are shy, timid, afraid to speak out," she said, echoing how the new president, Richard Nixon, a Republican, described the white middle class. "We have nothing against those women who are fulfilled by a home and children. It's just the ones who are unhappy we're trying to help." She assured them that signing up was safe. "We don't want to change our own social status," Burnett said. "We like being feminine." She promised that NOW would take pains not to appear threatening in order to protect members from their husbands' and friends' disapproval.

Burnett might have overestimated her guests' conservatism. The room was visibly moved when abortion advocates spoke. Some attendees were already involved in a movement to legalize the procedure in Michigan, where an 1846 law banned abortion except to save the mother's life and a 1931 statute enhanced the penalties faced by providers. As Burnett learned, abortion rights increasingly appealed to women's advocates across identities and perspectives. The sexual revolution was in full swing. Birth control pills that first became available in 1960 gave weight to the notion that sex need not always lead to pregnancy. In this light, many viewed the state's interference as prudish and outdated. Radical feminists had joined NOW's 1967 call for reproductive rights, declaring women's absolute right to bodily autonomy. When, in 1973, the U.S. Supreme Court asserted the constitutional right to abortion in *Roe v. Wade*, seventeen states had already legalized abortion.

Burnett's pitch won over the lunching ladies; they "passed the feathered hat," and nearly everyone joined NOW on the spot. She collected $120 and decided to give the money to Friedan in person. Her trip to New York alone cost more than this, but she wanted to go "partly for the symbolism of the Michigan chapter using its first dues to affirm solidarity with the national group—and maybe even more, because I sort of idolized Betty as my feminist guru." This was the occasion on which Burnett arrived, overdressed, at Friedan's doorstep. "So how was I to know that your average feminist didn't show up at NOW meetings in a chinchilla hat and muff?" she asked.

Inside, Burnett discovered that the author's apartment was crammed with cameras and lights, reporters and photographers. As it happened, Friedan was about to host a TV news conference with Beulah Sanders, a Black leader of the National Welfare Rights Organization, and a white nineteen-year-old from the radical feminist Redstockings, "in a ragged t-shirt and jeans, defiantly nursing her baby," Burnett observed. "You're going to fill this group out perfectly," Friedan told her. She made sure Burnett "*said* she was a Republican and had been 'Miss Michigan,' in front of the press," Friedan wrote later, because "the 'bra-burning' innuendoes had begun to build." The reporter's first question was, "Do you mean to say you dames have anything in common?" And Burnett was surprised when each of them answered in the affirmative. Friedan left a lasting impression on her. "The moment that press conference ended, I was ready to follow her anywhere," Burnett said.

As Burnett intended, the Michigan chapter started out as a slice of the Detroit area's prominent women. Burnett was its first president, and she continued to describe NOW around town as "the most conservative of the feminist movements," a journalist recounted. "No bra burning or radical action for them."

One of their first protests hewed closely to Burnett's own concerns. Her husband belonged to the Detroit Athletic Club, where the city's elite men rubbed elbows. Insulted by the club's "nasty little rule" that women could not enter the front door, she organized a protest. The women stepped out of their comfort zone when they gathered on the club's front steps. Burnett thought, "'You know, my husband is just going to have a complete total nervous breakdown over this. It might cost me my marriage.' Then I thought, 'well, what the hell!' and went on in." They marched, singing, into "this sacrosanct area with all their fine paintings, where women have hardly ever set foot, except unless you were a cleaning woman," Burnett said. Once inside the club, a group of her woman friends called out to her, confused and upset to see her in this group interrupting the tranquil atmosphere. The protest was front-page news, and the club changed its policy.

For another of the chapter's first acts, this one suggested by national leaders, members protested the conference of Roman Catholic bishops in the city. Burnett and seven other chapter members, a few of whom were Catholic, "stealthily sewed squares of torn-up white sheets on our dresses, front and back." They had written slogans on the squares: "The Catholic Church is unfair to women! Why are there no women bishops? Christ's mother was a woman!" They placed their coats over their "propaganda outfits," Burnett recalled, "and donned frivolous little hats and thoroughly respectable white gloves, before happily trotting into the hotel." Riding the elevator, one of the bishops asked them why they were "unescorted by men so late at night." Ignoring him, they crashed the conference, choosing a dramatic moment to remove their coats in unison.

Reflecting another of Burnett's budding interests, the Michigan chapter worked on the ERA and electoral politics. Both major parties had included the amendment in their official platforms for decades, so the issue was legitimately bipartisan. Michigan NOW convened an ERA committee to inform the public about its benefits and sent out a questionnaire on the amendment and other issues to all of the candidates running for office in the area. The chapter also interviewed political candidates from both parties, then worked to defeat those they deemed "too chauvinistic." As part of this effort, Burnett hosted an annual picnic for NOW members, inviting mostly Republican candidates for local, state, and national office. Unanimously reelected president in 1970, Burnett began traveling around the state to set up new chapters.

Burnett's efforts to position NOW against the radicals did not last long. Through Levin's media connections, the chapter attracted "great press." More women found their way to the group, including radicals from the robust Michigan Women's Liberation Coalition, which had been convening meetings of several hundred women at the downtown YWCA. Within the next few years, both Detroit NOW and the Women's Liberation Coalition could boast a thousand members apiece, with many drawn from the suburbs. The Detroit Feminist Women's Health Center, created by Valerie Angers, Joanne Parrent, and Cathy Courtney, feminist health activists in the city, opened in 1973 in a working-class neighborhood. It offered a range of sexual health services and educational workshops. Some of its founders also started the nation's first feminist federal credit union, and the two shared a building. Feminism caught on all over the city.

As the boundaries separating feminists in the city weakened, new NOW members were younger and less elite, and they included some women of color. These newcomers broadened the group's agenda and Burnett's own horizons when they started holding consciousness-raising sessions. "We'd go one by one," Burnett said, "and a woman would start telling what had happened to her lately that really upset her." For Burnett, the sessions were "a kind of free therapy" and "the equivalent of several college educations." They taught her "to relate to women on all levels—and they learned to relate to me, too, for I was very open with them about my problems." These conversations changed her life. "After hearing and seeing women come in with bruises all over their bodies and faces from being battered," Burnett said, she saw women's vulnerability and her own relative comfort in a new light.

These women exposed Burnett to a side of the city that segregation, poor public transit, and her own wealth had shielded her from. Detroit was increasingly polarized as Black nationalists and other leftists vied to transform the city's power structures and white conservatives attempted to shore up their authority. Their liberal counterparts pursued an optimistic vision of integration and mutual prosperity. But liberal hopes had been dimmed when the city burned in July 1967. The rebellion started at an evening celebration to honor a Black veteran's homecoming from Vietnam. When police began arresting the revelers, eventually capturing eighty-two people, two hundred others threw objects at police cars and started fires. The mayor and governor summoned ninety-two hundred members of the national guard and eight hundred state troopers. Although Detroit's was just one of 164 rebellions in 128 American cities that year, it hit especially hard. Jobs had been declining there since the 1950s, but the retail and manufacturing economy shrank by half in the wake of the unrest in 1967. Amid these challenges, many Detroiters felt the urgent need to shape their city's future.

With Burnett's blessing, Detroit NOW dove into the city's political tinderbox. The chapter grew and shifted, working side by side with radical feminists. Members held press conferences in the morgue to protest abortion-related deaths. They lobbied lawmakers to legalize abortion in the state and nearly won in 1970, missing by one vote. Burnett's awareness of the city's problems grew through her involvement in activism, and she expressed it in her own way. As chapter president, she helped organize a march in Lansing, the state capital, for abortion law reform. "We need to keep the pressure on—not with violence—but with constant letters, telegrams, polls, and verbalizing," she wrote to members, and "make it our personal NOW duty to get acquainted with our particular legislators."

The Detroiters also made their chapter a repository of information on child-care centers. They connected families with providers and helped to set up new centers. As of 1971, the Detroit chapter had committees on child care, employment, abortion, voter education, and more. The chapter held dozens of monthly meetings. NOW was the second largest of twenty feminist groups in Detroit, after Women's Liberation, whose members were generally younger. The chapter worked with them and joined "every major women's coalition in the state."

Like Collins, Burnett felt that feminism had woken her up. Everything looked different, if not always better. She met many kinds of women through NOW, but she believed that the wealthy wives who found feminism, like her, faced unique challenges. "It's easier to revolt when you are young, not so much to lose, not so brain washed. Your revolt appeals to your peers instead of frightening them," she journaled. Her new outlook transformed her social life. Her friends hated her "radical new ideas," which unsettled them. "If you are resentful, tortured, infuriated at the same set-up they are supposedly enjoying—you are telling them that they have wasted their lives." Dinner parties were insufferable, with their "uptight insulted men lying in wait to flaunt the latest anti-feminist cartoon or article in your face" and ready to sneer: "'You women never had it better.'"

Burnett's family, like her social circle, resisted her efforts to change her role within it. Harry could not relate to a wife who had had "the veil of intimidation, prejudice, carefully woven lies about mental and physical capabilities stripped from her eyes." On sex, she journaled, "It's almost impossible now to *fake it* like we used to." Suddenly she felt "like a whore fluttering around a man, twinkling + becoming, adoring + gushing when it's not sex but a new coat I really want." Her children, too, rejected her new self-assertion. She described their attitude: "*They* want to revolt not deal with one." Other relatives simply thought she was "cracking up" because she was "sick of being the family chauffeur, errand girl + whipping boy."

Still, Burnett could not fully reject elite white notions of femininity. She still believed that conventional beauty and domesticity were a woman's ultimate currency. "Being attractive is a marvelous weapon," she said. She saw the problems with how women like her were "brought up thinking they should wear lots of makeup, not be too bright, be charming, sparkle and all that stupid stuff. I discarded it for awhile. I tried wearing jeans." But she did not feel like herself without her fashionable clothes and the full complement of makeup. "The best thing I've painted is my face so I've gone back to that," she said. In spiral-bound notebooks, interspersed with her notes about NOW meetings were the extensive shopping lists and seating arrangements for her parties. Preoccupied with her own awakening, Burnett does not seem to have been concerned by the plight of the woman cooks and cleaners who helped her to host these affairs. "Can a liberated *housemaid* keep a really clean house?" she wrote. "The answer is NO."

Indeed, Burnett continued to interpret feminism in terms that accommodated her class position and the conservative aspects of her outlook. "Being a feminist is to believe that women should have completely equal rights to men in all fronts: home, socially and in business and politics," she said. Burnett believed that women had to "get inside and infiltrate the power structure." The structure she chose was the Republican Party, which to her stood for individual rights and personal freedom. She was a founding member, in 1972, of the Michigan Republican Women's Task Force. "I truly believe in the Republican concept that there should be less government, less bureaucracy, and less interference of the government in our lives and fewer taxes," she said. Neither political party in 1970 had endorsed an explicit women's agenda, so both were potential vehicles for women's rights, and Burnett believed NOW had to be bipartisan if it was going to live up to its promise to represent all women.

Burnett's Detroit chapter grew in a different direction from Collins's in Chicago, but she was equally devoted to her vision for the movement. Feminism taught Burnett that she was "a person rather than just a woman," she said. "I found my true identity. I found that I had a spine of iron, that nobody could crush."

———

As the chapters hit their stride, NOW had problems at the top. The issues were not just financial. Betty Friedan believed she had done a great job as the group's first leader. "I could have probably continued to be elected president of NOW forever," she reflected. "I wasn't very good at administrative stuff," but "you hire people to be administrators." In fact, the other officers, including Hernandez, wanted her out. Beyond her disorganization, Friedan had an "overpowering ego" and a short temper. "She was a screamer" and "verbally abusive," even of volunteers, said Dolores

Alexander, a New York chapter member who shouldered most of NOW's administrative work, working closely with Friedan. The other leaders began to "subtly accustom her to the idea that the Presidency of NOW may not be a life-time post." Friedan stepped down, likely because she needed more time to earn money after her 1969 divorce and she knew her credibility with NOW's members was waning.

Hernandez was "recruited" to run, unopposed, for the presidency in 1970. "I had been there from the beginning and Betty generally tended not to be hostile to me," Hernandez recalled, so the other officers "felt that this would be a transition that [Friedan] would accept." Hernandez was Friedan's opposite in many ways: organized, composed, and with deep personal experience and good relationships in the labor and civil rights movements and government. The L.A. NOW leader Toni Carabillo called Hernandez "the living example of what charisma can do for an organization—in that it turned so many people on, and the membership went up." "To watch her conduct a national NOW board meeting," claimed an L.A. NOW newsletter, "is to observe a brilliant woman at work."

Reporters could not help but contrast Hernandez with radical feminists, often favorably. They noted Hernandez's soft voice, subtle makeup, and conservative dress. She was quick to joke, retorting to the accusation that NOW wanted to destroy marriage, "Is it a howling success the way it is?" and the suspicion that the group hated men, "On the contrary, women want to enjoy sex too." Her demeanor gave her cover to lay out a sweeping agenda: transforming politics, the law, the labor force, universities, families, and popular culture to advance women's "checker" in "the big game—the real revolution, the Human Revolution" to end inequality in America.

To bring NOW up to this task, Hernandez sought to streamline procedures to accommodate growth. First she had to deal with the afterlife of Friedan's presidency. Several crises loomed. Friedan wanted NOW to put women on an equal footing with men, and she especially focused on relatively elite women who were shut out of male-dominated spaces. Early in her presidency, she had asked the Manhattan advertising executive Muriel Fox to start the New York chapter, its first. Fox selected a ritzy Upper East Side mansion, just off Fifth Avenue, for its inaugural meeting in April 1967. The three score attendees walked down a long hallway with marble floors and walls to a drawing room with rows of chairs. The gathered women included the law professor and future U.S. Supreme Court justice Ruth Bader Ginsburg and the historian Gerda Lerner. One by one, each stood up, introduced herself, and expressed her hopes for the new organization. It was "extraordinary," said one of them, to hear the stories about workplace and marital problems "just pouring out of people."

This meeting foreshadowed the tensions that would emerge in the New York chapter. Also in attendance was Florynce "Flo" Kennedy, a radical activist and one of the few Black woman lawyers practicing in the city. Kennedy saw strong connections among movements against sexism, racism, and imperialism. Fox and Friedan were incredulous when Kennedy suggested that NOW oppose the Vietnam War and back Black Power, the movement for Black self-determination, cultural freedom, and economic justice that had expanded since the southern civil rights movement peaked in the mid-1960s. By contrast, Fox and Friedan believed that the new group should first serve the interests of moderate professionals. Fox had her own recent experience in mind. She had tried to take clients to lunch at the Plaza Hotel's Oak Room. Her secretary had made reservations for the group, but they were turned away because the restaurant did not allow women at midday. Fox was mortified. She and the New York chapter soon occupied the Oak Room at lunch to protest its policy. "If you have a fur coat, wear it," she instructed. Fox was unusual. "Most of us didn't have mink coats," one member recalled.

New York became NOW's official epicenter in late 1968, when the national board moved its headquarters there. The chapter already comprised more than half of NOW's national membership, and Friedan, as president, expected to influence the city's outpost. At first, neither the professionals nor the radicals controlled the chapter. A reporter noted the heterogeneity at a regular chapter meeting in 1968. The members of the group, who were mostly women with jobs, ranged from their early twenties to middle age. "Their dress varied from the maxiest of minis to printed jersey with white pearl buttons." As the chapter grew and diversified, Ti-Grace Atkinson, a twenty-nine-year-old Columbia University graduate student from a wealthy Louisiana family, became its president in 1968. Friedan also named her to the national board, charmed by Atkinson's accent and hopeful that her connections might bring in new resources.

But Atkinson chafed against NOW's procedures and sought to radicalize its politics. A 1968 *New York Times* article identified her as president of New York NOW and quoted her comparing marriage to slavery. NOW's established leaders sought to reform marriage into "a fully equal partnership of the sexes," as written in the statement of purpose, not abolish the institution. A few months later, Barnard College's president, Martha Peterson, wrote to Kay Clarenbach to describe Atkinson's role in campus protests. Atkinson was part of a militant student left, buttressed by the antiwar movement, that was increasingly revolutionary in its approach. Clarenbach responded that she was "of course disturbed" by Atkinson's use of "far-in tactics in the name of NOW." In a "very, very painful" chapter meeting, Atkinson expressed her pride in the newspaper coverage she had drawn to NOW, but more moderate members countered that she had to "represent the group" as their leader. "We didn't want the newspaper printing that we support somebody who'd go and shoot somebody down."

This mention of shooting referred to the radical feminist Valerie Solanas, who had wounded the artist Andy Warhol in June 1968. Atkinson urged NOW to champion her case, and Flo Kennedy defended her in court wearing a "Freedom for Women" button. Friedan fretted that advocacy of violence against men could threaten NOW's very existence, especially in light of the recent assassinations of Martin Luther King Jr. and Robert Kennedy. Friedan called Mary Eastwood at the Justice Department to complain. "We've got to get rid of Ti-Grace," she said, in a tone that sounded to Eastwood like, "get the Mafia to rub her out or something." At the September 1968 board meeting in Louisville, the board agreed that the New York radicals posed a dire threat. Friedan began to retake power in the chapter, lecturing on NOW's founding principles and especially "the causes and dangers of the man-hating trap."

Hernandez took no position on the skirmishes in New York. But she was among the national leaders who objected when Atkinson sought to change the chapter's bylaws, proposing that presidents should be randomly selected and rotate often as "an experiment in participatory democracy." National officers responded that chapters had to use the standard bylaws, in part to preserve the group's tax-exempt status. The plan also posed practical challenges. "Imagine every member who joins NOW wanting to be president," said the chapter member Barbara Love. "Some people just couldn't handle it."

Atkinson's ideas often seemed so implausible that more moderate members feared "being, if not destroyed, completely discredited as a viable organization." At chapter meetings, "people would end up lying on the floor," Muriel Fox said. "Not only from sleepiness but from total stress." Frustrated in their efforts to transform the chapter, Kennedy and Atkinson left in November 1968 after less than two years. Atkinson formed the October 17th Movement, named after the date of their departure. She introduced the group as an "action coalition" of the student, Black Power, and feminist movements with "no officers and no structure." Plagued by internal turmoil, Atkinson's new group, which renamed itself The Feminists, lasted fewer than five years; she herself departed after two.

Hernandez was elected national NOW president just as a second crisis was threatening to destroy the New York chapter. This one was even more squarely of Friedan's making. The author believed that sexuality was a private matter. She viewed lesbian rights, which a budding lesbian feminism was increasingly demanding both through and apart from radical feminism, as an issue that would repel the kind of "everywoman" she knew growing up in Peoria, Illinois. Friedan also saw sexuality as a diversion from NOW's real business. "The name of the game is confrontation and action," Friedan explained her philosophy, "and equal employment is the gut issue."

A few open lesbians had been in the New York chapter since its inception, recalled the member Sidney Abbott, "on the liberal grounds that all women were accepted and that what one does in bed is one's own business." But most passed as straight and worked on other feminist causes within NOW. Over time, women in the chapter began to discuss the details of their personal lives through consciousness-raising meetings that mirrored Burnett and the Detroiters'. Some lesbians invented male partners, but most came out. "It was bad enough to have to hide from colleagues in the office, but to hide from other women in the movement was too much," Abbott and Love later wrote. They and some others were patient with the straight women in the chapter who had never met an open lesbian. "I thought, frankly, it was more courageous for them to struggle than it was for me," Abbott said. Straight women had "an economically comfortable alternative" in male partners and "a possible place to get regard and some approval from within a nuclear family." To Abbott, by contrast, feminism was a "struggle to save my life . . . I felt that I could not *not* do it."

As straight members came to know their lesbian sisters, they all debated the chapter's approach to matters of sexuality and identity. Some lesbians believed that the organization was too fragile to advocate on their behalf outright. Abbott, who had been educated at Smith College and Columbia University, felt comfortable in the group right away because her background resembled many NOW leaders'. She was reluctant to bring matters of sexuality to the forefront out of fear that she would be misunderstood as a "terrible radical" concerned with only one issue. But even relatively conservative lesbians like Abbott came to see the situation as untenable. While she was from the same "white glove background" as women like Fox and Friedan, she could not abide their polite scorn.

For her part, Friedan grew increasingly concerned that the presence of open lesbians, and what she viewed as their rejection of femininity, would undermine the movement. Friedan believed that NOW should combat the sexualization of women that shaped mid-century American culture and de-emphasize sex by hewing to narrow notions of respectability. Legal equality and economic independence would give women the leverage to change their private lives, Friedan argued. She accused the younger radicals of admonishing other women "to *make yourself ugly*, to stop shaving under your arms, to stop wearing makeup or pretty dresses—any skirts at all." Her paranoia about conformity was rooted in her own past. As a young adult, Friedan had been a "home-grown radical," according to her biographer Daniel Horowitz, in the antifascist movements of the 1930s. Later, amid the rigid expectations and suspicion of the McCarthy era, when federal officials persecuted political radicals as well as gays and lesbians, she took pains to conceal her years as a left-wing labor journalist.

One dramatic example of Friedan's efforts to steer NOW in her preferred direction occurred at the Second Congress to Unite Women, a gathering of women's organizations in New York City in May 1970. National NOW had proposed the periodic gatherings as a way to build coalitions with like-minded groups. Friedan especially believed the conferences should reach out to young women "who need a little more experience to understand the gut issues of this revolution involve employment and education and new social institutions, and not sexual fantasy." Friedan had prevented the Daughters of Bilitis (DOB), the nation's first social and advocacy group for lesbians, from being listed as a sponsor of the first congress; no open lesbians were listed on the program for the second gathering. The three-day conference included more than five hundred women from many organizations, and Friedan found that she could not control its agenda. On the first night, a handful of women from Female Liberation in Boston took center stage, and one woman cut another woman's hair to demonstrate her liberation from traditional beauty standards. The audience cheered; Friedan recoiled.

To the lesbian members of New York NOW, excluding open lesbians from the program was unacceptable. Rita Mae Brown, then an assistant in the NOW national office, and other lesbian feminists—many of whom were NOW members—decided to "kidnap the Congress." They bought forty T-shirts, stenciled them with "Lavender Menace"—Friedan's own slur against lesbians in the movement—and dyed them purple in a bathtub. On the first night of the conference, they slipped into the junior high auditorium where the conference was taking place, hiding their shirts and protest signs to blend in with the three-hundred-person audience. The New York chapter member Barbara Love was "sitting about in the middle with some NOW friends. My heart was pounding like crazy."

Just before the program was set to start, someone cut the lights and microphone. The protesters rushed down the aisles, fists raised, with some making rebel yells, and posted signs reading, WOMEN'S LIBERATION IS A LESBIAN PLOT, TAKE A LESBIAN TO LUNCH, and YOU'RE GOING TO LOVE THE LAVENDER MENACE. When they restored the lights, seventeen of them stood smiling onstage. Brown stepped up to the microphone and asked, "Does anyone want to join us?" As planned, Karla Jay, embedded in the audience, responded, "Yes, yes, sisters! I'm tired of being in the closet because of the women's movement." She started an exaggerated strip-tease, unbuttoning her blouse to uncover her Lavender Menace T-shirt. The others laughed and cheered her on as she went to the front of the auditorium.

Brown took center stage and started her own undressing routine, re-moving her Lavender Menace shirt to show a second one underneath. The audience roared with laughter; the whole room appeared to be on their side. Brown took a more serious tone. "This conference won't proceed until we talk about lesbians in the women's movement," she said. One by one, the protesters came forward, denounced Friedan, and testified to how antigay bias reinforced the gender roles that all feminists opposed.

The protest pushed matters of sexuality onto the conference agenda, as intended. The women in lavender asked lesbians and their allies in the audience to rise and move to the front of the auditorium, and at least thirty more women came forward. Even some of those straight women who welcomed lesbian participation recognized some of the protesters and were surprised to learn that women they knew were lesbians. The next day, spontaneous workshops on lesbian feminism were packed to over-flowing. That evening, some of the lesbians invited the straight women to a women-only dance. "After the refreshments were set up, there was an awful moment when the women thought no one would come. But then the women began to arrive, and the turnout was good," Abbott and Love remembered. "Nobody seemed overly concerned about who was gay and who straight." Unsurprisingly, Friedan left with a different impression. The Congresses to Unite Women "didn't really jell," she wrote, recapping the situation. "The radicals seemed to take over. Their tactics invited sabotage."

After the conference, lesbians and their specific concerns were more prominent in the New York chapter. Just weeks later, the burgeoning movement for gay and lesbian rights would enter the national conversation when a protracted confrontation erupted between police and a militant crowd of protestors that included lesbians, gay men, trans women, and drag queens at and around the Stonewall Inn bar in Greenwich Village. Ivy Bottini, a suburban housewife and mother of four, had been elected New York NOW president after the radicals Atkinson and Kennedy quit the group. Friedan might have been relieved, but Bottini came out as lesbian in 1970, still chapter president. "The first time I met her, she was in a little dress, a little Long Island . . . working woman," Collins said of Bottini. "She looked sort of middle aged and . . . housewifey," and "then she was in combat boots the next year."

Bottini and three New York NOW officers spoke at a Daughters of Bilitis meeting in November 1970. The NOW chapter president asked members of the lesbian rights group to join NOW "to work on our shared problems together and to get to know one another." Soon thereafter she and the chapter scheduled a panel discussion on the question "Is Lesbianism a Feminist Issue?" One speaker asked the women in the audience to stand if they had ever felt "erotic or strong emotional feelings toward another woman." Around two-thirds did so.

This was too much for Friedan and her crew. One such ally, the New York chapter officer Jacqui Ceballos, wrote to national leaders that NOW should sidestep matters of sexuality and "stick to our original goals." Friedan worked actively to ensure that Bottini was voted out of the leadership in 1971, and her comrades resigned in solidarity. "I happen to like Friedan, as much as she caused me pain," Bottini said later. "She was just too conservative." Bottini moved to L.A. and built the NOW chapter there.

Hernandez, as national president, attempted to settle the matter by forging a compromise. At a press conference in New York City in December 1970, she claimed that NOW had no formal position on lesbianism. "We do not prescribe a sexual preference test for applicants. We ask only that those who join do commit themselves to work for full equality for women." She blamed "frightened, unethical individuals in the media" for attempting to derail the women's movement by overemphasizing matters of sexuality, but she also asserted that NOW welcomed lesbian members. "Let us—involved in a movement which has the greatest potential for humanizing our total society—spend no more time with this sexual McCarthyism. We need to free all our sisters from the shackles of a society which insists on viewing us in terms of sex."

———

Hernandez also faced a third challenge as NOW's president. This one Friedan handed her directly at the March 1970 meeting where she stepped down from the presidency. Rather than gently give the reins over to Hernandez, she used the moment of her resignation to set up yet another burden for her successor to manage. She committed NOW to its most ambitious program ever.

Not long before, Friedan had learned that suffragists had planned a general strike of women toward the end of their campaign for the Nineteenth Amendment in the 1910s. They never held it, but Friedan, noting that the amendment's fiftieth anniversary was near, announced that NOW would host a national strike on August 26, 1970, to address "the unfinished business of women's equality." Mirroring her foiled plans for the Congresses to Unite Women, Friedan hoped that such protests would refocus media attention onto her priorities—away from "bra-burning actions," "radical rhetoric," and sexuality and toward feminism's "real goals": workplace rights, child-care centers, and free abortion available to all.

Hernandez was seated next to Friedan, prepared to settle in for the long-winded author's swan song. Instead, she heard Friedan pledge that NOW would hold a national day of action that Hernandez would have to carry out. As she was gripped by "a sinking feeling," her mouth fell open. "It was going to be very difficult for us to put any such thing together," Hernandez knew, because "our strength was less than the strength of millions." She also knew it was "kind of typical of Betty to have great ideas and leave the small details of instrumentation to others." The others would have to do much more than attend to details. Mary Jean Collins, seated in the audience, had a similar reaction. "We were all a little horrified. I mean we did have fewer than a hundred people in our chapter. I thought, 'how are we supposed to do this?'" Everyone returned to their chapters to figure it out.

Their first step was to try to walk back Friedan's promises, which she offered in sweeping terms to a national press that lapped up exciting news in a slow summer. Others in NOW reframed the national day of protest as an occasion for women to "do their own thing," even at work. "Wear a button to the office," Collins said. "Talk to other women about the working conditions you share and the changes that need to be made in pay, promotion and child care!" Hernandez echoed the theme of openness. Women might "refrain from all shopping in a visible rejection of our primary role as the nation's consumer." Wives could debate their husbands; students could sit out classes or raise issues of discrimination; secretaries could "stop typing" or slip away on a lunch break to attend a local rally.

Still, would anyone come? Friedan, freed from any accountability, was delighted when *The New York Times* covered her idea "not on the women's page, but on the news page." Still, even she had her doubts. "Every once in awhile I'd wake up in the middle of the night and think what if only three women came?" Members worked hard on publicity. In Chicago, they plastered posters all over town: "Women Strike for Women," "Worry Your Pretty Head—Strike August 26," and "Don't Iron While the Strike Is Hot." The chapter rented an answering service for the month so that women who saw the posters could call for more information about how to participate. Friedan's fears and the members' muscle reflected a basic fact about NOW's first four years. While the national organization remained disorganized, local networks were taking off. The leadership, preoccupied and under-resourced, had not kept up.

When the strike day arrived, it succeeded beyond any of their plans. There were demonstrations in forty cities, from Miami to Boston, Kansas City to San Francisco, where Hernandez addressed a noontime rally in Union Square. Women also picketed several U.S. embassies abroad. The New Orleans *States-Item* printed engagement announcements with photos of soon-to-be grooms rather than brides. Feminists in Rochester smashed teacups on the steps of Susan B. Anthony's former home. At college radio stations in Michigan, woman DJs bantered and chose the records while men attended to the office tasks. In Syracuse, feminists held a "guerilla theater in front of the charm school" downtown and read a "cute little script" to the businessmen who passed them. Nationwide, each of the three major television networks, whose serious and holistic coverage of the movement peaked that year, sent reporters to multiple cities to cover the demonstrations.

The protests far surpassed NOW's membership and priorities as activists of all stripes made their presence known. In Washington, D.C., the twelve hundred members of Federally Employed Women staged a noontime rally in Lafayette Park. They focused on combating job discrimination and on Senate approval of the ERA, which had recently passed in the House of Representatives. Secretaries in the Pentagon's Information Office held a smaller protest, throwing bras, girdles, lacy underpants, and a rolling pin into a trash can. Another one thousand protesters marched to Farragut Square, where speakers castigated sex discrimination and demanded an end to the Vietnam War and greater freedom for Black women. The Washington Teachers' Union leader Jean Wharton called on feminists to resist the "racist, capitalist system that oppresses all blacks, all women and all workers." Another one hundred picketed at the Women's Detention Center on North Capitol Street, demanding the release of "all women prisoners." Throngs of men also gathered at each of these sites. Some applauded or jeered, but most simply listened.

In Chicago, the chapter's extensive publicity campaign paid off. The chapter held two "informative and entertaining" rallies in prominent downtown sites designed to "allow us to communicate with the largest possible audience of sisters," Collins explained. The speakers came from the four main feminist groups in the city—the socialist-feminist Chicago Women's Liberation Union, the Equal Rights Alliance, Federally Employed Women, and NOW—and a labor leader and an open lesbian also addressed the masses.

The Chicagoans put their commitments right to work. As the first rally wound down, a woman emerged from the crowd of five thousand. She explained that she had just lost her job for bringing her child to work that day, encouraged by that morning's *Chicago Tribune*. ("One day of kids running around the office should be enough to motivate business" to subsidize day-care centers, the columnist asserted.) "We were exhausted by then," Collins said. "It was like 2 o'clock, and the program was finally over. We just wanted to go and have a beer." A lawyer stepped forward and offered to help. Soon, several thousand of the protesters were moving toward the nearby financial district, which held the city's tallest buildings. The crowd "trotted" down the street, their sound reverberating against the skyscrapers. They asked for a meeting with an official from the meat company that had fired the mother who was at the protest. "Of course they were totally freaked out," Collins said. "They took her back in a minute." Nationwide, the protests revealed women's strength to power brokers of all kinds—and to themselves.

———

In New York, Betty Friedan had risen early, eager to see how her grand idea would unfold that day. She called into a radio station. New Yorkers should "come in from the suburbs," she said. "Bring your children in. Come in from New Jersey. Take the subway." Stepping out of her apartment, she went to a hair salon. While women should strike that day, "you don't have to make yourself look ugly," she explained, "to be a woman for equality." She wanted to be ready for the spotlight that evening.

Across the city, the protests had already started. A bunch of feminists passed out leaflets to the morning commuters in the subways near Wall Street. One thousand others took their babies to city hall to protest the paucity of social services for mothers. "Repent, male chauvinists," they chanted. About fifteen hundred—half of them men—attended a noontime demonstration there, which included a temporary child-care center staffed with volunteers who watched several dozen children. That afternoon, others handed out leaflets titled "You and Your Marriage" to soon-to-be-brides at the Marriage Bureau. The pamphlet, which explained how marriage law affected women and men differently, was intended to "warn people about what they're getting into."

As the evening rush hour approached, women began marching down Fifth Avenue to Bryant Park. The police department assigned them to one side of the street, but they spilled over the barricades. Suffragists had marched down the same route to celebrate the passage of the Nineteenth Amendment fifty years earlier. Women had taken up the entire street then, Friedan said. "We can have it again." The demonstration blocked crosstown traffic, and the marchers shouted over honking horns as they surged forward, arm in arm and "in great swinging long lines, from sidewalk to sidewalk."

The protest grew as it moved. Suddenly there were thousands displaying their common resolve: waitresses, "Westchester matrons," nurses and telephone operators in uniform, office and factory workers, homemakers with babies in tow, Black and Puerto Rican activists, and elderly suffragists. "Every kind of woman you ever see in New York was there," marveled *The New York Times*. Some men carried "Men for Women's Rights" banners, representing the estimated one in ten marchers who were male.

The march ended in a rally where ten thousand people gushed into Bryant Park. Betty Friedan beamed out into the crowd from the stage. In its size and prominence, the strike had overwhelmed her vision for the organization she cofounded: the "absolute mass of women just as far as you could see," she said, was "like a sea, a whole sea." Friedan reveled in the attention. And yet this would also mark the moment when NOW left her behind.

4.

WE HAVE DIFFERENT
PROBLEMS

The Mary Tyler Moore Show, which started its eight-year run in 1970, starred a single career woman who reveled in her independence. That year, Germaine Greer's prescription of complete sexual revolution, The Female Eunuch, was an international bestseller. All three hundred thousand copies of the first issue of Ms. magazine, a feminist periodical founded by the journalist Gloria Steinem, sold out in eight days in 1972. Ideas about women's rights ricocheted across American culture and added to the wind at women's backs in the early 1970s. The broader movement, by then often called women's liberation, included national groups—with NOW the biggest and most broad—and independent local nodes. It reached millions more who never joined a group or attended a protest. "By the very force of its existence," noted The New York Times, the movement gave "moral support and credibility to every woman who sets out on her own to amend inequities in her marriage or in her job."

Feminists were pushing for gender equality in the law and politics in the early 1970s, with government officials mounting no strong opposition. Feminist lawyers framed new arguments and won key rulings, often on NOW's behalf. Joining with Steinem and Betty Friedan, the

Democratic congresswomen Shirley Chisholm and Bella Abzug and the prominent Republican Jill Ruckelshaus created the nonpartisan, non-government National Women's Political Caucus in 1971 to bring more women into elected office and make government more responsive to their concerns. In 1972 alone, both houses of Congress passed the Equal Employment Opportunity Act, which strengthened and extended Title VII, and Title IX of the Higher Education Act, which required gender equality in federally funded educational institutions, and the Senate passed the Equal Rights Amendment, which advanced that provision to state legislatures for final ratification.

Although NOW had pursued each of these provisions in coalition with longer-standing women's groups like the American Association of University Women and newer ones like the Women's Equity Action League, its loose structure and open-ended mission set it apart. "If somebody could think of it, NOW was going to try to do it, whatever it was," said Collins. Members protested sexism in churches, law, employment, beauty pageants, Little Leagues, advertising, toys, and more. NOW's co-filed charges persuaded the Department of Housing, Education, and Welfare to investigate sex discrimination at major universities in 1970. That same year, following two years of NOW's pickets, boycotts, and complaints, United Airlines ended its notorious men-only "executive" flights. In 1973, NOW won its challenge to sex-segregated job ads in the U.S. Supreme Court. And in 1974, responding to NOW's pressure, the Federal Communications Commission established new gender equality rules for television stations.

The 1970 Women's Strike for Equality had brought new attention and numbers to the organization, often the only outlet a striving feminist could find. As a Nebraska chapter president explained, "We're the only place in Omaha where a woman who has some gripes can come." NOW had eighteen thousand members and more than 250 chapters in cities, small towns, and college campuses nationwide in 1972. Two years later, there were forty thousand members and more than 700 chapters, including a strong presence in the South, although the region was home to just 14 percent of members. These newcomers often came from the radical feminist groups that had burned bright in the late 1960s but fizzled out.

They discovered that NOW was flexible and easy to join: any ten people who paid the national dues, which were raised to $10 in 1970, could form a chapter, elect officers, and dig into their chosen issues. As members brought varied priorities to the organization, they increased the national task forces from ten to thirty by 1973. The chapters, whether tiny or hundreds strong, incubated even more of members' ideas.

Organizing women and their male allies, as NOW's ambitious plans prescribed, required reaching across race, sexuality, gender, and nationality. "We have different problems," Hernandez said. "A women's movement has to include them all." She worked in the early 1970s to enhance NOW's appeal to women of color and lesbians. Meanwhile, Collins wanted men like her husband to be equal participants. And Burnett pushed a global approach, attracting three hundred activists from Africa, Asia, the Middle East, Latin America, and Canada to the international women's conference she organized for NOW in 1973. "We thought we were struggling alone," the Israeli feminist Sheila Prag marveled at the scene. Still, what did it mean to struggle together?

———

The groundswell of new members in the early 1970s brought a generational change. Some left, including Catherine Conroy. She believed NOW needed clearer lines of authority and a delegate system for voting at national conventions. Conroy "began to feel like a broken record," said a friend, as she continually raised the matter. The others wanted to plan campaigns, not tinker with bylaws. Sister Joel Read, by then the president of Alverno College, shared Conroy's fears that NOW "wasn't going to go anywhere," she said. "You just have a loose group of people," and anyone with the time and money to travel to a conference could "vote on the major issues of the day with no background, no preparation." Read too departed, along with most of the founders. They left because they disagreed with the group's direction, were occupied with other commitments, or had signed up in 1966 to signal their support but not their intention to be active in the new group. By 1974, just eight years after NOW's founding, less than one in five members had been there for more than two years.

Many who exited were women of color. In addition to Murray,

NOW's early Black supporters had included the labor and civil rights activists Addie Wyatt, a leader in Chicago's meatpackers' union, and Dollie Lowther Robinson, her fellow member of the Negro American Labor Council. Congresswoman Shirley Chisholm and the activists Septima Clark and Eleanor Holmes Norton, a future EEOC chair and member of Congress, also attended some of NOW's earliest meetings. "We had great women who were black," Hernandez said decades later. "But they were only there for a short period of time because they were already working in other places." Black women were busy, and white women's appeals to sisterhood often rang hollow. "Black women feel resentful that white women are raising issues of oppression," Norton explained in 1970, speaking in general terms, "because black women do not see white women in any kind of classic oppressed position." White women derived status from white men, and often, class privilege set them up to exploit Black women's labors as cooks, cleaners, and caregivers.

Racist slights and oversights cost NOW a more diverse organization from the beginning. The longtime civil rights activist Anna Arnold Hedgeman, who had briefly been NOW's vice president in Hernandez's stead and was the first chair of its Task Force on Women in Poverty, felt the pressure of serving as one of the few women of color in a leadership role. Pauli Murray pushed Hedgeman into the photographer's frame at their meetings. "You need a minority person there," she told the white women arranging a photograph at NOW's first conference in 1966. The founder and publicist Muriel Fox, ever attentive to the group's image, believed she had done enough by centering Inez Casiano, who worked for the Puerto Rican Community Development Project and was herself Puerto Rican and who Fox believed was "very pretty."

Friedan, also concerned with NOW's image, focused even less on racial representation. She foregrounded the Catholic nuns in their habits— Sisters Joel Read and Austin Doherty from Alverno College—not just to showcase the group's diversity but to symbolize how all women "were liberating themselves from the cloister," Friedan said. Hedgeman stuck it out for a while, lobbying the other leaders to understand that "the most serious victims of sex-discrimination" were "the women at the bottom," working "low-paying, marginal jobs" or unable to find work. But she resigned from NOW's board in 1968 rather than challenge its policy that board members should make major donations to cushion the organization's finances. Hedgeman was retired and in her late sixties, with scarce savings. Similarly, neither Casiano nor the civil rights attorney Graciela Olivárez, two Latinas among NOW's first board members, remained in a prominent role in the organization for long.

NOW's leaders' attention to regional variety over racial diversity created distinct problems for women of color. Eager to hold a board meeting in a southern city, they selected New Orleans in 1969. The white women in the group expressed shock when the hotel refused to honor Hernandez's reservation—"we had to threaten a riot," a white member recalled, "to have her registered" there—and when they saw openly racist job advertisements in local newspapers. At least one board member, Ollie Butler Moore, the longtime dean of women at Southern University nearby in Baton Rouge, refused to go, because she knew she would be treated this way.

The experience in New Orleans was one example of situations that diminished a feeling of sisterhood for Black women with white women, but the past was rife with others. Most notably, white suffragists had pursued sex-neutral voting rights half a century earlier that left race-based restrictions intact, rendering the Nineteenth Amendment ineffective for many women of color. In the amendment's wake, the white suffrage leader Alice Paul articulated the view of most of her associates: that southern Black women's continued disenfranchisement was a "racial" problem rather than a "feminist" issue that belonged on the agenda of her National Woman's Party. Black women continued to pursue the vote shoulder to shoulder with Black men. "Fifty years ago all women got suffrage," Dorothy I. Height, president of the National Council of Negro Women, reminded an audience in 1970, "but it took lynching, bombing, the civil-rights movement and then the Voting Rights Act of 1965 to get it for black women and black people."

"Feminist thinking" was catching on across demographic groups of women, announced one 1972 poll, and Black women viewed "women's liberation" more positively than white women. But Black women made their own calculations. Repelled by white women's pressure to disentangle their race and gender identities, most chose to work in Black-led groups, creating their own feminist associations or reshaping and leading existing organizations. They framed liberation in distinct terms, rejecting white women's "gender first" feminism and instead seeking to dismantle the "interlocking" systems of oppression that shaped their lives: racism, sexism, capitalism, and heterosexism. African Americans had spent more than a century organizing for political power and social justice, and their feminist consciousness developed independently. Chicana feminism also began to flourish in 1968, especially on California college campuses, where Chicana feminists formed consciousness-raising groups, pursued Chicano studies curricula, helped arrange illegal abortions, and critiqued machismo as a harmful response to white supremacy that the Chicano community should eradicate.

Hernandez believed that working with women across divisions would benefit women of color and that they especially needed feminism. All women were disadvantaged by comparison to men, she said, but women of color fared even worse. When she read the first batch of workers' EEOC complaints as a commissioner, she discovered that "there were 'ghetto sex' jobs just as there were 'ghetto race' jobs, and . . . very often minority women had the *worst* of all possible worlds." Because the women's movement sought to destroy these kinds of age-old patterns of dominance, it was "the most profound movement of our time, with a tremendous potential."

Hernandez remained in NOW. She believed that Black, white, and Latina women could work together. They cared about many of the same issues, but NOW had to approach them expansively. A tight focus on the challenges of managing both a marriage and a job, for example, would repel Black women who had always had to work for wages regardless of their marital status because racism curtailed Black men's employment. Middle-class whites often framed access to child care as a stepping-stone into paid work. But women receiving welfare might see the same child-care facility as a site where they were forced to leave their children in order to attend to other people for a pittance. Every mother deserved to choose "whether she wants to work," Hernandez claimed. And while white women viewed birth control as a matter of bodily autonomy, Black and Latina women recalled a history of abuse at the hands of early twentieth-century birth control advocates. Seeking to avert "the birth of defectives," including the poor, people of color, and disabled and queer people through forced sterilization, eugenicists including Margaret Sanger pursued reproductive freedom for the "fit" and violent sexual control for everyone else. Hernandez explained that women of color had also been the "most victimized by the antiabortion laws" because they were less likely than whites to have access to safe underground abortions. The right to abortion was one step, but access to reproductive health care for all women was a much longer road.

Other Black women in NOW expressed a similar mix of hope and realism about the issues that had the potential to unite or polarize women. "All women have problems to work on together," said Nancy Randolph, a dean at the University of Alabama's School of Social Work, in explaining her presence as the Tuscaloosa chapter's only Black member. But she also remarked, "Every time I'm at a NOW meeting, I think of all the blacks who are at home taking care of the members' children."

Hernandez rebutted NOW's reputation as white and middle class as inaccurate even as she pushed whites in the group to broaden their feminism. Black women were important members, she said. Some Black women saw NOW "as a dilettante organization, involved in frivolous things, not survival issues. But I think they're wrong." Even when she was one of a handful of women of color at a NOW meeting or rally, she expressed hope that the organization could become more diverse. She told a reporter in 1970 that NOW had more support among women who were not white and middle class than "one might suspect from looking at this conference." NOW had potential as a champion for all of them, she argued, if white members stopped viewing racism as "irrelevant" or "a side issue" to their concerns. NOW had to work "toward a better society," she said, not seek out "a place in an essentially corrupt society." This meant developing feminist positions on every issue: war, poverty, housing, and more. "All the issues out there are women's issues."

Hernandez believed that whites in NOW, including Friedan, "had the right motivations," and she was patient with them. When the leader of Berkeley NOW wrote that she and other white feminists had been

accused at a recent school board meeting of "subverting Black liberation" in their framing of women's concerns, Hernandez responded that
some members of NOW, "consciously or unconsciously," had "used arguments that could be termed racist." For example, some of the group's
statements on workplace rights declared it "insulting and degrading to
white females to earn less than black males." Hernandez suggested that
the insults cut both ways. "I am sure there have been comments by blacks
that sound 'sexist' and I think it is worth thinking through and clarify-
ing both problems." NOW's white leaders, in turn, saw Hernandez as a
bridge to Black women.

Some Black women criticized Hernandez's outreach to white feminists. The attorney and activist Inez Smith Reid asked "militant" Black
women about Hernandez in her nationwide survey of their attitudes and
activism in 1972. Reid analyzed the survey results in *"Together" Black
Women*, which she prepared for the Black Women's Community Development Foundation, the organization she led. It sought to uncover Black
women's "ideas on the major political and social issues that affect them."
Few of Reid's interviewees knew of Hernandez's work in NOW. Of those
who did, some believed she was "rendering a valuable service" to Black and
white women. Others argued that she was "totally on the wrong track" and
should instead work on projects "solely for the Black community."

Hernandez decided not to run for a second term as NOW president
in 1971, although Pauli Murray encouraged her to do so. "Your presidency has symbolic as well as organizational value," the older activist
prodded. But Hernandez was "not interested in being a permanent leader
of NOW." She wanted to "generate more and more people with the opportunity for leadership," both to eliminate the situation where "one person" was "doing everything, and everybody else was sitting back," and
because making space for more women could "demystify" leadership and
grow their skills and confidence. Hernandez believed in encouraging others, but she also expressed additional motives. NOW conferences spent
too much time on "obviously inept procedures" and not enough planning
"action on issues," she wrote in 1970. Most members were also too narrow in their outlook. "If this movement is to be successful at all," she said
in her final presidential address, feminists should not "make the mistake

of the women of the first wave of feminism who thought that they had won it at the time that we won the right to vote." NOW had to broaden its approach and "address itself to everything."

———

Hernandez was not finished trying to reshape NOW. Along with two other NOW members in San Francisco, both of whom were Black, she formed the NOW National Task Force on Minority Women. Patsy Fulcher, who worked as the deputy assistant secretary in the California Health and Welfare Agency, shared Hernández's belief that some women of color misunderstood NOW's purpose as advancing elite white interests: "We have to counteract it by being a part of the movement." Fulcher also blamed a biased media. "It is time for a positive article about black women and the women's liberation movement," she wrote to *Ebony* in 1973; the magazine had recently covered only Black women who were "anti-women's movement." Eleanor Spikes, who also worked in Hernandez's consulting business, was the task force's third leader.

This trio vowed to unite white women and women of color by teaching whites about racism and women of color about "the common problems faced by all women in a sexist society." Their task force would reach out to women of color not from the perspective "that NOW had all the answers," but instead to "make common cause" with them and their organizations, asking, "How can we help you?" Hernandez was heartened when NOW's 1973 national conference declared outreach to women of color a priority and when the fifty African American women and men who were present, out of twenty-one hundred registrants, formed a NOW Black caucus. The white women at the conference appeared to be "trying very hard to understand black women," the member Ruth W. Lee, who was Black, wrote in a follow-up survey. Fulcher agreed that the conference had gone well. The group was more diverse than she had expected, and everyone she met "seemed to be anxious for dialogue."

The white women who constituted about 90 percent of NOW's members did want dialogue, but on their terms. The first meeting of NOW's Black caucus at the national conference was limited to Blacks only—upsetting Dorothy Kemp, a white woman from the Baton Rouge chapter. "We're all women," she said. "Why can't we be all together?" A Black member of her chapter countered that until white women tried to understand "the depth, the intensity, the suffering and depravity of the real oppression blacks have experienced," she could have no sisterhood with those who faced "little more than boredom, general repression, and dish-pan hands." When some in the Twin Cities wanted to start a separate St. Paul chapter to focus more on outreach to women of color, the chapter president Virginia Watkins wrote to Hernandez to oppose it. "We don't recruit old, young, or any other select group of women," she wrote. Some white members called the task force "unnecessary" or "divisive," denying that racism existed in NOW.

But Hernandez saw white members alienate women of color first-hand. Some whites openly expressed racist attitudes; others made no effort to invite women of color in. The NOW Legal Defense and Education Fund (LDEF) president, Sylvia Roberts, claimed that it was wrong to actively recruit anyone. "If minority women don't feel a relevance, they don't feel a kinship to our issues," she said. Watkins took the sentiment even further. It was "patriarchal to declare that minority women 'should' be in the movement," she wrote in 1973. The Chicago NOW leader Anne Ladky later realized that the sense of openness she felt in joining her chapter had led her to assume that it was "welcoming to everybody," she said, "because it sure seem[ed] welcoming to me." Her chapter sought to cast a wide net by hosting drop-in "Help Every Woman" meetings that members advertised on flyers at train stations and bus stops to try to reach a wide cross section of women in the city, but it remained over-whelmingly white.

This was a major drawback of NOW's member-driven feminism: white feminists easily interpreted NOW's do-it-yourself feminism as do-it-for-yourself. Whites in NOW generally viewed racial justice struggles as laudable but distinct. Nearly half of the chapters claimed to work in coalition with civil rights groups, but less than 10 percent had their own task forces on minority women and women's rights. The white and more financially secure members in NOW were willing to add the specific concerns of women of color and poor women to the list of goals, but they resisted making them central.

Some in NOW, both whites and people of color, foregrounded the concerns of women who were not white. Hernandez's 1973 survey of NOW chapters revealed that members of color were active in more than half of western chapters, nearly half of midwestern chapters, and one-quarter of southern chapters. She noticed that chapter leaders "seldom" mentioned racism as a problem in their chapters, but women of color who sent their own responses referred to it "often." Several chapters translated NOW materials into different languages; others led boycotts in support of Latina farm and factory workers that NOW endorsed at the national level. More than a hundred chapters took independent action on behalf of Joan Little, an incarcerated Black woman who killed a prison guard when he attempted to rape her. As part of its support for Little, NOW sponsored a press conference in the U.S. Capitol with Representatives Shirley Chisholm and Yvonne Burke that called for a federally funded study of the conditions women endured in prison. And some women of color found separatism within NOW appealing. In San Diego, as in San Francisco, members of color departed the original chapter to form their own, second NOW chapter in the city.

Fighting women's poverty was another of NOW's stated goals, but the organization worked only intermittently on the issue. The planners of the 1970 national conference neglected to organize a workshop on women and poverty, but that task force worked primarily "at a local level," explained its leader, Merrillee Dolan, "because effective poverty fights . . . call for creativity" and "depend on the political 'ins' and 'outs' of your community." The National Welfare Rights Organization, a burgeoning site of working-class Black women's organizing, observed that NOW's declarations of support for welfare rights were largely symbolic.

Several NOW chapters did hold events dedicated to addressing women's poverty. The D.C. chapter co-hosted a 1972 "welfare dinner" that chapter members and welfare rights activists planned together. As the women ate "soul food," they listened to the featured speakers Gloria Steinem and Johnnie Tillmon of the NWRO. The conversation explored how, while their common oppression stemmed from "the inferior status of women in our society," they needed "to understand also how our problems are different." The Albuquerque chapter hosted a public meeting where women testified about the challenges of "trying to live on a welfare budget, getting shoved from one lousy job training program to another," and the poor "jail conditions and police treatment" they had endured.

NOW's chapter in Riverside, California, sponsored a welfare rights conference in 1971 that Lynne Tabb, an organizer with the United Farm Workers, helped to plan. The one hundred conference participants included between one-third and one-half welfare recipients, which "gave the conference the vitality and relevance that ours in Palo Alto only had tastes of," noted a Bay Area participant. As a featured speaker, Hernandez stressed "the marginal role of women in the economy," NOW's "alliance" with welfare rights activists, and the "unity of women." The Riverside chapter itself was split between a younger, "studentish" half that wanted to focus on poverty issues, and "ladies" who favored other concerns and less "militancy." Hernandez's "remarkable appeal to both groups made this unlikely situation work," members noted.

Hernandez also sought to change NOW at the grass roots. She found allies who shared her vision in San Francisco: a "wide open town" and a thriving center of radical politics and cultural nonconformity. Rich with bohemian subcultures and a vital refuge for gay and lesbian people, San Francisco hummed with Beat-inspired bookstores, coffee shops, and jazz clubs. Nearby were Berkeley, its University of California campus the birthplace of the free speech movement, and Oakland, a hub of Black nationalism. Through groups including the Black Panther Party for Self-Defense, which had formed in Oakland in 1966, Black residents there organized against unemployment, poverty, and police brutality and pursued full political participation.

Hernandez's local NOW outpost, the San Francisco chapter, helped build the thirty-group Bay Area Women's Coalition. But San Francisco NOW tended to focus narrowly on political change. This frustrated Hernandez as well as the chapter members and longtime lesbian rights activists Del Martin and Phyllis Lyon. That couple, who were then in their late forties, had founded the Daughters of Bilitis in 1955.

Like the Black women's groups that collaborated with the male-led civil rights organizations but also organized as women, the DOB worked closely with male-dominated "homophile" groups, but Martin and Lyon grew impatient with their polite tactics and focus on gay men. Lesbians wanted to emphasize their distinct priorities: child rearing, boosting salaries, and expanding job opportunities for gay women. Male homophile leaders tended to view their own concerns as universal. "What do you men know about Lesbians?" Martin asked those gathered at a gay rights conference in 1959. "Lesbians are *women*," she declared, and "not satisfied to be auxiliary members or second-class homosexuals." Because lesbians would still be disadvantaged even if the gay rights movement succeeded, Lyon later reflected, "we needed to do the women's thing also."

Lyon and Martin had been looking for an organization that would put women first and strike the right balance of assertiveness and respectability. Listening to the radio one day soon after NOW's creation, they heard Inka O'Hanrahan, one of its founders, describe the nascent group. Its possibilities excited them: "Finally the heterosexual women were getting it together." Lyon and Martin became the first open lesbians to join NOW and received the first couple's membership under the "husband-wife" dues category. The couple never hid their relationship. "There must be more of you," O'Hanrahan had told the pair, and asked them to "bring them around." Martin was soon elected San Francisco NOW's secretary.

As lesbians across the country were beginning to live more openly and demand specific rights, homophobia within NOW remained a problem. Martin and Lyon set out to change the minds of members who objected to lesbians' open involvement. Martin wrote to Kay Clarenbach in 1970, offering to draft a position paper and answer leaders' questions. "So many of their fears stem from myths, and it helps to know the facts," she wrote. Acknowledging that there were lesbians in NOW would end "the stickiness of the issue," Martin wrote to Friedan, as well as "unnecessary divisions and embarrassment." And if NOW was serious about building coalitions, the gay rights movement was a natural ally. However, most leaders relied heavily on media coverage for reaching new members, and they feared that committing NOW to lesbian rights would yield bad press.

Nearly 20 percent of NOW members identified as lesbian or bisexual by 1974. But lesbians were often closeted in women's circles. "If they knew the lesbians, they didn't know they knew lesbians," Collins said. The NOW founder Gene Boyer learned that "there were lesbians on the board and in the movement, and you know, I was more or less in their company all the time." Boyer's first reaction in 1971 was surprise. "Who? What? Where? What tree are they hiding behind here?" Then she was curious. Returning to rural Wisconsin, she asked her doctor "what it was that lesbians did"; it was "a whole new area of thought to contemplate." She was intrigued, but not hostile.

NOW's national leaders could not avoid addressing sexuality for long. Millions of American women were thinking critically about sex, regardless of whom they had it with. Influential radical feminist writings like "The Myth of the Vaginal Orgasm," Anne Koedt's well-circulated 1968 essay, exposed how female sexuality had been shaped by what pleased men. Women also discussed sex in their consciousness-raising groups and considered how male-centric sexuality structured power imbalances in heterosexual relationships and fed stigmas against lesbians. Sex was not a private affair or too taboo for polite conversation, many women insisted; it was political.

This climate affected NOW's membership—especially the California chapters. They felt "alienated and isolated from the rest of NOW," Hernandez reported. Western chapters began to develop independently and to absorb the perspectives and many members from defunct radical feminist groups. The Los Angeles NOW chapter hosted consciousness-raising sessions, fostering introspection and connection that attracted open lesbians to the chapter. They became some of its most dedicated members. The L.A. NOW president Toni Carabillo noticed that involvement in NOW reinforced the relationships of women who joined as couples, whereas it threatened the bonds of heterosexual partners.

The Californians began to spar with national officers, who expressed their biases without embarrassment. In a 1971 national officers' meeting, the Friedan ally and New Yorker Lucy Komisar accused the L.A. chapter of seeking to host the next national conference "so that lesbians could control it." She echoed the claim a few months later, writing to Hernandez that the L.A. chapter was being run by "a clique that share the same sexual persuasion." The western regional coordinator, Shirley

Bernard, responded that Komisar's "hideous" and "sick" charge was completely unfounded. Until NOW supported lesbians' right to live openly, "no two single women living together can afford to belong to NOW," an L.A. NOW officer wrote. The chapter passed a resolution condemning "the double oppression of women who are lesbians."

The tide began to turn when the L.A. chapter hosted the national conference several months later. Hernandez asked Martin and Lyon to organize a workshop on lesbianism. The couple was surprised when, as the sign-up list lengthened, the organizers kept postponing the workshop in order to find a larger room for it. Once the meeting began, "we didn't have to referee," Lyon said, "because nobody 'anti' was trying to talk." L.A. NOW proposed a lesbian rights resolution to the entire conference; it passed with near-unanimous support. Friedan, who tended to step to the microphone after the line ended so that she could have the last word, never showed up. The resolution committed NOW to "reassess the priorities that sacrifice principles to image." A second resolution, which vowed to help lesbian mothers keep custody of their children, also passed easily. After the conference, no one in NOW could deny that lesbians were among them or that lesbian rights related to their other goals.

But the resolutions were only the first steps. The chapters still varied in their openness to lesbian members and their priorities. Lesbian rights advocates in NOW began to push for a national task force that cemented the issue among the group's most prominent goals. The New Yorker Sidney Abbott asked the national board chair, Muriel Fox, about that possibility in 1972. Fox resisted: "Because of the expense involved in servicing task forces adequately, we are trying to practice 'birth control' regarding new ones." She urged Abbott to instead work within one of the thirty existing task forces. Fox also refused to commit NOW to taking a stand on "psychiatric opinions as to whether lesbianism is normal or neurotic." She wrote this the year before the American Psychiatric Association stopped classifying homosexuality as a disorder in itself.

National leaders began to budge a little. Several months after her rebuff to Abbott, Fox and other officers offered to fold lesbians' concerns into a task force on sexuality. They chose Shirley Nickols Fahey, a straight academic, to lead it. Lesbians accused the leaders of burying the issue by selecting someone with a scholarly approach rather than a personal one. "It is certainly time to have an out-front lesbian working with NOW, especially on this issue," Barbara Love, a lesbian and longtime member of the New York chapter, wrote to the board of directors in early 1973. Love and others persuaded the board to change the task force's name to "sexuality and lesbianism" in 1973 and to make Sidney Abbott, an open lesbian in the New York chapter, its co-coordinator. Abbott promised to move slowly. One of her first national newsletter articles profiled lesbians working, commuting, and grocery shopping. Its thrust, she said, was "please see us as people."

Lesbians in NOW kept up their pressure by forming their own caucus. They advertised a meeting at the March 1973 national conference in Washington. Of the two thousand conference goers, "200 strong were out of the closet and in that caucus room." The new caucus met nightly to set goals and craft resolutions for the plenary session. Its supporters attended other sessions to make sure lesbians' interests were represented. At the LDEF workshop, they prodded its director, Sylvia Roberts, to support the case of a lesbian mother in San Jose who had won custody on the condition that she would limit visits with her lover. When Roberts refused and tried to dismiss them—"this whole thing is taking a lot of time"—it was clear that "the ruling clique," not the membership, was the biggest obstacle. The caucus proposed a resolution condemning discrimination on account of sexual orientation, which the conference voted overwhelmingly to support.

The lesbian caucus also sought representation on the national board. Del Martin became the first open lesbian to win a seat, which she pursued not only to promote lesbians' specific concerns throughout NOW but to resolve a problem in her city of San Francisco. The leadership of her home chapter was "simply racist and homophobic," she said, and committed to pursuing a narrow notion of equal legal rights. "As a Lesbian, I could not just be a feminist," Martin said; "I had to be a full activist." Hernandez agreed. Since her time as NOW president, she had not been content to work solely through NOW, especially while her local chapter framed its issues rigidly. "I would find it impossible to decide that all my energies had to go to NOW—especially if NOW viewed its own interests so narrowly that it did not see a relevance in the struggle against racism and war," she had written in 1971.

Still, Martin, Lyon, and Hernandez wanted to start their own NOW chapter rather than secede. "For all of its faults, NOW had it going on," Hernandez explained, and Martin and Lyon agreed. Since NOW "had clout," they decided to "make NOW our own organization." National policy prohibited multiple chapters in the same location. As soon as Martin entered the board, she persuaded that body and the membership to change the rules so that she could cofound a more expansive chapter in San Francisco.

Their new chapter, Golden Gate NOW, flourished for several years as it pursued the kind of integrated feminism Hernandez had championed. The chapter president, Danette Mulrine, explained that its members would focus on the "multi-oppressed woman—the lesbian, older woman, handicapped, the black and Chicano woman." More than half of Golden Gate NOW's 250 members were lesbians and 10 percent were Black. The chapter anchored the growing Bay Area Women's Coalition, which comprised forty local women's groups. It also sought to set up a halfway house for formerly incarcerated women that operated a "feminist restaurant" and possibly a shoe store. "One of the reasons women are in jail today is because of the system," explained a formerly incarcerated woman and Golden Gate member. Most were poor women of color who lacked "the tools of society under the system the dudes have set up" and "the money to keep out of the joint." To dampen their class differences, wealthier members covered the dues for "welfare mothers" and anyone else who could not afford the $15 rate for the chapter.

Members of the Golden Gate chapter centered the lived experiences of both lesbians and women of color, but Hernandez made little progress in expanding NOW's appeal to the latter group. She resigned as national task force coordinator along with Spikes and Fulcher in 1974. Echoing Hernandez's departure from the presidency three years earlier, the trio cited their desire to give other women "the experience of functioning nationally." They might also have had other motives. The national board had just slashed task force budgets, and they stood to receive just over $100 of the $500 they had proposed spending for the year. To replace them, the trio recommended one Black woman, one woman of Asian descent, and one of Puerto Rican descent in order to bring perspectives that could boost those groups' tiny representation in the organization. Hernandez kept up her NOW membership but dove into other commitments. She took twice-monthly cross-country trips and shorter weekly trips for her consulting business. She also focused on different forms of activism. The previous year she had helped found Black Women Organized for Action, a Bay Area group that took a loose, grassroots approach to changing local politics.

Hernandez and other Californians had more success in changing NOW's approach to sexuality. The National Task Force on Sexuality and Lesbianism pursued civil rights legislation and custody rights for lesbian mothers and opposed discrimination in the military and within NOW itself. Chapters across the country also joined the fight. They organized workshops on sexuality and lesbian rights that were frequently the best-attended sessions at state and regional conferences. The Atlanta chapter's robust lesbian task force sponsored mixers and coffeehouse nights. Washington, D.C., NOW's sexuality task force sponsored activities such as dances, camping trips, and a weekly open house. The task force was instrumental in passing gay and lesbian rights protections in the District. Seattle NOW won in court on behalf of two lesbian mothers whose ex-husbands were suing for child custody. Louisville NOW challenged in federal court Kentucky's penal code, which punished consensual sex between women or men with imprisonment and a $500 fine.

Many in NOW began to shift their perspectives. Patricia Hill Burnett had once opposed embracing lesbian members and their specific concerns. She worried that the people in her social circles would assume all feminists were lesbians, an association that "gave men a wonderful handle, a wonderful stick to beat us over the head with." But she was losing faith in defensive respectability politics. "There was only a core group of women that would have been acceptable to the men; and even us, they didn't like very much." She also believed that excluding any women would undermine NOW's premise. They had invited all women to join them, and such inclusivity was their greatest strength. "We refuse to be divided," she wrote in her journal in 1971, responding to the passage of the lesbian rights resolution at the L.A. conference.

As lesbians gained more prominence in NOW, tensions also developed among them as the implosion of radical feminism brought young women into NOW chapters. At the founding meeting of the lesbian caucus in 1973, recounted Sidney Abbott, most of the women in the room dressed conservatively to blend in with other conference goers. "The women who were more openly lesbian-identified, and who dressed in more of an open-lesbian way—jeans and tee shirts and so forth—were in a very small minority." Two years later, Abbott was the one who felt out of place at the 1975 national conference. The throngs of "younger, much more radical women," she said, viewed her "sprinkled gray hair, and my little blazer and slacks, and Ivy League look as being right wing."

Yet members weathered these tensions over sexuality and broadened the organization's approach. Unlike the radical groups whose opposition to structures helped precipitate their collapse, NOW's structures gave it a better chance to sustain internal struggles, and, sometimes, to self-correct. Collins had once believed that a lesbian rights platform "would prevent us from organizing some people I thought needed to be organiz[ed]," persuading them and others "to discredit us before we could even get started." But when NOW shifted, "and when the showdown came and are you with us or against us, there weren't very many people who left," Collins said.

Those who evolved also included the eastern regional director, Karen DeCrow. She had written to Hernandez in 1971 that endorsing lesbian rights would force NOW into the old trap of identifying women by what they "do or do not do in bed." They should steer clear "not because we are uptight and hysterical" but "because it is just as relevant as what you eat for dinner." Four years later, DeCrow declared lesbianism "a civil rights issue" and "a genuine feminist issue." It was 1975, and she was on television stating NOW's official, uncontested position as its president.

———

As Black women and other women of color in NOW questioned whether whites could be real allies, and lesbians lobbied straight members to support them and their issues, women were also considering men's role in their movement. There had been outspoken male feminists in the nineteenth century, with the Black abolitionist Frederick Douglass most prominent among them, but he was one of a handful of such men. Early twentieth-century suffragists had to fend off the accusations that they were trying to turn women against men, or even to turn women into men. Half a century later, feminists debated anew whether men could be women's comrades.

Life was changing for men, too. Three basic norms of manhood were under threat in the late 1960s, writes the historian Robert Self: "bread-winning, soldiering, and heterosexuality." White men's command of high-paying, stable jobs that secured their authority within their families began to weaken, the antiwar movement dimmed the manly glow of military service, and a growing gay rights movement offered a new archetype for male identity. While many men moved to the right, others responded to these changes by declaring themselves part of the women's movement. More and more Americans believed that what they had understood to be facts about the sexes were instead "stereotypes supplied by society." Straight couples were having new discussions about their expectations of each other, especially regarding housework and birth control.

Many NOW women, in this shifting climate, were reconsidering their relationships to their male bosses, teachers, pastors, and brothers as well as their husbands. Some, like Hernandez, left unhappy marriages; others, like Burnett, wanted more power inside stifling unions; others, like Collins, were coupled with self-described feminist men. Still others came out as lesbian, which Collins would do in 1975. "Being in the women's movement, you could not help but confront" your own sexuality, Collins said. When the NOW founder and national treasurer Gene Boyer opened members' dues checks, she would sometimes find handwritten notes of thanks: "Since I've heard about NOW, I've left my husband. I deserted my children. I've gone off to become an astronaut," or to start a new relationship with a woman. Boyer found their gratitude unsettling. She felt that "we had to somehow stem the tide of the Pandora's box we had opened up" until "the world was ready."

Boyer herself was happily married to a man, and her fellow NOW founder Betty Friedan, although divorced, shared her more traditional approach to the opposite sex. During Hernandez's presidency, Friedan used her dwindling clout to settle her grudge with the New York chapter by fighting to move NOW's administrative services, and soon, its national headquarters, to Chicago. The author had recently struck up a friendship with Mary Jean Collins and her husband, Jim. "My first NOW conference was a mind-blowing experience," Jim wrote to Friedan in 1969. "I went to Atlanta with my head screwed on tight, and came back with the same head spinning like a top—as a duly baptized feminist." Jim, like his wife, sought to square his Catholic faith with his feminism. As the acting chair of a group called Men and Women United for Sexual Equality in the Church, he encouraged women to protest the formal ban on birth control by mailing each month's empty pill containers to their bishops: a "Pill In" to inform leaders of members' personal practices.

Friedan wanted men to have prominent roles in NOW, unlike radical feminists' approach. Identifying men as an oppressor class, those groups often called for separatism to create what the New York–based Redstockings called "female class consciousness." Friedan asked Jim Collins-Robson to serve on NOW's national board. He declined, citing the cost of traveling to meetings, but he was "very interested in helping NOW find ways to get the national 'grunt work' done." At Friedan's urging, he made good on his word and started a business in 1970, C-R Office Programs, to handle NOW's correspondence, printing, and record keeping. The board signed an initial eight-month agreement by contract that renewed annually. Soon Mary Jean volunteered full-time in the business, which brought in the couple's only income. It was more than a two-person job. "These duties are overwhelming and our Chicago office is *swamped* with work," the then president, Hernandez, noted. Swamped though Jim was, he was the only person earning a salary through NOW. Some members began to ask, why should a man pocket the money in a women's group?

NOW's 1966 statement of purpose had called for "a fully equal partnership of the sexes," reflecting the founders' demands for more power in their homes and at work. The first board of directors included the history professor Carl Degler, the Reverend Dean Lewis, and the attorney Phineas Indritz. Degler had resisted at first, echoing Friedan in his claim that he was "not much of an organization man." He soon assented: "I like to think that at least my name as a man brings something." Lewis, a leader in the Presbyterian Church, had attended the 1963 March on Washington and supported Black families fighting housing discrimination. He was "interested in equal rights for anybody who desires them," Lewis wrote to Friedan, but he did not want to be NOW's token man. Indritz was a civil rights lawyer who had attended the June 1966 conference on the status of women, where he handed out a hundred copies of a speech he wrote for Congresswoman Martha Griffiths: "a terrific attack upon the EEOC" for its approval of sex-segregated newspaper job ads.

The most committed of the first men involved, Richard Graham (one of NOW's first vice presidents), was a World War II veteran and engineer who had entered public service in his early forties. After a brief stint in the administration of the nascent Peace Corps, he was appointed one of the first five EEOC commissioners alongside Hernandez. Graham became especially focused on the problem of sex discrimination as he "learned on the job." He visited Alabama rubber plants where young men replaced women who had been hired during World War II. Union leaders and plant managers defended the practice, saying "they wouldn't want their wives taking jobs like that—moving those big pieces of rubber around," Graham said. He saw how this "misplaced chivalry" threatened women's economic foothold. Graham and Hernandez cast the dissenting votes on the commission's approval of sex-segregated job ads, which was likely why his one-year term was not renewed. Graham departed his role as one of NOW's vice presidents in 1968. "It doesn't seem right, or becoming," he said; a man could "help in the fight but . . . can't be a leader."

Many of the younger radicals Friedan sought to fend off flooded into NOW in the early 1970s, and they tended to see danger in granting men—who were 9 percent of members in 1974—full access to their movement. They shared the view of the Milwaukee chapter president, Sue Hester. "Although I agree with the spirit of the leaders' approach to men, i.e., that we should be able to enter into partnership with men as our brothers," she wrote, "I feel that such statements are decidedly premature. Equal partnerships do not exist between unequals." The L.A. chapter president, the journalism professor Jean Stapleton, agreed that women sometimes had to be alone—for example, in consciousness-raising sessions where they could "work out their feelings about men." Such demands for a distinct women's space within NOW paralleled those of the Black caucus, and to a lesser extent, the lesbian caucus, although the proponents of gendered separation never drew these connections.

This separatist impulse also formed the basis of transgender women's exclusion from many feminist spaces in the early 1970s, which marked a new era of repression for transgender people. Police began taking aggressive measures toward radical and antiestablishment groups and destroyed institutions serving the trans community. Most cis-gender feminists—those whose gender aligned with the sex assigned to them at birth—responded with hostility to trans issues if they considered them at all. Some argued that because men had built the gender system in order to oppress women, trans people's outward embrace of their gender identity would shore up a toxic system that should instead be dismantled. Others refused to accept trans women as women and excluded them from the spaces they created. There was little visibility of queer people who rejected the system of gender altogether. NOW's debate over gender and identity did not address the situation of trans people. Members held no public conversation about them in the 1970s, and if there were trans people among them, there is no record that they made themselves known.

While NOW viewed men narrowly, chapters experimented with different ways of including them. DuPage NOW, in suburban Chicago, held a "Mr. America contest," a humorous affair intended to highlight the harm in judging anyone by their appearance. L.A. NOW held a discussion titled "What Motivates a Male Feminist?" Three of the five male panelists were NOW members; four were married to NOW members. Chapter newsletters advertised feminist men's businesses when they peddled services women more often needed. "For vasectomy operations (Right On, NOW Men!)," Michigan NOW plugged the urologist Dr. Harvey Lewis. Burnett's chapter also held a special meeting to which husbands were invited to share their views on feminism. The men brought the refreshments; one prepared a hundred egg rolls. Cleveland NOW's president, Bob Johnson, took out an ad in his chapter's newsletter. He declared himself a "solid Feminist" who was "well trained and experienced in Home Maintenance and Repair. If you really can't do it yourself, he can—and possibly teach you how for the next time."

Meanwhile, a man ran for the office of information coordinator in Cincinnati NOW. A member for six months, Ken Onaitis was a self-described "househusband" with plenty of time and energy for the role, he wrote to the chapter. He also assured the others that he was not power hungry. Some woman members had asked him to run to make the race competitive, since there was only one other candidate. But two other women in the chapter asked him to withdraw, citing the "contradiction in philosophy" of having a male spokesperson. "How can we demand that our society promote women leaders, if we can't?" they asked, arguing that men should instead keep "a low profile." Onaitis refused. It would be unfair to subordinate men within the group, he said. Chapter leaders asked Collins, then NOW's Midwest regional director, whether men were prohibited from holding office. They reported her response: "There is no way that NOW can condone or favor a policy that discriminates against any NOW member in any way." Onaitis ran, but lost.

The most common way men participated in NOW was through their marriages. Some couples joined NOW together, like Mary Jean and Jim Collins-Robson; in other cases, husbands helped out in the background. But men also began coming to NOW with distinct goals in mind. The most prominent among them was Warren Farrell. As a college student, Farrell had begun to notice "that the women I was interested in, no matter how intelligent or exciting," soon offered to "type my papers or help me campaign for student office, giving up their own lives and centering around mine." When he was a graduate student in political science, his advisers pushed him to study national defense. He viewed that topic as rooted in an unexamined masculinity. Farrell's wife, Ursula, urged him to apply to be a White House fellow, but he persuaded her to apply herself and was surprised by his own jealousy when she was selected. "It was much harder than I expected to be introduced fifty or sixty times in a row" as the fellow's husband, he said.

Farrell began writing and speaking about how women's liberation would help men by loosening the expectations that masculinity imposed. "Men cannot cry, stay home, take care of children while their wife works, be soft or admit they are wrong without feeling part of that contempt for not being 'a real man,'" he wrote. Instead, they had to "conquer women, conquer countries, win in sports, and win in Vietnam." He outlined these ideas in his 1974 bestselling book, *The Liberated Man*, and appeared on *Today* and *The Phil Donahue Show* to discuss it.

Farrell joined NOW in the late 1960s and encouraged other men to do the same. At first, they were an awkward fit. "We were trying to dominate the meetings, telling the women what to wear to demonstrations and giving them hints on public speaking. Men don't know how to listen to women in meetings, how to learn from them," Farrell said. Other men treated NOW as a dating pool, attempting to impress the women with their "raised consciousness." L.A. NOW leaders reported that men tried to control meetings, spoke for the women present, and insisted that while other men oppressed women, they themselves did not. While some men demanded to be part of the solution with a bit too much authority, others arrived ready to listen. NOW meetings taught Dr. Ben Sheiner, one of ten male members of the northern New Jersey chapter in 1972, "that I had never looked at women as a human being." Instead, he had seen "good girls and bad girls and none of them were people."

To prepare men for feminism and highlight men's needs, Farrell shepherded the creation of NOW's Masculine Mystique Task Force in 1971. He had been attending mixed-gender consciousness-raising groups in New York NOW, but the chapter president, Ivy Bottini, asked him "to get the men together and have a separate meeting" because "the mixed groups aren't working—the women are too angry." The national conference resolution establishing the task force noted that men remained impediments to women's own advancement. But its premise was that men needed feminism just as much because sexism harmed them, too. Pressure to dominate conversations kept them from learning to listen. The expectation that they initiate sex with women forced them to always make the first move and endure the "pressure to outperform" a woman's previous partners, Farrell wrote. Years of athletic competition prepared men to commit violent crimes. Men were more likely to become alcoholics and to die by suicide.

Identifying feminism as the antidote to rigid sex roles gave these men a way to position themselves as women's allies and fellow victims. Many had been in the New Left and antiwar movements, and they saw themselves as on the side of social justice. "Men are in NOW because they believe sexism is a detriment to the full personhood of people," a young male member told a reporter in 1974, and also because "it's fun to rap the big guys": "corporate America, the power elite, politicians." Farrell argued that every NOW chapter and task force should address men's specific concerns: "the masculine aspect" of feminism. For example, the Image of Women Task Force should seek more varied media portrayals of men; advertising reform campaigns should target the stereotype of the macho man as much as the flighty female; and reproductive rights advocacy should include male birth control and paternity leave. Collins praised Farrell's proposal to hold the First National Conference on the Masculine Mystique, where men gathered at New York University in 1974.

But the task force's emphasis on making things more fair for men bothered many NOW women, who argued that their sex belonged at the center of the movement. Perhaps gender inequality hurt men, but it certainly hurt women more. Doubtful that men could ever surrender their privileges, they argued that NOW should emphasize the problems patriarchy caused for women and let the men fend for themselves. Influenced by radical feminism, some chapters began to emphasize single-sex consciousness-raising as a key movement-building tool. These intimate conversations could be vital havens from a male-dominated society: spaces for healing, bonding, and analysis. By the mid-1970s, rather than the focus on men's problems that Farrell and his task force had sought, some outposts hosted separate sessions for men intended not for "liberating" them, as Farrell had advocated, but to "help men get in touch with women's oppression."

The issue that best clarified NOW women's uneasiness with feminism for men was marriage and divorce. As no-fault divorce laws expanded across the states and former alimony requirements were loosened, NOW's approach remained deliberately gender conscious. A traditional marriage in which the man was "head of household" and the wife owed "housekeeping and sexual" services was far from an equal partnership. But making such a union easier to dissolve, on its own, could not compensate women for the unpaid labor they shouldered within their marriages or the greater likelihood that they could not independently earn enough to support themselves and their children. "Unilateral no-fault divorce" effectively "legalized desertion," NOW argued, by freeing husbands and fathers from their responsibilities. Married women needed more "safeguards built in all along the way" to ensure equality, such as "marriage contracts" that equitably divided labors and resources. If a husband did not meet his obligations in the contract, he would not deserve a no-fault or strictly equitable divorce.

Relatedly, some NOW members were also concerned about how sexism and ageism harmed the "displaced homemaker," a middle-aged housewife who was divorced or widowed. Divorced women rarely received alimony, while widows often struggled to access their husbands' pensions or Social Security, and both groups routinely lost their health insurance when a husband departed or died. NOW advocated for a federal bill to help such women find paid employment. The 1974 national conference resolved to pressure states to recognize "the value to society and to family life of the homemaker" and to protect "that job with all the employment benefits available to other jobs."

In response to these arguments, Farrell condemned policies that favored women and their advocates. "I couldn't believe the people I thought were pioneers in equality were saying that women should have the first option to have children or not to have children—that children should not have equal rights to their dad." New fathers' rights groups began to dispute policies that favored women in child custody. They joined forces with the seventy-five or so new divorced men's groups claiming that alimony was unfair and punitive.

Men were never kicked out of NOW, but Farrell and his allies departed to advance a "men's movement" that focused on one aspect of the "masculine mystique": how traditional masculinity harmed men. "These men meet weekly and concentrate on discussing (only) the negative aspects of their roles and the resultant pain," wrote an L.A. NOW member in 1975. Casting themselves as victims, they bonded "in the age-old manner of the men's club . . . the team . . . the gang," then went on to "obtain their PhD's, publish their books, give lectures, and, in short, are still telling women how to do it."

———

NOW members in the early 1970s also debated the meaning of the *N* in their name: Whom did "national" include? Women had long been gathering across national borders. North American and European women's transatlantic organizations pursued peace, suffrage, and temperance in the late nineteenth century. In those same years, women in North African and Middle Eastern networks debated "women's awakening." International efforts continued to grow and expand after World War I with the weakening of European global domination. Women formed internationalist networks that convened not only in groups focused on women but through Christian institutions, the International Labor Organization, and their own travels. Women's international organizing intensified again after World War II along with the creation of the United Nations. Two years after its 1945 charter asserted "the equal rights of men and women," the UN created the Commission on the Status of Women, fostering enduring networks.

But these new networks acted within the context of the expanding Cold War, which became explicit during the Vietnam War. This led women from the United States and Canada to work closely with Southeast Asian women to end that conflict. They couched their efforts in the shared belief that women had a mutual interest in global peace. Women of color in the United States embraced the label "Third World Women" to identify with women seeking independence for their nations in the post–World War II era of decolonization. They critiqued gender inequality as it intertwined with economic, racial, and colonial oppression.

NOW members did not acknowledge the long history of international women's activism, nor of the power imbalances that plagued it. White European and North American women often viewed their counterparts from elsewhere as coming from repressive, "underdeveloped" countries: victims who needed saving rather than true equals. They were often unwilling to acknowledge, let alone oppose, how their nation's imperialism shaped their assumptions and harmed women in other countries. But many Americans were thinking globally in new ways in the early 1970s. The Cold War dragged on and the Vietnam War ended in defeat, helping to expose the myth of American benevolence and inspiring a search for new kinds of connections with people abroad.

Patricia Hill Burnett, one of those global thinkers, proposed leading an international program for NOW. "If the time for revolution is now, it must be world-wide," Burnett told NOW's 1973 national convention, where she pursued and won a seat on the national board. Burnett attributed her interest in global feminism to Friedan, whom she had once asked what she should contribute to the organization. Friedan responded, "Well, you traveled all your life, and the women of the United States will never be free until women of the world are free. Go to these different countries and organize NOW chapters in these countries. Form an international committee, and get them to let you head it up."

Neither NOW's charter nor its bylaws addressed the possibility of a global dimension, but nothing prohibited it. When moneyed NOW members like Burnett returned from overseas, some reported back to their chapters on the women they met and the laws and customs they encountered. Members at the 1969 convention voted to explore holding international meetings and perhaps even to create a "world organization for women." They were ignorant of earlier and ongoing global feminist efforts, due in part to Cold War repression, but they were also earnest in their exploration.

Burnett became the head of the group's international committee from her perch on the national board. On NOW's behalf, she worked to obtain consultative status with the UN Economic and Social Council, which would permit NOW to attend its meetings and present position papers. She also became the most vocal advocate of international chapters. NOW's global nodes budded and spread as the national office began to field inquiries from women abroad. Some correspondents were Americans stationed overseas on military bases or serving in the Peace Corps; others were foreign citizens who sought to form a chapter in their country or simply wanted to learn about NOW. As of mid-1972, officers had received thirteen letters from women in Europe, Asia, Australia, and Canada. National leaders welcomed and took special care with this correspondence, which they viewed as evidence of NOW's expanding appeal.

From the national office, Jim Collins-Robson searched for the cheapest, quickest way to mail materials in response.

Paris soon emerged as a good place to plant NOW's first flag abroad. The city was *"ripe for NOW!"* Gene Boyer declared after a 1972 trip there. Feminist sentiment was palpable, and the city's existing feminist groups were disorganized and appeared to Boyer to be hard to find. Lucy Komisar, in that city a few months later, agreed with Boyer. Nothing in NOW's rules prevented international chapters, but there were no guidelines, either, so she forged ahead. Around eighty professionals, students, and housewives attended the first meeting at the U.S. government-run American Cultural Center. Paris NOW had about twenty active members six months later, more than thirty paid members, and fifty other sometime attendees—all mostly Americans. The chapter president wrote to her U.S.-based NOW contact that its five consciousness-raising groups were "stable and successful," and its employment committee was preparing a booklet on how to find work as a foreigner in Paris.

The mostly American composition of the Paris chapter spared it from cultural clashes, but the chapter soon encountered other problems. Members learned that their chapter would need to hire a lawyer to register them with the local police in order to be established as a "legal association." Their home addresses would become state property, their phones could be bugged, and chapter officers would bear legal responsibility for members' actions. Abortion was still illegal in France, for example, and if the chapter paid carfare to a ferry to England to procure the procedure, they could be jailed as accomplices. NOW's stateside leaders, when confronted with these problems, could not offer specific guidance. And because pay scales were higher in the United States, the women in France argued that membership dues were too costly for them. Stateside officials believed dues should be uniform. And although airmail was pricey, they wanted to keep in touch with the Paris members so that they would value their NOW affiliation.

If the group was serious about establishing an international presence, the Paris chapter leader, Marjorie Canja, wrote to stateside leaders, NOW needed to make some changes. She requested that chapters be allowed to make their own rules, "relevant to our local conditions." But the American officers refused to relax the rules and procedures, rejecting the chapter's proposals to create a dues-free local membership category and to limit membership to women. Less than two years after the branch's founding, Paris feminists voted to leave NOW in early 1974. Some could not accept NOW's bylaws, while others did not want to affiliate with an American group. Paris NOW renamed itself the Paris Organization of Women, written out in English. The Paris experience taught stateside officials that "actually forming an international organization was legally enormously complicated."

Meanwhile, Burnett planned for NOW to host an international women's conference. This "world convocation of women" would take place in the United States in 1973 and lay the groundwork for a larger European gathering several months later. "It was my idea to have it—my baby," she said. Burnett's thirty initial contacts sent the names of more women to invite. Her mailing list grew to five thousand in forty countries. Burnett and other NOW officials described the conference as a forum for mutual exchange: their group would host but not impose its "goals or political beliefs upon our visitors." Instead, as Burnett wrote to a Russian feminist, "the idea is to find common goals that will unite women all over the world." Most NOW leaders did not think to seek the support or expertise of women who had spent decades organizing women globally around the specific issues of peace, human rights, imperialism, and labor standards. Still, the Americans saw themselves as the vanguard: "As the world's largest feminist organization, it is our duty to extend ourselves to reach and help our sisters overseas."

The one exception was Hernandez, whose reaction to Burnett's plans also anticipated some of the problems to come. The conference idea was "fantastically exciting," Hernandez wrote to Burnett, but it should be "a serious, and fun, convention" rather than "a frivolous, media-oriented public relations gimmick." She was also concerned that American feminists not take too large a role. "I do *not* think NOW should be *the* conveners of the conference," she explained. Instead, they should "initiate contacts to international feminists (letters or personal) to join in a call for the convening." Hernandez also foresaw that finances would be a challenge, suggesting that NOW seek donations from "rich feminists." The budget should include subsidies or all-expenses-paid travel for women with less money, Hernandez suggested, to "lessen the 'elitist' quality of such a conference."

Money was indeed a major obstacle to a truly global gathering. On an initial list of twenty-four contacts, eleven responded that they either could not or might not attend due to the expense. Egly Psaltis of Athens, Greece, declined because "the distance and fare and other expenses are too high for me," compounded by the unfavorable exchange rate. Mercy Aguta of the All Africa Conference of Churches was "in sympathy with the goals and aspirations of your organization" but "cannot see my way through financially," since her own group was strapped for funds. In the end, most of the three hundred participants paid their own way, including the $35 registration fee ($209 today). Many "seemed to be quite the Elder Stateswomen of their worlds," a reporter noted. An Indian feminist turned up her diamond-studded nose at the accommodations—"I have never made a bed in my life," she told the organizers—but she stayed. Burnett herself donated more than $1,000 to the conference ($6,000 today). She called it "my gift to NOW for letting me have my dream come true."

NOW hosted the four-day conference in Cambridge, Massachusetts, in June 1973. The women hailed from two dozen countries, and they ranged in age from high school to retirement, although most were in their twenties and early thirties. The 300 attendees included 181 women from the United States, at least a few women from Canada, two dozen from countries in Europe, Latin America, the Middle East, and Asia, and one woman from what was then Swaziland. Its stated aims were "to discuss the common goals of the feminist movement and plan their implementation" and to build a network that could plan a second, larger conference. The musicians and activists Yoko Ono and John Lennon were the biggest celebrities there. Both were NOW members; Ono had recently donated $5,000. She was pleased that American women had convened the conference, she said, "because American women aren't really aware of the rest of the world." Lennon kept a low profile, "wander[ing] around in the background with a video camera." "He's been going through a lot of suffering because [he supports] the movement," Ono explained.

NOW's president, Wilma Scott Heide, the Pittsburgh sociologist who had succeeded Hernandez in 1971, welcomed the conference goers. Their gathering to "energize international feminism" was "not only necessary" but "imperative." As the women began discussing various topics in half-day sessions, an observer noted, it became "apparent that feminism means different things to different women throughout the world." Some wanted to target economic structures. The New Zealand trade unionist Connie Purdue called for a socialist revolution: "Capitalism . . . wastes the talents of women." Others, like Gool Sidhwa of Calcutta, framed more pragmatic concerns. In India, "women must first learn to read, then they must learn to keep from having 13 children, then they must be trained to work at a job," she said. Only then could they "sit around and . . . talk about philosophy." Mary Mdiniso agreed; women's most pressing problems in Swaziland were disease, hunger, and poverty.

Some conference goers criticized the gathering itself. A group of Europeans declared the meeting "too pale, too conservative and too chaotic." Objecting to men's modest presence among them, they did not want any men invited to the next conference, with a West German attendee claiming she would not participate if men were there. A NOW member countered that men should be welcome: "You have to remember that our movement is at a higher [level of] development than yours." The others shouted her down as she tried to explain herself.

Still, the conference had its high points. Ono's Saturday night concert at Old Cambridge Baptist Church had "all the color and excitement of a revival meeting." Indian and Russian women also led that audience in folk dances. Some wept when Sheila Prag of Israel claimed, "If I had known I was to have the opportunity to speak, I would have liked to have gotten together with my sister from Egypt," referencing the rising tensions between their nations that would soon culminate in the Yom Kippur War. Women like Prag had once felt so isolated, Prag said, "but we have discovered that everyone is going through the same awful experience we are."

Before they adjourned to the tune of the 1971 feminist anthem "I Am Woman" piped through the auditorium speakers, the conference goers approved several gestures of international solidarity. They committed to planning protests on behalf of "the three Marias," Portuguese women who struggled against a dictator-run government and strict Catholic patriarchy. The trio was facing trial in Lisbon for *New Portuguese Letters*, their four-hundred-page book of essays, poetry, and stories about Portuguese women's isolation and inequality. The conference also approved a message of support for a twenty-five-year-old Italian woman facing trial for her abortion eight years earlier. They agreed to plan a larger feminist conference in Europe, to raise $300,000, and to set up a global activist network.

To Burnett, the gathering proved that feminists were "starting brush fires on every continent" and created the momentum for a global organization. She was receiving two hundred letters each month from women all over the world, she told the other officers, including many requests for information on how to create NOW chapters. Burnett personally paid the $15 fee to start a chapter in New Delhi. Drawing from the contacts she made at the conference and the "friendship-by-mail" she had cultivated, Burnett planned her most ambitious undertaking yet: a three-month trip to fourteen countries to meet with feminists and form NOW chapters, sponsored by her husband to mark their twenty-fifth wedding anniversary.

Burnett began her voyage with two weeks in Moscow, then spent several days apiece in Beirut and Tehran. After remaining for more than a week in New Delhi, she traveled through Nepal, Bangkok, Singapore, and Bali. She stayed for one week apiece in Hong Kong and Japan and concluded the trip with eight days in Honolulu with her husband. Some in NOW questioned her motives, but they saw little downside. One described Burnett's trip as "a ten week tour (at her own expense) spreading American style feminism to our sisters in the Near and Far East." Burnett met with local feminists, visited tourist destinations, and purchased relics to decorate her home.

Burnett had the money to travel the world on NOW's behalf, but not the crucial understanding that movement building was a two-way process. In Hong Kong, near the end of the trip, she presented her "feminist impressions" to an audience of one hundred, hosted by the city's International Feminist League. In an unlabeled script in Burnett's archive that is likely this speech, she described her "super-deluxe treatment" in the U.S.S.R., where the Soviet Women's Committee hosted her. "The factories fascinated me with their colorful, cheerful interiors," she said. Her few days in Iran taught her that "women exist[ed] to serve men" there. Burnett had been "saddened . . . to see veiled faces everywhere." In India, she had painted Prime Minister Indira Gandhi's portrait, mastered wearing a sari, and learned "the Indian technique of eating rice." Nepal had impressed her with its "mountainous splendor" and "a savage heritage."

It is easy to imagine Burnett's hosts, a cosmopolitan group whose founding goals were "both Colony-wide and international," cringing at her words. Indeed, members of the International Feminist League wrote to NOW's national office after Burnett's visit. The Hong Kongers described her lecture as "a second-rate travelogue filled with misrepresentations" that made American feminists appear snobbish and provincial. Burnett "did not tell us about International Feminism," they wrote, and they doubted "she has any idea what the concept means." They urged NOW's leaders to be more careful in selecting its representatives abroad. Reading this criticism, Burnett was crushed. "You were all so friendly during the time that I was in Hong Kong," she protested, and she politely returned her hosts' rebuke. It was "so easy to tear each other down," she wrote to them, "instead of joining together to gain true equality."

Despite this disappointment, Burnett's trip advanced her mission. When she returned, NOW had twenty-seven overseas outposts in twenty-one countries; within two more years, she had convened twenty-five overseas chapters herself. The Washington, New York, and Detroit chapters sustained international task forces that translated feminist literature, welcomed feminists from other countries, and kept up correspondence. But like their approaches to men, to race, and to sexuality, the chapters' views of internationalism varied widely.

To become an international organization, NOW would have had to change beyond stretching to make room for more causes, as the Parisians had pointed out. The group's leaders and most members would not do it. In 1974, the board chose to adopt standards for international "affiliates" rather than chapters. These outposts would have to cover their own mailing costs and release NOW from liability for anything they did. The new kit for starting an overseas chapter included nothing specific about NOW's internationalism or what the organization could offer feminists abroad "except the chance to get together (which we have already been doing)," a U.S. service member wrote from her base in Germany in 1975. Some women on U.S. military bases built durable nodes of activism, and more than a hundred NOW members had promised to attend the United Nations' International Women's Year conference in 1975 in Mexico City. As other feminists deepened their global connections, some NOW members and chapters worked on international issues, but the officers kept their focus stateside.

———

When Burnett set out as NOW's self-appointed global ambassador, her organization was only seven years old. Realizing the founders' vision for a new women's politics now appeared both harder and more urgent. In years when American society appeared to be breaking apart and barreling toward an uncertain future, thousands of women turned to NOW. They hoped their gender could draw them together if they channeled their efforts through the same organization.

This work was challenging and often frustrating. Members sought to build power as a single group, but they were spread out geographically and their varied identities gave them different priorities. Along the way, they inevitably found one another's blind spots and prejudices. They also discovered that while NOW was an unstable coalition, it could bend without breaking.

5.

GETTING PAID

S ears Shortchanges Women." So shouted the flyers that Mary Jean Collins and other Chicago NOW members handed to women exiting the Sears Tower in the evenings in 1974. With the previous year's opening of that new corporate headquarters in the purpose-built world's tallest building, Sears, Roebuck had cemented its prominence in downtown Chicago and its reputation as a global giant. Sears was the world's largest retailer, twice the size of its nearest competitor, J. C. Penney. A trusted household name since 1892, Sears sold everything from baby clothes to car tires in thirty-seven hundred stores in all fifty states and in Latin America.

Behind Sears's burnished image, argued Collins and her allies, company officials increased their profits by exploiting women. NOW members campaigned to expose the retailer's practices and force it to change. They also reached out to the Sears clericals, salesclerks, and cleaners who knew firsthand the problems NOW described: low pay, no benefits, little room to advance. And woman shoppers all struggled to earn a store credit card—a lifeline for the poor, a boost into the middle class for the better off, and a status symbol for the wealthy—under the company's "arbitrary" system. Sears was "a notorious discriminator," but this was a new day, NOW asserted. As workers and consumers, "women won't buy it!"

Sears was just one business that had long cheated women, NOW claimed. Corporations, government programs, and patriarchal culture all treated their sex as dependents, their work as less valuable, and their security as best pursued through marriages to men. NOW reframed these customs as discrimination and used Title VII's workplace equality plank as an access point into the establishment's armor. Aileen Hernandez criticized the state laws that excluded women from jobs that required lifting much weight. Pointing out that her purse was often fifteen pounds or heavier, she retorted that society treated her sex as "frail and incapable" only "when women are getting paid." Hernandez and other members pushed the government to enforce Title VII and employers to follow it. More than that, their lawsuits, registered complaints, and protests sought to pry open the entire system of gender inequalities: a complex web that wove through regulations and statutes, tax codes and Social Security. At first, "[we] did our best on our own time and expense," explained the attorney Marguerite Rawalt, to hammer the bosses who underpaid and overcharged women. They had far fewer resources than their opponents, but before long, Collins said, "we had them on the run."

Focusing NOW on employment could make the organization "as effective as possible," Collins argued, with members "work[ing] together on a common thing" by targeting one national employer. But making labor that "common thing" spotlighted contradictions. The group's structure demanded constant upkeep through its members' unpaid work. Leading a chapter was "a non-stop job" that would have cost "more than anybody could pay," explained the Chicago chapter president, Mary-Ann Lupa. NOW thus championed working women's rights while dipping deep into its own free labor pool. The members in that pool then had less time to support themselves financially. This struck some as hypocritical. "Here I am, after ten years working for feminism," wrote the New York chapter president, Jacqui Ceballos, "still living off my husband!"

NOW's efforts to change work led its members to some hard questions. Was NOW taking advantage of them, just as corporations fleeced woman workers and consumers? Were their own comrades making money on their roles? Collins did NOW's clerical work for free through her husband's print shop while fending off attacks that she was "ripping off NOW" through that "profiteering" business. Hernandez took her own approach to reforming work. Unlike Collins and her allies, who sought to use Title VII as a stick for beating its offenders, Hernandez offered businesses the carrot of education and voluntary reform. Her consulting work, which advised employers on workplace equality laws, also raised some NOW members' eyebrows. Was she assisting well-meaning companies with following the law or helping violators to slither off the hook?

Given NOW's meager funds and vast workload, its members made their own judgments about how to participate and judged one another's choices, sometimes harshly. Many joined the campaign against Sears. The retailer was "eminently well qualified as a target," declared a 1974 NOW newsletter, because its enormous size, with outposts "in every community," was both a strength and a vulnerability. That was just as true of NOW.

———

Mary Jean Collins quit her job at the electronics company in 1970 to take two simultaneous roles in NOW. Appointed the group's first Midwest regional director, Collins received a $100 budget ($744 today) and thirteen states to cover. When someone from one of those states "called the national office and said they wanted to form a chapter, we would get in our car and go there." Their goal was "that every town in America would have a chapter of NOW." She "loved it," she recalled, even though the job "cost more than $100." Back home in Chicago, Collins volunteered around the clock in her husband's business, whose only client was NOW. But she also had to avoid the appearance of drawing monetary support from NOW while serving in its national leadership. Collins made it clear that she held no stake in C-R Office Programs: "a dangerous financial position" for her because "marriage is not necessarily forever," she reported to fellow members in 1973; indeed, her own marriage would soon collapse. "Jim was working but I was doing this full time," she said later, "even though I wasn't earning a salary."

Collins accepted these responsibilities because she was "committed to NOW." Serving as regional director and volunteering in the national office were both taxing and unpaid roles because, as NOW expanded in the late 1960s, its workload crept higher even as its funds stayed low. Things were so disorganized, Collins recalled, that "no one even knew where to send their dues." Officers moved the national headquarters three times in the first seven years. With every move, the organization lost records. "Nobody knew who belonged and who didn't," said Catherine Conroy. The group had grown to include hundreds of chapters and tens of thousands of members by the early 1970s, but it was still run by volunteers spread out across the country. Was it ethical to take ever more of members' time and energies in the fight to end the structures of inequality for everyone? Or should they give priority to raising money to pay staff, siphoning resources from an aggressive campaign for workplace rights?

Those questions had plagued them since the beginning. Reflecting many of their own experiences in institutions—government, unions, universities, and corporations—NOW's founders built a structure that took significant labor to maintain. The organization could not afford to pay much for that labor, but its first leaders were reluctant to shoulder much of the clerical work, and its volume soon became too much for them to handle anyway. "The one thing, by definition, we all hated to do was secretarial work," said Betty Friedan. In a cultural climate that often treated women's rights as a joke, she and the others wanted to emphasize their professional status. A few NOW officers funded part-time assistants from their own pockets. In December 1966, the national board voted to hire a secretary, Joan Simmons, who split her part-time hours between Muriel Fox's office at the Manhattan public relations firm Carl Byoir, Betty Friedan's apartment, and her own home.

Part-timers and volunteers could not keep up with all of the office tasks at hand: responding to inquiries, keeping accurate lists of members, making newsletters, and collecting dues. The leaders experimented with different ways to assign and compensate the work. In 1969, the New York NOW member Dolores Alexander, after a health scare, decided to leave her reporting job at *Newsday* and its $12,000 salary ($89,500 today). She approached NOW's national officers with a proposition: as a "gamble for the next six months," she would run the organization from her apartment in exchange for a "very nominal salary." After that, NOW would hopefully "be in a position to pay her what she's worth as full-time national executive director." Alexander expected to support herself through freelance writing and would draw down her savings if needed.

The officers debated whether it was fair to pay Alexander a pittance and make her home NOW's office. "It's much more of a gamble for her, of course, than it is for us," Friedan reasoned, "but I think she really wants to do it." She and the others agreed with Muriel Fox that NOW should "take this plunge while Dolores is willing to make the investment of her time and energy (and lack of higher salary)," Fox wrote. They "might never have such an opportunity with such a well-qualified person again."

The deal was made. As NOW's first paid employee in early 1969, Alexander moved to a larger apartment, with one room "devoted solely to NOW business" and with its own telephone line. She was "instantly snowed under with work" and "run ragged" as officers off-loaded their clerical duties onto her. "This organization has been given to me with the message: make it work," Alexander wrote to the national officers several months into her tenure. That meant "doing and being everything: mail clerk, typist, secretary, bookkeeper, publicity and public relations director, executive director, newsletter editor, membership coordinator and organizer, AND fundraiser." By contrast to the $250 per week plus benefits Alexander had earned at *Newsday*, NOW paid her $150 per week with no benefits. The organization paid for $2,000 worth of other "temporary help" in her office, and New York chapter members sometimes volunteered, but NOW could not be run by "one person, with occasional secretarial help." In this untenable situation, Alexander resigned after a little more than a year.

Some agreed with Alexander's claim that NOW could not continue "as a volunteer organization" because that structure undermined its broader fight for women's economic rights. Next to no one was being paid to work for NOW, but members like Mary Jean Collins were putting in full-time hours. Leaders' reliance upon members' unpaid work robbed those women of time to support themselves. "There can be little equality without economic independence," said the NOW Volunteerism Task Force leader, Pat McCormick. Her task force formed in 1971 to study how women's time and energy had long been sidelined into unpaid benevolent work. But did women's service to NOW depart from this tradition? Volunteering full-time for feminism "substituted service and self-sacrifice for a small group (i.e., the family) for that of a larger group (i.e., the women's movement)," McCormick warned.

The workload kept growing when national leaders moved NOW's business to Chicago in 1970. Jim Collins-Robson's modest operation received between 30 and 50 pieces of NOW mail per day in 1971; two years later, that figure was close to 150. Even with several assistants, he and Mary Jean could not keep up. Some chapters had no member willing to maintain their mailing list, prepare the newsletter, or answer the phone. "More charismatic leadership will be needed in the future," New York NOW leaders determined, "to induce women to do the 'shitwork' for NOW that they joined NOW in order to free themselves from."

They struggled to raise the funds to pay others to do those tasks. Wealthy white women had bankrolled earlier campaigns for suffrage, birth control, and more, but NOW leaders were not interested in cultivating a network of elite philanthropists. They wanted their organization to embody the egalitarian values they sought to promote in society. Membership had to be affordable, they insisted, even if that harmed the organization's bottom line. Regular annual dues in the early 1970s cost $10 per year (about $74 today), with a $5 "hardship" category, but everyone had to pay something. "You can't fight poverty with poverty," the board chair, Judy Lightfoot, wrote to a Pennsylvania chapter in 1973. "Although we all appreciate and share the desire to have as many feminists as possible become members of NOW, I know you realize the essential and urgent need to finance the revolution." Dues were the group's main funding stream, but they did not pay the bills. In 1973, for example, the organization anticipated $195,000 in income, including $161,000 from dues, $19,000 from contributions, and $2,500 from fundraising. But expenses topped $240,000, creating a deficit of nearly $45,000.

Such empty coffers meant that everyone was a volunteer and only a few could afford to be leaders. When Hernandez left the EEOC in late 1966, she walked away from a "fantastic" salary, especially "for a woman," she said. Unlike her predecessor, Betty Friedan, who earned book royalties and possibly alimony in the wake of her divorce, Hernandez was in a precarious position when she became NOW's president in 1970. It was "a real hardship" for her to "try and handle the presidency and still earn a living" through her consulting business, said a friend. Serving as NOW's president did not come with a wage; instead, it had cost her as much as

$6,000 ($44,670 today) for "travel to national meetings (at least four per year required), telephone, postage, supplies, [and] clerical assistance," as a newsletter story about NOW's national office explained. This expense likely factored into Hernandez's decision to preside for only one term.

NOW simply needed cash. In 1971, the leaders developed a tax-exempt arm, modeled on the NAACP's Legal Defense Fund, in hopes of attracting more donations to fund court battles. Already in its third decade, the NAACP's branch was the "legal arm of the civil rights movement," with fifty-one full-time staffers. It had raised more than $1.4 million in personal contributions and foundation support in 1964 alone.

But NOW's Legal Defense and Education Fund did not have its own version of the civil rights movement's access to African Americans' tradition of community uplift or institutions like Black churches and newspapers to trumpet their mission. And women might not have seen funding NOW as a matter of survival, as many African Americans viewed groups like the NAACP. The LDEF faced distinct challenges in advocating for women: swimming against the current of paternalist attitudes that had long closed their sex out of the financial sector, undervalued their labor, denied them access to economic institutions, and assumed they were a man's dependent.

The LDEF eked by on members' modest donations, unable to "take the helm and guide the destiny of the cases" it pursued. The fund's new director in the early 1970s, Mary Jean Tully, was married to an executive whose salary permitted her to work for NOW without one. Thus as NOW sought to erode the myth that men were always or should be the breadwinners, it had to take advantage of the fraction of its members for whom it was true.

Taking office, Tully discovered that the fund had done "practically nothing" due to lack of funds. The "whole world was out there," she said, "and we were going after a jungle full of animals with a pea shooter." NOW was not attached to a preexisting institution with its own resources like the American Civil Liberties Union, whose Women's Rights Project formed in 1972 and looked out for cases that could overturn precedents and force appeals. NOW instead turned away from litigation, due partly to its cost. Some members criticized Tully for soliciting donations from businesses; she responded that any funds she raised "were reparations I was getting on behalf of all women." NOW faced an "inherent contradiction," members saw, between the organization's need for money and its members' reluctance to sacrifice their "purity" by "toadying to" the same businesses that "hurt us so badly" as employers and creditors.

———

Even as NOW's structure came to parallel the corporations it targeted—a national headquarters with multiplying local outposts—its battlefield was steeply tilted. For generations, the law had been on employers' side. America's labor force was a racist, sex-caste system, buttressed by gendered state laws that locked women into a narrow range of occupations in the clerical and service sectors. Even those feminized jobs in offices, schools, shops, and hospitals were mostly out of reach for women of color. They typically worked for the lowest wages in stockrooms, factories, or restaurant kitchens, as janitors, or in white women's homes. Under these conditions, women of color often sought to remain at home to care for their own families. Some of NOW's founders understood the range of women's relationships to paid labor, but most were white women who viewed wage earning as a desirable route to independence. Their perspective shaped NOW's approach.

Hernandez had been gone from the EEOC for nearly a year when, in 1967, a quartet of Washington, D.C., attorneys—Pauli Murray, Mary Eastwood, Phineas Indritz, and Marguerite Rawalt—quietly began meeting after work in the library of the U.S. Department of Labor. Like Hernandez, they had observed officials' anemic approach to Title VII, and they viewed its stated promise of workplace equality for women as their best leverage point. Declaring themselves NOW's Legal Committee, they held a nightly review of the letters women had sent to NOW describing their workplace problems. Many of these correspondents had already petitioned the EEOC and received no relief. Sonia Pressman Fuentes, an attorney inside the agency, supported NOW's work more covertly as "a kind of double agent."

The Legal Committee attorneys appealed the cases of three working-class women who had lost Title VII claims in federal district courts. The first was that of the California assembly-line worker Velma Mengelkoch, whose employer, North American Aviation, built supplies for space travel. Mengelkoch challenged a state law that prevented women from working more than eight hours per day. Hernandez, who was then an EEOC commissioner, met with Mengelkoch and encouraged her to file a complaint with the agency in 1965. Months later, as the commissioner assigned to Mengelkoch's case, Hernandez ruled that Mengelkoch had experienced discrimination. But when Hernandez presented her finding to the other commissioners, they overruled her. The EEOC instead informed Mengelkoch that she could sue North American Aviation on her own.

NOW agreed to represent Mengelkoch in 1967, and with the group's support she became the first plaintiff whose sex discrimination claim reached the U.S. Supreme Court. The court declined to hear Mengelkoch's case "for want of jurisdiction" but permitted her to appeal to the Ninth Circuit Court of Appeals. The lower court threw out the state's limit on women's hours in 1971. With it, employers could no longer hide behind such laws to keep women out "of working as supervisors and of earning extra overtime pay," NOW boasted.

The next year, NOW represented women at an Indiana factory. They had accused their employer, Colgate-Palmolive, and their union of conspiring to uphold a company policy that excluded women from jobs that required lifting more than thirty-five pounds and left them vulnerable to layoffs. Unlike Mengelkoch's employer, theirs was a well-known brand. Betty Friedan, who was NOW's president at the time, threatened Colgate's president with a nationwide boycott. Not only would the group's members refrain from buying anything on "the complete list of your 60 consumer items," Friedan claimed; those members were ready to "go on the air and in the press in every city" and urge "the 28 million American women who today work for a living, the millions of girls now in high school and college, and the millions of young and older housewives" to close their wallets to Colgate.

The New York chapter took this indignation to the streets. Members dumped toothpaste, detergent, and powdered soap into a toilet at a public "flush in" outside the Colgate-Palmolive building in Manhattan in 1968 as they chanted, "Colgate is a sex offender!" In planning the protest, the chapter member Flo Kennedy made sure that all different kinds of women were there: especially those in respectable dress. When someone at a planning meeting expressed concerns about being arrested, Kennedy retorted, "You are the woman consumer," a population the company would take pains not to alienate. "They'll probably get on the phone to the precinct and tell them, 'please, baby, don't make any arrests,'" she predicted. A company spokesman confirmed Kennedy's point that Colgate would handle the protesters with some care. "We didn't realize that women wanted to carry around 50 to 100 pounds," he told a reporter. "I seriously doubt if the women picketing know what it's all about," adding, "We still love the ladies."

Colgate's love did not extend to the "ladies" it employed. NOW fought the company on their behalf and won in court. In *Bowe v. Colgate-Palmolive*, the Seventh Circuit Court of Appeals ruled in 1969 that employers could not explicitly separate workers by sex and that weight-lifting limits had to be gender neutral. All women at the plant received back pay, set at "the highest rate of pay" of the male-typed jobs for which they would have qualified if Colgate had had a "non-discriminatory seniority scheme." The three NOW attorneys donated their time, but NOW's copying and court costs amounted to $5,000 ($36,700 today), which was "a fortune" for NOW to absorb, but "not even peanuts" to Colgate. "It was imperative that we win," Kay Clarenbach said later, but "the funding looked hopeless" as the appeal wore on. She sent "an SOS" to national board members "pleading" for $100 from each "to be collected in any legal way she could get it." Board members chipped in enough cash, NOW succeeded, "and one more industrial Goliath began to get a message."

NOW's third Title VII case was steered by Sylvia Roberts, the Louisiana attorney who became the architect of its litigation strategy. Roberts had never seen a woman lawyer when she set her sights on the career as a teenager. After she earned high grades at Tulane University Law School, the state supreme court's chief justice, John B. Fournet, hired her as a clerk. It was a position with "schoolteacher hours" that allowed its mostly female workers to continue to manage their households. Roberts agreed to be "on standby" for NOW for a ripe Title VII case. One soon appeared.

Lorena Weeks was a nineteen-year employee of Southern Bell, a

Georgia subsidiary of the massive telephone company AT&T. Weeks, who was white, had read about Title VII in her union newsletter and applied for her boss's job when he retired in 1966. His switchman position paid nearly double her $78 weekly salary as an operator. The company instead gave the job to a man with much less experience, pointing to a Georgia law that banned women from lifting more than thirty pounds at work. Weeks believed that the ban served to protect men's control over the best jobs, not least because she defied it each morning to lift her typewriter from under her desk. A union official told her as much, explaining that men had families to support. "My daddy died in a boiler explosion at a sawmill when I was nine years old," Weeks said, and "my momma worked herself to death at age 38. I *knew* the man wasn't [always] the breadwinner."

Weeks sued in 1967 to force Southern Bell to open the switchman job to women. Waiting for her case to unfold while enduring the bosses' daily harassment was awful. When she refused to lift her typewriter and instead began handwriting her reports, the company suspended her. "I hated to keep being a troublemaker over and over and over," she said, but she held firm for four years, selling her house and borrowing from the company's credit union at a punishing 12 percent rate to keep her three kids in college.

When Weeks could not afford to appeal after losing in federal district court, NOW came to her defense. During the oral argument, Sylvia Roberts, who weighed about ninety pounds, lifted a workbench over her head as a visual rebuke to state lawmakers and employers who "ma[de] decisions for women about what they could lift." Hernandez, then NOW president, wrote to Southern Bell's president, Frank M. Malone, as the appeal wore on, declaring herself "appalled . . . as a former EEOC commissioner" that the company continued to throw "roadblock after roadblock into Ms. Weeks' path" because she challenged "an illogical practice" of the company. Hernandez asked the officials to consider their company's image: "What does the continued intransigence of Southern Bell convey to the public about the company's sense of law and justice?"

The Fifth Circuit Court of Appeals overturned the Georgia law in 1971 and ordered Southern Bell to change its policies, promote Weeks into the switchman's job, and pay her nearly $32,000 ($219,000 today), the gap between her wages and what she would have earned if she had been promoted in the first place. Commenting on the case's significance, Hernandez pointed to the amount of back pay Weeks won: "The court has established the principle that individuals who are the victims of discrimination may get full back pay to the time when their complaint was filed." NOW could barely scrape together the dollars it took to fight these corporations in court, but its Title VII strategy was changing the terms of American work.

The Weeks case victory not only gave NOW "a real solid achievement"; it vindicated members' position that the law was a vital "avenue for bringing about changes" for working women, Roberts said. And by allying with blue- and pink-collar workers, NOW "couldn't just be classified as being interested in elitist, professional women." But NOW's attorneys did make choices that favored some working women over others. By asserting an analogy between race discrimination and sex discrimination, they convinced judges that sex-based distinctions hurt women rather than protecting them. This strategy linked feminism to the broader fights against inequality and segregation. But it also positioned racism and sexism as merely parallel oppressions, failing to acknowledge their compound effects for women of color. The law was one of NOW's most successful vehicles for creating change, but creating that change nevertheless strained the resources of the group and narrowed its vision.

———

NOW soon found creative ways to pressure corporations outside the courtroom. Hernandez contributed key expertise and stature as a former EEOC commissioner. Other members set up a national compliance and enforcement task force that assembled an ambitious list of long-range goals aimed at making working men and women more equal. Enforcing sex equality laws and reevaluating state protections were top of mind, but they also wanted to open up industries and professions to women, upgrade jobs for low-wage earners, eliminate discrimination against mothers and older women, and win tax breaks for child-care expenses. These demands were not new, but their fusion was.

They started with the enforcement agencies. Women had new rights "on paper," said the compliance task force coordinator Ann Scott. But "our experience shows that our first struggle to realize these rights will not be with industry or organized labor so much as with the federal government," she said, referring to the EEOC's disinterest in Title VII's sex provision. In one instance, NOW confronted Houston industrialists at EEOC-sponsored hearings in 1970. The planners focused on "race and national origin," Sylvia Roberts reported. Those officials ducked Houston NOW's efforts to learn "how the hearings would be conducted" and resisted granting them "time to testify." Only after the Houston chapter produced its own research report on sex discrimination in local industries and publicly demanded to participate did NOW receive a ninety-minute session to put "the facts before the public" during the three-day gathering.

At the hearings, Sylvia Roberts took the lead, accusing business leaders of perpetuating male supremacy. Several industrialists had testified that women refused to perform strenuous tasks. "Women do hard work at home or on the farm," Roberts countered, including "lift[ing]" children who weighed thirty pounds or more. "There's no concern of protecting them—until a paycheck is involved." To the claim that men were breadwinners and women were "working as a hobby," she noted that "the fact that a man is a bachelor" never mattered to employers. In the session, EEOC officials asked "few searching questions on sex discrimination," although Commissioner Elizabeth Kuck, who had been the first woman appointed to the EEOC after Hernandez left, praised "the NOW group" for its "very impressive presentation," which had been "well grounded" in "basic information." The Houston hearings confirmed Roberts's impression that "institutional bias" was "truly present" in the EEOC, which was also "virtually the only government agency with a mandate to eradicate sex discrimination." But the agency appeared movable, and NOW kept pushing it.

NOW found another angle of attack in the amended Executive Order 11246, which banned workplace discrimination by federal contractors. Unlike the EEOC, which initially could do little more than try to persuade employers to respect its recommendations, the Office of Federal Contract Compliance (OFCC) could force a company to reform and cancel federal contracts with those that refused. And unlike NOW's litigation strategy, the OFCC did not require long, expensive court procedures: any group or individual could file a complaint with minimal evidence, and just one complaint could trigger a top-to-bottom investigation of an employer's policies. The amended executive order required employers to take affirmative action to ensure that workers were treated without regard to personal attributes such as race and sex, to submit a written plan of action analyzing their entire labor force in order to explain which groups were "underutilized," and to report their goals and timetables for fixing any imbalances.

Like the EEOC, the OFCC initially held sex and race discrimination to different standards. Secretary of Labor James D. Hodgson told NOW's leaders in a July 1970 meeting that he had "no intention of applying exactly the same approach to women" under a provision that had been "designed for racial minorities." Hernandez announced in 1970 that NOW was filing OFCC complaints against more than thirteen hundred American corporations that included the nation's largest industrial companies, commercial banks, insurance firms, transportation companies, and utilities. Together these businesses employed more than twenty-two million people.

Hernandez seized upon this opening. NOW was "outraged," she declared, that the OFCC was "accepting affirmative action programs that do not contain equal opportunity for women." Ann Scott wrote to that agency's new director the following year. "NOW knows the difficult tasks that lie ahead of you," and "we intend to be with you every step of the way. That should encourage either your comfort or your paranoia." She demanded access to figures on women's complaints and how they were handled by every federal agency that granted contracts. The days of business noncompliance and bureaucratic foot-dragging, Scott said, were over.

Through this public pressure and personal maneuvering, NOW learned that "a bunch of females," as a Miami EEOC official put it, could overcome government resistance. NOW leaders criticized the OFCC's reporting form for employers, which requested information on women's jobs and wages compared with men's but did not require employers to list workers of color by sex. By double counting women of color, the form made a company's workforce appear more diverse than it was. Confronted by NOW, officials corrected the process. The EEOC also promoted more women within its own offices because of the group's pressure. NOW celebrated when the Department of Labor issued Revised Order No. 4 in 1971, which laid out new OFCC affirmative action requirements for women that were "frankly stronger than we expected," Scott said.

Hernandez also leveraged her personal connections. She wrote to the EEOC chairman, William H. Brown, in early 1971, enclosing a description of a recent panel of government experts who spoke on equal employment opportunity to about six hundred Wisconsin business leaders. Not only were women's rights "alternately ignored, dismissed as unimportant or ridiculed," but the EEOC's executive director, Joseph Fagan, "showed an irresponsible disregard" of its own policies and "treated the entire matter as a joke." The situation was "particularly annoying," Hernandez explained, "because I recall similar actions by a previous EEOC executive director." She also took the opportunity to declare NOW "appalled" at the small number of women in high positions at the EEOC, including the "blatant tokenism" of having only one woman commissioner out of five. Brown soon met with Hernandez, and she expressed a range of NOW's concerns about the agency's inadequate actions on women's behalf.

Members also boycotted the products sold by employers who treated their workers poorly. In 1972, NOW launched a nationwide boycott of Farah, a manufacturer of men's pants based in Texas and New Mexico that was terrorizing its mostly female Mexican American workforce for trying to form a union. "It Doesn't Matter Who Wears the Pants," claimed a NOW flyer. "If They're Farah Pants, Take 'Em Off and Take 'Em Back." NOW also joined a boycott of General Mills, whose "products [were] used and known by all," that the National Urban League had organized. Workers of color had been fighting for equal opportunities at General Mills since 1964, supported by the NAACP.

Hernandez, by then NOW's immediate past president, was encouraged that the "women's movement and the black movement were finally identifying similar goals." But boycotts showed less promise than pressuring government agencies to enforce and strengthen laws. Such protests took "tremendous community cooperation and organizational resources," members realized. "An unsuccessful [boycott] is much worse than none at all" because it revealed the company's power and NOW's relative impotence to both the company and the women involved. The General Mills campaign, for example, had not dented the company's profits. Employment advocates in the group decided to refocus their efforts on sex discrimination law rather than consumer activism.

Through all of these avenues, members' workplace rights activism was creative and effective. Any chapter or individual could file a charge in NOW's name with a local agency or the EEOC. Some chapters made employment rights their main issue, using kits created by the leaders that explained how to gather evidence and file official complaints. Soon they discovered much more they could do: visiting local employers and agencies, demanding public hearings, and pressing elected officials to hold resistant companies accountable. Organizing around workplace rights focused members' efforts, gave chapters results they could see, and helped build their ranks.

———

Collins steered her Chicago chapter toward a focus on work. She knew, from her mother's experiences as a secretary and her own brief stint in teaching, that employers exploited stereotypes to keep working women poor. From her blue-collar roots, she also took the belief that government should help. Collins recalled her grandparents' fierce loyalty to FDR, forged through the New Deal programs that had kept their family afloat four decades earlier. A hard-boiled pragmatist, she had little time to theorize. "I came in as a Democrat," she said, recalling a meeting of radical feminists where the others "said to me, 'Are you a Leninist?' I didn't know but I said I must be because I was there." (She was not.)

Along with other advocates in Chicago, Collins viewed working women as an impoverished class and set out to help them. The leverage they needed was in plain sight. "We have these laws," Collins recalled their thinking. "Now how do we get them enforced" on behalf of "the whole mass of women?" They respected the elites who were shut out of the professions and could sue as individuals. "But I also felt that those kinds of strategies wouldn't work for everybody," Collins said. "Most women were going to work in very everyday jobs, secretarial jobs, clerical jobs, nursing, retail, education."

Other NOW members shared Collins's perspective. The recent Northwestern University graduate Anne Ladky joined a Chicago-area carpool of women who would "debate the issues of the women's movement" on the ride to their jobs in publishing. They recruited her to NOW, where she was amazed that "women were just taking things into their own hands and doing them." Collins's Alverno classmate and close friend Mary-Ann Lupa grew up in west suburban Chicago, the daughter of a Polish immigrant grocer. After college, she worked as a layout artist at Montgomery Ward. "They slotted me into the charm school ads and women's clothing ads," which were not especially engaging. After a pregnancy she hid from her conservative parents, she felt that she "needed to get some power" in her life, so she joined NOW.

The local feminist reporter Karen Fishman watched the Chicago chapter become "a very impressive group of women who could get a lot of people to a meeting and who were smart and appealing." The chapter raised enough money to open an office and became the first in the nation to hire a full-time staffer in 1973. Because the group had "a budget and staff and a place, you could find them," Fishman said. She attributed their focus and efficiency in part to the city's well-oiled Democratic political machine, which offered "organization to go up against." The chapter was especially focused on confronting employers. Members "jumped in a cab and went to lunchtime actions," Lupa said, then returned to work for the afternoon. Members like Lupa, stuck in jobs that did not exhaust their abilities, had plenty of energy to work a second shift for the movement.

For these members, the movement itself was sustained labor. "I think I went to a meeting every night," said Collins. "We met constantly." After doing their "full time jobs," they "came home and did NOW stuff until midnight." Some who worked in offices secretly did the group's clerical work, drafting memos and making photocopies under their bosses' noses. For chapter officers, the work, untethered from the regular workday, demanded personal sacrifices. When the mother of then Chicago chapter president Mary-Ann Lupa wrote to tell her daughter that her cancer had advanced, the letter was buried for weeks in the "piles of mail" covering her dining room table.

A seasoned local organizer began to help the Chicago chapter become more efficient. Heather Booth was an antiwar and civil rights activist and the founder of the underground abortion collective known as Jane. She had spent years convening women around shared issues through the socialist-feminist Chicago Women's Liberation Union and the Action Committee for Decent Childcare. Booth had recently attended the Industrial Areas Foundation training, created by the legendary Chicago community organizer Saul Alinsky. Its goal was to help mobilize working-class people or, as Alinsky wrote, "to create mass organizations to seize power and give it to the people." The trainers were tough on Booth, who believed she was only the third woman to ever take the course. Booth countered their skepticism, asserting that "women could be organized and organizers." The August 26 strike convinced her that NOW was "where the mass movement was going to occur."

Booth decided to teach NOW members and other woman activists to organize the way the men did. With money from a back pay suit she won against her employer, she opened the Midwest Academy in 1973. Its first class aimed to equip women with movement-building skills and connect them across their divisions. "Forces against women work 24 hours a day and are paid full-time salaries to keep the status quo," Booth told a reporter. "We're up against the most sophisticated government and corporate combination which is designed to keep women where they are. But there's room to maneuver."

A group like NOW could do that maneuvering for women, Booth believed, if its members could be disciplined. She wrote to the NOW president, Wilma Scott Heide, to introduce the academy in early 1973. "Now is the time to move from emphasizing much needed changes in consciousness to changes in our real power." She believed that she could help NOW become that structure and win that power, sparking a movement "that reflected and spoke to the majority of women in the country" by connecting them around their varied labors and shared experiences.

Collins and several other members of Chicago NOW eagerly took the first Midwest Academy training session in the summer of 1973: a two-week boot camp to open up the city's storied organizing tradition to women. The training promised to offer "conceptual and technical skills to help students build powerful organizations so that women workers— paid and unpaid—may receive the full fruits of their work." For fourteen hours each day and $500 "tuition" apiece, Collins and the other trainees crowded into a Presbyterian church north of downtown. They studied labor history and discussed how to grow their ranks and build campaigns they could win. Anne Ladky, who was then the Chicago chapter president, had outlined some of NOW's weaknesses in her application: "I think we lack a specific strategy, including timetables, to accomplish goals." The academy taught them that campaigns should "do the job, strengthen NOW through increased members, funds and press, build a base of power," and "be catchy for press value."

Chicago NOW began to adopt the Midwest Academy tactics. Booth held extra trainings for the chapter itself and for NOW's national board, for which the group paid her. More than that of other chapters, the Chicago members' premise became "'What are we going to organize around?' not 'What are we going to research, what are we going to study? And how are we going to get attention for this concern?'" said Ladky. "We became much more efficient" after the training, Lupa agreed. She "always had a printed agenda" for meetings and ran them on time. Collins explained the chapter's new focus in 1974. "We live in a city with a highly sophisticated and organized political machine," she declared, "so we've learned organization, too."

————

As Collins made her NOW chapter more like a corporation, with its discipline and coordination, the corporations NOW confronted steeled themselves for the fight. NOW helped shape the EEOC's 1973 settlement with AT&T, the nationwide telephone monopoly and America's largest employer of women. That $38 million accord revealed a new landscape of enforcement for businesses and their critics. It also signaled the shifts to come.

The settlement demonstrated that the EEOC was gaining strength. Congress had fortified Title VII in 1972, extending the commission's ability to enforce its findings through litigation and expanding its reach to cover state and local governments and educational institutions. William H. Brown III, appointed EEOC chairman in 1969, was a Black Republican attorney who began to target large businesses and entire industries rather than investigating charges one by one. Brown earmarked 60 percent of EEOC resources to fight high-priority "Track I" cases against the nation's largest employers and pushed to extract massive financial settlements.

The AT&T settlement also showed NOW's increasing sway with the EEOC. Commission officials "took more or less hook, line and sinker" NOW's "view of institutionalized sex discrimination," said the EEOC attorney and NOW LDEF board member David Copus, to root out "the whole sociology and psychology of sexual stereotypes." NOW's president, Wilma Scott Heide, persuaded Copus to include in the settlement a requirement for AT&T to place men in traditionally female jobs.

NOW's approach relied upon the strongest tools at hand, but by treating women as a single class and leaning so heavily on government mechanisms, NOW implicitly foregrounded white women. This was in part due to the EEOC's own policies. According to EEOC guidelines, when a worker filed a claim, she had to declare herself the victim of either race *or* sex discrimination. The AT&T settlement's mandate for men to take clerical positions previously held by white women created new competition for Black women who had just gained a foothold there. The settlement also overlooked Black women's experiences of intertwined race and sex discrimination in calculating back pay awards.

Meanwhile, businesses like AT&T began to change themselves to evade NOW's pressure. Seismic economic shifts gave them new justifications. A series of crises ended decades of postwar growth, undermined corporate confidence, and bred uncertainty. This loss of faith opened space for conservative intellectuals and shrewd consultants to peddle a new approach to the American economy. Corporations should be nimble and lean, they said, and refitted to deliver value to stockholders rather than stability to workers. These shifts began to erode the jobs and security many Americans took for granted.

The service sector weathered this upheaval more easily than heavy industry, which was battered by capital flight, offshoring, and outsourcing. But businesses of all kinds created a national narrative of austerity to justify squeezing their own workers, particularly the women. This language of financial hardship had new currency in the turbulent mid-1970s and offered the perfect cover for cutting costs and shoring up male supremacy in their labor forces. If white men could no longer count on claiming good jobs, the bosses argued, then no one should.

Some feminists sounded the alarm. "A crunch is coming down politically and economically," said the Midwest Academy's Heather Booth in 1974. "Concessions have been won, but the future will be rough." She and other activists saw that employers and political leaders were using the economic climate to wiggle out of their new legal obligations. "Certain economic decisions, made in the name of 'austerity,' are inflicting unfair penalties on women," a NOW leader wrote in 1976. Members could do little to stop these changes, not least because they disagreed over how much they mattered. While union members in NOW pointed out what these corporations were doing, other, more financially secure women in the group approached the same corporations for donations.

Hernandez crafted her own approach to employers. She believed that the government had to hold them accountable to new equal rights provisions, but she had begun exploring less confrontational tactics after leaving her post at the EEOC in 1966. When still NOW president, she invited the AT&T subsidiary Pacific Telephone and Telegraph to send a representative to a NOW conference and even invited the company to join the organization. (The national board would soon ban such corporate memberships.) Hernandez increasingly embraced education and common ground in tandem with external pressure.

To develop these techniques, Hernandez had begun consulting soon after arriving in San Francisco in late 1966, and she founded her small firm, Aileen C. Hernandez Associates, in 1974. She began building a roster of clients that eventually included businesses, state and federal agencies, universities, and advocacy groups. Her firm offered "personalized services from experienced professionals with a wide range of skills" who could "deal comprehensively with the complexities of the urban scene." Trainings could change the attitudes of the white men who made personnel decisions and spare their companies from lawsuits, Hernandez asserted. The seminars she ran on "inclusionary personnel practices" for her client companies were intended to "heighten our awareness of attitudinal and behavioral patterns that keep us from meeting the spirit as well as technicalities of equal employment opportunity laws."

Some of Hernandez's clients hired her to help diversify their labor forces; others wanted to avoid the financial pressure and bad publicity of a lawsuit. Still, civil rights remedies for workers appeared to be in short supply in this new era of declared scarcity and with the more conservative Nixon administration in office. This reinforced potential rivalries between white feminists and people of color and paved the road for corporations to outflank both groups. After helping to broker the EEOC's 1973 settlement with AT&T, NOW watched with dismay as the company made a $3 billion overhaul of its technology to shrink its need for operators, folding women into blue-collar jobs that were already slated for elimination—allegedly to cut labor costs. But the telephone monopoly was flush: its 1974 profits topped $2.5 billion, more than the combined profits of a dozen other major corporations.

AT&T had publicly accepted the settlement and opened previously all-male jobs to women, but restructuring its capital deflected the blow and allowed the company to shimmy women out the door legally. Male union leaders did not seem to care that "women's work is being eliminated faster than we move into men's work," Sally Hacker, the leader of NOW's AT&T Task Force, wrote to the president of a Communications Workers of America local union in 1974.

NOW's influence in the AT&T settlement and well-placed friends at the EEOC persuaded many of its members to plow ahead on employment. NOW was becoming a power broker, but a blinkered one. And its targets were retooling.

———

As Collins's Chicago chapter honed its workplace strategy, one employer came into focus. Through "telephone calls, notes, letters or comments made at membership and organizing meetings," members discovered women's many problems with the retailer Sears, Roebuck. "It was obvious to anyone who walked into Sears to see there was a problem," said Collins. "All the people selling hosiery were women and all the people selling refrigerators were men." On the sales floor, women barely scraped by on meager hourly wages while the men took home generous commissions. Black women and men were mostly hidden from customers in warehouse, cleaning, and food service jobs. Sears was also notorious for denying woman shoppers credit, a store-specific version of today's credit cards and a financial necessity in the booming consumer economy. Black woman shoppers, like their male counterparts, were not only denied credit but often surveilled and refused services.

Company officials had spent decades cultivating Sears's reputation as "a really truly good neighbor," according to Collins. The company "had always been associated with superlatives," crowed a *BusinessWeek* profile: "biggest, best, and sharpest." It was "the envy of its competitors" and "second to none in its ability to ferret out innovative products and to get suppliers to provide them at the lowest cost. Its mail-order catalog was the largest of its kind," and its suburban stores "represented the epitome of convenience." With four hundred thousand workers, credit accounts with one-third of American adults, and annual sales that constituted 2 percent of the nation's gross national product, Sears, Roebuck had taken a hefty slice of the U.S. retail industry.

Sears was known for its quality goods and fair prices, but it was far from being a generous employer. The company was fiercely anti-union. Its longtime head of employee relations, Nathan W. Shefferman, had spent decades devising new ways to prevent workers from organizing. Shefferman had once eliminated an entire department to prevent the National Labor Relations Board from ruling that a single worker in it had been wrongly fired for his union activities.

Sears met new sex equality laws with confidence. Companies like Sears were legally required to adopt an affirmative action plan. Federal enforcement agencies were supposed to monitor employers' compliance with their own such plans and cancel contracts with discriminating companies. "In reality, enforcement is practically non-existent," NOW members discovered, because compliance agencies were understaffed and often undermotivated. They declared Sears "a charter member of the Old (White)

Boys Club where Government officials and rich businessmen would sit quietly scratching each other's backs forever if we didn't act."

Many in NOW believed that Sears was breaking the law. The company had set up its legally mandated affirmative action plan in 1968. Such plans were supposed to be public information, but Sears refused to release any details, and members thought they knew why. The company was making steady progress in hiring and promoting men of color but had "fallen far short of its even modest goals of promoting women," according to a retail industry report. Eighty-six percent of women there were in office clerical or sales jobs in 1969. Four years later, more than 83 percent of those workers were still in those jobs. Women were nearly half of full-time employees but only 9 percent of salaried workers and just over 20 percent of the big-ticket commission sales force. Only 4 out of 840 store managers were women. The company was patriarchal from top to bottom.

Women faced discrimination even before they first clocked in. Human resources officials gave woman applicants typing tests while evaluating similarly qualified men for their management potential. Interviewers asked female applicants such questions about their families as "What does your husband think of you working outside the home?" and "what arrangements have you made for the care of your children?" New employees learned that they could be fired if they ever discussed their pay at work. As NOW discovered, personnel officials "refused to tell some women their job classifications"—a ranking system within the company—so that they had "no clear understanding of what other jobs might be open to them." Managers shunted white women into dead-end clerical and hourly sales jobs and funneled women of color into the lowest-status positions behind the scenes and in the warehouse, away from customers.

Sears's sexist approach also shaped its credit policies. Credit was an essential tool in the booming postwar economy, but all women in the early 1970s, regardless of their class, race, or marital status, struggled to independently obtain and use it. Creditors like Sears treated women as men's appendages or locked them out entirely. Sears refused to grant credit to women receiving public assistance. The National Welfare Rights

Organization had spent years protesting that policy through its "Sock it to Sears" campaign. The company held out even as other department stores relented, not wanting to face the public pressure Sears had. In addition, Sears's credit department identified married female customers as "Mrs." followed by their husbands' full names. The company defended the policy as a benefit to customers that would prevent clerical errors at the credit bureau. Perhaps it did help married men, but it also prevented their wives from creating their own economic identities.

Wealthy wives like Patricia Hill Burnett experienced the denial of credit as an insult to their class status. It highlighted the fact that husbands were both the font of their abundant wealth and its stingy guardian. Burnett's husband refused to tell her his income, let alone permit her to control much of it. She admired a friend who would get $5 from her husband to tip a bathroom attendant at a fancy club, then stash all but two quarters for herself. "The most important thing a woman can accumulate is cash," Burnett claimed, since "it carries the power to be truly independent." She had fired off a complaint when the posh Chicago department store Marshall Field and Company rejected her credit application. It had happened, she surmised, because she had listed only the money she earned painting portraits and not her "yearly allowance and income from other sources": more than double the amount she had written. Burnett had credit accounts at "at least 20 major stores," she wrote to Marshall Field's president. Like him, her husband was the "president of a large corporation" and "in the highest income bracket."

Sears's poor treatment of women as both workers and shoppers, Chicago NOW deduced, was part of a larger strategy to make the company more profitable at its laborers' expense. Company officials announced a plan to convert at least 60 percent of its sales force to part-time. But like AT&T, its business was booming. Sears's net sales in 1973 topped $12.3 billion—a 12 percent increase over the previous year—and its 1974 annual report boasted "record" sales of $13 billion. The retailer had added 3.5 million square feet of retail space in the past year and recently opened more than 150 new stores. Company officials hoped to accelerate this growth by reshaping their sales force to keep ascendant discounters like

Kmart from peeling off their customers. Those discounters were under-cutting Sears's prices by replacing skilled sellers with cashiers and stock-ers who worked part-time hours and received few or no benefits.

In competing with the new discounters, Sears officials also borrowed from their playbook. They made deeper investments in technology and advertising while slashing prices and labor costs. Less than 5 percent of the company's American employees pocketed a salary; the rest, including commission salesmen, took home an hourly wage. Personnel departments set out to drive this fraction even lower by laying off full-timers and re-placing them with part-timers who were denied benefits and job security. Sears cut its ranks of "professionals," its highest job category, by more than 50 percent between 1968 and 1974. Company officials discovered that they could elevate the perceived status of downwardly mobile male store managers and salesmen by keeping women out of "their" jobs. This gave company officials breathing room to devise "new ways to maintain the status quo of cheap female labor," the Chicagoans noted.

NOW lobbed this accusation in public. At the 1974 U.S. Commission on Civil Rights hearings on women and poverty, Anne Ladky testified that Sears's new part-time jobs were identical to full-time positions in all but pay, benefits, and flexibility. The job types' key differences: part-timers derived no sales commissions, "no substantial benefits, no promotability, no participation in Sears' famous profit-sharing plan." Working part-time at Sears "means being paid less than a living wage," Ladky declared. "It means you can be required to work 40 hours a week and still be classified as part time." Sears's policy was not "intended as a service to provide the convenience of part-time work for women," as company officials claimed, Ladky argued, but to cut labor costs.

The Sears CEO, Arthur Wood, scoffed at feminists' accusation that his company was, in his words, "against women." Wood, a sixty-two-year-old World War II veteran known for his hard-nosed style, instead attempted to pit women against one another, noting that a sex discrimi-nation settlement would raise prices for woman shoppers. He claimed that his corporation was doing as much as it reasonably could. Sears was "bringing women into our company," he said, but its rightful first priority was "maintaining a successful enterprise." In other words, the company should be able to comply with civil rights laws on its own terms. Privately, however, company officials feared that NOW's legal strategy could cost them dearly.

Sears officials rebuffed accusations of deliberate sexism. Defending their practices, they appealed to the old family wage idea that cast men as breadwinners and framed women's labors as inherently less valuable. Wood told a reporter that salesmen were "heads of families" who had "chosen a career in retail." Men's domination of the most lucrative sales jobs was "not a question of discrimination," he said, but the result of their "persuasive" style. Because saleswomen were naturally "a little more reticent," they deserved to earn low pay selling buttons and baby clothes. To these men, such gendered logic expressed differences so obvious they hardly needed to be spoken—at least until NOW pushed its way through Sears's revolving glass doors.

The Chicago chapter's past experience fighting national corporations had linked up with broader NOW actions. Picketing their local AT&T branch in 1971 as part of a national NOW campaign had taught Chicago members that focusing on one large corporation was more productive than "spreading our efforts over many smaller employers," said Ladky. Alongside Collins, she began to publicly label Sears "a notorious discriminator in every aspect of employment." While the company's size gave it power, its reliance upon consumers was a weak spot. "Who do you think goes and buys the underwear? It's the women," Collins said. "We knew that if we could damage their credibility with their customers, they would have to change." NOW sought to embarrass offending companies. Its national Image Committee gave out "Old Hat" awards, which "dishonored" ten brands each year for their offensive advertisements. Major newspapers covered the awards in 1971, which went to Mattel, Skinny Dip cologne, and Virginia Slims, to those companies' alarm.

Beyond shoppers, there were many other constituencies who could join a campaign against the company: credit applicants, shareholders, and retail unions. Work itself was a somewhat limited avenue of attack, given welfare rights advocates' fight for economic security as they cared for their own families, but targeting Sears could draw them in as consumers. Even the general public, whose taxes subsidized wages so low that many Sears employees could draw food stamps, might help block the construction of new stores and favorable tax assessments. The Chicagoans also believed that a campaign against Sears could spread nationally within NOW: "In every chapter there are probably women who have or want Sears credit, have jobs or want jobs with promotional opportunities at Sears stores and offices." The campaign's architects might have known that African Americans had already dedicated decades of activism to department stores, including Sears, pursuing equal access as shoppers and employees, but Chicago NOW envisioned an independent effort led by woman workers and consumers.

To many in NOW, Sears was the ultimate white whale. In going after it, they had accused the leading U.S. retailer of sex discrimination on every front the new federal policies had opened, and had the rare chance to set attention-getting precedents and push an expansive definition of women's economic rights onto the national stage.

———

Collins and Ladky dove into the Chicago chapter's Sears campaign. They made their first contact with Sears Tower workers with the flyers they handed to women leaving work. Such women, they learned, were "relegated to the same deadening jobs for years, without recourse, as men are promoted past them." Chapter members interviewed more than a hundred women "from a cross-section of departments." They learned that women made up most of the "timecard" employees who were "paid weekly, receive[d] few fringe benefits, and earn[ed] considerably less" than the male-dominated category of "checklist" workers. Then the members began doing head counts. "How many women; how many men; how many black; how many white?" NOW members nationwide were soon carrying the same discreet "charts" to fill out inside their local Sears.

NOW members' conspicuous counting and picketing flummoxed store managers. Not only did it block the flow of shoppers; it challenged Sears's carefully built reputation as a good place to shop. "This store is their store, it's not a fair store," the protesters sang to the tune of "This Land Is Your Land" as they amassed outside Sears outposts in their cities and towns. "They do not pay us all that we work for. They do not sell us all that we pay for. This store is not for you and me."

Some Sears women were willing to talk with NOW members about their working conditions as they pretended to shop. Often those women refused to give their names, but their inside information was valuable. One eleven-year employee had taken several management training programs and had heard from a friend that a better job had opened. The personnel department denied the opening existed, but she noticed that three new people were soon hired. Another woman told NOW that Sears's flagship State Street store had only one Black male manager and one Black female assistant manager across its more than eighty departments.

Collins and Ladky encouraged members across the nation to improvise in "exert[ing] pressure on Sears on as many different fronts as we can with as many different tactics as we can." They told customers about Sears's sexism when handing out candy canes outside the downtown store before Christmas. Purchasing Sears stock as individuals permitted them to attend and protest at the annual stockholders meeting. For an elaborate 1974 action at Sears Bank in Chicago, NOW members divided into three groups. A few met with a banker as a dozen NOW members waited outside. When a chapter member emerged from the brief meeting, she yelled, "That does it for me, I'm closing my account with this bank." The others rushed to the teller windows to do the same. That alerted the "consumers," waiting in line ahead of time, to loudly express their surprise and do the same. They leafleted the lobby as they left, adding their voices to the protest outside.

Reflecting feminists' confidence in the mid-1970s that the law was on their side and that direct action could make it work, Chicago members traveled to NOW's 1974 national convention determined to make their integrated campaign against Sears a national priority. The conference voted to adopt the Sears effort as one of dozens of its task forces. Next Ladky and Collins devised a loosely coordinated national campaign from their Chicago base. They printed a monthly newsletter that offered suggestions and updates for participating chapters. The campaign asked those chapters to select a Sears coordinator, convene a Sears action committee, and research their local Sears stores and compliance agencies.

Fostered by Collins and Ladky, the campaign continued to expand. Fifty NOW chapters participated in the National Sears Action Day on December 14, 1974, which was scheduled on a pre-Christmas weekend to deflate the company's holiday profits. Some chapters wrote press releases and complaint letters; others picketed and engaged in street theater. A Wisconsin member dressed as Mrs. Santa Claus and stood outside a Sears asking shoppers to go elsewhere. The Chicagoans held an in-store ceremony in which an Ebenezer Scrooge character received a Sears "discredit card" from the chapter president. By the end of that year, more than a hundred NOW chapters were taking some form of action against Sears in their communities. The Chicago chapter alone had filed thirteen EEOC class-action charges on behalf of women in the Tower offices and the downtown Chicago store.

This focused campaign needed activists with free time and discipline. Chicago members had found their Midwest Academy training essential. They had previously had "a very vague idea of how to begin attacking a power structure such as Sears," one member wrote, and the academy had helped them in "choosing an issue and mapping a campaign." Booth brought these tactics to the national organization. About two hundred NOW members attended her confrontation clinic, where she led them through role-playing exercises to challenge "Snears Doughbuck" on its employment and credit discrimination. Bobby D. Doctor, the director of the southern field office of the U.S. Commission on Civil Rights, dropped in and was impressed by its "*action* oriented" angle. The clinic started with facts about women's treatment at "Snears," then moved to forming an action plan that could expand NOW's membership and build its power. This was textbook Midwest Academy stuff, and officials like Doctor took notice.

NOW members believed that their campaign "came at Sears from almost every conceivable angle." But this described their range of leverage points. Their approach, pressuring government officials to enforce the law against Sears, and Sears to follow it, was deliberately focused. It was an approach that emphasized inequalities between women and men rather than inequalities among women. NOW sought to upgrade feminized clerical and sales jobs and move women into male-dominated positions.

That goal offered little to the people of color whom employers shut out of those jobs in the first place. Black women's confidential EEOC complaints about Sears described compounded race and sex discrimination. Despite their higher levels of education, training, and seniority than their white counterparts, Black women were pushed into "dirty" and "lower rated" manual labor even when they qualified for office jobs. Supervisors reserved those clerical positions for "white girls," as the Philadelphia Sears employee Shirley Mims wrote in her 1972 complaint to the EEOC. Mims's claim, like others filed by Black women, did not describe sex discrimination alone, but that was how the EEOC classified it.

NOW's tactics would only reinforce this divide among women. Members believed that building a united front of women that partnered with civil rights groups would deliver victory for everyone. "In the Chicago chapter, we work with different coalitions of action groups," a chapter leader explained in 1970. "We believe people can work under their own banners." But such partnerships did not guarantee that the concerns of women of color would be heard, especially where racial and ethnic groups did not advance their own feminist agenda. Some Black women from the Sears warehouse did write to NOW. But the group's main research technique, counting public-facing workers, did not reach women of color whose labor was kept invisible to customers.

NOW claimed to speak for all women in pressuring government officials to act against Sears. Unlike the OFCC, which members noticed was "virtually worthless as an enforcement agency these days," the EEOC was gaining strength. NOW's powerful allies inside the agency included David Copus, deputy chief of the national programs division. Copus steered the EEOC investigations into NOW's targets while advising members on how to engage the EEOC's regional offices. The members saw nothing wrong with this collaboration. "We thought the government should be on the side of the people who were being discriminated against," Collins said later.

The EEOC and NOW had grown close. Copus's romantic partner was Whitney Adams, the leader of NOW's campaign to compel the Federal Communications Commission to crack down on sexism in the media and an active member of the D.C. chapter. Adams helped the Chicagoans strategize. She urged them in a mid-1973 letter to file charges against Sears in order to gain access to discovery materials. The EEOC would soon announce Sears as the target of a Track I, highest-priority investigation, she wrote. NOW should "file charges as soon as possible" so as "not to be obvious" that members knew that the investigation was coming.

The EEOC launched that Track I investigation of Sears the following year, due largely to NOW's pressure. Sears fought back with a new set of legal maneuvers that would stretch into the mid-1980s. Still, the members believed they would beat Sears and keep going. The campaign offered a map for NOW's future, Collins claimed, by giving chapters "a national program they can link up with for unified power." Some, especially Sears workers, saw the campaign as a means to put cash in their pockets and access better jobs. And still others believed it could transform the economy and make work more fair. The campaign tried to do all of these things. Collins and her allies expected Sears to settle for at least $100 million—the largest-ever payout of its kind.

But NOW's own labor issues caught up to those members. When company officials wanted to meet in late 1974, Collins and four other NOW leaders traveled downtown to the Sears Tower, confident that victory was near. The top brass was waiting for them in force, including the company's president, the CEO, and half a dozen department leaders. Seated beside these corporate officials was NOW's past president and current board member Aileen Hernandez. She had sent the letter requesting the meeting, which had also informed them of her new role, but her presence across the table made it real. Collins and the others looked around the "magnificent boardroom" in horror: "That's when we realized that she worked for them."

———

Hernandez had first made contact with Sears leaders four years earlier, when, as NOW president, she had run for the company's board of directors. She did not win a seat, but officials noticed her, and they hired her to address Sears's Southern Territorial Personnel Conference the following year. In her remarks there, Hernandez struck an empathetic tone. "Those of us in the business of people frequently find ourselves viewing those who come before us as if they were carbon copies of ourselves," she said. But this was a problem when white men were the decision makers, she explained, urging her audience to see the obvious sexism at Sears. "Just look at where the women are and what they sell." After calling for "a revolution which has to also involve both men and women, all racial and ethnic groups, and all people who care about what kind of society we should have," Hernandez ended by inviting everyone in the audience to join NOW.

As NOW's campaign against Sears expanded over the next few years, company officials approached Hernandez again. She met with them before the Houston conference that made Sears a national NOW target, and she worked with company officials over the next few months to hammer out an annual contract. In their correspondence over the terms of the contract, Sears officials framed a narrow mission that had Hernandez helping Sears beat NOW, which Hernandez tried to broaden. While she contracted to review confidential data on women's working conditions and the company's affirmative action plan, Sears's draft contract had her looking for "weaknesses" in these. Hernandez changed the wording to "possible areas of change." Hernandez also pledged to help Sears establish "meaningful dialogue" with activist groups. Sears's proposed contract wanted that dialogue to be with "the National Organization for Women and other women's groups." Hernandez changed the wording to "minority and women's groups and organizations."

Once Hernandez signed on in late 1974, Sears officials made it clear that they wanted the first meeting Hernandez brokered to be with NOW, and she agreed to arrange it. She told company leaders it would "give Sears an opportunity to talk about what is happening with affirmative action and to give these women a chance to raise questions, make suggestions, offer assistance." Some of the officials fretted that inviting the leaders of NOW's Sears campaign into the Sears Tower was like letting "the enemy within the gates," but they followed her lead.

Hernandez was "pleased" with the meeting between NOW and Sears officials. She wrote to NOW leaders that she hoped it had opened up a fruitful conversation. From the other members' perspective, company officials had merely professed good intentions and evaded their questions. Hernandez conveyed to Sears officials her sense of the company's vulnerabilities. Officials should prepare more specific statistics on employment at various Sears stores, create more diverse advertisements, and open up opportunities for older women. "If you are not already monitoring practices in the area of age discrimination, you should be doing that immediately," she wrote to them after the meeting. She also encouraged officials to set "a written and specific policy on credit," and, as part of creating that policy, "look over the credit complaints gathered by NOW and give specific data on the reasons for refusing" it in each case.

As Hernandez's work for Sears expanded and continued into the 1980s, the retailer became one of her most important clients. Her tasks included reviewing the company's plans and data and offering her recommendations and leading seminars for Sears employees, more than a thousand of whom had attended one by 1978. In these meetings, Hernandez surveyed workers about their attitudes, gave an overview of antidiscrimination laws, and tried to change their behavior. "Each of us has prejudices," Hernandez was quoted as saying in a Sears employee publication. "Don't let your prejudices trap you into committing a discriminatory act."

The Sears campaign strategists understood why the company wanted to work with Hernandez, but her work for the company confused them, and NOW's racial politics complicated the situation. The St. Louis chapter leader, national board member, and Collins ally Mary Anne Sedey explained that Hernandez's status as a Black woman and a former EEOC commissioner deepened the controversy. "We didn't have a lot of African American leaders," she said. Sedey herself believed that Hernandez "sold her soul to Sears," but "everything got all balled up. If you were against Aileen, maybe you were racist. If you weren't for the Sears campaign, maybe you were ridiculous and didn't know what was important."

Hernandez made her motives clear. Far from seeing her work as a betrayal, she perceived lots of terrain between NOW and Sears where they could work toward a good outcome. "It seems to me appropriate for NOW people to meet with Sears," Hernandez wrote to the campaign leaders, "as a facet of the announced national action on Sears . . . That has certainly been an approach in past attempts to move on NOW programs." She also expressed her belief that incremental progress with Sears could help the women there, which was the stated purpose of NOW's campaign. "I hope that the dialogue begun last week," Hernandez wrote to Lynne Darcy, NOW's compliance director, after the Sears Tower meeting, "will result in some positive benefit for the thousands of women who now work at Sears and the many others who may decide to seek work and/or credit there." Hernandez might also have doubted the EEOC would come through for Sears women, drawing from her own experience, whereas the Sears campaign leaders' inside information and influence convinced them it would.

While Hernandez described her collaboration with Sears as potentially serving NOW's purposes, she also appears to have felt a growing distance from those in NOW who had shown little concern for her priorities. Hernandez's activism had never adhered to most white feminists' understanding of their movement. She kept up her connections to the civil rights and labor movements, and she supported the creation of the National Black Feminist Organization (NBFO) in August 1973. NOW leaders hoped that the groups would collaborate, and there was some early cross-pollination, but Black women had started the NBFO in part because white feminists in groups like NOW did not address racism and sexism with equal vigor. When Hernandez left the presidency in 1971, recalled the NOW founder and treasurer Gene Boyer, she cautioned the other leaders that employment issues should not take precedence over antiracist work. Hernandez wanted NOW to "identify with all oppressed peoples," but for most white members "the consciousness was not there," Boyer said. By the end, "she didn't quite trust us."

Having influence with a major corporation like Sears also gave Hernandez a new leverage point in her community's fight against racism. For decades, department stores had been debating whether to keep their footprint in changing urban centers as whites left for booming suburbs. Soon after Hernandez's work for Sears began, the retailer accelerated plans to close a downtown San Francisco store that served and employed many people of color. Sears was "an important facet in the economic well-being" of "inner city residents" there, Hernandez wrote to Ray Graham, the company's director of equal employment opportunity, in a letter that began with an update about planning Sears's meeting with NOW, which would take place several weeks later. Hernandez explained to Graham that workers and shoppers from shuttered Sears stores in the city would "have a very difficult time traveling to the other Sears locations—almost all of which are in suburbia." She asked corporate officials to delay for six months and offered to help with "some innovative things that can be done" and that would "involve the community in solutions." Officials moved forward with their plans to close down the store.

Hernandez may have had multiple reasons to work for Sears. The company became a lucrative client. Her consulting work paid the bills that her activist volunteer work could never cover, and her time as NOW president might have left her with significant debts. Hernandez paid more than $1,400 ($5,800 today) in interest on twenty-five credit cards and charge accounts in 1978, four years after the Equal Credit Opportunity Act had outlawed sex and race discrimination by credit-granting institutions, even though her business was thriving. She started out in 1974 earning $50 per hour or $350 per day ($252 and $1,764, respectively, today) from Sears. Three years later, the company paid her firm just under $46,000 (about $205,000 today)—close to half of her business's total income that year. Hernandez had two other employees and considerable overhead, but she made a good living. Her 1978 salary—not all of which came from Sears—was $26,700, or about $102,000 today.

Hernandez's Sears connection paid dividends when company officials put her in touch with the leaders of Celanese Corporation, which became another major client, as did the United Parcel Service. Over the years, she worked for many government agencies, universities, and corporations. For corporate employers, Hernandez's firm reviewed affirmative action programs and ran "sensitivity training[s]" for managers and "assertiveness and career counseling sessions" for women and workers of color. For those companies' broader pool of employees, she ran large and small "awareness" seminars about the "attitudinal and behavioral patterns that keep us from meeting the spirit as well as technicalities of equal employment opportunity laws." She described these seminars as "a forum for dialogue, and an arena in which knowledge can be shared, concerns can be raised and individuals can begin to understand their own roles in developing long-postponed solutions to the problem of inequity." Hernandez's public sector consulting included projects funded by the U.S. Departments of Transportation and Housing and Urban Development that proposed improvements for transportation and housing equity in the Bay Area.

Amid Hernandez's work for Sears, some in NOW began to argue that a sitting board member could not be employed by a major campaign target. Collins reported to her fellow officers that Hernandez "was a consultant for Sears, set up the meeting that was held, and sat on management's side of the table." NOW's legal vice president, Judith Lonnquist, tapped the board member Stuart Herzog to investigate whether Hernandez's work for a "national action target" represented a conflict of interest. Hernandez's Golden Gate chapter responded one week later with a supportive resolution that called her actions part of a "two pronged attack on Sears—working from within as well as from without." At a national board meeting several days later, Herzog reported that Hernandez's allies Del Martin and Phyllis Lyon responded to his "hello" by calling him "the enemy." Herzog's internal inquiry fizzled after a few months, when Hernandez's many allies on the national board countered by proposing a hearing on whether the initial investigation of Hernandez's relationship with Sears had "violated" her own "rights." The board dropped the matter. Sears fought the discrimination charges in court for most of the next decade. NOW members mostly focused elsewhere.

———

"*All* women are poor in a male-dominated society," NOW's president, Wilma Scott Heide, claimed in 1972. When its members resolved to change work six years earlier, they shouldered an enormous task. In concert with sympathetic officials and combining the tactics of litigation, lobbying, and street protests, they chipped away at the age-old gendered division of labor and cracked open the logical edifice that framed women's work as inherently less valuable. NOW's pressure moved officials to enforce the new principle of equality, which changed American culture by offering women an expanded sense of their own possibilities and, for the most fortunate, a foothold in areas of the labor force previously reserved for men.

NOW's saga with Sears unfolded amid the broad shifts in work and citizenship of the 1970s, when men of color and women tried to pry their way into the security white men had shored up decades earlier through the New Deal. The rise of feminism and allied social justice movements, which coincided with the broader decline of organized labor, required excluded groups to seek "citizenship outside of the realm of collective economic rights" through "a desperately needed progressive version of individualism," according to one prominent historian. Yet NOW's challenge in advancing women's collective economic rights was not an atomistic vision but the fact that women were an incoherent class. "While *all* women are poor vis a vis men," Hernandez corrected Heide's claim the year after she spoke, "the minority woman is by far in the worst economic plight." If women were disadvantaged on the whole, it was not to the same degree, and not in the same way. All they had in common was their lack of equality.

This was the puzzle NOW could not solve: the two strongest pieces of its push for workplace rights, the structures members built and the laws they weaponized, also stressed the weaknesses in their own organization. In NOW's pursuit of enough power to stop the world's largest businesses from ripping women off, the group threatened to violate its members in a similar way. Those members, in seeking to make new laws work for women, tended to accept government officials' terms as they positioned women as a solid legal class and sharpened their focus. Unable to square their urge to universalize about their sex with the fact of their own differences—especially their different relationships to work—they undermined their own efforts to strengthen women's economic standing.

6.

THE CHICAGO MACHINE VS. THE PENNSYLVANIA RAILROAD

Patricia Hill Burnett traveled to Chicago in May 1973 for NOW's national board meeting. The board had hired Heather Booth, the Chicago organizer and Midwest Academy leader, to run a training for the twenty-seven members who were present. Although the exercises were collaborative, Booth designed the training to teach board members "that each has to organize to exercise their power and points of view" and offer them "some skills to do this." Booth urged the board members to rely upon "pre-planning" rather than "spontaneity" to advance their priorities and to have open "political discussion and distinctions drawn" among them. She reported to her colleagues at the Midwest Academy that the latter point "was well taken but was initially greatly resisted" both because board members did not believe "there were political differences" among them and because they did "not want . . . to address them."

The participants left Booth's training with stark impressions. Burnett enjoyed learning about "the most dramatic possible way, almost left-wing way of handling the establishment." She was fascinated by the lessons in "how to get media attention, how to run strikes," and how to confront resistant politicians and businessmen. Others on the board found Booth's session unhelpful and even alarming. "We came away from [the training] furious" at the proposed tactics and suggestions, recalled the eastern regional co-director Jean Conger. Collins believed the problem was that Booth's "style was much too harsh for them." But others sensed that the organizers were not being transparent. "Something was going on," recalled the board member Toni Carabillo, "and it was hostile to Wilma," the newly elected president who had just run unopposed but was not present for Booth's training. Carabillo, a Californian, suspected that Booth was also working separately with the Chicagoans to help them advance their priorities through the national organization. She was right.

NOW's internal tensions in the mid-1970s took most members by surprise. They erupted into open controversy at the 1974 national conference in Houston. That gathering was not the celebration of united sisterhood most had expected but the site of the organization's first hotly contested elections. Never before had NOW seen real competition over its leadership. There had always been elections, but "if there was an empty position, and you looked at all like a live body, you were it," said one longtime officer. In fact, the earliest leaders, eager to project unity, would personally intercept would-be challengers to block them from the convention floor. But in Houston, two caucuses came together and started what would become a two-year battle for NOW's future. Stunned onlookers inside and beyond NOW puzzled over what divided the sides and how their bonds could fray so quickly. Surely, some whispered, the FBI or CIA was involved.

The battle was sparked by a practical problem: how to manage NOW's freewheeling growth. But the core of the conflict was a deeper question about how to organize. Should members emphasize looking outward, disciplining themselves, and narrowing their focus to contend for influence in the wider world? Or should they give priority to their internal work, building democracy and diversity inside their ranks? Over time, mounting grudges bred mutual distrust that made it impossible to mention, let alone debate, these issues. NOW was far from alone in facing these challenges. All of the democratic social movement groups of the 1960s—for example, civil rights, farmworkers', and antiwar organizations—struggled to balance inclusive practices with effective action. Most fell apart.

NOW's turbulence contributed to the national mood in the mid-1970s. As the economy sputtered and blue-collar jobs dried up, some men accused feminists of cutting them down on the job and at home. Americans became newly suspicious of institutions and their leaders amid political scandals at home and frustrations abroad. And with violence seemingly escalating in urban uprisings, on college campuses, and from the threat of political terrorism, many turned away from civic life, giving rise to the nickname "the me decade."

But not conservative activists. Angered by America's humiliating defeat in Vietnam, alarmed by liberal policies, and outraged by social justice movements' gains, they tapped into some white women's political networks and further galvanized them around cultural issues that fused gendered and racialized grievances: opposition to abortion, integrated classrooms, and affirmative action and support for school prayer. These women were part of the broad constituency NOW claimed, but their positions inverted that organization's. NOW's once-favorable press coverage began to turn as reporters asked whether the women's movement was "in serious trouble."

Confidence in America's potential collided with a new reality of limitation in the mid-1970s, a sense of scarcity that also shaped NOW's conflicts over its direction and leadership. That unrest distracted the members in charge from the conservative forces sprouting at the grass roots. This New Right was starting to reshape the nation's politics by demonizing feminists like them. Focused squarely on each other, NOW's two factions, one led by Collins and her allies in Chicago and the other anchored in Pittsburgh, did agree on one thing: NOW did not have enough power for its members to share with one another.

———

As NOW passed its fifth birthday in 1971, its federated structure groaned under old stresses and new scrutiny. Recent members brought diverse feminist perspectives and ideas for restructuring the organization. The founder and early leader Gene Boyer acknowledged that NOW's architecture did have a masculine style, with authority stuck at the top. "Every organization chart that you ever looked at, that a male had created, was a pyramid." Should NOW be like a labor union, with members who paid dues and who were represented in elections by their chosen delegates? A corporation, with power that was centralized but accountable to share-holders? Or a political party, with local and national components that cooperated toward a common agenda?

Other democratic movements were also struggling to determine their shape and direction in the early 1970s. For example, Students for a Democratic Society (SDS) had driven the national conversation about the Vietnam War in the mid-1960s. But explosive growth and high turnover also made it vulnerable to fissures. An insurgent sect remade that loosely coordinated organization into a revolutionary underground network called the Weathermen. By 1969, most SDS members, who could not relate to the Weathermen's goals or tactics, had simply walked away. In those same years, the United Farm Workers became the voice of California agricultural laborers by blending organizing and consumer boycotts. But in the mid-1970s, its leader, Cesar Chavez, put all of the union's resources into the uphill struggle to fix farm labor laws. When Californians voted down his effort, Chavez began to change the union's culture, instigating fights, purges, and defections that caused its membership and power to decline. And radical feminists' insistence on extreme democracy, with no official leaders or hierarchy, left them with few ways to ease disputes and no figures accountable for driving an agenda and forging consensus. Their groups, too, tended to collapse.

The structure NOW's founders selected—local chapters with national leadership that mirrored the labor unions and civil rights groups to which many of them belonged—offered members "a focal point," "a coordinated voice," and ways "to mobilize people when something needed to be done," said Hernandez. But that structure also had flaws that soon became obvious. While it freed the chapters to pursue their own interests, it also added to the disorder. The chapters, left alone by overburdened and under-resourced national leaders, took off in many directions and developed distinct priorities. Some members ignored even the minimal guidance from above, their chapters declining to appoint officers and improvising for reasons of principle rather than efficiency. Others wanted more engagement from the women in charge. Those overtaxed volunteers did not always answer correspondence, fill requests for membership materials, or promptly send the newsletter.

National leaders addressed both kinds of concerns by adding layers of bureaucracy. They divided the country into four official regions in 1970, four years into NOW's life span, and assigned each one its own regular conference, director, and representatives on the national board. Twelve states had also formed their own structures by 1972. A member could belong to a chapter, a state, and a region. And national leaders set up task forces to help members organize around NOW's issues. They began with ten in 1970, but members could propose more. Four years later, there were thirty-one. All of these units needed tending, and each contributed to NOW's complexity. "When I would stand up at a Board meeting and hand out a financial report, everybody's eyes would glaze over," recalled the finance vice president Gene Boyer. "This isn't a business," her fellow officers responded; "this is a Civil Rights organization." Boyer understood their point, but NOW had "to run like a business" in order to pursue its goals.

This additional apparatus was intended to make the organization more democratic, but it sidestepped the biggest problem. NOW's national conference, which happened every eighteen months in a different city, did not capture the will of its members. Any member who showed up could vote, but no one could vote remotely. The region that hosted a conference effectively controlled NOW until the next one.

This casual approach to democracy left power clumped rather than spread. When twelve members of the L.A. chapter, the nation's second largest, traveled at "extraordinary effort and expense" to the 1970 national conference in Chicago, they were vastly outnumbered by members from elsewhere. The meeting elected thirty-three board members from the eastern half of the country and just six from out west. Some officers identified the problem. They developed competing plans for a delegate system in 1973, but neither proposal won enough support from members in a vote by mail to take effect. NOW's apparatus had gotten them off the ground and held them together where other groups had broken apart, but it could take them only so far.

————

Under NOW's lax oversight and loose governance in the early 1970s, one chapter thrived more than any other: Chicago's. Mary Jean Collins, who rose from chapter president to become the organization's first Midwest regional director in 1970, had been making headway against Sears while volunteering full-time at her husband Jim's business, C-R Office Programs. Meanwhile, Jim's annual contract with NOW, his sole client, became more lucrative as that organization grew. Under the 1971 contract, which paid nearly $20,700 (just under $140,000 today), C-R took in an average of 40 pieces of mail per day and printed 500,000 impressions. Two years later, the contract paid out more than $50,500 and covered the handling of 150 pieces of daily mail and the printing of 1 million impressions. NOW had no other national office. C-R's storefront and telephone line were NOW's mailing address and phone number.

While the Collins-Robsons ran the business, they also advocated for the creation of a separate national NOW office in Chicago in order to "get out from what would be perceived by a lot of people," Mary Jean said later, "as a conflict of interest." If she pursued and won the national presidency, her critics could accuse her of continuing to steer NOW's business to Jim and indirectly profiting from it. The board agreed to open a new national office in Chicago in mid-1973. Mary Jean was part of a team that hired Jane Plitt, a Rochester resident in her early thirties, to be NOW's first full-time, salaried executive director. The finances would be tight, but the leaders vowed to make it work.

A skilled manager as well as a feminist activist, Plitt had the perfect profile for the job. After finishing her undergraduate degree in three years at Cornell University's School of Industrial and Labor Relations, Plitt had ascended through the ranks at Rochester Telephone, where she reached the male-typed position of personnel manager for labor relations. Plitt had been "shocked" to be barred from lunching with her colleagues at local "men's only grills," but what drew her to NOW's Genesee Valley chapter was her rejected Sears credit card application. Her husband at the time, a graduate student whom she was supporting, easily secured one.

Plitt had been looking for work in Chicago after her second husband took a job there. When the NOW position opened up, she said, "I couldn't imagine a dream job better than that one." Still, she was surprised by how much heavy lifting was needed right away. Beyond the empty office NOW had rented, "there was absolutely nothing." Plitt furnished and staffed the operation herself. She never joined Chicago NOW, but some of the other workers did. "We knew what our roles were," said the chapter member and national office worker Suzanne Doty. "We were clearly delineated from the Chicago NOW people." Members from elsewhere became less certain of this separation as the organization's power began to centralize in that city.

Many others in NOW, unlike the Chicagoans, sought to decentralize the group's power. In particular, they believed it was beneficial to have many chapters in a single area. "Large metropolitan chapters tend to stymie [the] growth of individual members," wrote Patricia Hill Burnett. To have several chapter listings in the *N* section of the telephone book would display their strength and popularity, she believed. Aileen Hernandez agreed, noting that members with different priorities could work in parallel chapters. "An amicable divorce is perhaps better than a hostile marriage" among disparate feminists, she said; this was an approach her Golden Gate chapter would adopt. For women of color and lesbians in particular, separate chapters could be vital havens, allowing members to benefit from their connection to the national organization while surrounded by others who would not dismiss their experiences and concerns.

The Chicago members disagreed. Their perspective, inspired by labor organizing, held that concentrated power could create the leverage to force opponents to the table. They argued that too many chapters in one place would dilute NOW, which should instead be a large and unified collective to maximize its influence. Perhaps multiple chapters could work elsewhere, some conceded, but their city was "not that kind of town," said the Chicago chapter president and Sears campaign co-leader Anne Ladky. "You had to contend for power, and you can't do that if it's ten people in ten chapters in ten neighborhoods." They defeated another group's attempt to form a second chapter there. To the national leaders, whose approach amounted to "What's the big deal? The more the merrier," Ladky and her allies responded that if the upstarts succeeded, their city would be left with "two weak chapters."

As the Chicago members expanded their influence in their city and in NOW, a phalanx of one dozen Pittsburgh chapters built enough strength to rival them. Wilma Scott Heide, NOW's national president from 1971 to 1974, hailed from the city. So too did Eleanor Smeal, a fiery housewife and political scientist whose feminist profile was on the rise. Smeal and other Pittsburgh feminists gravitated to the large Victorian home of the psychologist JoAnn Evansgardner and the businessman Gerald Gardner. The couple turned their house into a feminist center, installing one dozen telephone lines for their political work as well as a printing press in the garage. That press became the small nonprofit feminist printing operation KNOW Inc. After some modest success creating pamphlets and college course materials, the collective decided that they were not "comfortable" with the "philosophy" of "volunteerism." They agreed that "people should be paid" to work in "a very loving environment." To cover those salaries, the press needed to expand its output.

The Pittsburgh printers were also NOW members like the Collins-Robsons. Eyeing the national printing contract, they asked why a man should take in so much of their group's money. Jim Collins-Robson was C-R's sole owner and benefactor, as he and Mary Jean took pains to demonstrate. KNOW, by contrast, was a "feminist business" whose workers—mostly women—were "paid equally for their work." At the national board meeting in November 1973, C-R and KNOW both bid on the contract for NOW's printing needs. C-R's bid was higher, but the board voted 6–3 to keep NOW's business there. Some said they found the KNOW bid unrealistically low. Others raised doubts about the details of KNOW's proposal. The Pittsburghers responded by accusing the board of "unconscious sexism" in favoring C-R. The board broke off a piece of the work for KNOW, but it was "a shotgun wedding," said one board member. "They hated each other by then."

Pittsburgh members such as JoAnn Evansgardner saw the Chicago organizer Heather Booth as a "malevolent force" in NOW, Booth surmised. But Booth saw nothing wrong with better organizing members' efforts, whether on the chapter, state, regional, or national scale. As her Midwest Academy instructed, well-run campaigns were how everyday people built the power to pressure elites. Booth helped the Chicagoans prepare for the national conference in Houston with a series of half-day trainings in early 1974. The meetings would teach members to "start with the notion that you are there to organize a community of 3,000 people in a weekend," claimed a flyer.

In these sessions, women role-played through exercises that anticipated various scenarios at the upcoming conference. In each encounter, a member should "listen, try to understand where they're at so you can tie your opinions to what they care about," as Anne Ladky jotted down in her notes. But where there were "*strong* disagreements, can't convince, *don't* waste time, move on." Another NOW leader who attended called these tactics "confrontational" and "very pushy, very macho, very establishment," suggesting that "all we wanted to do was teach women men's tricks." "It hardened a lot of people," she said.

The allegation that the Chicagoans were "macho" reflected a new turn in feminist politics. Cultural feminism, an offshoot of radical feminism, held that women possessed distinct values and should honor them by fostering their own "women's culture." Rather than participating in institutions built by men—especially the economy, whose struggles they coded as masculine and thus "irrelevant to women"—their sex should carve out their own spaces and institutions where they could build community with one another. NOW generally resisted the separatist impulse of cultural feminism. But some members began to point its lens, which coded power structures as masculine, toward their own organization.

What some criticized as a masculine style, the Chicagoans saw as productive. Women had to be tough to change society. The training had given them "the nuts and bolts of things to improve people's lives," said a chapter member who claimed she could not understand why anyone objected. Their neighbors understood. Chicago "was without a doubt the preeminent NOW chapter," said the St. Louis member Mary Anne Sedey. Its members "were really, really good at what they were about, but there was an arrogance to them" that "pissed people off." "I doubt if you know how bad things can be if you don't play it Chicago's way," the head of the chapter in suburban Elgin, Illinois, wrote to national leaders, objecting to the city women's influence across the state. The urbanites accused them of bearing an anti-city bias "that is part of living in the suburbs, whether it crops up on the subject of mass transportation, crime control or whatever." Such regional skirmishes were a warning signal that no one heeded.

Brighter signs of danger for NOW also flashed beyond its membership. Downstate from Chicago, a housewife and political operator in suburban St. Louis had begun to activate conservative women. Phyllis Schlafly capitalized on two of feminists' recent victories—the 1973 U.S. Supreme Court opinion in *Roe v. Wade*, which established a constitutional right to abortion, and the Equal Rights Amendment's undeniable momentum on its path to ratification in state legislatures—to frame feminism as an attack on mainstream society. As NOW members prepared to gather in Houston, political leaders were brokering an end to the monthslong Arab oil embargo, which had doubled gasoline and oil prices and sent inflation soaring. Drivers lined up at gas pumps for rationed fuel that had once been bountiful and cheap. This economic instability buttressed Schlafly's insistence that the traditional family was in peril.

NOW had taken a bold position in endorsing legalized abortion in 1967, and the organization continued to pursue it as an issue of importance and broad appeal to women. Throughout the late 1960s, NOW members worked on the issue at the state and local levels. Chapters formed "abortion repeal" task forces to study their local restrictions and protested them in their communities. NOW co-sponsored an abortion rights ballot initiative in California in 1970 and rallied its members to collect signatures for it. Members in Massachusetts, Georgia, Illinois, New York, and elsewhere worked, often in coalitions with other women's organizations in their states, to urge members to testify in support of measures to repeal restrictive abortion laws and to lobby legislators to rescind them. "NOW can take a lot of credit for the significant changes in the abortion laws in many states," Aileen Hernandez said as president in 1970—sixteen states liberalized their laws between 1966 and 1972—and NOW was one of seven women's organizations to co-file an amicus brief with the U.S. Supreme Court in 1971 in the case that became *Roe v. Wade*. The brief declared abortion "a fundamental constitutional right of a personal nature." Abortion was always one among NOW's many priorities.

NOW members did not yet see women who opposed abortion, or any other group of women, as a potential threat to their organization. Confident that conservative women represented a tiny fringe, they believed that feminists drove the only legitimate conversation about women's politics and that their group was at the helm. Chicago NOW members decided not to rent beepers to help them stay connected during the upcoming convention, but they did reserve fifty seats together on a Delta flight. They were ready for Houston.

————

The Chicagoans prepared so strenuously for NOW's 1974 convention because one of their own, Mary Jean Collins, was running for national president of the rapidly expanding organization. It had grown from 120 in late 1966 to nearly 20,000 in 1972, then more than doubled by 1974. In previous years, a nominating committee of national board members had pored over applications and prepared a list of chosen candidates who almost always won. But NOW was growing too big to be run by a tight cohort of acquaintances. Members were less likely to know one another personally; the number of chapters tripled from 1972 to 1975 as the organization approached its tenth birthday. Those newcomers were generally younger than their predecessors in the group (62 percent of members in 1974 were in their twenties or thirties). They discarded the previous assumption that NOW was too moderate to bother with, both because other groups fell apart and because NOW was more open to their priorities. The organization appeared to many as a ready vehicle for driving a feminist agenda.

Hernandez, a member of the nominating committee for Houston, proposed a more democratic approach to the elections. She held that organizations had to "broaden" and foster new leaders rather than propping up existing ones. The committee should be less "autocratic," she wrote to the others, and work as "facilitators rather than as a power bloc." This call for small-scale democracy echoed the national mood in the mid-1970s as many Americans demanded more transparent governance given political leaders' newly exposed lies. The nominating committee adopted Hernandez's proposal: every interested candidate who had been a dues-paying member for at least six months would appear on the ballot. For the first time, contenders would work openly to defeat one another in an election.

Anticipating this competition, Collins remained confident. "There was not much question that I was going to come out of there being president," she said later. She outlined a pragmatic vision that involved translating NOW's "good policies and ideals" into effective programs, as she had done in the Sears campaign. The heart of her philosophy was that NOW, like a labor union, should focus its members' shared grievances against a common adversary. Fighting that adversary could unite members across their differences, build their organization, and win results, she argued. Collins thus saw her "formal training in organization building" through the Midwest Academy as just as strong an asset to her candidacy as her service on NOW's national board and the elbow grease she had applied to its clerical work through Jim's business. But Collins's self-assurance rubbed some the wrong way. And when the outgoing president, Wilma Scott Heide, openly backed her, this fed what the Californian Toni Carabillo and others saw as Collins's "self-righteous[ness] about the fact that she was entitled to win."

Collins also had a major weakness as a candidate, and she knew it: the appearance that she was "getting fat off the organization's dough" through her husband's print shop. Toni Carabillo had contemplated running for president herself, but she could not have kept her full-time job, run NOW, and shelled out the thousands of dollars it cost to be president. Jim Collins-Robson had no business "outside of the NOW contract," Carabillo said, and "it all seemed like a closed loop," with his outfit posing as legitimate but in reality milking NOW for cash. If Collins won the presidency, she would protect her husband's contract, effectively drawing a salary from NOW. "The rest of us didn't have that advantage," Carabillo pointed out. "It certainly was a fair point," Collins conceded much later. She and Jim vowed that he would give up the contract he had held for four years if she won.

Collins hoped that their promise would put the controversy to rest. Touching down in Houston, she and her fellow Chicagoans began working the conference, systematically, to push their agenda and Collins's campaign. In matching T-shirts that read, "$100 million and nothing less," a widely recognizable reference to the settlement they believed their Sears effort would soon deliver, they handed out buttons and position papers that introduced their issues and their slate. "We were fierce," the Chicagoan Suzanne Doty said, "very protective of each other," and "ready to go to war."

The Chicagoans "came in like thunder," Carabillo said, using techniques that were "meant to be used against the enemy." It was "devastating" and "shocking" to be confronted by so-called sisters. She and others viewed the national conference as a site of deliberation, sharing, and bonding: a crucible for NOW's democracy. Instead, the Chicagoans treated other members as either allies or enemies of their own fully formed agenda. Some East and West Coast members threw together a makeshift countercampaign. They redoubled their support for the presidential candidate Karen DeCrow, a thirty-six-year-old attorney from Syracuse. DeCrow was the only one in their network willing to run against Collins because of the financial cost of serving, but also, likely, because they all knew that challenging the front-runner would be a tough fight if not a lost cause. DeCrow's supporters rented a separate hotel room to serve as her campaign headquarters. Carabillo "hauled our Californians in there," she said, "and then we began organizing together."

DeCrow and Collins, the most prominent of the four candidates for national president in Houston, also had similar profiles. DeCrow had helped create her local NOW chapter in 1967, then became its president. Where the Chicago chapter's main issue was employment, Syracuse NOW focused on public accommodations. Many bars and eateries in town banned "unescorted" women. Title II of the 1964 Civil Rights Act outlawed discrimination in public accommodations, but sex was not among its protected categories. To change their city's laws, Syracuse chapter members picketed outside bars and frustrated the bartenders inside by continually going up to order a drink and getting turned down. They sought to be arrested, but bar owners chose to close instead, accepting a short-term financial loss rather than courting bad publicity by calling the cops to "arrest white, middle-class women," DeCrow recalled.

DeCrow's ascent into NOW's leadership paralleled Collins's. She served as national membership chair and eastern regional director in the early 1970s, when Collins held the same role in the Midwest. DeCrow used her own money to travel to board meetings, "very much against" her husband's approval. Her marriage strained and severed. When she sued Roger DeCrow for divorce in 1971, he countersued, contending that she "had lost interest in being a good wife," she recalled. He cited the fact that she had spent one Thanksgiving away at a NOW board meeting. Karen had found that experience liberating. She gazed down at her city while her plane ascended. "Every woman in every house that I am flying over, is making the stuffing, and I am going to a hotel in Chicago to eat club sandwiches. And boy, am I happy!"

Competing for NOW's presidency in Houston, DeCrow and Collins presented approaches with limited overlap. The candidates agreed that chapters were NOW's most important unit and that the national organization existed mostly to support them. Both claimed that national elections needed to be more representative. But while both wanted to boost the participation of working-class women and women of color, they outlined different strategies. Collins sought to unite women around the employment issue and against Sears; DeCrow believed that acknowledging women's differences could draw more of them in. DeCrow sought to focus NOW on how feminism connected to "the oppression of other groups" and cultivate methods for "changing the mainstream of society" through a "behavioral and social-practice revolution." The two disagreed over whether to first work to change culture or institutions and whether to broaden or tighten NOW's focus.

DeCrow's agenda was far less formed, and she had presumed "that it was going to be another NOW election, the way it had always been," said her ally Carabillo. "She and Mary Jean were going to get up and make speeches, and the best speech" would win the most votes. While DeCrow "spent no money" on her campaign, she and her allies did distill their criticism of Collins's approach into a nickname that had a local twist: the "Chicago Machine." This was an obvious reference to Chicago's mayor, Richard J. Daley, whose muscular style included patronage, corruption, and cigar-smoking backroom dealing. Collins's opponents claimed that her association with Heather Booth and the Midwest Academy made her too radical, but they also tarred Collins as too conservative because she foregrounded economic issues over identity-based concerns related to sexuality and race. Collins viewed the accusations as bizarre and contradictory. "One day we're communists; the next day we're thugs," she said with a shrug.

These attacks on Collins from within NOW, inconsistent as she found them, dovetailed with efforts by another group of women to weaken her from the outside. Sears, the target of her hallmark campaign, lobbied members in Houston. When Collins and her fellow Chicagoan Anne Ladky began leading a workshop on their Sears campaign, about thirty-five overdressed "ladies in suits"—nearly half of the women in the room—stood up to challenge them and hand out pro-Sears literature. "We started counting them and realized that it was serious," Collins said, "but we didn't realize how serious."

Sears soon made its new tactic clear. Company employees spoke out against the Sears campaign throughout the conference. NOW had an explicit policy not to "cooperate with any commercial venture known to exploit or denigrate women," but Sears had still managed to take out a full-page ad in the conference program. That promotion declared the company a model employer of women and urged them to apply for commission sales jobs—the same jobs that the Sears campaign accused the company of preserving for men. Right after the conference, company officials began contacting NOW members and chapters with credit card offers and invitations to meet.

Among NOW members at the conference, opposition to Collins began to fuse with opposition to the Sears campaign. Collins had to hand it to Sears officials. Their brilliant tactic of "sending women to a women's meeting" caused others in the room to ask, "Well, these are women too. Why would they argue against this?" Collins believed that DeCrow and her supporters began to oppose the Sears campaign because she was its face, but also because they did not see changing work as the paramount goal of the organization.

While DeCrow and her supporters offered a more varied and less concrete agenda, they also took a different approach to employment: changing attitudes about work rather than its structures. DeCrow described "being a housewife" as "a respectable occupation" that should have "economic security" and "be open to men." DeCrow's allies in Pittsburgh agreed that Collins's focus was misplaced. "There's nothing wrong with corporations," the Pittsburgh member and KNOW press cofounder Gerald Gardner told Collins in Houston. "That's not where the problem is. We're not socialists." His Pittsburgh chapter, through a coalition with the local NAACP, had been making "real progress with getting women and minority males into" better jobs at Sears by using gentler tactics than the Chicagoans', recalled his wife, JoAnn Evansgardner. When national NOW adopted the Chicago campaign, it "totally screwed up what we were trying to do." Collins suspected Sears was secretly helping her rivals in Houston, a charge Toni Carabillo denied. "I think Mary Jean began to see Sears everywhere."

As Collins and DeCrow faced off for the presidency, Aileen Hernandez chaired the candidate forum. Members' marijuana smoke swirled around the crystal chandeliers that evening in the twelve-hundred-seat grand ballroom. Over the stage hovered a huge square sign with the NOW logo in black and white. Hernandez hung back, according to Collins, as the other three candidates teamed up against her "and created enough doubt in the membership about whether I was stealing from the organization." Collins was "psychologically unprepared for it," she said, and "just couldn't believe that feminists were doing this to me." Afterward members confronted her, demanding, "Is it true that you made a million dollars out of NOW last year?"

When the voting started, NOW's procedures added to the acrimony. Every race in which no candidate won a 50 percent majority had to be rerun until someone did. The voting and revoting continued into the next day. Over "24 hours of hell," members were "shuffling their way between hotel and convention center unsure of whether they were coming or going." DeCrow beat Collins on the third ballot by a vote of 512–448. The new president called her win a triumph for internal democracy: the first time NOW's members, rather than its leaders, chose the officers. The national board election was held next, and there DeCrow had less to celebrate. Anyone who lost an earlier race could run for a seat. Collins won one, along with enough of her allies to gain control of the new board.

Many members left Houston surprised and confused by the infighting. Two who had recently joined wrote to the national board that they had expected unity and sisterhood, but instead they felt "angry, manipulated, wasted and generally disgusted" by the "endless political jockeying and petty bickering." Others were mystified by what separated the two sides. Patricia Hill Burnett suggested that NOW had been infiltrated by "devious groups intent on destroying" the organization. Indeed, the FBI had collected information about its chapters and campaigns, sent agents to its demonstrations, and received information from "sources" about planned protests in the late 1960s. But by 1973, the agency had determined that NOW had "no known subversive or violent background," nor was it "dominated by revolutionary groups." The FBI was also changing. The Justice Department had begun reining in its rampant domestic spying through new guidelines that focused on "quality over quantity" of cases. While Burnett had her suspicions about subversion, she also saw the conflict inside the organization as a battle for influence. "NOW had a great deal of power in the media, which women craved." Many "would love to [be] president of NOW, and be on T.V." The NOW founding member Muriel Fox agreed. "There were ideological differences," she said, but the disputes were mostly "just plain power struggles."

But there were real disparities between the emerging factions, however hard they were to see. The Chicagoans sought to streamline NOW to fight for influence beyond it. They were less concerned with rebalancing power inside the group, which others viewed as essential. In Houston, Hernandez's fellow Golden Gate chapter member Del Martin led an "affirmative-action program" to boost women of color and open lesbians into NOW's leadership. She noted with pride that their numbers grew from three to six on the thirty-eight-member national board. "We passed beyond tokenism and started to really tackle the problem," Martin exclaimed.

As the Chicagoans seethed at Collins's loss, their vantage point also obscured some insights into why it had happened. Reflecting on Houston, Ladky wrote, "Appreciation of skill—whether in leadership, organizing, successful action, or even knowledge of the organization—was rejected in favor of glorification of amateurism and anti-leadership rhetoric." She and her allies did not see how NOW's culture and membership were changing.

NOW's structures could accommodate the test of its rules and norms that happened in Houston, but the conference portended danger ahead.

That danger stemmed from the inherent challenges facing democratic advocacy organizations, according to the sociologist Francesca Polletta. Majority rule, while efficient, creates winners and losers. Groups can counterbalance this through processes that emphasize deliberation and by fomenting inclusive decision making that helps those who have been left out of political participation gain the skills to engage with authorities and experience their own power. NOW's chapters were typically small enough to serve this purpose, and newer members often found consensus building and personal support there. Conference goers in Houston affirmed their loyalty to their own place and the members they knew by wearing buttons declaring their support for "chapter rights."

But that conference itself struck a much different tone. Unlike chapter meetings, which were generally informal, NOW's national gathering ran according to *Robert's Rules of Order*. That system, which organizations that held conferences had been using "more and more" since the mid-1960s, was designed to promote fairness and efficiency. The rules protected the "rights of the majority, the minority, the absentees, the entire body and the individual," explained a professional parliamentarian, and not the kind of flexible deliberation that could fortify trust and friendship. Complex and laden with jargon, the rules gave significant authority to one parliamentarian, who interpreted the bylaws and determined who could speak, when, and for how long. Like the layers of bureaucracy national leaders recently added, procedures intended to make NOW more democratic did not address the challenges produced by its growth.

NOW resembled other social movement groups in its struggle to keep order as it grew. But inside a feminist organization, the accusation of overtly political, "masculine" tactics cut deep. Collins came to believe that the accusation was grounded in truth. "I was very enamored with this sort of, 'Let's get organized. Let's get something done' philosophy," she said, decades later, "and it was running flat up against the feminist 'Let's do things in a feminist way, and not in a traditional male way.'" But no one considered how to square the desire for a kinder, more empathetic politics with the need for a well-running organization that won results. And soon both sides would sacrifice any appeal to that gentler approach as they battled each other.

NOW's problems were not just internal. While members in Houston attacked one another in a hotel ballroom, emissaries of the evangelical group Happiness of Womankind picketed outside. They were a subset of the conservative women's movement that was emerging as a national political force. Its supporters' motivations ranged from anti-Communism and religious fundamentalism to the changes wrought by recent social justice movements. A feminist gathering in their city was a boon: an opportunity to draw media attention and to disprove, by their very presence, NOW's premise that women shared a program. "We believe NOW is atheistic and anti-God," one protester told a reporter. A smaller group calling itself the Coalition of Pro-Life Feminists held signs reading, UNBORN WOMEN HAVE RIGHTS, TOO, and PICK ON SOMEONE YOUR OWN SIZE. The feminists inside the hall scoffed at this meager display, but antifeminist women undermined NOW's claim to be the standard-bearer of women's united agenda.

An existential challenge from conservative women was just a few years away, but they were far from Collins's mind as she left Houston. She was focused on the enemies inside NOW's gates. "It was devastating to lose, just devastating," Collins said, "and just a miserable, nasty couple of months of feeling terrible." She had been defeated, but her agenda still had legs. "We had total control of the organization outside of the presidency," she said, and "we assumed our power."

———

The conflict continued to simmer as Karen DeCrow took over NOW's leadership in the summer of 1974. Just after her victory, she had outlined a vague agenda to the press that included "equal pay for equal work, education," and "emphasizing women's role in family development." But at the convention, she had openly pursued and helped to pass one specific item: a resolution calling for President Richard Nixon's impeachment. It was the furthest the organization had ever waded into electoral politics, but DeCrow argued that the stand was "within the responsibility of N.O.W. as a large national organization."

Nixon's embattled presidency shifted national sentiments in ways that also signaled danger for DeCrow. Nixon, ensnared by the Watergate scandal, resigned in August. His successor, Gerald Ford, soon pardoned him. The ordeal compounded many Americans' sense that power corrupted, that the corrupt escaped accountability, and that their nation was no longer fit to offer moral leadership to the rest of the world. Many were outraged that Nixon and his predecessors had lied to the public about the trajectory of the Vietnam War and tried to cover it up, as the leaked Pentagon Papers had revealed three years earlier. This obfuscation had not prevented America's spiral into a humiliating defeat in Vietnam, already underway in mid-1974. The moment when DeCrow stepped up and Nixon stepped down was marked by suspicion of authority in all forms.

DeCrow tried, grudgingly, to work with the national office in Chicago. But that office, like much else after the Houston conference, became a football in the fight to control NOW. The Chicagoans adored the executive director, Jane Plitt, praising her professionalism and work ethic, but DeCrow and her allies eyed her with suspicion. Plitt was unlikely to "transfer her services (much less her loyalties) to her new leader," Toni Carabillo wrote to DeCrow after her victory. Carabillo feared that Collins would run the organization through Plitt, rendering DeCrow a powerless "figurehead." DeCrow and Plitt sparred almost immediately, and each blamed the other for their struggles to communicate. DeCrow lodged a formal complaint with the national board, which had the power to start the process to fire Plitt, in November 1974.

Even though DeCrow accused Plitt of inefficiency, NOW's administrative work was simply overwhelming, as earlier leaders and members had discovered. The national board wound down the contracts with KNOW and C-R and shifted their work to the national office in Chicago when it opened several months before the Houston meeting. The officers began to off-load their administrative tasks onto the new paid staff—the half a dozen employees whom Plitt supervised in a costlier arrangement that was meant to be more centralized and professional—to free themselves to be the political activists they wanted to be. Soon the office was receiving five hundred pieces of mail per day. Suzanne Doty, the executive secretary, helped field this correspondence and did other "secretarial stuff, assistant stuff, putting board packets together," she said. These tasks made little use of her recent bachelor's degree from Wells College, a women's college in upstate New York, but "it was probably the most satisfying work I've done," she said later. "I knew it was for a larger cause."

Members' high expectations amplified the stress. Plitt, Doty, and the others did their best, but some members began to complain that their work was not prompt or thorough enough to justify their $10 annual dues ($53 today). "People were just infuriated if they didn't get the mailing," and they were "sure" it was "purposeful," Plitt said. The members treated them like "servants." Even before DeCrow took over the presidency, the national office staff was "worn thin, emotionally, mentally and physically," Plitt wrote to the outgoing president, Wilma Scott Heide, in mid-1974. They "wonder[ed] about NOW's sense of humaneness, its fairness as an employer, and its consistency with its own principles."

Once DeCrow took office, the growing tension with Plitt ruptured the national board at its December 1974 meeting in New Orleans. The board's personnel and procedures committee had asked DeCrow to send Plitt a written job evaluation. The committee agreed to keep the evaluation confidential until the next scheduled board meeting, in New Orleans, and asked Plitt to travel to the meeting to discuss it. The committee told Plitt that "this was not an adversarial situation or a hearing," but instead a forum for "informal discussion and resolution," but she did not trust that claim. Instead, she hired a former NOW legal vice president to represent her. The night before the board meeting started, Plitt and her lawyer distributed a hundred pages of materials: copies of correspondence, commendations of her work, and phone logs meant to demonstrate Plitt's efficiency and, she believed, help save her job.

The Chicagoans suspected that DeCrow was attacking Plitt to damage them. The next morning, they struck first. The board, dominated by the Chicagoans and their allies, placed Plitt's case at the top of the agenda. It was time to resolve the matter and end Plitt's "inhumane treatment," Collins said. After more debate, the group passed a motion to compel DeCrow to make a thirty-minute presentation to outline her case against the executive director. Plitt's allies controlled the room. "I remember standing behind her at the board meeting with my arms crossed like a sergeant at arms," said Suzanne Doty, who went to the meeting to support her beloved boss. "It was like, you bitches, you try to come to her, you have to go through me first."

DeCrow and her allies were appalled. At first, they struggled to understand what was happening. Del Martin had gotten a 2:00 a.m. call from her fellow board member Eleanor Smeal that a "kangaroo court" was going to "try to hang Karen DeCrow at 8 o'clock that morning." Toni Carabillo, another board member, took a principled stand when she realized that they were "ordering the president to essentially stand trial" for her treatment of Plitt. She pointed out that DeCrow had not even brought her own evidence of Plitt's performance. DeCrow had hoped to keep the matter in the personnel and procedures committee and avoid "an open, hostile, organization dividing hearing" before the entire board. But the board plowed ahead by voting to hear DeCrow's charges against Plitt and denying her request for more time to prepare. DeCrow would have to respond to the materials Plitt had distributed the night before. Martin recalled Hernandez "sitting there, and saying, 'I can't believe this. I just can't believe this.'" The Chicagoans and their allies were weaponizing procedures that were meant to keep the peace.

DeCrow and thirteen supporters walked out in protest. They included Hernandez, Smeal, Martin, and others from California, Pennsylvania, New York, and elsewhere. As the national secretary, Charlene Suneson, left, she picked up the equipment that had been recording their meeting. "I had no idea when anyone would be back," she said. "It wasn't like I was going to the bathroom." Some tried to physically restrain her, and others shouted, "'Stop her!' 'don't touch her!' 'get those tapes!'" The defectors gathered outside and proclaimed themselves a new subunit of NOW: the Majority Caucus. They made up a minority of the board, but through their commitment to "returning control of NOW's policies, funds and programs to the membership," they believed they represented the majority of NOW members. Hailing their departure an "exodus," they never returned to that meeting.

Meanwhile, the end of 1974 capped off a roller-coaster year for women. There were two sweeping legal victories: passage of the Equal Credit Opportunity Act, which banned discrimination in credit on the basis of personal characteristics, including sex, and which NOW had advocated; and the addition of sex to the Fair Housing Act, which banned discrimination in the rental or sale of housing. But victories were drying up. The Republican president, Richard Nixon, had replaced liberals in the federal government with conservatives. The previous year, he had vetoed a bipartisan bill to fund universal child care. Conservatives were already uniting in new ways to undermine abortion rights.

Even as problems outside NOW demanded robust action, the group's ability to respond was weakening. Its leaders continued to project strength and issue bold statements, so members refused to accept that their organization might not accomplish its entire agenda. NOW's ambitious plans dwarfed its tiny 1973 budget of $290,000, which was a lot of money to the average member. The cost of membership services rose while per member income from dues fell, creating a national budget deficit of $38,000 in 1974. Meanwhile, the number of national task forces multiplied so that the puny fund for action programs was split into ever smaller parcels.

As their organization became less productive, with no obvious villain, members and especially leaders started to blame one another. For many, the movement had taken over their lives with an intensity that was exhilarating but also difficult to sustain. Their expectations for what was possible expanded to match the size of their sacrifices. Sensing their power beyond NOW might be shrinking, the would-be leaders grasped for clout within it.

———

The feud ripped across the organization that winter and spring of 1975. It was fitting that the Caucus's walkout had happened on Pearl Harbor Day, wrote New York State's NOW president, Eileen Kelly. "A surprise attack on the national president, leaving due process by the wayside, has forced the creation in its wake of a political party within NOW." But the problem was much deeper than the blowup in New Orleans. Their leadership was stymied, Kelly wrote, "by a small group of persons centered around the power of the Chairone"—the national board chair and Chicagoans' ally Judith Lightfoot—"and the Chicago office." "National NOW has become a huge vacuum pump," wrote Bev Jones of Pennsylvania, "that sucks up the energies, money and personnel of the truly functional and combative units in the national organization": the state and local outposts that did "most of the real work" with "miniscule amounts of money." Of course, the women toiling in the national office could have described themselves in the same terms.

To redistribute NOW's power, Caucus leaders asserted, they should be in charge. NOW should become "a revolutionary feminist organization controlled by the membership," who the Caucus believed sided with them. It was time for those members, led by the Caucus, to "organize to recapture the organization, which we felt was out of control," said Toni Carabillo. A first step in this direction would be to eliminate the new executive director position. NOW's bylaws meant the elected leadership turned over quickly, Smeal later explained, but an executive director could serve forever and wield "the real power." NOW's executive director at that time would have scoffed at this suggestion: Plitt felt like the least powerful person in the organization as she worked to appease the hardening factions and support the members and officers on a shoestring budget.

Caucus members linked the projects of rebalancing power within NOW and drawing more diverse groups of women to it. Hernandez believed the Caucus could advance multiple social justice issues under NOW's umbrella, her longtime goal for the organization. She backed the Caucus's slogan "Out of the mainstream, into the revolution." As Hernandez explained it, "'Mainstream America' did not fit our definition of a humane society and we were anxious to start thinking through how to divert the mainstream into a non-sexist, non-racist, non-classist, non-ageist society." Hernandez believed NOW should be "a training ground for those who want to be involved in major social change," as her Golden Gate chapter had become. She was not a Caucus leader, but she organized at least one of its mailings to the national membership.

To capture members' support and pressure the enemy board, the Caucus pressed its case in person. Its leaders visited with members in their regions. "We would go to a hotel for a weekend," said the eastern regional co-director Jean Conger, and "anywhere from 50–200 people would show up. We would talk to them, and then play the tape" of the New Orleans board meeting. The tape was an effective piece of evidence. The national treasurer, Bonnie Howard, Collins's only East Coast ally on the board, recalled describing the "painful" New Orleans board meeting to a fellow member of Eastern Massachusetts NOW. She attended one of the Majority Caucus meetings "where they played the tape," Howard said, and "she never spoke to me again." Caucus leaders also used the tape to frame their discussion of "strategies for returning NOW to the membership," as Hernandez described it. In a "financial squeeze play," they encouraged chapters to divert into escrow accounts the portion of members' dues that chapters were required to send to the national organization. It was an "economic boycott" of their own organization. Pennsylvania NOW's board, led by Eleanor Smeal, voted overwhelmingly to escrow. At least five state organizations and many chapters, encompassing more than twelve thousand members, followed suit.

As the schism widened, NOW's members took varied approaches to the divide. Some chapters, like Patricia Hill Burnett's in Detroit, voted against escrowing. Not only were dues needed to support a "strong national structure," but according to the bylaws "persons who do not pay dues are no longer NOW members." Burnett wrote to her Detroit chapter that while the organization needed some changes, like delegate voting, escrowing dues could be catastrophic. "I'm not sure that NOW will survive until the next National Convention," she confessed. Others, unsure of the root of the quarrel, blamed its participants. "No members authorized an oligarchy to practice pork-barrel politics or conduct personal vendettas," the New York City chapter's board admonished the national leaders.

While the factions feuded over their group's economics in the spring of 1975, the nation's economy seized and contracted. NOW's efforts to chip away at male authority dovetailed with a recession that pushed men's 1975 unemployment rate above 6 percent. Overall unemployment peaked in May at 9 percent, a postwar record. Eight million unemployed Americans were seeking to enter the labor force, and another half a million had simply stopped looking. Such economic turmoil offered new ammunition to critics of feminism and other social movements that sought to redistribute wages, services, and jobs. With their presumption of economic security in peril, fewer white men were in a sharing mood. This climate of scarcity squeezed many of their wives between seeking to shore up their husbands' breadwinning status and advocating for their own job rights and earning potential.

NOW leaders certainly felt these changes in their own wallets, but they channeled their frustrations toward one another. Mary Jean Collins and her backers focused on fending off the Caucus's challenge. Striking a conciliatory tone, they still sought to maintain influence. Their board majority was at risk with the 1975 Philadelphia conference on the horizon. Both Pennsylvania and Philadelphia NOW were Caucus strongholds whose members' dues were in escrow. The midwesterners who controlled the board highlighted this fact and proposed moving the conference to St. Louis. Major time and expense had already been laid out for Philadelphia, responded the Caucus. The Tulsa chapter proposed changing the bylaws to create a delegate voting system before the Philadelphia convention, and the board voted, by a one-vote margin, to ask members to vote on the issue by mail. To the Caucus, this was another "divisive" power play by the Chicagoans. They pointed out that mail-in ballots had only ever been used for routine matters.

The Caucus beat back both challenges. DeCrow and twenty other officers took the board majority to court. They won their suit to halt the delegate system ballot from going out to the members because mail ballots violated recent changes to the code of Washington, D.C., which governed NOW as its site of incorporation. In an attempt to build goodwill, the Chicago-aligned board majority voted to rescind the New Orleans motion to pay Plitt's legal fees. The board also accepted DeCrow's refusal to write a letter retracting her charges against Plitt, who had continued to serve as executive director. Those months were "definitely awkward," Plitt said. She ended up resigning in September 1975.

The two sides brokered other compromises. The issue of moving the upcoming conference from Philadelphia to St. Louis never came up for a vote, largely because of Collins, who feared that forcing the change would cause permanent damage. Some from the Caucus, including DeCrow, paid their dues and agreed to urge other escrowers to pay up, too, and many of them did so to ensure that they would be members "in good standing" and thus eligible to vote at the upcoming convention. "I believe we have come out of a difficult situation as friends and respected opponents," wrote Flora Crater of Virginia NOW. But she and others knew that the tensions had eased but not disappeared. "I expect the next election to be highly contested," Crater predicted.

———

Over the summer of 1975, the Majority Caucus made scrupulous preparations for the upcoming conference in Philadelphia. Their opponents, by contrast, were scattered, with Collins denying her loyalty to any faction. Caucus leaders studied *Robert's Rules of Order* and found a professional parliamentarian to preside over the conference. They made sure there would be enough of "our own legal experts to be on the floor at all times." Their "alternative press room" would allow them to issue their own news reports if necessary. All Caucus candidates were expected to arrive early in Philadelphia to rehearse tactics and speeches. Each candidate selected a "campaign aide" to handle materials, run her schedule, and defuse "hostile situations." Caucus leaders directed candidates who received fewer votes in the first round to withdraw and support other allied members' campaigns. They discouraged supporters from making plans to socialize or sleep during any early-morning or late-night sessions.

The Caucus's extensive planning for the elections far exceeded what the Chicagoans had done for Houston. Their slate comprised thirty-four candidates, one for every office and many for the national board. Those candidates hailed from every region of the country, and each candidate had signed a pledge to work toward specific Caucus goals: ending "internal and external oppression" in NOW; working with equal vigor against sexism, racism, ageism, and classism; building "a more democratic NOW"; moving the organization's office from Chicago to Washington, D.C.; and holding a constitutional convention that would bring about "a total reordering of the NOW organizational structure."

In its sleek yellow booklet for all Philadelphia conference goers, the Caucus presented its platform and candidates' short biographies, as well as a compact "voter scorecard" that listed all Caucus contenders. The faction's leaders could create and distribute these materials because the national board had ended the limits on campaign spending, which for previous conferences had been around $10 (about $70 today). The main conference organizers did not print any introduction to all of the candidates and their backgrounds, so the Caucus's guide was the only election-related material that conference goers received.

Topping the Caucus ticket was the incumbent president, Karen DeCrow. She proposed to broaden NOW's issues in order to appeal to more groups, by contrast to the Chicagoans, whose approach the previous year had sought to organize disparate women around the issue of work. In terms that echoed her predecessor Hernandez, DeCrow claimed that NOW had been too slow to realize that "this is not a women's movement. This is a people's movement," and thus the organization should "use its resources to fight against racism in America," which was "not a separate problem." Challenging "gender role stereotypes" required understanding "the homosexual issue" and refusing to put lesbian rights "in the closet." And she argued that NOW should applaud and recruit housewives rather than encouraging them to enter paid work. In the past, DeCrow explained, "we fell into the trap of thinking what men did was good and what women did was bad."

But DeCrow did not want to win on her own, as she had last time. Electing her Caucus's full slate, DeCrow claimed, would give her "the opportunity to work with persons who are once again the cutting edge of the feminist movement." To be on that cutting edge, she believed, NOW should back political candidates. The Internal Revenue Service had recently changed the rules for tax-exempt groups like NOW, freeing them to make endorsements if they devoted less than half of their efforts to political activities. The board had issued NOW's first national endorsement several months earlier, backing the New York congresswoman Bella Abzug in her race for the U.S. Senate in 1976. Members debated whether their organization should plunge deeper into national politics, but the pull was undeniable. In the month after the rule change, nearly two dozen male candidates, including several members of Congress and a Democratic senator planning to run for president, approached NOW for its official support. "This is an indication that we are going to be taken seriously at the higher levels," DeCrow said. "Imagine, they're arguing with each other about who's more feminist."

In Philadelphia, Collins and five others challenged DeCrow for the presidency. Some of Collins's fellow Chicago chapter members tried to talk her out of it, she said, "but I thought I had a vision"—a vision of unity. Collins repudiated her former tough tactics and abandoned the faction she helped organize. "We Need Each Other," declared her campaign poster, which featured a large photo of her smiling. There were well-intentioned members on both sides of the conflict, she claimed. NOW needed a president to heal the wounds and forge compromises. They had to end the infighting, Collins stressed, because their "well-organized and well-financed" enemies were toiling "to expose a powerless women's movement that cannot achieve its goals."

To dramatize members' solidarity and power and to spread her message, Collins set out from Chicago in August 1975 to travel "some 17,000 miles" by Greyhound bus. She was thirty-five years old and a candidate for NOW's national presidency. Her four opponents dominated the West and the Northeast, so she started in Florida, then traversed the Carolinas and Appalachia before trekking up the eastern shore. Her campaign route hit twenty-three states in total. "Each night was a new chapter," Collins said, describing her grueling routine. "You would get somebody to organize a meeting, someone to put you up, and then boom, boom to the next one." She carried eight shirts, four pairs of pants, one bandanna, toothpaste, and a toothbrush.

Collins ended the trip two months later, road weary and with "saddle sores," but hopeful. At every stop she had found chapters engaged in "a lot of activity, hard work, solidarity, and incredible goodwill." The members she met did not care about the turmoil that had gripped the national leadership; they just wanted it ended. "The full power of NOW is yet to be felt," she declared. Privately, Collins worried that her crusade for unity came too late to save NOW and feared that she bore some of the blame. Her rivals blamed her entirely.

That campaign trip marked a turning point in her life. When her Sears campaign co-director Anne Ladky joined her for part of the tour, "that solidified our relationship," Collins said. "I had always been attracted to women, but kind of suppressed that side of myself—got married in 1968 to a perfectly decent guy, but discovered over time that my attraction and my emotional attraction was really to women." Returning home to Chicago, Collins left her marriage and moved in with Ladky. She began to live openly as a lesbian, but she still believed that explicit advocacy for lesbian rights would be divisive. Instead, she highlighted the economic issues she believed could unite "vast numbers of women" in a focused struggle.

————

NOW had sixty thousand members in 1975—its ranks had tripled in the previous three years—and three thousand of them went to Philadelphia that October. As in Houston, the conference contained two gatherings at once. One was celebratory, with poetry readings, reunions, and booths selling feminist T-shirts. The other was the bitter faction fight, which the Caucus made impossible to ignore. Its supporters' "bright yellow tee shirts" were "very visible on the floor." Their side had made "a quantum leap in 'professionalization' over the relatively primitive organization and materials of the 'Chicago slate' at Houston," boasted Carabillo, with banners, buttons, and "signs marking state delegations" that were all "infinitely more colorful and highly visual" than anything a NOW conference had seen before.

Caucus supporters controlled the event, and the Chicagoans cringed at feeling their own tactics deployed against them. "This is what factions produce," Collins told a reporter disgustedly. "Little t-shirts! We cannot have an organization within an organization." She and her supporters wore arm bandages that read, "Factionalism hurts." Something else that hurt: the Chicagoans' opponents hosted a workshop titled "Saul Alinsky and the Poverty of His 'Rent-a-Radical' Proxy Approach." The conference program promised that the session would explore "the implications of Alinsky-ism for organized feminism" and whether "we want or need professional feminist organizers." It was an open swipe at Booth and the Midwest Academy.

The Caucus revived their old name for their enemies, the "Chicago Machine," who in turn labeled them the "Pennsylvania Railroad." Everything her Caucus did in Philadelphia was fair, said Carabillo. The Chicagoans had started the conflict by creating "the first internal political 'party' in NOW." Her side's response was "an inevitable reaction." Once again, the nominating committee, chaired by the Caucus member Del Martin, simply advanced all the names of qualified and interested candidates. The Caucus offered the only real slate.

The meeting's rigid emphasis on rules and procedures highlighted the tension and slowed the proceedings to a crawl. It was nearly impossible to hear the debaters, whose remarks were drowned out by "frantic" calls of "point of privilege" and "point of information" from the crowd. There was a twenty-minute debate over whether to call a thirty-minute recess. The rules required Karen DeCrow to hand the gavel to the national board chair, Judith Lightfoot, prior to her own election, but the conference voted that she could instead "yield to a person of her choice." DeCrow, having endured months of acrimony with Lightfoot, the Chicagoans' ally, chose the Caucus supporter Aileen Hernandez to preside in her place.

Because Pennsylvania was Caucus turf, that faction could shore up its advantage by persuading the conference goers to credential 300 women who joined NOW on the spot and who had "no organizational ties." The meeting also voted to permit another 150 local women to vote who did not even pay the $30 registration fee, let alone membership dues. Many of these newcomers looked to be about sixteen years old, noted the midwesterner Catherine Conroy. "They must have recruited them from some high school," she said. "The thing was stacked." Chairing the meeting, DeCrow said, "Don't worry, no one is trying to do anything terrible." A shouted chant erupted from the back of the hall: "Bullshit."

The accusations of foul play escalated when the voting began. The leaders had intended to avoid any hint of scandal by securing voting machines and hiring the American Arbitration Association for oversight. Before the elections were scheduled to start at dinnertime on Friday, officials learned that someone had removed one of the twenty logs of credentialed voters from a locked suite, which threw everyone's voting eligibility into doubt. Both sides denied the theft, but the election was delayed until 3:30 a.m. to allow everyone to be re-credentialed. Some voters received more than one set of credentials; others were never given any. People whose national dues were in escrow—Majority Caucus leaders and supporters—got to vote on whether they themselves should be able to vote in the elections. (They won.) Members somehow cast hundreds more ballots in the second round than in the first. Some candidates' names were left off ballots. The voting machines broke.

The voting took all night. Some women were crying as they shuffled to the polls and "fainting on the mezzanine stairs" from sheer exhaustion. DeCrow was ahead on the first ballot but had not reached a majority. Collins came in third and dropped out. DeCrow won the presidency on the second ballot. Eleanor Smeal, DeCrow's "chief theoretician," was elected national board chair. After the officers' ballot, Caucus members immediately began "working the floor" to get their supporters elected to the board. Many midwesterners had to leave to catch flights home, missing the long-delayed board vote. The Caucus secured sixteen of twenty-five board spots and eight of nine national executive positions. DeCrow beamed at the election results, quoting the philosopher Albert Camus: "I have not changed. It is just that I am not alone."

DeCrow's ally Carabillo called Houston and Philadelphia "nearly inevitable stages in the process of NOW's organizational and political maturation." But many members left surprised and demoralized. The Wisconsin NOW president and future national president Judy Goldsmith went to Philadelphia with her "sweet little" chapter "looking for sisterhood. We ran head-on into a buzz saw." There were a few bright spots, such as the members' vote to take up the cause of the poisoned and possibly murdered nuclear technician Karen Silkwood, but the conference could hardly be called productive. Members adopted only four of the hundreds of proposed resolutions due to the "endless power playing," a reporter noted. "Everybody who could get to the microphone screamed at the top of her lungs, vilifying somebody else."

The members were so busy fighting that they squandered the influence they had worked hard to build. Two U.S. presidential candidates—the U.S. senator Birch Bayh and Pennsylvania's governor, Milton Shapp—had arrived for a scheduled forum. Both waited for several hours, then left without addressing the gathering. "They're talking about running a woman for President," someone overheard a male journalist say at the conference, "and they can't even run a little convention." Of course, many political conventions featured bitter disputes. But the negative press coverage underscored the fragility of women's power in the eyes of many onlookers.

At NOW's inaugural conference in Washington, D.C., on October 29 and 30, 1966, thirty founders (twenty-five of whom sat for this photograph) elected the first officers and adopted a statement of purpose. Some of those featured here: Inez Casiano and Betty Friedan sit on the left and right ends of the front row; the back row, from left to right, includes Pauli Murray, Sister Joel Read, Dorothy Haener, and Anna Arnold Hedgeman. (Photograph by Vince Graas, Schlesinger Library, Harvard Radcliffe Institute)

Pauli Murray, one of NOW's cofounders, believed that women needed a united front to create social change and pressure federal officials. She was a visiting professor in the American Civilization program at Brandeis University, where this photo was taken in 1970. (Associated Press)

The campus newspaper at Alverno College printed photographs of its 1963 graduates, including the history major Mary Jean Collins. (Alverno College Archives)

In 1965, Aileen Hernandez was working as the assistant director of the California State Division of Fair Employment Practices when President Lyndon Johnson appointed her to the Equal Employment Opportunity Commission.
(Associated Press)

Betty Friedan proposed the Women's Strike for Equality, which took place on August 26, 1970. In forty cities across the country, her fellow protesters, including the sign bearer behind her, ignored her call to pivot away from "bra-burning actions" and "radical rhetoric." (Photograph by Fred W. McDarrah, Getty Images)

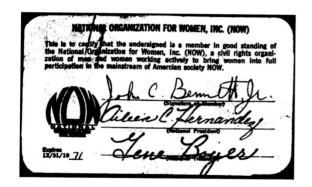

When Aileen Hernandez became NOW's national president in 1970, she standardized their procedures and issued membership cards. (Special Collections Research Center, George Washington University)

A talented portrait artist, Patricia Hill Burnett "piece-mealed" her career around her family obligations by painting oil portraits in her kitchen alcove. She sold them for $50 each. (*Detroit News*)

Aileen Hernandez used her organizing skills to build NOW and lead rallies like this one in 1970, in her adopted home of San Francisco. (*San Francisco Chronicle* / Polaris)

This bulletin board, posted at NOW's 1972 national conference in Washington, D.C., advertised a workshop on forming chapters, encouraged members to write to their senators to ask them to vote for the ERA, and promoted feminist T-shirts, literature, and postcards for sale. (Photograph by Bettye Lane, Rubenstein Library, Duke University)

As NOW's Midwest regional director, Mary Jean Collins had just met with Chicago's mayor, Richard J. Daley, when reporters interviewed her in 1971. (Photograph by Joe Kordick, PARS International)

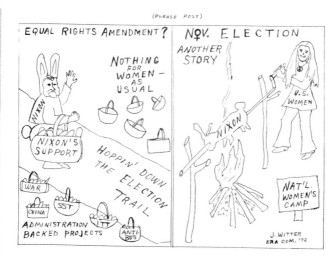

The Pittsburgh member Jean Witter framed NOW's ERA strategy in the late 1960s and early 1970s. In this cartoon, which was likely intended for public posting and reprinting in chapter newsletters, she predicted that women would oust President Richard Nixon in 1972 over his inattention to their specific concerns. (Schlesinger Library, Harvard Radcliffe Institute)

Men supported NOW as members, partners, and protesters, such as at the group's eastern regional conference in Atlantic City in 1974. (Photograph by Bettye Lane, Rubenstein Library, Duke University)

In pieces like this one (artist unknown) from NOW's 1973 national conference, members made visual their concerns and commitments. This mannequin wears a clock around her neck and a NOW name tag on her chest while holding a typewriter, a shoehorn, hand tools, a mirror, a baby, a saucepan, and an iron. (Photograph by Bettye Lane, Rubenstein Library, Duke University)

Nine members of NOW's executive board protested at the U.S. Supreme Court in 1973. Pictured from left to right: JoAnn Evansgardner, Roberta Benjamin, Muriel Fox, Jacqui Ceballos, Wilma Scott Heide, Karen DeCrow, Nola Claire, Dorothy Haener, and Toni Carabillo. (Photograph by Bettmann, Getty Images)

Women of color organized separately at some NOW gatherings, such as in the minority workshop at the 1974 national conference in Houston. (Photograph by Bettye Lane, Rubenstein Library, Duke University)

Lesbian feminists, who asserted distinct politics in both the feminist and gay liberation movements, marched behind their own banner at this 1981 Gay Pride March in New York City. (Photograph by Bettye Lane, Rubenstein Library, Duke University)

Patricia Hill Burnett, a feminist and a Republican Party activist in the 1970s, cultivated ties with powerful Michigan Republicans including President Gerald Ford (pictured here). (Bentley Historical Library, University of Michigan)

Karen DeCrow, shown here addressing the parade that kicked off NOW's 1975 national conference in Philadelphia, led NOW through its most fractious era. She was the group's national president from 1974 to 1977. (Photograph by Bill Ingraham, Associated Press)

Members voted at NOW's national conference in Philadelphia in 1975, where, after eighteen months of brutal infighting, "sisterly love" was scant. (Photograph by Bettye Lane, Rubenstein Library, Duke University)

Mary Jean Collins projected confidence in NOW's campaign against Sears, Roebuck in 1975 at the Philadelphia national conference, but Sears's sustained and savvy resistance kept victory out of reach. (Photograph by Bettye Lane, Rubenstein Library, Duke University)

After their elections at the 1977 national conference, officers Martha Buck, Arlie Scott, Eleanor Smeal, Eve Norman, and Sandy Roth posed in the "NOW salute," with their right arms arched overhead and three fingers extended. (Photograph by Lona O'Connor, USA Today Network)

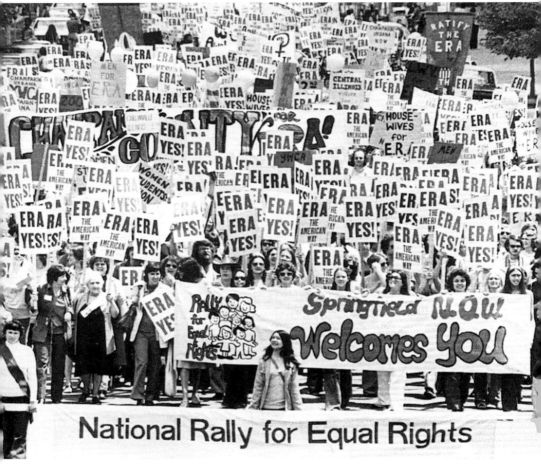

National Rally for Equal Rights

Ten thousand people rallied for the ERA at the Illinois State Capitol in 1976. Members also lobbied, canvassed, and protested across that state, which became an epicenter of NOW's ERA campaign. (Associated Press)

THE EQUAL RIGHTS AMENDMENT

equality of rights
under law shall not
be denied or abridged
by the United States
or by any State
on account of sex........ is for Everyone!

Won't you please help us?

Join the Missouri ERA Coalition, NOW!

AS A MEMBER, I AM ENTITLED TO VOTE AT THE QUARTERLY MEMBERSHIP MEETING, *NNN*
AND RECEIVE THE MONTHLY NEWSLETTER.

NAME_____

ADDRESS_____

TELEPHONE (home)_____(work)_____

SENATE DISTRICT_____HOUSE DISTRICT_____

_____$10.00 Individual Membership $50.00 Sponsoring Membership_____

_____I also wish to make a contribution. I want to pledge $_____per_____.

I WOULD LIKE TO HELP THE RATIFICATION EFFORT BY:

_____Hosting meetings in my home   _____Helping with mailings
_____Helping at the Coalition Office   _____Giving talks
_____Telephoning   _____Helping with fund raising events
_____Typing   _____Personal finance calls
Other, please specify_____

Please mail to: THE MO. ERA COALITION, 6668 BERTHOLD, APT. D, ST. LOUIS, MO. 63139

Sign-up sheets, like this one from unratified Missouri, advertised the state's broad ERA coalition and informed supporters about opportunities to contribute their time and money to the cause. (Schlesinger Library, Harvard Radcliffe Institute)

This receipt for a donation to the Sacramento ERA Task Force points out that those funds were not spent in the unratified state of Nevada. The NOW-led economic boycott of the fifteen states that had not ratified the ERA by 1977 deprived those states of $200 million in tourism revenue, according to state and local officials, as well as funds from the organizations that relocated their conventions. (Schlesinger Library, Harvard Radcliffe Institute)

As national president from 1977 to 1982 and from 1985 to 1987, Eleanor Smeal focused and expanded NOW's resources while shepherding its campaign to ratify the ERA. Smeal addressed a press conference in Washington, D.C., in January 1982. (Photograph by Bettmann, Getty Images)

Judy Goldsmith, NOW's national president from 1982 to 1985, spoke at the March on Washington in 1983 alongside the civil rights leader Coretta Scott King. (USA Today Network)

NOW drew more bad press just days later. Distracted by the infighting, the leaders had not fully committed to planning and publicizing the nationwide protest they had scheduled for October 29, 1975. NOW chapters in California had proposed the event as a sequel to the blockbuster 1970 Women's Strike for Equality. Five years later, the organizers called upon women once more to refuse to work, shop, volunteer, or parent on "Alice Doesn't Day" as a way "to show the nation how much it depends on them." The title was a nod to *Alice Doesn't Live Here Anymore*, a 1974 film about a determined single mother.

Alice Doesn't Day was a bust. Antifeminists stole attention by storming NOW rallies in frilly dresses to protest and "support American manhood." Chapters in New York and New Jersey did not publicize the strike at all, worried about negative press that would spoil the votes on state Equal Rights Amendment referenda that were just days away. Participating chapters fielded calls from women who wanted to strike for Alice Doesn't Day but feared losing their jobs. The press contacted employers nationwide, and none reported any elevated absenteeism. Most women treated the day like any other. It was a startling contrast to the action they had staged five years earlier. NOW's call to strike was "out of touch," explained a Chicago office worker: "Alice did—because she had to."

———

Shaking off the debris from Philadelphia and Alice Doesn't Day, NOW's new leaders got to work in late 1975. Within months, they closed the national office in Chicago and opened the new "National Action Center" in Washington, D.C. The center's five staffers would answer to the elected officers, with no executive director. These changes marked "a redirection of NOW's energies and resources," Smeal wrote. NOW would take advantage of the proximity to the federal government, as well as to "virtually every major lobby and public interest group," all headquartered in the capital. "Our staff requirements in Washington will not be so great as they are now," Smeal informed the workers from the shuttered Chicago office. "You are, however, cordially invited to apply for one of the new positions." Some might have applied, but none were apparently hired.

While the Caucus had enough power to make such sweeping changes, some dissenters still remained. Patricia Hill Burnett helped lead a faction of former NOW officers, half of whom had just lost in Philadelphia, who sought to retake control in 1976. In a meeting that Burnett hoped would "become as historical as the convening of NOW," they adopted the name Womansurge and pledged to counter the new leadership's "ruinously revolutionary drift." "If you have any political sense, you don't talk about revolution in America today," Womansurge's backer Mordeca Pollock told a reporter. "Look at Eldridge Cleaver," the former Black Panther Party leader who had renounced violence and returned to the United States after seven years in exile to face attempted murder charges stemming from a 1968 shoot-out with police. Womansurge's cofounder Shelley Fernandez agreed. "The movement has started to go in a direction that will frighten most women," she claimed in calling the Caucus "a small minority" of NOW members. Her new faction claimed to speak for most members. That majority wanted to "build . . . coalitions on bread-and-butter issues," she said, and steer clear of issues that might stir controversy. Womansurge wanted NOW to keep open the potential to work with social conservatives by endorsing lesbian rights but not foregrounding that issue, for example.

DeCrow countered that she did represent the majority of NOW members, and they wanted a nimble, grassroots-driven organization with a bold and expansive agenda. The Caucus had formed in the first place because "huge numbers of us" believed that NOW was "bogging down" and unable "to effect the changes we wanted," DeCrow said. Her side did not represent "some small elite"; the Philadelphia conference that swept them into power had been "no less representative of NOW members than any that preceded it." The Caucus's expansive approach to social justice and acknowledgment of women's differences was "the intellectually correct direction and the politically correct direction," she said. Her opponents, by contrast, appeared to believe that "if the feminist movement pays attention to anyone but white middle-class straight women, we will somehow deviate from [our] course." She dismissed the new faction as "the last gasp of a very small group with a condescending view of what feminism is like."

Burnett, Betty Friedan, and the dozen other Womansurge founders laid the groundwork to form a new organization. But they never presented an agenda beyond regaining control, and they were already stretched thin across their other personal and activist commitments. Womansurge fizzled, having accomplished little beyond garnering some media coverage.

Burnett's vision for NOW as a global network of women also faded. Two years had passed since her round-the-world tour. Several months after her return, the Houston conference voted for NOW to "go international" by accepting official overseas chapters, but the organization put few resources toward building them. Burnett had come to believe that international work "was not important" to most of NOW's leaders. And when the Majority Caucus emerged, Burnett felt that they saw her as a wealthy conservative, "a symbol of everything they didn't like about the right-wing." Even Burnett's friends saw that she increasingly stuck out. "I remember her well at the national NOW meetings," Friedan said of Burnett, "in her big hats, fashionable clothes and all that jewelry."

The new leaders diluted Burnett's power to craft an international agenda for NOW by assigning her a co-chair of the international committee, the New Yorker Arlie Scott. Scott took over the committee's budget and correspondence. Upon learning that Burnett had been sending her own money to help women start NOW chapters overseas, Scott told her to seek mental help for her "rich woman syndrome." Burnett requested about $1,500 to cover clerical assistance and travel in 1974 and more than $3,800 in 1975, but she did not receive it, nor was she reimbursed for the funds she had chipped in herself. NOW's international work "has been my life for the last four years," Burnett remarked, but she decided it was time to "ease out of this miserable situation."

At the same time, Burnett saw others run with her ideas. She had been "instrumental" to NOW's receiving official NGO status with the United Nations in 1974, and she openly lobbied to be the group's UN ambassador. DeCrow wanted Hernandez in the role, although the position does not appear to have been created. Meanwhile, global feminism flourished around NOW as the UN had declared 1975 International Women's Year and held a major multinational conference in Mexico City. DeCrow and Scott had wanted NOW to send an official delegation, but board meetings in the months after the late 1974 blowup in New Orleans had been so contentious that they "never got to our agenda item," DeCrow wrote to Burnett. Those two and about a hundred other NOW members went to Mexico City as individuals. Burnett remained involved in international feminism on her own terms, although the "world conference of feminists" she helped plan in Cambridge never materialized, and NOW had moved on. While Burnett left the national board in late 1975, she found that she could still pursue her ideals locally through NOW. She stayed on as the Detroit chapter's international coordinator.

NOW's leaders focused on their organization's internal work. One of the group's few tangible achievements in Philadelphia was the vote, by a wide margin, to hold a constitutional convention in 1976. It was fitting to establish new bylaws in the nation's bicentennial year. DeCrow appointed Smeal to chair the event and created a constitutional commission that comprised one delegate from each state, modeled on the U.S. Senate, itself an iconic but imperfect vessel for democracy. In nationwide hearings before the convention, members debated open-ended questions that scrutinized every aspect of the organization. These members generally wanted NOW to be more efficient and flexible, decentralized, and fiscally sound, and for leaders to be more accountable.

The organization had changed its bylaws a few times before, each time adding more internal structures in hopes of accommodating its growth. The original 1967 bylaws were adopted when NOW had few members and no chapters. Amendments in 1970 increased the number of national officers from five to thirteen and divided the country into four regions, each with its own director, bylaws, board, and officers. Members adopted another amendment in 1974 to allow for state organizations. Smeal promised that the upcoming constitutional convention would do more than tinker. NOW needed "streamlining and reorganizing" to accommodate its growth.

The convention hammered out bylaws that democratized the organization in some ways, as members wanted. The new rules created a delegate system for national conferences and gave members the power to elect national board members from their own regions rather than in one open contest at the national conference. But there would be nine regions rather than four, diluting each region's influence. These bylaws also replaced the executive committee, which had comprised thirteen volunteers, with five full-time, salaried officers. New officers could serve for longer stints: up to two consecutive two-year terms. Smeal and her allies had pushed for the salaried officers. They wanted NOW to be "not like a 'once a month thing'" that members could "work . . . into [their] spare time," Smeal said. "We saw this far more as a consuming cause."

"We can not afford to return to ground zero," warned a report that accompanied the bylaws ballot each member received. The membership voted to accept the changes. "We will never again be able to afford one entire year"—the time they spent preparing for the constitutional convention—"or such a major outlay of time and money." Indeed, some doubted that outlay had been worth it. In the two years members spent in internal combat, the national political landscape had become far more hostile to feminists. When they stopped fighting one another, they were forced into a defensive crouch together.

———

The women's movement entered a less confident stage in the mid-1970s. Its organizations had helped pass laws and raised expectations, with NOW at the forefront, but turning abstract principles into concrete change was expensive and time-consuming. Enforcement agencies were inconsistent and under-resourced, and the gendered wage gap expanded under economic pressures that workplace equality laws could not directly reach. NOW members understood that the tasks ahead diverged from what had come before. "In the early days, we had to discuss and define sexism, and we did that spectacularly well," a NOW official would tell a reporter in 1977. "Today the problems are more difficult. We have to ensure passage and compliance of the laws. It's not glamorous work, but it's essential."

NOW took on that unglamorous work amid major shifts in American life: scarcity replaced abundance in the nation's economy and cynicism pushed out trust in its politics. This gloomy climate shaped NOW's conflicts and their aftermath. The leaders' focused determination began to close off the kind of openness that had once characterized their group's mission as well as its potential. They had less patience for deliberation and more skepticism that all women could collaborate even if they tried. To Hernandez, the "internal battles" had been a "disaster." No one felt their effects more personally than Collins, who had once anchored the faction opposite Hernandez's. Burnett, whom the fights also left feeling unsettled and demoralized, would make one last attempt to frame a universal women's agenda: this time, in the realm of American electoral politics.

The emergence of organized antifeminism compounded many members' sense that women's politics was a magnet that could repel as often as it connected. NOW chapters in Ohio and California ousted members who opposed abortion. "It's ironic that I can't be for equal pay and the other issues and still be against abortion," said a woman who was "hounded out" of the Fresno chapter. The leaders defended their motives. "We are not a government that has to include all views," DeCrow told a reporter in late 1975, inviting feminists who did not approve of any of NOW's positions to join some other group. "I'm not trying to be president of the United States or president of an industry-wide union where I have to appeal to a lot of people," she said. "We cannot compromise with our consciences on what is the feminist point of view."

Internal friction was likely unavoidable in the mid-1970s, given NOW's explosive growth—membership more than doubled between 1972 and 1974 alone, rising from eighteen thousand to forty thousand—as well as its ambition, organizational youth, and external challenges. The conflict obscured real differences of emphasis through escalating power plays that also began to shrink members' own common ground. All of the factions correctly identified members' need to focus efforts to win results beyond their organization and the need to give a more diverse constituency greater influence within it. Unlike many of the other social movement groups of the 1960s, NOW did not collapse due to ideological splintering, a radical insurgency, government persecution, or a cult of personality. The organization survived its ordeal but emerged transformed.

———

Caught in NOW's mid-1970s cross fire was Collins's passion project, the Sears campaign. Collins, Ladky, and their allies, in ongoing negotiations with the corporation, gambled with the fate of women who worked at Sears in their crusade to crush the company and receive the credit. As the EEOC and Sears pursued a settlement in late 1975, the two sides agreed on most of the terms. But NOW persuaded the EEOC lawyers, led by its collaborator David Copus, to reject Sears's offer of $34 million for back pay and affirmative action programs. A similar consent decree brokered with AT&T several years earlier had been larger. Given Sears's size, a $100 million settlement would be both reasonable and attention grabbing. Instead, the negotiations fell apart and there was no settlement. Around this time, NOW's new leaders, who "hated" the Sears campaign, "dropped it" from the agenda, according to Collins.

The EEOC's showdown with Sears outlived NOW's involvement. The agency continued investigating and wrote a report that found Sears guilty of breaking workplace discrimination laws in seventy-four instances. The company won in court to delay the report's publication and kept up its fight. The two sides settled the race discrimination cases with no monetary damages in 1981, but the EEOC took the sex case to trial. Sears won in court in 1986, when the EEOC, led by the future Supreme Court justice Clarence Thomas, deliberately put up a weak case. Even a modest settlement would have benefited the women who worked at Sears.

NOW could have helped deliver a different outcome to Sears women, the group's attorney told NOW's president, Eleanor Smeal, in 1981. He believed there was a good chance that NOW could influence "both the issues and the relief" and ultimately "assist in the reshaping of certain facets of the second largest private employer in the country." Collins, back in Chicago, offered to dedicate significant time to the effort to finally hold Sears accountable. Smeal declined. She and other new leaders refused even to update the board on the Sears case. They were focused on the fight of NOW's life: fending off a rising conservative movement that took direct aim at the organization and its goals.

7.

PUT IT ON THE LINE NOW
FOR EQUALITY

History is being made here today," NOW's outgoing leader, Karen DeCrow, declared in 1977. The national convention, meeting in Detroit, had just elected her successor. "You have a former president and a current president standing here on the same platform together," she said, "who are going to smile at each other and get along." Standing beside DeCrow, Eleanor Smeal agreed that NOW's era of internal strife was over. Smeal took her landslide victory as a mandate for her plan to channel NOW's resources toward one goal: ratifying the Equal Rights Amendment. The ERA was "obviously the most important issue facing women in this country," Smeal said. To win it, NOW would build "an integrated national campaign directed by a national strike force" that used "many tactics," from massive protests to personal lobbying. Such a varied approach would rally the masses. "There are many women in this country who are not militant," DeCrow explained, "but they are ready now to speak out and work for the ERA."

When NOW's leaders held up the ERA as a unifying issue, others were sharpening it into a potent wedge. The amendment seemed to be cruising to the finish line after clearing both houses of Congress by 1972 and quickly passing in thirty of the needed thirty-eight state legislatures.

Both major political parties had long endorsed it. But women were not united under the banner of sex equality. Some who embraced traditional gender roles and condemned equal rights were, inspired by NOW's example, fervently organizing and advocating for their own conservative values. Commanding attention from the media and Republican Party power brokers, women who rejected feminism insisted that the ERA was not a benign expression of American values but a ticking bomb poised to explode American life.

Women who opposed the ERA, which stood to cement gender equality as the foundation of social policy and root out laws that positioned women as dependent family members, forced NOW to a crossroads. Equality was the organization's bedrock principle: a principle its founders believed that women could broadly share. NOW's leaders and bylaws did not strictly define that equality. Members could interpret it for themselves and pursue it through their chapters. The women's rights movement of the previous century had cultivated a similar kind of "functional ambiguity," according to the historian Nancy Cott, that helped suffragists build a broad, albeit racially circumscribed, coalition that won the Nineteenth Amendment in 1920. But the proposed ERA sundered that coalition after that amendment's passage. While some advocates pursued the amendment, others warned that the provision would end legal protections that took gender into account, thereby deepening the most vulnerable women's disadvantages.

By the 1970s, feminists generally favored the ERA as one of many objectives, and NOW pursued legal equality among dozens of its goals. The organization's flexible approach to equality, which was both attractive and productive, was meant to appeal to women across their differences. But NOW had no way to accommodate women who rejected equality itself. Those women's very existence threatened to undermine NOW's claim to advocate for all women. The group's leaders and members faced a choice: they could surrender the ERA or stand their ground. Most decided to dig in their heels. They reinterpreted the ERA in the late 1970s as "the bottom line issue for the feminist movement" and pledged to take any measure to bring it to life. This meant hustling to streamline operations, raise money, and pressure state legislators. By the end of the 1970s,

NOW was at the forefront of a coalition of women's, professional, religious, labor, and other organizations pushing for the amendment.

But that leadership came with a price. As NOW helped to make the ERA the turf where feminists and antifeminists battled over competing visions of society, the group's leaders asked its members for total allegiance. Some raised objections that went unheard. "I'm begging you and begging us not to save this organization or ourselves for something else," Smeal said in 1980, as NOW and other advocates pursued three more state ratifications before the 1982 deadline, "but to put it on the line now for equality." A win would be momentous, but what might it cost?

———

Ratifying the ERA had been one of NOW's earliest goals, but it was controversial even among feminists in the mid-1960s. After a year of internal debate, NOW's ERA supporters had overcome objections from members who favored more flexible approaches to women's rights to win their organization's official endorsement in 1967. It was time, the group had announced, to overturn thousands of sexist state and federal laws and equalize women's "service to the state and to the nation" through jury and military service. The ERA soon topped the group's legislative priorities, but it was accompanied by a host of other legal changes and government programs that would make equal rights broadly beneficial: state-funded child care, repeal of abortion laws, supports for women in poverty, and protected access to maternity leave, education, and employment.

As NOW president in the early 1970s, Aileen Hernandez had strongly supported the ERA. "We are going to have to organize politically (but non-partisan) to persuade our legislators that we mean what we say about equality," she wrote to other NOW leaders as the ERA languished in Congress in 1970. Due largely to feminist pressure, legislators began to consider the amendment, and some proposed carving out exceptions to equality for the military draft and labor laws. Hernandez urged women to reject both. By then, her mentor Pauli Murray had also come to see the ERA as "not only necessary but also politically wise," overcoming her earlier reservations as advocates lined up behind it. Murray returned to NOW after a three-year absence to join the ERA fight.

While members of Congress debated the ERA's merits, members of NOW contested its meaning. The amendment's language was plain: "Equality of rights under the law shall not be denied or abridged by the United States or by any state on account of sex." Black feminists, including Murray and Hernandez, viewed the amendment as one piece of a broader agenda for sex-, race-, and class-based justice. And to Patricia Hill Burnett, the ERA aligned with conservative values. Far from leveling hierarchies, the ERA, she believed, would help women ascend them. Burnett welcomed the military draft for her daughters as long as they could be officers. She also highlighted how the ERA would benefit men by democratizing workplace protections and making divorce laws sex neutral.

Burnett had taken part in NOW's earliest ERA action back in 1970: a campaign to muscle it through Congress. The amendment had been in both major-party platforms since the 1940s, but no member of Congress had brought it to the floor for a vote. Assisted by feminist lawmakers, the activists devised creative strategies to pressure state and federal legislatures. Burnett had traveled to Washington when Congresswoman Martha Griffiths, a Michigan Democrat, encouraged Michigan NOW to hold a vigil on the Capitol steps until the ERA was voted out of the House Judiciary Committee. "We literally stayed all night—day and night," Burnett said, cheering their fortitude.

Drawing strength from her fellow advocates' optimism, Burnett confronted Emanuel Celler, the Democrat who had kept the ERA tied up in the committee for years out of solidarity with the labor movement, whose leaders generally opposed the provision. Burnett breezed past Celler's secretary, she recounted, found the congressman at his desk, and perched on it to lecture him about supporting the ERA "as if he were a puppy that had peed on the rug." He would not relent for another two years, but she and other ERA advocates viewed their opposition as negligible, even pathetic. A 1970 Senate subcommittee hearing room packed with ERA supporters had "rocked with laughter," a reporter noted, when a solo union spokesman presented his objections.

The pressure had worked. The ERA passed in the U.S. House of Representatives in 1971 by a vote of 354–24. After a similar campaign to move the amendment out of the Senate Judiciary Committee and onto the floor, the ERA survived a last-ditch effort by some senators to weaken it through amendments. It cleared the Senate by a vote of 84–8 in 1972. Senators took the unusual step of adding an expiration date for ratification by the required thirty-eight state legislatures, but ERA backers were not worried. Hawaii's legislature ratified it that same day without a single dissenting vote. Advocates had seven years to win the same result in thirty-seven more states.

Burnett was one of those advocates. She believed the ERA was a good policy with broad appeal. Just weeks after the amendment cleared Congress in 1972, she testified before her state's Republican Party platform committee to dole out some tough love. "Some-one has to say this," she told them, and as a longtime donor and proud party "workhorse" she felt qualified to be that someone. Burnett accused her fellow Michigan Republicans of abandoning their historic commitment to "the right of the individual to pursue his or her own way in this society" by ignoring the new women's movement. The movement's values paralleled this party's, which stood for free enterprise and small government, by promoting women's personal potential, she explained. "So why is it," Burnett asked, "that people assume that because I am working for the cause of women, I must automatically be a Democrat?"

Republican Party leaders had been "remarkably slow in recognizing women's rights," Burnett warned, and had sent women "flocking to the Democratic Party." But the Democrats did not yet have the female vote sewn up. She told her allies that they had a "golden opportunity" to "make the Republican Party the 'Women's Party'" by championing the ERA. As a "staunch Republican feminist," Burnett believed that the ERA could fuse her movement and her politics. Women's rights advocates across the political spectrum held out similar hopes that fighting for constitutional equality could unify women and that achieving it would bring sweeping benefits.

———

To help push the ERA over the finish line in the mid-1970s, NOW's leaders devised a grassroots-driven strategy with notable but short-lived success. Chapters would research their lawmakers and their districts, then collaborate to make a plan for their own state. NOW's leaders saw that their organization was "weak in statehouse lobbying," but members could try to "force lawmakers to come out as for or against women" by "trad[ing the] threat of adverse publicity for ERA votes." NOW members felt the wind at their backs when thirty states ratified the amendment within the first year, including Burnett's state of Michigan. But progress slowed with eight out of fifteen states to go in early 1973, among them Arizona, Utah, and most of the South. The remaining states were the most conservative and the hardest to win, but the real problem was that they began "hitting well-organized, well-financed opposition," a NOW spokesperson said.

This opposition had a public face: Phyllis Schlafly, a conservative activist from St. Louis. The anti-Communist hawk, author, and former candidate for Congress was already well known, but she gained more notoriety by challenging the ERA's basic premise: that legal equality would benefit women. Too extreme even for the Republican Party, Schlafly was still stinging from her 1967 loss to a more moderate candidate for the presidency of the National Federation of Republican Women. Several months later, she had started a newsletter, *The Phyllis Schlafly Report*, which kept her donors abreast of her positions and, increasingly, set out to turn public opinion against the ERA.

Schlafly declared that the amendment was not a positive affirmation of women's value to the nation; instead, it would destroy their "right" to special treatment. Schlafly began to tap and fuse older networks of conservative white women, then reached out to younger, evangelical, and previously apolitical women by ginning up fears that the ERA threatened them personally. In 1972, she founded a new organization, STOP ERA, that had local committees in twenty-six states by the following year. That group presented itself as NOW's mirror image: a "spontaneous grass-roots" network whose very existence proved that women did not share the same goals and priorities.

Schlafly might have been on the GOP's conservative fringe, but pressure from her and other women was compounding an existential crisis for the party of old money, small government, and anti-Communism. Some Republican women, like Burnett, sought to ascend within the male-dominated establishment. Others like Schlafly organized separately, framing their issues as moral crusades that women were best suited to drive. Both types expressed frustration that women shouldered the "housework of government," providing crucial support but never tapped for leadership. "The time is past," Schlafly said, "when the women of the Republican Party are merely doorbell pushers. We have earned our right to participate in the making of policies at the top."

Schlafly never would have admitted it, but NOW had helped propel her rise. NOW was at the forefront of the feminist effort to normalize a new kind of woman: outspoken, political, and fearless. Schlafly's acolytes elevated her in these precise terms. They also borrowed from NOW even more specifically. Thousands crowded into organizations whose names, like NOW's, were acronyms: NEVER (No Equality via Equal Rights), WWWW (Women Who Want to Be Women), and, in the most direct reference to NOW, HOW (Happiness of Womanhood). Schlafly fostered this assortment of groups and acronyms to make her supporters seem like an unprompted, organic movement. These women also pulled strategies directly from NOW's playbook in how they spoke and organized. They made expansive claims about women, formed local cells with national coordination, and showed up en masse to lobby and protest. But the centerpiece of their agenda was the opposite of NOW's loosely defined equality: that equality itself was dangerous.

Schlafly's followers joined a sea of social and economic conservatives that was beginning to force the GOP further right by weaponizing gender and racial issues. Shifting and widening the party's long-standing commitment to protecting business prerogatives and promoting anti-Communism, this grassroots-powered New Right embraced cultural concerns. Its proponents addressed the threats conservatives saw around them—the shameful end of the Vietnam War, economic convulsions, and the civil rights movement's victories—through race-baiting, nostalgia, and anti-elitism. Joining these conservatives were some Roman Catholics, Protestants, Mormons, and Jews who were inflamed by liberalizing state abortion laws and *Roe v. Wade*. These abortion foes began to channel their outrage into stopping the ERA, claiming that both that provision and abortion rights would harm women by undermining the traditional family. They linked the ERA's mandate for equality to recent federal interventions to democratize public education and the workplace. As one North Carolina woman put it, "Forced busing, forced mixing, forced hiring. Now forced women. No thank you."

Conservative men began to see newly engaged antifeminist women less as pushy boundary crossers than as political assets. Feminism had so shifted the nation's consciousness by the mid-1970s that even conservatives had to tamp down on overt misogyny. *The New York Times* noted in 1977 that few men of the day would describe feminism the way one comedian had a few years earlier: "Sure, my wife joined the feminists. Why not? They all want somebody to help with the dishes." Conservatives thus packaged their aversion to gender equality in a new rhetoric of cherishing women by protecting the traditional family—areas where women could claim unique authority. Aiming squarely at feminism, they pointed to women's increased presence in college and the labor force and liberalized divorce and abortion laws as omens of societal collapse. Jacquie Davison, the founder and president of Happiness of Womanhood and its new offshoot, the League of Housewives, described those groups' members as "real women" who "want to be loved and protected by our men" and "defend our homes."

Despite this groundswell of social conservatism, a Republican feminist like Burnett could feel comfortable claiming both identities in the early 1970s. Historically, Republicans were friendlier than Democrats to women's rights, although neither party had done much specifically for women for decades. NOW was officially nonpartisan because its founders believed that both major parties represented an unacceptable status quo. Yet both parties were newly open to feminism in the early 1970s.

On the left side of American politics, the Democrats were wrapping up a process of internal party reform. The violent and disorderly Democratic National Convention in Chicago in 1968 persuaded party leaders to ask the liberal senator George McGovern to chair a commission to reform the party's procedure for choosing delegates. The commission issued a new requirement that women, young people, and people of color be appointed convention delegates in proportion to their representation in their state's population. It went into effect for the Democrats' 1972 convention, where women's percentage of delegates more than tripled over 1968, rising from 13 to 40 percent. That convention nominated McGovern for president. He helped pull his party to the left, endorsing abortion rights, an immediate end to the Vietnam War, and an expanded social safety net funded by new taxes on corporations and the wealthy.

On the right side, Republican President Richard Nixon waffled on women's rights, but the feminists in his party leveraged their clout. Eventually, Nixon appointed more women to federal positions than any predecessor, and he publicly stated his support for the ERA, although he did not fight for it. The 1972 GOP platform endorsed the ERA and federal support for child care, and it committed to "endeavor" to reach gender parity among convention delegates, 70 percent of whom were men that year. NOW's president, Wilma Scott Heide, criticized Nixon's "insensitivity and misogyny" in neglecting the ERA and opposing abortion rights. She urged members to write to Nixon and tell him "if you are still Republican," hoping to pressure his party with the fact that feminists were leaving it. Just over half of NOW members were Democrats in 1974, 15 percent were Republicans, and one-quarter described themselves as independents.

Burnett was in the minority as a NOW Republican, but she wanted to merge her causes. NOW taught her "to operate from the outside, to beat down the walls, and demand a change," she said. But she also saw value in being a party insider. "Men love us for tokens," but women like her were "very subversive, and will try to take power and then use that power to make changes." Burnett spent decades volunteering in various roles in the local and state GOP, including a stint as secretary of the party's ways and means committee in Michigan. As in her 1972 testimony before the platform committee, she often urged party officials to heed women's concerns and warned NOW not to "give up on millions of Republican women as a lost cause." When understood her way, Burnett's causes overlapped. Abortion was "a matter of personal choice" whose accessibility would lower public spending. Affordable child care would not "weaken the influence of the home"; it would unleash the "tremendous potential work-force" of mothers. An advocate of fiscal conservatism and small government, Burnett believed that the ERA, a shield for individual rights, could bring feminism and Republicanism closer together.

Republican feminists were especially prominent in Michigan. The state had back-to-back moderate Republican governors from 1963 to 1982, starting with the celebrated centrist George Romney. Republican women flourished in state politics, and First Lady Lenore Romney routinely campaigned in each of the state's eighty-three counties. The Detroit NOW member Lorraine Beebe, the only woman in the state senate, was a proud "Romney Republican." Governor Romney opposed the ERA, but his successor in 1969, William Milliken, backed it as part of his effort to build an open and inclusive party. Milliken appointed Burnett to the state's fifteen-member women's commission in 1973.

Burnett wrote to her governor in 1975 that their party offered "a special place to the modern woman who seeks equality before the law." This was a hope, not a fact, because conservatives were hyping the ERA's alleged dangers to turn the GOP against feminism.

———

Just as NOW had changed the right, the right started to change NOW. The ERA's momentum had noticeably slowed by mid-decade. Twenty-two states ratified in 1972, eight in 1973, and three in 1974. With five states to go, and with Schlafly's influence on the rise, the ratifications stopped coming. NOW's leaders tried to finish the job with a firmer hand. They focused on five states—Nevada, Missouri, Florida, Indiana, and Illinois—and studied up on state government, which was "hidden in character" and rooted in personal relationships and political favors. NOW had to learn this game to win it, they realized. No longer would the individual states run their own disparate campaigns; no longer would the ERA be one among many coequal priorities that members could choose to pursue through their chapters or the national task force.

When the national board declared a "state of emergency on the ERA" in early 1978, those leaders vowed to devote "almost all the organization's resources" to the fight. The board's emergency resolutions directed national officers, board members, and "chapters, states and regions and all members" to pull back from working on "all other issue areas," "turn their total attention" to the ERA, and "devote as much effort as possible" to winning it.

The main proponent of this strategy was the Pittsburgh housewife

Eleanor Smeal. The longtime NOW stalwart had helped steer the Majority Caucus insurgency that had defeated Mary Jean Collins and her allies a few years earlier. The thirty-seven-year-old Smeal had short graying hair, dark eyes, and a steely magnetism. Her middle-class image obscured her frugal upbringing. The daughter of working-class Italian immigrants in Erie, Pennsylvania, Smeal grew up debating at the dinner table with her father and three older brothers. She left a doctoral program in political science at the University of Florida in the mid-1960s to marry the metallurgist Charlie Smeal, and they moved to the Pittsburgh area to raise their two children. Ellie discovered feminism when, bedridden from a back injury, she found the writings of women's suffragists.

Smeal's local Pittsburgh-area NOW chapters were especially focused on legal change, including driving the challenge to sex-segregated classified job advertisements that triumphed in the U.S. Supreme Court in 1973. An area member, Jean Witter, was so important to NOW's efforts to shepherd the ERA through Congress that her fellow Pittsburghers called it "Jean's Amendment." The Pittsburgh members continued to emphasize the ERA. "We were winning," Smeal said, "but there were those cases that we were losing," and "a lot of our stuff was going nowhere." Smeal recalled the suffragists' persistence over many years to pass the Nineteenth Amendment in 1920 and their decades-long commitment to the ERA, still unrealized. The remaining veterans of the suffrage struggle, Smeal believed, viewed NOW members as their "reinforcements." Running for NOW national president in 1977, Smeal had called the ERA "the unfinished business for which NOW was created." But she also understood that constitutional equality could not solve every problem: while the ERA would "underpin all other gains for women's rights," Smeal said, "it cannot be a panacea."

Smeal won NOW's presidency at a relatively unified, upbeat conference in 1977. She defeated the San Francisco chapter president, Shelley Fernandez, who also backed the ERA but believed their strategy should develop "from the bottom up instead of the top down." Smeal pointed to her huge margin of victory, by a vote of 526–66, as evidence of united support for her focused ERA strategy. "We will all have to make many sacrifices for that drive," she said in her acceptance speech. Members would need "high visibility and militancy" as they assumed "the burden of ratifi-cation" themselves. NOW had recently proposed an economic boycott of states that had not ratified the ERA. Eventually, that initiative included hundreds of groups and cost those states around $200 million in tourism revenue. NOW would enter alliances, Smeal told the Detroit meeting, but their group would chart its own course. That conference also set up NOW's first political action committee to fundraise for its favored can-didates. Smeal, who would chair both the NOW PAC and the new ERA strike force, would have the authority to lead a national effort.

Smeal might have felt less powerful when she arrived at NOW's Washington, D.C., headquarters and reviewed the measly budget. "It was clear that we could not be a massive organization without having a finan-cial reality" to match, she said later. "How could you talk about a strong political movement if you were not able to raise your first million?" Amid the economic recession and dwindling donations, NOW's income had plummeted along with its ranks. National membership dropped from fifty-five thousand in 1975 to thirty-five thousand in 1976. Paying the new officers' salaries would be a stretch, as would covering board mem-bers' travel to meetings. The monthly office telephone bill alone reached $10,000 ($47,900 today). Smeal stepped up existing fundraising efforts. Members hawked everything from magazine subscriptions to bumper stickers to pints of their own blood in a "Blood Money for the ERA" campaign. "We usually had five to six avenues of money," Smeal said.

Before long, NOW hit the mother lode. That windfall was direct mail, a new method of targeted advertising and fundraising developed by NOW's enemies. The right-wing strategist Richard Viguerie sought to create a communications approach that would enable conservative pop-ulists to overthrow the elitist GOP establishment and overcome what he saw as a biased media and a liberal consensus in both parties. Starting with publicly available information about donors who had contributed more than $50 ($446 today) to the conservative Barry Goldwater's 1964 presidential campaign, Viguerie began to create and code lists of support-ers of different conservative causes. A group or candidate would buy that information to create a new mailing list and send out carefully crafted letters. Solicitors could be more provocative in these precise appeals than they would when facing the general public. "The shriller you are" in direct-mail appeals, said one Republican, "the easier it is to raise money." In 1980 alone, Viguerie brought in between $35 and $40 million for his clients.

Liberals wanted in on this money game. Smeal struck up a close partnership with the direct mailer Roger Craver, who ran with Viguerie's ideas in the opposite direction. Craver believed the best direct-mail letters were eye-catching and set up a problem that the reader could quickly grasp and help to solve, typically by writing a check. Other civil rights groups were already using direct mail with astonishing results. The United Negro College Fund, for example, raised $750,000 through direct mail in 1972, spending less than $20 per one thousand names and addresses—"a phenomenal success." Amnesty International expanded its budget from $140,000 in 1974 to $2 million in 1980, nearly all from direct mail.

NOW leaders already knew they could fundraise on the ERA, but direct mail accelerated those donations and lifted the organization out of its financial rut. At first, NOW's entire budget came from dues. Increasing income meant expanding the membership, which raised administrative costs in kind. ERA fundraising freed NOW from this pattern. NOW's net income in 1973 was $48,900, but the ERA Emergency Fund, a separate financial stream created by one of the organization's first direct-mail appeals, netted $139,000 that year. By contrast to a similar reproductive rights mailing, that ERA solicitation drew more money but fewer members. Smeal and her fellow officers "went big into direct mail" on the ERA, she said, and the money rolled in. NOW mailed 565,000 pieces on the ERA between 1973 and mid-1975. It cost about $95,000 and yielded $269,000, a "phenomenal" return rate of nearly triple what was typical for direct mail. That program also helped boost NOW's membership from fifty thousand in early 1977 to eighty thousand at year's end. The next year NOW netted $650,000 from direct mail.

This solicitation program not only expanded NOW's size and budget; it also started to change the organization itself. The letters invited recipients to join, donate, or both. Direct-mail joiners tended to become "at-large members" detached from any chapter. Before, most members had paid dues to chapters, which remitted a portion to the national office.

Once direct-mail money poured in, chapters started to look to headquarters for "a piece of the national pie," Mary Jean Collins said, eroding their independence. Collins also believed that the new fundraising method homogenized NOW, which began "tapping in, and tapping in, and tapping into the same white, upper-middle class people" whose names were already on the lists that NOW purchased from fellow activist groups. Other members saw direct mail as a success. They praised Smeal for ending an approach to money that "was going to keep us little" and for bringing in resources that "enhanced us immensely." Smeal believed she was fortifying NOW by growing its budget and tightening its focus. The ERA was "a gateway issue," she said. "It closes nothing off and it unites people."

In moving its national office to Washington, D.C., and emphasizing lobbying and fundraising, NOW resembled many other advocacy organizations in the 1970s. For a century, American civic life had featured membership groups that were anchored in local communities and reached the national policy debate, but those groups were waning. The new organizations that replaced them were more specialized. Rather than building massive memberships in order to claim authority and members' dues, they conveyed their messages and solicited contributions through the media. A professionally managed staff of lobbyists and researchers performed these groups' work. NOW began to ride this wave. It remained a membership organization, but its emphasis changed. As NOW and other advocacy groups were learning, direct-mail donors gave more and meddled less. The leaders now had the incentive to pursue larger checks and fewer engaged members.

———

When NOW started to unite behind the ERA push, Mary Jean Collins was on the outside. She had left the group's leadership, although she kept up her membership, and remade her life in the wake of the bruising faction fights. Living with her partner, Anne Ladky, Collins found work in Chicago as an organizer for the Illinois Nurses Association.

Collins noticed that Illinois was one of NOW's targeted states for the ERA, but she was conflicted on the issue. While she supported the amendment, she also viewed economic security as more important than legal rights to women like her mother, yoked to "an on-again, off-again kind of provider." She had explained her position on the ERA during her second campaign for NOW president in 1975. While the amendment would not "win many concrete changes in women's lives," neither should NOW sit back and watch conservatives weaponize it "to try to stop our organization's progress" and make their movement appear weak. Several years later, Collins decided she had to join the struggle. The ERA would help women. To pass it, advocates "needed to bring back the big guns," and she counted herself among them.

The ERA fight would be an uphill battle, Collins saw. The seven-year deadline was short. The unratified states, which were in the most conservative regions where NOW had the fewest members, "were the very places that we had to go," she said. Collins also believed that the organization was simply not set up for this kind of campaign. "In 1970, I was organizing my little chapters," she said. "This is two years later, and now I'm supposed to have the capacity to pass a statewide referendum?" Collins shared Smeal's assessment that NOW would have to focus their resources and find more. She began helping to coordinate political canvassing and massive protests in Springfield, the Illinois state capital.

ERA advocates faced a steep learning curve in Illinois, where they "got caught right away in the internal politics of the state," Collins said. A key sponsor in the Illinois House of Representatives, Eugenia Chapman, had angered Chicago's mayor, Richard J. Daley, when she backed another politician to lead the Illinois delegation to the Democratic National Convention in 1972. Some of Daley's allies retaliated by opposing the ERA. Other state legislators publicly claimed to support the amendment but were privately opposed or indifferent. Some voted for it only once party leaders could assure them that it would lose. And while the ERA won majority votes in both the state house and the state senate, a 1971 rule change required a three-fifths supermajority for constitutional amendments. Advocates introduced the ERA year after year. They were often confident it would pass, then embarrassed when it failed.

The ERA fight in Illinois became the bitterest in the late 1970s, when STOP ERA installed a coordinator in each of the fifty-nine legislative districts. Illinois was Schlafly's state, too; she lived on that side of the

Mississippi River outside St. Louis. "The one thing we could not get away from was her voice," said the Chicago chapter leader Mary-Ann Lupa. Several members of the chapter debated Schlafly. Kathy Rand was just twenty-six. "It was terrifying but sort of exhilarating," she said, and afterward the antifeminist complimented her performance. "I was so flattered and then so mad at myself that I was so flattered." Suzanne Doty faced off with Schlafly on local radio. "She never got up for water or coffee; she just sat there with her little pursed lips," she said. "We wished we'd had magnets so we could pull the hairpins out of her hair." Schlafly did well in these debates, according to her biographer Donald T. Critchlow, because feminists often "turned to personal attacks on her" rather than "exploiting inconsistencies in the anti-ERA movement." Indeed, they hated her. She was an opponent who seemed to benefit from their activism even as she decried it.

Collins saw antifeminists translate the ERA's abstract principle of equality into immediate fears for Illinois lawmakers. Young women from each state legislative district traveled to an ERA hearing. The women "got up one at a time" and said, "'I'm Suzie Q. I'm from district 43, I don't want to be drafted.' Then, 'I'm Lulu Belle, I'm from district 42, I don't want to be drafted.' Boom, boom, boom, boom, boom," said Collins. It was so effective because, on the heels of the Vietnam War, most feminists "weren't so hot on the idea of women being drafted either." STOP ERA brought three thousand women to the state capitol in March 1975 before an ERA vote. Schlafly held a bullhorn and pulled two toy wagons brimming with leaflets and buttons. Her supporters wore long dresses and delivered homemade baked goods to the lawmakers they targeted for lobbying. Their "femininity tactics" were well suited to the middle-aged white men who predominated in southern and midwestern state legislatures. They feared upsetting these women, who were becoming more informed about politics, mobilizing their community networks, and making ERA opposition their main issue.

Patricia Hill Burnett did not have STOP ERA's leader in her backyard, but antifeminists were also making inroads in her state. Burnett noted with alarm that local "pseudo" Phyllis Schlaflys were "carving a career out of denying women's rights." She was referring to women like Patt Barbour, who led the Michigan chapter of Happiness of Womanhood before becoming that organization's national leader in 1975. Barbour claimed that the ERA would "do nothing for women but put a federal noose around their neck," and she wrote to Governor Milliken that the Republican Party had abandoned women like her.

Soon after Burnett was appointed chair of the bipartisan Michigan Women's Commission in 1976, STOP ERA accused the group of "only representing the feminist viewpoint." The moderate Republican governor, Milliken, responded by adding two anti-ERA women. Democrats criticized the commission from the other side as "a convenient clubhouse for white, middle class Republican busybodies" that had no Black members. After a year of stalemates, Burnett doubted there was "a single issue that we can address that no one can take issue with." She responded to conservative women's gains by cofounding the Women's Republican Caucus, an "organization within the Republican Party for Progressive women" that struggled for funds and members. Burnett and other Republican feminists tried to hold a vanishing center between women's liberationists and conservative women.

Burnett also saw the national GOP changing. In 1974, after the Watergate scandal that ended in the Republican president Richard Nixon's resignation, only 18 percent of American voters identified as Republicans. Although feminists in the party pressured the leaders to rebuild by endorsing a women's rights agenda, GOP officials took the opposite approach, taking up antifeminism as a route back to power. The presidential candidates Gerald Ford and Ronald Reagan both refused to publicly back *Roe v. Wade* in 1976. That year, feminist members of the GOP Platform Committee noticed the momentum shifting against them, and they did not openly object to the antiabortion plank added to the platform. Burnett wrote to the RNC co-chair Mary Dent Crisp to protest that the two upcoming RNC women's meetings were planned in states that had not ratified the ERA. Crisp refused to move the meetings, explaining that the party could not "let one issue alone determine the sites." Burnett also believed the GOP was attempting to cultivate racial diversity at her expense. She had expected to be appointed a delegate to the 1976 RNC, but the state party asked her majority-Black district to send an all-Black delegation. "It's awful being a WASP minority these days!" she quipped.

Although their influence dwindled, Republican feminists still held enough clout in the Ford administration to bring about the National Women's Conference (NWC), a stateside observance of the United Nations' International Women's Year. The conference, scheduled for Houston in late 1977, would be a federally sponsored gathering of and about women. Each state held its own conference in the months before the national event, to debate priorities and select delegates. The state conferences represented a rare moment in women's history when a federally backed gathering invited women to tell officials what they wanted.

Burnett and the state's First Lady, Helen Milliken, helped organize Michigan's conference. Burnett helped broker the bipartisan Unity Caucus, which selected "a unified group of delegates for equal rights" to represent the state. Three hundred of the twenty-one hundred participants in the conference were conservatives, and they protested the fact that feminists had swept all forty-eight delegate positions, although the four elected alternates were conservatives. "It was all outrageous," said Elaine Donnelly of STOP ERA. "International Women's Year is nothing more than a yearlong joke and an insult to the intelligence of women."

The Michigan delegates joined two thousand other delegates elected from their states who traveled to Houston to forge a national women's agenda. Three First Ladies were also there along with scores of luminaries: the tennis champion Billie Jean King, the writer Maya Angelou, the activist Coretta Scott King, and the *All in the Family* television star Jean Stapleton. Smeal headed NOW's delegation to the conference, which included more than two hundred official delegates from the states, and she also helped steer the proceedings. Herself a delegate, Burnett believed the Michigan women made a strong impression. First Lady Helen Milliken was their "shining star," "always wise, always cheerful," and among the most well-known Republicans in attendance. Collins was also present. She gazed onto the conference stage: a "beautiful" sign that read WOMAN was layered over a royal blue curtain. The scene cemented her conviction that "the establishment was on our side." Collins had chaired Illinois's conference, where conservatives captured 40 percent of delegate spots. They would "have done better," Schlafly explained, "but our women didn't want to leave their families for an entire weekend and spend it with a group of lesbians."

Over several days in Houston in 1977, the National Women's Conference delegates debated and adopted a progressive platform that included reproductive rights, protections for gays and lesbians, the ERA, and federal child-care programs. The 130,000 participants and viewers included the nation's best-known journalists, more than 1,500 of whom had sought press passes. In an atmosphere that resembled a national political party convention, the meeting created a plan of action that comprised twenty-six sweeping planks and advanced a consensus that the federal government should promote gender equality. NOW played a strong role. The Columbus chapter leader, Anne Saunier, had been "tempered in the fires of NOW," gaining a thorough knowledge of *Robert's Rules of Order*. She so successfully chaired the NWC meeting in Ohio that the NWC asked her to chair the national proceedings. The night before the conference began, Saunier "went around to all the mic monitors, the parliamentarians, and the timekeepers separately" to make sure everything was in order. When the conference started, Saunier perceived "that NOW was running the tactics on the floor."

The NWC helped unite feminists, but it also gave the conservative women's movement a target to organize against. Livid at feminists' progress, antifeminists staged an energetic and attention-grabbing "Pro-life, Pro-family Rally" across town that focused especially on the ERA's threat to traditional families. The amendment had once seemed innocuous, even inevitable. Now it was a point of debate: Was it a recognition of basic rights or a radical intervention?

———

As the ERA's clock ran down, NOW pressured Congress to extend the ratification deadline and further tightened its own focus on several states. One was Illinois, the largest statewide campaign, where the Chicago chapter similarly concentrated its efforts. The state legislative season determined the chapter's pace, tactics, and schedule. Members set up a new office in the downtown Loop with more than a dozen phones installed on giant tables. "We ran phone banks every night of the week," Collins said. They also analyzed local politics, lobbied persuadable legislators, and sought challengers for resolute opponents. "All of these records had to be maintained by hand," Collins said. "We had file cards, and then file cards based on file cards." Members invited those from out of state to call or write to Illinois lawmakers or send "in bulk" handwritten, unsigned letters to lawmakers that local residents could sign and address. Some rode long-distance "freedom trains" to rallies in Springfield.

There were a few key ways to contribute to the ERA battle: canvassing, lobbying, protesting, and especially fundraising. The effort demanded "more resources than ever before," Collins wrote to her chapter. "NOW is the time for serious personal and financial commitments." The chapter raised more than $30,000 for the ERA in 1979 and increased its membership by 40 percent. In addition to leading the Chicago chapter, Collins co-directed NOW's ERA campaign in Illinois, overseeing a staff of fifty and "a sizeable budget" that covered staff and field organizers, phone banks, volunteer expenses, and printing.

The Illinois campaign cost NOW $35,000 monthly, with "full-time nerve centers" in Chicago and Springfield and "massive organizing and lobbying campaigns all across the state." While the amendment had received a majority vote in the legislature since 1972, it kept falling short of the 60 percent threshold, losing by just two votes in 1978. "Illinois is the crucial state for 1980," Collins wrote to members. "We must break through the inertia of the last several years." That year, more than ninety thousand ERA supporters marched in Chicago on May 10. They hailed from all over the country and represented more than three hundred groups and delegations. Phyllis Schlafly had claimed that each participant was paid $10 in order to create a massive turnout to impress the media. "I'm sorry you didn't get your checks," Smeal said, addressing the crowd, which broke into laughter.

The national leadership was also buckling down. In 1976, NOW joined ERAmerica, a national coalition of 120 pro-ERA organizations, but pulled out two years later. ERAmerica "had no money essentially," Smeal explained. "It was not reasonable to be one voice among many around a table when we were . . . putting that much money in" to the ratification fight. It was time to face "harsh political realities," Smeal had written in NOW's 1978 declaration of an ERA emergency, which the national board had unanimously adopted. Both major political parties claimed to back the ERA "while sabotaging its ratification by political deals, trade-offs and do-nothingness." NOW had to do more to win the amendment, which was "the foundation on which all our gains rest." The ERA demanded all of the group's capital and more. "To dilute and diffuse our resources is to yield a crucial advantage to the opposition," wrote another leader. Not every chapter gave priority to the ERA, but the campaign transformed the national organization and many chapters.

NOW needed even more money. The leaders intensified their use of direct mail to raise it. A typical letter from Smeal contained many facts, short paragraphs, and lots of emphasis. It was "*our LAST CHANCE for securing passage of the Equal Rights Amendment in our lifetime*," she wrote in an undated letter from the late 1970s. NOW's strategy to defeat "those who scorn the dream of constitutional equality for women" was "broad, many-faceted and expensive." These appeals brought in the checks, but NOW kept spending all of it. The leaders raised annual dues from $15 to $20 ($54 to $72 today) in 1979 and courted celebrities like Jacqueline Kennedy Onassis and First Lady Rosalynn Carter to headline fundraisers. They also organized annual walkathons, which took in $170,000 in 1978, $180,000 in 1979, and $200,000 in 1980.

Lobbying and protesting rounded out NOW's ERA emergency strategy. The group organized a lobby day on the Capitol in 1979 where thousands of activists "flooded the halls of Congress" to deliver three hundred thousand pro-ERA "mailgrams" to legislators. Across the country, as in Chicago, ERA organizers set up phone banks and tables in public places to solicit signatures and permissions for other volunteers to re-sign them on future mailings. National NOW brought 1 million printed postcards to members of Congress using those signatures. "If every NOW member generates 100 such cards and letters," members plotted, "Congress will be deluged by about 7 million of them—14,000 per congressperson." Some hosted parties where guests brought ERA mail as "payment" or held outdoor "type-ins."

NOW's leaders also planned massive protests. Smeal believed that her organization, like the earlier suffrage groups, had to "get people in the streets ourselves." One hundred thousand supporters from all fifty states took part in the NOW National ERA March on the National Mall in 1978. They walked in more than 325 delegations bearing yellow, purple, and white signs, a nod to the suffrage movement's colors. Participants wore white to honor the suffragists, which also made the march look bigger and like a blank canvas so that "anybody could visualize" herself there, Smeal said. There were thirty-five speakers from interest groups, government agencies, and celebrity circles. The group's newsletter bragged that the event had shown "not only NOW's preeminent leadership of the feminist movement, but the massive dimensions of our base of power."

This targeted pressure helped to win ERA advocates more time. As NOW drummed up support to extend the amendment's clock, its ratification drive grew into a coalition of labor, civil rights, academic, church, and other women's groups whose members also marched, contacted lawmakers, and testified before Congress. But the ERA's fate looked increasingly uncertain. The three-year extension Congress approved in late 1978 was shorter than the seven years NOW sought, and it passed by much narrower margins than those by which the ERA had won six years earlier. The extension also gave opponents new grounds for arguing procedural points in court. Smeal saw both the potential and the risks ahead. In response to the extension, she pledged to run an even bigger and more focused effort. NOW would "create a campaign of such massive size that it cannot be denied," Smeal said. "We pledge to be everywhere and to do everything necessary." NOW's leaders introduced a new program: ERA action teams. Paralleling local chapters, action teams were grassroots battalions of activists prepared to generate mail, phone bank, canvass, and lobby.

With everything on the line, building their campaign became more important than preserving their organization's character. To some in NOW, these shifts were not benign.

———

Aileen Hernandez looked on with alarm from her home in San Francisco. She remained active in Golden Gate NOW until it dissolved in

1977, when its members had departed the city or left or moved into other forms of local activism. The Golden Gate members had worked in local Bay Area coalitions that linked race, class, and sexuality in the kind of multiracial, social-justice-oriented feminism that was expanding nationwide.

Hernandez still prized legal rights. But she believed that "the ERA was symbolic more than anything else," and she always embedded equality within a broad activist agenda. Women of color could not "afford the luxury of a 'single issue' focus," she wrote. "The passing of the ERA is a very important thing for the women's movement," she said in 1975, "but it is not the only thing that needs to be done." One of these other things the movement had to do, which she worked on for a decade, was to make NOW more appealing to women of color. "We will deserve the labels of 'racist' and 'classist,'" she wrote, "if NOW views outreach to minorities and the poor as a recruiting drive for members, rather than as a chance to link with others, as equals in a two-way learning process."

Hernandez had also spent years warning about the dangers of charismatic leadership, despite her own undeniable charisma. Her approach echoed that of Ella Baker, a driving force in the Black freedom movement who sought to empower others to make change—especially working-class African Americans—rather than pursue the spotlight herself. "My theory is, strong people don't need strong leaders," Baker said. Hernandez pointed out how the assassination of Dr. Martin Luther King Jr., who was widely seen as the leader of the civil rights movement, disrupted that struggle. She told her fellow NOW members that the power of the women's movement should not rest in one person. A glance through the organization's newsletter or media coverage in the late 1970s reveals precisely the kind of tight focus on leadership that Hernandez criticized. The consistent message was that NOW had many members, but Smeal was NOW personified.

When Hernandez had stepped down as co-chair of the National Task Force on Minority Women and Women's Rights in 1974, other women of color stepped up to build upon her earlier work. They found white members generally preoccupied with other struggles, uninterested in or even hostile to the idea that they could be perpetrators as well as victims of discrimination. While the factions had battered each other at the Philadelphia conference in 1975, members of color had held a workshop on "combating racism, sexism and classism." Collaborating with the task force on rape, the minority women's task force held a workshop with the attorney of Joan Little, the formerly incarcerated North Carolina woman who killed her jailer in self-defense. "NOW belongs to minority women," the task force's co-leader Del Dobbins said there. "We are here working with our non-minority sisters and we will continue to work" and "make our demands known." Sharon Parker, a member of D.C. NOW and an African American and Native American woman, established a new national Minority Women's Committee.

While white leaders narrowed the organization's focus, women of color took up anew the work of fighting racism inside and beyond NOW. Parker studied the efforts of Hernandez and her predecessors. Learning that "there was a history within the movement and organization to be all inclusive from the very beginning" made her "more charged about what I was doing." Parker believed that NOW "had great potential" to foster "cross-racial and ethnic" solidarities by "involv[ing]" rather than "recruit[ing]" diverse women. The leaders of her committee endorsed the ERA alongside issues of critical importance to them: labor rights, incarceration, affordable housing, and "reproductive freedom" that encompassed both abortion rights and an end to the sterilization abuse of Latinas, African Americans, and Native Americans. Members of the Minority Women's Committee worked to persuade women of color to join NOW by helping to set up a Native American Women NOW chapter in 1977 in North Dakota and proposing mini-conferences across the country to bring members of different races into dialogue and chart NOW's future together.

By contrast, white leaders mostly approached women of color as foot soldiers for the ERA struggle. They printed materials that pointed out how women of color "suffer greater discrimination because of sexism and racism," and explained how the ERA could help. Members of the Minority Women's Committee met with Smeal in 1978 to seek her support for their varied priorities: "minority women's visibility, leadership training, brochures, conferences, [and] recruitment." Rather than offering NOW's resources, Smeal urged them to hold their own walkathon fundraiser "to highlight minority women's contributions."

Nevertheless, the Minority Women's Committee pressed on with its agenda. Its leaders invited Aileen Hernandez to be the keynote speaker at a 1979 conference at her alma mater, Howard University. The meeting's theme was "racism and sexism—a shared struggle for equal rights." Only one of the seven workshops was on the ERA. Hernandez assessed the diversity of the attendees with pride and noted that when she was NOW president nearly a decade earlier, a similar gathering "probably would have been done in a phone booth." She explained that while she supported the ERA, addressing it "so specifically and with such priority" implied "that this is the *only* thing with which we are concerned." Their very gathering proved otherwise, she said. Women of color in NOW were "so lost in a NOW convention that we appear insignificant, and we are not!" Hernandez urged them to "take back from this conference into NOW the issues that are of deep concern to us as minority people." But only months later, at NOW's national conference in Los Angeles, she would lose hope that the organization she once led could be a home for her feminism.

At that October 1979 conference, a reporter noted the "corporate tone," underscored by the delegates' uniform green and white dress and their buttons that read "59 Cents." That NOW ERA slogan, which referenced the gap between men's and women's average wages, was a powerful symbol of inequality. "Essentially, the bottom line of the Equal Rights Amendment is money," Smeal said. "Someone profits from underpaying women, and that opposition is real and is gaining." But the ERA could only ever partially succeed in rebalancing the American economy. While the provision could have forced insurance companies to end sexism in rate pricing and strengthened legal protections for caregivers and pregnant people, for example, it also would have fortified existing laws that were already proving inadequate to remedy structural and interconnected inequities. As an NYU student told the activists selling "59 Cents" buttons on her campus, their buttons did not represent her: "Black women earn only 54 cents."

Smeal ran unopposed for reelection as president in 1979, part of a slate of five straight white women. Slate members emphasized their efficiency, mutual respect, and dedication to the ERA. Its ratification was their first priority, but they also promised to "mobilize a broad reproductive rights action campaign," "dramatically increase minority participation and action in NOW," create a "strong and visible action campaign for lesbian rights," and "focus on the impact of economic issues on women." Smeal pointed out that in her two years as president she had grown NOW's annual financial base from $700,000 to $3.4 million. She and the other leaders had used the money to build a sophisticated ERA campaign that hired field organizers, supported volunteers, prepared kits and materials, researched, and litigated.

Meanwhile, the only candidate of color at the conference was Sharon Parker. In her campaign for national secretary, Parker emphasized the importance of grassroots diversity and strength; she opened her address to the conference in Spanish. Her Washington, D.C., chapter was especially vocal about all of the things the ERA could not do: deliver affordable child care, end discrimination against lesbians, or ensure that health insurance covered abortion.

Smeal and her allies swept the election. She was pleased by their conference's discipline and efficiency. It was a stark contrast to NOW's earliest conventions, she said, when "we were so happy just to be among people who thought the way we did" that "we let anybody vote who walked in. Now we have real conventions." Parker interpreted Smeal's campaign message in this way: "if you really want the ERA, you'll give me the people I want," a clique "which did not include me and other women of color." Parker did not believe the fight had been fair. "We put campaign literature out and it disappeared. You call a meeting and the room's not available. Rumors were circulating. It's not the kind of thing that we expected of feminists working for the cause."

The slate's victory ensured that NOW's officer corps would remain all white. Some whites in NOW said they felt electing Parker would be tokenism. "Members of NOW apparently find exclusionism more acceptable," Hernandez retorted. She was "furious" that Smeal ran "a white woman's slate all the way down the line" and that she proposed "an outreach program to set up NOW chapters in ghetto communities" rather than endorsing Black women for positions of power. Hernandez accused the organization of ignoring "almost any issue that deals with the inequity of society more than the inequity of being female." NOW's approach to women of color was intended not to support them but rather "to indoctrinate" them to support the ERA, Hernandez said, as if they were "the present stumbling block" to its passage. In refusing to address a broader range of issues on equal terms, NOW seemed "to be going backwards." Hernandez, disgusted by the state of the organization, publicly urged Black women to avoid NOW or "turn in their membership cards."

Smeal responded that NOW's membership was diverse, although she did not know its specific demographics. She blamed biased coverage from newspapers whose publishers were still steamed at having been forced to desegregate their job ads years earlier. "We have been addressing issues" that mattered to women of color, she said, "but people have got to know about it, so we've got to go out there and recruit." Black women knew otherwise. Pauli Murray wrote to Smeal after Hernandez's public stand to declare that she would not renew her NOW membership either. "All of this has distressed me more than I can express," she wrote, "because underneath everything we are all sisters."

Del Martin, one of NOW's first lesbian rights activists, was also disturbed by the 1979 conference. "The racism was evident, and the slate business was anti-lesbian, anti-minority women, and so on." The new leadership had transformed their grassroots-driven sisterhood into "a million dollar corporation," she declared. Martin and her partner, Phyllis Lyon, had spent years working within NOW to make it live up to its public pledge to promote lesbian rights, sometimes criticizing other chapters and national leaders. But they had still seen benefit to remaining in NOW, despite its flaws, because they could work toward their own version of equality from within it. The ERA campaign narrowed this possibility. Martin and Lyon left NOW in solidarity with Hernandez.

As Martin made clear, NOW's ERA-or-bust approach alienated many lesbians as well as women of color. Like the Minority Women's Committee, NOW's Lesbian Rights Committee in the late 1970s developed an expansive agenda that included legal protections for consensual sex between same-sex partners, child custody rights for lesbian mothers, and nondiscrimination laws to protect gays and lesbians in employment, housing, and more. And like the women of color in NOW, lesbians were working within the group to educate other members about their own biases.

But NOW's leaders undermined those efforts in their attempts to deflect conservative women's barbs. Schlafly had called NOW "a destructive, anti-family organization" that was "trying to make perversion acceptable as an alternative lifestyle." Antifeminists cultivated conservative evangelicals' and Catholics' anger at abortion rights by linking abortion to the ERA and homosexuality to label feminism a three-headed threat to the traditional family. This move united a diverse coalition of social conservatives and exploited shifts in American life. The traditional breadwinner-homemaker family was becoming a thing of the past as deindustrialization weakened men's earning potential and divorce laws loosened.

Antifeminists thus stoked many women's economic fears and obscured their real causes. Their movement pitted equal rights against family values and declared the traditional family in moral peril. An emerging "right to life" strand of the New Right won its first legislative victory in 1976 with the passage of the Hyde Amendment, which banned the use of federal funds for abortion in most circumstances and had an immediate detrimental effect on low-income women. "Dismayed bystanders who had hoped, without reference to their own sentiments, that abortion could become a matter of individual conscience, are dreamers," a reporter wrote about the rising conflict in 1979. "One side sees abortion as a crime and the other regards it as a right; there is no middle ground."

NOW's leaders grew frustrated by antifeminists' accusation that they were trying to ruin the nation's families. They began to emphasize the amendment's appeal to the same white housewives whom antifeminists claimed to represent. Homemakers, who constituted 30 percent of NOW's membership in 1974, were "active adult[s]," with rich lives "outside the home," Smeal declared. "We have the American homemaker on our side." NOW's materials promoted the ERA as "the embodiment of traditional American values." The provision would strengthen domestic life, NOW claimed, by extending legal protections for homemakers and making marriage a more equal partnership.

Antifeminists' rising profile also shaped NOW's messaging on abortion. In the wake of the 1973 *Roe v. Wade* opinion, NOW members had worked to expand the new federal right to abortion. NOW's Task Force on Reproduction and Population demanded that all people have "easy access" to contraception and abortion at public hospitals; urged the government to fund research on "safer methods" for both and make them "easily available"; and called for the "repeal of all laws prohibiting or restricting abortions." Three years later, NOW's ERA campaign leaders insisted that the ERA and abortion rights were separate issues. Alongside other feminist groups, they started to shift their rhetoric, emphasizing "reproductive rights" more than abortion access, seeking to downplay an increasingly polarizing issue and frame their opponents as enemies of women's autonomy. Smeal reached out to antiabortion groups in 1979 to try to find areas of agreement. Some interpreted this move as a suggestion that NOW would sacrifice its work on abortion rights in exchange for conservative politicians' support for the ERA. This olive branch only hardened her opponents. The leader of March for Life, a nascent group that organized annual protests on *Roe v. Wade*'s anniversary, declined Smeal's invitation to a "summit meeting on abortion" in dramatic fashion: "I will not negotiate with babykillers."

Inside NOW, the ERA-first strategy also "put a whole damper on all discussions of lesbianism, all meaningful work on lesbianism," said the longtime member and lesbian rights advocate Barbara Love. The leaders of NOW's ERA coalition publicly asserted that the amendment would not pave the way to same-sex marriage and refused to refute antifeminist claims that it would. Inside NOW, lesbians received the message that their specific concerns—and even just being open and themselves—could undermine the ERA push. When NOW's leaders instructed all of the internal committees to "mobilize their constituencies around the ERA," the Lesbian Rights Committee prepared "a general mailing . . . on ERA." Although they sent it to the national office along with a list of addresses of gay and lesbian organizations, the mailing never went out. Committee members were left to wonder "whether this was due to lack of womanpower, or for other reasons." In the ERA battleground state of Illinois, the national office told Chicago lesbians to take care not to appear "dyke-y" in ERA

actions; march organizers banned signs with any "form of lesbian identification"; and Betty Friedan was tapped to address a NOW-sponsored rally
in Springfield despite her history of homophobic statements.

Some in the organization continued to work on lesbian rights, especially at the state and local levels, but conservatives' "lesbian-baiting"
seemed to shape Smeal's approach. In at least two fundraising letters in
the early 1980s, Smeal outlined NOW's priorities without mentioning
lesbian rights. This was "unconscionable," responded the Lesbian Rights
Committee chair, Susan Russell. Lesbian rights were an established tenet
of the organization, which benefited from the loyal efforts of lesbians
who "worked on every single issue that NOW has put before us even
when it did not immediately affect us." Russell noted that issues of "family planning, contraception or abortion" bore little "personal meaning" for
her, but she had devoted many hours to them.

Lesbians in NOW agreed that the ERA was an important goal, but
they argued that the New Right's rising attacks on gay men and lesbians,
following several years of progress in expanding state and local antidiscrimination laws, demanded the same "'crisis' attention." Members of the
National Gay Task Force brought a letter of concern to NOW's 1981
conference co-signed by lesbian feminists including Sidney Abbott, who
had co-chaired NOW's first sexuality task force. "We feel the impact of
the Right Wing's bigotry daily," they wrote, and "just when we are most in
jeopardy, many in the women's movement give the impression of having
decided to 'let the gay rights issue go'" in "a pattern of 'benign neglect.'"
Smeal continued to counter antifeminist allegations with more conservatism: "The ERA does not give homosexuals any additional rights."

NOW's official endorsements of lesbian rights and abortion rights
gave weight to opponents' argument that the organization and its goals,
including ratifying the ERA, threatened family values. But within a few
years, pursuing the amendment was nearly all national NOW was doing
while emphasizing the provision's inherent conservatism. "I'll never ask
nor be a part of suspending activities on vitally important matters for
human dignity or human rights," Smeal declared in 1980. "But I will ask
that if we do something for other issues during this period that we do just
something more for ratification" and "that we give more."

Sidelining the concerns of women of color and lesbians did not win NOW any ground. Not only did ERA advocates remain stuck three states short, but conservatives were working in a dozen states to rescind their earlier ratifications and casting doubt on the legal legitimacy of the three-year extension. Four state legislatures passed rescission bills. STOP ERA in Michigan had been trying to repeal the ERA in the state since its passage. Antifeminists there held coffee hours, printed yard signs and bumper stickers, and even handwrote "rescindograms" to the lawmakers they were lobbying: an obvious counterpoint to the "ERA-grams" NOW members had been sending to the White House by the thousands. Congress had never honored such rescissions before, but NOW could not be certain. The national leaders diverted resources from battleground states and doubled back to lobby, phone bank, and protest in states they had already won. Conservatives also expanded the fight to other fronts. State attorneys general in Nevada and Missouri used antitrust laws to sue NOW over its economic boycott in their states. NOW ultimately won, but the fight took time and money.

NOW members struggled to grasp that their side was losing. It was hard to believe that any well-informed woman would oppose her own equality. NOW's position continued to reflect the 1973 comments by its then president, Wilma Scott Heide, when feminists first learned of the anti-ERA movement: "These efforts are not funded by women or those who ever had any interest in women as people. They prey on their fears, uncertainty and misinformation." Polls taken in the late 1970s showed that 80 percent of Americans supported the ERA and less than 20 percent were strongly antifeminist. *The Phyllis Schlafly Report* had a circulation of under sixteen thousand; the *National NOW Times* went to seventy-five thousand. "Phyllis Schlafly is a little doll put up by the men to distract us," Collins wrote to her chapter in 1980, "but there is money and misogyny behind the effort to defeat ERA and keep women in their place." Schlafly and her allies were insulted by NOW's insistence that they must be ignorant, deluded, or brainwashed by men. They denied accusations that they took in funds from the conservative John Birch

Society or big business. "We don't need much money because we haven't done anything expensive," Schlafly asserted.

But ERA advocates noticed that industries profiting from discrimination seemed to be working against the provision, especially the state-regulated field of insurance. Companies had installed lobbyists in state legislatures to protect sexist practices that boosted profits, such as over-charging women for stingier health and life insurance coverage. The Farm Bureau, the owner of dozens of insurance companies, publicly opposed the ERA and fueled its defeat in several states. The companies denied that there was any industry-wide campaign, although NOW discovered that their lobbyists coordinated across states through the National Association of Insurance Commissioners and the National Conference of Insurance Legislators. Powerful insurance lobbyists had "well established systems" for "influenc[ing] legislation *quietly* when overt opposition" might harm their industries' reputations. The feminists declared that this was a scandal and "another 'Watergate,'" but they could not prove it. They called for a congressional investigation that never came.

As the 1980 presidential election approached, and with the ERA on the line, NOW's national officers tightened their grip on power. The conference voted by two to one in 1980 to extend their terms by one year so that elections would not disrupt the ERA fight. Smeal brushed aside accusations that she was power hungry. "If I *had* been a little dictator," she said later, "I would have said to the board, 'Don't just extend my term, remove the term limitation entirely.'" She and the other leaders plunged NOW deeper into party politics. "It took women a while to learn what labor unions and other groups have known all along," the national news-letter noted: "You have to throw your weight around at election time if you want to be taken seriously by the politicians." NOW members trained to run as party delegates at national political conferences. Smeal pledged to build "the massive campaign treasuries needed to protect our interests at the ballot box." She kept her promise: feminist groups including NOW PAC raised and spent more than $2 million in state and federal elections in 1980.

NOW also turned a critical eye on the incumbent president, Jimmy Carter. He had been elected in 1976 with the help of both liberal feminists and social conservatives, but he soon seemed to realize that it would be hard to keep the support of both groups. Not a single state had ratified the ERA in his four years in office, and as president he did little to help. Carter mentioned the amendment in a major speech only twice. He also fired the former congresswoman and longtime NOW supporter Bella Abzug from co-chairing his National Advisory Committee for Women after the committee released a report criticizing his economic policies followed by a meeting in which Abzug "attempted to lecture the President on the duties of the committee and its role," a White House official explained. Later that day, twenty-three out of thirty-nine committee members resigned in solidarity with Abzug. Still, Carter had appointed a record number of women to executive branch roles and federal judgeships, including appointing Ruth Bader Ginsburg to an appellate court.

"We know the President could have delivered the ERA by now, if he had wanted to," said a NOW board member in early 1980, citing the close votes in state legislatures where Carter's support might have made a difference. After two days of deliberation, NOW's national board voted unanimously to recommend that the NOW PAC oppose Carter in 1980 no matter who ran against him, and the PAC unanimously accepted. One board member accused Carter of having "placed women's concerns at the very bottom of his domestic priorities." He "must be held accountable," another explained. President Carter took note. Several days after NOW's public snub, he invited members of sixteen women's groups to the White House for an ERA strategy meeting, but not NOW. Leaders of those groups denied Smeal's request to boycott the meeting in solidarity. A bunch of NOW members picketed outside it, holding an ERA banner aloft in the cold December rain.

Those other women's organizations had generally looked to NOW for leadership on the amendment, and they questioned its stand on Carter. None followed suit in opposing the president, although they tended to agree with NOW's criticisms of him. The announcement seemed premature since the general election was almost a year away. To some women of color, NOW's move also smacked of elitism. "We Puerto Rican women have had so little input in any other administration," explained the president of the National Conference of Puerto Rican Women, who had attended the meeting with Carter. "We do not want to cut ourselves out." The president of the National Council of Jewish Women called NOW's pronouncement "very bad strategy," explaining, "When you isolate yourself there's very little you can do. I really think they've hurt the cause." The leaders of the Coalition of Labor Union Women, the National Women's Political Caucus, and the National Abortion Rights Action League (NARAL) also offered thinly veiled criticism.

NOW had publicly condemned the party's leader, but the Democrats had moved steadily left on social and economic issues in the 1970s. It showed at the 1980 Democratic National Convention in New York City, where feminist pamphlets and "ERA YES" buttons circulated widely. Women were 50 percent of the voting delegates, and about two hundred of the approximately thirty-four hundred delegates and alternates were NOW members. The feminist delegates fought for planks in the party platform that would withhold support from anti-ERA candidates and affirm reproductive rights as human rights, in part by backing Medicaid funding for abortion. Carter's delegation tried to block the planks, but Senator Ted Kennedy's people backed them, and both were added to the platform. NOW called them "the strongest ERA and reproductive rights planks in party history."

In the meantime, the Republican Party drifted further rightward. While President Richard Nixon had been ambivalent about the ERA earlier in the decade, his successor, Gerald Ford, pursued it openly, in part because he believed it would inevitably pass. First Lady Betty Ford was especially outspoken in favor of the amendment. Republican feminists in 1976 used personal connections with the Ford campaign to prevent an anti-ERA vote by the entire platform committee. To prove their loyalty to party over gender, Republican feminists asked members of NOW, whom party leaders disparaged as a "special interest" group, to leave the conference. Ford's centrism and his eventual defeat by Jimmy Carter in 1976 opened more space in the Republican Party for the New Right's influence. This grassroots alliance between religious and political conservatives had begun with specific issues such as opposition to the ERA. By 1980, it was a durable coalition with clout and a wide agenda. The national GOP still officially supported the ERA in early 1980, but Republicans were blocking it in their states. NOW leaders eyed this "wildcat Republican defection from equality" with alarm.

Governor William Milliken brought the 1980 Republican National Convention (RNC) to Detroit, where feminists found little traction. ERA advocates, led by the Michigan delegates, were far outnumbered. The platform committee had replaced the ERA with language that affirmed "equal rights and equal opportunities" as well as the "traditional rights of women" and opposed anything that gave "the federal government more power over families." Some of the party's most prominent feminists resigned in protest. Unlike the more open DNC, the RNC was "so tightly controlled" that there could be no "intelligent discussion of the ERA," NOW leaders noted. Patricia Hill Burnett also saw that abortion rights had no chance. "I asked to be on the agenda," she said, "and they couldn't say, 'No,'" given her decades of service. In brief remarks, she laid out the relative costs of abortion and welfare, and the two-thousand-person audience booed her. It was "sexism in an unholy alliance with religion," she said. "There are a lot of men who are not comfortable with the idea of women having control over their own bodies."

Chicago NOW sent forty members by bus to Detroit, joining approximately thirteen thousand others who had traveled to Detroit for a NOW-sponsored protest there. Along the mile-long route past the GOP's convention center, marchers dressed in white chanted, "Keep it in the platform . . . ERA." Michigan's First Lady, Helen Milliken, skipped the convention's opening ceremonies to attend the march. She told the protesters that without the ERA "we are kidding ourselves if we think that small little privileges, small steps toward righting a particular law, token women in token jobs, means we have achieved our goal of equality."

The elections that November brought big wins for Republicans nationwide, sweeping Ronald Reagan into the White House and more Republican lawmakers into the legislatures of unratified states. Those states included Illinois, where Republicans took control of the state senate and doomed the ERA's chances. "The election will make our task harder," Smeal acknowledged.

But for the first time since the Nineteenth Amendment had enfranchised millions of women in 1920, the 1980 election results showed a real gender gap; millions more women than men voted for Carter. And after the election, NOW had its largest growth in a single month, gaining twelve thousand new members in November 1980 alone. "Women *will* vote in their self-interest," Smeal wrote, and NOW gave them "somewhere to turn."

This new political landscape orphaned Republican feminists. Burnett had largely abandoned her hopes for her Republican Women's Commission as "a strong haven for liberal Republican women." Of her state party, she wrote, "If it weren't for Milliken, I'd find it hard to hang in there." Not even Milliken himself could hang on. He retired in 1982 when state party leaders vowed to purge him. The next year, the Michigan GOP endorsed an opponent of the ERA and abortion rights for governor. Prominent Republican feminists in the state backed his Democratic challenger. Burnett had "happily voted for Reagan and cheered when he crushed Jimmy Carter." But as antifeminism captured her party, Burnett became "a thorn under their saddle" and saw that "they'd be so glad if I were a Democrat."

There was also little room by the 1980s for a Republican in NOW. Burnett felt the others dismiss her as "hopelessly right-wing and out of touch." She decided to run for president of the National Association of Commissions on Women, an umbrella group of state and local women's commissions. Her longtime friend in NOW Muriel Fox offered to solicit support from the group's leadership on her behalf. Burnett sent Fox her résumé, and Fox excised all of Burnett's Republican Party credentials in order to highlight "the feminist part of her biography." But Burnett did not view her Republican Party experience as un-feminist. She wanted to make the point "that feminists are needed in every major organization, particularly those dominated by conservative men." Ultimately, she decided not to accept NOW's endorsement, since it might not help her in more rural states. She won her election and broke with NOW.

As the ERA became a partisan issue, NOW pursued it with all its might. In mid-1981, with one year to go before the clock would run out on ratification, NOW opened new "ERA countdown campaign offices" in nine cities. Each launched its own phone banks, message brigades, and other forms of "massive outreach." NOW and allied groups held enormous rallies in unratified states and at the U.S. Capitol. ERA walkathons in 160 cities raised nearly $1 million that August. NOW increased the scale of direct-mail appeals, earning more and more each time. A single solicitation raised nearly $450,000 in late 1981. The organization raised $1.3 million *each month* from December 1981 to May 1982. By contrast, the Democratic Party raised $2.5 million in those six months combined, and STOP ERA spent only $49,774 in all of 1981. "I think now the politicians see us like they see labor unions," Smeal declared: "a group of people who are organized" and "can deliver." When she spoke, unions had begun to lose some of that power.

NOW's efforts reached a fever pitch. "We are literally mailing millions of pieces of mail, phoning thousands of individuals, printing millions of pieces of ERA information, but we must do more," Smeal told NOW's 1981 conference. "We must launch a nationwide media campaign which will enter as many living rooms as possible." NOW hired an agency and made its first two national television ads, then spent big to blanket the airwaves. A two-week, sixty-second spot in eleven cities cost $43,800. Molly Yard, one of Smeal's lieutenants as the director of NOW PAC, recounted the last few years of the struggle. "We literally emptied the national office. We left two officers, and everyone else took off" for the "tiring, all-consuming battle." The Florida NOW leader Patricia Ireland described the end of the ERA fight in similar terms. "The last two years we did almost nothing else."

But none of it won them another state. In Illinois, the ERA became a football in the house of representatives. Black representatives from Chicago voted against the provision, frustrated that the city's white Democratic Party leaders had traded their support for the amendment in a deal to elevate their preferred candidates for house leadership. There and elsewhere, state lawmakers noticed that many calls and letters on the ERA came from outside their districts, so they did not reflect their constituents' interests. Even some supportive state lawmakers grew weary of returning to the ERA and believed it sapped their time from more important matters.

In the summer of 1980, after the ERA failed in Illinois for the eighth time in eight years, Collins told her chapter of her "intense anger and frustration" that "we are up against a solid opposition." She and the other chapter leaders added abortion as a second priority issue not because members wanted to divert their energy from the ERA but because the leaders wanted to keep the members active on something else once it became clear that the ERA would not succeed. "It was a very good campaign but we didn't win," Collins said later. "If it didn't pass in '80, it wasn't going to pass. But we just had to drag ourselves along for two more years."

ERA proponents crossed the finish line still three states short in June 1982. If just seven state lawmakers in three states had switched their votes, the ERA would have been ratified. Instead, it became the first proposed amendment since a 1924 measure to "limit, regulate and prohibit" child labor to expire after winning congressional approval.

———

Eleanor Smeal led a protest near the White House on June 30, 1982, hours before the ERA's deadline. "We knew (the odds against ratifying ERA) better than anybody," especially after the 1980 election, she had told a reporter several days earlier, when the loss was imminent. "But we also knew we have a burden in history" to see it through. Her organization and others had not created enough pressure to move the levers of political machinery. The Republican Party had abandoned women's rights and begun attacking them, Smeal told the crowd. The Democrats offered encouragement but little muscle. But rather than retreat from the political arena, Smeal promised the gathered protesters that she would dig in. NOW was "telling male politicians to move over and make room for women," she said. It was time to stop "begging men for our rights." This anger at the ERA defeat stung, and it lingered. It would shape the rest of NOW's history.

Even before Smeal addressed those ERA supporters, scholars and pundits had begun debating the provision's trajectory, and they continue to this day. Some have argued that support waned in the 1970s because the amendment would have had few substantive effects; others point to the power of conservative arguments that the amendment would be transformative and their canny strategy to yoke it to abortion politics and gay rights. The ERA's failure to be ratified in 1982 can also be tied to unrelated and even random forces: shifts in the politics and perceptions of the Supreme Court, the timing of state legislative sessions, and even the Soviet Union's invasion of Afghanistan. Some have rightly emphasized the challenge of amending the Constitution toward any end.

Whatever the reason for the ERA's expiration, NOW's all-out campaign for it cut against the organization's own strengths. The less centralized, more freewheeling structure of the mid-1970s, however flawed, promoted internal dialogue, fostered personal and collective liberation through grassroots power and creativity, and nurtured campaigns that had many pressure points and definitions of success. "It was very hard," Collins said, "to keep women organized around the Equal Rights Amendment." The provision "had a lot of appeal to a lot of women," but women who were not white, straight, and middle class were less likely to see it as a singular priority, just as Pauli Murray had anticipated more than a decade earlier. Smeal and her fellow leaders, on the other hand, believed that maintaining their earlier wide focus, with the ERA just one of many objectives, would hamper their campaign to ratify it. Both views were correct.

The ERA's expiration was a crushing blow, but NOW lost in another way by transforming itself to try to achieve it. Once engaged in many forms of feminism at the local, state, and national levels, the organization gave priority to a single goal—a goal that had once coexisted easily with other aims and approaches—and concentrated more power among a few leaders in its pursuit. Under pressure from the amendment's ticking clock and a savvy opposition, NOW came to measure success in funds raised, petitions signed, lawmakers met, doors knocked, marchers in the streets, ads bought, and states ratified, putting its fate in the hands of a few state legislators. These changes were profound and long-lasting.

Moreover, as the partisan divide widened under members' feet, NOW's ERA campaign exposed it to attacks from the right and the left, wedging the organization between conservative women fearful of a "unisex society" and the women of color and lesbians whose distinct concerns the ERA campaign submerged. With the ERA's defeat, NOW also had to give up its idea that pursuing legal equality could unite women across their differences. NOW members had converted their organization to chase that equality. They arrived at a crossroads in a hostile new era.

8.

YOU BETTER BE *IN* THE THRONE

On a sweltering August day in 1983, Mary Jean Collins packed into the National Mall with 250,000 others. The masses hailed from hundreds of cities nationwide and overseas, descending upon the capital from "freedom trains," planes, and thousands of chartered buses. To the speakers who addressed them from the steps of the Lincoln Memorial, the crowd was a bright mosaic in T-shirts that boasted their more than seven hundred labor union, church, and movement groups. Many also wore buttons whose message affirmed their intention that day to look forward and back: "We Still Have a Dream."

The 1983 March on Washington marked the twentieth anniversary of the 1963 March on Washington for Jobs and Freedom where Dr. Martin Luther King Jr. gave his electrifying "I Have a Dream" speech. Pauli Murray had criticized that event for its lack of women at the podium, an insult that nudged her toward the need for a national organization of women. Two decades later, the organization she cofounded was an official sponsor of its sequel. Mary Jean Collins, recently elected NOW's vice president, helped lead its delegation. They had worked for months, she said, to get "as many people there as we could."

While its size rivaled that of the 1963 march, the 1983 march attracted a more diverse crowd and embraced a broader agenda. In addition to racial and economic justice, this gathering endorsed women's, gay, and lesbian rights, peace, environmentalism, and more. The scene reflected how the nation's activist landscape had changed. "Twenty years ago we came as individuals," announced Andrew Young, the Atlanta mayor who had been Dr. King's aide. "We came back as organizations. There were many women here then, but no women's organizations; many Hispanics, many members of organized labor, many handicapped, but none nearly so organized as they are now." The event's marquee organizer, Coretta Scott King, a renowned activist and Dr. King's widow, acknowledged their diversity in affirming their common purpose. "We are united by adversity," she declared; "we are united by love."

But what united them more concretely, the five dozen speakers made clear, was their mutual opposition to President Ronald Reagan. The first-term Republican was dismantling the federal programs and agencies that helped so many Americans out of his belief that government was "not the solution to our problem," but was the problem itself. Reagan's approach "demonstrated an insensitivity almost beyond belief," pronounced the Atlanta city councilman and future congressman John Lewis. "Turn on Reagan," admonished Jesse Jackson, the high-profile Chicago community organizer who would soon announce his bid for president. "Turn to each other."

Reagan was a kind of magnet in the early 1980s. His policies repelled liberal organizations and pushed them toward one another. NOW's new president, the Wisconsinite Judy Goldsmith, had reached out to Mrs. King after learning of her plans for the 1983 march. King named Goldsmith its co-chair, and the pair traveled the East Coast by bus to promote it. The march disrupted NOW's calendar. It was scheduled for August 27, one day after Women's Equality Day, which NOW members had observed each year since the 1970 Strike for Equality. By the early 1980s, chapters marked the day with massive walkathon fundraisers. But NOW "yielded" the symbolic and lucrative August 26 that year, Goldsmith told the sea of protesters at the march, by forgoing its typical events. She instead urged her members to affirm "our commitment to civil rights for all people" by supporting the march. "We are tired of

Ronald Reagan, who gives women only sweet nothings and bitter realities," she said. It was time to end the "insidious 'battle between the sexes'" and other efforts to turn Americans against one another. "Those who wish to divide and conquer us do so because they know that if we see each other as the enemy, we won't see them."

Goldsmith projected confidence about NOW's priorities and its place in a progressive coalition, but her organization's path was less certain than ever. On the one hand, while the ERA's 1982 expiration had been a devastating defeat, NOW had nearly 250,000 members and more visibility than ever, and its goals were increasingly mainstream. Anyone who wanted to alter gender relations in demanding social equality could be called a feminist, regardless of whether they welcomed the label or signed up for anything. On the other hand, the New Right's recent progress was undeniable. Reflecting both how much feminists had changed the national conversation and how easily its terms could be seized from them, conservatives had begun to weaponize a warped strain of equality: women's equal right to hold power as antifeminists.

NOW's leaders in the early 1980s faced difficult choices. Collins, Goldsmith, and others wanted to re-stretch its agenda, attract a broader membership, and ensure it was a good coalition partner. But, sharpening the sting of the ERA defeat, the conservatives ensconced in government were blocking liberal efforts to accomplish anything. NOW cleaved more tightly to the Democratic Party because the New Right had been so successful in enacting its agenda through the GOP. This move reflected a shift in the leaders' approach to clout: pursuing it at the top more than nurturing a wide grassroots base. By 1982, NOW's founder Gene Boyer had sharpened her political instincts in the sixteen years since she had found herself lost in the Washington Hilton, and explained this stark new outlook: "If you cannot achieve what you want by being the power behind the throne," Boyer said, "you better be *in* the throne. Or at least next to it."

———

When the ERA expired in June 1982, Eleanor Smeal had a few months left as NOW president. She predicted that women would punish the lawmakers who had strangled the amendment. It was a "tragedy," Smeal declared, that women would have "to spend more of our lives fighting for what should have been our birthright." But NOW had "turned a disgraceful defeat . . . into a base of political activity," and the group's ERA efforts had helped make feminism "a majority movement." She claimed, "You can't look at what we've done and say we've lost." NOW had thousands and thousands of activists nationwide who knew how to do door-to-door and phone canvassing, public speaking, fundraising, and community outreach, explained the Florida NOW leader and future national president Patricia Ireland, and "they were pissed."

As the midterm election approached, NOW turned its ERA apparatus—750 phone banks, million-name mailing lists, and sixty-seven hundred full-time volunteers—into a lobbying and fundraising machine. Chapters held walkathons to fundraise for NOW PACs, which netted more than $2 million and sent 4.5 million pieces of mail that fall. The PACs funded 109 congressional candidates, 61 percent of whom won. A new era was dawning, Smeal said: "from women's voting rights to a women's voting bloc."

Smeal brimmed with energy and ideas, but she had served two consecutive terms, NOW's limit. To succeed her, Smeal endorsed Judy Goldsmith, then a member of NOW's five-member officer corps as vice president for administration. The forty-three-year-old Goldsmith came from a "poor working class" family in rural Wisconsin. Her single mother had raised five kids with no child support and earned much less than the men working beside her at the factory. Goldsmith described herself as "strongly pragmatic with a no-frills political and economic approach to contemporary issues." As she rose through NOW's ranks, she taught English literature, most recently at the University of Wisconsin at Manitowoc. Her eleven-year-old daughter, Rachel, helped persuade her to run for NOW president by calling her mom's office line each day and humming "Hail to the Chief."

Although Smeal had tapped Goldsmith, Collins, energized by the ERA fight and angered by the rise of the New Right, intended to run for NOW president for the third time. "I wasn't inside enough to know that [the candidates] had already been decided," she said. "It used to be that people just ran." Smeal instead urged Collins to run for one of the two vice presidential roles: vice president for action. (Her counterpart was the vice president for administration.) As Goldsmith's running mate on the Smeal-backed "Ellie slate," Collins presented herself as a "grassroots activist for NOW." Collins and Goldsmith credited the ERA campaign for establishing NOW as "the preeminent feminist organization in this country." They would continue to work on electoral politics, they promised, because "the assaults of the Right Wing on women's rights will only be halted with the defeat of the Reagan Right at the voting booth." But they also framed the ERA's defeat as an opportunity "to reshape our program" and "build on NOW's strengths."

Assuming their new offices, Goldsmith and Collins discovered that changing the organization would require a heavy lift. Goldsmith soon tired of fielding the same misguided inquiry. "We had people calling NOW headquarters saying 'I want to join ERA,'" she said. "That's what they thought we were." NOW was "synonymous" with the ratification drive, reporters remarked; a *Los Angeles Times* headline even referred to "ERA President Goldsmith." Collins pointed out that NOW's distorted reputation reflected a deeper crisis. It was "the nightmare that everyone predicted," she said. "If you lose the ERA, you got nothing, you have to start over. And I was the issues person." The organization had $1.1 million of debt (a figure that Smeal contested), an expensive national office to support, salaries to pay, and, since the ERA had expired, no message with which to fundraise.

Goldsmith and Collins were both elected at NOW's conference in Indianapolis in late 1982. They called their victory "a strong mandate" for their plan to blend political work with renewed action on more of NOW's longtime priorities. As Collins started her NOW comeback, her glee faded. "I realized, my God, I've got to leave Chicago," she said. She dreaded the move, which ended her seven-year relationship with Anne Ladky. Ladky stayed in the city to continue as executive director of the local advocacy group Women Employed. Leaving the familiar Midwest, Collins entered a new activist environment. "I didn't fit in well with these Washington people," she said. For one thing, she refused to live in the Arlington apartment building where Smeal had persuaded her officer corps to reside so that they could carpool and collaborate at any hour. Not a "suburban person," Collins moved in with a friend on Capitol Hill. At work, becoming NOW's action person meant learning "a whole other ballgame" in terms of understanding existing groups, how they worked together, and where NOW fit in.

Still, Collins went right to work, and Goldsmith backed her plans to broaden NOW's agenda and refocus on the grass roots. The board assigned more resources to local chapters, "the primary units of involvement for the membership." Chapters would be asked to hold at least one event per year devoted to either racism, lesbian rights, or reproductive rights and to "guarantee all members access to decision making." The new secretary Kathy Webb praised the changes. "We really did focus on chapter development," she said. Webb traveled the country to help them organize and offer her support, "not me telling them what to do." Diane Pollack, NOW's new lobbyist, appreciated that after the ERA, NOW had "a broader field of action from which we could choose to focus our energy." The reproductive rights organizer Maureen Anderson found "totally post-ERA" NOW "an exciting place to be."

One of their first goals was to build upon the earlier work by Hernandez and others to broaden NOW's agenda and better engage with women of color. The 1982 conference that elected Collins and Goldsmith passed a resolution acknowledging that NOW's "outreach" to women of color had "continually been superseded by other priority programs," and even NOW's official policies had not been implemented. That resolution created a full-time staff position to "promote the interests of minority women in all aspects of the organization." Collins saw Goldsmith work aggressively "to try to overcome the barrier between black women and white women" and spend "real time on the phone with black leaders, men and women." Co-sponsoring the 1983 March on Washington was one such effort, as was NOW's support for the campaign to make Martin Luther King Jr. Day a national holiday.

Lesbians in NOW also demanded more concerted effort on their agenda, and Collins made sure that their concerns were a priority. She hired the longtime Chicago activist Chris Riddiough to be NOW's first full-time lesbian rights organizer, "one of the most effective leaders" of that city's gay and lesbian community, according to the local newspaper *Gay Life*. Riddiough found "general acceptance" of lesbian issues among the members. Most seemed to understand that there had always been lesbians among them, and "it was maybe time to not be so surreptitious about it." Riddiough planned a well-attended conference in Milwaukee, "Lesbian Rights: Power and Politics in '84," to connect NOW members with gay and lesbian activists and forge a mutual agenda. Riddiough strengthened alliances with their groups including the National Gay Task Force to lobby Congress to build support for a civil rights bill, enhance AIDS research funding, and block antigay provisions.

Riddiough started to build real momentum on state gay rights legislation. Nearly half of state legislatures had considered laws banning anti-LGBT discrimination by 1983, but because activists were not coordinated, "each state lesbian and gay rights organization wound up reinventing the wheel," said Collins. NOW built a state pilot program starting with New Jersey. Allies in the state assembly introduced a bill to amend antidiscrimination laws to include sexual orientation. NOW-NJ hired a lobbyist, built a coalition of supporters, and kicked off a grassroots campaign of lobbying, letter writing, and fundraising. The bill passed in the state senate, and the governor was expected to sign it. NOW intended the successful New Jersey campaign to be the first of many, with transferable lessons for chapters around the country.

Collins and Goldsmith, together with their new staffers, worked to enlarge NOW's agenda and harness grassroots creativity in the wake of the ERA defeat. But events outside their control—conservatives' shifting tactics, the ERA's continued popularity, and the organization's own perilous financial standing—would shape their choices and narrow their options.

———

As NOW's leaders sought to expand their group's activism, they felt how much more treacherous the political climate had grown in the years the organization had spent focused on the ERA. The New Right had secured its grip on the Republican Party, which held the U.S. Senate and the presidency. Those conservatives initiated seismic shifts in the national budget. They cut taxes and ramped up military spending, stoked Cold War tensions and reversed peacemaking that Democratic Congresses had steered in the wake of Vietnam. And Democrats approved these hawkish budgets in the early 1980s, fearful of being criticized as weak.

Republicans tightened the domestic purse strings in ways that disproportionately harmed women. The budget cuts in Reagan's first four years plunged almost five million women and two million female-headed households into poverty by rolling back social programs. One-third of the cuts were to programs that mostly served women—including Food Stamps, Aid to Families with Dependent Children, and Medicaid—and that accounted for just 10 percent of the federal budget. The budget cuts and economic instability especially harmed the women of color who were more likely to be living in poverty and working "at the bottom of the job ladder." Women's unemployment soared, with Black women's rate more than double their white counterparts'. In place of social programs, Congress passed punitive provisions, such as a 1984 law that toughened child support enforcement. The law would, Reagan declared in signing it, promote "responsible behavior" rather than "creating more dependency on government."

Conservatives in Washington also took explicit aim at women's rights. In the Reagan administration's only policy speech on American women, the spokesperson Faith Whittlesey called feminism a "straitjacket" for women. Reagan himself called upon the Supreme Court to overturn *Roe v. Wade*. The officials he appointed took a scalpel to federal commissions and departments, replacing feminists with opponents of civil rights and affirmative action. At the same time, congressional Republicans began a legislative push to limit reproductive freedoms and gay and lesbian rights. All of this placed feminists on the defensive, their recent gains tenuous and reversible.

This hostile climate reset the landscape for liberal and progressive organizations. Some groups benefited from liberals' outrage, which many expressed with their checkbooks. Fundraising appeals dedicated to preserving abortion rights drew in $5 million in 1980 alone. The National Abortion Rights Action League's membership rose from 85,000 to 135,000 in the year after Reagan's election, and NOW's membership doubled to 220,000 in the two years after Reagan took office.

Many organizations suffered. While NOW's ERA blitz had drawn unprecedented cash—up to $500,000 from a single mailing—other groups, like the NAACP, had fallen into debt because inflation had skyrocketed their operating costs. Reagan's spending cuts deepened the pain for groups like the National Council of Negro Women, which had relied on government grants, and forced them to divert energy from programs to fundraising. Some smaller feminist groups folded, destroyed by declining income and membership; others responded to the harsh politics at home by turning to international work. Labor unions, especially those in blue-collar sectors, were under siege. They were muscled into concessions due to competition with foreign products and pummeled by new union-busting consulting firms. Gay and lesbian activists defended against legislative assaults and day-to-day persecution fueled by the nascent AIDS crisis.

Liberal and progressive groups faced these challenges by cooperating in new ways. The 1983 March on Washington was an especially visible collaboration, and its list of participating organizations and issues grew rapidly in the organizing stages. The Leadership Conference on Civil Rights, which helped to plan it, had expanded from 79 member organizations in 1963 to 165 in 1983. At the press conference just before the March, Judy Goldsmith sat alongside Coretta Scott King and the leaders of the Southern Christian Leadership Conference, the National Gay Task Force, and the National Coalition of Black Gays to announce that the March would endorse gay and lesbian rights and support pending legislation in Congress that would add sexual orientation to the list of protected categories under the Civil Rights Act of 1964. This affirmation marked a major milestone, but such expansive coalitions were also unwieldy. Black and Latino groups clashed on immigration reform in planning the march. Jewish and Black leaders sparred over the fractious politics in the Middle East. A focus on defeating Reagan was often their only point of consensus.

The New Right also shaped feminist organizations' own priorities.

National surveys in the early 1980s revealed that most Americans did not favor banning abortion, but abortion rights advocates agreed that their movement was on the defensive. In the first month of 1981 alone, Republicans in Congress introduced several constitutional amendments designed to effectively nullify *Roe v. Wade*. Single-issue antiabortion organizations allied with the broader right wing in a powerful coalition that approached the family in conservative terms. "The crisis is upon us and the danger is clear," NARAL's executive director told her group's national conference in 1981.

Inside NOW, Collins started monitoring efforts to pass state abortion restrictions and trying to build momentum to secure Medicaid funding for the procedure by overturning the Hyde Amendment. Conservatives' activism soon convinced her that abortion rights deserved even higher priority. Antiabortion terrorists bombed a Delaware abortion clinic in January 1984. They went on to assault two dozen clinics in subsequent months, always on nights and weekends in efforts to destroy the facilities without killing anyone. NOW began a campaign to publicize and end the violence. Goldsmith demanded an FBI investigation and called upon President Reagan to "immediately and publicly condemn these terrorist acts in the same strong terms you use to condemn the attacks of international terrorists upon American citizens." Reagan did not speak out against the violence for months.

Collins hatched a plan to recruit NOW members to sit in at the clinics. Every chapter the national office contacted agreed to participate. "They're not going to bomb us if we're there, so it was an act of defiance," Collins said, to "dare them to come and get us." Planned Parenthood and other abortion rights groups "went batshit" over the confrontational tactic, Collins said, but the clinics and the press "just loved us." At NOW's sit-ins at twenty-five clinics in eighteen states, journalists found the activists singing songs, eating pizza, and happily camping out. In one instance, federal officials asked NOW to stay out of a specific clinic so they could catch the bombers red-handed. "They didn't care if another abortion clinic blew up," the NOW staffer Maureen Anderson said, but she told them NOW was not willing to stand by "so that you guys can have a glorious bust." Battling conservatives on the fronts where conservatives were gaining ground was necessary, gave advocates focus and new points for cooperation, and yielded some wins, but it also gave conservatives a measure of control over NOW's agenda.

Collins was also drawn into ongoing struggles for the ERA, which still had considerable momentum. The time limit had expired on the version that cleared Congress in the early 1970s, but lawmakers could challenge the constitutionality of its time limit or reintroduce the provision. Collins would have preferred to shelve it for a time. The architect of the Sears effort knew the power of a focused campaign, so she had pushed hard for the ERA until 1982, "in part to get it off the goddamn agenda." While it seemed fruitless to pour in much time or money considering the strong conservative headwinds, she understood that many of NOW's members cared deeply about the ERA, lured in by "the mystique of the suffragists" who kept up their dogged fight for decades. Collins told the others, "fine, introduce the damn thing every year, but don't work on it." Members of the Democratic-controlled House of Representatives reintroduced the ERA on January 3, 1983, as the new session's first order of business. The 222 co-sponsors in the House "were not hard to get," Goldsmith noted.

As Smeal had done with the 59 Cents campaign, Goldsmith and Collins framed the ERA as an economic issue. They pointed to the insurance industry as "the silent lobby against ERA." Single adult women together overpaid for auto insurance almost $1 billion each year. Over their lifetimes, women paid as much as $16,000 more for insurance than men. Insurers frequently excluded maternity coverage or offered benefits that were lower than its costs. More than half of new health insurance policies excluded maternity outright. Those that included it covered less than half of the actual costs. Insurance was a state-regulated industry with a "corps of lobbyists" in the legislatures protecting their bottom line, so "opposition to ERA was all in a day's work for them," NOW alleged. Industry officials responded that eliminating the sex-based categories would "totally disrupt" the insurance market and end up raising women's premiums by more than $1 billion per year.

Phyllis Schlafly and her followers sided with the insurance industry. "These people want a gender-free society," Schlafly declared. "Having failed in their No. 1 effort—a gender-free draft and military—now they're trying insurance" and "ignoring the realities of gender differences." Goldsmith responded by framing the ERA and insurance discrimination in economic terms in her testimony before several congressional sub-committees in 1983. "Discrimination is about money," she said. A good salesperson could tell customers that a "price reflects 'sex-based costs' and chances are they'll believe it." Members phone banked, lobbied, and fundraised to support both a federal fair insurance bill and the revived ERA.

Once again, the prospects for help from political leaders faded when even Democratic support started to soften. In January 1983, the ERA looked likely to pass in the House of Representatives. But later that year, the ERA failed in the chamber by six votes. Even some of the original co-sponsors voted against it to protest Speaker Tip O'Neill's decision to bring up the amendment under special House rules that prohibited amendments and limited the time for debate and that were typically re-served for uncontroversial items. In those same months, the House and Senate considered bills that would have banned sex-based classifications in insurance pricing and risk assessment. The House bill eventually died in a committee after intense lobbying from the industry. Many in NOW seethed with anger at these men who stood in the way of equality. They wanted them gone.

NOW's financial problems also pulled the organization toward the ERA and electoral politics. The group's sophisticated direct-mail program had raised millions of dollars, and the direct-mail guru Roger Craver urged Goldsmith to keep fundraising on the amendment because it was so consistently lucrative. Craver outlined his approach to organization building at NARAL's 1981 convention. "The money you raise is in danger of being, if not misspent, then diffusely spent," and thus "the problem isn't raising money, it's finding a focus." Collins wanted to pivot NOW's fundraising focus to abortion, and she suspected that Craver kept pushing the ERA despite its poor prospects because he was already fundraising on abortion for his other clients, NARAL and Planned Parenthood.

NOW needed direct mail. The fundraising letters were bringing gobs of money into the organization, but NOW was spending even more. In the first half of 1983, NOW took in nearly $3,059,000, but spent $3,162,000 for a net loss of more than $100,000. NOW paid Craver's firm a $15,000 monthly fee for "full-service consulting" to expand its list of donors, "upgrade" those donors' "giving level," shape an overall strategy, and create and analyze fundraising campaigns.

Only direct mail could bring in the needed cash, but it was an expensive strategy that no longer paid for itself. For each of three mailings between early 1983 and mid-1984, the average gift was between $21 and $25, but the percent returns declined from 4.0 to 2.5 to 1.8. In early 1984, direct mail brought in 85 percent of NOW's income, the group's combined debts approached $400,000, and its monthly overhead cost $250,000. NOW's other sources of money paled in comparison. Plotting NOW's fundraisers for 1984, officers expected that two receptions in Washington would cost $18,000 and bring in $50,000; walkathons would cost $8,000 to raise $50,000. An advertising "blitz" to recruit new members was projected to break even. Goldsmith shrank the "cold prospecting program," which pursued new members through unsolicited mailings to people on purchased lists, because previous direct-mail campaigns had saddled NOW with a mail debt of $250,000. NOW's finances were in a downward spiral.

Campaigning for national office in 1982, Goldsmith and Collins had highlighted the importance of national politics, but these financial pressures tightened their focus on fundraising around the ERA and the upcoming 1984 elections. The organization had to fundraise for both their congressional and their state PACS "from basically the same sources," who were being targeted by many other activist groups, Goldsmith wrote to the board. She penned a solicitation claiming that the next sixty days were critical to the ERA's future. "You can count on NOW to do everything possible," she wrote, "but we simply cannot do what needs to be done without your immediate and generous support." Goldsmith's letter brought in the predicted cash infusion, but it was her last one on the ERA. "I wasn't comfortable raising money on an issue that can't legitimately be moved," she said soon after. "We aren't interested in any more exercises in futility."

Yet electoral politics appeared to be the path to progress on any issue and the best way to attack "the establishment" as the New Right pushed its priorities through all three branches of government. And President

Reagan offered them a person and an agenda to organize against. "Ronald Reagan has been a disaster for women," Collins told an Indiana NOW banquet in mid-1983. "Are you any better off now than you were 2½ years ago?" she asked, and the audience shouted back, "No!" Soon they were fighting on many fronts, because Reagan continued to slash government programs and fill courts and federal agencies with archconservatives.

NOW's leaders also felt their group had real political leverage and sought to position their organization as the voice of their sex. Since the first national election in which women voted, their votes roughly mirrored men's. But an examination of the 1980 electorate revealed an 8 percent difference between Reagan's support from women and men. Fifty-five percent of men voted for Reagan by comparison with 47 percent of women. Goldsmith believed that feminists had created the disparity. "Ronald Reagan is directly responsible for emergence of the gender gap" because he "appeared intent on sending women back to the 19th century."

Women's anti-Reagan sentiment, NOW hoped, could fuel a major membership drive. The organization spent $250,000 in late 1982 on a new advertising campaign, part of a fundraising and membership drive, which asserted that it had helped create and could expand that gender gap. One television ad showed a man placing a drink, cigarettes, and a gun on a table. A feminine voice pointed out that there were eleven thousand lobbyists representing various interests in Washington. "But who speaks for women?" she asked as a woman's hand replaced the items with a NOW button. "NOW, the National Organization for Women."

———

NOW's confident assertion aside, the matter of who spoke for women was hotly contested. Political experts, newly focused on women's behavior, debated whether the gender gap was the last gasp of the past decade's feminist resurgence or the dawn of an era shaped by women's clout. Women were registering and voting at high rates, and women's groups, including NOW, had more political influence than ever. "Five years ago, even right-thinking Democrats could assign a lower priority to women's issues," *The Boston Globe* noted several weeks before the 1982 elections. "That's no longer the case. NOW has the money, the leadership, the determination

and the skill." NOW gained up to nine thousand members per month in
the two years after Reagan was elected and raised nearly $2 million for
1982 candidates by October of that year. No rust had settled on its ERA
machine of organizers, canvassers, and letter writers. NOW women had
long been politically active, said the New York City chapter president,
Denise Fuge, "but we were like little brown field mice; nobody knew we
were there." She boasted, "Now candidates are coming to us."

As those candidates discovered, women's politics were more complex
than ever. A decade earlier, women's advocates across the political spectrum
generally supported the goal of electing women to office. The few woman
candidates had little money or establishment support, and they ran against
men. In the early 1980s, women were running against women, moderate
women ran against progressive men, and antifeminist women ran against
feminist men. The rise of antifeminism left little common ground in
women's politics; even explicitly nonpartisan, centrist groups began to
choose sides. In 1983, the League of Women Voters asserted its support
for abortion rights after years of avoiding weighing in on the issue. The
group took the stand after polling its own chapters, 92 percent of which
backed a reproductive rights position.

This fragmented landscape forced women's organizations to decide:
Did advocating for women in politics mean helping all women gain
office, or was it more important to support feminist candidates no matter
their gender? The National Women's Political Caucus chose to strictly
support woman candidates. Its gender-first, bipartisan politics sometimes
cut against feminists' priorities. "The failure of our success is that as more
women run they are not always running against targeted men," its president said. "We are also running against our friends."

NOW took the opposite approach, choosing ideology over identity.
The organization supported several male Democrats over female Republicans in the 1982 midterms. In one such race, the Connecticut Republican
Nancy Johnson criticized NOW for backing her opponent, William
Curry, in their race for the U.S. House of Representatives. Johnson had
supported child-care subsidies, abortion rights, and the ERA as a state as-
semblywoman. NOW seemed to be "only concerned about a partisan fight
to keep Republicans out of office," Johnson said. Smeal acknowledged

that strategy. "If all things are the same we would rather see more women in office," but her group believed that "a Democratic Congress, a Democratic leadership is better." Conservative Republicans embraced NOW's opposition as a point of pride. "Let them be my guest," Congressman Carlos Moorhead of California responded to NOW's threat to find a "viable candidate" to challenge him. "They consistently support liberal Democratic candidates. I don't expect them to support me. They never have."

As the 1984 presidential race approached, Ronald Reagan wrapped himself in the American flag. His campaign embraced the hopeful theme of "Morning in America." He claimed that he had turned the page on the turbulent 1970s in his main television advertisement titled "Prouder, Stronger, Better." As nostalgic music played, families greeted the day on their immaculate suburban lawns and strode confidently out to work as paperboys cycled past. The narrator crowed that on Reagan's watch more Americans held paid jobs than ever before, interest rates had fallen by half, and homeownership was on the rise.

Returning to an earlier time, or at least the late 1970s, seemed possible in the form of an early front-runner in the Democratic Party primaries: Walter Mondale, the former U.S. senator from Minnesota who had served as Carter's vice president. Mondale had spent four decades brokering political compromises and demonstrating his loyalty to the Democratic Party, climbing its ladder by paying his dues. A centrist in temperament, Mondale was liberal on civil rights, but he also wanted to regain the working-class white support that Reagan had peeled away from the Democrats in 1980. His most prominent early opponent was the U.S. senator from Colorado Gary Hart. In his nearly ten years in the Senate, Hart distinguished himself as a champion of a new "neoliberalism" that pursued liberal priorities through the free market.

The Democratic Party rewarded NOW's support in the 1982 midterms by embracing its key issues. Mondale and Hart agreed on women's issues when narrowly interpreted: both sought to extend the deadline for passing the ERA, called for opening Medicaid funding for abortion, and backed affirmative action and the new pay equity movement known as comparable worth. Both vowed to appoint women to powerful roles in their administrations. Mondale promised to reverse Reagan's cuts to social services, while Hart ruled out making dramatic cuts to military spending or mounting a muscular assault on poverty. Critics on the left accused both candidates of watering down Reaganism rather than rejecting it.

One of those critics became a late entry to the Democratic primary who unsettled the race: the civil rights and economic justice activist Jesse Jackson of Chicago. A former associate of Dr. Martin Luther King Jr.'s, Jackson was the forty-two-year-old leader of Operation PUSH (People United to Save Humanity). Jackson rode a nationwide surge of Black political activism in the early 1980s, and he described his campaign as "growing out of the black experience and seen through the eyes of a black perspective—which is the experience and the perspective of the rejected." At the same time, he framed his candidacy in broad terms: he vowed to represent the interests of a new "rainbow coalition" made up of everyone who was excluded from the political process. Jackson's political rallies featured panels of Blacks and Latinos, Asian Americans, gays and lesbians, and disabled people. If these groups locked arms, Jackson claimed, they could win. His coalition kicked off a massive voter-registration drive that reached many people of color, received national attention, and raised people's hopes about what a broad progressive coalition could accomplish.

Mondale, Hart, and Jackson advanced different visions for the future of the Democratic Party. At one of several debates in the heat of the primaries, Hart accused Mondale of being beholden to interest groups, especially organized labor, and too committed to simply refunding the federal government programs Reagan had cut. The private sector could often be more efficient, Hart claimed. Mondale criticized Hart's embrace of free enterprise, promising that he would stand up "*against* special interests" and "support Social Security and Medicare." Jackson accused all of his opponents of wanting "new leadership that replaces old leadership basically going in the same direction," and "not sharing parity with farmers, not sharing the ticket with a woman, increasing the military budget, resisting a real commitment to enforce the Voting Rights Act." Jackson argued that his competitors wanted to make the Democrats the "new name of an old game" rather than a "party of conscience" that centered the concerns of the nation's most marginalized.

Amid this ferment, and with four more years of Reagan's rule at stake, NOW announced to the press that it would make its first-ever presidential endorsement. Those reporters had already begun to treat NOW like one of several major power brokers in a liberal landscape of national interest groups, including organized labor and teachers' associations, that pursued their members' will through political endorsements. NOW's coffers could not match the major campaign contributions from unions and teachers' groups. But NOW was a national network of seasoned organizers, and its approval carried symbolic weight. According to a Mondale aide, "their support says the candidate is good on the issues."

"We have a new role in the political arena, and it is a central one," Goldsmith told NOW's 1983 conference, less than four months before the first primary election. "Our priority for 1984 is to get rid of Ronald Reagan." Six of the seven major Democratic candidates addressed that gathering to seek the group's endorsement. Each man proclaimed his support for the ERA, abortion rights, and equal pay. Goldsmith asked each whether he would choose a "feminist woman" as his running mate; none agreed, but each promised to consider it. Mondale was clearly the crowd favorite. The room roared when he declared, "I am a feminist." By contrast, the delegates booed the Ohio senator John Glenn for his explanation of why the ERA had not been ratified by enough states: "we all loafed" while the opposition "outhustled us."

Glenn's remark might have ruined his bid for their group's endorsement. Reflecting NOW's clout, the candidate's aides fired off a written "clarification": "Certainly no organization has worked harder or done more for the passage of the amendment than NOW." A West Virginia delegate denounced Glenn from the podium. "I was not loafing during the ERA campaign," she said, "and I want a candidate that can speak 'feminist' without a script."

Their conference was a success, the delegates agreed, and many also viewed it as a turning point for their organization. One member explained that when she joined NOW ten years earlier, "we were extremely naïve" for believing that "if we pointed out inequities to our leaders, things would change. We learned we have to change our leaders." For the first time, a critical mass of the men contending to lead the nation came to them. "I think what we saw here were the candidates speaking to us as a *constituency*," declared California NOW's president. The leader of Indiana NOW agreed: "We have recognized where our power lies, and it lies in our vote." So determined were the gathered members to maximize the potency of their endorsement that they voted to pressure NOW PACs not to support any independent or third-party candidates if Reagan won the Republican endorsement, which was all but inevitable.

Jackson's candidacy tested NOW's commitments. He personally opposed abortion and had once criticized the women's movement in general as being led by "upper middle-class white females." But Jackson was also the only candidate who promised to pick a woman running mate—"very significant," according to Goldsmith—and vowed to hire women for half of his campaign jobs. Jackson's appeal to voters of color was also important to those in NOW who sought to expand the mostly white, middle-class composition that Jackson had criticized. In energetic pursuit of NOW's endorsement, Jackson met twice with Goldsmith and sent surrogates to lobby her, including Maxine Waters, the California State Assembly's majority whip and future congresswoman. Women should choose Jackson, argued one staffer, because he was "the only candidate that acknowledges the institutionalization of sexism." A different aide identified women as natural members of Jackson's coalition: "another group that has been traditionally ignored in the political process."

But as NOW's 1983 convention revealed, many in the organization saw themselves less as one piece of a progressive coalition than as an independent force with the hard-won power to make candidates curry their favor. Jackson's candidacy compelled NOW to choose between its stated goals: electing women, pursuing antiracism and grassroots militancy alongside its allies, broadening its membership, and doing whatever it took to defeat Reagan. All of this attention from the Democratic candidates compounded NOW leaders' sense that their organization spoke with women's voice, that their group's endorsement could reshape the race, and that electoral politics deserved the bulk of their energies. Each of these assumptions soon proved dangerous.

———

NOW's national board held a marathon meeting in December 1983 to debate their endorsement. Mondale's supporters emphasized his electability, while Jackson's warned that backing Mondale would put a wedge between the feminist and the Black agendas. After six hours of debate, the group nearly reached consensus. Mondale received thirty-two of the board members' thirty-seven votes. The choice sent "a message to the majority of the women of this nation that Walter Mondale is the candidate who will be best for women and who can defeat Ronald Reagan," Goldsmith said in a post-meeting press conference. She described Mondale as the most electable candidate and a champion of women's issues. While he promised to select a "feminist" running mate, Goldsmith estimated that there was a "50-50 chance" that he would pick a woman.

NOW's endorsement expressed a commitment to pragmatism over progressive principles. Black women took notice. Donna Brazile, Jackson's director of constituent mobilization, described NOW's choice as "very disappointing." It was Jackson who "represent[ed]" NOW's "activist tradition," she pointed out. Jackson's wife expressed her frustration to Goldsmith in vivid terms, Goldsmith recalled later (without repeating those terms), and the Black poet Maya Angelou "was just as cursory and curt as she could be" when introducing NOW's president at an event. Goldsmith "felt really bad," but she did not believe they should endorse Jackson. "He was simply not viable," and compared with his campaign, which juggled the concerns of many constituencies, Mondale's people had "bent over backwards" for NOW. "The commitments have been very specific," she said. "I will be in the room." This promised access to Mondale intensified NOW leaders' sense that they were power brokers on behalf of all women.

With their endorsement driven by stark calculations, NOW's leaders spent the next six months lobbying Mondale to choose a woman running mate. They couched this move as another way to help oust Reagan. NOW could not "deliver the women's vote," Goldsmith acknowledged, but the organization was "in touch with the realities of the way women vote." A female vice presidential candidate would energize women across the spectrum and create the margin of victory. "We aren't saying, 'if there isn't a woman, we won't play,'" Goldsmith said. "We're saying, 'if there isn't a woman we don't win.'"

Mondale addressed NOW's 1984 conference in Miami Beach, held just weeks before the Democratic National Convention that would officially nominate him and his yet-unchosen running mate. Before he began, the twelve hundred delegates chanted at him, "Run with a woman, win with a woman." Many wore decals that read, "Woman VP NOW." The potential vice presidential candidates Representatives Barbara Mikulski, Patricia Schroeder, and Geraldine Ferraro all gave speeches to the delegates. The New Jersey member Mary Roche Eidsvik voiced the only objection to the resolution urging Mondale to choose "a woman who is strong on women's issues," expressing her fears that NOW was turning into an "auxiliary unit of the Democratic Party" and a "vote-getting machine." The other delegates shouted her down.

NOW's leaders pushed the limits of their clout in Miami Beach. At a press conference, Goldsmith pointed out that women would be half of the delegates at the next month's Democratic National Convention. In what Goldsmith called "a prediction," not "a threat," she pointed out that those woman delegates could nominate their own vice presidential candidate from the floor, rousing bad memories of the fractious 1968 DNC.

NOW was effectively challenging the Democratic Party to choose which constituency it valued more: women or African Americans. Mondale began interviewing possible running mates, including Jesse Jackson, who had conceded his own presidential bid. There had never been a Black vice president either, and Jackson called it a "step in the right direction" when Mondale interviewed him and the mayors of Los Angeles and Philadelphia, all of whom were Black men. But once it became clear that Mondale would choose a white woman, Jackson accused Mondale's campaign of racist treatment. He pointed to recent polls on voters' preferences as well as his strong performance in early primaries. "If there was any scientific basis for making a vice presidential choice, it would be me." Jackson accused "white women" and especially NOW of co-opting a central issue of his campaign: that a woman should be vice president.

Days before the Democratic National Convention, Mondale chose the candidate who was also NOW's favorite: the three-term New York congresswoman Geraldine Ferraro, a Roman Catholic and Italian American from Queens who was married and had teenage children. While Ferraro would be the first woman on a major party's presidential ticket, she was in many ways a conservative choice: liberal rather than progressive in her politics, like Mondale, and backed by party leaders including her mentor, the powerful House Speaker, Tip O'Neill. Mondale's advisers downplayed Ferraro's gender, insisting that she would help Mondale win blue-collar voters in the industrial Midwest. "She's a woman, she's ethnic, she's Catholic," said a Mondale adviser. "She will energize, not just women, but a lot of men who have fallen away from the Democrats." In their first press conference together, Ferraro couched her biography in terms of her Italian immigrant father's life story.

After the DNC nominated Mondale and Ferraro days later in San Francisco, both candidates continued to downplay her historic presence on the ticket. They seemed concerned about a backlash by men and confident that her presence alone would attract women's votes. Reporters noted that Mondale was angered and embarrassed by the public pressure to choose a woman running mate at NOW's 1984 conference. Nor did party officials "like the image of the feminists pushing [Mondale] around, telling the Democrats what to do," observed the Florida NOW leader and future NOW president Patricia Ireland. Mondale's campaign never gave women's groups the funds to set up a national voter-registration drive, and it was slow to establish a hotline for woman volunteers. His team asked Ferraro not to highlight women's issues. She was happy to comply. "I wanted people to vote for me not because I was a woman," she said, "but because they thought I would make the best Vice President."

But this approach did not shield Ferraro from sexist jabs and personal attacks. *Newsweek* framed Mondale as having "popp[ed] the question" to her. *People* described the press conference where Mondale introduced her as his pick: Ferraro "clenched and unclenched her hands," "bit her lip, kept her head modestly bowed, as unexpectedly overwhelmed as a bride."When the campaign put out *The Mondale Family Cookbook*, reporters asked why none of the recipes were Ferraro's. A *Meet the Press* reporter asked her if she had the nerve to launch nuclear weapons. Republicans also hyped legitimate concerns about her tax returns and her husband John Zaccaro's real estate business.

Mondale and his staff created distance from NOW, but the organization still backed him, and the Democratic Party fostered a closer collaboration, eager to tap NOW's networks of energetic organizers. Once Mondale named Ferraro, "all we did was electoral," said NOW's reproductive rights organizer Maureen Anderson. "The whole staff was just working for the campaign." NOW's office workers "felt like we were the Mondale campaign in some states."Members raised $2.5 million in 1984 at "Mondale house parties" and another $1 million for "Super Tuesday–Mondale house parties." NOW made 1984 its "most active year politically," with members registering 250,000 new voters between January and mid-October, nearly all of them women. NOW PACs alone raised more than $1 million. Unlike their standard-bearer that year, Democratic Party officials embraced feminists' concerns and wrote them into the party platform, which Goldsmith praised as "strong, specific, and clearly supportive of our issues": "the ERA, reproductive rights and abortion funding, pay equity, affirmative action, child care . . . and gay and lesbian rights."NOW members teamed up with local Democratic candidates, helping with outreach and fundraising on behalf of their organization.

NOW predicted victory. Its members posited that the gender gap was driven by feminist woman voters. Gambling that women were a political constituency that would hold together, NOW created a "women's truth squad on Reagan" to publicize his "devastating social and economic implications for women."Its premise was that women who learned the truth would oppose the president in solidarity with their gender.

But just what was good for women, and what it meant for women to influence politics, were open questions. As in the ERA campaign of the previous decade, conservative women found NOW to be a useful force to organize against. The Republican National Committee sponsored the creation of the National Women's Coalition (NWC), which billed itself as

NOW's "flip side." A tiny but effective foil, the NWC convened polished woman professionals in the fields of business, law, education, and politics. These well-heeled spokeswomen declared Reagan's policies to be good for women. They argued that the president, by bringing down inflation, unemployment, and interest rates, had afforded women "an unprecedented opportunity" to "better care for ourselves and our families."

Other Republican women appealed to the same tokenism NOW pushed in pursuing a woman vice president: Reagan had appointed the first woman to the U.S. Supreme Court, Justice Sandra Day O'Connor, and installed two women on his cabinet. Women against abortion opposed Ferraro's nomination because she had consistently voted pro-choice as a member of Congress. They argued that abortion rights were antiwoman by definition.

Black women were more united against Reagan, who had caricatured the poor among them as undeserving "welfare queens" to ground his social spending cuts, but they were conflicted over Ferraro's nomination. They wanted the leaders of NOW and the National Women's Political Caucus to acknowledge that Jackson had paved the way to a woman nominee, and they felt that white women ignored their frustration that no Black woman was even considered for the role. "Feminists continue to send the message that their agenda—sexism—is closed, and will not be expanded to include a fuller picture of the multiplicity of oppression which includes racism and classism," said Ruth Sykes, the longtime assistant to the president of the National Council of Negro Women. But when cameras were rolling, white feminists "rel[ied] heavily on civil rights rhetoric." Black feminists pointed out that Jackson's campaign embodied a feminist politics that white women tended to reject. His approach insisted upon the multiplicity of oppressions rather than boiling all political issues down to matters of gender alone.

Other critics offered their own perspectives. NOW's endorsement unnecessarily sacrificed political leverage, they said, and improperly substituted its leaders' judgment of who would be best for women for that of women themselves, who had many points of view. Some in NOW felt uneasy about the endorsement. "I didn't ever want NOW to be viewed as an arm of the Democratic Party," the future national president Patricia

Ireland said later. But NOW had limited political options. "The Republicans partly made that our choice."

———

The 1984 elections were a bloodbath for the Democrats. Reagan took 525 of 538 Electoral College votes, winning every state but Minnesota (Mondale's home state) and Washington, D.C. Republicans kept the Senate and gained seats in the House. The Democrats' crushing losses reflected their struggles to respond to the Reagan revolution. Since the 1970s, their party had been retreating from its earlier embrace of a kind of economic populism rooted in direct federal government support for the working class. The party had become increasingly beholden to more conservative corporate funders and PACs. These changes positioned most Democratic candidates in 1984 to package themselves as weaker Reaganites rather than rejecting Reagan's conservatism. As a party insider and a centrist by nature, Mondale sought a nebulous middle ground between progressives' efforts to reinvigorate and expand the New Deal and neoliberals' efforts to move beyond it.

The election results also disproved NOW's theory of women's solidarity. The gender gap had shrunk and shifted, with white married women mostly voting Republican. Fifty-seven percent of all women voted for Reagan in 1984, up from 47 percent in 1980. The incumbent had captured so much of the women's vote by dividing it. Reagan targeted older women with advertisements emphasizing how he had lowered inflation. To younger married women, he highlighted the expansion of the child tax credit. He also won support from many white men and women, previously Democrats, who rejected the party's appeals to civil rights and feminism. "We came out of '84 with greater strengths than we have ever had," Collins wrote, "but also with an opposition that has never been better financed or more determined."

By emphasizing Ferraro's importance as a symbol, NOW had unwittingly helped set the stage for the conservative triumph in 1984 and the Democrats' pain that followed. The organization had opened the door for Republicans to run conservative women for Congress and call that progress for women. The GOP condemned feminism but elected women—

conservative women who opposed abortion rights and the ERA—like never before. Postelection postmortems estimated that Ferraro gave Mondale a modest boost typical of any vice presidential running mate.

But many Democrats blamed Ferraro for the loss. "We can't afford to have a party so feminized that it has no appeal to males," warned one Democratic consultant after the election. NOW members' close collaboration with the Democrats fed conservative attacks on Mondale as beholden to "special interest" groups while making NOW activists resent their supportive labor for a party that seemed to downplay their group's influence, especially in southern states. The mistrust and animosity lingered, and just like after the ERA expiration, NOW had no clear path forward.

Black women's groups were similarly scarred by Reagan's reelection as well as NOW's recent behavior. "Our white sisters and white organizations failed to support us," said C. Delores Tucker, the vice-chairperson of the DNC's Black Caucus. Before the convention, white feminists, including NOW's leaders, had promised to back the proposed minority plank, which called for cutbacks in defense spending and reinvestments in health resources, job training, and racial justice. "But when we got there," Tucker said, "we found we were all alone." Most white feminists explained that they had reversed course out of loyalty to Mondale—he did not support the plank—but they were also distracted by their own "exuberance" over Ferraro's nomination, posited the U.S. Civil Rights Commission member Mary Frances Berry.

After the Democrats' nominating convention, a group of thirty-six Black women formed the National Black Women's Political Caucus, whose founding conference drew almost four hundred women from thirty-four states in mid-1985. They criticized both major parties for failing Black women. "The time has come when all of us can no longer be the complacent, armchair recipients of whatever morals or politics this country decrees for us," said the former congresswoman Shirley Chisholm, the group's cofounder and inaugural chair. The new caucus would collaborate with NOW when expedient but pledged to remain independent.

Reproductive justice organizations also moved away from NOW. The Reproductive Rights National Network (R2N2) was a loose-knit network of more than seventy-five local organizations founded in 1979 after the Hyde Amendment banned the use of Medicaid funding for abortion. R2N2 viewed abortion rights as merely a first step toward women's liberation, arguing that women also needed adequate social and economic supports to make the choice meaningful. The organization emphasized women's race and class differences in calling for accessible and comprehensive health care, affordable child care, workplace protections, and an end to racialized sterilization abuse—surpassing NOW's agenda.

For the second time in three years, NOW's leaders tried to pivot after a major loss. They made abortion rights the group's most visible program. NOW helped organize a major reproductive rights march that brought 155,000 to the capital, and Collins coordinated abortion rights lobby days, press conferences, speak-outs, and a fundraiser, as well as thirty overnight vigils against clinic violence in eighteen states over a single 1985 weekend. Goldsmith condemned antiabortion violence at dedicated House subcommittee hearings that NOW had been working to arrange for more than a year. Americans outraged by both the clinic bombings and conservatives' advances opened their wallets and made NOW's direct-mail program profitable once more.

Yet the organization seemed to be playing defense on every front. Some NOW members blamed their lack of progress on their leaders, who seemed impotent to make headway against the massive power of the Reagan administration. Those leaders worked regular business hours in an "orderly and strangely tranquil" office suite just steps from the White House. None of it implied that NOW had "the momentum to toss out a sitting President," said a California NOW leader. Seeing little chance for "forward progress," NOW's lesbian rights organizer Chris Riddiough took a job with the Gay Democrats.

Eleanor Smeal, just two years out of her time as NOW president, was also frustrated. She believed NOW needed more members, money, and visibility. "This is not the time for behind-the-scenes activity," Smeal said. "We can see where low-key has gotten us: people think we've gone away." She mentioned several action areas, but her main goal was to take the ERA "out of the deep freeze and turn up the heat on those who profit from sex discrimination." As an activist group, she said, NOW's "political clout is the ability to galvanize public opinion," and the ERA could help do it. It was "a wonderful organizing tool and consciousness raiser" that made "good dollars and cents."

Smeal decided to challenge Goldsmith for her old job. Her allies believed she had done Collins and Goldsmith a favor two years earlier in endorsing their slate, which they nicknamed "the oatmeal caucus" for its blandness, and that they had spurned Smeal's efforts to help them succeed. After this, according to Smeal's ally Toni Carabillo, she decided to turn away from Goldsmith and Collins. "There's a limit to how many times you're going to go back to the same people, and be nice," said Carabillo. "Ellie kept rescuing the organization," said her fellow former Californian and Majority Caucus member Judith Meuli. "Her role has been to make sure that NOW doesn't die."

Goldsmith and Smeal began to lay out different accounts of the last two years. Goldsmith refuted Smeal's charge that NOW had been passive and invisible, which "denies reality and demeans all of the hard work done." The group finally had a surplus of income over expenses despite more than $1 million of remaining debt, and ninety thousand new members in 1984. Goldsmith promised to build on that success through "a style of leadership that is true to feminist principles, that includes, empowers and respects our chapter and state activists for their ideas, experience and expertise." They now had a wider range of issues and tactics. "At times it can be radical to lobby and conventional to demonstrate," Goldsmith claimed. The candidates' differences were more tactical than substantive, but the stakes were real. "Ellie's answer to every problem is to raise hell," said one member. "Judy's is to negotiate." Everyone agreed that their showdown would be ugly, with some recalling the last decade's brawls. A Smeal supporter warned conference goers to prepare for battle: "These elections aren't known for their niceties."

Like many past NOW conventions, the New Orleans gathering in July 1985 seemed to contain two events at once. The scene looked like a political convention. In the hall, thousands of women wore scarves, T-shirts, and stickers printed with "Ellie" or "Judy." Emphasizing this focus on powerful individuals, reporters wrote deep profiles of the two candidates. Collins reminded journalists that feminism was a mass movement, not a clash of icons. "The women's movement is not a one-woman show, a two-woman show or a three-woman show," she said. "We all have to be involved."

The turmoil in New Orleans "gave everybody who was there something to equal the stories of people who were at the '75 conference in Philadelphia," recalled the Michigan NOW president Barbara Hays. At workshops on issues, each candidate's supporters crowded the microphones with questions designed to embarrass the opponent. Smeal's campaign distributed a sample ballot that listed the candidates in a different order from what was printed on the official ballot. Fearing voting errors, election officials reopened the polls and scrambled to track down the delegates. NOW members were "feeling real frustrated," said a former Mondale-Ferraro staffer who backed Goldsmith. The tension between the candidates "may be a reflection of that kind of fury."

Although the conference was not as rough as Collins's last messy election, she was beaten, and Goldsmith also lost to Smeal, 839–703. "They killed us in New Orleans," said Collins, describing their despair despite the relatively close vote tallies. "They just killed us." After the defeat, she left NOW for good, like Hernandez and Burnett six years earlier. Smeal's campaign manager, Patricia Ireland, who would step into the presidency herself in six years, later expressed some regret about how Goldsmith's presidency ended. "I was so driven by passion for change and so eager to succeed, it was like life or death, and if it's life or death you can beat people up if they're in the way." In the national office, the transition was tense. The employees "joked about how from now on we'd need two seats for everyone at the board meetings," said an outgoing officer: "one for each board member and one for each of their attorneys."

The delegates campaigned fiercely against one another, but they agreed on what had happened in the previous year's race for the U.S. presidency. With an air of self-congratulation, the gathered members expressed their common view that they had put Ferraro on the ticket and that their accomplishment had benefited all women. Ferraro herself was overseas with her family, but she addressed the conference in a prerecorded video. She told them that her candidacy had realized feminists' decades-old dream of being "on the inside" of American politics. "NOW has helped open wonderful doors for women," she declared. "With your help, I know we will go through them."

———

Eleanor Smeal retook NOW's presidency in September 1985 with the energy and focus she had promised. NOW spearheaded massive abortion rights marches, including one that brought eighty-five thousand protesters to the capital: "the largest march in women's rights history," Smeal boasted. She viewed such protests as a key movement-building tool. They drew media attention, energized the masses, and "touch[ed] their hearts," she said. But some in the organization disagreed. "I think feminism is more significant than getting on a bus and marching on Washington," a member told a reporter in 1987. "We need to talk about day care in my hometown." Smeal also renewed the group's focus on the ERA, as promised. NOW was nearly $2 million in debt, and abortion and the ERA were hot media issues; the leaders calculated that emphasizing them would limit the amount NOW had to spend on publicizing its own agenda.

That agenda was largely stuck. Direct-mail campaigns could still bring in vast sums, but the ERA had faded further. Not only were the powerful business lobby and the Republican Party united against it, but elected Democrats were distancing themselves from constituency groups like NOW. Many had learned from Mondale's bloody defeat that appearing to yield to such "special interests" could expose them to stinging Republican attacks. Nevertheless, the Democratic Party had become the party of NOW's issues—reproductive rights, workplace parity, and the ERA—and NOW raised millions to help Senate Democrats regain the majority in 1986. However, when the group sought more direct influence, "it was as if nothing had happened," Smeal said. Their only hope, she believed, was to "flood the ticket" with progressive women from their ranks.

When Smeal spoke in 1987, NOW had taken the shape it would keep. The organization had centralized leadership with an expensive headquarters in the capital, local chapters with the autonomy to pursue their own projects but little influence to reshape the national organization, and an insider-outsider strategy of lobbying and confronting political officials. That strategy had already proved effective; NOW's consistent pressure changed the Democratic Party. But the Democratic Party also changed NOW by persuading enough of its leaders and members to focus on politics—a focus that tethered the group to the government's rules and rhythms. On that terrain, NOW's well-placed allies offered the organization some of what it sought, but always at a price, as Republicans fought back every step of the way.

NOW had other battles to fight toward the end of the 1980s. Many young white women argued that feminism had finished its work of opening the workplace and changing American law and culture, but overlooked the gendered and racialized poverty and discrimination that remained. Conservatives continued their long game to roll feminism back, asserting that women's liberation was the real source of women's problems. Social critics replaced praise for feminists' vision and courage with the message that feminism had made women unhappy. The popular conservative talk radio host Rush Limbaugh gained popularity by declaring "feminazis" responsible for a range of social problems.

NOW's two decades of activism had transformed American life and sparked a mighty backlash. But its future looked uncertain in the late 1980s. Membership dropped from 200,000 in the mid-1980s to 140,000 at the end of the decade. Other groups began to capture some of NOW's long-held territory in the feminist landscape. Some, like the Fund for the Feminist Majority (now the Feminist Majority Foundation), which Smeal cofounded when she departed NOW's presidency for good in 1987, were multi-issue but relied on donations rather than a membership base. Others focused on reproductive health care, foregrounded the concerns of women of color and queer people, or worked overseas. These women's advocacy groups narrowed their notions of women's issues.

Feminists also advanced their agendas through all of the organizations they were part of: religious groups, universities, labor unions, professional associations, and more. To women on NOW's right, gender equality was a radical threat to the social order. To women to the left, gender equality was not enough to deliver justice. All that remained to seize was a rapidly shrinking center.

The former congresswoman Shirley Chisholm addressed this problem at NOW's 1988 convention, offering her hard-won wisdom. As one of the group's earliest board members and a 1972 candidate for the Democratic Party's presidential nomination, Chisholm understood activism and its vital role in politics. She urged the gathered leaders and members to "accept constructive criticism" by acknowledging that they falsely equated NOW's well-being with that of all women. Chisholm beseeched them not to use their organization's influence in the upcoming elections for "intimidation and threats," as they had four years earlier, but to use those elections to make a fresh start. Jesse Jackson was back on the ballot, she reminded them, and as before, he interpreted women's issues more expansively and embraced them more firmly than his rivals.

Chisholm also pointed beyond the next election: NOW needed to work broadly, not vertically, to make women a real political force. "If we're talking about power," she said, "we'll have to organize all women—black women, white women . . . all women—into the movement."

EPILOGUE:
IT WAS PERSONAL, POLITICAL,
EVERYTHING

S oon after starting this project, I met with Mary Jean Collins over sandwiches in her sunny kitchen in the Adams Morgan neighborhood of Northwest D.C. We sat less than a mile from the Washington Hilton where NOW was founded half a century earlier. Collins clearly relished recounting the details of her feminist career. She had adored traveling across the Midwest in the late 1960s, meeting different women and setting up chapters. She was still so proud of the Sears campaign. After departing NOW in 1985, Collins worked for seven years at Catholics for a Free Choice and fifteen at People for the American Way, retiring in 2008. Through it all, NOW remained closest to her heart. "There's no other organization that I've ever been a part of that is exactly the model of organizing that I subscribe to," she said. "It was personal, political, everything."

NOW was an effort to organize women for power, an idea hatched by Collins's mentors and raised up by her generation. After she left, Collins looked on as Smeal's successors kept up the focus on attention-grabbing direct action, lobbying, and fundraising with a top-heavy structure, despite

Shirley Chisholm's warnings. The group also began mobilizing around U.S. Supreme Court nominees as *Roe v. Wade* came under new threat. NOW was no longer the freewheeling and flexible grassroots-driven magnet it had been in Collins's first years there.

"Keeping something going for forty years is really not easy, to keep it new," Collins reflected in 2019. When NOW formed in the 1960s, women were already gathered in groups like the League of Women Voters. "We could have joined them," Collins said, but "we didn't want to do it their way. When you see these young people organizing and they don't want to come to you, fine," she added. "They should do their own thing."

———

Back in the Midwest, Patricia Hill Burnett had moved on and stayed active. She continued to support reproductive rights and cultivated her personal global network of five thousand feminists. When her painting career peaked in the 1980s, she was creating fifteen portraits per year. The Michigan Women's Hall of Fame inducted her in 1987. After spending a decade as a "socialite widow," she married the business consultant Robert Siler. In her first-ever "equal, loving relationship," she kept her last name, which was also that of her second husband, Harry Burnett. When Burnett left Detroit for a comfortable suburb, she sold the family home to the legendary musician Aretha Franklin.

Although Burnett was content, she still reflected on the paths her life had not taken. Right after she won the Miss Michigan title in 1942, local GOP officials had lobbied her to run for a safe seat in the state legislature. "It would have been a snap," she said, "but I didn't have any interest then." Her political awakening had come decades later, when she struggled to pursue her ambitions while meeting society's expectations for a moneyed white wife. On the eve of Burnett's ninety-fourth birthday, a few months before her death in 2014, a reporter found her still firmly pro-ERA, pro-choice, and Republican. She lamented that few younger women knew about Betty Ford, the former First Lady from Michigan whose portrait Burnett had painted: an "open and feisty" Republican woman like herself.

Burnett had left NOW behind, but the new feminism of the 1990s, which insisted that the straight, white, middle-class experience should not be its core, took up some of her ideas in surprising ways. Younger American feminists strengthened international connections, although they rejected Burnett's evangelizing approach. Tens of thousands met in Beijing in 1995 for the United Nations' Fourth World Conference on Women. That gathering crafted the Beijing Platform for Action, an expansive statement on gender equality. American feminism became even more global with the rise of the internet as activists cultivated new international networks online. NOW had gone to Beijing but seemed retrograde in this new context. The group's bare-bones website gave users few ways to connect, unlike the younger, nimbler groups that also raised funds online.

As NOW increasingly focused on electoral politics, another of Burnett's priorities, she kept arguing that the Democrats were no better for women; they "just give lip-service" to their issues, she said. NOW continued to focus on the GOP as its major impediment, but its leaders came to agree with Burnett that neither major party was a true ally. NOW even briefly helped to launch a new political party, which its founders called the 21st Century Party, in 1992. Feminist allies, including the National Abortion Rights Action League and the National Women's Political Caucus, criticized this effort for squandering the movement's limited resources and alienating friendly members of Congress.

Most Senate Democrats had voted against confirming Clarence Thomas to the U.S. Supreme Court the previous year, but feminists accused all of them of mistreating Thomas's former colleague Anita Hill when she testified that he had sexually harassed her. "Women have been the most loyal of the Democratic voters," said the NOW board member Jeanne Clarke in 1991. "We gave them our votes. We gave them our money. And they gave us Clarence Thomas." The ascent of a nominally feminist president in 1993, the Democrat Bill Clinton, only complicated matters. NOW sought to hold him accountable for campaign promises to advance feminist issues but also hesitated to risk alienating him. Members were excited, explained NOW's president, Patricia Ireland, that "we didn't have to just play defense" anymore.

But Clinton made it clear that the Democratic Party no longer feared feminist pressure or felt the need to court groups like NOW. Although he nominated the first feminist justice to the U.S. Supreme Court, Ruth Bader Ginsburg, and helped shepherd passage of the Violence Against Women Act in 1994, Clinton also responded to the GOP's pressure and midterm gains by reinventing himself as an enemy of government programs by helping Congress to gut welfare. His mounting sexual scandals squeezed NOW's leaders between guarding their access to him and protecting their own credibility. Burnett wrote to Detroit NOW in 1995 urging her onetime organization to distance itself from Clinton and the Democrats and instead try to recover "the common views in all women."

———

Aileen Hernandez agreed that NOW had become too narrow. She had also kept busy after leaving the organization in 1979. She consulted for local government agencies and continued her hallmark "awareness seminars" for corporate clients, which she framed as helping everyone understand the behaviors "that keep us from meeting the spirit as well as technicalities of equal employment opportunity laws." She charged $121 per hour for her services in 1990 ($235 today). By mid-decade, she had shrunk her firm and worked on a range of causes, from electoral politics to pesticide awareness. The latter stemmed in part from her 1998 breast cancer diagnosis, which she believed came from "something in this environment," she wrote to her brothers. Hernandez dove into the grassroots-driven Black feminist networks that thrived in the 1990s, working from the premise that "race, class, gender and sexuality are codependent variables," as the scholar and activist Barbara Ransby described Black feminism at century's end. Hernandez certainly agreed. Black women had to organize, she explained, "so that we can play a role in designating policy for the 21st century rather than passively accepting someone else's plan."

Perhaps Hernandez, in referencing others' plans, was thinking of NOW. "It has been bad for a long period of time," she said of the organization in 1996. NOW continued to launch projects intended to reach women of color while handing them little real power and attracting few to the membership. Those women of color who did join NOW still had to fight for much of what Hernandez had pursued there in the mid-1970s: a broader agenda that engaged related liberation struggles, more funding for those programs, outreach to women of color that proved that NOW was centering their concerns, and education about racism for members. Hernandez offered measured praise to mark NOW's fortieth birthday in 2006, eleven years before her death from complications of dementia. NOW was "not THE LEADER of a women's movement," she said, but "a strong partner in a very diverse coalition . . . We've still got a long way to go!"

Those who came to NOW in the 1990s also noticed other tensions. Most veteran members had stuck with it since the 1970s, sustained by memories of their early wins. By contrast, newcomers in the 1980s generally "didn't stay long term," said Kim Gandy, a longtime NOW officeholder and the group's president from 2001 to 2009, because of all the "losing." NOW's protests in the 1990s rallied a new generation of feminists who felt a stark generational gap. Smeal's successor as president, Molly Yard, explained that she visited college campuses as "a way to make money for NOW" through speaker's fees rather than build the membership. The California teen Shauna Shames attended the national conference in 1996, and she sensed "a lot of anger, or misunderstanding, or resentment, or annoyance directed at young women," she said, "like 'you don't appreciate how hard we worked.'" Several years later, she became Gandy's assistant in the national office. Younger women like her "worked out in the cubicles and got paid shit wages," while many of the officers had been in NOW for decades and "were so incompetent," Shames said. "They were making double or more, triple what we were making," although she and her peers did much of the work.

In this new era, NOW's problems were also structural. The organization attracted four thousand new members in the week after Anita Hill's powerful 1991 testimony before the U.S. Senate Judiciary Committee, seemingly without a concerted membership drive, but it was no longer primed to turn women's renewed interest in organized feminism into a sustained movement. NOW's March for Women's Lives the following year drew 750,000 participants—an unprecedented mobilization, but they lacked a locally driven infrastructure that could keep all of these women organized and engaged across the country once they returned home.

Only a few hundred of NOW's hundreds of thousands of members were meaningfully involved in general. The other members sent dues to the national office, where the leaders found that "you could get a lot done" with a "friendly" White House or Congress, said Gandy. But liberal organizations also saw their bottom lines improve when Republicans were in charge. Clinton's election depressed donations to NOW and abortion rights groups like NARAL; the NAACP's fundraising had also plummeted, because many Black people came to see its long-standing approaches of litigation and legislation ineffective to address their most pressing problems. Because NOW took no corporate, government, or foundation funds, membership dues and personal donations made up the entire budget, and the nation's economic fluctuations hit the organization especially hard.

NOW was still the mainstream media's idea of the center of feminism in the 1990s as "the McDonald's of the women's movement: recognizable and accessible to millions," as described by the feminist writer Paula Kamen, a member of "the twentysomething generation of young women." But many new organizations and ideas had entered the scene. The number of national feminist groups had risen from 75 in 1982 to 140 in the mid-1990s. NOW was increasingly displaced by a coalition of organizations that included professional women's clubs and associations, foundations, and groups focused on politics, law, and labor. NOW's membership dropped by about 10 percent each year in the last eight years of the twentieth century. Its most vital and influential era seemed to be over.

———

In 1971, the writer and activist Gloria Steinem, often misremembered as a leader of NOW, introduced the new feminism in a *New York Times* article. "The first problem for all of us, men and women, is not to learn, but to unlearn," she wrote. "Part of living this revolution is having the scales fall from our eyes." Steinem understood that old certainties must be uprooted to create a seedbed for real change.

I kept returning to Steinem's idea as I wrote this history of NOW, which has required both learning and unlearning. Growing up in a middle-class white environment in the 1990s, I saw nothing but opportunities ahead. I watched my mother, who had graduated from law school in the late 1970s, ascend the ranks of a top Chicago firm. Her career was possible because of NOW's campaigns to change the laws and tame the stereotypes that blocked women from jobs that were once men's domains.

NOW's efforts benefited me even more. In school I sat in classes, joined clubs, and played sports alongside the boys. Later I wrote college and doctoral theses on women's history, by then a respected field of study. No one called me an old maid when I turned thirty, still single. The man I later married holds the same job that I do. And so when I began to study NOW's history, my first instinct was to celebrate those brave women who had stood up to sexism and often won.

Over time, I understood how the blind spots and biases of NOW's members shaped the organization they built and infused my own out-look. When I peered back at my life through a more critical lens, different things came into view. Perhaps my mom's career represented the triumph of a kind of gender equality, but even so, she struggled mightily, enduring all the stresses of law firm life plus being the primary parent of three daughters. Neither set of responsibilities would have been manageable without other women, often women of color and immigrants, whose low-paid labors sustained us. Women of color did not just play this support-ing role in our lives; they had been erased and excluded from visions of women's leadership even though they were instrumental in securing our freedoms. We would live in a better world if white feminists of the past had not diminished the work of those women.

Furthermore, my life's advantages did not exist in the same way for many who grew up alongside me. The 1990s economic boom further stratified the wealthiest and the poorest Americans. The wage gap be-tween white and Black women surged from just below 5 percent in 1979 to 12 percent in the mid-1990s. The playing field also tilted further against children who were not white. The percentage of Black children who grew up in poverty soared at century's end, and children of color continued to receive far fewer public educational resources than their white counter-parts. Prisons overflowed with Black and Latino men and, increasingly, women, the result of several decades of tough and targeted incarcera-tion policies that were intensified by the 1994 crime bill. Another of that decade's landmark policies, the Personal Responsibility and Work

Opportunity Act of 1996, set up strict new limits on welfare and drained the pool of eligible adults. Two decades into that diminished program, it was pulling two-thirds fewer participating families out of "deep poverty" than its predecessor program, Aid to Families with Dependent Children. Conservatives in the 1990s attacked affirmative action and uprooted gay rights protections through local ballot initiatives. The Defense of Marriage Act, passed in 1996, permitted states to deny the validity of the marriages of same-sex couples who had wed elsewhere. Some of these inequalities have lessened since the 1990s, but others have held firm or expanded. America still falls far short of its stated values of equality and justice for everyone.

We cannot blame NOW for failing to bridge all of women's complex divisions or fix every problem we face today, but neither should we overlook how NOW's history—its failures and achievements—has shaped our world: a world of utterly transformed expectations around sex, family, work, and education; a world where elite women can scale the heights of influence while their sisters suffer crushing inequality and insecurity; a world where sexism thrives, but often in disguise; a world whose backlash to feminism is evidence of the movement's continued power.

———

Despite these limitations, no one should doubt that NOW transformed America. It played a key role in creating the feminist identity, making that identity mainstream and, most important, one that can be easily enacted. NOW provided a structure for feminists to launch and sustain campaigns against sexism at work, at school, at home, and in the law and culture. It inspired countless people to imagine and then pursue a more just world. It eroded the ancient consensus that women should not control their own lives, much less link arms in pursuit of equality. It took important steps to make citizenship more equitable and America's democratic promise more real. And crucially, for a time, it held down a center that permitted many feminists and feminisms to coexist in tension and collaboration. Those successes also galvanized an antifeminist response that modeled itself as NOW's mirror. They were much smaller in numbers but effective enough to batter the feminist organization by undermining its premise that women could share one agenda. NOW's sustained pressure and organizing remade both the Democratic and the Republican Parties and reshaped the nation's political landscape.

The organization was so susceptible to antifeminist attack because it fashioned itself as a nation inside the nation, a democracy for women. NOW thus had all of the potential, as well as the vulnerabilities, of any democracy: the power to broker group-based consensus as well as the need for its constituents to accept its legitimacy. Its members discovered that while the identity of "woman" holds the potential to unify, the diversity of those who claim that identity makes it inherently volatile. Strong and adaptable, customizable and universal, the organization sustained local improvisation while building national clout. As NOW revealed in its heyday, determining whether women have anything in common is less important than what they can achieve when they behave as though they do, shouldering the hard work of collaboration.

Members had to push on many fronts at once as they addressed their own internal conflicts and fought powerful opponents. Blindsided by antifeminist women and obstinate corporations in the mid-1970s, NOW forfeited its versatility by tightening its focus. The leaders turned the organization into a machine streamlined to pursue the ERA. They reframed equal political rights as the font from which all of women's gains would flow, no longer one goal within a vast and open-ended agenda that members themselves had real power to shape. This shift not only foregrounded the most privileged among them, for whom legal rights were most likely to yield meaningful benefits; it also ceded ground to their enemies. NOW had no effective counterattack against women claiming to advocate for their sex by opposing equality.

NOW's battle with conservative forces ended its most ambitious efforts and diminished its potential. As women's divisions continued to deepen, the 1960s-era vision of a feminism for all women evaporated, and the notion of uniting women across hardening lines of politics and identity went from dangerous and unorthodox to effectively unthinkable. We have forgotten that there was once an expansive and flexible membership organization that aspired to be for all women: one whose leaders included a Republican beauty queen enmeshed in elite Detroit society who tried to bridge women's differences, a Jamaican American federal official with roots in Brooklyn and the Bay Area who framed an inclusive agenda, and an Irish Catholic labor activist from blue-collar Milwaukee who led a disciplined battle against feminism's foes. As NOW sought to take seriously the full spectrum of problems women faced and advocate for them through a national mass movement, it needed this range of approaches to grow and endure.

———

In the twenty-first century, the multi-issue, membership-focused, and policy-driven feminism of NOW's golden years has yielded to a more fragmented landscape. Today feminism is diffuse, both globally and locally. The movement has many perspectives and goals, and some see its lack of cohesion as part of its power. Single-issue organizations have taken much of the space NOW once held. In feminism and other social justice efforts, the older national multi-issue organizations, especially those that were federated and had chapters, have been replaced by single-issue groups with no local outposts. Meanwhile, conservative women have fortified their own national groups, appealing to a gendered world where white heterosexual men lead and protect their families and, by extension, the nation.

Our nation is perilously divided, but there are also glimmers that the identity of "woman" can draw women together. In the wake of Donald Trump's ascent to the presidency in 2017, millions of feminists took to the streets for the Women's March, the largest one-day protest in U.S. history: an event that echoed the 1983 March on Washington's anti-Republican sentiment. The Me Too movement, which Tarana Burke started in 2006 to support sexual assault survivors, especially Black girls and women, has helped bring down some of the most influential abusers in America. Me Too gave women models for fighting back and made us less tolerant of exploitive behavior. Women and queer people of color have been the leaders and builders of grassroots power in both of these events while also leading other key efforts to end racial violence, such as Black Lives Matter. There are also women-led, issue-specific campaigns on education reform, health care, gun control, and much more. A reenergized coalition of women's rights activists and state and federal lawmakers seeks to ratify the ERA. The amendment was recently affirmed by the thirty-eighth state legislature needed for ratification, but the provision still faces legal challenges before it can be added to the Constitution. The labor movement, which was so central to NOW's rise, is itself resurgent.

An expansive national feminist organization could command the kind of prominence and grassroots strength that NOW held in its prime, but would NOW itself be the right vehicle? Today NOW calls itself "the largest organization of feminist grassroots activists in the United States," and some of its state and local chapters are thriving. NOW's website describes its "holistic," "multi-issue," and "multi-strategy" approach to feminism on six core issues: economic justice; reproductive rights and health care; the ERA; and fighting racism, anti-LGBTQ bigotry, and violence against women. In framing NOW's historic accomplishments, the site emphasizes the size of its largest rallies in Washington, D.C.: 100,000 people at its 1978 ERA march; 750,000 at the 1992 March for Women's Lives; and a record 1.15 million at the 2004 March for Women's Lives, which was then "the largest mass action of any kind in U.S. history." More recently, the organization has faced accusations of racism, ageism, and a toxic environment in its chapters, conferences, and national office. No one from that office responded to my multiple requests to be interviewed for this book.

NOW's website features prominent purple buttons inviting visitors to donate or join. I did speak with two women who recently did so and who have risen in the organization's ranks: the Massachusetts chapter president Sasha Goodfriend and the Florida chapter president Kim Porteous. Both discovered the group's long-standing problems, which range from inconsistent administration and shaky finances to generational tensions and contrasts between what NOW claims to be and what it actually accomplishes. But both activists also joined other state leaders working to forge a new era for the group that reckons honestly with its past and attempts to de-center white women like them.

Both women see potential in NOW. Like the founders and subsequent generations of members who shouldered the hard work of building NOW, which so easily could have collapsed, they have done their part to keep it standing. To Porteous, the organization is like "a great old house or an estate. It probably doesn't have the heating system working, let alone the internet. And it's going to need to be reworked. But it has great structure and it has room for everyone." Goodfriend also finds "a lot of opportunity in the bones and the structure of NOW" as an intersectional and multi-issue feminist project. "Standing up for marginalized people is the way forward," agreed Porteous. She sees herself as "holding the door open" for the next generation of feminists.

———

NOW will be theirs to claim, if they choose it.

AFTERWORD:
WHAT IT TAKES TO BEGIN AGAIN

On June 24, 2022, the U.S. Supreme Court struck down *Roe v. Wade*, which had upheld a constitutional right to abortion for forty-nine years. Some states immediately activated dormant antiabortion provisions; others advanced new ones. The majority opinion and concurrences in the case, *Dobbs v. Jackson Women's Health Organization*, also outlined rejections of the rights to interracial marriage and access to contraception, which the court has sustained since the 1960s, as well as the more recent right to marriage equality. Less than two months after the decision, Alabama's attorney general justified a state law that criminalized medical treatment for transgender youth by citing the majority's assertion that the U.S. Constitution did not protect rights that were "not deeply rooted in the nation's history and traditions." Alabama's provision builds upon a wave of recent laws, some of which predate *Dobbs*, that permit state governments to regulate gender and sexuality.

Many Americans expressed concern and anger at longtime rights—rights won by determined activists organizing during NOW's heyday—being menaced and revoked. "I'm just reeling," said the thirty-four-year-old Chicagoan Jamie Macpherson two days after the *Dobbs* decision. "It makes me afraid for what else they can take away." Some predicted practical problems in a post-*Roe* world. "People won't ever stop needing abortion," said the professor of health policy and management Jacqueline Ellison; *Dobbs* would only "further stigmatize and criminalize this essential health care that people need." Others reflected upon their own decades in the fight for protections that subsequent generations seemed to take for granted. The women's health activist and self-described "second wave feminist" Elayne Clift noted that younger women "who never experienced a pregnancy scare in pre–*Roe v. Wade* times," struggled to obtain equal credit, or suffered workplace discrimination or unchecked domestic violence were "sadly . . . about to find out what it's like and what it takes to begin again from the ground up."

Liberals and progressives, divided on how to handle that post-*Roe* world, have taken part in self-criticism and debate. Some argue that mainstream feminism became too focused on personal achievements and symbolic wins. The writer and cultural critic Susan Faludi contrasts the sustained organizing of 1970s feminists with contemporary "pop feminism's . . . faith in the power of the individual star turn over communal action." Some point to electoral politics as the way forward. "The failure of folks to pick up the shovel and fight this on the state level is why we're in the position that we're in right now," according to the Georgia voting rights advocate Nsé Ufot. Laurie Bertram Roberts, cofounder and executive director of the Mississippi Reproductive Freedom Fund, instead highlighted "the power of civil disobedience." People have different "level[s] of comfort in the movement and in risk-taking," Bertram Roberts explained, "but that doesn't mean you sit on your hands and comply in advance."

Today's NOW has engaged with this shift through a range of approaches. Chapters organized local demonstrations in the days after the *Dobbs* opinion, including one in Fayetteville, North Carolina. "I have been out here for years," said the protester Ethelyn Holden Baker, who is in her late eighties. "I have a lot to fight about, and so do you." In West Virginia, Morgantown NOW urged abortion rights supporters to voice their concerns at a public hearing in the state legislature as it considered banning abortion in the state. A few states north, Delaware NOW vowed "to continue to work with community partners to ensure that everyone in

Delaware is able to access abortion services," declared the chapter president, Melissa B. Froemming. Later that summer, NOW linked up with the Women's March, Planned Parenthood, Black Feminist Future, and other groups to co-sponsor the Women's Convention in Houston. Unlike NOW's landmark 1974 conference in that city, this convention was a multigroup gathering. It sought to build "a community with purpose" and help both longtime activists and newcomers "gain the tools needed for the fight and get a glimpse of the feminist future that they are hoping to create."

————

In this era of backlash and uncertainty, feminists have resources: in particular, long-lasting infrastructure and lessons from the past. NOW's history offers several insights that might guide us today.

NOW's decades-long presence and durable components are assets in current struggles to preserve and extend democracy. For more than half a century, NOW has worked in the background when that was more effective and returned to the headlines in moments of crisis and opportunity. In both kinds of moments, NOW's enduring armature has facilitated the work of forging consensus and advancing an agenda. NOW members, since their group's founding, have used as models the institutions they knew, taken action on the problems they saw in front of them, and employed the tools they had in hand. There is power in this flexibility, pragmatism, and institutional memory. And as a large, mainstream, and seemingly permanent feminist organization, NOW has also been a seedbed for more focused groups and has shaped a broader feminist ecosystem.

NOW's history also reveals the potential and challenge of uniting women and their allies across differences. Women from diverse backgrounds—class, race, political affiliation, region, and religion—can organize together to change American culture, politics, and institutions. They have done it before, and they have done it through NOW. The group's past missteps also have much to teach us about hard trade-offs, the damage of internal conflicts, and the perils of sacrificing grassroots agency for centralized control.

The greatest lesson NOW provides, though, may be that even large organizations can change. NOW itself can continue to adjust to meet the needs of its members today. It has adapted many times before. Women whose priorities were sidelined within the organization have called attention to its promise to stand for all women and demanded inclusion and reform. Generations of members have believed enough in NOW—in its core mission, in its power through coalition—to insist that it live up to its promise to broadly advocate for women.

And NOW is still here, both as an organization and as a wellspring of ideas and practices. It is still framing conversations about how to transform America into a more just nation. In this, we might find some reassurance despite the challenges ahead of us. History brings the comfort that we are not starting from scratch.

APPENDIX A

THE FOUNDERS OF NOW

These twenty-eight women broke away from the Third National Conference of Commissions on the Status of Women to form NOW. They signed their names, and most paid $5 membership dues, at the Washington Hilton in Washington, D.C., on June 30, 1966.

Ada Allness

Mary Evelyn Benbow

Gene Boyer

Analoyce Clapp

Kathryn "Kay" Clarenbach

Catherine Conroy

Caroline Davis

Mary Eastwood

Edith Finlayson

Betty Friedan

Dorothy Haener

Anna Roosevelt Halstead

Lorene Harrington

Mary Lou Hill

Esther Johnson

Nancy Knaak

Min Matheson

Helen Moreland

Dr. Pauli Murray (later Rev.)

Ruth Murray

Inka O'Hanrahan

Pauline A. Parish

Eve Purvis

Edna Schwartz

Mary-jane Ryan Snyder

Gretchen Squires

Betty Talkington

Dr. Caroline Ware

At NOW's first national conference, held on October 29–30, 1966, these twenty-one women and men comprised a second set of founders. They gathered at the Washington Post Building in Washington, D.C., joined by nine of

the original founders, to endorse the group's Statement of Purpose and elect its officers.

Caruthers Berger
Colleen Boland
Inez Casiano
Carl Degler
Elizabeth Drews
Muriel Fox
Dr. Mary Esther Gaulden
   (later Jagger)
Ruth Gober
Richard Graham
Anna Arnold Hedgeman

Lucille Kapplinger (later Hazell)
Bessie Margolin
Margorie Palmer
Sonia Pressman (later Fuentes)
Sister Joel Read
Amy Robinson
Charlotte Roe
Alice Rossi
Claire R. Salmond
Morag Simchak
Clara Wells

See "Honoring Our Founders & Pioneers," National Organization for Women, accessed August 10, 2022, now.org/about/history/honoring-our-founders-pioneers.

APPENDIX B

NOW IN 1974

In late 1973, NOW's national office sent a detailed survey to a random sample of five hundred of the group's approximately forty thousand members. The national office tabulated the responses and made them available to members and the media at NOW's May 1974 national conference in Houston.

The survey offers a unique snapshot of the group's membership in its mid-1970s heyday.

Sex: Female: 91%; Male: 9%.

Age: Under 20: 5%; 20–29: 42%; 30–39: 20%; 40–49: 21%; 50–59: 9%; Over 60: 3%.

Marital Status: Single: 34%; Married: 55%; Divorced: 4%; Widowed: 5%.

Racial Background: White: 90%; Black: 5%; Asian: 1%; Puerto Rican: 2%; Mexican/Spanish American: 1%; Other: 1%.

Sexual Orientation: Heterosexual: 81%; Lesbian: 8%; Bisexual: 9%; Celibate: 2%.

Highest Grade of School Completed: 8th Grade or Less: 1%; Some High School: 3%; High School Graduate: 8%; Some College: 16%; 2-Year College Graduate: 5%; 4-Year College Graduate: 36%; Master's Degree: 21%; Doctoral Degree: 9%; Trade School: 1%.

Where Do You Live?: Rural: 8%; Farm: 2%; Non-farm: 2%; Urban:

23%; City or Village of 2,500–50,000: 27%; City of 50,000 or More: 36%; Suburb: 2%.

Work for Pay Outside the Home: Full-Time: 63%; Part-Time: 15%; Not at All: 22%.

Primary Occupation: Homemaker: 17%; Working in the Feminist Movement: 2%; Student: 14%; Professional: 25%; Teacher: 11%; Artist: 5%; Executive: 9%; Clerical: 8%; Sales: 3%; Service Worker: 3%.

Union Member: Yes: 16%; No: 84%.

How Many Children Do You Have?: None: 27%; One: 14%; Two: 24%; Three: 17%; Four: 6%; Five: 3%; Six or More: 9%.

Spouse's Occupation (if Married): Homemaker: 3%; Working in the Feminist Movement: 0%; Student: 4%; Professional: 35%; Teacher: 12%; Artist: 1%; Executive: 18%; Clerical: 17%; Sales: 4%; Service Worker: 1%; Skilled Craft Worker: 5%.

Total 1972 Household Income: Under $2,500 ($14,270 today): 5%; between $2,500 and $4,999 ($14,270–$28,500 today): 5%; between $5,000 and $9,999 ($28,500–$57,100 today): 20%; between $10,000 and $14,999 ($57,100–$85,600 today): 21%; between $15,000 and $19,999 ($85,600–$114,200 today): 6%; between $20,000 and $29,999 ($114,200–$171,200 today): 18%; between $30,000 and $39,999 ($171,200–$228,300 today): 19%; $40,000 or more ($228,300 today): 6%.

Political Orientation: Democrat: 53%; Republican: 15%; Independent: 25%.

Political Philosophy: Radical Left: 9%; Liberal: 62%; Middle of the Road: 12%; Conservative: 8%; Radical Right: 4%.

Have You Ever Had an Abortion?: Yes: 20%; No: 80%.

Do You Belong to a NOW Chapter?: Yes: 69%; No: 31%.

How Did You First Learn About NOW?: Through Friends: 32%; News Coverage of NOW: 34%; NOW Advertising: 9%; Public Meeting or Conference: 5%; Feminist Literature: 16%; NOW Speaker at Non-NOW Meeting: 4%.

Other Organizations You Belong To: Business or Professional Groups: 39%; League of Women Voters: 13%; American Association of University Women: 6%; National Women's Political Caucus: 16%; Environmental Groups: 22%; Consumer Groups: 14%; Civil Rights Groups: 23%; Gay Liberation Groups: 3%; Abortion Repeal or Reform Groups: 6%; Church- or Synagogue-Sponsored Groups: 21%; Student Activist Groups: 4%; Other Feminist Groups: 12%.

How Long Have You Been a NOW Member?: Less Than One Year: 13%; One Year: 47%; Two Years: 27%; Three Years: 7%; Four Years: 4%; Five Years: 1%; Six Years: 1%.

Do You Want NOW to Provide Services to Members Such as Insurance, Credit Unions, Travel Agencies, Etc.?: Yes: 66%; No: 34%.

Which of the Following Should Receive Greatest Emphasis from NOW? (respondents could choose more than one): Legislation: 57%; Image of Women: 48%; Business Industry Compliance and Enforcement: 41%; Child Care: 29%; Credit and Insurance: 28%; Elementary and Secondary Education: 27%. (The published results did not include all of the categories listed in the survey.) Receiving the fewest responses were: Sexuality and Lesbianism: 9%; Volunteerism: 6%; Women and Sports: 6%; Ecumenism: 6%; Labor Unions: 5%; Women and Arts: 4%; Stockholders Action Program: 4%.

See "Summary of Questionnaire for NOW," ca. early 1974, folder 4, box 45, Karen DeCrow (1937–2014) Papers, 31/6/94, Northwestern University Archive; "Who Are We? Results of Survey of NOW's Membership," *Do It NOW*, July 1974, 15; and Marsha Dubrow, "Urge Ban of Little League Baseball: Feminists Would Alter Male's Role in Society," *Globe and Mail*, June 8, 1974, 15.

NOTES

PROLOGUE: YOU CAN'T STOP NOW

3 *The economy was contracting*: Nelson Lichtenstein, *State of the Union: A Century of American Labor* (Princeton, N.J.: Princeton University Press, 2013), 212–13; Judith Stein, *Pivotal Decade: How the United States Traded Factories for Finance in the Seventies* (Princeton, N.J.: Princeton University Press, 2010), 101–17.

3 *The Watergate scandal had*: Kevin M. Kruse and Julian E. Zelizer, *Fault Lines: A History of the United States Since 1974* (New York: Norton, 2019), 8–10.

3 *The Vietnam War*: Robert Self, *All in the Family: The Realignment of American Democracy Since the 1960s* (New York: Hill and Wang, 2012), 47–74.

3 *The nonviolent interracial*: Kruse and Zelizer, *Fault Lines*, 26–30, 48.

3 *A clear majority*: Mark R. Daniels, Robert Darcy, and Joseph W. Westphal, "The ERA Won. At Least in the Opinion Polls," *PS* 15, no. 4 (Autumn 1982): 578; Civil Rights Act of 1964 § 7, 42 U.S.C. § 2000e et seq. (1964); Education Amendments Act of 1972, 20 U.S.C. §§1681–1688 (2018).

3 *The previous year*: *Roe v. Wade*, 410 U.S. 113 (1973).

4 *"scores of musical accents"*: Vicki Giella, "Impressions of the National Conference," *NOW Newsletter* [Los Angeles chapter], July 1974, 5, "California–Los Angeles" folder, box 2, NOW Chapter Newsletters Collection, Schlesinger Library, Harvard Radcliffe Institute.

4 *"the barefoot to"*: Laurie Johnston, "NOW Expands the List of What It's For and What It's Against," *New York Times*, June 1, 1974, 18.

4 *"working women, housewives"*: Giella, "Impressions of the National Conference," 5.

4 *"It Was a Man's"*: Marsha Dubrow, "Urge Ban of Little League Baseball: Feminists Would Alter Male's Role in Society," *Globe and Mail*, June 8, 1974, 15.

4 *"older" women*: Johnston, "NOW Expands the List of What It's For and What It's Against," 18.

4 *trimming their agenda*: "Resolutions from the 1974 NOW National Conference," *Do It NOW*, July 1974, 14.

4 *thirty-seven thousand additional members*: "Election and Debate on Agenda as NOW Begins Convention," *New York Times*, May 26, 1974, 35; Dubrow, "Urge Ban of Little League Baseball," 15.

4 *"You Can't Stop NOW"*: "Women's Fate Affects Men Also—NOW Head," *Los Angeles Times*, May 26, 1974, 6.

4 *Only eight years earlier*: NOW Statement of Purpose, adopted Oct. 29, 1966, accessed Oct. 24, 2021, now.org/about/history/statement-of-purpose.

6 *"not prepared to do"*: "Aileen Hernandez, Former President, NOW," Makers, Oct. 26, 2012, www.makers.com/profiles/591f2765bea17771623a7f48/554890e6e4b0f61941d18562.

6 *"that our society is"*: Aileen Hernandez, "Remarks," Frankel Lecture Series, University of Houston Law School, Feb. 14, 1975, 3, unlabeled folder, box 122, Aileen Hernandez Papers, Sophia Smith Collection, Smith College.

6 *"everything little girls"*: Betty J. Blair, "A Liberated Miss Michigan Looks to New Challenges for the Women's Movement," *Detroit News*, April 22, 1977, folder 31, box 24, NOW Records, Schlesinger Library.

6 *At fifty years old*: Patricia Hill Burnett résumé, n.d., ca. Jan. 1974, folder 15, box 22, Wilma Scott Heide Papers, 1968–85, Schlesinger Library; Patricia Hill Burnett, *True Colors: An Artist's Journey from Beauty Queen to Feminist* (Troy, Mich.: Momentum Books, 1995), 1, 4.

7 *"the Democrats were"*: Collins, interview by author, Oct. 30–31, 2015, 1.

7 *"lesbian feelings"*: Collins, interview by author, Feb. 22, 2019, 1, 8.

7 *"clique-iness and passive aggression"*: "Michelle Goldberg Grapples with Feminism After Roe," *The Ezra Klein Show*, July 8, 2022, www.nytimes.com/2022/07/08/opinion/ezra-klein-podcast-michelle-goldberg.html?showTranscript=1.

7 *"fatally privileged"*: Rachel Cooke, "Amia Srinivasan: 'Sex as a Subject Isn't Weird. It's Very, Very Serious,'" *Guardian*, Aug. 8, 2021, www.theguardian.com/world/2021/aug/08/amia-srinivasan-the-right-to-sex-interview.

7 *"oblivious to race and class"*: Susan Faludi, "Feminism Made a Faustian Bargain with Celebrity Culture. Now It's Paying the Price," *New York Times*, June 20, 2022, www.nytimes.com/2022/06/20/opinion/roe-heard-feminism-backlash.html. Faludi outlines and argues against this common criticism of 1970s feminism.

7 *"second-wave feminism"*: Although the term "second-wave feminism" persists in popular culture, scholars have critiqued it as simplistic and exclusionary. See, for example, the essays in *No Permanent Waves: Recasting Histories of U.S. Feminism*, ed. Nancy A. Hewitt (New Brunswick, N.J.: Rutgers University Press, 2010). For a nuanced history of feminism from the late 1960s to the early 1980s, see Sara Evans, *Tidal Wave: How Women Changed America at Century's End* (New York: Free Press, 2004). Histories of feminism that take a longer view include Dorothy Sue Cobble, Linda Gordon, and Astrid Henry, *Feminism Unfinished: A Short, Surprising History of Women's Movements* (New York: Liveright, 2014); Estelle B. Freedman, *No Turning Back: The History of Feminism and the Future of Women* (New York: Ballantine, 2002); Annelise Orleck, *Rethinking American Women's Activism* (New York: Routledge, 2015); and Christine Stansell, *The Feminist Promise, 1792 to the Present* (New York: Modern Library, 2010).

7 *Some pit NOW members*: On NOW's treatment in historical overviews of feminism, see, for example, Cobble, Gordon, and Henry, *Feminism Unfinished*, 69, 90–92, 107–10; Evans, *Tidal Wave*, 24–26, 40–46, 61–97; Orleck, *Rethinking American Women's Activism*, 84–87; and Stansell, *Feminist Promise*, 211–17, 275–84, 297.

8 *In stressing women's differences*: Fine-grained accounts of local feminism include Melissa Estes Blair, *Revolutionizing Expectations: Women's Organizations, Feminism, and American Politics, 1965–1980* (Athens: University of Georgia Press, 2014); Finn Enke, *Finding the Movement: Sexuality, Contested Space, and Feminist Activism* (Durham, N.C.: Duke University Press, 2007); and Stephanie Gilmore, *Groundswell: Grassroots Feminist Activism in Postwar America* (New York: Routledge, 2013). Histories of feminism that examine the movement's internal divides

include Benita Roth, *Separate Roads to Feminism: Black, Chicana, and White Feminist Movements During the 1960s and 1970s* (Cambridge, U.K.: Cambridge University Press, 2003); Stansell, *Feminist Promise*; and Kirsten Swinth, *Feminism's Forgotten Fight: The Unfinished Struggle for Work and Family* (Cambridge, Mass.: Harvard University Press, 2018).

8 *dovetails with broader*: Jefferson Cowie, *The Great Exception: The New Deal and the Limits of American Politics* (Princeton, N.J.: Princeton University Press, 2016), 27–28, 190; Kruse and Zelizer, *Fault Lines*, esp. 5–6; Mark Lilla, *The Once and Future Liberal* (New York: Harper, 2017), 35–36; Daniel T. Rodgers, *Age of Fracture* (Cambridge, Mass.: Belknap Press of Harvard University Press, 2011), 3, 12, 145–46; and Self, *All in the Family*, 7–11. Lane Windham, *Knocking on Labor's Door: Union Organizing in the 1970s and the Roots of a New Economic Divide* (Chapel Hill: University of North Carolina Press, 2017), is an important exception to this narrative of decline.

8 *To trace NOW's longer arc*: On local NOW chapters, see Judith Ezekiel, *Feminism in the Heartland* (Columbus: Ohio State University Press, 2002); Gilmore, *Groundswell*; Stephanie Gilmore and Elizabeth Kaminski, "A Part and Apart: Lesbian and Straight Feminist Activists Negotiate Identity in a Second-Wave Organization," *Journal of the History of Sexuality* 16, no. 1 (Jan. 2007): 95–113; Stephanie Gilmore, "The Dynamics of Second-Wave Feminist Activism in Memphis, 1971–1982: Rethinking the Liberal/Radical Divide," *NWSA Journal* 15, no. 1 (Spring 2003): 94–117; Jo Reger and Suzanne Staggenborg, "Patterns of Mobilization in Local Movement Organizations: Leadership and Strategy in Four National Organization for Women Chapters," *Sociological Perspectives* 49 (Fall 2006): 297–323; Suzanne Staggenborg, "Stability and Innovation in the Women's Movement: A Comparison of Two Movement Organizations," *Social Problems* 36 (Feb. 1989): 710–27. On single issues, see Marisa Chappell, "Rethinking Women's Politics in the 1970s: The League of Women Voters and the National Organization for Women Confront Poverty," *Journal of Women's History* 13, no. 4 (Jan. 2002): 115–79; Deborah Dinner, "The Universal Childcare Debate: Rights Mobilization, Social Policy, and the Dynamics of Feminist Activism, 1966–1974," *Law and History Review* 28 (Aug. 2010): 577–628; Lisa Levenstein, "'Don't Agonize, Organize!': The Displaced Homemakers Campaign and the Contested Goals of 1970s Feminism," *Journal of American History* 100 (March 2014): 144–68; Nancy MacLean, *Freedom Is Not Enough: The Opening of the American Workplace* (Cambridge, Mass.: Russell Sage Foundation Books at Harvard University Press, 2006), 117–54; Katherine Turk, "Out of the Revolution, into the Mainstream: Employment Activism in the NOW Sears Campaign and the Growing Pains of Liberal Feminism," *Journal of American History* 97 (Sept. 2010): 399–423. Biographies of NOW founders and leaders include Patricia Bell-Scott, *The Firebrand and the First Lady: Portrait of a Friendship: Pauli Murray, Eleanor Roosevelt, and the Struggle for Justice* (New York: Knopf, 2016); Eleanor Humes Haney, *A Feminist Legacy: The Ethics of Wilma Scott Heide and Company* (Buffalo, N.Y.: Margaretdaughters, 1985); Daniel Horowitz, *Betty Friedan and the Making of "The Feminine Mystique"* (Amherst: University of Massachusetts Press, 2000); Susan Oliver, *Betty Friedan: The Personal Is Political* (New York: Pearson, 2007); Judith Paterson, *Be Somebody: A Biography of Marguerite Rawalt* (Fort Worth, Tex.: Eakin Press, 1986); Rosalind Rosenberg, *Jane Crow: The Life of Pauli Murray* (Oxford: Oxford University Press, 2017); Troy R. Saxby, *Pauli Murray: A Personal and Political Life* (Chapel Hill: University of North Carolina Press, 2020); and Jennifer Scanlon, *Until There Is Justice: The Life of Anna Arnold Hedgeman* (Oxford: Oxford University Press, 2016). In dozens of volumes, scholars and participants have recounted NOW's founding moment. See, for example, Cobble, Gordon, and Henry, *Feminism Unfinished*, 59–62; Gilmore, *Groundswell*, 21–33; Stansell, *Feminist Promise*, 211–17; Cynthia Harrison, *On Account of Sex: The Politics of Women's Issues, 1945–1968* (Berkeley: University of California Press, 1988), 192–209. Firsthand accounts

include Betty Friedan, *"It Changed My Life": Writings on the Women's Movement* (New York: Random House, 1976), 75–86; Pauli Murray, *Song in a Weary Throat: Memoir of an American Pilgrimage* (New York: HarperCollins, 1987), 359–68; and several of the interviews curated in Brigid O'Farrell and Joyce L. Kornbluh, *Rocking the Boat: Union Women's Voices, 1915–1975* (New Brunswick, N.J.: Rutgers University Press, 1996). See Maryann Barakso, *Governing NOW* (Ithaca, N.Y.: Cornell University Press, 2004), for an analysis of NOW's governance structures.

1. WE RECOGNIZED THE HONEST FIRE

11 *At ten o'clock*: Murray, *Song in a Weary Throat*, 366–67. Several other sources date the meeting in Friedan's room to June 28, 1966, and NOW's founding to the following day. See, for example, Marcia Cohen, *The Sisterhood: The True Story of the Women Who Changed the World* (New York: Simon and Schuster, 1988), 137; Toni Carabillo, Judith Meuli, and June Bundy Csida, *Feminist Chronicles, 1953–1993* (Los Angeles: Women's Graphics, 1993), 24; and NOW's own website: "Honoring Our Founders & Pioneers," National Organization for Women, accessed Aug. 10, 2022, now.org/about/history/honoring-our-founders-pioneers. But according to the official program (*Targets for Action: The Report of the Third Annual National Conference of Commissions on the Status of Women* [Washington, D.C.: U.S. Women's Bureau, 1966], v–vii) and contemporary newspaper accounts ("Washington Proceedings," *New York Times*, June 28, 1966, 39; "Delegates Attend Washington Meeting," *Los Angeles Times*, June 30, 1966, WS9; and "Women Are Poverty War Force: Johnson," *Chicago Tribune*, June 29, 1966, B7), the conference spanned Tuesday, June 28, to Thursday, June 30. Firsthand accounts and secondary sources concur that the meeting in Friedan's room happened on the second night of the conference and NOW's founders established the organization the next day during and after the closing luncheon. See, for example, Murray, *Song in a Weary Throat*, 366; Friedan, *"It Changed My Life,"* 83; Carabillo, Meuli, and Csida, *Feminist Chronicles*, 24; and Cohen, *Sisterhood*, 133, 136.

11 *"reception and buffet"*: Mattie Belle Davis, "Third National Conference of Commissions on the Status of Women," *Women Lawyers Journal* 52 (Summer 1966), 109; Catherine Conroy, interview by Elizabeth Balanoff, Aug./Dec. 1976, Institute of Labor and Industrial Relations, University of Michigan (Sanford, N.C.: Microfilming Corp. of America, 1978), 50–51; Carabillo, Meuli, and Csida, *Feminist Chronicles*, 21.

11 *the women passed through*: "Nostalgic Décor Spells Welcome," *Washington Post*, March 10, 1965, B5.

11 *they filled paper cups*: Carabillo, Meuli, and Csida, *Feminist Chronicles*, 21.

11 *"little bar"*: Mary Eastwood, interview by Muriel Fox, March 7, 1992, 6, 10, folder 4, box 3, Tully-Crenshaw Feminist Oral History Project, Schlesinger Library.

11 *some folding their legs*: Cohen, *Sisterhood*, 133.

11 *"long, long" day*: Eastwood, interview by Fox, 10.

11 *Pauli Murray surveyed*: Troy R. Saxby, *Pauli Murray: A Personal and Political Life* (Chapel Hill: University of North Carolina Press, 2020), 3–16.

12 *In her view*: MacLean, *Freedom Is Not Enough*, 122.

12 *Women's activism was*: On suffrage activism and its racial politics, see Cathleen Cahill, *Recasting the Vote: How Women of Color Transformed the Suffrage Movement* (Chapel Hill: University of North Carolina Press, 2020); and Martha Jones, *Vanguard: How Black Women Broke Barriers, Won the Vote, and Insisted on Equality for All* (New York: Basic Books, 2020).

12 *Murray was on a mission*: Serena Mayeri, *Reasoning from Race: Feminism, Law, and the Civil Rights Revolution* (Cambridge, Mass.: Harvard University Press, 2011), 3–4.

12 *She and her co-author*: Pauli Murray and Mary O. Eastwood, "Jane Crow and the Law:

Sex Discrimination and Title VII," *George Washington Law Review* 34, no. 2 (Dec. 1965): 232–56.

12 *She waited somewhat impatiently*: Murray, *Song in a Weary Throat*, 366–67.

12 *After several minutes*: Carabillo, Meuli, and Csida, *Feminist Chronicles*, 21–24.

12 *"an independent national"*: Murray, *Song in a Weary Throat*, 366.

12 *Those East Coast lawyers*: Friedan, *"It Changed My Life,"* 75, 80–82.

12 *Fearful that outspoken activism*: Paterson, *Be Somebody*, 159.

12 *Wisconsin labor leader*: O'Farrell and Kornbluh, *Rocking the Boat*, 231–35; Jamakaya, *Like Our Sisters Before Us: Women of Wisconsin Labor* (Milwaukee: Wisconsin Labor History Society, 1998), 28–29.

12 *Conroy was "built square"*: Gene Boyer, interview by Muriel Fox, June 12, 1991, 42, folder 8, box 1, Tully-Crenshaw Feminist Oral History Project.

13 *The daughter of*: Jamakaya, *Like Our Sisters Before Us*, 23–29; O'Farrell and Kornbluh, *Rocking the Boat*, 233–35. On the history of telephone work—especially its race and gender politics—see Venus Green, *Race on the Line: Gender, Labor, and Technology in the Bell System, 1880–1980* (Durham, N.C.: Duke University Press, 2001).

13 *But Conroy and*: Conroy, interview by Balanoff, 49; Genevieve G. McBride, ed., *Women's Wisconsin: From Native Matriarchies to the New Millennium* (Madison: Wisconsin Historical Society Press, 2005), 437.

13 *Murray tried to*: Carabillo, Meuli, and Csida, *Feminist Chronicles*, 20–23.

13 *Many Americans in*: Nancy MacLean, *The American Women's Movement, 1945–2000: A Brief History with Documents* (Boston: Bedford/St. Martin's, 2009), 9–14; Van Gosse, *Rethinking the New Left: An Interpretive History* (New York: Palgrave Macmillan, 2005), 10.

14 *Many states forced*: Stephanie Coontz, *A Strange Stirring: "The Feminine Mystique" and American Women at the Dawn of the 1960s* (New York: Basic Books, 2010), 6.

14 *"stitch rule"*: Coontz, *Strange Stirring*, 13.

14 *the U.S. Supreme Court*: *Hoyt v. Florida*, 368 U.S. 57 (1961).

14 *For women of color*: *Loving v. Virginia*, 388 U.S. 1 (1967).

14 *Some states prohibited women*: MacLean, *American Women's Movement*, 11.

14 *"the perfect follower"*: Coontz, *Strange Stirring*, 15.

15 *Turning on her television*: Ruth Rosen, *The World Split Open: How the Modern Women's Movement Changed America* (New York: Penguin, 2001), xi–xii; Coontz, *Strange Stirring*, 17.

15 *some proprietors denied women*: Deborah Dinner and Elizabeth Sepper, "Sex in Public," *Yale Law Journal* 129, no. 1 (2019): 86–87. See also Georgina Hickey, "Barred from the Barroom: Second Wave Feminists and Public Accommodations in U.S. Cities," *Feminist Studies* 34 (Fall 2008): 382–408.

15 *"It's men only at lunch"*: "Viewpoint," *Hospitality*, Feb. 1970, 10C, folder 14, box 15, Mary Jean Collins NOW Officer Papers, Schlesinger Library.

15 *Groups ranging from*: Dinner and Sepper, "Sex in Public," 81.

15 *"executive flight"*: Joseph Boyce, "Friendly Skies Thunder with Gals' Protest," *Chicago Tribune*, Feb. 15, 1969, W5.

15 *To test the policy*: Karen DeCrow, interview by Frances Arick Kolb, Feb. 15, 1981, 11, folder 10, box 2, Tully-Crenshaw Feminist Oral History Project.

15 *"business woman"*: Mary Jean Collins, interview by Rebecca Davison, n.d., 3.

15 *Political leadership too*: Through the 1950s, "the face of political power was still male," write Stacie Taranto and Leandra Zarnow; while women could lobby and volunteer, their political influence was "indirect" at best. Taranto and Zarnow, *Suffrage at 100: Women in American Politics Since 1920* (Baltimore: Johns Hopkins University Press, 2020), 6, 7. Melissa Estes Blair argues that the presidential campaigns of Franklin D. Roosevelt, Harry S. Truman, and

Dwight D. Eisenhower made robust efforts to motivate and persuade women as voters. Estes Blair, "'I Have Talked to You Not as Women but as American Citizens': The Gender Ideology of Presidential Campaigns, 1940-1956," in *Suffrage at 100*, ed. Taranto and Zarnow, 183–198. See also Catherine Rymph, *Republican Women: Feminism and Conservatism from Suffrage Through the Rise of the New Right* (Chapel Hill: University of North Carolina Press, 2006), 4.

15 *The breadwinner-homemaker model*: Alice Kessler-Harris, *Out to Work: A History of Wage-Earning Women in the United States* (Oxford: Oxford University Press, 1982), 300–302; Gail Collins, *When Everything Changed: The Amazing Journey of American Women from 1960 to the Present* (New York: Little, Brown, 2009), 15–17.

15 *Classified ads in newspapers*: Rosen, *World Split Open*, xi.

16 *This separation previewed*: Kessler-Harris, *Out to Work*, 303.

16 *Sexual harassment*: Carrie N. Baker, *The Women's Movement Against Sexual Harassment* (Cambridge, U.K.: Cambridge University Press, 2007), 1.

16 *the U.S. Supreme Court*: *Meritor Savings Bank v. Vinson*, 477 U.S. 57 (1986).

16 *pundits accused them*: Mayeri, *Reasoning from Race*, 23–25.

16 *women who were not attached*: Premilla Nadasen, *Rethinking the Welfare Rights Movement* (New York: Routledge, 2012), 5–6; Alison Lefkovitz, "Men in the House: Race, Welfare, and the Regulation of Men's Sexuality in the United States, 1961–1972," *Journal of the History of Sexuality* 20, no. 3 (Sept. 2011): 594–614.

16 *"Hell yes, we have a quota"*: Collins, *When Everything Changed*, 20.

16 *Women were 7 percent*: Martha Weinman Lear, "The Second Feminist Wave," *New York Times*, March 10, 1968, SM24.

16 *Even in the rare case*: Louis Hyman, "Ending Discrimination, Legitimating Debt: The Political Economy of Race, Gender, and Credit Access in the 1960s and 1970s," *Enterprise and Society* 12, no. 1 (March 2011): 202.

16 *After the early*: Stansell, *Feminist Promise*, 179–80.

16 *women remained active*: Evans, *Tidal Wave*, 6; Gosse, *Rethinking the New Left*, 75.

16 *Since the nineteenth century*: There is a vast literature on women's reform movements. For an overview focused on the United States, see Orleck, *Rethinking American Women's Activism*. For an analysis of American activist women's international campaigns, see Dorothy Sue Cobble, *For the Many: American Feminists and the Global Fight for Democratic Equality* (Princeton, N.J.: Princeton University Press, 2021).

17 *Young women in the early 1960s*: Compared with their parents, they married older, bore fewer children, divorced more often, and were more likely to live in a two-earner household. See Alison Lefkovitz, *Strange Bedfellows: Marriage in the Age of Women's Liberation* (Philadelphia: University of Pennsylvania Press, 2018), 11.

17 *Their most important official*: Kathleen A. Laughlin, *Women's Work and Public Policy: A History of the Women's Bureau, 1945–1970* (Boston: Northeastern University Press, 2000), esp. 6–9; Judith Sealander, *As Minority Becomes Majority: Federal Reaction to the Phenomenon of Women in the Work Force, 1920–1963* (Westport, Conn.: Greenwood, 1983), 22–23.

17 *These laws put a floor*: Nancy Woloch, *A Class by Herself: Protective Laws for Women Workers, 1890s–1990s* (Princeton, N.J.: Princeton University Press, 2015), 1–2.

17 *The bureau struck*: Kessler-Harris, *Out to Work*, 313; Woloch, *Class by Herself*, 190.

17 *The first chairperson*: Bell-Scott, *The Firebrand and the First Lady*, 192–93; "Global Issues: Gender Equality," United Nations, accessed May 20, 2021, www.un.org/en/global -issues/gender-equality.

17 *More than a decade*: Dorothy Sue Cobble, *The Other Women's Movement: Workplace Justice and Social Rights in Modern America* (Princeton, N.J.: Princeton University Press, 2005), 159–61.

18 *"the most significant"*: Murray, *Song in a Weary Throat*, 347.

18 *The commission's final report*: The President's Commission on the Status of Women, *American Women* (Washington, D.C.: U.S. Government Printing Office, 1963).

18 *March on Washington*: William G. Nunn, "'I Have a Dream . . . Today!': Negroes Given Rallying Cry by Dr. M. L. King Jr.," *Pittsburgh Courier*, Sept. 7, 1963, 1. Some estimate the number of participants at the March on Washington at 250,000. See, for example, Bell-Scott, *The Firebrand and the First Lady*, 321.

18 *Its authors encouraged employers*: Stansell, *Feminist Promise*, 198–203; Cobble, *Other Women's Movement*, 168–73.

18 *The reformers on*: Stansell, *Feminist Promise*, 206–8; Cobble, *For the Many*, 351.

18 *Smith believed that*: Gillian Thomas, *Because of Sex: One Law, Ten Cases, and Fifty Years That Changed American Women's Lives* (New York: St. Martin's Press, 2016), 2. Congresswoman Martha Griffiths, a women's rights advocate, had considered proposing the "sex" amendment. Once she heard that Smith was considering the same move, she let him go ahead in hopes that his advocacy would motivate his conservative allies to support the amendment. Rebecca Onion, "The Real Story Behind 'Because of Sex,'" *Slate*, June 16, 2020, www.slate .com/news-and-politics/2020/06/title-vii-because-of-sex-howard-smith-history.html.

18 *Born in Baltimore*: Rosenberg, *Jane Crow*, 1–4. For more on Murray's life, see Glenda Gilmore, *Defying Dixie: The Radical Roots of Civil Rights* (New York: Norton, 2008); Saxby, *Pauli Murray*; Bell-Scott, *The Firebrand and the First Lady*; and Murray's autobiographies, *Proud Shoes: The Story of an American Family* (Boston: Beacon Press, 1956) and *Song in a Weary Throat*.

19 *"The harsh reality"*: Murray quoted in Mayeri, *Reasoning from Race*, 15.

19 *"one of nature's experiments"*: Kathryn Schulz, "The Many Lives of Pauli Murray," *New Yorker*, April 10, 2017, www.newyorker.com/magazine/2017/04/17/the-many-lives-of-pauli -murray. Transgender studies and shifts in our culture have transformed how we think about language and identity. Historians now sometimes identify queer subjects with the pronoun "they" when their subjects did not use that pronoun. They have pointed out that those subjects might not have been able to freely claim a nonbinary or trans identity in their own era. See Jen Manion, *Female Husbands: A Trans History* (Cambridge, U.K.: Cambridge University Press, 2020), 11–14, for more discussion. More specifically, scholars have debated whether to refer to Murray as "she" or "they" in light of evidence that she sometimes trans-ed her gender and explored medically changing the sex she was assigned at birth. Rosenberg explains her rationale for referring to Murray as "she" in *Jane Crow*, xvii. I, too, have chosen to refer to Murray as "she," which was the pronoun she used in her lifetime.

19 *"the civil rights bill"*: MacLean, *Freedom Is Not Enough*, 121.

19 *Lawmakers signed the Civil Rights Act*: Pub.L. 88–352, 78 Stat. 241, enacted July 2, 1964.

19 *They feared that*: Cobble, *Other Women's Movement*, 171.

19 *Leaders of the*: Louis Menand, "How Women Got in on the Civil Rights Act," *New Yorker*, July 21, 2014, www.newyorker.com/magazine/2014/07/21/sex-amendment.

19 *Among them were members*: Harrison, *On Account of Sex*, 192–93; Cobble, *Other Women's Movement*, 182–84; Katherine Turk, *Equality on Trial: Gender and Rights in the Modern American Workplace* (Philadelphia: University of Pennsylvania Press, 2016), 12–42.

20 *Nearly one-third of complaints*: Menand, "How Women Got in on the Civil Rights Act."

20 *Presidents Dwight D. Eisenhower and Kennedy*: Gosse, *Rethinking the New Left*, 3.

20 *"How did we know"*: Friedan, *"It Changed My Life,"* 81.

20 *they had been central*: Daina Ramey Berry and Kali Nicole Gross, *A Black Women's History of the United States* (Boston: Beacon Press, 2020), 164–84, esp. 164. See also Barbara Ransby, *Ella Baker and the Black Freedom Movement: A Radical Democratic Vision* (Chapel Hill:

University of North Carolina Press, 2005); Keisha Blain, *Until I Am Free: Fannie Lou Hamer's Enduring Message to America* (Boston: Beacon Press, 2021); and Kate Clifford Larson, *Walk with Me: A Biography of Fannie Lou Hamer* (Oxford: Oxford University Press, 2021).

21 *The Women's Bureau attorney*: Murray, *Song in a Weary Throat*, 347; Cobble, *Other Women's Movement*, 185.

21 *"What we need"*: O'Farrell and Kornbluh, *Rocking the Boat*, 179.

21 *"sex-based discrimination"*: Murray, *Song in a Weary Throat*, 353. On the "sexism and authoritarianism" that limited Black women's access to prominent, public roles despite their essential leadership in and contributions to the civil rights and Black nationalist movements, see Kimberly Springer, *Living for the Revolution: Black Feminist Organizations, 1968–1980* (Durham, N.C.: Duke University Press, 2005), 21–28, quotation on p. 23.

21 *"It is as humiliating"*: Dinner and Sepper, "Sex in Public," 98–99.

21 *"can no longer postpone"*: Murray quoted in MacLean, *Freedom Is Not Enough*, 123.

21 *"It should not be necessary"*: Murray, *Song in a Weary Throat*, 365.

21 *Murray joined a secretive network*: Friedan, *"It Changed My Life,"* 76–80.

21 *Her closest tie*: "Mary Eastwood," Veteran Feminists of America, accessed Sept. 12, 2016, www.vfa.us/Mary_Eastwood_Obituary.htm; Murray and Eastwood, "Jane Crow and the Law."

22 *"Deep Throat"*: Anthony Ramirez, "Catherine East, 80, Inspiration for National Women's Group," *New York Times*, Aug. 20, 1996, 6.

22 *These and other white-collar*: On the history of women in the legal profession, see Virginia G. Drachman, *Sisters in Law: Women Lawyers in Modern American History* (Cambridge, Mass.: Harvard University Press, 1998). On the history of race and gender in federal employment, see Margaret Rung, *Servants of the State: Managing Diversity and Democracy in the Federal Workforce, 1933–1953* (Athens: University of Georgia Press, 2002); John Thomas McGuire, "'The Most Unjust Piece of Legislation': Section 213 of the Economy Act of 1932 and Feminism During the New Deal," *Journal of Policy History* 20 (2008): 516–41.

22 *Friedan had contacted Murray*: Friedan, *"It Changed My Life,"* 77; Murray, *Song in a Weary Throat*, 365–66.

22 *"a powerful, haunting attractiveness"*: Friedan's unnamed colleague is quoted in Horowitz, *Betty Friedan and the Making of "The Feminine Mystique,"* 229–30.

22 *"I don't even like organizations"*: Cohen, *Sisterhood*, 132.

22 *Friedan had long obscured*: Horowitz, *Betty Friedan and the Making of "The Feminine Mystique."*

22 *Friedan warmed to the idea*: Friedan, *"It Changed My Life,"* 77–81.

22 *East and Eastwood flattered*: Oliver, *Betty Friedan*, 90–91.

22 *"If you ever start"*: "Founders' Reception," Sept. 4, 1971, *NOW Acts* 4 (Sept. 1971): 7.

22 *Friedan signed up*: Murray, *Song in a Weary Throat*, 366.

23 *The "lavish" Washington Hilton*: Geoffrey Wolff, "New Hilton Can Serve 3200 Diners," *Washington Post*, Feb. 6, 1965, B1.

23 *"an international status-symbol"*: "The New Hilton," *Washington Post*, March 18, 1965, A24.

23 *"clean, noble and impressive"*: Wolff, "New Hilton Can Serve 3200 Diners."

23 *"with a hushed reverence"*: "New Hilton," *Washington Post*, March 18, 1965.

23 *"I might as well"*: Boyer, interview by Fox, June 12, 1991, 35.

23 *Hundreds of women traveled*: Harrison, *On Account of Sex*, 160–61.

23 *The women who convened*: *Targets for Action*, iii.

23 *the states' bodies varied*: *Targets for Action*, 4–10.

23 *"We weren't able to get"*: Louise R. Noun, *More Strong-Minded Women: Iowa Feminists Tell Their Stories* (Ames: Iowa State University Press, 1992), 207.

24 *Its chair, the political scientist*: McBride, *Women's Wisconsin*, 433–35; Collins, email to author, July 28, 2016.

24 *With Clarenbach at the helm*: Jamakaya, *Like Our Sisters Before Us*, 30; McBride, *Women's Wisconsin*, 437; *Targets for Action*, 9.

24 *"very vigorous"*: Conroy, interview by Balanoff, 49.

24 *"truly representative"*: Jamakaya, *Like Our Sisters Before Us*, 30.

24 *"until education and understanding"*: *Targets for Action*, 3.

24 *"Labor Standards and Equal Employment"*: *Targets for Action*, 16–18, vi.

24 *"Creating Positive Attitudes"*: *Targets for Action*, 40–41.

25 *"That was really a shame"*: Conroy, interview by Balanoff, 49.

25 *"the ladylike rows"*: Friedan, *"It Changed My Life,"* 82.

25 *"just loaded with anger"*: "Founders' Reception," Sept. 4, 1971, 6.

25 *"anyone we met"*: Friedan, *"It Changed My Life,"* 81.

25 *"we had pretty well"*: O'Farrell and Kornbluh, *Rocking the Boat*, 179.

25 *The author was so inspired*: Friedan, *"It Changed My Life,"* 81.

25 *She, in turn, invited*: Conroy, interview by Balanoff, 51.

26 *"an informal affair"*: Carabillo, Meuli, and Csida, *Feminist Chronicles*, 21.

26 *"going up the escalators"*: Transcript of NOW "Herstory" Session, Jan. 10, 1992, 8–9, 15, folder 7, box 7, Tully-Crenshaw Feminist Oral History Project.

26 *twenty-odd women "jammed"*: Conroy, interview by Balanoff, 51.

26 *Those women sipped water*: Carabillo, Meuli, and Csida, *Feminist Chronicles*, 21.

26 *Cigarette smoke swirled*: Eastwood, interview by Fox, 10.

26 *"Everybody was feeling"*: Conroy, interview by Balanoff, 51.

26 *"were strangers to one another"*: Murray, *Song in a Weary Throat*, 367.

26 *"This was no random group"*: Carabillo, Meuli, and Csida, *Feminist Chronicles*, 21.

26 *They proposed the NOW acronym*: Carabillo, Meuli, and Csida, *Feminist Chronicles*, 21. There is some debate among those present in Friedan's room that night about who—Friedan or Clarenbach—proposed the name, and whether Friedan wrote it on a cocktail napkin or Clarenbach suggested it aloud.

26 *forty-nine of them*: *Targets for Action*, 86–87.

26 *"all-out shouting match"*: Carabillo, Meuli, and Csida, *Feminist Chronicles*, 21.

26 *"talked to us"*: Kornbluh and O'Farrell, *Rocking the Boat*, 180.

27 *"came to this cold"*: Eastwood, interview by Fox, 12.

27 *"very unpleasant"*: Eastwood, interview by Fox, 12.

27 *"Who in the hell invited you?"*: Conroy, interview by Balanoff, 51.

27 *"You know, this is my room"*: Carabillo, Meuli, and Csida, *Feminist Chronicles*, 20.

27 *"Get out! Get out!"*: Carabillo, Meuli, and Csida, *Feminist Chronicles*, 22.

27 *"flowing, brightly colored cape"*: Cohen, *Sisterhood*, 135.

27 *"Perhaps I really didn't"*: Carabillo, Meuli, and Csida, *Feminist Chronicles*, 22.

27 *Clarenbach echoed Knaak's suggestion*: Carabillo, Meuli, and Csida, *Feminist Chronicles*, 23; Friedan, *"It Changed My Life,"* 82.

27 *"just work within"*: Carabillo, Meuli, and Csida, *Feminist Chronicles*, 20.

27 *"very strong convictions"*: O'Farrell and Kornbluh, *Rocking the Boat*, 179–80.

27 *"Well, let them try"*: Carabillo, Meuli, and Csida, *Feminist Chronicles*, 21.

27 *When Friedan emerged*: Cohen, *Sisterhood*, 135.

27 *"just looked at one another"*: Friedan, *"It Changed My Life,"* 82.

28 *"was thoroughly discouraged"*: Murray, *Song in a Weary Throat*, 368.

28 *In the morning*: Harrison, *On Account of Sex*, 194; O'Farrell and Kornbluh, *Rocking the Boat*, 246.

28 *"was absolutely outraged"*: Friedan, *"It Changed My Life,"* 83.

28 *"a pretty conservative gang"*: O'Farrell and Kornbluh, *Rocking the Boat*, 245–46.

28 *"My job requires"*: Catherine Conroy testimony, *Report of the Wisconsin Governor's Commission on the Changing Status of Women* (Washington, D.C.: Women's Bureau, U.S. Department of Labor, 1964), 21, 23.

28 *"padded-dashboard motif"*: Wolff, "New Hilton Can Serve 3200 Diners."

29 *"They had the head table"*: O'Farrell and Kornbluh, *Rocking the Boat*, 246.

29 *Congresswoman Martha Griffiths proposed*: *Targets for Action*, 75.

29 *"where the action is"*: *Targets for Action*, 77.

29 *The women who had*: Friedan, *"It Changed My Life,"* 83.

29 *Conroy began the discussion*: Eastwood, interview by Fox, 16.

29 *the women whispered "agitatedly"*: Friedan, *"It Changed My Life,"* 83.

29 *"sound[ed] kind of blah"*: Eastwood, interview by Fox, 24.

29 *"brilliant women must have"*: "Founders' Reception," 6.

29 *As lunch ended*: Noun, *More Strong-Minded Women*, 209.

29 *"Shall we choose our colors?"*: Eastwood, interview by Fox, 23.

29 *"I just knew"*: Boyer, interview by Fox, June 12, 1991, 35.

29 *"bring women into full participation"*: Oliver, *Betty Friedan*, 92.

29 *NOW would be*: "Board Meeting Minutes," June 29, 1966, folder 1, box 2, National Organization for Women Papers, Schlesinger Library.

29 *Their first act*: Harrison, *On Account of Sex*, 195; Murray, *Song in a Weary Throat*, 368.

30 *They sketched a plan*: Oliver, *Betty Friedan*, 92.

30 *"everybody who was"*: Muriel Fox, phone interview by author, July 15, 2016, 3.

30 *"pulled out $5"*: "Founders' Reception," 7.

30 *NOW opened its treasury*: McBride, *Women's Wisconsin*, 437. Many sources confirm that 28 women each paid $5 and that NOW's first treasury contained $135. Thus one of these founders signed her name but did not pay dues that day.

30 *Yet these founders shattered*: Harrison, *On Account of Sex*, 195.

2. BE WHAT YOU ARE, A WOMAN

33 *"be what you are"*: "What Alverno Is," Alverno College Student Handbook, 1962, 3, Alverno College Archives, Milwaukee.

34 *William Burr Hill*: Burnett, *True Colors*, 6.

34 *"just shone"*: Burnett, interview by Gene Boyer, Aug. 19, 1991, 1, folder 20, box 7, Tully-Crenshaw Feminist Oral History Project.

34 *member of the elite*: Burnett, *True Colors*, 6.

34 *Patricia's mother, Myrtle*: Burnett, *True Colors*, 9.

34 *Uline's daughter Myrtle*: Burnett, *True Colors*, 6.

34 *The young couple married*: Burnett, interview by Boyer, 1, folder 20, box 7; Burnett, *True Colors*, 8.

34 *Located where the Maumee*: Tana Mosier Porter, *Toledo Profile: A Sesquicentennial History* (Toledo: Toledo Sesquicentennial Commission, 1987), 67–80, 91.

35 *"glass capital of the world"*: Porter, *Toledo Profile*, 78.

35 *Myrtle expected her husband*: Burnett, *True Colors*, 8.

35 *Divorce remained relatively rare*: Samuel A. Stouffer and Lyle M. Spencer, "Marriage and Divorce in Recent Years," *Annals of the American Academy of Political and Social Science* 188 (Nov. 1936): 58.

35 *Myrtle's father blamed his daughter*: Burnett, *True Colors*, 9.

35 *"It's 80–90% your job"*: Burnett, interview by Boyer, 181, folder 20, box 8.

35 *Patricia recalled her mother writing*: Jack Lessenberry, "She's Painted Her Life with Bold Strokes," *Toledo Magazine*, Sept. 17, 1995, 6, "Biographical + Artistic, 4 of 5" folder, box 1, Patricia Hill Burnett Papers, Bentley Historical Library, University of Michigan, Ann Arbor.

35 *"genteel poverty"*: Burnett, *True Colors*, 12.

35 *She persuaded a sixteen-year-old*: Burnett, *True Colors*, 12. It's not clear where Claudis went to college, but a 1934 U.S. Office of Education survey of the nation's colleges found that an academic year cost $630, or nearly $14,000 today. A public university would have been significantly cheaper. Lily Rothman, "Putting the Rising Cost of College in Perspective," *Time*, Aug. 31, 2016, time.com/4472261/college-cost-history.

35 *"grew up in a sort"*: Burnett, *True Colors*, 12.

35 *"I was something"*: Lessenberry, "She's Painted Her Life with Bold Strokes," 6.

35 *When Patricia was ten*: Burnett, *True Colors*, 12–13.

36 *"be charming, be agreeable"*: Patricia Hill Burnett, "Having It All—and Loving It," n.d., 1, "PHB—Feminist Speeches" folder, box 10, Burnett Papers.

36 *At age twelve*: Burnett, interview by Boyer, 18, folder 20, box 7.

36 *soon she was selling*: Patricia Hill Burnett, "Marketing Your Talent," March 7, 2001, 2, Independent Women's Forum Tenth Annual Business Leadership Program, Oklahoma State University, "Talks" folder, box 7, Burnett Papers.

36 *"I learned to use make-up"*: Burnett, interview by Boyer, 4, folder 20, box 7.

36 *Women's use of makeup*: Kathy Peiss, *Hope in a Jar: The Making of America's Beauty Culture* (New York: Henry Holt, 1998), 97–98, 144, 154, 171.

36 *Myrtle dressed her daughter*: Lessenberry, "She's Painted Her Life with Bold Strokes," 6; Burnett, interview by Boyer, 4, folder 20, box 7.

36 *"It was my pride"*: Burnett, "Having It All—and Loving It," 1.

36 *Migiel Uline, by then divorced*: Burnett, *True Colors*, 18.

37 *Uline had expanded*: Burnett, *True Colors*, 10; Jack Walsh, "Sports Arena Sold by Ulines," *Washington Post*, Dec. 18, 1959, C1.

37 *With her grandfather's connections*: Lessenberry, "She's Painted Her Life with Bold Strokes," 6; Burnett, *True Colors*, 18.

37 *"intensive training"*: Burnett, *True Colors*, 18.

37 *Aileen Hernandez had been born*: "Aileen Hernandez, Former President, NOW."

37 *a craftsman who made*: Shelley Gross, "NOW York Woman: Aileen Hernandez," May 29, 1971, newspaper clipping, "Aileen Clippings" folder, box 29, Hernandez Papers.

37 *Ethel and Charles, both born*: "Remembering Norris Walton Clarke," ca. April 2004, "Aileen Personal" folder, box 80, Hernandez Papers.

37 *"world's greatest Negro city"*: Floyd J. Calvin, "West Indians Vital Factors in Harlem Leadership," *Pittsburgh Courier*, June 11, 1927, 4.

37 *Tens of thousands*: Kelly Miller, "After Marcus Garvey—What: U.N.I.A. Founder Called Black John the Baptist," *New York Amsterdam News*, April 20, 1927, 16. See also Dorsey E. Walker, "A Half Century of Jamaican Migration," *Negro History Bulletin* 11 (May 1948): 179.

37 *"The West Indian Negro"*: Miller, "After Marcus Garvey—What."

38 *Bazil O. Parks*: "America Not Like Jamaica," *Baltimore Afro-American*, Dec. 2, 1921, 1, 5.

38 *"The Jamaicans who moved"*: Janet Dewart Bell, *Lighting the Fires of Freedom: African American Women in the Civil Rights Movement* (New York: New Press, 2018), 70.

38 *Charles, earned enough*: Hernandez, interview by Sherri Mora, 1999, ed. Susanna Cohen, 2002, 2, "Aileen" folder, box 19, Hernandez Papers; "Aileen Clarke Hernandez," Black Biography, Answers.com, "Bio" folder, box 1, Hernandez Papers.

38 *"I was always beautifully dressed"*: Hernandez, interview by Mora, 2.

38 *They named their daughter*: "Aileen Hernandez, Former President, NOW."

38 *Aileen's parents nicknamed her*: Janice Cobb, "Aileen Hernandez: A Profile," "Aileen Clippings" folder, box 29, Hernandez Papers.

38 *All three kids learned*: Gross, "NOW York Woman: Aileen Hernandez."

38 *"always told when I was growing up"*: "Aileen Hernandez," Makers.com.

39 *"A small town"*: Pamela Gwyn Kripke, "Bay Ridge, Brooklyn, a 'Small Town' in a Big City," *New York Times*, April 6, 2016, www.nytimes.com/2016/04/10/realestate/living-in-bay -ridge-brooklyn.html; Eleanora W. Schoenebaum, "Emerging Neighborhoods: The Development of Brooklyn's Fringe Areas, 1850–1930" (PhD diss., Columbia University, 1977), 227.

39 *The neighborhood's population density*: Schoenebaum, "Emerging Neighborhoods," 203.

39 *"white attitudes, which"*: Harold Xavier Connolly, "Blacks in Brooklyn from 1900 to 1960" (PhD diss., New York University, 1972), 143.

39 *To help offset*: Connolly, "Blacks in Brooklyn from 1900 to 1960," 145.

39 *This was the world*: Bell, *Lighting the Fires of Freedom*, 70.

39 *"the neighborhood would deteriorate"*: Hernandez, "Remarks," Frankel Lecture Series, 2.

39 *With the help*: Hernandez, interview by Mora, 2.

39 *"kind of a novelty"*: Hernandez, "Remarks," Frankel Lecture Series, 2.

39 *"Having come from Jamaica"*: Bell, *Lighting the Fires of Freedom*, 70.

40 *"gave him a lecture"*: "Aileen Hernandez," Makers.com.

40 *Ethel and Charles channeled*: Bell, *Lighting the Fires of Freedom*, 70.

40 *"a lot of support"*: Hernandez, "Remarks," Frankel Lecture Series, 3.

40 *Aileen established herself*: Gross, "NOW York Woman."

40 *"dainty little bolero"*: "Women's Lib," *Urban West*, n.d., ca. late 1970, folder 43, box 1, NOW Records.

40 *"got along fine"*: Hernandez, interview by Mora, 1.

40 *"We were the black people"*: Bell, *Lighting the Fires of Freedom*, 72.

40 *"educational excellence"*: Hernandez, "Remarks," Frankel Lecture Series, 2.

40 *"enthusiastic participant"*: "Aileen Clarke," "Bay Ridge High School" folder, box 19, Hernandez Papers.

41 *"became air raid wardens"*: Aileen Clarke, Graduation Speech, "Bay Ridge High School" folder, box 19, Hernandez Papers.

41 *Aileen's own mother*: Hernandez, interview by Mora, 2.

41 *"great advisor"*: Hernandez, interview by Mora, 1.

41 *"learn what I was all about"*: "Women's Lib," *Urban West*.

41 *"the detour"*: Hernandez, "Remarks," Frankel Lecture Series, 2.

41 *"lace-curtain middle-class"*: Collins, interview by author, 2015, 1.

42 *"patchwork of tight-knit"*: Patrick D. Jones, *The Selma of the North: Civil Rights Insurgency in Milwaukee* (Cambridge, Mass.: Harvard University Press, 2009), 16.

42 *A heavily industrial city*: Jones, *Selma of the North*, 15–17.

42 *"the Germans and the Poles"*: Collins, interview by author, 2015, 1.

42 *Most Milwaukee Catholics*: Jones, *Selma of the North*, 85.

42 *"People would talk about"*: Collins, interview by Noreen Connell, Feb. 1992, 15, folder 6, box 8, Tully-Crenshaw Feminist Oral History Project.

42 *They had their grade-school-age*: Collins, interview by Connell, 2, folder 6, box 8.

43 *"It was a big deal"*: Collins, interview by author, 2015, 1.

43 *"Growing up what I saw"*: Collins, interview by Connell, 3, 2, 14, folder 6, box 8.

43 *When Emmett's condition worsened*: Collins, interview by author, 2015, 1.

43 *"not a valued thing"*: Collins, interview by author, 2015, 1. See also Collins, interview by Connell, 1, folder 6, box 8.

43 *"our grade school nuns"*: Collins, interview by author, 2015, 2.

43 *"very positive on higher education"*: Collins, interview by Connell, 4, folder 6, box 8.

43 *"it always bothered"*: Collins, interview by author, 2015, 2.

43 *at the University of St. Thomas*: Collins, email to author, Nov. 4, 2021.

44 *Lucille suddenly entered*: Collins, interview by author, 2015, 2.

44 *She died the next morning*: Collins, email to author, Nov. 4, 2021.

44 *"pretty shocking"*: Collins, interview by author, 2015, 2.

45 *Patricia enrolled in 1937*: "Patricia Hill Burnett," biography, ca. 2009, "Talks" folder, box 7, Burnett Papers.

45 *Most of Patricia's classmates*: *Donnybrook Fair* [Goucher College Student Yearbook], 1938, Goucher College Special Collections and Archives, Baltimore.

45 *one of her two roommates*: Terrill Burnett, interview by author, April 29, 2021, 1.

45 *About one-third of students*: Anna Heubeck Knipp and Thaddeus P. Thomas, *The History of Goucher College* (Baltimore: Goucher College, 1938), 446.

45 *Goucher had been established*: "The First 100 Years: Goucher College, 1885–1985," *Goucher Quarterly* 62, no. 4 (Summer 1984): 1; *Stone and Spirit: Building Goucher College, 1885–1954* (Baltimore: Goucher College, 2000), 1.

45 *"equal advantages in the business"*: *Stone and Spirit*, 1.

45 *The school's curriculum*: *Stone and Spirit*, 1, 4.

45 *The college's graduates enrolled*: "The First 100 Years: Goucher College," 2.

45 *As time went on*: "The First 100 Years: Goucher College," 20.

45 *"to the question"*: Frederic O. Musser, *The History of Goucher College, 1930–1985* (Baltimore: Johns Hopkins University Press, 1990), 15, 16, 19.

46 *According to turn-of-the-century*: Paul Aikinson, "The Feminist Physique: Physical Education and the Medicalization of Women's Education," in *From "Fair Sex" to Feminism: Sport and the Socialization of Women in the Industrial and Post-industrial Eras*, ed. J. A. Mangan and Roberta J. Park (London: Frank Cass, 1987), 41–43.

46 *"to make athletes"*: Knipp and Thomas, *History of Goucher College*, 471.

46 *administrators built what they boasted*: "First 100 Years: Goucher College," 5; Musser, *History of Goucher College*, 24.

46 *They also recruited*: Musser, *History of Goucher College*, 24.

46 *Required to attend*: Knipp and Thomas, *History of Goucher College*, 439–40.

46 *A group petitioned in 1932*: Musser, *History of Goucher College*, 25–26; Knipp and Thomas, *History of Goucher College*, 450.

46 *"problems incidental to repeal"*: Musser, *History of Goucher College*, 27.

47 *"adequate social center"*: Knipp and Thomas, *History of Goucher College*, 450.

47 *"minor liberties"*: Knipp and Thomas, *History of Goucher College*, 447.

47 *When Patricia arrived*: "Evening Rites Unite Couple in Marriage," *Washington Post*, May 6, 1945, S1; Knipp and Thomas, *History of Goucher College*, 491.

47 *"sufficiently high"*: Knipp and Thomas, *History of Goucher College*, 492.

47 *The students took frequent trips*: Knipp and Thomas, *History of Goucher College*, 446.

47 *The college also began*: Musser, *History of Goucher College*, 34.

47 *"chapel talks especially"*: Musser, *History of Goucher College*, 24.

47 *The college newspaper printed*: Musser, *History of Goucher College*, 25.

47 *There were also more men*: Musser, *History of Goucher College*, 27.

47 *"Colleges for women"*: Burnett to Mrs. Charles C. Clagett Jr., Feb. 2, 1979, "Correspondence Jan.–June 1979" folder, box 2, Burnett Papers.

48 *even her children*: Hillary Burnett, interview by author, April 29, 2021, 1; Terrill Burnett, interview by author, April 29, 2021, 1.

48 *Patricia stayed close*: Hillary Burnett, interview by author, April 29, 2021, 1; Terrill Burnett, interview by author, April 29, 2021, 1.

48 *"recognition for studies"*: Burnett to Rhoda M. Dorsey, June 12, 1978, "Correspondence, 1976–1978" folder, box 7, Burnett Papers.

48 *"finishing school"*: Burnett, *True Colors*, 18.

48 *All of the sleeping car porters*: Hernandez, interview by Mora, 3.

48 *"You'll have to get the black taxi"*: Bell, *Lighting the Fires of Freedom*, 71–72.

48 *"It had nothing to do"*: Hernandez, "Remarks," Frankel Lecture Series, 2–3.

48 *"I could not believe"*: Bell, *Lighting the Fires of Freedom*, 70.

49 *Riding up to campus*: Bell, *Lighting the Fires of Freedom*, 72.

49 *"America's Leading Negro University"*: Rayford Whittingham Logan, *Howard University: The First Hundred Years, 1867–1967* (New York: New York University Press, 1969), 401.

49 *The school, coeducational*: Logan, *Howard University*, 25–26.

49 *Howard's liberal arts college*: Logan, *Howard University*, 361.

49 *There were students*: Murray, *Song in a Weary Throat*, 200–201.

49 *"they were a generation"*: Pauli Murray, "A Blueprint for First Class Citizenship," *Crisis*, Nov. 1944, folder 3, box 1, Pauli Murray Papers, Moorland-Spingarn Research Center, Howard University.

49 *"bevy of Howard beauties"*: "'Life' Magazine Comes to HU Homecoming," *Hilltop*, Oct. 23, 1946, 1.

49 *"People sent their daughters"*: Bell, *Lighting the Fires of Freedom*, 73.

49 *"a very uninvolved campus"*: Hernandez, interview by Vincent J. Brown, March 1968, 49, "Interview w/ACH, Civil Rights Documentation Proj." folder, box 29, Hernandez Papers.

49 *"the great days of Howard"*: Murray, interview by Robert Martin, Aug. 15–17, 1968, 45, Ralph Bunche Oral History Collection, Moorland-Spingarn Research Center, Howard University.

50 *"the training ground"*: Murray, interview by Martin, 75.

50 *"outstanding student organization"*: "NAACP Elects New Head," *Hilltop*, Feb. 4, 1945, 1.

50 *"The fact that an accident"*: Murray, *Song in a Weary Throat*, 205.

50 *Aileen, whose own older brother*: Bell, *Lighting the Fires of Freedom*, 72.

50 *"nonviolence in our racial struggle"*: Murray, *Song in a Weary Throat*, 201.

50 *"attractively dressed coeds"*: Murray, interview by Martin, 51.

50 *"little restaurant across the road"*: Bell, *Lighting the Fires of Freedom*, 74.

50 *"one of the most precious"*: "Civil Rights Committee H.U. Chapter NAACP Pledge," May 1, 1944, folder 9, box 1, Murray Collection.

50 *Through their protests*: Saxby, *Pauli Murray*, 117.

50 *"proved that intelligent"*: Murray, *Song in a Weary Throat*, 208.

50 *"could do things"*: Bell, *Lighting the Fires of Freedom*, 73.

50 *"as most girls did"*: Bell, *Lighting the Fires of Freedom*, 74.

50 *She wanted to understand*: "Aileen Hernandez, Former President, NOW"; Bell, *Lighting the Fires of Freedom*, 74.

50 *"One of the values"*: Hernandez, interview by Mora, 2.

51 *"we were living"*: Bell, *Lighting the Fires of Freedom*, 74.

51 *Howard's history department*: Linda M. Perkins, "Merze Tate and the Quest for Gender Equity at Howard University: 1942–1977," *History of Education Quarterly* 54, no. 4 (Nov. 2014): 526.

51 *"bulging" with the school's*: "Record Enrollment," *Hilltop*, Oct. 23, 1946, 1.

51 *"at any Negro institution"*: John Plummer, "From GI to CI," *Hilltop*, Oct. 23, 1946, 2.

51 *The vets coming to Howard*: "Aileen Clarke Hernandez," Black Biography.

51 *With two male schoolmates and another female*: "Lisner Bars H.U. Students," *Hilltop*, Nov. 6, 1946, 1.

51 *picket[ing] for four years*: "Aileen Hernandez, Former President, NOW."

52 *Mary Jean's chosen college*: Tracy Schier and Cynthia Eagle Russet, *Catholic Women's Colleges in America* (Baltimore: Johns Hopkins University Press, 2002), 253–54.

52 *Most Catholic women's colleges*: Schier and Russet, *Catholic Women's Colleges in America*, 5.

52 *"concerned with full"*: "What Alverno Is," *Alverno College Student Handbook*, 1962, 3, Alverno College Archives.

52 *In 1960, Mary Jean's*: Peggy House, "Fulltime Students Total 844," *Alverno Campus News*, Oct. 18, 1960, 4.

52 *When Mary Jean graduated*: Margaret Freeman, "112 Will Receive Degrees," *Alverno Campus News*, May 20, 1963, 1.

52 *"working to pay"*: Margaret Hennen, "Summer Programs Promise Enrichment," *Alverno Campus News*, May 20, 1963, 1.

52 *The college offered*: Sister Joel Read and Collins, interview by author, Sept. 3, 2016, 5.

52 *Alverno also administered*: "What Alverno Asks of You," *Alverno College Student Handbook*, 1962, 17, Alverno College Archives.

52 *"You just didn't see that"*: Collins, interview by Connell, 14, folder 6, box 8.

52 *The sisters who led*: Schier and Russet, *Catholic Women's Colleges in America*, 4.

52 *"There were male professors"*: Read and Collins, interview by author, 11.

52 *"an organization we could"*: Read and Collins, interview by author, 8.

52 *"lesser-known liberal arts"*: Howard Benoist and Robert Gibbons, "The Competence Movement and the Liberal Arts Tradition: Enemies or Allies?," *Journal of Higher Education* 51, no. 6 (Nov.–Dec. 1980): 688.

52 *"life-related outcomes"*: Benoist and Gibbons, "Competence Movement and the Liberal Arts Tradition," 685.

53 *Alverno leaders' reforms*: Robert C. Doty, "Pope Paul Closes Vatican Council amid Pageantry," *New York Times*, Dec. 9, 1965, 1.

53 *"The whole intent"*: Joel Read, "Letter from Alverno College," *Women's Studies Newsletter* 1, no. 5 (Fall 1973): 3.

53 *"didn't overemphasize" women's history*: Read and Collins, interview by author, 7.

53 *student life was convent-like*: *Alverno College Resident Student Handbook*, 1962–63, 5, 7–10, 12, Alverno College Archives.

53 *"Me and My Gal"*: Alverno College Class of 1963, 50th Anniversary Commemorative Program, Alverno College Archives.

53 *"blouses, sweaters, skirts"*: "What Alverno Asks of You," *Alverno College Resident Student Handbook*, 1962, 16, Alverno College Archives.

53 *"student-postulants"*: Photo and caption, *Alverno Campus News*, Feb. 19, 1962, 2.

53 *"I was really concerned"*: Read and Collins, interview by author, 2.

53 *Read helped bring*: "Alverno Group Plans for Goal: 2 African Students Next Year," *Alverno Campus News*, Oct. 18, 1961, 4.

53 *made sure the student newspaper*: "6 to Continue Study, Training for Service," *Alverno Campus News*, May 20, 1963, 1.

53 *"spacious reading room"*: "What Alverno Offers You," *Alverno College Student Handbook*, 1962, 4.

53 *College leaders like Read*: "What Alverno Offers You," 4–6; "Alumnae Act as Cooperating Teachers," *Alverno Campus News*, Oct. 18, 1961, 3.

54 *She thrived, serving*: Collins, interview by author, 2015, 2.

54 *Her Alverno professors connected her*: Read and Collins, interview by author, 1–2, 5.

54 *"Conroy was the kind"*: Collins, interview by author, 2015, 3.

54 *"from some of the religious"*: Collins, interview by Connell, Feb. 1992, 3, folder 6, box 8.

54 *"led me not to become"*: Collins, interview by author, 2015, 2.

54 *"a naturally curly"*: Kathleen Powell, "NOW Candidate Campaigns Here," *Fort Myers (Fla.) News-Press*, Aug. 23, 1975, 1D, folder 5, box 24, Collins NOW Officer Papers.

54 *The two women had switched places*: Burnett, *True Colors*, 25, 36.

55 *"combin[ing] Northern efficiency"*: Burnett, *True Colors*, 20–21.

55 *1942 Miss Michigan pageant*: Burnett, *True Colors*, 26, 27, 28.

55 *Atlantic City, the home*: Margot Mifflin, *Looking for Miss America: A Pageant's 100-Year Quest to Define Womanhood* (Berkeley, Calif.: Counterpoint, 2020), 13, 12, 57–58, 5.

56 *When Patricia arrived*: Mifflin, *Looking for Miss America*, 59–60.

56 *The pageant was its own education*: Burnett, *True Colors*, 29, 30, 28.

56 *The comedians hit on her*: Susan E. Harrison, "Beauty Queen Trades Tiara for Feminism," news clipping, n.d., "Burnett, Patricia Hill" folder, box 6, Burnett Papers.

56 *"My virginity was seen"*: Burnett, *True Colors*, 30.

56 *she worked as a model*: Burnett, "Marketing Your Talent."

56 *"I was ambitious"*: "Patricia Hill Burnett . . . from Beauty Queen to Leading Feminist," *Muskegon (Mich.) Chronicle*, April 21, 1973, "Articles" folder, box 2, Burnett Papers.

56 *Finally, at age twenty-four*: "The Art and Times of Patricia Burnett," clipping, n.d., "Speeches, Articles, Interviews, 1973–1987 and Undated" folder, box 2, Burnett Papers.

56 *Myrtle adored him*: Burnett, *True Colors*, 38.

56 *They married in 1945*: "Evening Rites Unite Couple in Marriage."

56 The New York Times *also announced*: Preston Sweet, "Patricia Hill Wed to Maj. W. A. Lange," *New York Times*, May 6, 1945, 33.

57 *"I barely knew him"*: Burnett, interview by Boyer, Aug. 19, 1991, 7–8, folder 20, box 7.

57 *She missed her busy life*: Burnett, *True Colors*, 38–39, 41, 40.

57 *Harry Burnett, a bachelor*: Burnett, *True Colors*, 41–43, 45.

57 *Detroit had the nation's*: Thomas J. Sugrue, *Origins of the Urban Crisis: Race and Inequality in Postwar Detroit* (Princeton, N.J.: Princeton University Press, 1996), 1.

57 *The city was bursting*: Sugrue, *Origins of the Urban Crisis*, 23.

57 *But most whites remained*: Heather Ann Thompson, *Whose Detroit? Politics, Labor, and Race in a Modern American City* (Ithaca, N.Y.: Cornell University Press, 2001), 26.

58 *Many white Detroiters demanded*: Sugrue, *Origins of the Urban Crisis*, 10, 231–35.

58 *"Message to the Grass Roots"*: Gosse, *Rethinking the New Left*, 51.

58 *While there were white segregationists*: Thompson, *Whose Detroit?*, 71–102.

58 *tucked away in pockets*: Sugrue, *Origins of the Urban Crisis*, 235.

58 *They lived in*: Clipping, n.d., ca. 1988, Detroit Monthly City Guide, "Biographical + Artistic, 4 of 5" folder, box 1, Burnett Papers.

58 *a replica English manor*: "Pat Burnett/Close-Up," news clipping, n.d., "Burnett, Patricia Hill" folder, box 6, Burnett Papers.

58 *"wealth of raven hair"*: Jean Whitehead, "Miss Michigan of '42 Still Walks in Beauty," *Detroit News*, Dec. 24, 1961, 7A, "Biographical + Artistic, 3 of 5" folder, Burnett Papers.

58 *Their child-care provider*: Terrill Burnett, interview by author, April 29, 2021, 1, 2.

58 *"a fine Victorian gentleman"*: Burnett, *True Colors*, 45.

59 *she chose to mirror*: Joanne Omang, "Not So Congenial Anymore," *Washington Post*, Feb. 20, 1973, A3.

59 *"total dedication"*: "Notebook: NOW August 1970 to January 1971," "Burnett Notebooks" folder, box 6, Burnett Papers.

59 *A psychiatrist advised her*: Burnett, *True Colors*, 46.

59 *"only as a background"*: Burnett, "Having It All—and Loving It," 1.

59 *"just slid down to nothing"*: Burnett, interview by Boyer, 35, folder 20, box 7.

59 *"considered appropriate for lady-like"*: Burnett, interview by Boyer, 62, folder 20, box 7.

59 *For a decade*: "Art and Times of Patricia Burnett," 3.

59 *"a perfect arrangement"*: Whitehead, "Miss Michigan of '42 Still Walks in Beauty."

59 *"My career was piece-mealed"*: Cobey Black, "Patricia Hill Burnett," *Honolulu Advertiser*, n.d., "Biographical + Artistic, 2 of 5" folder, box 1, Burnett Papers.

59 *"She was someone"*: "Patricia & Hillary Burnett," Oct. 27, 2014, Ellis Rourk Production, YouTube, accessed April 29, 2021, www.youtube.com/watch?v=yR43-2mozZw&t=231s.

59 *Patricia decided to set up*: Noel Osment, "She Makes a Point as She Paints," *San Diego Union News*, n.d., "Biographical + Artistic, 2 of 5" folder, box 1, Burnett Papers.

59 *In 1962, she sought*: Burnett, *True Colors*, 50; "Meet Patricia Burnette [*sic*] at Women of Wayne's Studio Tour & Luncheon," clipping, n.d., ca. 1976, "Biographical/Art Career, 1 of 5" folder, box 1, Burnett Papers.

59 *When the members received*: Dorothy Austin, "Battle Discrimination with Happy Artist," clipping, n.d., "Articles" folder, box 2, Burnett Papers; Burnett, *True Colors*, 51–52.

59 *"nearly assaulted"*: Omang, "Not So Congenial Anymore."

59 *"please sign your name"*: Transcript of NOW "Herstory" Session, 39–40.

60 *"A woman can paint"*: "Art and Times of Patricia Burnett."

60 *"Her love of people"*: Rita Simmons, "Featured on Program for Art Specialists," n.d., "Biographical/Art Career, 1 of 5" folder, box 1, Burnett Papers.

60 *she traveled to Norway*: Hernandez, interview by Brown, 1.

60 *"doesn't pay a lot"*: "Aileen Hernandez, Former President, NOW."

60 *"They're talking to me"*: Bell, *Lighting the Fires of Freedom*, 75.

60 *It was formed*: Gus Tyler, *Look for the Union Label: A History of the International Ladies' Garment Workers' Union* (Armonk, N.Y.: M. E. Sharpe, 1995), 11, 23–29.

60 *Most of the union's*: On the ILGWU's mostly male leadership and female membership, and the union as a wellspring of "industrial feminism," see Annelise Orleck, *Common Sense and a Little Fire: Women and Working-Class Politics in the United States, 1900–1965* (Chapel Hill: University of North Carolina Press, 1995), esp. 75–76.

60 *"the importance of"*: Susan Stone Wong, "From Soul to Strawberries: The International Ladies' Garment Workers' Union and Workers' Education, 1914–1950," in *Sisterhood and Solidarity: Workers' Education for Women, 1914–1984*, ed. Joyce L. Kornbluh and Mary Frederickson (Philadelphia: Temple University Press, 1984), 40.

60 *The garment trade flourished*: Tyler, *Look for the Union Label*, 262.

60 *"falling behind"*: Hernandez, interview by Mora, 2.

61 *"We knew right away"*: Hernandez, interview by Mora, 3.

61 *"excellent people"*: Bell, *Lighting the Fires of Freedom*, 76.

61 *The activist and former First Lady*: Hernandez, interview by Mora, 9.

61 *"appalled" when their educated*: Hernandez, interview by Mora, 3.

61 *After finishing the training*: Aileen Hernandez, "Personal History," May 1970, folder 43, box 1, NOW Records; "Women's Lib," *Urban West*.

61 *"very simple"*: "Aileen Hernandez, Former President, NOW."

61 *After Aileen had worked*: Joan Wolverton, "NOW Wants Equal Pay and 'a Choice,' Says President," *Seattle Times*, Aug. 15, 1971, "NOW" folder, box 1, Hernandez Papers.

61 *"I soon found myself"*: Hernandez to David Dubinsky, July 6, 1961, "International Ladies' Garment Workers' Union" folder, box 113, Hernandez Papers.

62 *"every racial group"*: Hernandez, interview by Mora, 3.

62 *"I've seen some marriages"*: "Women's Lib," *Urban West*.

62 *They divorced in 1961*: "Aileen Clarke Hernandez," Black Biography.

62 *"definitely represents"*: Wolverton, "NOW Wants Equal Pay and 'a Choice.'"

62 *By her mid-forties*: Lacey Fosburgh, "Dealing with Feminism in Black and White," *Los Angeles Times*, March 20, 1974, E1.

62 *resigned from the union*: "Biographical Data: Ms. Aileen C. Hernandez," June 1970, folder 43, box 1, NOW Records.

62 *The agency was pressuring*: Hernandez, interview by Mora, 5.

62 *"the state of California"*: Wolverton, "NOW Wants Equal Pay and 'a Choice.'"

62 *"had met a lot of people"*: Hernandez, interview by Mora, 4.

62 *"it would be"*: Vera Glaser, "Mrs. Hernandez Works with FDR, Jr.," *Washington Sunday Star*, Aug. 1, 1967, "Aileen Personal" folder, box 77, Hernandez Papers.

63 *Her salary of $26,000*: "Aileen Hernandez Gets $26,000 Commission," *Berkeley Post*, May 15, 1965, "Aileen Clippings" folder, box 29, Hernandez Papers.

63 *"attractive and smartly dressed"*: Glaser, "Mrs. Hernandez Works with FDR, Jr."

63 *"queenly stride"*: "Women's Lib," *Urban West*.

63 *"tall, arrow-postured"*: Helen Dudar, "NOW—a Leader," *Post Weekend Magazine*, May 16, 1970, 19, "NOW 1970" folder, box 26, Hernandez Papers.

63 *"appointed by a computer"*: Hernandez, interview by Mora, 5.

63 *"Don't wear that kind of hat"*: Glaser, "Mrs. Hernandez Works with FDR, Jr."

63 *"If you are in Washington"*: Aileen Hernandez, "How to File a Job Complaint with the EEOC," *Crisis*, Nov. 1965, 575.

64 *She described its thorough process*: Hernandez, "How to File a Job Complaint with the EEOC," 575, 605.

64 *"I would be pleased"*: Glaser, "Mrs. Hernandez Works with FDR, Jr."

64 *"aided and abetted"*: Hernandez, "Remarks," Frankel Lecture Series, 4.

64 *Jet's March 1966*: "FDR, Jr. Fights Job Bias," *Jet*, March 3, 1966.

64 *"no valid reason"*: Hernandez, "Remarks," Frankel Lecture Series, 4.

65 *"felt that a 'little'"*: Hernandez, "Remarks," Frankel Lecture Series, 5.

65 *"were there to fight"*: Sonia Pressman Fuentes, "Representing Women," *Frontiers: A Journal of Women's Studies* 18, no. 3 (1997): 97.

65 *Luther Holcomb*: Turk, *Equality on Trial*, 19; Fuentes, "Representing Women," 98.

65 *"conservative" commissioner*: Fuentes, "Representing Women," 98.

65 *"had no real interest"*: Fuentes, "Representing Women," 99.

65 *"the most political person"*: Richard Graham, interview by Cynthia Harrison, July 31, 1985, 1, folder 44, box 26, Catherine Shipe East Papers, Schlesinger Library.

65 *"were dealing with the race issues"*: "Aileen Hernandez, Former President, NOW."

65 *"a sea of male faces"*: "Chapter 3" of book draft, 109, folder 11, box 2, Papers of Frances Arick Kolb, Schlesinger Library.

65 *"any real teeth"*: Ida Lewis and Aileen Hernandez, "Conversation," *Essence*, Feb. 1971, 22.

65 *"more useful as an activist"*: Hernandez, "Remarks," Frankel Lecture Series, 6.

66 *"If you wanted to be"*: Collins, interview by author, 2015, 5.

66 *"I didn't really feel"*: Collins, interview by Connell, Feb. 1992, 5, folder 6, box 8.

66 *After one year teaching history*: Collins, interview by author, 2015, 4.

66 *"I went through the 'men' door"*: Collins, interview by author, 2015, 5.

66 *"a little better"*: Collins, interview by author, Oct. 31, 2019, 1.

66 *"I went in there"*: Collins, interview by Connell, 5, folder 6, box 8.

66 *Milwaukee's racial tensions*: Jones, *Selma of the North*, 20, 27.

66 *Father James Groppi*: Jones, *Selma of the North*, 93–94.

67 *Groppi attended St. Francis Seminary*: Stuart Stotts, *Father Groppi: Marching for Civil Rights* (Madison: Wisconsin Historical Society Press, 2013), 17.

67 *"a conversion experience"*: Groppi quoted in Jones, *Selma of the North*, 98.

67 *Groppi and other civil rights activists*: Jones, *Selma of the North*, 179–200.

67 *"the ugliest display"*: Newspaperman quoted in Jones, *Selma of the North*, 183.

67 *"I never went to the South"*: Collins, interview by author, 2015, 2.

67 *"It was terrifying"*: Collins, interview by author, Oct. 31, 2019, 1.

67 *"bottles, eggs, rocks, wood"*: Jones, *Selma of the North*, 2.

68 *"I saw what systematic"*: Collins, interview by Connell, Feb. 1992, 14, folder 6, box 8.

68 *Mary Jean helped Lupa*: Lupa, interview by author, Dec. 10, 2015, 4.

68 *They married in June 1968*: Collins, interview by Connell, 5–6, folder 6, box 8; Collins, interview by author, 2015, 4.

68 *The bestseller prompted*: Burnett, *True Colors*, 4; Omang, "Not So Congenial Anymore."

68 *"forget my aspirations"*: Burnett, *True Colors*, 46.

68 *"like a child"*: Burnett, *True Colors*, 55.

69 *"I knocked on the door"*: Transcript of NOW "Herstory" Session, 40.

69 *"very little was happening"*: Hernandez, interview by Mora, 13.

69 *"The women who came"*: Bell, *Lighting the Fires of Freedom*, 80.

69 *She kept a low profile*: Targets for Action, vi, 88.

69 *"I'm basically an organizer"*: "Aileen Clarke Hernandez," Black Biography.

69 *Aileen left her post*: "Aileen Hernandez, Former President, NOW."

69 *Inspired by this new chance*: Bell, *Lighting the Fires of Freedom*, 81.

69 *They moved to the racially mixed*: Collins, interview by author, 2015, 4.

70 *"tried to really live"*: Collins, interview by Connell, 9, folder 6, box 8.

3. WOMEN ARE GOING TO HAVE TO ORGANIZE

71 *"Don't do anything"*: Hernandez, interview by Rebecca Davison, Nov. 1995, 1.

71 *the nation's vanguard*: Stansell, *Feminist Promise*, 216.

71 *"charitable, but unauthorized gesture"*: Aileen C. Hernandez, "EEOC and the Women's Movement (1965–1975)" (paper for the Symposium on the Tenth Anniversary of the U.S. Equal Employment Opportunity Commission, Rutgers University Law School, Nov. 28–29, 1975), 26, in author's possession.

71 *"sounded very impressive"*: "Aileen Hernandez Speaks at the VFA Celebrates 40 Years of Title VII Conference," May 1, 2004, Veteran Feminists of America Pioneer Histories: Aileen Hernandez, accessed Dec. 17, 2021, www.youtube.com/watch?v=myAr_kn2gLQ.

71 *"penniless" to pay*: Kathryn Clarenbach comments, NOW National Conference, May 25, 1974, 5, folder 1, box 25, Marguerite Rawalt Papers, 1870s–1989, Schlesinger Library.

71 *"made my life miserable"*: "Aileen Hernandez Speaks at the VFA Celebrates 40 Years of Title VII Conference."

72 *"I decided I had enough"*: "Aileen Clarke Hernandez," "Bio" folder, box 1, Hernandez Papers.

72 *Hernandez finally agreed*: "Report of Aileen Hernandez, Vice President West," NOW Third Annual Conference, Dec. 6–8, 1968, "NOW-1966-7" folder, box 26, Hernandez Papers.

72 *"There was no money"*: Hernandez, interview by Mora, 14.

72 *"All we had was"*: Clarenbach, interview by Margaret Andreasen, Nov. 17, 1987, ninth session, tape 9, interview no. 466, University of Wisconsin–Madison Archives Oral History Project.

72 *"We're not building"*: "Chapter 2" of book draft, 67, folder 10, box 2, Kolb Papers.

73 *"It was much harder"*: Bell, *Lighting the Fires of Freedom*, 82.

73 *"women are going to"*: Friedan, *"It Changed My Life,"* 149.

73 *"a loner"*: Friedan, *"It Changed My Life,"* 81.

74 *"If she says NOW"*: Eastwood to Murray, n.d., ca. late summer or early fall 1966, folder 893, box 50, Murray Papers.

74 *She also oversaw*: McBride, *Women's Wisconsin*, 438.

74 *"much of the printing"*: Collins, *When Everything Changed*, 86.

74 *While the committee*: Carabillo, Meuli, and Csida, *Feminist Chronicles*, 165.

74 *Friedan convinced a few*: Eastwood, interview by Fox, 19; Oliver, *Betty Friedan*, 93–94.

74 *"paranoid" bunch included*: Eastwood, interview by Fox, 17.

74 *That position reflected*: O'Farrell and Kornbluh, *Rocking the Boat*, 180.

74 *"slow-witted Midwesterner"*: McBride, *Women's Wisconsin*, 437.

75 *Clarenbach agreed that NOW*: Oliver, *Betty Friedan*, 93–94.

75 *Over time, they learned*: Clarenbach, interview by Andreasen.

75 *"elite cadre"*: Muriel Fox, interview by author, July 15, 2016, 3.

75 *"a kind of NAACP"*: Friedan to Gerda Lerner, Sept. 1, 1966, folder 1495, Betty Friedan Papers, 1933–85, Schlesinger Library.

75 *"wast[ing] time arguing"*: Friedan to Reverend Dean Lewis, Aug. 23, 1966, folder 1495, Friedan Papers.

75 *even asking the U.S. representative*: Griffiths to Murray, Sept. 13, 1966, folder 893, box 50, Murray Papers.

75 *A phalanx of like-minded elites*: Friedan to Lewis, Aug. 23, 1966.

75 *Early documents noted*: Clarenbach to NOW Steering Committee, Sept. 9, 1966, folder 1477, Friedan Papers.

75 *"community room"*: Eastwood, interview by Fox, 28.

75 *Those thirty people included*: Friedan, *"It Changed My Life,"* 84. Scholars and participants contest the number of people who attended this meeting. Friedan recounts that NOW had three hundred members by late October 1966 but there were thirty present. Photographs of the meeting support her more modest tally. Some contend that there were three hundred present at the meeting; see "NOW Origins Workshop Souvenir Journal," NOW National Conference, 1974, folder 1, box 7, Tully-Crenshaw Feminist Oral History Project. The historian Stephanie Gilmore places that figure at "more than 200." Gilmore, *Groundswell*, 27. The confusion may result in part from NOW's first press release, issued at the end of this gathering, which asserted that "more than 300 men and women today formed a new action organization." See NOW, press release, Oct. 31, 1966, folder 1482, Friedan Papers. But that press release might have been referring to NOW's total membership rather than the number of people present in the Washington Post building that October weekend. As Ruth Rosen writes, "Of these three hundred members, only thirty could be present." Rosen, *World Split Open*, 78. Pauli Murray counted thirty-two members present. Murray, *Song in a Weary Throat*, 368.

75 *"It was a relative handful"*: Collins, interview by author, 2015, 4, 5.

76 *NOW's statement vowed to move*: NOW Statement of Purpose, reprinted in Carabillo, Meuli, and Csida, *Feminist Chronicles*, 159, 161.

76 *Women's limited workforce prospects*: Stansell, *Feminist Promise*, 214–15.

76 *"many broader questions"*: Rosenberg, *Jane Crow*, 299–300.

76 *The group did not take*: NOW Board Meeting Minutes, Oct. 29–30, 1966, Attachment C: Targets for Action 1966–67, folder 1, box 2, NOW Records.

76 *Friedan proposed asserting*: Friedan, *"It Changed My Life,"* 84.

76 *The $5 annual membership*: NOW Board Meeting Minutes, Oct. 29–30, 1966, 2.

76 *All five of the candidates*: "NOW's First Election Ballot," reprinted in Carabillo, Meuli, and Csida, *Feminist Chronicles*, 165.

76 *The new board included*: Harrison, *On Account of Sex*, 196.

76 *To hold the vice presidency*: Scanlon, *Until There Is Justice*, 208; Eastwood, interview by Fox, 39–40.

76 *When the board of directors*: NOW Board Meeting Minutes, Nov. 20, 1966, folder 1, box 2, NOW Records.

76 *In fact, she had just accepted*: Rosenberg, *Jane Crow*, 300.

77 *"Well, you, this liberal"*: Eastwood, interview by Fox, 39. While this was Fox's interview of Eastwood, Fox made this point about Murray.

77 *Stepping back her efforts*: Scanlon, *Until There Is Justice*, 209–10; Rosenberg, *Jane Crow*, 307–8; Murray, handwritten notes, Oct. 29, 1966, folder 894, box 50, Murray Papers.

77 *"The male White House staff"*: Murray to Bess Abell (White House social secretary), "Personal and Confidential," Dec. 11, 1966, folder 893, box 50, Murray Papers.

77 *"Through the years"*: Fox to "Editor," n.d., ca. Nov. 1966, folder 1500, Friedan Papers.

77 *"gravelly alto"*: Lisa Hammel, "They Meet in Victorian Parlor to Demand 'True Equality'—NOW," *New York Times*, Nov. 22, 1966, 44.

77 The New York Times: Jean Hewitt, "And Here Are Three Untraditional Stuffing Recipes," *New York Times*, Nov. 22, 1966, 44.

77 *"The one thing"*: Jean M. White, "NOW—'New Woman' Demands to Be Heard," *Washington Post*, Jan. 14, 1967, A3.

78 *In November 1966*: Dolores Alexander, "Idea Is Old, the Group Is NOW," *Newsday*, Nov. 23, 1966, 2B.

78 *A NOW delegation*: White, "NOW—'New Woman' Demands to Be Heard."

78 *"We are off"*: Murray to Clarenbach, Nov. 1, 1966, folder 895, box 50, Murray Papers.

78 *which took place*: Paterson, *Be Somebody*, 180.

78 *NOW membership had grown*: "NOW Origins Workshop Souvenir Journal," 1, folder 1, box 7, Tully-Crenshaw Feminist Oral History Project.

78 *Aileen Hernandez, who was reelected*: 1967 National Conference of National Organization for Women Agenda, folder 23, box 2, NOW Records.

78 *cost about $230*: Ken Kaye, "1959 L.A.–N.Y. Flight Kicks Off the Jet Age," *South Florida Sun-Sentinel*, Dec. 24, 2001, www.sun-sentinel.com/news/fl-xpm-2001-12-24-0112230419 -story.html.

78 *the organization had just*: Caroline Davis, "Financial Report for November 1966 thru November 1967," folder 3, box 23, NOW Records.

78 *Catherine Conroy's union*: Collins, email to author, Nov. 11, 2021; Conroy, interview by Balanoff, 52.

78 *"I had never been"*: Collins, interview by Connell, 17, folder 6, box 8.

78 *"fancy people"*: Collins, interview by author, 2015, 3.

78 *"fascinated by the process"*: Collins, interview by author, 2015, 3.

78 *105 members present*: Friedan to All Members of NOW, Jan. 15, 1968, folder 3, box 23, NOW Records.

78 *Bill of Rights for Women*: "NOW Bill of Rights for 1968," folder 53, box 26, East Papers.

79 *National Welfare Rights Organization*: Cobble, Gordon, and Henry, *Feminism Unfinished*, 72.

79 *"kept her in line"*: Eastwood, interview by Fox, 51.

79 *at the time the procedure*: Leslie Reagan, *When Abortion Was a Crime: Women, Medicine, and Law in the United States, 1867–1973* (Berkeley: University of California Press, 1997), 2, 216–18.

79 *Women suffering from*: Stansell, *Feminist Promise*, 313–15.

79 *the U.S. Supreme Court*: *Griswold v. Connecticut*, 381 U.S. 479 (1965).

79 *Abortion rights advocates*: Stansell, *Feminist Promise*, 317.

79 *"the fundamental human right"*: Carabillo, Meuli, and Csida, *Feminist Chronicles*, 191.

79 *"sweating and wondering"*: Collins, interview by author, 2015, 3.

79 *Friedan made clear*: Fox, interview by author, 7.

79 *In a vote*: Friedan to All Members of NOW, Jan. 15, 1968.

80 *A contingent of Ohio members*: NOW Board Meeting Minutes, Jan. 27–28, 1968, 7, folder 3, box 2, NOW Records; Evans, *Personal Politics*, 25; Collins, interview by author, 2015, 3.

80 *"old hat"*: Discussion of the Founding of NOW Legal Defense and Education Fund, 5, folder 14, box 10, Tully-Crenshaw Feminist Oral History Project.

80 *a committee Murray*: Rosenberg, *Jane Crow*, 307.

80 *"Human Rights Amendments"*: Mayeri, *Reasoning from Race*, 34–35.

80 *Instead, she argued*: Rosenberg, *Jane Crow*, 248–49.

80 *"designed to protect"*: Murray quoted in Mayeri, *Reasoning from Race*, 18.

80 *"unite civil rights"*: Mayeri, *Reasoning from Race*, 19.

80 *Murray was also concerned*: Rosenberg, *Jane Crow*, 250.

80 *Murray was also especially attentive*: Rosenberg, *Jane Crow*, 308.

81 *The recently issued Moynihan Report*: Daniel Patrick Moynihan, *The Negro Family: The Case for National Action* (Washington, D.C.: U.S. Department of Labor, 1965).

81 *portrayed Black single mothers*: Berry and Gross, *Black Women's History of the United States*, 188.

81 *Hedgeman and Murray*: Rosenberg, *Jane Crow*, 308.

81 *"in force"*: Clarenbach, interview by Andreasen.

81 *"alienate organizations who have"*: Rosenberg, *Jane Crow*, 309.

81 *The civil rights attorney*: Paterson, *Be Somebody*, 180.

81 *"I do not see"*: Eastwood to Murray, n.d., ca. late 1966, folder 893, box 50, Murray Papers.

81 *"a row of suffragists"*: Paterson, *Be Somebody*, 180.

81 *When the conference voted*: Friedan to All Members of NOW, Jan. 15, 1968, 2.

81 *"had no idea why"*: Collins, interview by author, 2015, 3.

81 *"you have to keep your eye"*: Collins, interview by Connell, 19, folder 6, box 8.

82 *Her stint at the EEOC*: Rosenberg, *Jane Crow*, 305.

82 *She meant for her strategy*: Mayeri, *Reasoning from Race*, 39–40.

82 *"members who had other loyalties"*: Murray to Clarenbach, Nov. 21, 1967, folder 899, box 50, Murray Papers.

82 *She would return*: "NOW Caucus," June 11, 1970, folder 901, box 51, Murray Papers.

82 *"I've always been distressed"*: "Women's Lib," *Urban West*.

82 *They persuaded the EEOC*: Friedan to All Members of NOW, Jan. 15, 1968.

82 *NOW also publicly supported*: Friedan to All Members of NOW, Jan. 15, 1968, 4; Mac-Lean, *Freedom Is Not Enough*, 129.

82 *At a national board meeting*: NOW Board of Directors Meeting Minutes, May 4–5, 1968, 4–5, folder 3, box 2, NOW Records.

83 *"Can't serve you ladies"*: Friedan, *"It Changed My Life,"* 107.

83 *New chapters were sprouting up*: Oliver, *Betty Friedan*, 99.

83 *NOW's tiny national office*: "Report on Operation of the National Headquarters," May 1, 1968, folder 38, box 7, NOW Records.

83 *The D.C. chapter president*: Barbara Ireton to Friedan, Oct. 29, 1968, folder 1536b, Friedan Papers.

83 *"an excellent machine"*: Friedan to Clarenbach, Feb. 14, 1968, folder 1477, Friedan Papers.

83 *"suffer[ed] from a great deal"*: Aileen Hernandez, "Suggestions to the National Board of NOW," Dec. 1, 1968, folder 14, box 1, Muriel Fox Papers, Schlesinger Library.

83 *In several instances*: Jo Freeman, *The Politics of Women's Liberation: A Case Study of an Emerging Social Movement and Its Relation to the Policy Process* (London: Longman, 1975), 87.

83 *"hardly covered anything"*: Clarenbach, interview by Andreasen.

83 *"finance our own 'revolution'"*: Hernandez, "Suggestions to the National Board of NOW."

83 *"If we are not to become"*: Hernandez to Clarenbach and Friedan, re: Many and Varied, July 5, 1967, "NOW-1966–7" folder, box 26, Hernandez Papers.

84 *Only one-third of NOW's members*: NOW Board Meeting Minutes, Jan. 27–28, 1968, 2.

84 *The leaders debated fundraising*: Fox Papers; NOW Board Meeting Minutes, Dec. 6, 1969, 3, folder 5, box 2, NOW Records.

84 *"I don't know"*: Betty Friedan, "Our Revolution Is Unique: President's Report to the National Conference of NOW," Dec. 6, 1968, 3, folder 1568, Friedan Papers.

84 *"I was a kid"*: Read and Collins, interview by author, 5.

84 *"It turned out"*: Collins, interview by Connell, 7, folder 6, box 8.

84 *"big, ugly" hats*: Collins, interview by Davison, n.d., 10.

85 *"No, not there"*: Collins, interview by Connell, 7, folder 6, box 8.

85 *The secretarial skills*: Carol Kleiman, "Executive Wins in Man's World," *Chicago Tribune*, May 22, 1969, B6.

85 *Collins was there*: Lupa, interview by author, 5; Collins, interview by Connell, 7, folder 6, box 8.

85 *Chicago was an epicenter*: Mark Kurlansky, *1968: The Year That Rocked the World* (New York: Ballantine Books, 2004), 9, 269–86.

85 *This bloody showdown*: Stansell, *Feminist Promise*, 234.

85 *New Left women criticized*: Stansell, *Feminist Promise*, 222–27.

85 *"probably made it inevitable"*: Collins, interview by Connell, 15, folder 6, box 8.

86 *"NOW was more pragmatist"*: Collins, interview by Connell, 41, folder 6, box 8.

86 *"I was a radical feminist"*: Collins, interview by Connell, 42, folder 6, box 8.

86 *"All of us"*: Marian McBride, "OWLs Flock to NOW Leader," Feb. 5, 1970, news clipping, folder 14, box 15, Collins NOW Officer Papers.

86 *"the underwear question"*: "In Short: What Are Feminists' Aims?," *Newsday*, April 11, 1974, 13A.

86 *"Society has chosen"*: Barbara Strain, "Oppression Blocks Women's Liberation, Speaker Says," *Milwaukee Journal*, March 12, 1970, folder 14, box 15, Collins NOW Officer Papers.

86 *"They say women"*: Kleiman, "Executive Wins in Man's World."

87 *Despite their mutual critiques*: Gosse, *Rethinking the New Left*, 161.

87 *At many newspapers*: Stansell, *Feminist Promise*, 237.

87 *"women's lib" groups*: Kit Barrett, "Women's Rights: Where Have All the Shrinking Violets Gone?," *Chicago Tribune*, May 17, 1970, W4.

87 *"The women who"*: "The Seventies May Usher in Woman Power," *Hartford Courant*, Feb. 25, 1970, 42C.

87 *Papers printed the occasional letter*: Mrs. Clayton C. Moore, "Too Oppressed to Attend Lib Rally," *Chicago Tribune*, Sept. 4, 1970, 12.

87 *"If the old dragon-slayer"*: Dick West, "Ladies Demand Equality—So Who Needs Men?," *New Journal and Guide*, June 3, 1967, 6.

87 *"So the nuclear age"*: Ken Botwright, "Wives Scoff at 'Cook-for-Husband' Law," *Boston Globe*, Dec. 13, 1969, 1.

88 *The chapter had*: Collins, interview by Connell, 10, folder 6, box 8; Lupa, interview by author, 11; Karen Fishman and Anne Ladky, interview by author, Feb. 26, 2018, 1–2.

88 *"that economic issues"*: Collins, interview by Connell, 24–25, folder 6, box 8.

88 *"I was a kid"*: Collins, interview by author, 2015, 7.

88 *By the summer of 1969*: Aleta D. Steyers to NOW National Board Meeting, June 28–30, 1969, re: Chicago Area Chapter Report, folder 1629, Friedan Papers.

88 *"We had 150 people"*: Collins, interview by author, 2015, 9.

88 *Some organized sit-ins*: "Women Break Bars at Men's Tavern," clipping, n.d., folder 14, box 15, Collins NOW Officer Papers.

88 *"It's kind of like"*: "Viewpoint," *Hospitality World*, Feb. 1970, 10C, folder 14, box 15, Collins NOW Officer Papers.

88 *"This insults women"*: Collins, interview by Connell, 56, folder 6, box 8.

88 *"like waking up"*: Collins, interview by Connell, 56, folder 6, box 8.

89 *"all the power"*: Burnett, interview by Boyer, 45, folder 20, box 7.

89 *Many in the group*: Helen Fogel, "Michigan NOW Organizes, Seeks the 'Silent Majority,'" *Detroit Free Press*, Jan. 9, 1970, 1C.

89 *"a wide variety"*: Marj Jackson Levin, "The Beginning—1969," Metropolitan Detroit NOW Newsletter clipping, n.d., ca. 1981, "Recollections of NOW" folder, box 10, Burnett Papers.

89 *She and Burnett invited*: Barbara Hitsky, "Detroit Feminists Map Strategy—NOW," *Detroit News*, Jan. 9, 1970, 2D.

89 *"chic" gathering began*: Fogel, "Michigan NOW Organizes, Seeks the 'Silent Majority.'"

89 *"We're trying to reach"*: Hitsky, "Detroit Feminists Map Strategy—NOW."

89 *"We don't want to change"*: Barbara Hitsky, "Now Is the Time: Women of the World, Unite for Your Rights," *Detroit News*, n.d., ca. 1969, "Correspondence, 1966–2002" folder, box 7, Burnett Papers.

89 *The room was visibly moved*: Levin, "Beginning—1969."

89 *Michigan, where an 1846 law*: Michigan's penal code made it a felony to give a pregnant woman "any medicine, drug, substance," or use "any instrument or other means whatever, with intent thereby to procure the miscarriage of any such woman," unless it was necessary to save her life. If the pregnant woman died in an attempted abortion, anyone who helped with that abortion could be charged with manslaughter. Andrew Howell, *The General Statutes of the State of Michigan* (Chicago: Callaghan, 1883), 2:2211; "750.14: Miscarriage; administering with intent to procure; felony, penalty," *Michigan Penal Code*, Act 328 of 1931, Section 750.14, www.legislature.mi.gov/(S(55flms3egf14nti4r5yiatrc))/mileg.aspx?page=GetObject&objectname=mcl-750-14.

90 *The sexual revolution*: Stansell, *Feminist Promise*, 317.

90 *Radical feminists had joined*: Stansell, *Feminist Promise*, 323.

90 *When, in 1973, the U.S. Supreme Court*: Cobble, Gordon, and Henry, *Feminism Unfinished*, 72.

90 *"passed the feathered hat"*: Burnett to Detroit NOW, "NOW Was My Time," May 26, 1995, 1, "Speeches, Publications & Interviews" folder, box 10, Burnett Papers.

90 *Friedan was about to host*: Friedan, *"It Changed My Life,"* 130.

90 *"in a ragged t-shirt and jeans"*: Burnett to Detroit NOW, "NOW Was My Time," 2.

90 *"said she was a Republican"*: Friedan, *"It Changed My Life,"* 130.

90 *And Burnett was surprised*: Burnett to Detroit NOW, "NOW Was My Time," 2.

90 *"The moment that press"*: Burnett to Detroit NOW, "NOW Was My Time," 3.

91 *"the most conservative"*: Margaret Weisenberger, "Motor City Lions Hear Women's Lib President," Michigan NOW Newsletter, Nov. 1970, 3, folder 4, box 1, Marjorie Jackson Levin Papers, Walter Reuther Library, Wayne State University.

91 *One of their first protests*: Burnett, interview by Boyer, 184–86, folder 2, box 8.

91 *"stealthily sewed squares"*: Burnett to Detroit NOW, "NOW Was My Time," 3.

91 *"unescorted by men"*: Burnett to Detroit NOW, "NOW Was My Time," 4.

91 *Michigan NOW convened*: Bonnie Calvin, "Political Action Committee," *As We See It NOW* (Detroit), Oct. 1970, 3, NOW Chapter Newsletters Collection.

92 *"too chauvinistic"*: "NOW Meeting Agenda," Jan. 14, 1971, "Burnett Notebooks: Michigan NOW, 1969–1974" folder, box 6, Burnett Papers.

92 *As part of this effort*: "PICNIC!! At: Patricia Burnett's," *As We See It NOW*, Aug. 1972, 5, NOW Chapter Newsletters Collection.

92 *Unanimously reelected president*: "Michigan NOW in the News," *As We See It NOW*, Nov. 1970, 3–4, NOW Chapter Newsletters Collection.

92 *"great press"*: Burnett, interview by Boyer, 53, folder 20, box 7.

92 *More women found*: "Detroit Chapter of NOW," n.d., folder 1628, Friedan Papers.

92 *Michigan Women's Liberation Coalition*: Enke, *Finding the Movement*, 237.

92 *Within the next few years*: Enke, *Finding the Movement*, 243.

92 *Detroit Feminist Women's Health Center*: Enke, *Finding the Movement*, 179, 201.

92 *"We'd go one by one"*: Burnett, interview by Boyer, 55, folder 20, box 7.

92 *"a kind of free therapy"*: Burnett to Detroit NOW, "NOW Was My Time," 6–7.

92 *"After hearing and seeing"*: Burnett, interview by Boyer, 53, folder 20, box 7.

93 *Detroit was increasingly polarized*: Thompson, *Whose Detroit?*, 2–3.

93 *But liberal hopes*: Thompson, *Whose Detroit?*, 29, 46–47.

93 *Jobs had been declining*: Enke, *Finding the Movement*, 14.

93 *Members held press conferences*: "Detroit Chapter of NOW," n.d., "Patricia Hill Burnett NOW, 1974–5 and Undated," box 3, Burnett Papers.

93 *"We need to keep the pressure"*: *As We See It NOW*, April 1971, 3, NOW Chapter Newsletters Collection.

93 *The Detroiters also made*: "Detroit Chapter of NOW," n.d., "Patricia Hill Burnett NOW, 1974–5 and Undated," box 3, Burnett Papers.

93 *As of 1971*: "List of Michigan NOW Officers," *As We See It NOW*, March 1971, 5, NOW Chapter Newsletters Collection.

93 *NOW was the second largest*: Marjory [sic] Jackson, "A Detroit Feminist Speaks Out," Spring 1970, 5, folder 4, box 1, Levin Papers.

94 *"every major women's coalition"*: "Detroit Chapter of NOW," n.d., "Patricia Hill Burnett NOW, 1974–5 and Undated," box 3, Burnett Papers.

94 *"It's easier to revolt"*: "Notebook: NOW August 1970 to January 1971."

94 *"the veil of intimidation"*: "Notebook: NOW August 1970 to January 1971."

94 *"Being attractive is"*: "Surprise, Surprise," *She Magazine*, clipping, n.d., ca. 1980, 84, "Biographical + Artistic, 3 of 5" folder, box 1, Burnett Papers.

94 *In spiral-bound notebooks*: "P.H.B. Notebook," Nov. 1969 to Feb. 1970, "Burnett Notebooks" folder, box 6, Burnett Papers.

95 *"Can a liberated housemaid"*: "Notebook: NOW August 1970 to January 1971."

95 *"Being a feminist"*: Patricia Hill Burnett, notes, n.d., ca. 1990s, "Talks" folder, box 7, Burnett Papers.

95 *"get inside and infiltrate"*: "Patricia Hill Burnett . . . from Beauty Queen to Leading Feminist."

95 *She was a founding member*: Harriet B. Rotter to National Women's Political Caucus

Founders, re: Michigan Chapter, n.d., "Correspondence, 1966–2002" folder, box 7, Burnett Papers.

95 *"I truly believe"*: Burnett, interview by Boyer, 82, folder 1, box 8.

95 *"a person rather than"*: Burnett, interview by Boyer, 133, folder 1, box 8.

95 *"I could have probably"*: Friedan, interview by Marlene Sanders, Dec. 21, 1993, 8, folder 4, box 9, Tully-Crenshaw Feminist Oral History Project.

95 *"overpowering ego"*: Oliver, *Betty Friedan*, 110.

95 *"She was a screamer"*: Alexander, interview by Kelly Anderson, video recording, March 20, 2004, and Oct. 22, 2005, Voices of Feminism Oral History Project, Sophia Smith Collection, Smith College.

96 *"subtly accustom her"*: Jean Witter to Wilma Scott Heide, Feb. 7, 1969, folder 1, box 1, Jean Witter Papers, University of Pittsburgh Library Special Collections.

96 *Friedan stepped down*: Oliver, *Betty Friedan*, 109–10.

96 *"recruited" to run*: Hernandez, interview by Davison, June 30, 1997, 3.

96 *"the living example"*: Carabillo, interview by Muriel Fox, May 1997, 123, folder 2, box 12, Tully-Crenshaw Feminist Oral History Project.

96 *"To watch her conduct"*: "Meet NOW National President," *NOW News* (Los Angeles), May 1970, 1, folder 43, box 1, NOW Records.

96 *They noted Hernandez's soft voice*: Frances Cerra, "Feminist President Speaks Softly," *Newsday*, May 13, 1970, 17A.

96 *"Is it a howling success"*: Maggie Savoy, "NOW Lib Group Leader Too Busy to Be Angry," *Los Angeles Times*, June 3, 1970, E1.

96 *Early in her presidency*: Fox, interview by author, 3.

97 *It was "extraordinary"*: Alexander, interview by Anderson, March 20, 2004, and Oct. 22, 2005.

97 *Also in attendance*: Sherie Randolph, *Florynce "Flo" Kennedy: The Life of a Black Feminist Radical* (Chapel Hill: University of North Carolina Press, 2015), 101, 113.

97 *Black Power, the movement*: Gosse, *Rethinking the New Left*, 112–15.

97 *She had tried to take clients*: Michele Ingrassia, "NOW and Then," *New York Newsday*, Oct. 29, 1991, 59.

97 *"If you have a fur coat"*: Fox, interview by author, 3.

97 *"Most of us didn't have"*: Alexander, interview by Davison, n.d., 3.

97 *New York became NOW's*: NOW National Board Meeting Minutes, Dec. 6, 1968, 1, folder 3, box 2, NOW Records.

97 *The chapter already comprised*: Preliminary Report of the Nominating Committee, Nov. 6, 1968, folder 1, box 5, Heide Papers.

98 *"Their dress varied"*: Lisa Hammel, "A Class of Fledgling Pickets Gets the Word: 'Make It Exciting, Make It Swing!,'" *New York Times*, Aug. 24, 1968, 33.

98 *As the chapter grew*: Collins, *When Everything Changed*, 191; Friedan to Atkinson, Sept. 20, 1967, folder 1507, Friedan Papers.

98 *A 1968 New York Times article*: Martha Weinman Lear, "The Second Feminist Wave," *New York Times*, March 10, 1968, SM24.

98 *"a fully equal partnership"*: Carabillo, Meuli, and Csida, *Feminist Chronicles*, 159.

98 *Barnard College's president*: Peterson to Clarenbach, May 7, 1968, folder 1477, Friedan Papers.

98 *part of a militant*: Gosse, *Rethinking the New Left*, 100.

98 *"of course disturbed"*: Clarenbach to Peterson, May 17, 1968, folder 1477, Friedan Papers.

98 *"very, very painful"*: Jean Faust, interview by Julie Altman, June 20, 1990, 31, folder 5, box 4, Tully-Crenshaw Feminist Oral History Project.

98 *"Freedom for Women" button*: Randolph, *Florynce "Flo" Kennedy*, 145.

98 *Friedan fretted that advocacy*: Friedan to Faith A. Seidenberg, June 25, 1968, folder 1536b, Friedan Papers.

98 *"We've got to get rid of"*: Eastwood, interview by Fox, 54.

98 *At the September 1968*: NOW Board Meeting Minutes, Sept. 14–15, 1968, 4, folder 3, box 2, NOW Records.

98 *"the causes and dangers"*: Friedan to Seidenberg, June 25, 1968.

99 *But she was among*: Excerpt from Minutes of NOW Board Meeting, Sept. 14–15, 1968, folder 3, box 2, Marcia Cohen Papers, 1967–87, Schlesinger Library.

99 *"an experiment in participatory democracy"*: Florynce Kennedy to "The Officialdom of NOW, National and New York," Nov. 18, 1968, folder 1536b, Friedan Papers.

99 *"Imagine every member"*: Love, interview by Sidney Abbott, July 1993, 15, folder 12, box 5, Tully-Crenshaw Feminist Oral History Project.

99 *"being, if not destroyed"*: Jean Faust to Clarenbach, Oct. 2, 1968, folder 1536b, Friedan Papers.

99 *"people would end up"*: Collins, *When Everything Changed*, 192.

99 *Frustrated in their efforts*: Randolph, *Florynce "Flo" Kennedy*, 160–64.

99 *Atkinson formed the October 17th Movement*: "'Young, Black, and Beautiful' Organize," *Los Angeles Times*, Oct. 31, 1968, C4.

99 *"The name of the game"*: "Why Women Complain," *New York Times*, July 26, 1970, 119.

99 *"on the liberal grounds"*: Sidney Abbott and Barbara Love, *Sappho Was a Right-On Woman* (New York: Stein and Day, 1972), 109.

99 *Over time, women in the chapter*: Abbott and Love, *Sappho Was a Right-On Woman*, 110.

100 *"It was bad enough"*: Flora Davis, *Moving the Mountain: The Women's Movement in America Since 1960* (New York: Simon & Schuster, 1991), 262.

100 *"I thought, frankly"*: Abbott, interview by Barbara Love, July 1993, 31, folder 1, box 1, Tully-Crenshaw Feminist Oral History Project.

100 *Some lesbians believed*: Davis, *Moving the Mountain*, 262–63.

100 *"terrible radical"*: Abbott, interview by Love, 21, folder 1, box 1.

100 *"white glove background"*: Abbott, interview by Love, 20, folder 1, box 1.

100 *Friedan believed that NOW*: Stansell, *Feminist Promise*, 253–54.

100 *"to make yourself ugly"*: Rosen, *World Split Open*, 87.

100 *"home-grown radical"*: Horowitz, *Betty Friedan and the Making of "The Feminine Mystique,"* 10.

101 *Later, amid the rigid*: Margot Canaday, *Queer Career: Sexuality and Work in Modern America* (Princeton, N.J.: Princeton University Press, 2023).

101 *"who need a little more experience"*: "Chapter 6" of book draft, 16–17, folder 1, box 3, Kolb Papers.

101 *Friedan had prevented*: Lillian Faderman, *The Gay Revolution* (New York: Simon & Schuster, 2015), 235.

101 *The three-day conference*: Rosen, *World Split Open*, 86.

101 *"kidnap the Congress"*: Faderman, *Gay Revolution*, 235.

101 *"sitting about in the middle"*: Love, interview by Abbott, 27, folder 12, box 5.

102 WOMEN'S LIBERATION IS: Faderman, *Gay Revolution*, 236.

102 *"Does anyone want"*: Sara Warner, *Acts of Gaiety: LGBT Performance and the Politics of Pleasure* (Ann Arbor: University of Michigan Press, 2012), ix.

102 *"Yes, yes, sisters!"*: Faderman, *Gay Revolution*, 236.

102 *"This conference won't proceed"*: Faderman, *Gay Revolution*, 236.

102 *"After the refreshments"*: Abbott and Love, *Sappho Was a Right-On Woman*, 114.

102 *"didn't really jell"*: Freidan, *"It Changed My Life,"* 138.

102 *Just weeks later*: Gosse, *Rethinking the New Left*, 4.

103 *Ivy Bottini, a suburban*: David Mixner and Dennis Bailey, *Brave Journeys: Profiles in Gay and Lesbian Courage* (New York: Bantam Books, 2000), 48.

103 *Bottini came out*: Mixner and Bailey, *Brave Journeys*, 70.

103 *"The first time I met her"*: Collins, interview by Connell, 44, folder 6, box 8.

103 *"to work on our shared"*: Abbott and Love, *Sappho Was a Right-On Woman*, 119.

103 *"Is Lesbianism a Feminist Issue?"*: Abbott and Love, *Sappho Was a Right-On Woman*, 120.

103 *"stick to our original"*: Jacqui Ceballos, "Letter Number 2," Jan. 31, 1971, "NOW-NYC Founding Documents" folder, NOW Chapter Newsletters Collection.

103 *Friedan worked actively*: "Minutes from the General Membership Meeting," March 16, 1971, folder 11, box 2, National Organization for Women, New York City Chapter Records, Tamiment Library & Robert F. Wagner Labor Archives, New York University.

103 *her allies resigned*: Bottini, interview by Davison, 1994, 6.

103 *"I happen to like"*: Mixner and Bailey, *Brave Journeys*, 49.

103 *"We do not prescribe"*: *As We See It NOW*, April 1971, 10–11, folder 1628, Friedan Papers.

104 *"the unfinished business"*: Friedan, *"It Changed My Life,"* 141.

104 *"bra-burning actions"*: "Betty Friedan's Recollections," 1, folder 8, box 1, Shirley Bernard Papers, Schlesinger Library.

104 *"a sinking feeling"*: "Aileen Hernandez," folder 8, box 1, Bernard Papers.

104 *"We were all"*: Collins, interview by Connell, 20–21, folder 6, box 8.

105 *"do their own thing"*: NOW Board of Directors Meeting Minutes, May 2–3, 1970, folder 7, box 2, NOW Records.

105 *"Wear a button"*: "Women's Lib Strikes Again, 'Strike for Women' Is Set," *Chicago Daily Defender*, Aug. 22, 1970, 20.

105 *"refrain from all shopping"*: Elizabeth Shelton, "Women's Strike Planned Aug. 26," *Washington Post*, May 5, 1970, D6.

105 *"not on the women's page"*: "Betty Friedan's Recollections," 2.

105 *"Women Strike for Women"*: "Women's Lib Strikes Again, 'Strike for Women' Is Set."

105 *There were demonstrations*: "It Was a Great Day for Women on the March," *New York Times*, Aug. 30, 1970, 125.

105 *Hernandez addressed a noontime rally*: Dorothy Townsend, "Women's 'Lib' Group Plans Nationwide Strike," *Los Angeles Times*, Aug. 23, 1970, B1.

105 *Women also picketed*: "Betty Friedan's Recollections," 4.

105 *The New Orleans States-Item printed*: "Ad Policies Rapped by Striking Women," *Guild Reporter*, Sept. 11, 1970, 12.

105 *Feminists in Rochester*: Townsend, "Women's 'Lib' Group Plans Nationwide Strike."

105 *At college radio stations*: Muriel Dobbin, "In the Nation," *Baltimore Sun*, Aug. 27, 1970, A1.

105 *"cute little script"*: "Karen DeCrow," 4, folder 8, box 1, Bernard Papers.

105 *Nationwide, each of the three*: Bonnie J. Dow, *Watching Women's Liberation 1970: Feminism's Pivotal Year on the Network News* (Urbana: University of Illinois Press, 2014), 144–67.

106 *In Washington, D.C., the twelve hundred*: Elizabeth Shelton, "Women's Rally," *Washington Post*, July 24, 1970, B1.

106 *Secretaries in the Pentagon's*: Dobbin, "In the Nation," A8.

106 *Another one thousand protesters*: Claudia Levy and Alex Wald, "Women Rally to Publicize Grievances," *Washington Post*, Aug. 27, 1970, A1, A7.

106 *"informative and entertaining"*: "Women's Lib Strikes Again, 'Strike for Women' Is Set."

106 *The speakers came from*: "Women's Lib Strikes Again, 'Strike for Women' Is Set"; Collins, interview by Connell, 21, folder 6, box 8.

106 *As the first rally*: Bonne J. Nesbitt, "No Bra Burning in Rally," *Chicago Daily Defender*, Aug. 27, 1970, 3.

106 *"One day of kids"*: Carol Kleiman, "American Women, Today Is Your Day!," *Chicago Tribune*, Aug. 26, 1970, B1.

106 *"We were exhausted"*: Collins, interview by Connell, 21–22, folder 6, box 8.

107 *"come in from"*: "Betty Friedan's Recollections," 2.

107 *A group of feminists*: Linda Charlton, "Women Seeking Equality March on 5th Ave. Today," *New York Times*, Aug. 26, 1970, 44.

107 *"Repent, male chauvinists"*: Dobbin, "In the Nation."

107 *"You and Your Marriage"*: Charlton, "Women Seeking Equality March on 5th Ave. Today."

107 *"warn people about"*: Linda Charlton, "Women March Down Fifth in Equality Drive," *New York Times*, Aug. 27, 1970, 1.

107 *The police department assigned*: "It Was a Great Day for Women on the March," *New York Times*, Aug. 30, 1970, 125.

107 *"We can have it again"*: Dobbin, "In the Nation."

108 *"in great swinging"*: Friedan, *"It Changed My Life,"* 151.

108 *Suddenly there were thousands*: "It Was a Great Day for Women on the March."

108 *"Men for Women's Rights"*: Charlton, "Women March Down Fifth in Equality Drive."

108 *"absolute mass of women"*: "Betty Friedan's Recollections," 3.

4. WE HAVE DIFFERENT PROBLEMS

109 The Mary Tyler Moore Show: Don Page, "New Time, New Show for Mary Tyler Moore," *Los Angeles Times*, Sept. 21, 1970, E22.

109 *That year, Germaine Greer's*: Germaine Greer, *The Female Eunuch* (London: MacGibbon & Kee, 1970).

109 *All three hundred thousand copies*: Gosse, *Rethinking the New Left*, 162.

109 *"By the very force"*: Deirdre Carmody, "Feminists Shifting Emphasis from Persons to Politics," *New York Times*, Aug. 22, 1972, 47.

109 *Feminist lawyers framed*: Evans, *Tidal Wave*, 62–63.

109 *Joining with Steinem*: Gosse, *Rethinking the New Left*, 162; Stansell, *Feminist Promise*, 282–83.

110 *In 1972 alone*: Evans, *Tidal Wave*, 67.

110 *Although NOW had pursued*: Rebecca Davison, "The Hot Years," 7–14, unpublished manuscript, in author's possession; Gosse, *Rethinking the New Left*, 163. On feminist coalitions in the early 1970s, see also Blair, *Revolutionizing Expectations*, esp. 63; Anne M. Valk, *Radical Sisters: Second-Wave Feminism and Black Liberation in Washington, D.C.* (Urbana: University of Illinois Press, 2008), esp. 5; Stephanie Gilmore, ed., *Feminist Coalitions: Historical Perspectives on Second-Wave Feminism in the United States* (Urbana: University of Illinois Press, 2008).

110 *"If somebody could think"*: Collins, interview by author, 2015, 12.

110 *Members protested sexism*: "NOW to Protest 'Sex in Toys,'" *Atlanta Constitution*, April 5, 1973, 28A; "Image, Action, and NOW," *Washington Post*, Aug. 25, 1973, B3; Marjorie Hyer, "Women's Group Asks Reform of Churches," *Washington Post*, Oct. 29, 1973, C1; "3-Month Battle: College Places Ban on Campus Beauty Contests," *Los Angeles Times*, Jan. 26, 1972, 3.

110 *NOW's co-filed charges*: "Women's Rights Study Begun at Universities," *New York Times*, April 5, 1970, 43.

110 *That same year*: Fred Bruning, "Wings of Man Are Clipped," *Newsday*, Jan. 8, 1970, 15.

110 *In 1973, NOW won*: Pittsburgh Press Co. v. Pittsburgh Commission on Human Relations, 413 U.S. 276 (1973).

110 *And in 1974*: Kay Mills, "NOW Campaigns for TV Reform," *Atlanta Constitution*,

June 11, 1974, 9B; Patricia Shelton, "NOW Broadens Its Attack," *Christian Science Monitor*, Sept. 18, 1970, 18; "FCC Sets Pro Woman Rule," *Boston Globe*, Dec. 21, 1971, 32.

110 *often the only outlet*: Gilmore, *Groundswell*, 15.

110 *"We're the only place"*: Lisa Hammel, "NOW Still Growing—but It's Still White and Middle-Class . . . ," *New York Times*, Jan. 24, 1976, 35.

110 *NOW had eighteen thousand members*: "The New Woman, 1972," *Time*, March 20, 1972, 29.

110 *Two years later*: MacLean, *American Women's Movement*, 16; Kim Gandy, interview by author, May 3, 2021, 1; "NOW Membership's Characteristics Told," *Los Angeles Times*, May 26, 1974, 6.

110 *the radical feminist groups*: Evans, *Tidal Wave*, 45–46; Freeman, *Politics of Women's Liberation*, 142–46.

111 *any ten people*: "Standards for Provisional Chapters," ca. Aug. 1970, folder 1, box 5, Bernard Papers; M. L. Myers, "Administrative Policies and Procedures, Assumptions and Delegations of Authority, 1966–1972," July 30, 1972, 5, folder 9, box 1, NOW Records.

111 *As members brought varied*: "Action: NCAC-NOW Task Forces Briefly Noted," *Vocal Majority*, June 1973, 7, folder 3, box 1, NOW Washington, D.C., Chapter and Capitol Hill Chapter Records, Special Collections Research Center, George Washington University. On the variety of NOW chapters, see, for example, Gilmore, *Groundswell*, 44; Jo Reger, "Organizational Dynamics and Construction of Multiple Feminist Identities in the National Organization for Women," *Gender and Society* 16 (Oct. 2002): 710–27; and Stansell, *Feminist Promise*, 276–79.

111 *"We have different problems"*: Fosburgh, "Dealing with Feminism in Black and White."

111 *"We thought we were"*: Maria Karagianis, "Feminists of 27 Nations Vow 'to Change Society,'" *Boston Globe*, June 5, 1973, 29.

111 *"began to feel like"*: Clarenbach, interview by Andreasen.

111 *"wasn't going to go"*: Read and Collins, interview by author, 6.

111 *By 1974, just eight years*: "Summary of Questionnaire for NOW," n.d., ca. 1974, folder 4, box 45, Karen DeCrow Papers, Special Collections, Charles Deering McCormick Library, Northwestern University.

111 *In addition to Murray*: Scanlon, *Until There Is Justice*, 209.

112 *"We had great women"*: Bell, *Lighting the Fires of Freedom*, 83.

112 *"Black women feel resentful"*: Charlayne Hunter, "Black Members Are Few in Women's Lib Groups," *Atlanta Constitution*, Nov. 21, 1970, 2B.

112 *"You need a minority"*: Eastwood, interview by Fox, 37.

112 *Inez Casiano, who worked*: "Inez Casiano Feminist of the Month—July 2011," accessed Aug. 3, 2022, www.veteranfeministsofamerica.org/legacy/INEZ%20CASIANO2.htm.

112 *"very pretty"*: Eastwood, interview by Fox, 37. Fox made this comment while interviewing Eastwood.

112 *She foregrounded the Catholic*: Anne Braude, "Faith, Feminism, and History," in *The Religious History of American Women: Reimagining the Past*, ed. Catherine A. Brekus (Chapel Hill: University of North Carolina Press, 2007), 240.

112 *"were liberating themselves"*: Friedan, *"It Changed My Life,"* 85.

112 *"the most serious victims"*: Anna Arnold Hedgeman, "Task Force on Women in Poverty Report," n.d., ca. 1966–67, folder 30, box 48, NOW Records.

113 *But she resigned*: Scanlon, *Until There Is Justice*, 212.

113 *Neither Casiano nor*: Loretta J. Ross, "Combating Racism: Chronology of Women of Color Events in NOW History," Oct. 1987, folder 20, box 48, NOW Records. Jennifer Scanlon notes that Casiano remained involved with NOW until her death in 2011. Scanlon, *Until There Is Justice*, 210.

113 *"we had to threaten"*: Carabillo, interview by Fox, 20, folder 1, box 2.

113 *Ollie Butler Moore*: Carabillo, interview by Fox, 20, folder 1, box 2; Barbara J. Love, ed., *Feminists Who Changed America, 1963–1975* (Urbana: University of Illinois Press, 2006), 321.

113 *the past was rife*: On the longer history of racial tensions among women, see, most recently, Kyla Schuller, *The Trouble with White Women: A Counterhistory of Feminism* (New York: Bold Type Books, 2021).

113 *Most notably, white suffragists*: Schuller, *Trouble with White Women*, 44.

113 *"racial" problem rather than*: Alice Paul quoted in Nancy F. Cott, *The Grounding of Modern Feminism* (New Haven, Conn.: Yale University Press, 1987), 69.

113 *"Fifty years ago"*: Hunter, "Black Members Are Few in Women's Lib Groups."

113 *"Feminist thinking"*: Gilmore, *Groundswell*, 32.

113 *"women's liberation"*: Gilmore, *Groundswell*, 34.

114 *Repelled by white women's pressure*: Springer, *Living for the Revolution*, 31; Ashley Farmer, *Remaking Black Power: How Black Women Transformed an Era* (Chapel Hill: University of North Carolina Press, 2017), esp. 6–11; Berry and Gross, *Black Women's History of the United States*, 188–94; Spencer, *Revolution Has Come*, 45–48.

114 *"gender first" feminism*: On "gender first" feminism, see Venus Green, "Flawed Remedies: EEOC, AT&T, and Sears Outcomes Reconsidered," *Black Women, Gender, and Families* 6, no. 1 (Spring 2012): 43–70.

114 *"interlocking" systems of oppression*: The Combahee River Collective (CRC), a Black feminist group that began meeting in 1974 as a radical offshoot of the National Black Feminist Organization, which was itself created in response to white-led feminist groups' anemic treatment of racism, theorized that forms of oppression were "interlocking" and took place "simultaneously." See Keeanga-Yamahtta Taylor, ed., *How We Get Free: Black Feminism and the Combahee River Collective* (Chicago: Haymarket Books, 2017), esp. 4. The CRC's 1977 statement is reprinted on pp. 15–27.

114 *African Americans had spent*: See, for example, Elsa Barkley Brown, "To Catch the Vision of Freedom: Reconstructing Southern Black Women's Political History, 1865–1880," in *African American Women and the Vote, 1837–1960*, ed. Ann Gordon et al. (Amherst: University of Massachusetts Press, 1997); Martha S. Jones, *Vanguard: How Black Women Broke Barriers, Won the Vote, and Insisted on Equality for All* (New York: Basic Books, 2020); Premilla Nadasen, *Welfare Warriors: The Welfare Rights Movement in the United States* (New York: Routledge, 2005); Felicia Kornbluh, *The Battle for Welfare Rights: Politics and Poverty in Modern America* (Philadelphia: University of Pennsylvania Press, 2007); Annelise Orleck, *Storming Caesar's Palace: How Black Mothers Fought Their Own War on Poverty* (Boston: Beacon Press, 2006); Kimberly Springer, *Living for the Revolution: Black Feminist Organizations, 1968–1980* (Durham, N.C.: Duke University Press, 2005), 19–21; Rebecca Tuuri, *Strategic Sisterhood: The National Council of Negro Women in the Black Freedom Struggle* (Chapel Hill: University of North Carolina Press, 2018). On how Black, Chicana, and white women emerged from different political traditions and cultural contexts, thus coming to feminism by "separate roads," see Benita Roth, *Separate Roads to Feminism: Black, Chicana, and White Feminist Movements in America's Second Wave* (Cambridge, U.K.: Cambridge University Press, 2012); on Black and white women's conflict and cooperation in the civil rights movement, which contributed to tensions in feminist movement building, see Winifred Breines, *The Trouble Between Us: An Uneasy History of White and Black Women in the Feminist Movement* (Oxford: Oxford University Press, 2006).

114 *Chicana feminism also began*: Roth, *Separate Roads to Feminism*, 129–40.

114 *"there were 'ghetto sex' jobs"*: Aileen C. Hernandez, "Equal Employment Opportunities

for Women: Problems, Facts & Answers," *Contact* 3, no. 10 (Fall 1973): 11, "Aileen" folder, box 19, Hernandez Papers.

114 *"the most profound movement"*: Maggie Crum, "NOW President Speaks for Women's Lib," *Contra Costa Times*, Oct. 30, 1970, 1B, "NOW 1970" folder, box 26, Hernandez Papers.

114 *A tight focus*: Judy Klemesrud, "NOW's New President Sees Men Helped, Too," *New York Times*, May 2, 1970, 36.

114 *"whether she wants to work"*: "NOW Head Asserts: Black Women Think Birth Control Is Aimed at Them," *Chicago Daily Defender*, Feb. 2, 1971, 17.

115 *Black women recalled a history*: Schuller, *Trouble with White Women*, 115–47.

115 *"the birth of defectives"*: Sanger quoted in Schuller, *Trouble with White Women*, 118.

115 *"most victimized by"*: Fosburgh, "Dealing with Feminism in Black and White."

115 *"All women have problems"*: "With Consciousness Raised, NOW Focusing on Economy and Politics," *Baltimore Sun*, Oct. 29, 1974, B6.

115 *"as a dilettante organization"*: Fosburgh, "Dealing with Feminism in Black and White."

115 *"one might suspect"*: Helen Fogel, "NOW Changes Focus . . . Action, Not Words," *Detroit Free Press*, March 24, 1970, 1-C.

115 *"irrelevant" or "a side issue"*: Valerie Jo Bradley, "Black Woman Heads Drive to Liberate Women," *Jet*, n.d., ca. 1970, 48, "Aileen Clippings" folder, box 29, Hernandez Papers.

115 *"toward a better society"*: Toni Carabillo, "Meet NOW National President," *NOW News* (Los Angeles), May 1970, 4, folder 43, box 1, NOW Chapter Newsletters Collection.

115 *This meant developing*: Aileen Hernandez, "Revolution: From the Doll's House to the White House!," Sept. 4, 1971, folder 17, box 23, NOW Records.

115 *"All the issues"*: Hernandez, interview by Davison, Nov. 1995, 2.

115 *"had the right motivations"*: Hernandez quoted in Roth, *Separate Roads to Feminism*, 106.

116 *"subverting Black liberation"*: Marijean Suelzle to Hernandez, Sept. 8, 1970, "NOW Chapter Corr. West" folder, box 27, Hernandez Papers.

116 *"consciously or unconsciously"*: Hernandez to Suelzle, Sept. 25, 1970, "NOW Chapter Corr. West" folder, box 27, Hernandez Papers.

116 *"militant" Black women*: Inez Smith Reid, *"Together" Black Women* (New York: Emerson Hall Publishers, 1972), x.

116 *"ideas on the major"*: Joseph Jenkins, "'Together' Shoots Down Myths," *Afro-American*, Feb. 10, 1973, A1.

116 *Of those who did*: Reid, *"Together" Black Women*, 50, 51.

116 *"Your presidency has symbolic"*: Murray to Hernandez, Aug. 7, 1971, folder 902, Murray Papers.

116 *"not interested in being"*: Hernandez, interview by Davison, June 30, 1997, 3–4.

116 *"one person"*: Bell, *Lighting the Fires of Freedom*, 84–85.

116 *"obviously inept procedures"*: Hernandez to Casey Eicke, April 7, 1970, "NOW 1970" folder, box 26, Hernandez Papers.

116 *"If this movement"*: "Keynote Address—Aileen C. Hernandez," NOW National Conference, Los Angeles, Sept. 3–6, 1972, 4, "NOW Minority Wm/Wm's Rights Task Force" folder, box 22, Hernandez Papers.

117 *Patsy Fulcher*: "Patsy Fulcher," *Do It NOW*, May–June 1975, 7; "Patsy Fulcher," in Love, *Feminists Who Changed America*, 164.

117 *"We have to counteract it"*: "Sharing the Work and the Glory," news clipping, n.d., folder 9, box 6, Collins NOW Officer Papers.

117 *"It is time for"*: Fulcher to Louie Robinson, July 31, 1973, folder 1, box 31, NOW Records.

117 *Eleanor Spikes*: Wilma Scott Heide, "An Open Letter to Sisters of the National Black Feminist Organization," Aug. 27, 1973, folder 7, box 8, Heide Papers.

117 *"the common problems"*: Report of the Task Force on Minority Women and Women's Rights, May 1974, folder 18, box 48, NOW Records.

117 *"that NOW had"*: Hernandez, interview by Davison, June 30, 1997, 9.

117 *Hernandez was heartened*: Report of the Task Force on Minority Women and Women's Rights, May 1974, folder 18, box 48, NOW Records.

117 *out of twenty-one hundred registrants*: "Report from the National Conference," *Do It NOW*, March 1973, 1.

117 *"trying very hard"*: Ruth W. Lee, NOW Black Caucus Survey Response, "NOW Black Caucus Questionnaire Responses, May 1973" folder, box 12, Hernandez Papers.

117 *"seemed to be anxious"*: Patsy Gayle Fulcher, NOW Black Caucus Survey, March 29, 1973, "NOW Black Caucus Questionnaire Responses, May 1973" folder, box 12, Hernandez Papers.

117 *The white women*: "Summary of Questionnaire for NOW," n.d., ca. 1974, folder 4, box 45, DeCrow Papers.

118 *"We're all women"*: Fulcher, Hernandez, and Spikes to Chapter Presidents, Task Force Coordinators, and National Board Members, re: Newsletter, Sept. 1973, folder 1, box 31, NOW Records.

118 *"We don't recruit old"*: Watkins to Hernandez, June 5, 1973, "Memoranda" folder, box 88, Hernandez Papers.

118 *"unnecessary" or "divisive"*: Report of the Task Force on Minority Women and Women's Rights, May 1974, 2, folder 18, box 48, NOW Records.

118 *Some whites openly expressed*: Omaha NOW President [signature page missing] to Hernandez, May 23, 1973, "NOW Minority Women Task Force, 1973" folder, box 17, Hernandez Papers.

118 *"If minority women"*: Roberts, interview by Jacqui Ceballos, 114–15, folder 3, box 10, Tully-Crenshaw Feminist Oral History Project.

118 *"patriarchal to declare"*: Watkins to Hernandez, June 5, 1973, "Memoranda" folder, box 88, Hernandez Papers.

118 *"welcoming to everybody"*: Fishman and Ladky, interview by author, 7–8.

118 *"Help Every Woman"*: "Chicago NOW Sets 2-Day 'Help Every Woman,'" *Chicago Daily Defender*, May 10, 1971, 18.

118 *Nearly half of the chapters*: Report of the Task Force on Minority Women and Women's Rights, May 1974, folder 18, box 48, NOW Records.

119 *Hernandez's 1973 survey*: Results of Survey of Chapters, Sept. 1973, folder 18, box 48, NOW Records.

119 *"seldom" mentioned racism*: Hernandez, interview by Davison, Nov. 1995, 5.

119 *Several chapters translated*: Report of the Task Force on Minority Women and Women's Rights, May 1974, folder 18, box 48, NOW Records.

119 *More than a hundred chapters*: "Bulletin: Joann [*sic*] Little's Case," *Priorities*, June 1975, 4–5, "Minority Women (3) Minority Women and Women's Rights, 1975" folder, San Diego NOW Records, Special Collections, San Diego State University Library.

119 *In San Diego*: "California NOW Report of Task Force on Minority Women and Women's Rights," "Minority Women (3) Minority Women and Women's Rights, 1975" folder, San Diego NOW Records.

119 *The planners of*: Chappell, "Rethinking Women's Politics in the 1970s," 158.

119 *"at a local level"*: Merrillee Dolan, "Welcome to the Women and Poverty Task Force!," n.d., ca. 1972, from Dolan's personal collection, via Marisa Chappell, in author's possession.

119 *The National Welfare Rights Organization*: Nadasen, *Welfare Warriors*, 219–21.

119 *"welfare dinner"*: Mary Vogel to Dolan, March 10, 1972, from Dolan's personal collection, via Marisa Chappell, in author's possession.

120 *"trying to live"*: Albuquerque NOW Chapter Report for 1972, from Dolan's personal collection, via Marisa Chappell, in author's possession.

120 *NOW's chapter in Riverside*: Tabb to Tish Sommers, n.d., ca. Aug. 1971, from Dolan's personal collection, via Marisa Chappell, in author's possession; Dolan, email to Chappell, May 16, 2005, printout, via Chappell, in author's possession.

120 *The one hundred conference participants*: Tish Sommers to Dolan, re: Riverside Conference, June 5, 1971, from Dolan's personal collection, via Chappell, in author's possession.

120 *"wide open town"*: Gilmore, *Groundswell*, 98; Gosse, *Rethinking the New Left*, 66–68.

120 *Through groups including*: Robyn C. Spencer, *The Revolution Has Come: Black Power, Gender, and the Black Panther Party in Oakland* (Durham, N.C.: Duke University Press, 2016), 10–14, 19–25.

120 *Hernandez's local NOW outpost*: Gilmore, *Groundswell*, 99–101, 114.

120 *That couple, who were*: John D'Emilio, *Sexual Politics, Sexual Communities: The Making of a Homosexual Minority in the United States, 1940–1970* (Chicago: University of Chicago Press, 1998), 100–102.

121 *"What do you men"*: D'Emilio, *Sexual Politics, Sexual Communities*, 105.

121 *"we needed to do"*: Lyon and Martin interview, part 3, 39, folder 7, box 9, Tully-Crenshaw Feminist Oral History Project.

121 *Lyon and Martin had*: Self, *All in the Family*, 164.

121 *"Finally the heterosexual women were getting"*: Lyon and Martin interview, part 3, 34, folder 7, box 9.

121 *Lyon and Martin became*: Lyon and Martin interview, part 3, 35, folder 7, box 9; Marcia Gallo, *Different Daughters: A History of the Daughters of Bilitis and the Rise of the Lesbian Rights Movement* (Emeryville, Calif.: Seal Press, 2007), 135–36.

121 *"husband–wife" dues category*: Myers, "Administrative Policies and Procedures, Assumptions and Delegations of Authority, 1966–1972," 5.

121 *"There must be more"*: Vern L. Bullough, *Before Stonewall: Activists for Gay and Lesbian Rights in Historical Context* (New York: Harrington Park Press, 2002), 165.

121 *Martin was soon elected*: Davis, *Moving the Mountain*, 261.

121 *As lesbians across*: On lesbian feminism's origins and trajectory in the United States, see Orleck, *Rethinking American Women's Activism*, 172–81.

121 *"So many of their fears"*: Martin to Clarenbach, Feb. 19, 1970, in Ladky's possession.

121 *"the stickiness of"*: Martin to Friedan, Feb. 11, 1970, folder 1523, Friedan Papers.

121 *Nearly 20 percent*: "Summary of Questionnaire for NOW," n.d., ca. 1974, folder 4, box 45, DeCrow Papers.

121 *"If they knew"*: Collins, interview by Connell, 99, folder 7, box 8.

122 *"there were lesbians"*: Boyer, interview by Fox, 125, folder 9, box 1.

122 *Women also discussed sex*: Cobble, Gordon, and Henry, *Feminism Unfinished*, 79–81.

122 *"alienated and isolated"*: "National NOW Board Meeting," Southern California NOW Newsletter, June 1969, 1, "California–Los Angeles" folder, box 2, NOW Chapter Newsletters Collection.

122 *"so that lesbians"*: Shirley Bernard to Komisar, Jan. 18, 1971, folder 21, box 23, NOW Records.

122 *"a clique that share"*: Komisar to Hernandez et al., March 8, 1971, folder 17, box 37, NOW Records.

123 *"hideous" and "sick"*: Bernard to Komisar, Jan. 18, 1971, folder 21, box 23, NOW Records.

123 *"no two single women"*: Judith Meuli to Boyer, Jan. 28, 1971, folder 17, box 37, NOW Records.

123 *"the double oppression"*: "LA NOW Resolution," May 18, 1971, folder 27, box 23, Toni Carabillo and Judith Meuli Papers, Schlesinger Library.

123 *The tide began*: "Summary Report of the Conference Coordinator," 1971, folder 17, box 23, NOW Records.

123 *Hernandez asked Martin*: Lyon and Martin interview, part 3, 57, folder 7, box 9.

123 *"we didn't have"*: Lyon and Martin interview, part 3, 59, folder 7, box 9.

123 *"reassess the priorities"*: "Resolutions of the 1971 Conference," folder 17, box 23, NOW Records.

123 *After the conference*: Abbott and Love, *Sappho Was a Right-On Woman*, 130–31.

123 *The chapters still varied*: Gilmore and Kaminski, "A Part and Apart," esp. 97.

123 *"Because of the expense"*: Fox to Abbott, March 3, 1972, folder 12, box 47, NOW Records.

123 *She wrote this*: Henry L. Minton, *Departing from Deviance: A History of Homosexual Rights and Emancipatory Science in America* (Chicago: University of Chicago Press, 2002), 2.

124 *"It is certainly time"*: Love to NOW Board of Directors, re: Lesbianism and a NOW Task Force, Jan. 6, 1973, folder 12, box 47, NOW Records.

124 *"sexuality and lesbianism"*: Fahey to Judy Lightfoot, Kathy Rand, and NOW National Office, re: Task Force on Sexuality and Lesbianism, Jan. 15, 1973, folder 9, box 31, NOW Records.

124 *"please see us"*: Abbott, interview by Love, 43, folder 1, box 1.

124 *"200 strong were out"*: Fran Pollner, "Lesbian Dynamics," *Off Our Backs*, Feb./March 1973, 7.

124 *The caucus proposed*: Lesbian Liberation Newsletter, Des Moines, Jan. 23, 1973, 7–8, folder 3, box 19, Sally Hacker Papers, 1951–91, Schlesinger Library.

124 *"simply racist and homophobic"*: Gilmore, *Groundswell*, 117.

124 *"I would find it impossible"*: Hernandez to Eve Norman, April 29, 1971, folder 20, box 169, NOW Records.

125 *Martin, Lyon, and Hernandez wanted*: Gilmore, *Groundswell*, 120, 121, 117.

125 *"multi-oppressed woman"*: "Beyond Bra Burning: NOW Vanguard Shifts Focus," *Los Angeles Times*, April 20, 1975, 3.

125 *The chapter anchored*: Gilmore, *Groundswell*, 119.

125 *set up a halfway house*: "Beyond Bra Burning."

125 *"the experience of functioning"*: Hernandez, Fulcher, and Spikes to Karen DeCrow, July 31, 1974, "NOW Task Force on Minority Wm + Wms Rts," box 96, Hernandez Papers.

125 *they stood to receive*: Collins-Robson to Hernandez and Spikes, March 20, 1974, "NOW Minority Women Task Force, 1974" folder, box 17, Hernandez Papers.

125 *To replace them*: Hernandez, Fulcher, and Spikes to DeCrow, July 31, 1974.

126 *She took twice-monthly*: Fosburgh, "Dealing with Feminism in Black and White."

126 *The previous year*: Springer, *Living for the Revolution*, 61–63.

126 *The National Task Force*: NOW National Task Force on Sexuality and Lesbianism, "Proposed 1976 Program of Action," folder 12, box 47, NOW Records.

126 *They organized workshops*: Abbott and Jan Welch to Sexuality and Lesbianism Task Force Chairs, Legislative Committee Heads, and Chapter Presidents, re: Federal Legislation, NOW National Conference, Task Force News, Liaison with the National Gay Task Force, May 1975, folder 12, box 47, NOW Records.

126 *The Atlanta chapter's robust*: "Connections Is Having a Christmas Party," flyer, n.d., folder 20,

box 8, Atlanta Lesbian Feminist Alliance Archives, Sallie Bingham Center, Rubenstein Library, Duke University; "NOW Atlanta Connections—Lesbian Task Force of Atlanta NOW," flyer, n.d., folder 20, box 8, Atlanta Lesbian Feminist Alliance Archives.

126 *The task force was*: A Sister, "Editorial Page," *Washington Equal Times*, May 1979, 1, folder 2, box 4, NOW Washington, D.C., Chapter and Capitol Hill Chapter Records.

126 *Seattle NOW won*: "More NOW Victories," *Do It NOW*, Nov. 1974, 1.

126 *Louisville NOW challenged*: Patricia Wenzel to Dian Terry, April 12, 1975, folder 12, box 47, NOW Records.

126 *"gave men a wonderful"*: Burnett, interview by Boyer, 111, folder 1, box 8.

126 *"There was only"*: Burnett, interview by Boyer, 113, folder 1, box 8.

126 *"We refuse to be divided"*: Burnett, journal entry, n.d., ca. 1971, 4, "Burnett Notebooks, Michigan NOW, 1969–1974" folder, box 6, Burnett Papers.

127 *"The women who were"*: Abbott, interview by Love, 25, folder 1, box 1.

127 *"would prevent us"*: Collins, interview by author, Feb. 22, 2019, 8.

127 *"do or do not"*: DeCrow to Hernandez, March 28, 1971, folder 12, box 47, NOW Records.

127 *"a civil rights issue"*: DeCrow, interviewed on "Controversies Within the Women's Movement," *Woman*, WNED, Buffalo Public Television, taped Dec. 1975, 9–10, folder 5, box 16, Kolb Papers.

127 *There had been outspoken*: See, for example, David W. Blight, *Frederick Douglass: Prophet of Freedom* (New York: Simon & Schuster, 2020); and Stacey M. Robertson, *Parker Pillsbury: Radical Abolitionist, Male Feminist* (Ithaca, N.Y.: Cornell University Press, 2000).

128 *Turn-of-the-century suffragists*: Cott, *Grounding of Modern Feminism*, 271. There were also men among them; see Brooke Kroeger, *The Suffragents: How Women Used Men to Get the Vote* (Albany: State University of New York Press, 2017).

128 *"breadwinning, soldiering, and heterosexuality"*: Self, *All in the Family*, 8. On challenges to men's authority within their families, see also Deborah Dinner, "The Divorce Bargain: The Fathers' Rights Movement and Family Inequalities," *Virginia Law Review* 102, no. 1 (2016): 79–152, esp. 87–104.

128 *"stereotypes supplied by society"*: Fred Bruning, "Male and Female: The Differences Are Changing," *Newsday*, July 8, 1974, 4A.

128 *Couples were having*: "Let George Do It: Women's Lib Movement Inspires More Couples to Strive for Equality," *Wall Street Journal*, Aug. 4, 1970, 1.

128 *"Being in the women's movement"*: Collins, interview by author, Feb. 22, 2019, 1.

128 *she would sometimes find*: Boyer, interview by Fox, 79, 80, folder 9, box 1.

129 *"My first NOW conference"*: James Collins-Robson to Friedan, Jan. 3, 1969, folder 1, box 19, Collins NOW Officer Records.

129 *"Pill In"*: Jim Collins-Robson to "Friends," n.d., ca. 1968, folder 13, box 6, Collins NOW Officer Records.

129 *"female class consciousness"*: "Redstockings Manifesto," 1968, accessed June 9, 2021, www .redstockings.org/index.php/rs-manifesto.

129 *He declined, citing*: Collins-Robson to Friedan, Jan. 3, 1969.

129 *"very interested in helping"*: Jim Collins-Robson, "NOW Member Information Form," April 22, 1970, folder 38, box 1, NOW Records.

129 *The board signed*: Hernandez to Fox, May 18, 1970, folder 12, box 1, Fox Papers; *As We See It NOW*, April 1971, 12.

129 *Soon Mary Jean volunteered*: Collins, interview by author, 2015, 12.

129 *"These duties are overwhelming"*: Hernandez to NOW Board Members, Chapter Presidents and Conveners, and National Coordinators, Feb. 26, 1971, "NOW" folder, box 96, Hernandez Papers.

129 *"a fully equal partnership"*: NOW Statement of Purpose, reprinted in Carabillo, Meuli, and Csida, *Feminist Chronicles*, 159.

129 *The first board*: "National Organization for Women: An Invitation to Join," Nov. 1966, folder 2, box 1, NOW Records.

130 *"not much of an organization man"*: Degler to Friedan, Oct. 19, 1966, folder 1479, Friedan Papers.

130 *"I like to think"*: Degler to Friedan, July 14, 1967, folder 1504, Friedan Papers.

130 *Lewis, a leader*: Reverend Dean H. Lewis, "The Crowd Would Roar and Then Fall Silent," Reflections of the March on Washington, 1963, 18, accessed Nov. 9, 2022, https://phs -app-media.s3.amazonaws.com/s3fs-public/Civil_Rights_reminiscences_optimized.pdf.

130 *"interested in equal rights"*: Lewis to Friedan, Nov. 2, 1966, folder 1496, Friedan Papers.

130 *"a terrific attack"*: Transcript of NOW "Herstory" Session, 28; Wolfgang Saxon, "Phineas Indritz, 81, Counsel to Several House Committees," *New York Times*, Oct. 26, 1997.

130 *"learned on the job"*: Adam Bernstein, "Richard Graham, Early EEOC, Teacher Corps Leader," *Washington Post*, Sept. 29, 2007, B6.

130 *"they wouldn't want their wives"*: Transcript of NOW "Herstory" Session, 25.

130 *"misplaced chivalry"*: Bernstein, "Richard Graham, Early EEOC, Teacher Corps Leader."

130 *Graham and Hernandez cast*: Margalit Fox, "Richard Graham, Equal Rights Leader, Dies at 86," *New York Times*, Oct. 8, 2007, B6.

130 *Graham departed his role*: NOW Board Meeting Minutes, Sept. 14–15, 1968, 8.

130 *"It doesn't seem right"*: Graham, interview by Cynthia Harrison, July 31, 1985, 7, folder 44, box 26, East Papers.

130 *who were 9 percent*: "Summary of Questionnaire for NOW," n.d., ca. 1974, folder 4, box 45, DeCrow Papers.

130 *"Although I agree"*: "Chapter Views on the Conference," *NOW Acts* 6, no. 1 (1973): 19.

131 *"work out their feelings"*: Jean Stapleton, "Are Men the Enemy?," Los Angeles Chapter NOW News, June 1970, 1, "California–Los Angeles" folder, box 2, NOW Chapter Newsletters Collection.

131 *a new era of repression*: Susan Stryker, *Transgender History*, rev. ed. (New York: Seal Press, 2017), 115–16.

131 *Some argued that because*: Stryker, *Transgender History*, 127–38.

131 *"Mr. America contest"*: "Chapter News," *Illinois NOW*, July 1976, 1, folder 7, box 58, Chicago NOW Collection, Richard J. Daley Library, University of Illinois at Chicago.

131 *"What Motivates a Male"*: "What Motivates a Male Feminist?," *Los Angeles Chapter of NOW News*, Nov. 1971, 1, "California–Los Angeles" folder, box 2, NOW Chapter Newsletters Collection.

131 *"For vasectomy operations"*: *As We See It NOW*, April 1971, 2, folder 1628, Friedan Papers.

131 *one prepared a hundred*: Harriet Alpern, "Reminiscences of the Beginnings of Michigan NOW," 7, Metropolitan Detroit NOW Newsletter, n.d., ca. 1981, "Recollections of NOW" folder, box 10, Burnett Papers.

131 *"solid Feminist"*: "Help Available," *Women Unite NOW* (Cleveland), June 1973, 7, folder 4, box 2, Philadelphia NOW Records, Pennsylvania Historical Society.

132 *"househusband" with plenty*: "Statements from the Candidates," Cincinnati NOW Election, folder 8, box 6, Collins NOW Officer Papers.

132 *"contradiction in philosophy"*: Maggie Quinn and Charlene Ventura, "Statement of Philosophy . . . ," Nov. 19, 1973, folder 8, box 6, Collins NOW Officer Papers.

132 *"There is no way"*: Maggie Quinn to Kathy Rand, Dec. 3, 1973, folder 8, box 6, Collins NOW Officer Papers.

132 *The most prominent*: Swinth, *Feminism's Forgotten Fight*, 42–45.

132 *"that the women"*: Jay Molishever, "Group Leaders Trained: Masculine Mystique Is Now Spotlighted," news clipping, n.d., ca. 1973, folder 5, box 216, NOW Records.

132 *"It was much harder"*: Copley News Service, press release, Aug. 23, 1973, folder 3, box 48, NOW Records.

132 *"Men cannot cry"*: Warren Farrell, "NOW Task Force on the Masculine Mystique," Nov. 1973, folder 3, box 48, NOW Records.

133 *"conquer women, conquer countries"*: Warren T. Farrell, "The Resocialization of Men's Attitudes Toward Women's Role in Society," Sept. 9, 1970, 9, folder 22, box 210, NOW Records.

133 *He outlined these ideas*: Warren Farrell, *The Liberated Man: Beyond Masculinity: Freeing Men and Their Relationships with Women* (New York: Random House, 1974); "Background with Women's and Men's Liberation," folder 3, box 48, NOW Records.

133 *"We were trying to dominate"*: Molishever, "Group Leaders Trained."

133 *"raised consciousness"*: "Men: Guidelines for Consciousness-Raising," *Ms.*, Feb. 1973, 12.

133 *L.A. NOW leaders reported*: Jane Wagner, "Men's Liberation Backlash to Feminist Movement—Part I," *NOW!* (Los Angeles), Aug. 1975, 1, 4, NOW Chapter Newsletters Collection.

133 *"that I had never looked"*: Norma Harrison, "Men Sign Up in Women's Rights Fight," *New York Times*, Feb. 20, 1972, 94.

133 *Farrell shepherded the creation*: Warren Farrell, "The Liberated Man," folder 3, box 48, NOW Records.

133 *"to get the men"*: Bottini, interview by Davison, 1994, 3.

133 *The national conference resolution*: "Resolutions of the 1971 National Conference," *NOW Acts* 4, no. 3 (1971): 14.

133 *"pressure to outperform"*: Warren T. Farrell, "The Human Lib Movement: I," *New York Times*, June 17, 1971, 41.

134 *Many had been in the New Left*: Swinth, *Feminism's Forgotten Fight*, 47.

134 *"Men are in NOW"*: Bruning, "Men Helping Women Help Themselves," *Newsday*, May 31, 1974, 3A.

134 *"the masculine aspect"*: Farrell form letter, May 1, 1974, folder 2, box 48, NOW Records.

134 *Image of Women Task Force*: Warren Farrell, NOW Task Force on the Masculine Mystique, Nov. 1973, folder 3, box 48, NOW Records; Warren Farrell, "An Open Letter to NOW Members," folder 3, box 48, NOW Records.

134 *Collins praised Farrell's proposal*: Collins to Farrell, Nov. 26, 1973, folder 6, box 8, Collins NOW Officer Papers; "First National Conference on the Masculine Mystique: Training Laboratory for Men's and Joint Consciousness-Raising Facilitators," n.d., ca. early 1974, folder 6, box 8, Collins NOW Officer Papers.

134 *Influenced by radical feminism*: Neil Habermehl, letter to the editor, *What NOW* (Milwaukee), March 1980, 13, folder 3, box 3, Milwaukee NOW Records, Special Collections, University of Wisconsin–Milwaukee; Jane Wagner, "Dear Sisters," n.d., ca. 1976, folder 28, box 23, Carabillo and Meuli Papers.

134 *not for "liberating" them*: Harriet Perl and Gay Abarbanell, "Guidelines to Feminist Consciousness Raising, 1975, 1976," 40–41, folder 3, box 326, NOW Additional Records, Schlesinger Library.

134 *As no-fault divorce laws*: Lefkovitz, *Strange Bedfellows*, esp. 40–41.

134 *"head of household"*: Nan Wood, "The Marriage Contract," n.d., folder 1, box 48, NOW Records.

135 *"Unilateral no-fault divorce"*: Ann Scott and Betty Berry to Legislative Task Force, re:

Legislative Recommendations from the Task Force on Marriage and Divorce, n.d., folder 43, box 47, NOW Records.

135 *"safeguards built in"*: Wood, "Marriage Contract."

135 *"marriage contracts"*: Nan Wood to Dian Terry, Sept. 3, 1974, folder 68, box 30, NOW Records.

135 *If a husband did not meet*: "Proposed Resolution on the Marriage Contract," n.d., ca. Aug. 1975, folder 43, box 47, NOW Records.

135 *"displaced homemaker"*: Levenstein, "'Don't Agonize, Organize!,'" 1117–18, 1121–31.

135 *"the value to society"*: Elizabeth Coxe Spalding, Statement of NOW Task Force on Marriage and Divorce, n.d., folder 68, box 30, NOW Records.

135 *"I couldn't believe"*: J. Steven Svoboda, "An Interview with Warren Farrell," 1997, accessed Dec. 14, 2012, www.menweb.org/svofarre.htm.

135 *New fathers' rights groups*: Dinner, "Divorce Bargain," 112–15.

135 *They joined forces*: Levenstein, "'Don't Agonize, Organize!,'" 1118.

135 *"men's movement"*: Svoboda, "Interview with Warren Farrell."

135 *"These men meet weekly"*: Wagner, "Men's Liberation Backlash to Feminist Movement— Part I," 1.

136 *North American and European*: Judy Tzu-Chun Wu, "US Feminisms and Their Global Connections," in *The Oxford Handbook of American Women's and Gender History*, ed. Ellen Hartigan-O'Connor and Lisa G. Materson (Oxford: Oxford University Press, 2018), 492; Leila J. Rupp, *Worlds of Women: The Making of an International Women's Movement* (Princeton, N.J.: Princeton University Press, 1997).

136 *"women's awakening"*: Lucy Delap, *Feminisms: A Global History* (Chicago: University of Chicago Press, 2020), 10.

136 *International efforts continued*: Freedman, *No Turning Back*, 105; Mona Siegel, *Peace on Our Terms: The Global Battle for Women's Rights After the First World War* (New York: Columbia University Press, 2021).

136 *Women formed internationalist networks*: On these networks, see Keisha N. Blain, *Set the World on Fire: Black Nationalist Women and the Global Struggle for Freedom* (Philadelphia: University of Pennsylvania Press, 2018); Eileen Boris, *Making the Woman Worker: Precarious Labor and the Fight for Global Standards, 1919–2019* (Oxford: Oxford University Press, 2019); Cobble, *For the Many*; Katherine M. Marino, *Feminism for the Americas: The Making of an International Human Rights Movement* (Chapel Hill: University of North Carolina Press, 2019).

136 *"the equal rights"*: Freedman, *No Turning Back*, 107.

136 *More recently, women*: Judy Tzu-Chun Wu, *Radicals on the Road: Internationalism, Orientalism, and Feminism During the Vietnam Era* (Ithaca, N.Y.: Cornell University Press, 2013), 193–95.

136 *"Third World Women"*: Wu, "US Feminisms and Their Global Connections," 490.

136 *White European and North American*: See, for example, Boris, *Making the Woman Worker*, 95–98; Delap, *Feminisms*, 252–56; Marino, *Feminism for the Americas*, 75, 160–62; Jocelyn Olcott, *International Women's Year: The Greatest Consciousness-Raising Event in History* (Oxford: Oxford University Press, 2017), 121; and Wu, *Radicals on the Road*, 4–5.

136 *But many Americans*: Wu, *Radicals on the Road*.

137 *"If the time for revolution"*: "Revised Standard Information Form for Candidates for NOW National Elections for Office," n.d., ca. 1973, "Biographical/Art Career 1 of 5" folder, box 1, Burnett Papers.

137 *"Well, you traveled"*: Burnett, interview by Boyer, 50, folder 20, box 7.

137 *When moneyed NOW members*: New York NOW Membership Meeting Minutes, June 15, 1972, folder 12, box 2, National Organization for Women, New York City Chapter Records.

137 *voted to explore*: "NOW Legislative Program, 1969," folder 7, box 1, NOW Records.

137 *"world organization for women"*: Betty Friedan, "Our Revolution Is Unique: President's Report to the National Conference of NOW," Dec. 6, 1968, 4, folder 7, box 1, NOW Records.

137 *She worked to obtain*: Olcott, *International Women's Year*, 117; Patricia Hill Burnett résumé, n.d., ca. Jan. 1974, folder 15, box 22, Heide Papers; "Report on NOW's International Conference, 1973," n.d., ca. 1973, 2, folder 1, box 8, NOW Records.

137 *Some correspondents were Americans*: Elizabeth Drahman to NOW, Sept. 12, 1973, "NOW-NIA-International Chapters," box 3, Burnett Papers; Sheila Ford to NOW, May 3, 1973, folder 21, box 9, NOW Records; Betty Newcomb to Dian Terry, Nov. 5, 1973, "NOW-International Committee [1973]" folder, box 3, Burnett Papers; Deirdre Milne, Auckland, New Zealand, to NOW, Sept. 4, 1972, folder 21, box 9, NOW Records; Mrs. Dharini Anaud to "The Secretary" of the National Organization for Women, n.d., ca. Aug. 1974, "NOW-NIA-International Chapters," box 3, Burnett Papers.

137 *As of mid-1972*: Marijean Suelzle to National NOW Board Meeting, Feb. 19–21, 1972, "NOW-International Committee [1970–72]" folder, box 3, Burnett Papers.

137 *National leaders welcomed*: Betty Newcomb to Jane Plitt, Oct. 14, 1973, "NOW-International Committee [1973]" folder, box 3, Burnett Papers.

138 *"ripe for NOW!"*: Gene Boyer, "Notes on International Conference and Chapter Organization from Trip to Denmark and France—May, 1972," n.d., ca. May 1972, folder 23, box 36, NOW Records.

138 *Around eighty professionals*: Marjorie Canja, Paris NOW President, "Some Problems Encountered in Setting Up a NOW Chapter in a Foreign Country: Some Proposals for NOW United States," n.d., ca. 1973, 1, folder 59, box 26, NOW Records.

138 *Paris NOW had*: "International NOW 'Chapters': Background Information for NOW National Board," July 15, 1973, folder 59, box 26, NOW Records.

138 *"stable and successful"*: Nikki D. Economos (Paris NOW president) to Komisar, April 25, 1973, folder 12, box 22, Heide Papers.

138 *"legal association"*: Leader of Paris NOW to Wilma Scott Heide, Jan. 8, 1973, folder 14, box 22, Heide Papers.

138 *NOW's stateside leaders*: Betty Newcomb (international convener) to Marjorie Canja, Jan. 8, 1974, folder 7, box 3, Judith Lightfoot NOW Officer Papers, Schlesinger Library.

138 *And because pay scales*: "Taking Stock," *NOW or Never* (Paris), May 1973, 2, "France-Paris" folder, box 7, NOW Chapter Newsletters Collection.

138 *For stateside officials*: Komisar to Jim Collins-Robson and Mary Jean Collins-Robson, June 22, 1972, folder 20, box 9, NOW Records; "International NOW 'Chapters.'"

138 *"relevant to our local"*: Canja, "Some Problems Encountered," 3.

138 *But the American officers*: Leader of Paris NOW to Wilma Scott Heide, Jan. 8, 1973, folder 14, box 22, Heide Papers.

139 *Less than two years*: Canja to Judy Lightfoot, Jan. 12, 1974, folder 7, box 3, Lightfoot NOW Officer Papers.

139 *Some could not accept*: "No NOW Affiliation," *POW: Paris Organization of Women*, Nov. 1973, 2, "Paris-France" folder, box 7, NOW Chapter Newsletters Collection.

139 *"actually forming an international"*: "International NOW 'Chapters,'" 1.

139 *"world convocation of women"*: Nan Wood, "Chronological Summary of NOW Board Decisions and Actions," folder 7, box 1, NOW Records.

139 *"It was my idea"*: Burnett, interview by Boyer, 116, folder 1, box 8.

139 *"goals or political beliefs"*: Wilma Scott Heide, Betty Friedan, and Patricia Hill Burnett, "Dear Ms.," n.d., ca. 1972, folder 57, box 26, NOW Records.

139 *"the idea is to find"*: Burnett to Ms. Proskurnikova (vice president, Soviet Women's Committee), Feb. 5, 1973, "Correspondence 1973" folder, box 1, Burnett Papers.

139 *"As the world's largest"*: "Report on NOW's International Conference, 1973," n.d., ca. 1973, folder 1, box 8, NOW Records.

139 *"fantastically exciting"*: Hernandez to Burnett, Feb. 22, 1972, "Correspondence, 1972" folder, box 1, Burnett Papers.

140 *On an initial list*: "Answers to Letters Sent Out for the International Feminist Planning Conference," n.d., ca. 1973, "International Feminist Planning Conf., 1973" folder, box 13, Burnett Papers.

140 *"the distance and fare"*: Psaltis to Burnett, April 17, 1973, "NOW-International Feminist Planning Conference" folder, box 3, Burnett Papers.

140 *"in sympathy with the goals"*: Aguta to Burnett, "NOW NIA International Chapters—Africa," Burnett Papers.

140 *"seemed to be quite"*: Gill Gaze, "International Feminists: A Small World?," *Boston Phoenix*, June 11, 1973, 5, folder 61, box 26, NOW Records.

140 *"I have never made a bed"*: Transcript of NOW "'Herstory' Session," 41.

140 *"my gift to NOW"*: Burnett to Wilma Scott Heide, July 2, 1973, "NOW-International Committee [1973]" folder, box 3, Burnett Papers.

140 *NOW hosted the four-day*: Patricia McCormack, "Feminists World Wide 'Together' on Issues," *Las Vegas Sun*, Aug. 26, 1975, folder 2, box 216, NOW Records; List of Participants in the Cambridge Feminist Planning Conference (not complete), n.d., ca. 1973, folder 15, box 22, Heide Papers; Transcript of NOW "Herstory" Session, 41–42.

140 *"to discuss the common"*: "International Feminist Planning Conference," n.d., ca. 1973, folder 16, box 22, Heide Papers.

140 *Both were NOW members*: Betty Danfield, "'Mr. and Ms. Lennon' Back NOW with Love," *Detroit News*, n.d., ca. July 1973, folder 1, box 22, NOW Records.

140 *"because American women"*: Gaze, "International Feminists: A Small World?"

141 *"energize international feminism"*: Wilma Scott Heide, "Welcoming Remarks," ca. June 1, 1973, folder 1, box 22, NOW Records.

141 *"apparent that feminism means"*: Betty Danfield, "Lib Goals Differ Around the World," *Detroit News*, June 10, 1973, folder 1, box 22, NOW Records.

141 *"women must first learn"*: Betty Danfield, "World Lib Session Fails in Harmony Dept.," *Detroit News*, June 4, 1973, 1D, folder 2, box 216, NOW Records.

141 *Mary Mdiniso agreed*: Dorothy Austin, "Is There a Common Denominator?," *Milwaukee Sentinel*, June 13, 1973, folder 61, box 26, NOW Records.

141 *"too pale, too conservative"*: Dorothy Austin, "No Male Feminists, Conference Decrees," *Milwaukee Sentinel*, June 4, 1973, 6.

141 *"You have to remember"*: Danfield, "World Lib Session Fails in Harmony Dept."

141 *"all the color"*: Austin, "No Male Feminists, Conference Decrees."

141 *"If I had known"*: Dorothy Austin, "Feminists Part in Peace," *Milwaukee Sentinel*, June 5, 1973, folder 2043, Friedan Papers.

141 *"but we have discovered"*: Maria Karagianis, "Feminists of 27 Nations Vow 'to Change Society,'" *Boston Globe*, June 5, 1973, 29.

141 *"I Am Woman"*: Austin, "Feminists Part in Peace."

141 *"the three Marias"*: "How to Demonstrate Against [the] Portuguese Embassy," n.d., ca. 1973, folder 65, box 26, NOW Records.

142 *The conference also approved*: Patricia Hill Burnett, "Report on the International Feminist Planning Conference," n.d., ca. June 1973, "NOW-International Committee-Undated" folder, box 3, Burnett Papers.

142 *They agreed to plan*: Burnett, "Report on the International Feminist Planning Conference"; "Over 300 Women Met in Cambridge," n.d., ca. 1973, folder 64, box 26, NOW Records.

142 *"starting brush fires"*: Sue Marx, "She's Taking the Women's Word to Russia," magazine clipping, n.d., ca. 1973, 33, "Biographical + Artistic, 3 of 5" folder, box 1, Burnett Papers.

142 *She was receiving*: Patricia Hill Burnett, "The Winds of Change Are Blowing" (address to Zonta Club of Detroit Luncheon, Oct. 26, 1974), 1–2, "PHB—Speeches" folder, box 10, Burnett Papers.

142 *Burnett personally paid*: Burnett to Dr. W. S. Subrahmaryan, April 18, 1974, "NOW-NIA-International Chapters-India" folder, box 3, Burnett Papers.

142 *"friendship-by-mail"*: Patricia Hill Burnett, address to the NOW International Planning Conference, n.d., ca. June 1973, 4, "Speeches, Articles, Interviews, 1973–1987" folder, box 2, Burnett Papers.

142 *a three-month trip*: Burnett, *True Colors*, 80, 87.

142 *Burnett began with two weeks*: "Itinerary—Patricia Hill Burnett," n.d., ca. 1973, "Trips—Russia, 1973, October 1–15" folder, box 5, Burnett Papers; Linda LaMarre, "Feminist Battle Continues on All World Fronts," clipping, n.d., "Burnett, Patricia Hill" folder, box 6, Burnett Papers.

142 *"a ten week tour"*: Betty Newcomb to Stella O'Leary, Nov. 5, 1973, "NOW—International Committee [1973]" folder, box 3, Burnett Papers.

142 *Burnett met with*: Burnett to Ms. K. Proskurnikova, Sept. 22, 1973, "Correspondence 1973" folder, box 1, Burnett Papers; Burnett, handwritten notes, n.d., "Patricia Hill Burnett Around the World Trip, Oct. 1–Dec. 10, 1973" folder, box 5, Burnett Papers; Lorraine Smith, *Hong Kong Standard* clipping, n.d., ca. 1973, "Biographical + Artistic, 2 of 5" folder, box 1, Burnett Papers; Burnett to Florence Lyon, Aug. 7, 1974, "Correspondence 1974, August–December" folder, box 1, Burnett Papers; Eleanor Breitmeyer, "Pat Burnett Libs Life to the Fullest," clipping, n.d., "Articles" folder, box 2, Burnett Papers.

142 *"feminist impressions"*: Burnett to International Feminist League of Hong Kong, April 20, 1974, folder 16, box 22, Heide NOW Officer Papers.

142 *"super-deluxe treatment"*: Patricia Hill Burnett, untitled address, n.d., ca. 1973, 4, 5, 6, 7, 10, "Speeches, Articles, Interviews, 1973–1987" folder, box 2, Burnett Papers.

143 *"both Colony-wide and international"*: Diane M. Behrenhausen, "The International Feminist League of Hong Kong," news clipping, n.d., ca. 1973, 59, "International Feminist Planning Conf., 1973" folder, box 13, Burnett Papers.

143 *"a second-rate travelogue"*: International Feminist League of Hong Kong to National Organization for Women, Feb. 3, 1974, folder 16, box 22, Heide NOW Officer Papers.

143 *"You were all so friendly"*: Burnett to International Feminist League of Hong Kong, April 20, 1974, folder 16, box 22, Heide NOW Officer Papers.

143 *When she returned*: Detroit NOW Newsletter, Jan. 1976, 4, NOW Chapter Newsletters Collection.

143 *The Washington, New York*: Burnett to NOW National Board, re: Activities of the NOW International Committee, n.d., ca. Aug. 1974, folder 46, box 2, NOW Records.

143 *"affiliates" rather than chapters*: "Standards for NOW International Affiliates, Adopted by National NOW Board of Directors," Feb. 23, 1974, folder 23, box 9, NOW Records;

"Application for Provisional International Affiliate Chapter Charter," n.d., ca. April 1974, folder 7, box 3, Lightfoot NOW Officer Papers.

143 *The new kit*: NOW International Affiliate Convener Kit and Cover Letter, n.d., ca. 1975, folder 23, box 9, NOW Records.

144 *"except the chance"*: Private First Class Kathleen A. Kooi to Jane Plitt, April 21, 1975, folder 23, box 9, NOW Records.

144 *Some women on U.S. military bases*: Burnett to Fran P. Hosken, April 17, 1977, "Correspondence, 1976–1978" folder, box 7, Burnett Papers; Claudia Nichols, "How We Got Started," *Right NOW* (Clark Air Base), Nov. 1982, 2, "Philippines: Right NOW" folder, box 24, NOW Newsletters Collection.

144 *more than a hundred*: Olcott, *International Women's Year*, 121.

144 *As other feminists*: Cobble, *For the Many*, 388–91; Olcott, *International Women's Year*.

5. GETTING PAID

145 *"Sears Shortchanges Women"*: "Sears Shortchanges Women," *Retail Reader*, July 27, 1974, folder 8, box 246, Chicago NOW Collection.

145 *With the previous*: Carolyn Colwell, "Towering Controversy: Sears vs. NOW Tests the Teeth of Civil Rights Laws," *Chicago Tribune*, July 22, 1975, B1, B2.

145 *low pay, no benefits*: Colwell, "Towering Controversy," B2.

145 *"arbitrary" system*: "Sears Christmas Special?," flyer, n.d., ca. Dec. 1974, folder 8, box 246, Chicago NOW Collection.

145 *"a notorious discriminator"*: "Look Out, Sears—You Can't Stop NOW!," *NOW Compliance Newsletter*, July 1974, folder 1, box 245, Chicago NOW Collection.

145 *"women won't buy it!"*: "Sears Christmas Special?"

146 *"frail and incapable"*: Ms. Aileen Hernandez's Remarks—Sears Roebuck & Co. Southern Territorial Personnel Conference, May 31, 1972, tape, side B, unknown creator, Hernandez Papers.

146 *"[we] did our best"*: Report of the Legal Committee to Board of Directors and Members of NOW at the First Annual Conference, Nov. 18–19, 1967, 2, folder 3, box 51, NOW Records.

146 *"we had them"*: Collins, interview by Connell, 27, folder 6, box 8.

146 *"as effective as possible"*: Collins, interview by Connell, 26, folder 6, box 8.

146 *"a non-stop job"*: Lupa, interview by Turk, 8.

146 *"Here I am"*: Ceballos to Burnett, March 21, 1979, "Correspondence Jan.–June, 1979" folder, box 2, Burnett Papers.

146 *"ripping off NOW"*: Mary Jean Collins-Robson, "Report on C-R Office Programs," April 1973, folder 6, box 1, Chicago NOW Collection.

147 *"eminently well qualified"*: "Look Out, Sears—You Can't Stop NOW!"

147 *"in every community"*: Collins, interview by Connell, 26, folder 6, box 8.

147 *"called the national office"*: Collins, interview by author, 2015, 10.

147 *"that every town"*: Collins interview, Documenting the Midwestern Origins of the Twentieth-Century Women's Movement, 1987–92, tape 128, side B, Wisconsin Historical Society.

147 *"Jim was working"*: Collins, interview by author, 2015, 10.

147 *"committed to NOW"*: Collins-Robson, "Report on C-R Office Programs."

147 *"no one even knew"*: Collins, interview by author, 2015, 7.

148 *"Nobody knew who belonged"*: Conroy, interview by Balanoff, 54.

148 *"The one thing"*: Friedan, *"It Changed My Life,"* 84.

148 *A few NOW officers*: Clarenbach to Friedan, O'Hanrahan, and Hernandez, Sept. 30, 1968, "NOW Secretary-Treasurer Corr., 1968" folder, box 27, Hernandez Papers; Wilma Scott Heide, "From the President," *Do It NOW*, June 1972, 4.

148 *In December 1966*: Friedan to NOW Board Members, Dec. 6, 1966, folder 1499, Friedan Papers.

148 *"gamble for the next six months"*: Friedan to NOW Executive Committee, Jan. 18, 1969, folder 12, box 1, Fox Papers.

149 *"It's much more"*: Friedan to NOW Executive Committee, Jan. 18, 1969.

149 *"take this plunge"*: Fox to Friedan, Jan. 21, 1969, folder 12, box 1, Fox Papers.

149 *"devoted solely to NOW"*: Alexander to All NOW National Officers, Board Members, Chapter Presidents and Conveners, n.d., folder 1523, Friedan Papers; Alexander to Friedan, Jan. 17, 1969, folder 12, box 1, Fox Papers.

149 *"instantly snowed under"*: Alexander to O'Hanrahan, Feb. 17, 1969, folder 12, box 1, Fox Papers.

149 *"run ragged"*: Bottini, interview by Davison, 1994, 4.

149 *as officers off-loaded*: Friedan to All Members of the Executive Committee of NOW, March 3, 1969, folder 12, box 1, Fox Papers.

149 *"This organization has been"*: Alexander to Clarenbach et al., Nov. 14, 1969, folder 1473, Friedan Papers.

149 *By contrast to the $250*: Bottini, interview by Davison, 1994, 6.

149 *"temporary help"*: "NOW Inc.—Financial Report from 2/10/69 to 12/12/69 from National Office," folder 12, box 1, Fox Papers.

149 *Alexander resigned*: Hernandez to Alexander, May 16, 1970, folder 12, box 1, Fox Papers.

149 *"as a volunteer organization"*: Alexander to Clarenbach et al., Nov. 14, 1969.

149 *"There can be little"*: Pat McCormick, "Full-Time Volunteering Within NOW," n.d., folder 7, box 328, NOW Additional Records.

150 *Jim Collins-Robson's modest*: "C-R Office Programs Report," Oct. 1972, "General Corr. 1970" folder, box 105, Hernandez Papers.

150 *"More charismatic leadership"*: "Review and Evaluation of NOW-NY 1972 Achievements and Problems, and Ideas for 1973," 2–3, folder 12, box 2, National Organization for Women, New York City Chapter Records.

150 *Wealthy white women*: Joan Johnson, *Funding Feminism: Monied Women, Philanthropy, and the Women's Movement, 1870–1967* (Chapel Hill: University of North Carolina Press, 2018), 9–15.

150 *Regular annual dues*: Jane Plitt, "The Inside Story: How NOW Operates," July 1974, folder 26, box 18, Carabillo and Meuli Papers.

150 *"You can't fight poverty"*: Lightfoot to Sisters and Brothers of Lebanon NOW, Aug. 28, 1973, folder 32, box 2, JoAnn Evansgardner Papers, Special Collections Library, University of Pittsburgh.

150 *In 1973, for example*: "National Organization for Women 1973 Budget," n.d., ca. 1972, folder 48, box 7, NOW Records.

150 *a "fantastic" salary*: Hernandez, "Remarks," Frankel Lecture Series, 6.

150 *"a real hardship"*: Carabillo, interview by Fox, 118, folder 2, box 2.

151 *"travel to national meetings"*: "Capsule Descriptions of NOW National Offices," *Do It NOW*, Aug. 1972, 6.

151 *In 1971, the leaders*: "NLDEF Incorporation Sequence," n.d., folder 1, box 25, Rawalt Papers.

151 *"legal arm of the civil rights movement"*: "NAACP Legal Defense Fund Handles Record Case Load," *Cleveland Call and Post*, May 22, 1965, 1C.

151 *the civil rights movement's access*: On Black women's uplift work, see, for example, Berry and Gross, *Black Women's History of the United States*, esp. 113, 138–41; Jacquelyn Jones, *Labor of Love, Labor of Sorrow: Black Women, Work, and the Family, from Slavery to the Present* (New York: Basic Books, 2010), esp. 1–2; Victoria Wolcott, *Remaking Respectability: African American Women in Interwar Detroit* (Chapel Hill: University of North Carolina Press, 2001).

151 *"take the helm"*: Roberts, interview by Ceballos, 94, folder 3, box 10.

151 *The fund's new director*: Tully, interview by Collins, March 14–15, 1992, 64, 77, folder 11, box 6, Tully-Crenshaw Feminist Oral History Project.

151 *Taking office, Tully discovered*: Discussion of Founding of NOW LDEF, 27, 28, folder 14, box 10, Tully-Crenshaw Feminist Oral History Project.

151 *NOW was not attached*: Stansell, *Feminist Promise*, 303–4.

151 *"were reparations I was"*: Tully, interview by Collins, 83, folder 11, box 6.

152 *NOW faced an "inherent contradiction"*: Discussion of Founding of NOW LDEF, 32, folder 15, box 10.

152 *America's labor force*: For statistics, see Women's Bureau, U.S. Department of Labor, "Background Facts on Women Workers in the United States," Jan. 1962, 1, "President's Commission on the Status of Women 1962" folder, box 38, Women's Bureau Division of Legislation and Standards, General Records 1920–66, National Archives and Records Administration, College Park, Md. On the longer history of laboring women, see also Kessler-Harris, *Out to Work*.

152 *Even those feminized jobs*: Jones, *Labor of Love, Labor of Sorrow*, esp. 2, 201–5.

152 *a quartet of Washington, D.C., attorneys*: Report of the Legal Committee, Nov. 18–19, 1967, folder 2, box 2, NOW Records.

152 *Declaring themselves NOW's*: "Marguerite Rawalt's Career with NOW," n.d., folder 1, box 25, Rawalt Papers; "Chapter 3" of book draft, 139–40, folder 11, box 2, Kolb Papers.

152 *"a kind of double agent"*: MacLean, *Freedom Is Not Enough*, 128.

152 *The first was that*: "Report of the Legal Committee to Board of Directors and Members of NOW at the First Annual Conference," Nov. 18–19, 1967, folder 3, box 51, NOW Records.

153 *Hernandez, who was then*: "Chapter 3" of book draft, 142–44, folder 11, box 2, Kolb Papers.

153 *NOW agreed to represent*: *Velma L. Mengelkoch et al. v. Industrial Welfare Commission and North American Aviation Inc.*, 442 F.2d 1119 (9th Cir. 1971); "Chapter 3" of book draft, 142–44, folder 11, box 2, Kolb Papers; Marguerite Rawalt, "NOW Legal Committee Precedent Setting Court Decisions," n.d., ca. Sept. 1968, 7, folder 2, box 25, Rawalt Papers.

153 *"for want of jurisdiction"*: "Supreme Court Actions," *New York Times*, Oct. 29, 1968, 75.

153 *"of working as supervisors"*: "NOW Is First in Civil Rights for Women," n.d., ca. 1968, folder 1670, box 133, Friedan Papers.

153 *They had accused their employer*: Rawalt, "NOW Legal Committee Precedent Setting Court Decisions."

153 *"the complete list"*: Friedan to George H. Lesch, May 13, 1968, folder 12, box 40, DeCrow Papers.

153 *"flush in"*: Rhoda Amon, "Ladies Flush with Anger," Sept. 10, 1968, news clipping, folder 3, box 1, Jean Faust NOW Officer Papers, Schlesinger Library.

154 *"You are the woman consumer"*: Hammel, "Class of Fledgling Pickets Gets the Word."

154 *"We didn't realize"*: Amon, "Ladies Flush with Anger."

154 *All women at*: Rawalt, "NOW Legal Committee Precedent Setting Court Decisions."

154 *"the highest rate"*: Thomas H. Barnard, "Title VII Class Actions: The 'Recovery Stage,'" *William and Mary Law Review* 16, no. 3 (1974–75): 516.

154 *The three NOW attorneys*: The case wound on as the plaintiffs disagreed about how disparities in seniority and transfers should be resolved. The district court does not seem to have required Colgate to reimburse any of the women's attorneys for fees or other expenses until the case concluded in 1977, after eleven years, two appeals, and nearly four thousand pages of trial transcript. See *Bowe et al. v. Colgate-Palmolive Company et al.*, 443 F. Supp. 696 (S.D. Ind. 1977).

154 *"a fortune"*: Kathryn Clarenbach Comments, May 25, 1974, 5, folder 1, box 25, Rawalt Papers.

154 *It was a position*: Roberts, interview by Ceballos, 32, 48.

154 *Lorena Weeks*: Paterson, *Be Somebody*, 184.

155 *"My daddy died"*: Martha Brannigan, "The Pioneers: Women Who Fought Sex Bias on Job Prove to Be a Varied Group," *Wall Street Journal*, June 8, 1987, 1.

155 *"I hated to keep"*: Trustman Senger, "Rawalt in Review: At 90, a Feminist Lawyer Takes a Look Back," *Washington Post*, Aug. 28, 1986, G1.

155 *selling her house*: Carol Kleiman, "Changing Things Legally," *Chicago Tribune*, May 19, 1971, C3.

155 *"ma[de] decisions for women"*: Roberts, interview by Ceballos, 58, folder 2, box 10.

155 *"appalled . . . as a former"*: Hernandez to Malone, Feb. 18, 1971, folder 34, box 10, Rawalt Papers.

155 *The Fifth Circuit Court of Appeals*: Kleiman, "Changing Things Legally."

156 *"a real solid achievement"*: Discussion of the Founding of the NOW Legal Defense and Education Fund, 18, 19, folder 14, box 10, Tully-Crenshaw Feminist Oral History Project.

156 *By asserting an analogy*: Mayeri, *Reasoning from Race*, 30, 33.

156 *Other members set up*: "NOW Task Force on Compliance and Enforcement History and Statement of Policy," n.d., ca. 1972, folder 16, box 44, NOW Records. On NOW's activism on behalf of older women and "displaced homemakers," see Levenstein, "'Don't Agonize, Organize!'"

157 *Women had new rights*: "Chapter 10" of book draft, 2, folder 3, box 3, Kolb Papers.

157 *"race and national origin"*: Roberts to Hernandez et al., re: EEOC Hearings–Houston, June 2, 3, 4, 1970, May 31, 1970, folder 7, box 5, Bernard Papers.

157 *Only after the Houston*: Roberts to Catherine East, re: EEOC Hearings in Houston, May 31, 1970, folder 20, box 2, East Papers.

157 *"the facts before"*: Roberts to Hernandez et al., May 31, 1970.

157 *"Women do hard work"*: Mary Lu Zuber, "Silence No More, NOW Says," *Houston Chronicle*, June 3, 1970, sec. 3, p. 3.

157 *"working as a hobby"*: Sylvia Roberts Statement Before EEOC Hearings in Houston, n.d., ca. June 5, 1970, folder 7, box 5, East Papers.

157 *"few searching questions"*: Roberts to Hernandez et al., June 5, 1970, folder 7, box 5, Bernard Papers.

157 *"the NOW group"*: Martha Liebrum, "To Make It in a Man's Job, Women Must Work Like a Man," *Houston Post*, June 8, 1970, folder 20, box 2, East Papers.

157 *"institutional bias"*: Roberts to Hernandez et al., June 5, 1970.

157 *Unlike the EEOC*: Komisar to Aleta Steyers and Faith Seidenberg, April 4, 1970, folder 5, box 5, Heide NOW Officer Papers.

158 *And unlike NOW's*: Ann Scott, "Feminism vs. the Feds," *Issues in Industrial Society* 2, no. 1 (1971): 9, folder 44, box 37, NOW Records.

158 *"underutilized," and to report*: Bernard E. Anderson, "The Ebb and Flow of Enforcing Executive Order 11246," *American Economic Review* 86 (May 1996): 300.

158 *"no intention of applying"*: Scott, "Feminism vs. the Feds," 2.

158 *Hernandez announced in 1970*: Pittsburgh NOW, press release, June 25, 1970, folder 14, box 44, NOW Records.

158 *"outraged," she declared*: Pittsburgh NOW, press release.

158 *"NOW knows the difficult"*: Scott to George Holland, March 8, 1972, folder 44, box 42, NOW Records.

158 *"a bunch of females"*: Von Kirk to William H. Brown III, Nov. 13, 1973, folder 8, box 19, Heide NOW Officer Papers.

158 *NOW leaders criticized*: "Federal Compliance Committee Report: OFCC's Form A," n.d., ca. 1970–72, folder 44, box 37, NOW Records.

159 *The EEOC also promoted*: Eliza Paschal to Heide, n.d., ca. 1970, folder 3, box 19, Heide NOW Officer Papers.

159 *"frankly stronger than"*: Scott to Senator Harrison Williams, Sept. 20, 1971, folder 43, box 42, NOW Records.

159 *"alternately ignored, dismissed"*: Hernandez to Brown, Jan. 4, 1971, folder 4, box 19, Heide Papers.

159 *"blatant tokenism"*: Hernandez to Brown, March 15, 1971, folder 4, box 19, Heide Papers.

159 *"It Doesn't Matter"*: "It Doesn't Matter Who Wears the Pants. If They're Farah Pants, Take 'Em Off and Take 'Em Back," n.d., ca. 1973, folder 19, box 44, NOW Records.

159 *"products [were] used and known"*: Joan Hull to Judith G. Stowers, Feb. 10, 1973, folder 1, box 2, Lynne Darcy Papers, Schlesinger Library.

159 *that the National Urban League*: "NOW Asks Food Firm 'Boycott,'" *St. Paul Pioneer Press*, Aug. 29, 1972, 7.

159 *Workers of color*: St. Paul Urban League, "Fact Sheet: The Case Against General Mills," Sept. 15, 1972, folder 13, box 1, Darcy Papers.

159 *"women's movement"*: Hernandez to Vernon Jordan, Nov. 7, 1972, folder 12, box 1, Darcy Papers.

159 *"An unsuccessful [boycott]"*: Lightfoot to Lani J. Stacks, Jan. 17, 1974, folder 9, box 1, Darcy Papers.

160 *The General Mills campaign*: Lani J. Stacks to Lightfoot, Jan. 3, 1974, folder 9, box 1, Darcy Papers.

160 *Any chapter or individual*: "Legal Procedures in Job Discrimination Cases," n.d., ca. 1970, folder 14, box 44, NOW Records.

160 *Some chapters made*: Lynne Darcy to Ruth Householder, June 24, 1973, folder 5, box 1, Darcy Papers.

160 *Soon they discovered*: "Suggested NOW Chapter Employment Activities to Help Those Filing Sex Discrimination Complaints," n.d., ca. 1970, folder 14, box 44, NOW Records.

160 *"I came in"*: Collins, interview by author, 2015, 11.

160 *Along with other advocates*: Emily Zuckerman, "The Cooperative Origins of EEOC v. Sears," in Gilmore, *Feminist Coalitions*, 227–32.

160 *"We have these laws"*: Collins, interview by Connell, 25, 26, folder 6, box 8.

161 *"debate the issues"*: Fishman and Ladky, interview by author, 1, 2.

161 *"They slotted me"*: Lupa, interview by author, 2, 5.

161 *"a very impressive group"*: Fishman and Ladky, interview by author, 3.

161 *The chapter raised*: Lupa to Chicago NOW Membership, July 20, 1973, folder 5, box 38, Chicago NOW Collection; "Volunteers Needed," *Act NOW*, Feb. 1974, 3, folder 3, box 247, Chicago NOW Collection.

161 *"a budget and staff"*: Fishman and Ladky, interview by author, 4.

161 *"jumped in a cab"*: Lupa, interview by author, 11.

161 *"I think I went"*: Collins, interview by author, 2015, 7, 8, 9.

162 *"piles of mail"*: Lupa, interview by author, 8.

162 *She had spent years*: Day Creamer and Heather Booth, "Action Committee for Decent Childcare: Organizing for Power," 2–3, "Women-Action Committee for Decent Childcare-1972" folder, box 48, Midwest Academy Records, Chicago History Museum.

162 *"to create mass organizations"*: Saul Alinsky, *Rules for Radicals: A Pragmatic Primer for Realistic Radicals* (New York: Vintage, 1971), 3.

162 *"women could be organized"*: Booth, interview by author, March 26, 2018, 2, 1.

162 *With money from*: Booth, interview by author, 3.

162 *Its first class aimed*: Booth, email to author, Feb. 20, 2022.

162 *"Forces against women"*: Carol Kleiman, "Learn to Organize," *Chicago Tribune*, Oct. 6, 1974, D4.

162 *"Now is the time"*: Booth to Heide, Jan. 23, 1973, "NOW, 1974–9" folder, box 29, Midwest Academy Records.

162 *"that reflected and spoke"*: Booth, interview by author, 2.

163 *"conceptual and technical skills"*: "Midwest Academy Summer Session 1973," "Historical, 1972–1973" folder, box 3, Midwest Academy Records.

163 *$500 "tuition"*: "Midwest Academy Session Fact Sheet," "Historical, 1972–3" folder, box 3, Midwest Academy Records.

163 *Collins and the other*: Kleiman, "Learn to Organize."

163 *They studied labor history*: "Daily Outline, Midwest Academy, Summer 1973," "Summer Classes 7/73" folder, box 81, Midwest Academy Records.

163 *"I think we lack"*: Anne Ladky Midwest Academy Application Form, n.d., ca. Winter 1973, "Anne Ladky" folder, box 67, Midwest Academy Records.

163 *"do the job"*: "NOW Action Planning Sheet, Leadership Training, March 24, 1973," "Chicago NOW, 3/24/73" folder, box 80, Midwest Academy Records.

163 *Booth held extra trainings*: "Leadership Training," *Act NOW*, Sept. 1974, 3, folder 3, box 247, Chicago NOW Collection; Midwest Academy Staff Report, May 16, 1973, "Board Meeting-May 1973" folder, box 1, Midwest Academy Records.

163 *"what are we going"*: Fishman and Ladky, interview by author, 5.

163 *"We became much more efficient"*: Lupa, interview by author, 11.

163 *"We live in a city"*: Carol Kleiman, "Where the Women's Movement Is Today," *Chicago Tribune*, Oct. 6, 1974, D1.

163 *That $38 million accord*: "Largest Bias Settlement: A.T.&T. Signs $38 Million Agreement on Worker Rights," *Chicago Tribune*, Jan. 19, 1973, 1.

163 *Congress had fortified*: "Equal Employment Act Signed by President," *Atlanta Daily World*, April 14, 1972, 3.

164 *Brown earmarked 60 percent*: Emily Zuckerman, "EEOC Politics and Limits on Reagan's Civil Rights Legacy," in *Freedom Rights: New Perspectives on the Civil Rights Movement*, ed. Danielle L. McGuire and John Dittmer (Lexington: University Press of Kentucky, 2011), 248.

164 *"took more or less"*: Haney, *Feminist Legacy*, 77–78.

164 *According to EEOC guidelines*: Green, "Flawed Remedies," esp. 44. On this EEOC policy and how it has harmed Black women, see also Kimberlé Crenshaw, "Demarginalizing the Intersection of Race and Sex: A Black Feminist Critique of Antidiscrimination Doctrine, Feminist Theory, and Antiracist Politics," *University of Chicago Legal Forum* 1989, no. 1 (1989), article 8, 139–67; and Traci Parker, "'Sears Discriminated Against Me Because of My

Sex and Race': African American Women Workers, Title VII, and the Sears Sex Discrimination Case," *Journal of Women's History* 33 (Spring 2021): 12–36.

164 *The AT&T settlement's mandate*: Green, "Flawed Remedies," 52–55.

164 *A series of crises*: Louis Hyman, *Temp: How American Work, American Business, and the American Dream Became Temporary* (New York: Viking, 2018), 3–6, 161–63; Kruse and Zelizer, *Fault Lines*, 5–6, 26–31; and Stein, *Pivotal Decade*, esp. xi–xii.

164 *The service sector*: Jefferson Cowie, *Stayin' Alive: The 1970s and the Last Days of the Working Class* (New York: New Press, 2012), 12; Windham, *Knocking on Labor's Door*, 58–61; Bethany Moreton, *To Serve God and Wal-Mart: The Making of Christian Free Enterprise* (Cambridge, Mass.: Harvard University Press, 2010), esp. 2–5; Gabriel Winant, *The Next Shift: The Fall of Industry and the Rise of Health Care in Rust Belt America* (Cambridge, Mass.: Harvard University Press, 2021), esp. 16–19.

165 *"A crunch is coming"*: Kleiman, "Where the Women's Movement Is Today."

165 *"Certain economic decisions"*: Karen DeCrow to "Friend," May 12, 1976, folder 20, box 9, Atlanta Lesbian Feminist Alliance Archives.

165 *When still NOW president*: Hernandez to William Mobraten (VP-Personnel, Pacific Telephone), Feb. 3, 1971, "PT and T Minority Consulting Group" folder, box 9, Hernandez Papers.

165 *She began building*: Aileen C. Hernandez Associates, Statement of Services, n.d., ca. Jan. 1975, "Reading File January 1975" folder, box 55, Hernandez Papers.

165 *"personalized services from experienced"*: "Aileen C. Hernandez Associates," Dec. 1983, "Aileen" folder, box 19, Hernandez Papers.

166 *"inclusionary personnel practices"*: Hernandez and Associates, "Seminars in Inclusionary Personnel Practices," for United Parcel Service Southwest Region, Dallas, Oct. 22, 1982, "Writings" folder, box 20, Hernandez Papers.

166 *This reinforced potential rivalries*: Mayeri, *Reasoning from Race*, 3; MacLean, *Freedom Is Not Enough*, 151–52.

166 *the company made*: "Electronics Bringing a Quiet Revolution in the Nation's Telephone Service," *New York Times*, April 6, 1975, 1, 50.

166 *But the telephone monopoly*: Neil D. Klotz, "The Affirmative Action You Have Reached Is Not in Service," *Straight Creek Journal*, Feb. 18–24, 1975, folder 1, box 19, Hacker Papers.

166 *AT&T had publicly accepted*: On the EEOC's case against AT&T, see also Lois Kathryn Herr, *Women, Power, and AT&T: Winning Rights in the Workplace* (Boston: Northeastern University Press, 2002); and Green, *Race on the Line*.

166 *"women's work is being eliminated"*: Sally Hacker to Dutch Kleywegt, May 20, 1974, folder 1, box 19, Hacker Papers; Hacker to Ann Kelly, Oct. 1, 1974, folder 6, box 19, Hacker Papers.

166 *"telephone calls, notes"*: Affidavit of Anne Ladky, U.S. District Court for the Northern District of Illinois, Eastern Division, *EEOC v. Sears*, 1982, 2–3, in Ladky's possession.

166 *"It was obvious to anyone"*: Collins, interview by author, 2015, 13.

167 *Black women and men*: Traci Parker, *Department Stores and the Black Freedom Movement: Workers, Consumers, and Civil Rights from the 1930s to the 1980s* (Chapel Hill: University of North Carolina Press, 2019), 17.

167 *Sears was also notorious*: Hyman, "Ending Discrimination, Legitimating Debt," 216.

167 *Black woman shoppers*: Parker, *Department Stores and the Black Freedom Movement*, 17.

167 *"a really truly good"*: Collins, interview by Connell, 28, folder 6, box 8.

167 *"had always been associated"*: "How Sears Became a High-Cost Operator," *BusinessWeek*, Feb. 16, 1981, 52.

167 *With four hundred thousand workers*: Jad Mouawad, "Arthur Wood, Executive, 93, Who Led Sears," *New York Times*, June 22, 2006, C16; Gordon L. Weil, *Sears, Roebuck, U.S.A.:*

The Great American Catalog Store and How It Grew (Briarcliff Manor, N.Y.: Stein and Day, 1977), 2.

167 *Its longtime head*: Nathan W. Shefferman, *The Man in the Middle* (New York: Doubleday, 1961), 86–87.

167 *Companies like Sears*: Parker, *Department Stores and the Black Freedom Movement*, 204.

167 *"In reality, enforcement"*: "A Simplified Guide to Affirmative Action and Why the Sears Case Is Significant," n.d., ca. 1974, folder 19, box 44, NOW Records.

167 *"a charter member"*: "Look Out, Sears—You Can't Stop NOW!"

168 *"fallen far short"*: Council on Economic Priorities, *Economic Priorities Report* 5, no. 3 (Oct. 1974): 37, in Anne Ladky's possession.

168 *Eighty-six percent of women*: Research Report Prepared by Chicago NOW, May 1974, in Anne Ladky's possession.

168 *Women were nearly half*: Mary Jean Collins-Robson and Ladky to NOW Chapter Presidents, Sears Subcommittee, Board of Directors, and Task Force Coordinators, Nov. 9, 1974, 4, folder 1, box 245, Chicago NOW Collection.

168 *Human resources officials*: Research Report Prepared by Chicago NOW, May 1974.

168 *"what does your husband"*: Atlanta NOW Research Report, Nov. 1974, 5, folder 18, box 44, NOW Records.

168 *Managers shunted white women*: "NOW Sears Action—Why," n.d., ca. 1974, folder 20, box 9, Atlanta Lesbian Feminist Alliance Archives.

168 *Credit was an essential*: Hyman, "Ending Discrimination, Legitimating Debt," 213–18.

169 *"Sock it to Sears"*: Nadasen, *Welfare Warriors*, 110–11.

169 *Sears's credit department*: Hyman, "Ending Discrimination, Legitimating Debt," 216.

169 *Burnett's husband refused*: Burnett, *True Colors*, 46, 152.

169 *She admired a friend*: Burnett, *True Colors*, 15–16.

169 *"yearly allowance and income"*: Burnett to President (Marshall Field), n.d., ca. 1978, "Correspondence, 1976–1978" folder, box 7, Burnett Papers.

169 *Sears's net sales*: Research Report Prepared by Chicago NOW, May 1974; Sears, Roebuck and Company, *Annual Report*, 1974, i, 2, "Sears Action 1975" folder, box 10, National Organization for Women Michigan Conference Records, 1969–96, Bentley Historical Library.

170 *Those discounters were undercutting*: Parker, *Department Stores and the Black Freedom Movement*, 189–90.

170 *They made deeper investments*: Parker, *Department Stores and the Black Freedom Movement*, 191–92.

170 *Less than 5 percent*: Colwell, "Towering Controversy," B1.

170 *Personnel departments set out*: Lightfoot to Employment Committee, "Sears Ponce de Leon Store," Aug. 20, 1974, folder 12, box 3, Lightfoot NOW Officer Papers.

170 *"professionals," its highest job category*: Colwell, "Towering Controversy," B2.

170 *Company officials discovered*: On Wal-Mart officials' similar strategy, see Moreton, *To Serve God and Wal-Mart*, 49–66.

170 *"new ways to maintain"*: Mary Jean Collins-Robson and Ladky, memo to NOW Chapter Presidents, Sears Subcommittee, Board of Directors, and Task Force Coordinators, Nov. 9, 1974, folder 4, box 15, Collins NOW Officer Papers.

170 *"no substantial benefits"*: Testimony of Anne Ladky, *Hearings Before United States Commission on Civil Rights*, 2 vols. (Chicago, 1974), 2:50.

170 *"against women"*: Carolyn Colwell, "Sears' New Challenge: Bring in Women with Training," *Chicago Tribune*, July 23, 1975, B1.

170 *Wood, a sixty-two-year-old*: Mouawad, "Arthur Wood, Executive, 93, Who Led Sears."

171 *"heads of families"*: Colwell, "Sears' New Challenge."

171 *"spreading our efforts"*: Affidavit of Anne Ladky, U.S. District Court for the Northern District of Illinois, Eastern Division, *EEOC v. Sears*, 1982, 5, in Ladky's possession.

171 *"a notorious discriminator"*: "Look Out, Sears—You Can't Stop NOW!"

171 *"Who do you think"*: Collins, interview by Connell, 30, folder 6, box 8.

171 *"Old Hat" awards*: "N.O.W. Gives Out 'Old Hat' Awards," *Chicago Tribune*, Aug. 30, 1971, C8.

171 *Even the general public*: Collins, interview by Connell, 27, folder 8, box 6.

172 *"In every chapter"*: Sears Action Bulletin, no. 1 (July 1974): 3, folder 4, box 15, Collins NOW Officer Papers.

172 *The campaign's architects*: Parker, *Department Stores and the Black Freedom Movement*, esp. 81.

172 *"relegated to the same"*: Sears Action Bulletin, no. 2 (July 1974): 3, folder 4, box 15, Collins NOW Officer Papers.

172 *"paid weekly, receive[d]"*: NOW, Sears sample press release, May 1975, folder 4, box 15, Collins NOW Officer Papers.

172 *"How many women"*: Collins, interview by Connell, 29–30, folder 6, box 8.

172 *"This store is their store"*: "Songs," n.d., ca. 1974, folder 10, box 246, Chicago NOW Collection.

173 *Some Sears women*: Notes, n.d., ca. 1974, folder 3, box 245, Chicago NOW Collection.

173 *"exert[ing] pressure on Sears"*: "A Decade of Feminism: Chicago NOW Highlights of the 1970s," folder 17, box 58, Chicago NOW Collection.

173 *"That does it"*: "Today's Action Will Proceed as Follows," n.d., ca. 1974, folder 1, box 247, Chicago NOW Collection.

173 *They printed a monthly*: Sears Action Bulletin, no. 2 (Sept. 1974): 3.

174 *Fifty NOW chapters participated*: Sears Action Bulletin, no. 6 (Dec. 1974): 1, folder 4, box 15, Collins NOW Officer Papers.

174 *"discredit card"*: Sears Action Bulletin, no. 6 (Dec. 1974): 1.

174 *By the end*: Mary Jean Collins-Robson and Ladky to NOW Chapter Presidents, Sears Subcommittee, Board of Directors, and Task Force Coordinators, Nov. 9, 1974, folder 1, box 245, Chicago NOW Collection.

174 *The Chicago chapter alone*: "NOW Gears Up for Sears Campaign," *Spokeswoman*, Aug. 15, 1974, 1, folder 5, box 244, Chicago NOW Collection.

174 *"a very vague idea"*: Agnes Kelley to Chicago NOW, re: Midwest Academy, Spring 1974, folder 4, box 38, Chicago NOW Collection.

174 *"Snears Doughbuck"*: "Report on NOW Conference Training," n.d., ca. March 1973, "Board Meeting, March 1973" folder, box 1, Midwest Academy Records.

174 *"action oriented"*: Doctor to Carol Kummerfeld, re: National Conference of NOW Workshop Reports: Confrontation and Demonstration and Masculine Mystique, March 13, 1973, folder 3, box 244, Chicago NOW Collection.

174 *"Snears," then moved*: "Sixth NOW National Conference, Action Planning Sheet," Feb. 16, 1973, "NOW Training-April 1972," box 80, Midwest Academy Records.

174 *"came at Sears"*: "Decade of Feminism."

174 *NOW sought to upgrade*: Colwell, "Towering Controversy."

175 *Black women's confidential*: Green, "Flawed Remedies," 55–56; Parker, "'Sears Discriminated Against Me Because of My Sex and Race,'" 22–28.

175 *"dirty" and "lower rated"*: Mims quoted in Parker, *Department Stores and the Black Freedom Movement*, 213–14.

175 *"In the Chicago chapter"*: Barrett, "Women's Rights: Where Have All the Shrinking Violets Gone?"

175 *But such partnerships*: Zuckerman, "Cooperative Origins of EEOC v. Sears," 241–42; Parker, "'Sears Discriminated Against Me Because of My Sex and Race,'" 22; Green, "Flawed Remedies," 46–48.

175 *Some Black women*: Collins, interview by Connell, 29, folder 6, box 8.

175 *"virtually worthless"*: Lynne Darcy to Trudy Peterson, Oct. 17, 1973, folder 5, box 1, Darcy Papers.

175 *Copus steered the EEOC*: Green, "Flawed Remedies," 58.

175 *"We thought the government"*: Collins, interview by author, March 28, 2018, 3.

175 *Copus's romantic partner*: Paul Merrion, "EEOC Staffer's Connections Weaken Bias Suit Against Sears," *Crain's Chicago Business*, May 16, 1980, 3; Whitney Adams, "Report on the FCC Task Force," Oct. 5, 1972, folder 42, box 43, NOW Records.

176 *"file charges as soon"*: Adams to Lupa, April 25, 1973, folder 16, box 18, Heide NOW Officer Papers.

176 *Sears fought back*: Parker, "'Sears Discriminated Against Me Because of My Sex and Race,'" 24–26, 29.

176 *"a national program"*: Mary Jean Collins-Robson, "$100 Million and Nothing Less!," n.d., ca. 1974, folder 5, box 244, Chicago NOW Collection.

176 *Collins and her allies*: *Spokeswoman*, May 15, 1977, 1.

176 *When company officials wanted*: Lynne Darcy to DeCrow et al., re: Meeting with Sears, n.d., ca. Oct. 1974, folder 1, box 246, Chicago NOW Collection.

176 *The top brass*: "Top Management Feels the Pressure," *Sears Action Bulletin* 8 (April 1975): 1, folder 1, box 246, Chicago NOW Collection.

176 *She had sent*: Hernandez to DeCrow et al., re: Meeting with Sears Officials, Dec. 16, Oct. 24, 1974, folder 1, box 245, Chicago NOW Collection.

176 *"magnificent boardroom"*: Judith Lonnquist, interview by Davison, June 18, 1996, 2.

176 *"That's when we realized"*: Collins, interview by author, March 28, 2018, 2.

176 *Hernandez had first made*: Michael Harris, "Minority Protest on Large Firms," *San Francisco Chronicle*, Feb. 5, 1971, 6.

176 *In her remarks there*: Ms. Aileen Hernandez's Remarks—Sears Roebuck & Co. Southern Territorial Personnel Conference, May 31, 1972, tape, side A.

177 *She met with them*: Hernandez to A. Dean Swift, March 22, 1974, "Sears Correspondence, 1974–5" folder, box 74, Hernandez Papers; Hernandez to "Jim," Sept. 16, 1974, "Sears Correspondence, 1974–5" folder, box 74, Hernandez Papers.

177 *Sears's draft contract*: Draft contract between Hernandez and Sears, Roebuck, ca. Nov. 1974, "Sears Correspondence, 1974–5" folder, box 74, Hernandez Papers.

177 *"give Sears an opportunity"*: Hernandez to Ray Graham, Dec. 22, 1974, "Sears Correspondence, 1974–5" folder, box 74, Hernandez Papers.

177 *"the enemy within"*: Eleanor Spikes to Hernandez, memo on telephone call from Ray Graham, Jan. 13, 1975, "Sears Correspondence, 1974–5" folder, box 74, Hernandez Papers.

177 *"pleased" with the meeting*: Hernandez to Lynne Darcy, March 6, 1975, "Reading File, February 1975" folder, box 55, Hernandez Papers.

177 *From the other*: "Top Management Feels the Pressure," *Sears Action Bulletin*, no. 8 (April 1975): 1–2, folder 1, box 246, Chicago NOW Collection.

178 *"If you are not already"*: Hernandez to Ray Graham, re: Postscript to the Meeting with NOW, March 6, 1975, "Reading File, March 1975" folder, box 55, Hernandez Papers.

178 *As Hernandez's work*: Gene Harmon to Hernandez, June 8, 1982, "For Follow-Up" folder, box 40, Hernandez Papers.

178 *more than a thousand*: "Equality Is Not Just a Nice Idea . . . ," *Tower News: A Biweekly for Sears Headquarters Employees*, June 9, 1978, 3, "Sears Management Forum 1977" folder, box 74, Hernandez Papers.

178 *"We didn't have"*: Sedey, interview by author, Feb. 21, 2019, 3.

178 *"It seems to me"*: Hernandez to DeCrow et al., re: Meeting with Sears Officials, Dec. 16.

178 *"I hope that the dialogue"*: Hernandez to Darcy, March 6, 1975, "Reading File February 1975" folder, box 55, Hernandez Papers.

179 *the Sears campaign leaders'*: NOW's leaders would soon drop the Sears campaign, but the historian Venus Green argues that NOW's "pressure" persuaded the EEOC to walk away from Sears's offer of $34 million in 1978 and begin litigation. See Green, "Flawed Remedies," 59.

179 *She kept up*: Ricki Fulman, "Black Feminist Group Launched," *New York Daily News*, Aug. 16, 1973, folder 7, box 8, Heide Papers; Roth, *Separate Roads to Feminism*, 106.

179 *there was some early*: Doris Wright to Dian Terry, Aug. 18, 1973, folder 18, box 48, NOW Records; Wilma Scott Heide, "An Open Letter to Sisters of the National Black Feminist Organization," Aug. 27, 1973, folder 7, box 8, Heide Papers.

179 *Hernandez wanted NOW*: Boyer, interview by Fox, 115, 111, folder 9, box 1.

179 *For decades, department stores*: Parker, *Department Stores and the Black Freedom Movement*, 187–88.

179 *Soon after Hernandez's work*: "Head of Sears to Discuss Closing Store," *San Francisco Chronicle*, Jan. 8, 1975, "Reading File January 1975" folder, box 55, Hernandez Papers.

179 *"an important facet"*: Hernandez to Graham, Jan. 8, 1975, "Sears Correspondence, 1974–5" folder, box 74, Hernandez Papers.

180 *Officials moved forward*: Jerry Burns, "Sears Rejects Store Plea," *San Francisco Chronicle*, Jan. 22, 1975, "Reading File January 1975" folder, box 55, Hernandez Papers.

180 *Hernandez paid more than*: Aileen C. Hernandez, "Data for Personal Income Tax, 1978," "ACH Income Tax" folder, box 61, Hernandez Papers.

180 *four years after*: Stansell, *Feminist Promise*, 285.

180 *She started out*: Draft contract between Hernandez and Sears, Roebuck, ca. Nov. 1974.

180 *Three years later*: "Sears Fees," n.d., ca. 1980, "Sears—Fees, 1975–80" folder, box 74, Hernandez Papers; Hernandez and Associates, "Data for 1977 Tax Return," 1977, unlabeled folder, box 54, Hernandez Papers.

180 *Her 1978 salary*: Hernandez, "Data for Personal Income Tax, 1978."

180 *Hernandez's Sears connection*: Hernandez to Graham, April 4, 1975, "Sears Correspondence, 1974–5" folder, box 74, Hernandez Papers; Aileen to Eleanor, Jackie, and Patsy, re: Possible New Business, June 21, 1981, "BWOA-Pol.-Act.-Nove. Elections" folder, box 54, Hernandez Papers; Eleanor Spikes to Walter G. Hooke (National Personnel Manager, UPS), Jan. 22, 1975, "Reading File January 1975" folder, box 55, Hernandez Papers; "Aileen C. Hernandez Associates," n.d., "Hernandez + Associates" folder, box 22, Hernandez Papers.

180 *"sensitivity training[s]"*: Hernandez to Dr. Dorothy Gregg, June 23, 1975, "Reading File, June 1975" folder, box 55, Hernandez Papers.

180 *"awareness" seminars about*: Hernandez and Associates, "Seminars in Inclusionary Personnel Practices," for United Parcel Service Southwest Region.

180 *"a forum for dialogue"*: Hernandez to Marilyn Riegel, Aug. 20, 1980, unlabeled folder, box 70, Hernandez Papers.

180 *Hernandez's public sector consulting*: "Aileen C. Hernandez Associates," Dec. 1983, "Aileen" folder, box 19, Hernandez Papers.

181 *"was a consultant"*: NOW National Board Meeting Minutes, May 24–25, 1975, 9, folder 1, box 246, Chicago NOW Collection.

181 *"national action target"*: "Chronology: Aileen Hernandez/Sears Conflict of Interest," n.d., in Anne Ladky's possession.

181 *"two pronged attack"*: "Resolution Passed by Unanimous Vote of Golden Gate Chapter," Nov. 20, 1974, folder 1, box 46, DeCrow Papers.

181 *"hello" by calling him*: "Chronology: Aileen Hernandez/Sears Conflict of Interest."

181 *Herzog's internal inquiry*: NOW National Board Meeting Minutes, May 24–25, 1975, 9–10.

181 *"violated" her own "rights"*: NOW National Board Meeting Minutes, May 24–25, 1975, 10.

181 *"All women are poor"*: Wilma Scott Heide, "The Feminist Cause *Is the Common Cause*," March 27, 1972, 10–11, folder 21, box 2, Evansgardner Papers.

182 *The rise of feminism*: Cowie, *Great Exception*, 28, 27, 183.

182 *"While all women are"*: Hernandez, "Equal Employment Opportunities for Women: Problems, Facts & Answers."

6. THE CHICAGO MACHINE VS. THE PENNSYLVANIA RAILROAD

183 *"that each has to organize"*: Heather Booth, "NOW National Board Training: Midwest Academy Staff Report, May 16, 1973," "Board Meeting-May 1973" folder, box 1, Midwest Academy Records.

183 *"the most dramatic"*: Burnett, interview by Boyer, 90–91, folder 1, box 8. Burnett recalls this training having been run by Saul Alinsky himself, but he had died the previous year. Booth's training, which was heavily inspired by Alinsky's work, was the only training to which Burnett would have referred.

183 *"We came away"*: Conger, interview by Davison, April 21, 2003, 4.

184 *"style was much too harsh"*: Collins, interview by Connell, 40, folder 6, box 8.

184 *"Something was going on"*: Carabillo, interview by Fox, 96, folder 2, box 2.

184 *She was right*: "Report on Meeting with Judy Lightfoot, Chairone of the NOW National Board," 1, "Board Meeting, March 1973" folder, box 1, Midwest Academy Records.

184 *"if there was an empty position"*: Transcript of NOW "Herstory" Session, 34.

184 *In fact, the earliest leaders*: Lupa, email to author, April 28, 2016.

184 *Surely, some whispered*: Eleanor Smeal, "Womansurge Forms," *Pennsylvania NOW*, Dec. 1975, 4, folder 2, box 7, Philadelphia NOW Records. Betty Friedan advanced this view most prominently in a 1976 interview. When pressed on whether she had "direct proof," Friedan pointed to "certain women who seem to get from one place to another around the country and who seem to disrupt the NOW chapters wherever they go," yet lacked "visible means of support." Pat Huntington, "Interview with Betty Friedan," *Playgirl*, March 15, 1976, 129. Friedan and other feminists were not just being paranoid. According to the historian Ruth Rosen, regional FBI offices "paid dozens—more likely hundreds—of female informants to infiltrate the women's movement." Rosen, *World Split Open*, 241. On state scrutiny of the women's liberation movement in Canada in this era, see Christabelle Sethna and Steve Hewitt, *Just Watch Us: RCMP Surveillance of the Women's Liberation Movement in Cold War Canada* (Montreal: McGill-Queen's University Press, 2018).

185 *"the me decade"*: Evans, *Tidal Wave*, 98–99.

185 *Angered by America's humiliating defeat*: Evans, *Tidal Wave*, 111–12; Elizabeth Gillespie McRae, *Mothers of Massive Resistance: White Women and the Politics of White Supremacy* (Oxford: Oxford University Press, 2018), esp. 3–4.

185 *"in serious trouble"*: David Behrens, "What NOW for Women: And What Women for NOW?," *Newsday*, Nov. 26, 1975, 1A.

185 *Recent members brought*: Freeman, *Politics of Women's Liberation*, 92–93.

185 *"Every organization chart"*: Boyer, interview by Fox, 127, folder 9, box 1.

186 *Other democratic movements*: Francesca Polletta, *Freedom Is an Endless Meeting: Democracy in American Social Movements* (Chicago: University of Chicago Press, 2002), 2.

186 *For example, Students*: Gosse, *Rethinking the New Left*, 69–70, 100–101.

186 *In those same years*: Matthew Garcia, *From the Jaws of Victory: The Triumph and Tragedy of Cesar Chavez and the Farm Worker Movement* (Berkeley: University of California Press, 2011), esp. 2–4.

186 *radical feminists' insistence*: Freeman, *Politics of Women's Liberation*, 105, 118–29.

186 *"a focal point"*: Hernandez, interview by Davison, June 30, 1997, 2, 6.

186 *Some members ignored*: Freeman, *Politics of Women's Liberation*, 93, 87.

187 *They divided the country*: "Model Regional By-Laws," n.d., ca. 1970, folder 6, box 1, NOW Records.

187 *Twelve states had*: Fox to Suzanne Stocking, Nov. 13, 1972, folder 2, box 7, Heide Papers.

187 *They began with ten*: Ann Scott to Heide, Sept. 16, 1970, folder 6, box 14, Heide NOW Officer Papers; Task Forces Team to Board of Directors, re: Proposed National Task Force Guidelines, Oct. 28, 1974, folder 46, box 2, NOW Records.

187 *Four years later*: Task Forces Team to Board of Directors, re: Proposed National Task Force Guidelines, Oct. 11, 1974, 1, folder 5, box 22, Heide Papers.

187 *"When I would stand up"*: Boyer, interview by Marie Cantlon, March 8, 1997, 11.

187 *Any member who showed up*: Conroy, interview by Balanoff, 53.

187 *"extraordinary effort and expense"*: Jean Stapleton, "Chicago '70," *Los Angeles NOW Newsletter*, April 1970, 1, "California–Los Angeles" folder, box 2, NOW Chapter Newsletters Collection.

187 *They developed competing plans*: Catherine Conroy to Chapter President, Oct. 1, 1973, folder 4, box 45, DeCrow Papers; "Proceedings of the Sixth National Conference of NOW," Feb. 16–19, 1973, *NOW Acts* 6, no. 1 (1973): 16; Karen DeCrow, "An Open Letter to Members of Central New York NOW," Oct. 16, 1973, folder 4, box 45, DeCrow Papers; "To All Chapter Presidents," Oct. 25, 1973, folder 4, box 45, DeCrow Papers; Betty Newcomb, "Report on By-Laws Vote," *Do It NOW*, Jan. 1974, 8.

188 *Under the 1971 contract*: "C-R Office Programs Report," Oct. 1972, "Finances" folder, box 105, Hernandez Papers.

188 *C-R's storefront and telephone*: "Agreement," "General Corr. 1970" folder, box 105, Hernandez Papers.

188 *"get out from what"*: Collins, interview by author, March 28, 2018, 3.

188 *The board agreed*: NOW 7th National Conference Program, 1974, 17, folder 13, box 154, Chicago NOW Collection.

188 *Mary Jean was part*: Collins, interview by author, March 28, 2018, 3.

188 *After finishing her undergraduate*: Plitt to Nan Wood, July 9, 1973, folder 3, box 45, DeCrow Papers.

188 *"shocked" to be barred*: Plitt, interview by author, Nov. 29, 2018, 1.

188 *"I couldn't imagine"*: Plitt, interview by author, 2, 3.

189 *"We knew what our roles"*: Doty, interview by author, March 5, 2019, 4.

189 *"Large metropolitan chapters"*: Patricia Hill Burnett, "NOW Ideas from the National Board," *As We See It NOW*, June 1972, 5, "Detroit" folder, NOW Chapter Newsletters Collection.

189 *"An amicable divorce"*: Hernandez to Ollis Marie-Victoire, Oct. 30, 1973, unlabeled folder, box 85, Hernandez Papers.

189 *"not that kind of town"*: Fishman and Ladky, interview by author, 3.

190 *So too did Eleanor*: Claudia Dreifus, "Eleanor Smeal: What Made This Homemaker from Pittsburgh Move into the National Spotlight?," *Redbook*, April 1982, 60.

190 *Smeal and other*: Kathy Bonk, interview by author, July 26, 2019, 4.

190 *not "comfortable" with*: *KNOW News*, Sept. 1975, 1, folder 1, box 12, Atlanta Lesbian Feminist Alliance Archives.

190 *"people should be paid"*: *KNOW News*, Sept. 1975, 1, 3.

190 *"feminist business"*: *KNOW News*, Sept. 1975, 1, 3.

190 *At the national board*: Minutes of the NOW Board Meeting, St. Louis, Nov. 10–11, 1973, 3, folder 3, box 45, DeCrow Papers; Whitney Adams and Cathy Irwin, "To the Vocal Majority," *Vocal Majority* 5, no. 3, 1974, 11, folder 4, box 1, NOW Washington, D.C., Chapter and Capitol Hill Chapter Records.

190 *"unconscious sexism"*: Anne Pride, "To the Vocal Majority," *Vocal Majority*, 5, no. 4, 1974, 5, 10, folder 4, box 1, NOW Washington, D.C., Chapter and Capitol Hill Chapter Records.

190 *"a shotgun wedding"*: Carabillo, interview by Fox, 162, folder 2, box 2.

190 *"malevolent force"*: "July 5, 1973, Board Meeting Minutes," 2, "June Board Meeting, 1973" folder, box 1, Midwest Academy Records.

190 *"start with the notion"*: "NOW Pre-convention Planning Sessions," n.d., ca. Spring 1974, folder 19, box 154, Chicago NOW Collection.

191 *In these sessions*: "Agenda: Conference Planning Session #1," April 13, 1974, folder 19, box 154, Chicago NOW Collection.

191 *"listen, try to understand"*: Ladky, handwritten notes, n.d., ca. April 1974, in Ladky's possession.

191 *Another NOW leader who*: Lightfoot, interview by Boyer, 85, 86, 62, folder 7, box 2.

191 *"women's culture"*: Alice Echols, *Daring to Be Bad: Radical Feminism in America, 1967–1975* (Minneapolis: University of Minnesota Press, 1989), 7.

191 *"the nuts and bolts"*: Doty, interview by author, 3.

191 *"was without a doubt"*: Sedey, interview by author, 3.

191 *"I doubt if you know"*: Marline Rennels (Elgin, Ill., NOW coordinator) to Karen DeCrow, Sept. 24, 1974, folder 11, box 40, DeCrow Papers.

191 *"that is part of living"*: Chicago NOW Board to Marline Rennels, Aug. 29, 1974, folder 11, box 40, DeCrow Papers.

192 *the 1973 U.S. Supreme Court*: *Roe v. Wade*, 410 U.S. 113 (1973).

192 *This economic instability*: Self, *All in the Family*, 311.

192 *"abortion repeal" task forces*: Mary Lu Zuber, "Young Couple Initiates NOW Chapter in Houston," *Christian Science Monitor*, May 13, 1970, 14.

192 *protested them in their communities*: "NOW Asks Abortion Law Repeal," *Atlanta Constitution*, May 11, 1969, 2B. See also "Women's Protest Spoils Mother's Day for George," *NOW Acts* 2, no. 1 (Winter/Spring 1969): 5. On grassroots abortion rights activism in New York, see Felicia Kornbluh, *A Woman's Life is a Human Life: My Mother, Our Neighbor, and the Journey from Reproductive Rights to Reproductive Justice* (New York: Grove, 2023).

192 *NOW co-sponsored an abortion rights*: "Signature Campaign," *San Francisco Sun Reporter*, April 4, 1970, 14; Susan Berman, "West Coast Women Lead Fight; Legalize Abortion," *Atlanta Constitution*, Aug. 2, 1970, 7G.

192 *Members in Massachusetts*: Ann-Mary Currier, "Women Fighting Law on Abortion," *Boston Globe*, Feb. 15, 1970, 39; "Women Back Altering of Abortion Law," *Atlanta Constitution*, Feb. 1, 1970, 8B; *NOW Acts* 1, no. 1 (Fall 1968): 10; "Coalition Conferences," *NOW Acts* 1, no. 3 (Winter 1970): 15. See also Rebecca Davison, "Revolutionaries and Reformers," 9–17, unpublished manuscript, in author's possession.

192 *"NOW can take"*: Aileen Hernandez, "From the President," *NOW Acts* 3, no. 2 (July 1970): 3.

192 *"a fundamental constitutional right"*: "Abortion Laws Under Attack," *Washington Post*, Aug. 12, 1971, D13. The brief pertained to abortion restrictions in Texas and Georgia, and its other organizational co-sponsors were the American Association of University Women, the national board of the YWCA, the National Women's Conference of the American Ethical Union, the Professional Women's Caucus, the Unitarian Universalist Women's Federation, and the Women's Alliance of the First Unitarian Church of Dallas.

193 *Chicago NOW members*: Handout, April 28, 1974, folder 19, box 154, Chicago NOW Collection; Ladky to Fox Valley–Elgin NOW, Feb. 25, 1974, folder 5, box 156, Chicago NOW Collection.

193 *In previous years*: Boyer to Members of the 1972 Nominating Committee, Nov. 6, 1972, folder 27, box 7, NOW Records.

193 *Members were less likely*: Tracie Rozhon, "The Women Meet, and . . . Divide and Destroy," *Baltimore Sun*, Nov. 2, 1975, K3.

193 *Those newcomers, who were*: "Summary of Questionnaire for NOW," n.d., ca. 1974, folder 4, box 45, DeCrow Papers; Freeman, *Politics of Women's Liberation*, 92.

193 *"broaden" and foster*: Bell, *Lighting the Fires of Freedom*, 84.

193 *The committee should be*: Hernandez to Nominating Committee, re: Nominating Procedures, n.d., ca. early 1974, unlabeled folder, box 85, Hernandez Papers.

193 *The nominating committee adopted*: Nominating Committee, "Important Information from the Nominating Committee to All Candidates for NOW Office," Feb. 25, 1974, folder 8, box 5, Lightfoot NOW Officer Papers.

194 *"There was not much question"*: Collins, interview by author, 2018, 1.

194 *She outlined a pragmatic vision*: Mary Jean Collins-Robson, "Candidate Questionnaire," May 5, 1974, folder 19, box 154, Chicago NOW Collection.

194 *The outgoing president*: Carabillo, interview by Fox, 155, 143, folder 2, box 2.

194 *"getting fat off"*: NOW Split Roundtable Discussion, Sept. 12, 1991, 8, folder 7, box 11, Tully-Crenshaw Feminist Oral History Project.

194 *shelled out the thousands*: "Capsule Descriptions of NOW National Offices," *Do It NOW*, Aug. 1972, 6.

194 *"outside of the NOW"*: Carabillo, interview by Fox, 144, 152, folder 2, box 2.

194 *"It certainly was"*: Collins, interview by author, Feb. 22, 2019, 1.

194 *"$100 million and nothing less"*: Collins, interview by author, 2018, 1.

195 *"We were fierce"*: Doty, interview by author, 3.

195 *"meant to be used"*: Carabillo, interview by Fox, 95, folder 2, box 2.

195 *They redoubled their support*: Carabillo, interview by Fox, 150, folder 2, box 2.

195 *"hauled our Californians"*: Carabillo, interview by Fox, 154, folder 2, box 2.

195 *DeCrow had helped*: DeCrow, interview by Frances Arick Kolb, Feb. 15, 1981, 3, 5, 8, folder 10, box 2, Tully-Crenshaw Feminist Oral History Project.

195 *banned "unescorted" women*: Central New York NOW Meeting Minutes, Jan. 10, 1968, folder 8, box 40, DeCrow Papers; Minutes of NOW Meeting, May 15, 1968, DeCrow Papers.

195 *Title II of the 1964 Civil Rights Act*: Dinner and Sepper, "Sex in Public," 103.

195 *"arrest white, middle-class"*: DeCrow, interview by Kolb, 15, folder 10, box 2.

195 *She served as national*: Karen DeCrow, Membership Chairman Report to NOW National Conference, March 17, 1970, folder 1, box 45, DeCrow Papers; DeCrow to Hernandez, March 28, 1971, folder 14, box 51, DeCrow Papers.

195 *"very much against"*: DeCrow, interview by Kolb, 23, 24, folder 10, box 2.

196 *"the oppression of other groups"*: DeCrow, interviewed on "Controversies Within the Women's Movement," *Woman*.

196 *"changing the mainstream"*: Laurie Johnston, "NOW Expands the List of What It's For and What It's Against," *New York Times*, June 1, 1974, 18.

196 *"that it was going"*: Carabillo, interview by Fox, 154, folder 2, box 2.

196 *"spent no money"*: "Revamp Work Ethic: NOW Chief," *Chicago Tribune*, May 28, 1974, A2.

196 *"Chicago Machine"*: Collins, interview by Connell, 41, folder 6, box 8.

196 *This was an obvious*: On Daley, see, for example, Mike Royko, *Boss: Richard J. Daley of Chicago* (New York: E. P. Dutton, 1971).

196 *Collins's opponents claimed*: Collins, interview by Connell, 41, folder 6, box 8.

197 *"One day we're communists"*: Collins, interview by author, 2018, 2.

197 *"ladies in suits"*: Collins, interview by author, 2018, 1; Collins, interview by Connell, 31, folder 6, box 8.

197 *"We started counting them"*: Collins, interview by author, 2015, 14.

197 *"cooperate with any commercial"*: Gene Boyer, "Policies for NOW Chapter/Regional/National Relationships Regarding Finances and Fund-Raising," Feb. 19, 1972, 6, folder 9, box 1, NOW Records.

197 *That promotion declared*: NOW 7th National Conference Program, 1974, 4.

197 *Right after the conference*: "Chapter Alert—Sears Wants to Join NOW," n.d., ca. June 1974, folder 18, box 44, NOW Records.

197 *"sending women to"*: Collins, interview by Connell, 31, folder 6, box 8.

197 *"being a housewife"*: DeCrow, interviewed on "Controversies Within the Women's Movement," *Woman*.

197 *"There's nothing wrong"*: Collins, interview by author, 2019, 1.

198 *"real progress with"*: Evansgardner, interview by Davison, Dec. 13, 1995, 4.

198 *"I think Mary Jean"*: Carabillo, interview by Fox, 153, folder 2, box 2.

198 *Aileen Hernandez chaired*: NOW Split Roundtable Discussion, 9; "Comfortable Capacities of Rice Hotel Public Space," n.d., ca. 1974, folder 1, box 4, JoAnn Evansgardner and Gerald H. F. Gardner Papers, 1965–91, AIS.2001.09, Archives & Special Collections, University of Pittsburgh Library System.

198 *Members' marijuana smoke*: NOW Split Roundtable Discussion, 9.

198 *"and created enough doubt"*: Collins, interview by Connell, 39–40, folder 6, box 8.

198 *"24 hours of hell"*: NOW Split Roundtable Discussion, 9.

198 *"shuffling their way"*: TSK, "Don't Go Back to Houston," L.A. NOW Chapter Newsletter, July 1974, 4, "California–Los Angeles" folder, box 2, NOW Chapter Newsletters Collection.

198 *The new president*: Karen DeCrow, "Houston Acceptance Speech," May 1974, folder 4, box 40, DeCrow Papers.

198 *Collins took one*: "NOW Officers and Board of Directors," *Do It NOW*, July 1974, 3.

198 *"angry, manipulated, wasted"*: Susan Dillon and Ellen S. Agress to National Board, May 28, 1974, folder 1, box 43, DeCrow Papers.

199 *Others were mystified*: Chris Guerrero, "Internalizing the Struggle," *& Nothing Less* (St. Louis), July 1974, 2, folder 2, box 104, Chicago NOW Collection.

199 *"devious groups intent"*: Win Frederick of Detroit NOW to DeCrow, n.d., ca. late 1974, folder 1, box 43, DeCrow Papers.

199 *the FBI had collected*: FBI Records: The Vault, "National Organization for Women," part 3 of 3, 33, vault.fbi.gov/National%20Organization%20for%20Women%20%28NOW%29/National%20Organization%20for%20Women%20%28NOW%29%20Part%2017%20of%203/view.

199 *"sources" about planned protests*: FBI Records: The Vault, "National Organization for Women," part 2 of 3, 36, vault.fbi.gov/National%20Organization%20for%20Women%20%28NOW%29/National%20Organization%20for%20Women%20%28NOW%29%20Part%202%20of%203/view.

199 *"no known subversive"*: FBI Records: The Vault, "National Organization for Women," part 1 of 3, 46, vault.fbi.gov/National%20Organization%20for%20Women%20%28NOW%29/National%20Organization%20for%20Women%20%28NOW%29%20Part%201%20of%203/view.

199 *"quality over quantity"*: Ivan Greenberg, *The Dangers of Dissent: The FBI and Civil Liberties Since 1965* (Lanham, Md.: Lexington Books, 2010), 98.

199 *"NOW had a great deal"*: Burnett, interview by Boyer, 125, folder 1, box 8.

199 *"There were ideological differences"*: Fox, interview by author, 4.

199 *"affirmative-action program"*: Johnston, "NOW Expands the List of What It's For and What It's Against."

199 *"Appreciation of skill"*: Ladky quoted in Freeman, *Politics of Women's Liberation*, 95.

200 *That danger stemmed*: Polletta, *Freedom Is an Endless Meeting*, 8–10.

200 *NOW's chapters were typically*: Joanna Martin, "Factions in NOW, 1974," May 10, 1976, in Ladky's possession.

200 *"chapter rights"*: Johnston, "NOW Expands the List of What It's For and What It's Against."

200 *"more and more"*: David Fouquet, "She's a Referee of Robert's Rules," *Washington Post*, Sept. 12, 1965, T1.

200 *"I was very enamored"*: Collins, interview by Connell, 40, folder 6, box 8.

201 *"We believe NOW"*: "Feminists Urge Nixon Impeachment," *Courier-Journal*, May 28, 1974, A4.

201 UNBORN WOMEN HAVE: Chase Untermeyer, "NOW Is Urged to Be Bolder Against Bias," *Washington Post*, May 26, 1974, A3.

201 *"It was devastating"*: Collins, interview by author, 2019, 1.

201 *"We had total control"*: Collins, interview by author, 2019, 1. For an overview of the conflict, see also Evans, *Tidal Wave*, 109–10; and Kelsy Kretschmer, "Should We Stay or Should We Go? Local and National Factionalism in the National Organization for Women," *Qualitative Sociology* 40 (2017): 403–23.

201 *outlined a vague agenda*: "Revamp Work Ethic: NOW Chief."

202 *The Chicagoans adored*: Boyer, interview by Fox, 82, folder 9, box 1; Kathy Rand, interview by author, March 14, 2018, 5.

202 *"transfer her services"*: Carabillo to DeCrow, June 5, 1974, folder 1, box 43, DeCrow Papers.

202 *"figurehead"*: Carabillo, interview by Fox, 143, folder 2, box 2.

202 *DeCrow and Plitt sparred*: DeCrow to Plitt, Oct. 27, 1974, folder 33, box 38, NOW Records; Plitt to DeCrow, Nov. 1, 1974, folder 33, box 38, NOW Records.

202 *DeCrow lodged a formal*: DeCrow to Plitt, Nov. 14, 1974, folder 3, box 4, Lightfoot NOW Officer Papers.

202 *The national board wound down*: "Ask NOW," *Do It NOW*, Jan.–Feb. 1975, 12.

202 *Soon the office*: NOW 7th National Conference Program, 1974, 17.

202 *Suzanne Doty, the executive secretary*: Doty, interview by author, 3.

203 *Plitt, Doty, and the others*: Freeman, *Politics of Women's Liberation*, 89.

203 *"People were just infuriated"*: Plitt, interview by author, 5.

203 *"worn thin, emotionally"*: Plitt to Heide, April 17, 1974, 9, 11, folder 17, box 6, Heide NOW Officer Papers.

203 *"this was not an adversarial situation"*: "Open Letter to the Membership of NOW," n.d., ca. Dec. 1974, folder 35, box 38, NOW Records.

203 *The board, dominated*: "Open Letter to the Membership of NOW."

203 *"inhumane treatment"*: New Orleans Board Meeting Minutes Tape Transcript, Dec. 7, 1974, 3, folder 47, box 2, NOW Records.

203 *After more debate*: "Open Letter to the Membership of NOW."

203 *"I remember standing"*: Doty, interview by author, 2.

204 *"kangaroo court"*: Lyon and Martin, interview, part 4, 12, folder 7, box 9.

204 *"ordering the president"*: Carabillo, interview by Fox, 145, folder 2, box 2.

204 *DeCrow had not even*: NOW National Board Meeting Minutes Transcribed, Dec. 7–8, 1974, 3, 22, folder 44, box 2, NOW Records.

204 *But the board plowed ahead*: New Orleans Board Meeting Minutes Tape Transcript, Dec. 7, 1974, 24.

204 *DeCrow would have*: "Open Letter to the Membership of NOW."

204 *"sitting there, and saying"*: Lyon and Martin interview, part 4, 15, folder 7, box 9.

204 *DeCrow and thirteen*: NOW National Board Meeting Minutes Transcribed, Dec. 7–8, 1974, 3.

204 *"I had no idea"*: Suneson, interview by Davison, Dec. 13, 1999, 8.

204 *"Stop her!"*: "Open Letter to the Membership of NOW."

204 *the Majority Caucus*: "Open Letter to the Membership of NOW."

204 *Meanwhile, the end of 1974*: Abbye Atkinson, "Borrowing Equality," *Columbia Law Review* 120, no. 6 (Oct. 2020): 1424; Betsy Friedman, "Pioneering Approaches to Confront Sex Bias in Housing," *Cleveland State Law Review* 24, no. 1 (1975): 81.

205 *Richard Nixon*: Heide to NOW Members, Dec. 15, 1972, folder 21, box 2, Evansgardner and Gardner Papers.

205 *The previous year, he*: Dinner, "Universal Childcare Debate."

205 *Conservatives were already uniting*: Kruse and Zelizer, *Fault Lines*, 89–91; Self, *All in the Family*, 287–91.

205 *NOW's ambitious plans*: NOW National Board Meeting Minutes Transcribed, Dec. 7–8, 1974, 10.

205 *Meanwhile, the number*: Martin, "Factions in NOW, 1974."

205 *For many, the movement*: Evans, *Tidal Wave*, 104.

205 *"A surprise attack"*: Eileen Kelly, "December 7, 1974," NOW New York State Newsletter, March 1975, 1, folder 1, box 4, Kolb Papers.

205 *"National NOW has become"*: Bev Jones, "A Proposed Platform for the Majority Caucus," Jan. 6, 1975, 3, 2, folder 15, box 51, DeCrow Papers.

206 *"a revolutionary feminist organization"*: Majority Caucus, "To Every Member of NOW," n.d., ca. April 1975, 4, folder 32, box 38, NOW Records.

206 *"organize to recapture"*: Carabillo, interview by Fox, 148, folder 2, box 2.

206 *"the real power"*: Smeal and Bonk, interview by author, April 10, 2019, 12.

206 *"out of the mainstream"*: Beth Gillin Pombeiro, "NOW: City of Sisterly Love?," *Philadelphia Inquirer*, Oct. 25, 1975, 1.

206 *"'Mainstream America' did not fit"*: Hernandez to Geri Kenyon, June 18, 1976, "June 1976" folder, box 55, Hernandez Papers.

206 *"a training ground"*: Vera Glaser, "NOW Braces for Floor Fights in Convention Here Friday," *Philadelphia Inquirer*, Oct. 19, 1975, 7.

206 *She was not a Caucus leader*: James Field to Hernandez, June 17, 1975, "NOW" folder, box 7, Hernandez Papers.

206 *"We would go"*: Conger, interview by Davison, April 21, 2003, 8.

207 *"painful" New Orleans*: Howard, interview by Davison, May 21, 1997, 8.

207 *"strategies for returning NOW"*: "Summary of Discussion: Eastern Region Majority Caucus Meeting," May 18, 1975, "May 1975" folder, box 55, Hernandez Papers.

207 *"financial squeeze play"*: "Means of Fighting for the Majority Caucus," n.d., ca. early 1975, folder 4, box 16, Kolb Papers.

207 *"economic boycott"*: Jackie Starkey, "National NOW and the Majority Caucus," NOW New York State Newsletter, March 1975, 2, folder 1, box 4, Kolb Papers.

207 *Pennsylvania NOW's board*: Pennsylvania NOW State Board Meeting, Jan. 11–12, 1975, 5, folder 11, box 6, Evansgardner and Gardner Papers.

207 *At least five state organizations*: "Action Taken at State Board Meeting," L.A. NOW Chapter Newsletter, March 1975, 1, "California–Los Angeles" folder, box 2, NOW Chapter Newsletters Collection; Rosemary Belmont and Jean Conger to Chapter Presidents, National Board Members in the Eastern Region, Maryland, West Virginia, and Washington, D.C., n.d., ca. early 1975, folder 1, box 4, Kolb Papers; List of Chapters in Escrow, folder 8, box 40, DeCrow Papers.

207 *"strong national structure"*: "Board of Directors, Metropolitan Detroit Chapter," n.d., ca. 1975, 2, folder 14, box 3, Lightfoot NOW Officer Papers.

207 *"I'm not sure"*: Burnett to Members of the Detroit NOW Board, re: Problems of the National NOW Board, ca. Dec. 1974, "Correspondence 1974" folder, box 1, Burnett Papers.

207 *"No members authorized"*: Zalmar to All Officers and Board Members of National NOW, Jan. 28, 1975, folder 35, box 38, NOW Records.

207 *NOW's efforts to chip*: Carol Kleiman, "Women's Job Gains May Be Gone with the Recession," *Chicago Tribune*, March 20, 1975, B5.

207 *Overall unemployment peaked*: Tom Wicker, "Deficits, Jobs, and Democrats," *New York Times*, May 6, 1975, 39.

207 *Such economic turmoil*: Evans, *Tidal Wave*, 111–13.

207 *With their presumption*: Self, *All in the Family*, 296–99; Stacie Taranto, *Kitchen Table Politics: Conservative Women and Family Values in New York* (Philadelphia: University of Pennsylvania Press, 2017), esp. 5–6.

208 *Striking a conciliatory tone*: Judy Lightfoot et al., "Dear NOW Chapter Presidents and State Coordinators," n.d., ca. Winter 1975, folder 34, box 38, NOW Records.

208 *The midwesterners who controlled*: "Important Information About National NOW—Please Share with All NOW Members," ca. early 1975, folder 14, box 3, Lightfoot NOW Officer Papers.

208 *Major time and expense*: Eileen Kelly to Members of NOW National Board, May 23, 1975, folder 38, box 38, NOW Records.

208 *The Tulsa chapter proposed*: "Special Report: NOW and the Women's Movement," *Spokeswoman*, Dec. 15, 1975, 1.

208 *"divisive" power play*: Smeal to Board Members and Officers, Feb. 4, 1975, folder 35, box 38, NOW Records.

208 *DeCrow and twenty*: "Special Report: NOW and the Women's Movement," 1.

208 *The Chicago-aligned board majority*: "Notes Taken by Whitney Adams of the April 5–6, 1975, Meeting of the NOW Board of Directors, Kansas City," n.d., ca. April 1975, folder 2, box 4, Lightfoot NOW Officer Papers.

208 *"definitely awkward"*: Plitt, interview by author, 6.

208 *She ended up resigning*: Plitt to NOW Board Members, Aug. 26, 1975, folder 36, box 38, NOW Records.

208 *The issue of moving*: "Special Report: NOW and the Women's Movement," 3.

208 *"in good standing"*: Davelyn Jones to DeCrow and Smeal, re: Majority Caucus and the National NOW Convention, Aug. 1975, folder 15, box 51, DeCrow Papers.

208 *"I believe we have"*: Crater to Virginia NOW Chapter Presidents, State Coordinators, and Others, re: National Board Meeting, May 24–25, June 2, 1975, folder 14, box 3, Lightfoot NOW Officer Papers.

209 *Their opponents, by contrast*: "Special Report: NOW and the Women's Movement," 3.

209 *Caucus leaders studied*: Smeal to Lightfoot, March 6, 1975, folder 6, box 40, DeCrow Papers.

209 *"our own legal experts"*: "Western Majority Caucus Meeting 2," Aug. 16–17, 1975, 8, "Majority Caucus [?]" folder, box 89, Hernandez Papers.

209 *"alternative press room"*: Aileen Hernandez, "Summary of Discussion: Eastern Region Majority Caucus Meeting," May 18, 1975, "May 1975" folder, box 55, Hernandez Papers.

209 *"campaign aide"*: "Dear Majority Caucus Candidate," Oct. 13, 1975, folder 15, box 51, DeCrow Papers.

209 *Their slate comprised*: "Special Report: NOW and the Women's Movement," 4; Majority Caucus, "Out of the Mainstream, into the Revolution," 1975, 7, folder 5, box 24, NOW Records.

209 *"internal and external oppression"*: Majority Caucus, "Out of the Mainstream, into the Revolution," 2.

209 *"a more democratic NOW"*: "Majority Caucus: We're Doing It NOW," n.d., ca. Oct. 1975, 2, folder 18, box 36, Carabillo and Meuli Papers.

209 *In its sleek yellow*: Majority Caucus, "Out of the Mainstream, into the Revolution."

209 *"voter scorecard"*: "Vote Majority Caucus," n.d., ca. Oct. 1975, folder 5, box 24, NOW Records.

209 *The faction's leaders*: Beth Gillin Pombeiro, "NOW Reelects DeCrow," *Philadelphia Inquirer*, Oct. 27, 1975, 1.

210 *The main conference organizers*: Linda Nadle to DeCrow, Oct. 27, 1975, folder 36, box 38, NOW Records.

210 *"this is not a women's movement"*: Beth Gillin Pombeiro, "Snafus Delay Election at NOW's Convention," *Philadelphia Inquirer*, Oct. 26, 1975, 1.

210 *"gender role stereotypes"*: Enid Nemy, "NOW Leaders Form a Dissident 'Network,'" *New York Times*, Nov. 15, 1975, 1.

210 *"we fell into the trap"*: Pombeiro, "Snafus Delay Election at NOW's Convention."

210 *"the opportunity to work"*: Majority Caucus, "Out of the Mainstream, into the Revolution," 3.

210 *The Internal Revenue Service*: Marlene Cimons, "NOW, Permitted to Endorse Candidates, Bypasses Men," *Washington Post*, Sept. 8, 1975, A6.

210 *The board had issued*: Barakso, *Governing NOW*, 53.

210 *"This is an indication"*: Cimons, "NOW, Permitted to Endorse Candidates, Bypasses Men."

211 *In Philadelphia, Collins*: "Candidates for National Office," Sept. 24, 1975, folder 7, box 24, Collins NOW Officer Papers.

211 *"but I thought I had a vision"*: Collins, interview by author, 2019, 2.

211 *"We Need Each Other"*: Mary Jean Collins, "We Need Each Other," n.d., ca. 1975, folder 5, box 24, NOW Records.

211 *"well-organized and well-financed"*: "Mary Jean Collins-Robson, Candidate for NOW President," n.d., ca. 1975, folder 7, box 24, Collins NOW Officer Papers.

211 *"some 17,000 miles"*: Carol Kleiman, "N.O.W. Is the Goal of This Presidential Hopeful," *Chicago Tribune*, Sept. 6, 1975, N12.

211 *"Each night was a new chapter"*: Collins, interview by author, Feb. 22, 2019, 2.

211 *She carried eight shirts*: Kathleen Powell, "NOW Candidate Campaigns Here," *Fort Myers News-Press*, Aug. 23, 1975, folder 14, box 15, Collins NOW Officer Papers.

211 *"saddle sores"*: "Dear X," n.d., ca. 1975, folder 6, box 24, Collins NOW Officer Papers.

211 *"a lot of activity"*: Vera Glaser, "NOW Braces for Floor Fights in Convention Here Friday," *Philadelphia Inquirer*, Oct. 19, 1975, 7.

211 *"The full power"*: Kleiman, "NOW Is the Goal of This Presidential Hopeful."

211 *"that solidified our relationship"*: Collins, interview by author, 2019, 2.

211 *"I had always been attracted"*: Collins, interview by Connell, 42, folder 6, box 8.

212 *"vast numbers of women"*: Collins, interview by author, 2019, 1.

212 *NOW had sixty thousand members*: Rozhon, "Women Meet, and . . . Divide and Destroy"; "Special Report: NOW and the Women's Movement," 3; Judith Coburn, "Is NOW on the Brink of Becoming Then?," *Village Voice*, Nov. 17, 1975; Carol McCullough, "Philadelphia Revisited: A Report on the 1975 NOW National Conference," *Pennsylvania NOW*, December 1975, 2, folder 2, box 7, Philadelphia NOW Records.

212 *One was celebratory*: Coburn, "Is NOW on the Brink of Becoming Then?"

212 *"bright yellow tee shirts"*: McCullough, "Philadelphia Revisited," 2.

212 *"a quantum leap"*: Toni Carabillo, *Perspective for the NOW National Advisory Committee & Leadership*, vol. 1, no. 1 (1976): 1, folder 12, box 6, Evansgardner and Gardner Papers.

212 *"This is what factions"*: Pombeiro, "NOW: City of Sisterly Love?"

212 *"Saul Alinsky and the Poverty"*: 8th National NOW Conference Schedule, 1975, folder 1, box 154, Chicago NOW Collection.

212 *"Chicago Machine"*: Coburn, "Is NOW on the Brink of Becoming Then?"

212 *"the first internal political"*: Carabillo, *Perspective for the NOW National Advisory Committee & Leadership*, 1.

212 *Once again, the nominating*: "Conference Committee Reports Nominating Committee," *Do It NOW*, Sept.–Oct. 1975, 8.

213 *"frantic" calls*: Tracie Rozhon, "Moderates Defeated in Final NOW Vote," *Baltimore Sun*, Oct. 28, 1975, A6.

213 *There was a twenty-minute debate*: Beth Gillin Pombeiro, "NOW Takes a Turn Toward All Women," *Philadelphia Inquirer*, ca. Oct. 1975, folder 8, box 24, NOW Records.

213 *"yield to a person"*: "Minutes of the Eighth National Conference of the National Organization for Women," Oct. 23–27, 1975, 3, folder 7, box 24, NOW Records.

213 *Because Pennsylvania was*: "Special Report: NOW and the Women's Movement," 4.

213 *"They must have recruited"*: Conroy, interview by Balanoff, 61.

213 *"Don't worry, no one"*: Coburn, "Is NOW on the Brink of Becoming Then?"

213 *The leaders had intended*: Carabillo, *Perspective for the NOW National Advisory Committee & Leadership*, 2; "Martha Dickey," n.d., ca. June 1975, folder 6, box 24, NOW Records; "Minutes of the Eighth National Conference of the National Organization for Women," 1.

213 *Some voters received*: Pombeiro, "Snafus Delay Election at NOW's Convention."

213 *People whose national dues*: Judith Lonnquist to NOW Member, ca. Autumn 1975, folder 6, box 24, NOW Records.

214 *The voting took all night*: Rozhon, "Women Meet, and . . . Divide and Destroy."

214 *"fainting on the mezzanine"*: Rozhon, "Moderates Defeated in Final NOW Vote."

214 *DeCrow was ahead*: "Special Report: NOW and the Women's Movement," 4.

214 *DeCrow won the presidency*: "Minutes of the Eighth National Conference of the National Organization for Women," 3.

214 *"chief theoretician"*: David Behrens, "A Militant NOW Seen After Re-election Battle," *Newsday*, Oct. 27, 1975, 7.

214 *"working the floor"*: Beth Gillin Pombeiro, "NOW Presidency Is Karen DeCrow's by Narrow Margin," *Philadelphia Inquirer*, Oct. 27, 1975, 1.

214 *Many midwesterners had*: Rozhon, "Women Meet, and . . . Divide and Destroy."

214 *The Caucus secured sixteen*: "Special Report: NOW and the Women's Movement," 4.

214 *"I have not changed"*: Pombeiro, "NOW Presidency Is Karen DeCrow's by Narrow Margin."

214 *"nearly inevitable stages"*: Carabillo, *Perspective for the NOW National Advisory Committee & Leadership*, 1.

214 *"sweet little"*: Goldsmith, interview by author, Dec. 18, 2015, 12.

214 *"endless power playing"*: Georgie Anne Geyer, "Talking to One's Self About NOW," n.d., ca. Oct. 1975, clipping, folder 8, box 24, NOW Records.

214 *Two U.S. presidential candidates*: Coburn, "Is NOW on the Brink of Becoming Then?"

214 *"They're talking about running"*: Rozhon, "Women Meet, and . . . Divide and Destroy."

215 *"to show the nation"*: "NOW Calls for an All Woman National Strike Next Month," *Chicago Defender*, Sept. 17, 1975, 14.

215 *The title was a nod*: Mary Knoblauch, "N.O.W.'s Political Clout Turning Politicians into Instant Feminists," *Chicago Tribune*, Aug. 7, 1975, B2.

215 *Alice Doesn't Day*: Behrens, "What NOW for Women."

215 *"support American manhood"*: Judy Klemesrud, "Most of the Nation's 'Alices' Stay on Job, Ignoring NOW's Call for One-Day Strike," *New York Times*, Oct. 30, 1975, 44.

215 *"National Action Center"*: Mary Lynn Myers to NOW Chapter Presidents, State Coordinators, and Task Force Coordinators, re: Actions of the NOW National Board at the Dec. 6–7 Meeting in San Diego, Dec. 8, 1973, 3, Aileen Hernandez Folder, Bingham Center.

215 *"a redirection of NOW's"*: Smeal to NOW Employees, Dec. 22, 1975, folder 5, box 38, Chicago NOW Collection.

216 *"become as historical"*: Patricia Hill Burnett to Terrill Burnett, Jan. 18, 1976, "Correspondence January–June 1976" folder, box 1, Burnett Papers.

216 *"ruinously revolutionary drift"*: "Womenswar," *Time*, Dec. 1, 1975, 55.

216 *the former Black Panther*: John F. Burns, "Cleaver Seized on Return Here After 7-Year Exile," *New York Times*, Nov. 19, 1975, 20.

216 *"The movement has started"*: Nemy, "NOW Leaders Form a Dissident 'Network.'"

216 *"build . . . coalitions on"*: "Womenswar."

216 *"huge numbers of us"*: Nemy, "NOW Leaders Form a Dissident 'Network.'"

216 *"the last gasp"*: "Womenswar."

217 *already stretched thin*: Dorothy Howze to Steering Committee, Jan. 19, 1976, folder 6, box 4, Lightfoot NOW Officer Papers; "Womansurge Notes on Atlanta Meeting," n.d., ca. Jan. 11–12, 1976, folder 6, box 4, Lightfoot NOW Officer Papers.

217 *"go international"*: Johnston, "NOW Expands the List of What It's For and What It's Against."

217 *the organization put*: Transcript of NOW "Herstory" Session, 41.

217 *"was not important"*: Burnett, interview by Boyer, 118, 124, folder 1, box 8.

217 *"I remember her well"*: Lessenberry, "She's Painted Her Life with Bold Strokes," 6.

217 *The new leaders diluted*: Burnett to DeCrow and Nola Claire, Aug. 21, 1974, "Correspondence 1974, August–December" folder, box 1, Burnett Papers.

217 *"rich woman syndrome"*: "For Patricia Burnett," n.d., ca. late 1974, "National Organization for Women, 1974" folder, box 4, Burnett Papers.

217 *Burnett requested about*: NOW Budget Request Form for International Committee for the Period of Jan. 1, 1974, to Sept. 20, 1974, n.d., ca. late 1973, "NOW-International Com-

mittee [1974]" folder, box 3, Burnett Papers; NOW Budget Request Form for International Committee for the Period of Jan. 1, 1975, to Dec. 31, 1975, n.d., ca. late 1974, "NOW-International Committee [1975]" folder, box 3, Burnett Papers.

217 *"has been my life"*: Burnett to DeCrow, n.d., ca. mid-1974, "Correspondence 1974, August–December" folder, box 1, Burnett Papers.

217 *"ease out of this"*: Patricia Hill Burnett to Terrill Burnett, Nov. 15, 1974, "Correspondence 1974" folder, box 1, Burnett Papers.

217 *"instrumental" to NOW's receiving*: ". . . Pat Burnett Retires," *Detroit NOW Newsletter*, Jan. 1976, 4, NOW Chapter Newsletters Collection; Burnett to Curtis Roosevelt, Jan. 21, 1973, folder 14, box 22, Heide Papers; Olcott, *International Women's Year*, 117.

217 *DeCrow wanted Hernandez*: "For Patricia Burnett," n.d., ca. late 1974.

217 *Meanwhile, global feminism flourished*: "United Nations Calls on Member States to Make Significant Progress for Women During 1975—International Women's Year," 1, folder 4, box 22, Carabillo and Meuli Papers; Olcott, *International Women's Year*.

217 *"never got to"*: DeCrow to Burnett, May 6, 1975, "Correspondence 1975" folder, box 1, Burnett Papers.

218 *Those two and about a hundred*: Olcott, *International Women's Year*, 121.

218 *"world conference of feminists"*: Dorothy Austin, "Feminists Part in Peace," *Milwaukee Sentinel*, June 5, 1973, folder 2043, Friedan Papers.

218 *She stayed on*: ". . . Pat Burnett Retires."

218 *One of the group's*: 8th National Conference of NOW Meeting Minutes Appendix: Resolutions Passed by the Conference, 2, folder 7, box 24, NOW Records.

218 *DeCrow appointed Smeal*: Smeal to NOW State Coordinators, Constitutional Delegates and Alternates, "Call to the First Meeting of the National Constitutional Commission," Jan. 30, 1976, folder 10, box 24, NOW Records; "Constitutional Commission," *Do It NOW*, March 1976, 34; "NOW National Constitution Commission Begins Work," *Do It NOW*, Jan.–Feb. 1976, 9; "Eight Committee Reports on Issue Areas," n.d., ca. early 1976, folder 10, box 24, NOW Records.

218 *members debated*: "Pro Statement on National NOW Bylaws Change," n.d., ca. Oct. 1976, 2, folder 11, box 24, NOW Records.

218 *The original 1967 bylaws*: "NOW By-Laws Conference, October 9–11, 1976," *Do It NOW*, May 1976, 14; National Organization for Women By-Laws, adopted Feb. 23, 1967, folder 3, box 1, NOW Records.

218 *Amendments in 1970*: National Organization for Women By-Laws, 1970, folder 3, box 1, NOW Records.

218 *Members adopted another amendment*: National Organization for Women By-Laws, March 1974, folder 3, box 1, NOW Records.

218 *"streamlining and reorganizing"*: Smeal to Pennsylvania NOW Chapters, "Should You Go to Kansas in October?," n.d., ca. early 1976, folder 12, box 24, NOW Records.

218 *The new rules created*: NOW, "Streamlined NOW Enters Second Decade of Action," press release, Oct. 13, 1976, folder 15, box 24, NOW Records.

218 *These bylaws also replaced*: David Behrens, "NOW Opts for Compromise," *Newsday*, Oct. 13, 1976, 4A.

219 *New officers could serve*: Georgia Fuller to NOW Members in Virginia, re: Proposed Bylaws from the 1976 National NOW Conference, Oct. 9–11, Oct. 14, 1976, folder 11, box 24, NOW Records.

219 *"not like a 'once a month thing'"*: Smeal, interview by Davison, July 1997, 3.

219 *"We can not afford"*: "Pro Statement on National NOW Bylaws Change."

219 *Its organizations had changed*: For an overview, see Stansell, *Feminist Promise*, 307–8.

219 *"In the early days"*: Mary Bralove, "NOW and Then: The Feminists After 10 Years," *Wall Street Journal*, April 1, 1977, 12.

219 *"internal battles"*: DeCrow to Hernandez, March 28, 1971, DeCrow Papers.

220 *"It's ironic that I can't"*: Nick Thimmesch, "Who's Excommunicating NOW," *Newsday*, May 12, 1975, 38.

220 *"We are not a government"*: Kay Mills, "Feminists Broaden Outlook," *Atlanta Constitution*, Dec. 5, 1975, 15C.

220 *Collins, Ladky, and their allies*: Green, "Flawed Remedies," 58–59.

221 *"hated" the Sears campaign*: Collins, interview by author, 2018, 2.

221 *The agency continued investigating*: "'Secret' Sears Bias Charges Bared," *Chicago Sun-Times*, May 4, 1979, 77.

221 *The two sides settled*: Merrill Brown, "U.S. Settles Its Racial Bias Suits Against Sears," *Washington Post*, June 5, 1981, A1.

221 *Sears won in court*: On *EEOC v. Sears*, see, for example, Jacquelyn Dowd Hall and Sandi E. Cooper, "Women's History Goes to Trial: *EEOC v. Sears, Roebuck and Company*," *Signs* 11 (Summer 1986): 751–79; Parker, "'Sears Discriminated Against Me Because of My Sex and Race,'" esp. 29–31; and Joan Wallach Scott, *Gender and the Politics of History* (New York: Columbia University Press, 1999), 167–77.

221 *Even a modest settlement*: Green, "Flawed Remedies," 59–60.

221 *"both the issues"*: Thomas J. Hart to Smeal, re: Possible Intervention by NOW in *EEOC v. Sears, Roebuck and Co.*, Dec. 3, 1981, in Anne Ladky's possession.

221 *She and other new leaders*: Virginia Watkins to Sandy Roth, Jan. 23, 1978, folder 41, box 3, NOW Records.

7. PUT IT ON THE LINE NOW FOR EQUALITY

223 *"History is being made"*: Mary Thornton, "NOW Puts Aside Feuds to Push for ERA," *Boston Globe*, April 25, 1977, 2.

224 *"functional ambiguity"*: Cott, *Grounding of Modern Feminism*, 20.

224 *"the bottom line issue"*: "Major New Policies Included in Resolutions," *National NOW Times*, Nov. 1978, 12.

224 *By the end of the 1970s*: Leslie Bennetts, "Feminists Cool to NOW Stand Against Carter," *New York Times*, Dec. 21, 1979, B6.

225 *"I'm begging you"*: "Total ERA Mobilization Voted," *National NOW Times*, Nov. 1980, 5.

225 *"service to the state"*: NOW Information Memorandum, "Constitutional Protection Against Sex Discrimination," Nov. 1968, 10, folder 9, box 2, Witter Papers.

225 *The ERA soon topped*: "Report of Legislative Discussion," NOW National Conference, Dec. 7–8, 1968, folder 2, box 51, NOW Records.

225 *"We are going to"*: Hernandez to NOW Board Members, Chapter Presidents and Conveners, re: Immediate Action Items, Oct. 16, 1970, "NOW" folder, box 96, Hernandez Papers.

225 *Due largely to*: NOW Memo, "The Equal Rights Amendment and the Draft," Aug. 1971, folder 1, box 66, Bernice Resnick Sandler Papers, Schlesinger Library.

225 *Hernandez urged women*: Hernandez to NOW Members, n.d., ca. June 1971, folder 8, box 11, Betty Blaisdell Berry NOW Officer Papers, Schlesinger Library.

225 *"not only necessary"*: Murray to Senator Edward W. Brooke, Sept. 5, 1970, folder 67, Records of Boston NOW, Schlesinger Library.

225 *Murray returned to NOW*: Murray to Brooke, Sept. 5, 1970; Murray to Congressman David Nelson, Sept. 5, 1970, folder 67, Records of Boston NOW.

226 *"Equality of rights"*: ERA text reprinted in Julie C. Suk, *We the Women: The Unstoppable*

Mothers of the Equal Rights Amendment (New York: Skyhorse, 2020), 1. On the decades-long struggle to ratify the ERA, which began in the 1920s, see, for example, Cott, *Grounding of Modern Feminism*; Rebecca DeWolf, *Gendered Citizenship: The Original Conflict over the Equal Rights Amendment, 1920–1963* (Lincoln: University of Nebraska Press, 2021); and Suk, *We the Women*.

226 *Black feminists, including Murray*: Mayeri, *Reasoning from Race*, 194.

226 *Burnett welcomed the military*: "Q. Patricia Burnett, Will Women Be Drafted?," clipping, n.d., ca. late 1970s, "Clippings—Biographical + Artistic, 5 of 5" folder, box 1, Burnett Papers.

226 *She also highlighted*: Peggy Guthaus, "State NOW Founder Paints Picture of Discrimination Against Women," *Kalamazoo Gazette*, May 5, 1976, "Articles" folder, box 2, Burnett Papers; Burnett, untitled notebook entry, "NOW" Notebook, n.d., "Burnett Notebooks" folder, box 6, Burnett Papers.

226 *Assisted by feminist lawmakers*: Jean Witter, "Equal Rights Amendment Strategy," Sept. 13, 1968, folder 9, box 2, Witter Papers.

226 *"We literally stayed"*: Burnett to Detroit NOW, "NOW Was My Time," 5.

226 *"as if he were a puppy"*: Burnett to Detroit NOW, "NOW Was My Time," 5.

226 *"rocked with laughter"*: Isabelle Shelton, "Women Demand Equal Rights," *Baltimore Sun*, May 10, 1970, C3.

226 *The ERA passed*: "The Equal Rights Amendment: Achieving Constitutional Equality for All," *Hearing of the House Committee on Oversight and Reform*, Oct. 21, 2021, https://oversight.house.gov/legislation/hearings/the-equal-rights-amendment-achieving-constitutional-equality-for-all#:~:text=On%20October%2012%2C%201971%2C%20the,1970s%20fell%20three%20states%20short, accessed November 7, 2022.

227 *Hawaii's legislature ratified it*: Eileen Shanahan, "Equal Rights Amendment Is Approved by Congress," *New York Times*, March 23, 1972, 1; Steiner, *Constitutional Inequality*, 98.

227 *"Some-one has to say this"*: Patricia Hill Burnett, "Testimony for the Hearings on the Republican Platform," n.d., ca. 1972, 1, "Speeches, Articles, Interviews, 1973–1987 and Undated" folder, box 2, Burnett Papers.

227 *"workhorse" she felt qualified*: Burnett, *True Colors*, 147.

227 *"the right of the individual"*: Burnett, "Testimony for the Hearings on the Republican Platform," 1.

227 *"remarkably slow in recognizing"*: Burnett, "Testimony for the Hearings on the Republican Platform," 1, 2, 4.

227 *"staunch Republican feminist"*: Burnett, *True Colors*, 1.

227 *Chapters would research*: Ann London Scott and Elizabeth Cox to ERA State Coordinators, May 29, 1973, folder 474, box 51, Betty Friedan Additional Papers, Schlesinger Library.

228 *"weak in statehouse lobbying"*: "NOW ERA Timeline," n.d., 2, folder 62, box 54, NOW Records.

228 *But progress slowed*: Susanna McBee, "With 15 States Still to Go, Equal Rights Amendment Slows Down," *Washington Post*, Jan. 28, 1973, A2.

228 *The anti-Communist hawk*: Donald T. Critchlow, *Phyllis Schlafly and Grassroots Conservatism* (Princeton, N.J.: Princeton University Press, 2005), esp. 217–20.

228 *Too extreme even*: Carl Greenberg, "Mrs. Schlafly Pushes Demand for GOP Women's Vote Inquiry," *Los Angeles Times*, June 18, 1967, EB.

228 *Several months later*: Warren Weaver Jr., "Defeated Leader Sets Up a Rival Group for Republican Women," *New York Times*, Aug. 9, 1967, 21.

228 *Schlafly began to tap*: Critchlow, *Phyllis Schlafly and Grassroots Conservatism*, 220. Michelle Nickerson reveals that women were active participants in twentieth-century conservative

social movements, asserting rigid notions of what was "natural" to women's personalities and their bodies and insisting upon their special connection to children and their domestic roles. Michelle Nickerson, "Women, Gender, and Conservatism in Twentieth-Century America," in Hartigan-O'Connor and Materson, *Oxford Handbook of American Women's and Gender History*. On activism by conservative white women in the mid-twentieth century, see also Erin Kempker, *Big Sister: Feminism, Conservatism, and Conspiracy in the Heartland* (Urbana: University of Illinois Press, 2018), 15–63; McRae, *Mothers of Massive Resistance*; and Michelle Nickerson, *Mothers of Conservatism: Women and the Postwar Right* (Princeton, N.J.: Princeton University Press, 2014).

228 *In 1972, she founded*: Douglas Martin, "Phyllis Schlafly Dies at 92; Helped Steer the United States to the Right," *New York Times*, Sept. 6, 2016, A1; John Boland, "Phyllis Schlafly Leads Women Against ERA," *Twin Circle*, March 2, 1973, 10, folder 11, box 195, NOW Records.

228 *"spontaneous grassroots"*: Boland, "Phyllis Schlafly Leads Women Against ERA," 10.

229 *"housework of government"*: On this tension, see Rymph, *Republican Women*, quotation on p. 243.

229 *"The time is past"*: Critchlow, *Phyllis Schlafly and Grassroots Conservatism*, 139.

229 *That group was*: Tanya Melich, *The Republican War Against Women: An Insider's Report from Behind the Lines* (New York: Bantam, 1998), 45–46.

229 *Thousands crowded into organizations*: Self, *All in the Family*, 294; "Women Lobby Against 'Rights,'" *New York Times*, April 15, 1973, 82. Schlafly drew the parallel between NOW and HOW in a 1974 article on state and federal Status of Women Councils, which she criticized for their alleged feminist point of view and public funding: "Hence the acronym 'SOW,' which stands for Status of Women—just as 'NOW' stands for National Organization for Women, and 'HOW' stands for Happiness of Womanhood." Phyllis Schlafly, "Are You Financing Women's Lib and ERA?," *Human Events*, Feb. 23, 1974, 12.

229 *Schlafly fostered this assortment*: Marjorie J. Spruill, *Divided We Stand: The Battle over Women's Rights and Family Values That Polarized American Politics* (New York: Bloomsbury, 2017), 94.

229 *Its proponents addressed*: Heather Cox Richardson, *To Make Men Free: A History of the Republican Party* (New York: Basic Books, 2014), 273–74; Evans, *Tidal Wave*, 111–13.

229 *Joining these conservatives*: Donald T. Critchlow, *The Conservative Ascendency: How the GOP Right Made Political History* (Cambridge, Mass.: Harvard University Press, 2007), 134–35; Karissa Haugeberg, *Women Against Abortion: Inside the Largest Moral Reform Movement of the Twentieth Century* (Urbana: University of Illinois Press, 2017), esp. 2–4; Mary Ziegler, *After Roe: The Lost History of the Abortion Debate* (Cambridge, Mass.: Harvard University Press, 2015), 14–15. On the rise of grassroots antiabortion politics, see also Jennifer L. Holland, *Tiny You: A Western History of the Anti-abortion Movement* (Berkeley: University of California Press, 2020). The historian Daniel K. Williams argues that the antiabortion movement before *Roe v. Wade* stemmed from its members' interest in protecting life, not as a response to the women's movement. See Daniel K. Williams, *Defenders of the Unborn: The Pro-life Movement Before Roe v. Wade* (Oxford: Oxford University Press, 2016).

230 *"Forced busing, forced mixing"*: North Carolinian quoted in Stansell, *Feminist Promise*, 341. On southern white women's "grassroots resistance to racial equality" in the middle decades of the twentieth century, see McRae, *Mothers of Massive Resistance*, quotation on p. 4.

230 *Male conservatives began*: Melich, *Republican War Against Women*, 52.

230 *"Sure, my wife joined"*: "Feminism, Then and NOW," *New York Times*, May 3, 1977, 40.

230 *Conservatives thus packaged*: See Self, *All in the Family*.

230 *"real women"*: "They're Housewives and Proud of It," *New York Times*, April 3, 1972, 44.

230 *Historically, Republicans were friendlier*: Jo Freeman, "Whom You Know Versus Whom You Represent: Feminist Influence in the Democratic and Republican Parties," in *Women's Movements of the United States and Western Europe*, ed. Mary Fainsod Katzenstein and Carol McClurg Mueller (Philadelphia: Temple University Press, 1987), 216–18.

230 *NOW was officially nonpartisan*: "Keynote Address—Aileen C. Hernandez," NOW National Conference, Los Angeles, Sept. 3–6, 1972, 7, "NOW Minority Wm/Wm's Rights Task Force" folder, box 22, Hernandez Papers.

230 *The violent and disorderly*: "Democratic Reform," *Chicago Daily Defender*, April 5, 1969, 8.

230 *The commission issued*: "Democrats' Agony May Crest in Miami," *Atlanta Constitution*, May 4, 1972, 8C.

230 *It went into effect*: Evans, *Tidal Wave*, 72.

231 *He helped pull his party*: "Nixon, McGovern—Where They Stand," *Chicago Tribune*, Oct. 15, 1972, A1, A6; Critchlow, *Conservative Ascendency*, 98.

231 *Eventually, Nixon appointed*: Stansell, *Feminist Promise*, 280.

231 *"endeavor" to reach*: "Republican Feminists Prepare to Fight for Convention Delegates, Rights Amendment, and Abortion," *New York Times*, Feb. 19, 1976, 25.

231 *"insensitivity and misogyny"*: Heide to NOW Members, Dec. 15, 1972, folder 21, box 2, Evansgardner and Gardner Papers.

231 *Just over half of NOW members*: "Summary of Questionnaire for NOW," ca. 1974, folder 4, box 45, DeCrow Papers.

231 *"to operate from"*: Burnett, interview by Boyer, 176, folder 2, box 8.

231 *Burnett spent decades*: Patricia Hill Burnett, "To Registered Voters of District 14, Precinct 21," n.d., ca. 1976, "Correspondence, 1976, January–June" folder, box 1, Burnett Papers.

231 *she often urged*: John W. Dean III to Burnett, Oct. 9, 1971, "Correspondence, 1966–2002" folder, box 7, Burnett Papers.

231 *"give up on millions"*: Burnett to Detroit NOW, "NOW Was My Time," 10.

231 *"a matter of"*: Burnett, "Testimony for the Hearings on the Republican Platform," 2.

232 *The state had back-to-back*: Ann Marie Wambeke, "Republican Feminists and Feminist Republicans: The Search for the Sensible Center in Michigan, 1968 to 1984" (PhD diss., Wayne State University, 2017), 5, 19.

232 *Republican women flourished*: "Women on the Action Team," *Republican Women of Michigan Bulletin*, Sept. 1966, 4, Bentley Library.

232 *"Romney Republican"*: Michael Maharry, "Bouquets to New Senator Lorraine," *Republican Women of Michigan Bulletin*, Dec. 1966, 2, Bentley Library.

232 *Governor Romney opposed*: Dave Dempsey, *William G. Milliken: Michigan's Passionate Moderate* (Ann Arbor: University of Michigan Press, 2006), 223.

232 *Milliken appointed Burnett*: Burnett to Joyce Broithewaite, Feb. 5, 1973, "Correspondence 1973" folder, box 1, Burnett Papers.

232 *"a special place"*: Burnett to Milliken, Sept. 20, 1975, "Correspondence, 1975, July–September" folder, box 1, Burnett Papers.

232 *Just as NOW*: From abolition to suffrage to workers' rights, other progressive social movements have faced hard choices about strategy. Movement leaders have seen formal politics as necessary, but embracing it has often been conservatizing. On the tensions between working through and working outside political structures, see, for example, James Oakes, *The Radical and the Republican: Frederick Douglass, Abraham Lincoln, and the Triumph of Antislavery* (New York: W. W. Norton, 2008); and Jack Ross, *The Socialist Party of America: A Complete History* (Lincoln: University of Nebraska Press, 2015).

232 *"hidden in character"*: NOW Legislative Office, "NOW ERA Timeline," n.d., ca. 1975, 1, folder 62, box 54, NOW Records.

232 *"state of emergency"*: "NOW Declares State of Emergency on ERA; Extension Deemed Vital to Victory," *National NOW Times*, April 1978, 1.

232 *"chapters, states and regions"*: "Board's Emergency Resolutions," *National NOW Times*, April 1978, 2.

233 *The daughter of working-class*: Margaret Mason, "Ellie Smeal, the First Housewife President of NOW, Is a Complex and Powerful Personality, Driven Almost Singularly by the Feminist Cause," *Washington Post*, Nov. 17, 1977, C3.

233 *She left a doctoral program*: Ben A. Franklin, "A New President for NOW," *New York Times*, April 28, 1977, A18.

233 *Ellie discovered feminism*: Mason, "Ellie Smeal, the First Housewife President of NOW," C3.

233 *Smeal's local Pittsburgh-area*: "Sex-Telling Ads Banned," *New Pittsburgh Courier*, Aug. 1, 1970, 8; *Pittsburgh Press Co. v. Pittsburgh Commission on Human Relations*, 413 U.S. 276 (1973).

233 *"Jean's Amendment"*: Haney, *Feminist Legacy*, 65.

233 *"We were winning"*: Smeal and Bonk, interview by author, 8, 5.

233 *Smeal had called the ERA*: "Ellie's Campaign Speech," n.d., ca. 1977, 2, 3, folder 25, box 24, NOW Records.

233 *"it cannot be"*: Mason, "Ellie Smeal, the First Housewife President of NOW," C3.

233 *Smeal won NOW's presidency*: Reginald Stuart, "NOW Getting Organized to Fight for Amendment," *New York Times*, April 25, 1977, 57.

233 *"from the bottom up"*: NOW National Conference Transcript, April 23, 1977, 75, folder 27, box 24, NOW Records.

233 *Smeal recalled*: "NOW Plans to Work for ERA," clipping, n.d., ca. April 1977, folder 30, box 24, NOW Records.

233 *"We will all have"*: Smeal Acceptance Speech, n.d., ca. April 1977, folder 25, box 24, NOW Records.

234 *NOW had recently proposed*: "NOW Declares State of Emergency on ERA" 1; Janet K. Boles, "Building Support for the ERA: A Case of 'Too Much, Too Late,'" *PS* 15 (Autumn 1982), 574.

234 *Eventually, that initiative*: Mary Margaret Smith, "NOW in '78: A Retrospective," *National NOW Times*, Feb. 1979, 8; "The Boycott: Impact on States That Have Not Ratified the ERA," June 11, 1979, "NOW Boycott" folder, box 23, ERAmerica Records, Library of Congress, Washington, D.C.

234 *NOW would enter*: On Virginia NOW's work with coalitions to pursue the ERA in that state, see Megan Taylor Shockley, *Creating a Progressive Commonwealth: Women Activists, Feminism, and the Politics of Social Change in Virginia, 1970s–2000s* (Baton Rouge: Louisiana State University Press, 2018), 49–95.

234 *That conference also*: Stuart, "NOW Getting Organized to Fight for Amendment," 57. On some members' concerns about the creation of the NOW PAC, see Barakso, *Governing NOW*, 68.

234 *"It was clear"*: Smeal and Bonk, interview by author, 14.

234 *"How could you talk"*: Smeal, interview by Davison, July 1997, 2.

234 *National membership dropped*: Patricia Anstett, "11-Year-Old NOW Seeks Comeback," *Chicago Sun-Times*, April 21, 1977, 50.

234 *The monthly office*: Smeal and Bonk, interview by author, 14.

234 *Members hawked everything*: Gene Boyer, "Report of the Finance Vice-President to the NOW National Conference," May 1974, 14–15, folder 1, box 4, Evansgardner and Gardner Papers. On *Financing the Revolution*, NOW's "mail-order catalog of feminist products," see

also Joshua Clark Davis, *From Head Shops to Whole Foods: The Rise and Fall of Activist Entre-preneurs* (New York: Columbia University Press, 2017), 143–45, quotation on 143.

234 *"Blood Money for"*: McBee, "With 15 States Still to Go, Equal Rights Amendment Slows Down."

234 *"We usually had"*: Smeal and Bonk, interview by author, 14–15.

234 *Richard Viguerie*: Claire Bond Potter, *Political Junkies: From Talk Radio to Twitter, How Alternative Media Hooked Us on Politics and Broke Our Democracy* (New York: Basic Books, 2020), 66–69, 76.

234 *Starting with publicly available*: Potter, *Political Junkies*, 80; Critchlow, *Conservative Ascendency*, 130–31.

235 *"The shriller you are"*: Republican quoted in Kruse and Zelizer, *Fault Lines*, 96.

235 *In 1980 alone*: Ziegler, *After Roe*, 13.

235 *Craver believed the best*: Roger Craver, "The Direct Mailbox: Better Read Than Dead," *Campaigns and Elections* (Winter 1986): 64–65.

235 *"a phenomenal success"*: "Money Tight? It Ain't So Say Major Civil Rights Groups," *New York Amsterdam News*, Jan. 8, 1972, A4.

235 *Amnesty International expanded*: Kenneth Cmiel, "The Emergence of Human Rights Politics in the United States," *Journal of American History* 86, no. 3 (Dec. 1999): 1243.

235 *NOW's entire budget*: Freeman, *Politics of Women's Liberation*, 91; "NOW 1973 Budget," n.d., folder 34, box 2, Evansgardner and Gardner Papers.

235 *NOW's net income*: Boyer, "Report of the Finance Vice-President to the NOW National Conference," 1, 12.

235 *"went big into direct mail"*: Smeal and Bonk, interview by author, 14.

235 *"phenomenal" return rate*: Mary Lynn Myers, "Financial Development Report," *Do It NOW*, July–Aug. 1975, 9.

235 *That program also helped*: Toni Carabillo, "The First Year of NOW's Second Decade," *National NOW Times*, Feb. 1978, 7.

235 *The next year*: Smeal to Mary Jane Patterson, April 13, 1979, folder 33, box 194, NOW Records.

235 *"at-large members"*: Boyer, "Report of the Finance Vice-President to the NOW National Conference," 11.

236 *"a piece of the national pie"*: Collins, interview by Connell, 76, 77, folder 7, box 8.

236 *"was going to keep"*: Carabillo, interview by Fox, 124, folder 2, box 2.

236 *"enhanced us immensely"*: Patricia Ireland, interview by author, April 30, 2021, 3.

236 *"a gateway issue"*: Smeal and Bonk, interview by author, 10.

236 *For a century, American*: Theda Skocpol, *Diminished Democracy: From Membership to Management in American Civic Life* (Norman: University of Oklahoma Press, 2003), esp. 6, 161–63, 198–99.

236 *She had left the group's*: Collins, interview by author, May 2, 2022, 2.

236 *Living with her partner*: Collins, interview by author, 2019, 2; Charlotte Cooper and Karen Wellisch, "Collins for NOW Action Vice President," Sept. 13, 1982, folder 1, box 25, Collins NOW Officer Records.

237 *"an on-again, off-again"*: Collins, interview by Connell, 47, folder 6, box 8.

237 *"win many concrete changes"*: "Mary Jean Collins-Robson, Candidate for NOW President," n.d., ca. 1975.

237 *"needed to bring back"*: Collins, interview by Connell, 51, folder 6, box 8.

237 *"were the very places"*: Collins, interview by Connell, 60, folder 6, box 8.

237 *"In 1970, I was"*: Collins, interview by author, 2015, 16.

237 *Collins shared Smeal's assessment*: Collins, interview by Connell, 60, folder 6, box 8.

237 *She began helping*: "Michigan State NOW Action Alert," Oct. 29, 1978, "File-ERA-Correspondence (1975–1979)" folder, box 11, NOW Michigan Conference Records, 1969–96, Bentley Library; Carabillo, *Perspective for the NOW National Advisory Committee & Leadership*, 6.

237 *"got caught right away"*: Collins, interview by Connell, 23, folder 6, box 8.

237 *A key sponsor*: Critchlow, *Phyllis Schlafly and Grassroots Conservatism*, 237.

237 *And while the ERA*: Steiner, *Constitutional Inequality*, 99.

237 *ERA advocates introduced*: Critchlow, *Phyllis Schlafly and Grassroots Conservatism*, 235.

237 *ERA fight in Illinois*: Critchlow, *Phyllis Schlafly and Grassroots Conservatism*, 235.

238 *"The one thing"*: Lupa, interview by author, 15.

238 *"It was terrifying"*: Rand, interview by author, 6, 7.

238 *"She never got up"*: Doty, interview by author, 1.

238 *"turned to personal attacks"*: Critchlow, *Phyllis Schlafly and Grassroots Conservatism*, 226.

238 *"got up one at a time"*: Collins, interview by Connell, 61, folder 6, box 8.

238 *"femininity tactics"*: Judy Klemesrud, "Opponent of E.R.A. Confident of Its Defeat," *New York Times*, Dec. 15, 1975, 53; Critchlow, *Phyllis Schlafly and Grassroots Conservatism*, 224.

238 *Burnett noted with alarm*: Burnett to Elly M. Peterson, n.d., ca. Nov. 1977, "Correspondence, 1977, July–December" folder, box 1, Burnett Papers; Burnett to Midge Costanza, June 12, 1978, "Correspondence, 1976–1978" folder, box 7, Burnett Papers.

239 *"do nothing for women"*: Barbour quoted in Wambeke, "Republican Feminists and Feminist Republicans," 127.

239 *"only representing the feminist"*: Cheryl Pilate, "Women's Rights Meet Your Watchdogs," *Detroit Free Press*, May 27, 1976, 1-C.

239 *The moderate Republican governor*: Burnett to Shari Cohen, n.d., ca. Nov. 15, 1976, "Correspondence, 1976, July–December" folder, box 1, Burnett Papers.

239 *"a convenient clubhouse"*: Hugh McDiarmid, "Democrats Have One Act Together," *Detroit Free Press*, ca. 1977, "Correspondence, 1977, July–December" folder, box 1, Burnett Papers.

239 *"a single issue"*: Burnett to Barbara Timmer, Oct. 14, 1977, "Correspondence, 1977, July–December" folder, box 1, Burnett Papers.

239 *"organization within the Republican Party"*: Burnett, "To Registered Voters of District 14, Precinct 21," n.d., ca. 1976, "Correspondence, 1976, January–June" folder, box 1, Burnett Papers.

239 *In 1974, after the Watergate*: Critchlow, *Conservative Ascendency*, 103.

239 *Although feminists in the party*: Rymph, *Republican Women*, 1.

239 *The presidential candidates*: "Republican Feminists Prepare to Fight for Convention Delegates, Rights Amendment, and Abortion."

239 *That year, feminist members*: Rymph, *Republican Women*, 224.

239 *Burnett wrote to the RNC*: Burnett to Crisp, Dec. 9, 1977, "Correspondence" folder, box 8, Burnett Papers.

239 *"let one issue"*: Crisp to Burnett, Feb. 16, 1978, "Correspondence, January–June 1978" folder, box 1, Burnett Papers.

240 *"It's awful being"*: Burnett to Pat Goldman, June 23, 1976, "Correspondence, 1976, January–June" folder, box 1, Burnett Papers.

240 *The conference, scheduled for Houston*: On the National Women's Conference, see Spruill, *Divided We Stand*, esp. 1–2.

240 *"a unified group"*: "'Focus: Michigan Women' Conference Elects Unity Caucus Delegates," folder 14, box 1, Loretta Moore Papers, Reuther Library. See also Wambeke, "Republican Feminists and Feminist Republicans," 225–28.

240 *Three hundred of*: Spruill, *Divided We Stand*, 156–57.

240 *"It was all outrageous"*: Donnelly quoted in Spruill, *Divided We Stand*, 157.

240 *The Michigan delegates joined*: Spruill, *Divided We Stand*, 3.

240 *Three First Ladies*: Spruill, *Divided We Stand*, 4–5. Billie Jean King had run in the "Torch of Freedom" from Seneca Falls, New York, to Houston. Angelou, Stapleton, and Coretta Scott King were members of the presidentially appointed IWY Commission, which had planned the conference.

240 *Smeal headed NOW's delegation*: Mason, "Ellie Smeal, the First Housewife President of NOW"; Smeal to "NOW Delegate to the IWY Conference," Nov. 10, 1977, "International Women's Year Houston Conference, 1977" folder, box 2, Burnett Papers.

240 *"shining star"*: Patricia Hill Burnett, "Notes from the Chairwoman," *Michigan Women*, April 1978, 2, "Michigan Women's Commission, 1976–1979" folder, box 3, Burnett Papers.

240 *"beautiful" sign that read*: Collins interview, Documenting the Midwestern Origins of the Twentieth-Century Women's Movement, 1987–92, tape 128, side B.

240 *Collins had chaired*: Cooper and Wellisch, "Collins for NOW Action Vice President."

241 *"have done better"*: Spruill, *Divided We Stand*, 156.

241 *Over several days*: MacLean, *American Women's Movement, 1945–2000*, 1; Spruill, *Divided We Stand*, 3.

241 *"tempered in the fires"*: Saunier, interview by Davison, July 28, 2003, 3–4.

241 *"Pro-life, Pro-family Rally"*: Spruill, *Divided We Stand*, 11–12; Kruse and Zelizer, *Fault Lines*, 92.

241 *One was Illinois*: "Fact Sheet: ERA Ratification Campaign in Illinois, 1980," folder 36, box 194, NOW Records; Kem Kemmerer, "From the President," *Act NOW* (Chicago), April 1978, back page, NOW Chapter Newsletters Collection.

241 *The state legislative season*: "ERA Update," *Act NOW* (Chicago), July 1979, 1, NOW Chapter Newsletters Collection.

242 *"We ran phone banks"*: Collins, interview by Marie Scatena, June 14, 2019, University of Illinois at Chicago, in Collins's possession.

242 *"in bulk"*: Illinois NOW to "Sisters and Brothers," April 29, 1977, folder 405, Boston NOW Records, Schlesinger Library.

242 *"freedom trains"*: "Support the ERA: Ride the ERA Freedom Train to Illinois," May 14–17, 1976, folder 20, box 3, NOW Records.

242 *"more resources than ever"*: Mary Jean Collins, "From the President," *Act NOW* (Chicago), Aug. 1979, back page, NOW Chapter Newsletters Collection.

242 *The chapter raised*: Chicago ERA Ratification Project Fund Raising Campaigns, n.d., ca. 1979, folder 34, box 194, NOW Records.

242 *"a sizeable budget"*: "Smeal Draft Letter," n.d., ca. Sept. 1979, folder 34, box 194, NOW Records.

242 *"full-time nerve centers"*: Smeal to NOW Member, March 1980, folder 421, Boston NOW Records.

242 *While the amendment*: "Fact Sheet: ERA Ratification Campaign in Illinois," 1980, folder 36, box 194, NOW Records; "Thousands to Come to Chicago for National ERA March May 10," *National NOW Times*, April 1980, 1.

242 *"Illinois is the crucial state"*: Mary Jean Collins, "From the President," *Act NOW* (Chicago), April 1980, 1, NOW Chapter Newsletters Collection.

242 *That year, more than*: Sandy Roth, "Over 90,000 March in Chicago," *National NOW Times*, June 1980, 1, 3.

242 *In 1976, NOW joined*: Lawrence Van Gelder, "After the Early Rush, the E.R.A. Is Now

at a Standstill," *New York Times*, April 1, 1977, 34; Karen DeCrow to Liz Carpenter, April 23, 1976, "NOW" folder, box 117, ERAmerica Records; Eleanor Smeal to Elizabeth A. Johnson, March 16, 1978, "NOW" folder, box 117, ERAmerica Records.

242 *"had no money"*: Smeal, interview by Rebecca Davison, Aug. 10, 1997, 4.

243 *NOW's 1978 declaration*: NOW National Board Meeting Minutes, Feb. 25–26, 1978, 14, 15, folder 36, box 3, NOW Records.

243 *"To dilute and diffuse"*: Judy Goldsmith, "Dear Activists," Feb. 23, 1979, folder 33, box 194, NOW Records.

243 *Not every chapter*: Gilmore, *Groundswell*, esp. 15.

243 *A typical letter from Smeal*: Eleanor Smeal, "Dear Friend," n.d., ca. 1978, "NOW" folder, box 227, ERAmerica Records.

243 *These appeals brought*: Smeal to Patterson, April 13, 1979.

243 *The leaders raised annual dues*: "Dues Increase," *Act NOW* (Chicago), Dec. 1978, back page, NOW Chapter Newsletters Collection; Fox to Onassis, May 8, 1979, folder 33, box 194, NOW Records; Naomi Ross to Carter, May 14, 1979, folder 33, box 194, NOW Records.

243 *They also organized*: "Stepping Out for Equality," *National NOW Times*, Nov. 1979, 1; "Walk-a-Thons Raise Funds for ERA Campaign," *National NOW Times*, Oct. 1978, 1.

243 *"flooded the halls"*: Smeal to Patterson, April 13, 1979.

243 *Across the country*: ERA Emergency Extension National Field Organizing Manual, 1978, folder 44, box 138, NOW Records.

243 *"If every NOW member"*: Sandy Jenkins, "How You Can Help Ratify the ERA," *Washington Equal Times* 1, no. 2 (April 1978): 11, NOW Washington, D.C., Chapter and Capitol Hill Chapter Records.

243 *Some hosted parties*: "Action Alert Inventory," *National NOW Times*, Aug. 1978, 9.

244 *"get people in the streets"*: Smeal and Bonk, interview by author, 9.

244 *One hundred thousand supporters*: "100,000 March for ERA," *National NOW Times*, Aug. 1978, 1.

244 *"anybody could visualize"*: Smeal and Bonk, interview by author, 10.

244 *There were thirty-five speakers*: "100,000 March for ERA," 1.

244 *"not only NOW's preeminent"*: "On Power—in White Cotton," *National NOW Times*, Aug. 1978, 7.

244 *As NOW drummed up*: Sandy Roth, "111 Groups Declare 'No Time Limit on Equality,'" *National NOW Times*, June 1978, 1; Bennetts, "Feminists Cool to NOW Stand Against Carter."

244 *The three-year extension*: Sandra Reeves Roth, "We Did It! Senate Votes Extension 60–36," *National NOW Times*, Nov. 1978, 1.

244 *The extension also gave*: Steiner, *Constitutional Inequality*, 76–77.

244 *"create a campaign"*: Mary Margaret Smith, "ERA to Be Nationwide Effort: Leadership Conference Calls for Cohesive Campaign," *National NOW Times*, May 1979, 1.

244 *"We pledge to be everywhere"*: Smeal to Patterson, April 13, 1979.

244 *NOW's leaders introduced*: Smeal to NOW Activist, n.d., ca. 1979, folder 22, box 139, NOW Records; Smeal, handwritten notes, n.d., ca. 1979, folder 22, box 139, NOW Records.

244 *She remained active*: Golden Gate NOW Newsletter, Jan. 1976, 2, NOW Chapter Newsletters Collection; Golden Gate NOW Newsletter, May 1976, back page, NOW Chapter Newsletters Collection; Gilmore, *Groundswell*, 121.

245 *The Golden Gate members*: Gilmore, *Groundswell*, 118–21; Levenstein, "'Don't Agonize, Organize!,'" 1131. On Black feminism in the mid- to late 1970s, see, for example, Gross and Berry, *Black Women's History of the United States*, 197–205; Springer, *Living for the Revolution*; and Taylor, introduction to *How We Get Free*.

245 *"the ERA was symbolic"*: Hernandez, interview by Davison, Nov. 1995, 4.

245 *"afford the luxury"*: Hernandez, "Dear Friends," n.d., folder 903, box 51, Murray Papers.

245 *"The passing of the ERA"*: Draft Copy of Interview with Hernandez on the ERA, n.d., ca. April 1975, 9, "April 1975" folder, box 55, Hernandez Papers.

245 *One of these other things*: Ann Allen Shockley, "The New Black Feminists," *Northwest Journal of Africa and Black America Studies* 2 (Winter 1974): 1, 3, "Bay Area Black Women United" folder, box 8, Hernandez Papers.

245 *"We will deserve"*: Aileen Hernandez, "Notes from . . . the First Decade, Aileen Hernandez, President, March 1970 to September 1971," n.d., ca. 1977, "Aileen" folder, box 19, Hernandez Papers.

245 *Her approach echoed*: On Baker and her "radical democratic, humanistic worldview, her confidence in the wisdom of the black poor, and her emphasis on the importance of group-centered, grassroots leadership," see Ransby, *Ella Baker and the Black Freedom Movement*, quotation on p. 6.

245 *"My theory is"*: C. Gerald Fraser, "Ella Baker, Organizer for Groups in Civil-Rights Movement in South," *New York Times*, Dec. 17, 1986, B18.

245 *Hernandez pointed out*: Carabillo, interview by Fox, 123, folder 2, box 2.

246 *"combating racism, sexism"*: Del Dobbins, "Minority Women at the National Conference," *Do It NOW*, Jan./Feb. 1976, 16.

246 *Sharon Parker, a member*: NOW National Board Meeting Minutes, July 30–31, 1977, 8–9, folder 28, box 3, NOW Records.

246 *"there was a history"*: Parker, interview by Davison, June 1997, 4–5.

246 *The leaders of her committee*: NOW, press release, Oct. 2, 1977, folder 18, box 48, NOW Records; Dee Coleman, Recorder, Minority Women's Committee Meeting Notes, Jan. 14, 1978, 3, 6, folder 18, box 48, NOW Records.

246 *"reproductive freedom"*: Summary of Minority Women's Committee Meeting, Jan. 13–15, 1978, 2, folder 18, box 48, NOW Records.

246 *Members of the Minority*: Coleman, Minority Women's Committee Meeting Notes, Jan. 14, 1978, 2; Jackie Washington to "Brenda" and "Valerie," Feb. 16, 1978, folder 38, box 3, NOW Records.

246 *"suffer greater discrimination"*: NOW brochure, "Minority Women and the Equal Rights Amendment," 1977, folder 29, box 209, NOW Records.

246 *"minority women's visibility"*: Coleman, Minority Women's Committee Meeting Notes, Jan. 14, 1978, 7.

247 *"racism and sexism"*: Sharon Parker, "Minority Women's Leadership Conference," *National NOW Times*, Nov. 1979, 13.

247 *Hernandez assessed the diversity*: Aileen Hernandez, "Statement at NOW Minority Women's Leadership Conference," Aug. 25, 1979, 1, 8, 16, folder 18, box 48, NOW Records.

247 *"corporate tone"*: Pamela G. Hollie, "Mood at NOW Conference Is Businesslike as E.R.A. Is Pushed: Issues Before Convention," *New York Times*, Oct. 8, 1979, B11.

247 *read "59 Cents"*: Claire Spiegel, "NOW Seeks Candidate to Support ERA: Other Goals," *Los Angeles Times*, Oct. 9, 1979, C5.

247 *"Essentially, the bottom line"*: Beverly Beyette, "Women's Movement Under Attack: NOW President Sees Era of Truth," *Los Angeles Times*, March 5, 1981, F1.

247 *While the provision*: Caley Horan, *Insurance Era: Risk, Governance, and the Privatization of Security in Postwar America* (Chicago: University of Chicago Press, 2021), 179–81; Suk, *We the Women*, 178; Crenshaw, "Demarginalizing the Intersection of Race and Sex."

247 *"Black women earn"*: Beverly Stephen, "Options: Countdown on Campus for ERA," *Los Angeles Times*, Dec. 10, 1981, I7.

248 *Slate members emphasized*: "For NOW, Sandra Reeves Roth for National Secretary," n.d.,

ca. 1979, folder 3, box 25, NOW Records; "Judy Goldsmith for Vice President-Executive," n.d., ca. 1979, folder 3, box 25, NOW Records; "Organizing for Feminism: NOW Enters the '80s," n.d., ca. Oct. 1979, folder 4, box 25, Collins NOW Officer Records.

248 *"mobilize a broad"*: "Organizing for Feminism: NOW Enters the '80s."

248 *Meanwhile, the only candidate*: Sharon Parker, "Dear National Committee Member," June 20, 1979, folder 18, box 6, Evansgardner and Gardner Papers; "Vote Sharon Parker for Secretary Now," n.d., ca. 1979, folder 3, box 25, NOW Records; Nancy Day, "More Minorities Urged for NOW, Meeting in LA," *San Francisco Examiner*, Oct. 8, 1979, 8, "NOW" folder, box 22, Hernandez Papers.

248 *Her Washington, D.C., chapter*: "Resolution for the Mid-Atlantic Regional Conference, 1978," *Washington Equal Times*, April 1978, 15, folder 1, box 4, NOW Washington, D.C., Chapter and Capitol Hill Chapter Records; Grace Crunican, "Priorities," *Washington Equal Times*, Dec. 1980, 4, folder 1, box 4, NOW Washington, D.C., Chapter and Capitol Hill Chapter Records. On the sliver of ERA strategy opponents in NOW, see Barakso, *Governing NOW*, 64. On the rich grassroots feminism and movement "cross-fertilization" in Washington in the 1970s, see Valk, *Radical Sisters*, esp. 5.

248 *"we were so happy"*: Joanne Omang, "NOW Launching Political Push on Issues," *Washington Post*, Oct. 9, 1979, A12.

248 *"if you really want"*: Parker, interview by Davison, June 1997, 1–5.

248 *The slate's victory*: "National Officers Elected at 12th Conference: Team with Comprehensive Platform Takes All Five Seats," *National NOW Times*, Nov. 1979, 3.

248 *"Members of NOW"*: John L. Mitchell, "Young Urges Black, Jewish Discussions: Says Groups Must Work to Ease Tensions," *Los Angeles Times*, Oct. 15, 1979, B21.

248 *"furious" that Smeal*: Hernandez, interview by Davison, Nov. 1995, 5.

249 *"almost any issue"*: Paula Giddings, *When and Where I Enter: The Impact of Black Women on Race and Sex in America* (New York: Morrow, 1984), 344.

249 *"to indoctrinate" them*: Hernandez to "Friends," n.d., ca. Oct. 1979, folder 1, box 214, NOW Records.

249 *"to be going backwards"*: "Ex-president of NOW Calls Group 'Racist,'" *San Diego Union*, Oct. 28, 1979, folder 44, box 33, NOW Records.

249 *"turn in their"*: Mitchell, "Young Urges Black, Jewish Discussions," B21. Nancy Cott notes a similar dynamic in the National Woman's Party in the 1920s, whose "single-issue politics" and "top-down control" excluded Black women and their distinct concerns—in particular, their functional exclusion from the Nineteenth Amendment's protections in large swaths of the country. Cott, *Grounding of Modern Feminism*, 68–69.

249 *She blamed biased coverage*: Smeal and Bonk, interview by author, 11.

249 *"We have been addressing"*: "Ex-president of NOW Calls Group 'Racist.'"

249 *"All of this"*: Murray to Smeal, Feb. 13, 1980, folder 903, Murray Papers.

249 *"The racism was evident"*: Lyon and Martin interview, part 3, 80, folder 7, box 9.

249 *"a million dollar corporation"*: Lyon and Martin interview, part 4, 9, folder 7, box 9.

249 *Martin and her partner*: "NOW Leader Calls Bias Dehumanizing," *Baltimore Sun*, May 26, 1974, A8.

249 *Like the Minority*: "Proposal for Lesbian Rights Implementation Committee," n.d., ca. 1977, folder 13, box 47, NOW Records.

250 *And like the women*: Beth Leopold to Kay Whitlock, June 21, 1977, folder 13, box 47, NOW Records.

250 *"a destructive, anti-family organization"*: Klemesrud, "Opponent of E.R.A. Confident of Its Defeat," 53.

250 *Antifeminists cultivated conservative*: Ziegler, *After Roe*, 179–81; Kruse and Zelizer, *Fault Lines*, 88–89.

250 *The traditional breadwinner-homemaker*: Lefkovitz, *Strange Bedfellows*, esp. 75; Kruse and Zelizer, *Fault Lines*, 66.

250 *Antifeminists thus stoked*: Self, *All in the Family*, 3, 310–11; Lefkovitz, *Strange Bedfellows*, 76; Taranto, *Kitchen Table Politics*, esp. 6.

250 *"right to life"*: Nick Thimmesch, "Right-to-Life Group Claims Gains in Members and Money," *Chicago Tribune*, June 24, 1977, B2; Morton Mintz, "Medicaid Can Be Denied: Court Approves Hill Curb on Funding for Abortions," *Washington Post*, June 30, 1977, 1.

250 *"Dismayed bystanders who had"*: Mary McGrory, "Abortion: The Issue in 1980?," *Boston Globe*, Feb. 3, 1979, 19.

250 *NOW's leaders grew frustrated*: Swinth, *Feminism's Forgotten Fight*, 100–102; Levenstein, "'Don't Agonize, Organize!,'" 1131; Ziegler, *After Roe*, 135. Feminists pursuing ratification in conservative states like Indiana adopted a "low-key" strategy that "sought to present a single feminist identity that eschewed radicalism" in order to "appeal to Republican lawmakers," according to Erin Kempker. Kempker, *Big Sister*, 90–111, quotation on p. 90. On how Indiana NOW chapters pursued the ERA in coalition with "women's organizations" and "explicitly feminist groups," see Blair, *Revolutionizing Expectations*, 62–95, quotations on p. 65.

250 *Homemakers, who constituted*: "With Consciousness Raised, NOW Focusing on Economy and Politics," *Baltimore Sun*, Oct. 29, 1974, B6.

250 *"active adult[s]"*: Leonard Yourist and Betty Blair, "Feminists Pick Homemaker to Be Their New Leader," clipping, ca. April 1977, folder 31, box 24, NOW Records.

250 *"the embodiment of traditional"*: Esther Kaw and Nicki Burton to NOW Board of Directors, April 3, 1976, folder 20, box 3, NOW Records.

250 *The provision would strengthen*: "The E.R.A. and the Homemaker," Jan. 30, 1978, 4, folder 5, box 3, NOW Washington, D.C., Chapter and Capitol Hill Chapter Records.

251 *"easy access"*: "Programs for NOW: Task Force Summaries," Nov. 1973, folder 44, box 209, NOW Records.

251 *Three years later*: In the wake of *Roe v. Wade*, the U.S. Congress and a handful of state legislatures passed laws restricting public funding for abortion. In challenging these laws, some feminist attorneys believed that their best strategy was to assert that they violated protections including the Fourteenth Amendment's equal protection clause. But with state lawmakers increasingly asking about the ERA's practical effects (and the equal protection clause generally understood to offer weaker protections than the ERA would grant), some feminists feared repelling potential allies by directly linking the equal protection clause, and thus the ERA, to abortion. Smeal persuaded the attorneys waging the federal abortion funding case not to advance the equal protection argument. Jane J. Mansbridge, *Why We Lost the ERA* (Chicago: University of Chicago Press, 1986), 124–25.

251 *"reproductive rights"*: Dave Goldberg, "Clout in the '80s: Women in Politics: NOW's the Time," *Los Angeles Times*, Dec. 9, 1979, G35; Ziegler, *After Roe*, 137–38.

251 *Smeal reached out*: Brett Harvey, "Give 'Em Ellie: Is There NOW After ERA?," *Voice*, Feb. 11, 1986, 2, folder 6, box 23, Loretta Ross Papers, Sophia Smith Collection.

251 *"summit meeting on abortion"*: McGrory, "Abortion: The Issue in 1980?"

251 *"put a whole damper"*: Love, interview by Abbott, 38, folder 12, box 5.

251 *The leaders of NOW's*: Jean M. Krauskopf to ERA Coordinator, NOW Legislative Office, Nov. 4, 1974, folder 40, box 192, NOW Records; Constance Scott, "Sold Out? Turning the ERA Defeat into Victory," *Womanews*, Dec.–Jan. 1982–83, 1, folder 37, box 194, NOW Records.

251 *"mobilize their constituencies"*: Minutes from Lesbian Rights Committee Meeting, July 10, 1978, 1, folder 14, box 47, NOW Records.

251 *"dyke-y" in ERA actions*: Harvey, "Give 'Em Ellie," 2.

252 *"form of lesbian identification"*: Kay Whitlock to Lois Reckitt, June 2, 1976, folder 13, box 47, NOW Records.

252 *Some in the organization*: For example, the Allentown, Pennsylvania, NOW chapter worked with local gay rights organizers to push forward an antidiscrimination ordinance that protected gay rights. Bob Wittman Jr., "Gay Rights Movement Was Born 10 Years Ago," *Allentown (Pa.) Morning Call*, June 25, 1979, A8; and Arlie Scott, NOW vice president for action, addressed the 1979 National March on Washington for Lesbian and Gay Rights. "The 1979 National March on Washington for Gay and Lesbian Rights," Houston LGBT History, accessed Feb. 19, 2022, www.houstonlgbthistory.org/march1979LP.html.

252 *"lesbian-baiting"*: Kay Whitlock and Nancy Boyd, "Introduction to Proposed 1976 Program of Action, NOW National Task Force on Sexuality and Lesbianism," 5, folder 13, box 47, NOW Records.

252 *"unconscionable"*: Russell to Smeal, Nov. 2, 1982, folder 14, box 47, NOW Records.

252 *"'crisis' attention"*: Minutes from Lesbian Rights Committee Meeting, July 10, 1978, 1. In 1977, the Florida singer and evangelical Christian Anita Bryant had led a successful campaign to overturn a Dade County antidiscrimination law that protected lesbians and gay men. Bryant established Save Our Children, the first national organization against gays and lesbians. The following year, California state lawmakers proposed a ballot initiative that would have permitted local school boards to prohibit gay teachers, and the right-wing ideologue Dan White assassinated the San Francisco supervisor and gay rights activist Harvey Milk. The first fundraising appeals for Moral Majority, founded in 1979 to support Christian right political candidates, asserted a "Declaration of War" against homosexuality. See "History of the Anti-gay Movement Since 1977," *Intelligence Report of the Southern Poverty Law Center*, April 28, 2005, www.splcenter.org/fighting-hate/intelligence-report/2005/history-anti-gay-movement-1977.

252 *"We feel the impact"*: Sidney Abbott et al., "An Open Letter of Concern About Lesbian/Gay Rights to the National NOW Convention," Oct. 10, 1981, folder 55, box 2, Charlotte Bunch Papers, 1967–85, Schlesinger Library. See also Lisa M. Keen, "Lesbians Hold Ground at NOW Conference," *Washington Blade*, Oct. 23, 1981, A5, folder 55, box 2, Bunch Papers.

252 *"The ERA does not give"*: Brad Lemley, "Eleanor Smeal in Overdrive: Getting the Women of America Back into the Streets," *Washington Post*, Nov. 24, 1985, SM34.

252 *NOW's official endorsements*: Critchlow, *Conservative Ascendency*, 141.

252 *But within a few years*: Maryann Barakso cites the range of board resolutions passed during the ERA emergency to argue that NOW remained committed to "principles such as grassroots activism and participation and to a multi-issue, multitactical strategy." Barakso, *Governing NOW*, 70, 83–85. But while NOW's leadership declared their commitments to a range of goals and offered members different ways to contribute to the ERA fight, they undeniably focused the organization and its resources on pursuing the amendment.

252 *"I'll never ask"*: "Total ERA Mobilization Voted," *National NOW Times*, Oct.–Nov. 1980, 5.

253 *Not only did ERA advocates*: Eleanor Smeal, "Opposition's ERA Rescission Campaign Defeated," *National NOW Times*, Aug. 1979, 1, 4.

253 *"rescindograms" to the lawmakers*: Wambeke, "Republican Feminists and Feminist Republicans," 139–40.

253 *"ERA-grams" NOW members*: "ERA-Grams a Success," n.d., ca. 1977, folder 6, box 13, National Organization for Women, New York City Chapter Records.

253 *The national leaders diverted*: Judy Goldsmith, "Rescission Defeated in Five States," *National NOW Times*, April 1979, 1.

253 *NOW ultimately won*: Leonard Orland, "NOW Suit: A Constitutional Threat?," *New York Times*, March 26, 1978, F14; Sandy Roth, "NOW Wins Boycott Suit," *National NOW Times*, April 1979, 1, 5.

253 *"These efforts are not"*: "Women's Rights Attack Tied to Klan, Birchers," *Newsday*, Feb. 18, 1973, 6.

253 *Polls taken in the late 1970s*: Toni Carabillo, "The More Things Change . . . ," *National NOW Times*, Jan. 1978, 6.

253 *"Phyllis Schlafly is a little doll"*: Mary Jean Collins, "From the President," *Act NOW* (Chicago), July 1980, 2, NOW Chapter Newsletters Collection.

254 *"We don't need much money"*: Klemesrud, "Opponent of E.R.A. Confident of Its Defeat." Schlafly was secretive about STOP ERA's finances. Her sources of funding included subscribers and small contributions. She sold buttons, bumper stickers, and literature, and her husband, Fred, pitched in. Feminists insisted that her movement was being secretly funded and controlled by right-wing forces, but feminists, scholars, and reporters could not confirm it. Spruill, *Divided We Stand*, 106.

254 *But ERA advocates noticed*: Ann K. Justice, "The Insurance Connection with Stop ERA Forces," Sept. 1974, 5, folder 65, box 2, Ann London Scott Papers, Schlesinger Library; Twiss Butler, "Who Profits from Sex Discrimination?," *National NOW Times*, June–July 1982, 6; "Was the ERA Sacrificed for the Insurance Numbers Game?," *National NOW Times*, Aug. 1982, 6. See also Horan, *Insurance Era*, 167–89, esp. 180–81.

254 *"well established systems"*: "ERA/Insurance Connect," n.d., ca. 1983, folder 5, box 20, Collins NOW Officer Papers.

254 *"another 'Watergate'"*: Justice, "Insurance Connection with Stop ERA Forces," 1.

254 *The conference voted*: "Officer and Board Terms Extended One Year," *National NOW Times*, Oct.–Nov. 1980, 1.

254 *"If I had been"*: Ellen Hawkes, *Feminism on Trial: The Ginny Foat Case and the Future of the Women's Movement* (New York: William Morrow, 1986), 50.

254 *"It took women"*: "No More Ms. Nice NOW," *National NOW Times*, Dec. 1979–Jan. 1980, 11.

254 *NOW members trained*: "Feminists Display Convention Clout," *National NOW Times*, Sept. 1980, 4.

254 *"the massive campaign treasuries"*: Smeal to Friend, n.d., ca. 1981, folder 15, box 22, Downriver NOW Chapter Records, Reuther Library.

254 *He had been elected*: Spruill, *Divided We Stand*, 264.

255 *Carter mentioned the amendment*: "Record of President Carter on Women's Issues," *National NOW Times*, Dec. 1979–Jan. 1980, 3.

255 *and he fired*: On Abzug, see Leandra Ruth Zarnow, *Battling Bella: The Protest Politics of Bella Abzug* (Cambridge, Mass.: Harvard University Press, 2019), esp. 291–94.

255 *"attempted to lecture"*: Terence Smith, "Carter, in Angry Exchange, Ousts Bella Abzug from Women's Unit," *New York Times*, Jan. 13, 1979, 1.

255 *Later that day*: Richard Halloran, "23 Leave Committee over Abzug Dismissal," *New York Times*, Jan. 14, 1979, 1.

255 *Still, Carter had appointed*: "The Complaints of the Women's Lobby: When NOW Was Too Soon," *New York Times*, Dec. 19, 1979, A30.

255 *"We know the President"*: "NOW Members 'Blitz' Convention," *National NOW Times*, Feb. 1980, 4.

255 *After two days*: "NOW PAC Votes to Oppose Carter," *National NOW Times*, Dec.

1979–Jan. 1980, 1. National NOW did not endorse a candidate for president. California NOW voted to endorse Senator Ted Kennedy, a progressive Democrat from Massachusetts, in the Democratic primary. He was "excellent on feminist issues," one member noted, but he was also "the only viable alternative." "NOW Members 'Blitz' Convention."

255 *"placed women's concerns"*: "NOW to Oppose Carter Against Any Opponent," *Baltimore Sun*, Dec. 11, 1979, A12.

255 *Several days after*: Bennetts, "Feminists Cool to NOW Stand Against Carter"; "Carter Has No Time for NOW," *Washington Post*, Dec. 14, 1979, A7.

255 *None followed suit*: Leslie Bennetts, "NOW's Carter Stand Perplexes Feminists," *New York Times*, Dec. 12, 1979, B8; Bennetts, "Feminists Cool to NOW Stand Against Carter."

256 *feminist pamphlets and "ERA YES" buttons*: "Feminists Display Clout at Democratic Convention," *National NOW Times*, Sept. 1980, 1, 4–5.

256 *about two hundred*: Sources vary on the total number of delegates at the convention. Totaling the vote counts received by Kennedy and Carter, Hedrick Smith, "Democrats Back Carter on Nomination Rule; Kennedy Withdraws from Presidential Race," *New York Times*, Aug. 12, 1980, A1, places the total at 3,438.

256 *"the strongest ERA"*: "1980: The Highlights in Review," *National NOW Times*, Feb. 1981, 11.

256 *While President Richard Nixon*: Critchlow, *Conservative Ascendency*, 138.

256 *Republican feminists in 1976*: Freeman, "Whom You Know Versus Whom You Represent," 238–39.

256 *Ford's centrism and his eventual defeat*: Critchlow, *Conservative Ascendency*, 128; Evans, *Tidal Wave*, 112.

257 *"wildcat Republican defection"*: "Rescission: Fact Sheet & Analysis," *National NOW Times*, April 1979, 7.

257 *Governor William Milliken brought*: Dempsey, *William G. Milliken*, 140.

257 *ERA advocates, led by*: "GOP's ERA Stand Abandons Principle," *Port Huron (Mich.) Times Herald*, July 1980, "Talks" folder, box 8, Burnett Papers.

257 *"equal rights and equal opportunities"*: "History of the ERA and the GOP," n.d., 2, folder 60, box 158, NOW Records.

257 *"so tightly controlled"*: "Republican Convention in Detroit," *Joint Pittsburgh Area NOW Newsletter*, Aug. 1980, 1, NOW Chapter Newsletters Collection.

257 *"I asked to be"*: Burnett, interview by Boyer, 85–86, folder 1, box 8.

257 *"sexism in an unholy alliance"*: Burnett, *True Colors*, 34.

257 *Chicago NOW sent*: Vi Bingham, "ERA Protest at GOP," *Act NOW* (Chicago), Aug. 1980, 3, NOW Chapter Newsletters Collection.

257 *"Keep it in the platform"*: Nancy Thompson, "ERA Supporters March on Republican Convention," *National NOW Times*, Aug. 1980, 1.

257 *"we are kidding ourselves"*: Dempsey, *William G. Milliken*, 140.

257 *The elections that November*: David S. Broder, "Carter Yields Early in Night: Ronald Reagan Elected in a Landslide of Electoral Votes," *Washington Post*, Nov. 5, 1980, A1; "ERA Analysis on Elections in Unratified States," *National NOW Times*, Dec.–Jan. 1980–81, 3.

257 *"The election will make"*: Paw, "Election Returns," *Joint Pittsburgh Area NOW Newsletter*, Dec. 1980, 1, NOW Chapter Newsletters Collection.

257 *But for the first time*: "Women Vote Differently Than Men: Feminist Bloc Emerges in 1980 Elections," *National NOW Times*, Dec.–Jan. 1980–81, 1, 5.

258 *And after the election*: "1980 in Review," *National NOW Times*, Feb. 1981, 11.

258 *"Women will vote"*: Smeal to NOW Activist, *Joint Pittsburgh Area NOW Newsletter*, Jan. 1981, 1, NOW Chapter Newsletters Collection.

258 *"a strong haven"*: Burnett to Mae Junod, May 15, 1978, "Correspondence, January–June 1978" folder, box 1, Burnett Papers.

258 *"If it weren't for Milliken"*: Burnett to Elly M. Peterson, n.d., ca. Nov. 1977, "Correspondence, 1977, July–December" folder, box 1, Burnett Papers.

258 *He retired in 1982*: Dempsey, *William G. Milliken*, 177.

258 *Prominent Republican feminists*: Rymph, *Republican Women*, 237.

258 *"happily voted for Reagan"*: Burnett, *True Colors*, 33.

258 *"a thorn under their saddle"*: Burnett, interview by Boyer, 81, folder 20, box 7.

258 *"hopelessly right-wing"*: Burnett, *True Colors*, 71.

258 *She decided to run*: Handbook for Commissions on the Status of Women, 3rd ed., n.d., ca. early 1980s, "National Association of Commissions for Women" folder, box 3, Burnett Papers.

258 *"the feminist part"*: Fox to Smeal, March 21, 1979, "Correspondence Jan.–June 1979" folder, box 2, Burnett Papers.

258 *"that feminists are needed"*: Burnett to Mary Olsen, March 29, 1979, "Correspondence Jan.–June 1979" folder, box 2, Burnett Papers.

258 *Ultimately, she decided*: Burnett to "Pat," April 1, 1979, "Correspondence Jan.–June 1979" folder, box 2, Burnett Papers.

258 *She won her election*: NACW, national press release, Oct. 1981, "National Association of Commissions for Women" folder, box 3, Burnett Papers.

258 *"ERA countdown campaign offices"*: "ERA Offices Open," *National NOW Times*, Sept. 1981, 1.

258 *NOW and allied groups*: NOW to All Groups Supporting Ratification of the ERA, re: ERA Countdown Rallies, June 30, 1981, "NOW" folder, box 33, ERAmerica Records; "Thousands Lobby for Women's Rights in Nation's Capitol," *National NOW Times*, March 1981, 1; "Thousands at a Rally in Chicago Back Equal Rights Amendment," *New York Times*, May 11, 1980, 22.

258 *ERA walkathons in 160 cities*: Judy Goldsmith, "ERA Walks Raise $1 Million," *National NOW Times*, Sept. 1981, 1.

259 *A single solicitation*: "Special Appeal Statistics," n.d., ca. late 1981 or early 1982, folder 6, box 79, NOW Additional Records.

259 *The organization raised*: Jane Perlez, "NOW's Funds Soar Suggesting Extent of Women's Power," *New York Times*, May 20, 1982, C1.

259 *the Democratic Party raised*: Perlez, "NOW's Funds Soar Suggesting Extent of Women's Power," C12; Critchlow, *Phyllis Schlafly and Grassroots Conservatism*, 230.

259 *"I think now"*: Beverly Stephen, "The Arrival of Feminist Clout," *Los Angeles Times*, Feb. 17, 1980, I23.

259 *"We are literally"*: Smeal's Speaking Tour Speech, 14th Annual NOW Convention, 1981, 5, folder 3, box 140, NOW Records.

259 *NOW hired an agency*: Christine Terp Madsen, "NOW Pins Efforts on New Strategies," *Christian Science Monitor*, Oct. 20, 1981, 5; Bonk, interview by author, 3.

259 *A two-week, sixty-second spot*: Beber, Silverstein & Partners to Kathy Bonk, Feb. 11, 1982, folder 10, box 1, Kathy Bonk NOW Officer Papers, Schlesinger Library.

259 *"We literally emptied"*: Paula Kamen, *Feminist Fatale: Voices from the "Twentysomething" Generation Explore the Future of the "Women's Movement"* (New York: Donald I. Fine, 1991), 100.

259 *"The last two years"*: Ireland, interview by author, April 30, 2021, 4.

259 *In Illinois, the ERA*: Mary Frances Berry, *Why ERA Failed: Politics, Women's Rights, and the Amending Process of the Constitution* (Bloomington: Indiana University Press, 1986), 67.

259 *There and elsewhere*: Janet K. Boles, *The Politics of the Equal Rights Amendment: Conflict and the Decision Process* (New York: Longman, 1979), 130, 134.

259 *"intense anger and frustration"*: Collins, "From the President," *Act NOW* (Chicago), July 1980, 1, 2; Berry, *Why ERA Failed*, 74.

259 *She and the other*: Staggenborg, "Stability and Innovation in the Women's Movement," 86.

260 *"It was a very good campaign"*: Collins, interview by author, 2015, 17.

260 *If just seven state lawmakers*: Steiner, *Constitutional Inequality*, 3, 100.

260 *"limit, regulate and prohibit"*: William D. Guthrie et al., "The Federal Child Labor Amendment," *American Bar Association Journal* 21 (Jan. 1935): 11–18.

260 *Eleanor Smeal led a protest*: Barbara Toman, "With the ERA Dead, Even Eleanor Smeal Asks: 'What NOW?,'" *Wall Street Journal*, June 25, 1982, 1.

260 *The Republican Party*: Statement of Eleanor Smeal, June 24, 1982, folder 428, Boston NOW Records.

260 *"telling male politicians"*: NOW, "The GOP Has a Grand Old Problem—Women," press release, June 30, 1982, 2, folder 429, Boston NOW Records.

260 *Some have argued*: Mansbridge, *Why We Lost the ERA*, esp. 2, 6; Berry, *Why ERA Failed*, 83–84; Donald G. Mathews and Jane Sherron De Hart, *Sex, Gender, and the Politics of ERA: A State and the Nation* (Oxford: Oxford University Press, 1990), esp. xi.

260 *The ERA's failure*: Mansbridge, *Why We Lost the ERA*, 5–6; Steiner, *Constitutional Inequality*, 55, 70.

261 *Some have rightly emphasized*: Berry, *Why ERA Failed*, 4; Steiner, *Constitutional Inequality*, 28–29.

261 *"It was very hard"*: Collins, interview by Connell, 62, folder 6, box 8.

8. YOU BETTER BE *IN* THE THRONE

263 *On a sweltering*: Patrick Owens, "'We Still Have a Dream': 250,000 Rally to Fulfill an Old Dream," *Newsday*, Aug. 28, 1983, 1; Collins, email to author, June 26, 2021.

263 *"freedom trains"*: "Thousands Rally for 'Freedom March,'" *Indianapolis Star*, Aug. 27, 1983.

263 *To the speakers*: Simon Anekwe, "Stepoff and Liftoff Blast Off A-Okay," *New York Amsterdam News*, Sept. 3, 1983, 1.

263 *"We Still Have"*: William R. Doerner, "We Still Have a Dream," *Time*, Sept. 5, 1983, 14.

263 *"I Have a Dream"*: Kenneth B. Noble, "Rights Marchers Ask New Coalition for Social Change," *New York Times*, Aug. 28, 1983, A1.

263 *"as many people there"*: Collins, email to author, June 26, 2021.

264 *The scene reflected*: Noble, "Rights Marchers Ask New Coalition for Social Change."

264 *"not the solution"*: Lou Cannon, "Inaugural Address: Evocative Version of Campaign Message," *Washington Post*, Jan. 21, 1981, A29.

264 *"demonstrated an insensitivity"*: Anekwe, "Stepoff and Liftoff Blast Off A-Okay," 43.

264 *"Turn on Reagan"*: Doerner, "We Still Have a Dream."

264 *NOW's new president*: Goldsmith, interview by author, 11. On NOW's coalition building and engagement in electoral politics in the 1980s, see also Joe J. Ryan-Hume, "The National Organization for Women and the Democratic Party in Reagan's America," *Historical Journal* 64 (2021): 454–76.

264 *Goldsmith told the sea of protesters*: "Goldsmith Addresses 'We Still Have a Dream' March," *National NOW Times*, Nov. 1983, 6.

265 *NOW had nearly*: Joanne Omang, "NOW Convention Set to Elect President from Among Five Candidates," *Washington Post*, Oct. 10, 1982, A3.

265 *Anyone who wanted*: Freedman, *No Turning Back*, 5.

265 *"If you cannot achieve"*: Austin C. Wehrwein, "What Now, NOW?," *Boston Globe*, Oct. 12, 1982, 43.

265 *She predicted that women*: Eleanor Smeal, "Women's Equality Day: From Women's Voting Rights to a Women's Voting Bloc," Aug. 26, 1982, folder 28, box 200, NOW Records. On how NOW's approach to electoral politics between 1982 and 1985 shifted from a "tactic" to "an end in itself," see Barakso, *Governing NOW*, 92–100, quotation on p. 93.

266 *"tragedy," Smeal declared*: "Eleanor Smeal Muses on 5 Years," *New York Times*, Nov. 30, 1982, C10.

266 *"they were pissed"*: Ireland, interview by author, 1.

266 *As the midterm election*: Paul Taylor, "NOW Seeking $3 Million War Chest to Oust ERA Foes, Fight New Right," *Washington Post*, Aug. 27, 1982, A2.

266 *Chapters held walkathons*: Barakso, *Governing NOW*, 95; Smeal, "Women's Equality Day."

266 *The PACs funded*: NOW, "Progress for Women in 1982 Elections with Significant Gains in ERA States—A NOW Analysis," press release, Nov. 4, 1982, folder 29, box 200, NOW Records.

266 *"from women's voting rights"*: Smeal, "Women's Equality Day."

266 *"poor working class"*: Nadine Brozan, "A President with a Pragmatic Approach: Judith Becker Goldsmith," *New York Times*, Oct. 10, 1982, B6.

266 *Her single mother*: "Judy Goldsmith's Campaign Speech to 1985 National NOW Conference," n.d., ca. 1985, folder 15, box 7, Collins NOW Officer Papers.

266 *"strongly pragmatic with"*: Brozan, "President with a Pragmatic Approach."

266 *"I wasn't inside"*: Collins, interview by author, 2019, 4.

267 *"grassroots activist for NOW"*: "Mary Jean Collins for Action-Vice President," n.d., ca. Sept. 1982, folder 1, box 25, Collins NOW Officer Records.

267 *"the preeminent feminist organization"*: Judy Goldsmith et al., "A Strong NOW for a Feminist Future," n.d., ca. Sept. 1982, 1, folder 4, box 25, Collins NOW Officer Records.

267 *"to reshape our program"*: Mary Jean Collins, "Dear NOW Activist," n.d., ca. Sept. 1982, folder 1, box 25, Collins NOW Officer Records.

267 *"We had people calling"*: Brad Lemley, "Eleanor Smeal in Overdrive," *Washington Post*, Nov. 24, 1985, SM31.

267 *NOW was "synonymous"*: Bill Peterson, "Battle for NOW Presidency Focuses on Group's 'New Image,'" *Hartford Courant*, Oct. 7, 1982, A6.

267 *"ERA President Goldsmith"*: Beverly Stephen, "Options: New Role for ERA President Goldsmith," *Los Angeles Times*, Jan. 9, 1983, E8.

267 *"the nightmare that everyone"*: Collins, interview by author, 2019, 5.

267 *The organization had*: Goldsmith told a reporter in 1985 that she had inherited $1.1 million of debt from Smeal, who countered that much of it was an anonymous "donor loan" to subsidize NOW's television spots during that ERA campaign and which was "being forgiven as a gift." Bill Peterson, "NOW's Time of Choice: Leadership Fight Touches Group to Core," *Washington Post*, July 14, 1985, A20.

267 *"a strong mandate"*: Brozan, "President with a Pragmatic Approach."

267 *"I realized, my God"*: Collins, interview by author, 2019, 4, 1.

268 *"suburban person"*: Collins, interview by author, 2019, 1; Collins, email to author, Feb. 6, 2022.

268 *"a whole other ballgame"*: Collins, interview by author, 2019, 5.

268 *"the primary units"*: "Chapter Development Resolution," n.d., ca. Dec. 4–5, 1983, folder 22, box 5, NOW Records.

268 *"guarantee all members access"*: NOW National Board Meeting Minutes, April 23–24, 1983, folder 26, box 5, NOW Records.

268 *"We really did focus"*: Webb, interview by author, March 5, 2019, 2, 3.

268 *"a broader field"*: Pollack, interview by author, March 19, 2019, 3.

268 *"totally post-ERA"*: Anderson, interview by author, Feb. 26, 2019, 1.

268 *passed a resolution*: Rosemarie Pegueros, "My Sister's Keeper: NOW and the Issue of Race," Jan. 1988, 5, folder 20, box 48, NOW Records.

268 *"to try to overcome"*: Collins, interview by Connell, 77, folder 7, box 8.

268 *Co-sponsoring the 1983*: Collins to NOW National Board, "Minority Issues Update," July 22, 1983, folder 32, box 5, NOW Records.

268 *Lesbians in NOW*: Gilmore and Kaminski, "A Part and Apart," 101.

268 *"one of the most effective"*: "NOW Appoints Lesbian Liaison," May 1983, clipping, folder 5, box 12, Collins NOW Officer Records.

269 *"general acceptance"*: Riddiough, interview by author, March 5, 2019, 3.

269 *"Lesbian Rights: Power and Politics in '84"*: Collins and Riddiough to NOW Leadership List, re: 1984 Lesbian Rights Conference, Oct. 12, 1983, folder 15, box 12, Collins NOW Officer Papers; "Lesbian Rights Conference Held in Milwaukee," *What NOW* (Milwaukee), Feb. 1984, 6, folder 3, box 3, Records of the Milwaukee Chapter of the National Organization for Women, Milwaukee Area Research Center, University of Wisconsin–Milwaukee.

269 *Riddiough strengthened alliances*: "NOW Pledges Assistance to GRNL," May 25, 1983, folder 14, box 47, NOW Records; Riddiough to Collins, June 2, 1983, folder 3, box 12, Collins NOW Officer Papers; Riddiough, interview by author, 3.

269 *Riddiough started to build*: Riddiough, interview by author, 3.

269 *"each state lesbian and gay rights"*: Mary Jean Collins Keynote, Pro-PAC, April 6, 1984, 5, folder 7, box 1, Collins NOW Officer Papers.

269 *NOW built a state*: "Lesbian and Gay Rights Legislation Resolution," passed by 1983 NOW National Conference, folder 1, box 91, NOW Records.

269 *Allies in the state assembly*: Christine Carmody-Arey to Collins, re: NOW New Jersey Project and A1721, Jan. 10, 1985, folder 1, box 13, Collins NOW Officer Papers.

269 *NOW intended the successful*: Collins to NOW Leadership List, re: Lesbian and Gay Rights '84 Project, June 15, 1984, folder 20, box 47, NOW Records.

269 *Those conservatives initiated*: Doug Rossinow, *The Reagan Era: A History of the 1980s* (New York: Columbia University Press, 2015), 59–62, 66–83; Kruse and Zelizer, *Fault Lines*, 123.

270 *The budget cuts*: Susan Faludi, *Backlash: The Undeclared War Against American Women* (New York: Crown, 1991), xvii.

270 *including Food Stamps*: Sheldon Danziger and Robert Haveman, "The Reagan Administration's Budget Cuts: Their Impact on the Poor," *Focus*, Dec. 1, 1981, 13; Marilyn Power, "Falling Through the 'Safety Net': Women, Economic Crisis, and Reaganomics," *Feminist Studies* (Spring 1984): 36–37.

270 *"at the bottom"*: Power, "Falling Through the 'Safety Net,'" 32.

270 *Women's unemployment soared*: Mike Bayer, "Reaganomics and Working Women," *Atlanta Daily World*, March 22, 1984, 5-D.

270 *"responsible behavior"*: Don Irwin, "Reagan Signs Tough Child Support Law," *Los Angeles Times*, Aug. 17, 1984, B4.

270 *"straitjacket" for women*: Faludi, *Backlash*, xii.

270 *Reagan himself called upon*: "Reagan Writes Article Saying Abortion Is a Moral Wrong," *Baltimore Sun*, April 29, 1983, A12.

270 *The officials he appointed*: Evans, *Tidal Wave*, 177.

270 *All of this placed*: Lynn Hecht Schafran, "Reagan vs. Women," *New York Times*, Oct. 13, 1981, 23.

270 *Fundraising appeals dedicated*: Linda Greenhouse, "Abortion Rights Group Expects Hard Times," *New York Times*, Feb. 16, 1981, B6.

270 *The National Abortion Rights Action League's*: Michael Vitez, "Abortion Rights League Holds Benefit Swimathon," *Hartford Courant*, Dec. 5, 1981, B6; Wehrwein, "What Now, NOW?," 42.

271 *While NOW's ERA blitz*: Amanda Spake, "Goldsmith v. Smeal: The Debate of the Decade," *Washington Post*, Nov. 24, 1985, SM28.

271 *other groups, like the NAACP*: Steven V. Roberts, "Financial Crisis Perils Activities of N.A.A.C.P.," *New York Times*, Dec. 21, 1978, A1.

271 *Reagan's spending cuts*: "National Council of Negro Women Offers New Support Program," *Baltimore Afro-American*, Sept. 12, 1981, 12; "NCNW Raises $20,000 at Soiree for Black Families," *New York Amsterdam News*, May 1, 1982, 8.

271 *Some smaller feminist groups*: Evans, *Tidal Wave*, 186; Stansell, *Feminist Promise*, 355–94.

271 *They were muscled*: James Strong, "The Labor Movement: Is It Still Working? Unions Are Giving Up Past Gains," *Chicago Tribune*, Sept. 5, 1982, A1; Rossinow, *Reagan Era*, 85–88; Joseph McCartin, *Collision Course: Ronald Reagan, the Air Traffic Controllers, and the Strike That Changed America* (Oxford: Oxford University Press, 2013).

271 *Gay and lesbian activists*: Linda Greenhouse, "4-to-4 Vote Upholds Teachers on Homosexual Rights Issue," *New York Times*, March 27, 1985, A23; Robin Herman, "A Disease's Spread Provokes Anxiety," *New York Times*, Aug. 8, 1982, 31; "Rev. Falwell's Anti-gay Crusade," *Atlanta Constitution*, Sept. 4, 1984, 20A.

271 *The Leadership Conference on Civil Rights*: Lyle Denniston, "After 20 Years, 'We Still Have a Dream': 1983 March Broadly Focused," *Baltimore Sun*, Aug. 23, 1983, A12.

271 *At the press conference*: "Goldsmith Addresses 'We Still Have a Dream' March."

271 *Black and Latino groups*: Denniston, "After 20 Years, 'We Still Have a Dream.'"

272 *National surveys*: Greenhouse, "Abortion Rights Group Expects Hard Times."

272 *"The crisis is upon us"*: Greenhouse, "Abortion Rights Group Expects Hard Times."

272 *Inside NOW, Collins*: Collins to NOW National Board, re: Update on State Reproductive Rights Legislation, April 21, 1983, folder 7, box 2, Collins NOW Officer Papers; Collins to NOW National Board, re: Update on Congressional Activity on Abortion, July 22, 1983, folder 9, box 2, Collins NOW Officer Papers.

272 *Antiabortion terrorists bombed*: "The 30 Abortion Clinic Arson and Bombing Attacks Between May 29, 1982, and Jan. 3, 1985," UPI, Jan. 4, 1985, www.upi.com/Archives/1985/01/04/The-30-abortion-clinic-arson-and-bombing-attacks-between/6555473662800/. On antiabortion violence, see also Haugeberg, *Women Against Abortion*, 75–90.

272 *They went on to assault*: Joe Pichirallo and Ruth Marcus, "No Conspiracy Seen in Clinic Attacks," *Washington Post*, Jan. 6, 1985, A16.

272 *NOW began a campaign*: Collins to NOW National Board, re: Abortion, May 4, 1984, folder 50, box 5, NOW Records; NOW National Conference Resolutions, 1984, folder 40, box 25, NOW Records.

272 *"immediately and publicly condemn"*: "The National Organization for Women Today . . . ," March 2, 1984, folder 31, box 200, NOW Records.

272 *Reagan did not speak*: Ruth Marcus and Eric Pianin, "Reagan Strongly Condemns Abortion Clinic Bombings," *Washington Post*, Jan. 4, 1985, A1; Haugeberg, *Women Against Abortion*, 85–86.

272 *Every chapter the national office*: Anderson, interview by author, 3.

272 *"They're not going to bomb"*: Collins, interview by author, 2019, 6.

272 *At NOW's sit-ins*: "Rights Activists Plan Abortion Clinic Vigils," *Boston Globe*, Jan. 19, 1985, 6; Anderson, interview by author, 2.

273 *"in part to get"*: Collins, interview by author, 2019, 6.

273 *Members of the Democratic-controlled*: Collins to Goldsmith et al., re: Reintroduction of ERA, Jan. 3, 1983, folder 15, box 9, Collins NOW Officer Papers.

273 *"were not hard"*: Judy Mann, "ERA Again," *Washington Post*, Jan. 5, 1983, B1.

273 *As Smeal had done*: Mann, "ERA Again."

273 *"the silent lobby"*: Goldsmith to ERA Support Organizations, re: Progress on the Reintroduction of the ERA in the Congress of the United States, n.d., ca. 1983, 3, folder 37, box 194, NOW Records. On feminists' battle with the insurance industry in the early 1980s, see also Horan, *Insurance Era*, 168–89.

273 *Single adult women*: Pat Butler to Pennsylvania ERA—Auto Insurance Group, re: Insurers Discover That We Are Right, Jan. 14, 1985, 2, folder 10, box 11, Collins NOW Officer Papers.

273 *Over their lifetimes*: Barbara Mikulski, "Debate & Discussion: Insurance Rates for Women," *Baltimore Sun*, June 4, 1983, A10.

273 *Insurers frequently excluded*: Judy Mann, "Insurance," *Hartford Courant*, July 16, 1982, B1.

273 *"corps of lobbyists"*: "Will the ERA Be Sacrificed for the Insurance Numbers Game?," n.d., ca. 1982, folder 10, box 11, Collins NOW Officer Papers.

273 *"opposition to ERA"*: "ERA/Insurance Connect," n.d., ca. 1983, folder 5, box 20, Collins NOW Officer Papers.

273 *"totally disrupt"*: Joann S. Lublin, "Feminists to Push for Law Requiring Unisex Insurance: But Proponents Are Outspent by Insurers That Contend Bill Would Wreak Havoc," *Wall Street Journal*, June 3, 1983, 12.

273 *"These people want"*: Frances J. Flaherty, "Battle Lines Form in Unisex Insurance War," *Chicago Tribune*, April 10, 1983, K1.

274 *"Discrimination is about money"*: Judy Goldsmith, Statement to Accompany Testimony on S. 372, Fair Insurance Practices Act, Before the U.S. Senate Committee on Commerce, Science, and Transportation, April 12, 1983, 1, folder 7, box 2, Collins NOW Officer Papers.

274 *Members phone banked*: Collins to NOW Leadership List, re: Campaign to Pass H.R. 100, S. 372, Equal Rights Amendment, Aug. 12, 1982, folder 5, box 20, Collins NOW Officer Papers.

274 *In January 1983*: Mann, "ERA Again."

274 *But later that year*: T. R. Reid, "House Fails to Approve ERA: Sullen House Rejects Equal Rights Amendment," *Washington Post*, Nov. 16, 1983, A1.

274 *In those same months*: Horan, *Insurance Era*, 181.

274 *The House bill eventually*: Mary Jean Collins, "Non Discrimination in Insurance—Federal Level," Feb. 16, 1985, folder 3, box 3, Collins NOW Officer Papers; Horan, *Insurance Era*, 182–85.

274 *The group's sophisticated*: Jennie Thompson to NOW File, "Overview of the Growth of the NOW Direct Mail Program," March 7, 1984, folder 11, box 85, NOW Records.

274 *"The money you raise"*: Greenhouse, "Abortion Rights Group Expects Hard Times."

274 *Collins wanted to pivot*: Collins, interview by Connell, 111, folder 7, box 8.

274 *In the first half*: "Statement of Income and Loss," July 31, 1983, folder 43, box 5, NOW Records. This statement does not itemize NOW's expenses, but its monthly overhead in early 1984 was $250,000. Jennie Thompson to NOW File, re: Meeting at NOW Regarding Finances, Jan. 9, 1984, folder 6, box 79, NOW Additional Records.

275 *"full-service consulting"*: Jennie Thompson to Goldsmith, "Reviewed Letter of Proposal

and Agreement for Direct Mail Services Between July 1, 1983, and November 30, 1983," Sept. 14, 1983, folder 10, box 85, NOW Records; Craver to Goldsmith, July 15, 1983, folder 10, box 85, NOW Records.

275 *For each of three mailings*: "Special Appeal Statistics," n.d., ca. late 1984 or early 1985, folder 6, box 79, NOW Additional Records.

275 *In early 1984*: Thompson to NOW File, re: Meeting at NOW Regarding Finances, Jan. 9, 1984.

275 *Plotting NOW's fundraisers*: "Fundraising Programs for 1984," n.d., ca. late 1983, folder 3, box 4, Collins NOW Officer Papers.

275 *"cold prospecting program"*: Goldsmith to the National Board, Feb. 18, 1984, folder 3, box 4, Collins NOW Officer Papers; Peterson, "NOW's Time of Choice," A1.

275 *Campaigning for national office*: "Vows to Defeat 'Right Wing': Goldsmith Elected President of NOW," *Los Angeles Times*, Oct. 11, 1982, B14; NOW Board Meeting, Unapproved Minutes, May 5, 1984, folder 14, box 2, Collins NOW Officer Papers.

275 *"from basically the same"*: Goldsmith to the National Board, Feb. 18, 1984.

275 *"You can count on NOW"*: Goldsmith to Friend, n.d., ca. 1984, folder 37, box 194, NOW Records.

275 *"I wasn't comfortable"*: Peterson, "NOW's Time of Choice," A20.

275 *"the establishment"*: Barakso, *Governing NOW*, 93.

276 *"Ronald Reagan has been a disaster"*: Pat Rindle, "NOW Speaker Blasts Reagan," *Vidette-Messenger* (Valparaiso, Ind.), July 11, 1983, folder 2, box 1, Collins NOW Officer Papers.

276 *Soon they were fighting*: Kruse and Zelizer, *Fault Lines*, 112, 120–22.

276 *But an examination*: "Portrait of the Electorate," *New York Times*, Nov. 8, 1984, A19.

276 *"Ronald Reagan is directly responsible"*: "Nation/World: Reagan=Disaster, NOW Leader Says," *Chicago Tribune*, July 1, 1983, 5.

276 *The organization spent*: Joanne Omang, "NOW Seeks to Expand to 1 Million by 1984," *Washington Post*, Oct. 9, 1982, A3.

276 *"But who speaks"*: Omang, "NOW Seeks to Expand to 1 Million by 1984."

276 *Political experts, newly focused*: Jane Perlez, "Women, Power, and Politics: The 'Gender Gap' Worries Both Parties, as Presidential Candidates Woo Women Voters—with Mixed Results," *New York Times*, June 24, 1984, SM23.

276 *"Five years ago"*: "Power, Politics, and Women," *Boston Globe*, Oct. 12, 1982, 18.

277 *"but we were like"*: Nadine Brozan, "NOW Elects New Officers and Plots Its Future," *New York Times*, Oct. 11, 1982, B6.

277 *A decade earlier*: Ellen Goodman, "The Feminist's Choices Get Complicated," *Washington Post*, Oct. 26, 1982, A19.

277 *In 1983, the League*: "League of Women Voters Supports Abortion Rights," *Atlanta Constitution*, Jan. 20, 1983, 1A.

277 *"The failure of our success"*: Goodman, "Feminist's Choices Get Complicated."

277 *The organization supported*: Goodman, "Feminist's Choices Get Complicated."

277 *"only concerned about"*: "NOW Supporting Some Men Instead of Women for Office," *New York Times*, Oct. 3, 1982, 68.

278 *"Let them be my guest"*: Jan Klunder, "NOW Targets Foes of ERA for Defeat," *Los Angeles Times*, Dec. 4, 1983, GB2.

278 *"Morning in America"*: Kruse and Zelizer, *Fault Lines*, 128.

278 *Walter Mondale, the former*: Steven M. Gillon, *The Democrats' Dilemma: Walter F. Mondale and the Liberal Legacy* (New York: Columbia University Press, 1992).

278 *His most prominent early opponent*: Kruse and Zelizer, *Fault Lines*, 128.

278 *Mondale and Hart*: Sally Chew, "Running on Empty: Candidates Fail to Bridge 'Gender Gap,'" *Womanews*, April 1984, 4.

279 *Critics on the left*: Wendy Patterson, "Somewhere over the Rainbow: Ferraro's Legacy," *Womanews*, Oct. 1984, 2.

279 *A former associate*: David Lightman, "Jackson Rides Black Political Push," *Hartford Courant*, May 15, 1983, A1, A15.

279 *"growing out of"*: Jackson quoted in Kruse and Zelizer, *Fault Lines*, 129.

279 *"rainbow coalition"*: Patterson, "Somewhere over the Rainbow."

279 *At one of several debates*: George Lardner Jr. and Dan Balz, "Mondale Turns Combative, Clashes with Hart in Debate," *Washington Post*, March 12, 1984, A1, A6.

279 *"against special interests"*: Ann Woolner and Robin Toner, "Hart the Target in Debate," *Atlanta Constitution*, March 12, 1984, 14A.

279 *"new leadership that replaces"*: "Excerpts from Transcript of 5 Candidates' Debate in Atlanta," *New York Times*, March 12, 1984, B8.

280 *"new name of an old game"*: "Excerpts from Transcript of 5 Candidates' Debate in Atlanta."

280 *Those reporters had already*: Bill Peterson, "NOW to Endorse a Presidential Candidate Early," *Washington Post*, Oct. 1, 1983, A3.

280 *"their support says"*: Bernard Weinraub, "Women's Endorsement Seems a 2-Way Race," *New York Times*, Dec. 2, 1983, A24.

280 *"We have a new role"*: NOW National Conference Transcript, Oct. 2, 1983, 9, folder 34, box 25, NOW Records.

280 *"Our priority for 1984"*: Peterson, "NOW to Endorse a Presidential Candidate Early."

280 *"feminist woman"*: David Treadwell, "'84 Ticket May Include Women, 6 Democrats Say," *Los Angeles Times*, Oct. 3, 1983, 1. Jesse Jackson entered the Democratic presidential primary one month after NOW's 1983 convention, and he vowed to choose a woman running mate.

280 *"I am a feminist"*: Beverly Beyette, "NOW Flexing New Political Muscle," *Los Angeles Times*, Oct. 6, 1983, I3.

280 *"we all loafed"*: Andrew Mollison, "Democrats Back Woman as VP," *Atlanta Constitution*, Oct. 3, 1983, 3A.

280 *"Certainly no organization"*: Mollison, "Democrats Back Woman as VP."

280 *Their conference was a success*: Beyette, "NOW Flexing New Political Muscle," I2.

281 *Jackson's candidacy tested*: NOW National Board Meeting Unapproved Minutes, Dec. 10, 1983, 3, folder 12, box 2, Collins NOW Officer Papers.

281 *"upper middle-class white females"*: Weinraub, "Women's Endorsement Seems a 2-Way Race."

281 *"the only candidate"*: Chew, "Running on Empty."

281 *"another group that"*: Weinraub, "Women's Endorsement Seems a 2-Way Race."

282 *Mondale's supporters emphasized*: Bernard Weinraub, "NOW, in First Endorsement, Backs Mondale," *New York Times*, Dec. 11, 1983, 1, 39.

282 *After six hours of debate*: Bill Peterson, "Feminist Group Contends Mondale Is Most Likely to Defeat Reagan," *Washington Post*, Dec. 11, 1983, A2.

282 *"very disappointing"*: Peterson, "Feminist Group Contends Mondale Is Most Likely to Defeat Reagan."

282 *Jackson's wife expressed*: Goldsmith, interview by author, 11–12.

282 *"The commitments have been"*: Perlez, "Women, Power, and Politics," SM26.

282 *With their endorsement driven*: NOW, "1984 National NOW Conference to Focus on Woman Vice President, Women's Rights/Reagan's Wrongs," press release, June 15, 1984, folder 32, box 22, NOW Records.

283 *"deliver the women's vote"*: Bruce McCabe, "A Priority for NOW," *Boston Globe*, June 29, 1984, 46.

283 *A female vice presidential candidate*: "National Conference Resolutions, 1984," folder 40, box 25, NOW Records.

283 *"We aren't saying"*: Judy Goldsmith, Keynote Speech at 1984 NOW National Conference, Miami Beach, Fla., June 30, 1984, 8, folder 39, box 25, NOW Records.

283 *"Run with a woman"*: Bruce McCabe, "Women Pave Way for Fight over VP," *Boston Globe*, July 2, 1984, 4.

283 *"Woman VP NOW"*: Alison Muscatine, "NOW Is Confident Mondale Will Put Woman on Ticket," *Washington Post*, June 30, 1984, A7.

283 *The potential vice presidential candidates*: McCabe, "Priority for NOW."

283 *Mary Roche Eidsvik*: Bill Peterson, "Floor Fight Threatened by NOW: Convention Battle Vowed if Nominee Selects a Male," *Washington Post*, July 2, 1984, A1.

283 *"a prediction"*: Muscatine, "NOW Is Confident Mondale Will Put Woman on Ticket."

283 *Mondale began interviewing*: Fay S. Joyce, "Jackson, in a Concession, Suggests Study of Runoff Primaries," *New York Times*, May 4, 1984, A16.

283 *"step in the right"*: "NOW: Woman for VP Is a Must," *Newsday*, July 2, 1984, 6.

283 *"If there was any"*: "Jackson Blasts Jews, 'White Women,'" *Atlanta Constitution*, July 11, 1984, 1A.

284 *Days before the Democratic National Convention*: Davis, *Moving the Mountain*, 423.

284 *"She's a woman"*: Bernard Weinraub, "'Difficult' Decision: But Likely Nominee Says Representative from Queens Is 'Best,'" *New York Times*, July 13, 1984.

284 *Reporters noted that Mondale*: Jack W. Germond and Jules Witcover, "A Chilly Political Climate for NOW," *Boston Globe*, July 25, 1985, 15.

284 *"like the image"*: Ireland, interview by author, April 30, 2021, 5.

284 *Mondale's campaign never*: Davis, *Moving the Mountain*, 424.

284 *But this approach did not shield*: Jo Ognibene, "Gerry and the Gender Gap," *Womanews*, Oct. 1984, 2.

285 *A* Meet the Press *reporter*: Davis, *Moving the Mountain*, 425.

285 *Republicans also hyped*: Those concerns were rooted in real problems. Ferraro had failed to disclose required information about her husband's income and illegally overborrowed from him and her children to fund her 1978 congressional campaign. After she and Zaccaro publicized their tax returns, the IRS scrutinized them, discovering false disclosures and demanding payment of $53,000 in interest and back taxes. See Thomas Ferguson and Joel Rogers, *Right Turn: The Decline of the Democrats and the Future of American Politics* (New York: Hill and Wang, 1986), 187. Zaccaro pleaded guilty to a misdemeanor fraud charge in 1985 but was acquitted of bribery charges two years later. "Zaccaro Pleads Guilty in Fraud Case: Ferraro's Husband Gets Guarantee He Won't Go to Prison," *Los Angeles Times*, Jan. 7, 1985, A2; "Zaccaro Cleared of Bribe Charges: Ferraro Raps Prosecutor," *Washington Post*, Oct. 15, 1987, A3.

285 *"all we did"*: Anderson, interview by author, Feb. 26, 2019, 4.

285 *"Mondale house parties"*: "Budget/Fundraising Meeting," March 16, 1985, folder 4, box 4, Collins NOW Officer Papers.

285 *"most active year politically"*: NOW, "NOW PACs Raise More Than $1 Million," press release, Nov. 3, 1984, folder 31, box 200, NOW Records; NOW, "NOW Members Register a Quarter of a Million New Voters," press release, Oct. 18, 1984, folder 31, box 200, NOW Records.

285 *"strong, specific"*: Goldsmith, Keynote Speech at 1984 NOW National Conference, 7.

285 *NOW members teamed up*: Sharron Hannon, "Women and the Presidential Race: Fall-out from 1984," *Christian Science Monitor*, Feb. 4, 1988, 13.

285 *Its members posited*: Davis, *Moving the Mountain*, 418–19.

285 *"women's truth squad"*: "Women's Rights, Reagan's Wrongs: The Women's Truth Squad on Reagan," n.d., ca. early 1980s, folder 13, box 2, Collins NOW Officer Papers; Judy Goldsmith, press release, n.d., folder 30, box 200, NOW Records.

286 *NOW's "flip side"*: Victoria Irwin, "New GOP Women's Group Aims to Narrow Reagan Gender Gap," *Christian Science Monitor*, June 8, 1984, 7.

286 *Other Republican women appealed*: "Women's Clout, Cohesion Increasing," *Cincinnati Enquirer*, July 20, 1984, A8, A9.

286 *Women against abortion*: "Pro-life Group Opposes Ferraro Selection," *New Pittsburgh Courier*, July 28, 1984, 5.

286 *Black women were*: Pat Press, "What Do Black Women Want?" *Washington Post*, July 21, 1984, A17.

286 *"welfare queens"*: Premilla Nadasen, "From Widow to 'Welfare Queen': Welfare and the Politics of Race," *Black Women, Gender, and Families* 1, no. 2 (Fall 2007): 53.

286 *"Feminists continue to send"*: Pat Press, "Black Women, White Women: The Gap Is Growing," *Washington Post*, Oct. 13, 1983, A23.

286 *Black feminists pointed out*: Patterson, "Somewhere over the Rainbow."

286 *NOW's endorsement unnecessarily*: Chew, "Running on Empty."

286 *"I didn't ever want"*: Ireland, interview by author, 4–5.

287 *Reagan took 525 of 538*: "Reagan and Bush Are Re-elected in a Landside, 525 Votes to 13," *New York Times*, Jan. 8, 1985, 14.

287 *The Democrats' crushing losses*: Robert Kuttner, *The Life of the Party: Democratic Prospects in 1988 and Beyond* (New York: Viking, 1987), 10–15, 57–58.

287 *As a party insider*: Kuttner, *Life of the Party*, 26–27; Ferguson and Rogers, *Right Turn*, 185–89.

287 *The gender gap*: Davis, *Moving the Mountain*, 427–28; Spruill, *Divided We Stand*, 317; "Portrait of the Electorate," A19.

287 *He also won support*: Rymph, *Republican Women*, 231–32.

287 *"We came out of '84"*: Collins to NOW Board Members, Dec. 8, 1984, folder 2, box 3, Collins NOW Officer Papers.

287 *The organization had opened*: Rymph, *Republican Women*, 232.

288 *Postelection postmortems estimated*: Davis, *Moving the Mountain*, 428.

288 *"We can't afford"*: Maureen Dowd, "Reassessing Women's Political Role: The Lasting Impact of Geraldine Ferraro," *New York Times Magazine*, Dec. 30, 1984, 18.

288 *"special interest" groups*: Hannon, "Women and the Presidential Race."

288 *"Our white sisters"*: Diane R. Powell, "Call to Arms . . . : Women's Caucus Aims to Flex Muscle," *New Pittsburgh Courier*, Sept. 1, 1984, 1.

288 *"exuberance" over Ferraro's nomination*: Marilyn Milloy, "Black Women Gather to Create Clout," *Newsday*, June 9, 1985, 15.

288 *a group of thirty-six Black women*: "Afro-American Women Hold National Meeting," *Atlanta Daily World*, July 10, 1985, 10.

288 *Reproductive Rights National Network*: "Reproductive Rights National Network: Rough Road Ahead," *Off Our Backs*, Aug./Sept. 1981, 10, 17; Suzanne Staggenborg and Marie B. Skoczylas, "Battle over Abortion and Reproductive Rights: Movement Mobilization and Strategy," in *Oxford Handbook of U.S. Women's Social Movement Activism*, ed. Holly J. McCammon et al. (New York: Oxford University Press, 2017).

289 *The organization emphasized*: Tacie Dejanikus, "Abortion Strategies for 1983," *Off Our Backs*, Jan. 1983, 10–11; Ziegler, *After Roe*, 148.

289 *NOW helped organize*: Sheri O'Dell to National Board Members, re: Action Report, May 3, 1985, folder 1, box 2, Patricia Ireland Papers, Schlesinger Library; Mary Jean Collins, "NOW Campaign to Save Women's Lives," Feb. 16, 1985, folder 3, box 3, Collins NOW Officer Papers.

289 *Goldsmith condemned antiabortion violence*: Collins to NOW National Board Meeting, "Congressional Hearings on Clinic Violence," Feb. 16, 1985, folder 3, box 3, Collins NOW Officer Papers.

289 *Americans outraged by both the clinic bombings*: National Board Meeting Approved Minutes, May 5–6, 1984, folder 48, box 5, NOW Records.

289 *"orderly and strangely tranquil"*: Perlez, "Women, Power, and Politics," SM28.

289 *"forward progress"*: Riddiough, interview by author, 4.

289 *"This is not the time"*: Ellen Goodman, "Trying to Kick NOW Back to Life," *Boston Globe*, July 25, 1985, 15.

289 *"out of the deep freeze"*: "Ellie Smeal for President of NOW," July 19, 1985, folder 43, box 25, NOW Records.

289 *"political clout is the ability"*: Goodman, "Trying to Kick NOW Back to Life."

290 *"a wonderful organizing tool"*: Peterson, "NOW's Time of Choice," A20.

290 *"the oatmeal caucus"*: Johanna Ettin, interview by author, Sept. 5, 2019, 1.

290 *had spurned Smeal's efforts*: Carabillo, interview by Fox, 131–32, folder 2, box 2.

290 *"There's a limit"*: Carabillo, interview by Fox, 134, folder 2, box 2.

290 *"Ellie kept rescuing"*: Meuli comments in Carabillo, interview by Fox, 134, folder 2, box 2.

290 *"denies reality and demeans"*: "Judy Goldsmith's Campaign Speech to NOW National Conference, 1985," 2, folder 15, box 7, Collins NOW Officer Papers.

290 *The group finally*: "Judy Goldsmith's Campaign Speech to NOW National Conference, 1985," 2; Peterson, "NOW's Time of Choice," A20; Spake, "Goldsmith v. Smeal."

290 *"a style of leadership"*: "NOW 1985 Convention Candidate Information Sheet: Re-elect Judy Goldsmith," folder 43, box 25, NOW Records.

290 *"At times it can be radical"*: Lemley, "Eleanor Smeal in Overdrive," 31.

290 *"Ellie's answer to every problem"*: Peterson, "NOW's Time of Choice," A20.

290 *"Ellie" or "Judy"*: Marilyn Gardner, "Eleanor Smeal Elected NOW President After 'Intense' Campaign," *Christian Science Monitor*, July 22, 1985, 3.

291 *"gave everybody who"*: Hays, interview by Davison, Jan. 1998, 4.

291 *At workshops on issues*: Hawkes, *Feminism on Trial*, 401–2, 407–8.

291 *"feeling real frustrated"*: Beverly Beyette, "NOW at 19 Reaffirms Its Priorities: With Election of Eleanor Smeal, ERA Fight Will Resume," *Los Angeles Times*, July 24, 1985, E1.

291 *Goldsmith also lost to Smeal*: Gardner, "Eleanor Smeal Elected NOW President After 'Intense' Campaign," 3.

291 *"They killed us"*: Collins, interview by author, 2019, 6.

291 *Smeal's campaign manager*: Judy Klemesrud, "NOW's President: Assessing the Election," *New York Times*, July 27, 1985, 48.

291 *"I was so driven"*: Ireland, interview by author, 5.

291 *"joked about how"*: Spake, "Goldsmith v. Smeal," SM28.

291 *With an air*: Germond and Witcover, "Chilly Political Climate for NOW."

291 *she addressed the conference*: Beyette, "NOW at 19 Reaffirms Its Priorities."

292 *Eleanor Smeal retook*: Mary Schmich, "Eleanor Smeal: Taking NOW Beyond '80s," *Chicago Tribune*, Aug. 18, 1985, A1.

292 *NOW spearheaded massive*: Linda Wheeler and Lyle V. Harris, "80,000 March on Washington: Abortion Rights Supporters Counter Opponents' January Rally," *Washington Post*, March 10, 1986, A1.

292 *"the largest march"*: Beverly Beyette, "NOW to Lead L.A. Women's March: Smeal, Volunteers to Show Pro-choice Support Sunday," *Los Angeles Times*, March 14, 1986, H12.

292 *"touch[ed] their hearts"*: Smeal and Bonk, interview by author, 9. But mobilizing people does not necessarily organize them. "Organizing . . . involves creating ongoing groups that are mass-based in the sense that the people a group purports to represent have real impact on the group's direction. Mobilizing is more sporadic, involving large numbers of people for relatively short periods of time and probably for relatively dramatic activities." Charles Payne, "Ella Baker and Models of Social Change," *Signs* 14, no. 4 (Summer 1989): 897.

292 *"I think feminism"*: Victoria Irwin, "NOW's New Leader Makes Pat Schroeder's Candidacy a Priority," *Christian Science Monitor*, July 20, 1987, 3.

292 *Smeal also renewed*: Doug Struck, "NOW, 20 Years Old, Is Hoping to Grow," *Baltimore Sun*, June 16, 1986, 3A.

292 *Not only were*: Germond and Witcover, "Chilly Political Climate for NOW."

292 *"it was as if"*: Ellen Goodman, "Eleanor Smeal Is Ready for Battle," *Chicago Tribune*, July 19, 1987, 2.

292 *The organization had centralized*: Irwin, "NOW's New Leader Makes Pat Schroeder's Candidacy a Priority," 3.

293 *Many young white women*: Faludi, *Backlash*, x.

293 *Social critics replaced praise*: Jo Reger, *Everywhere and Nowhere: Contemporary Feminism in the United States* (New York: Oxford University Press, 2011), 13; see also Faludi, *Backlash*.

293 *declaring "feminazis" responsible*: Evans, *Tidal Wave*, 7.

293 *Membership dropped from 200,000*: "NOW President Molly Yard: 'Elect More Women Our Strategy,'" *Asbury Park Press*, Aug. 9, 1987, folder 1, box 26, NOW Records.

293 *Other groups began*: Reger, *Everywhere and Nowhere*, esp. 13–14; Lisa Levenstein, *They Didn't See Us Coming: The Hidden History of Feminism in the Nineties* (New York: Basic Books, 2020).

293 *Some, like the Fund*: Cecilie Ditlev-Simonsen, "NOW's Smeal Tells of Her New Battle Plans," *Los Angeles Times*, July 9, 1987; Beverly Beyette, "Candidate Backed by Smeal Elected President of NOW," *Los Angeles Times*, July 1987, A5.

293 *These women's advocacy groups*: Kirsten Goss, *The Paradox of Gender Equality: How American Women's Groups Gained and Lost Their Public Voice* (Ann Arbor: University of Michigan Press), esp. 182–83.

293 *Feminists also advanced*: Levenstein, *They Didn't See Us Coming*.

293 *Shirley Chisholm addressed this problem*: "Chisholm to NOW: 1988 Is Ripe for Political Influence," *Boston Globe*, June 27, 1988, 7.

EPILOGUE: IT WAS PERSONAL, POLITICAL, EVERYTHING

295 *Soon after starting*: Collins, interview by author, 2015.

295 *After departing NOW*: Collins, interview by author, 2019, 7, 29; Collins, interview by author, 2022, 5, 7.

295 *"There's no other organization"*: Collins, interview by author, 2019, 7.

295 *After she left*: Irwin, "NOW's New Leader Makes Pat Schroeder's Candidacy a Priority," 2–3; Rita Ciolli, "NOW Plans 'Stop Souter' Campaign," *Newsday*, Sept. 6, 1990, 13; Nadine Brozan, "Reporter's Notebook: NOW Bracing to Stop Bork," *New York Times*, July 20, 1987, A17; "NOW Opposes Kennedy as Women's Rights 'Disaster,'" *Los Angeles Times*, Nov. 19, 1987, 1. This focus on the U.S. Supreme Court produced a major win in the

1994 case *National Organization for Women v. Scheidler*, when the court ruled unanimously that abortion clinics could sue antiabortion protest organizations for damages using federal racketeering law. Linda Greenhouse, "Court Rules Abortion Clinics Can Use Rackets Law to Sue," *New York Times*, Jan. 25, 1994, A1.

296 *"Keeping something going"*: Collins, interview by author, 2019, 6.

296 *She continued to support*: Constance L. Jones and Susan K. Rogan to Burnett, Oct. 21, 1983, "Correspondence, 1966–2002" folder, box 7, Burnett Papers; Stephanie Hampton to Burnett, March 4, 1981, "Correspondence, April–June 1980" folder, box 2, Burnett Papers; Burnett to Margaret Papandreou, n.d., ca. 1984, "Correspondence, 1984" folder, box 2, Burnett Papers.

296 *When her painting career*: Burnett, interview by Boyer, 69; Burnett to Suzanne R. Parrott, Jan. 12, 1984, "Correspondence, 1984" folder, box 2, Burnett Papers; Laura Berman, "Unveiling of Betty Ford Portrait Also Spotlights Artist," *Detroit News*, July 8, 2014, "Biographical/ Art Career, 1 of 5" folder, box 1, Burnett Papers.

296 *Michigan Women's Hall of Fame*: Karen Douglas and Helen R. Clegg, "8 to Be Inducted into Hall of Fame," *Lansing State Journal*, Oct. 12, 1987, 1D, "Biographical + Artistic, 4 of 5" folder, box 1, Burnett Papers.

296 *"socialite widow"*: Burnett, "Marketing Your Talent."

296 *"equal, loving relationship"*: Harrison, "Beauty Queen Trades Tiara for Feminism."

296 *When Burnett left Detroit*: Hillary Burnett, interview by author, April 29, 2021, 1.

296 *"It would have been"*: Jack Lessenberry, "Old Age Is a State of Mind She's Not Ready to Enter Yet," *Oakland Press*, Sept. 22, 1997, "Biographical + Artistic, 4 of 5" folder, box 1, Burnett Papers.

296 *On the eve of*: Jack Lessenberry to Elaine Didier, July 8, 2014, "Remembering Betty Ford," "Biographical + Artistic, 1 of 5" folder, box 1, Burnett Papers.

296 *"open and feisty"*: Lessenberry to Didier, "Remembering Betty Ford."

296 *the new feminism*: Cobble, Gordon, and Henry, *Feminism Unfinished*, 151–67; see also Levenstein, *They Didn't See Us Coming*.

297 *Younger American feminists*: Levenstein, *They Didn't See Us Coming*, 4–7; Lisa Levenstein, "A Social Movement for a Global Age: U.S. Feminism and the Beijing Women's Conference of 1995," *Journal of American History* 105 (Sept. 2018): 337.

297 *Tens of thousands*: Levenstein, "Social Movement for a Global Age," 336.

297 *American feminism became*: Levenstein, "Social Movement for a Global Age," 364.

297 *NOW had gone to Beijing*: Levenstein, *They Didn't See Us Coming*, 62.

297 *"just give lip-service"*: Burnett, interview by Boyer, 84, folder 20, box 7.

297 *NOW even briefly helped*: Maralee Schwartz, "NOW Meeting Plans Vote on Support of '21st Century Party,'" *Washington Post*, June 28, 1992, A21.

297 *Feminist allies including*: In Defense of Marxism: Information, Education, Discussion Bulletin, April 1992, 16, www.marxists.org/history/etol/newspape/bidom/n95-apr-1992-bom .pdf; Dan Balz, "NOW's Talk of New Party Attacked as Self-Defeating," *Washington Post*, July 28, 1989, A5; Judy Mann, "NOW's Flirtation with Suicide," *Washington Post*, July 26, 1989, B3.

297 *"Women have been"*: Richard L. Berke, "Women Accusing Democrats of Betrayal," *New York Times*, Oct. 17, 1991, A1.

297 *NOW sought to hold him*: "Report Card: Bill Clinton, First 100 Days," folder 4, box 358, NOW Additional Records.

297 *"we didn't have to just"*: "Patricia Ireland, Past President," video interview transcript, 2006, 4, folder 21, box 434, NOW Additional Records.

297 *But Clinton made it*: Kruse and Zelizer, *Fault Lines*, 200–201, 209–10.

297 *Although he nominated*: "Ruth Bader Ginsburg Is Confirmed: Senate Votes 96–3 for Second Woman and 107th Supreme Court Justice," *Chicago Tribune*, Aug. 3, 1993, 1; Robert Shepard, "Female Agenda Takes Long Way to Become Law," *Chicago Tribune*, Sept. 25, 1994, F1; Felicia Kornbluh and Gwendolyn Mink, *Ensuring Poverty: Welfare Reform in Feminist Perspective* (Philadelphia: University of Pennsylvania Press, 2018).

298 *His mounting sexual scandals*: Kruse and Zelizer, *Fault Lines*, 226–27; Maureen Dowd, "Suit Sets Off Rush for High Ground," *New York Times*, May 8, 1994, 16; "Women Leaders to Take Action to Stop Impeachment, Warn What's at Stake for Women and Who's on Third to Succeed," *Feminist Majority Foundation Feminist News*, Sept. 24, 1998, folder 4, box 358, NOW Additional Records; Statement of NOW President Patricia Ireland, "Where Is Congress on Our Issues?," Sept. 24, 1998, folder 4, box 358, NOW Additional Records. See also Andrea Friedman, "The Price of Shame: Second-Wave Feminism and the Lewinsky-Clinton Scandal," in *Heterosexual Histories*, ed. Rebecca L. Davis and Michele Mitchell (New York: New York University Press, 2021), 358–86.

298 *"the common views"*: Burnett to Detroit NOW, "NOW Was My Time," 11.

298 *"awareness seminars"*: Hernandez and Associates, "Seminars in Inclusionary Personnel Practices," for United Parcel Service Southwest Region.

298 *She charged $121*: "1990 Fee Schedule," "Aileen C. Hernandez Assoc." folder, box 78, Hernandez Papers.

298 *By mid-decade, she had shrunk*: "Aileen Clarke Hernandez," Black Biography.

298 *"something in this environment"*: Hernandez to Charles H. Clarke Jr. and Norris W. Clarke, April 4, 1998, "Aileen Personal" folder, box 80, Hernandez Papers.

298 *"race, class, gender"*: Barbara Ransby, "Black Feminism at Twenty-One: Reflections on the Evolution of a National Community," *Signs* 25, no. 4 (Summer 2000): 1218.

298 *"so that we can play"*: "On the Move: Black Women in the Bay Area Make Their Influence Felt in Politics, Government, Business, Medicine, Education, and the Arts," *San Francisco Examiner*, Jan. 16, 1983, "Aileen Bio" folder, box 29, Hernandez Papers.

298 *"It has been bad"*: "Aileen Clarke Hernandez," Black Biography.

298 *NOW continued to launch*: Pegueros, "My Sister's Keeper"; Loretta J. Ross, "Women of Color and the Feminization of Power," July 16, 1987, folder 9, box 5, Ross Papers.

299 *eleven years before*: Richard Sandomir, "Aileen Hernandez, Ex–NOW President and Feminist Trailblazer, Dies at 90," *New York Times*, March 1, 2017, A28.

299 *"not THE LEADER"*: Aileen Hernandez, "NOW at Forty!," July 2006, "NOW" folder, box 77, Hernandez Papers.

299 *"didn't stay long term"*: Gandy, interview by author, May 3, 2021, 3.

299 *"a way to make money"*: Kamen, *Feminist Fatale*, 99.

299 *"a lot of anger"*: Shames, interview by author, Aug. 20, 2019, 1, 2.

299 *The organization attracted*: Maralee Schwartz, "NOW Meeting Plans Vote on Support of '21st Century Party,'" *Washington Post*, June 28, 1992, A21.

299 *NOW's March for Women's*: Cobble, Gordon, and Henry, *Feminism Unfinished*, 157.

300 *Only a few hundred*: Shames, interview by author, 3.

300 *"you could get a lot done"*: Gandy, interview by author, 4.

300 *Clinton's election depressed donations*: Ireland, interview by author, 3–4.

300 *the NAACP's fundraising*: James Brock, "NAACP Hopes Court Rulings Will Put Troubled Group Back on Familiar Turf," *Baltimore Sun*, July 9, 1995, 1A.

300 *Because NOW took*: Gandy, interview by author, 5.

300 *"the McDonald's of the women's movement"*: Kamen, *Feminist Fatale*, 1, 99.

300 *The number of national*: Levenstein, *They Didn't See Us Coming*, 12.

300 *NOW was increasingly displaced*: Nadine Brozan, "NOW Renews Equal Rights Battle: The Strategy Includes Putting Women in Office," *New York Times*, July 1, 1988, B6.

300 *NOW's membership dropped*: Barakso, *Governing NOW*, 125.

300 *often misremembered as a leader*: Steinem, interview by Carolyn Heilbrun, June 1991, 1, folder 8, box 6, Tully-Crenshaw Feminist Oral History Project.

300 *"The first problem"*: Gloria Steinem, "A New Egalitarian Life Style," *New York Times*, Aug. 26, 1971, 37.

301 *We would live*: For recent critiques of "white feminism," see Koa Beck, *White Feminism: From the Suffragettes to Influencers and Who They Leave Behind* (New York: Atria Books, 2021); and Rafia Zakaria, *Against White Feminism: Notes on Disruption* (New York: Norton, 2021). See also Schuller, *Trouble with White Women*.

301 *The 1990s economic boom*: Edmund L. Andrews, "Economic Inequality Grew in 90's Boom, Fed Reports," *New York Times*, Jan. 23, 2003, C1.

301 *The wage gap*: Becky Pettit and Stephanie Ewert, "Employment Gains and Wage Declines: The Erosion of Black Women's Relative Wages Since 1980," *Demography* 46 (2009), www.ncbi.nlm.nih.gov/pmc/articles/PMC2831350.

301 *The percentage of Black children*: Samuel L. Myers Jr., "'The Rich Get Richer and . . .': The Problem of Race and Inequality in the 1990s," *Minnesota Journal of Law and Inequality* 11 (Dec. 1993): 371–72.

301 *children of color*: Linda Darling-Hammond, "Unequal Opportunity: Race and Education," Brookings, March 1, 1998, www.brookings.edu/articles/unequal-opportunity-race-and-education.

301 *Prisons overflowed with*: Myers, "Rich Get Richer and . . . ," 371–72; German Lopez, "The Controversial 1994 Crime Law That Joe Biden Helped Write, Explained," *Vox*, Sept. 29, 2020, www.vox.com/policy-and-politics/2019/6/20/18677998/joe-biden-1994-crime-bill-law-mass-incarceration.

302 *"deep poverty"*: Vann R. Newkirk II, "The Real Lessons from Bill Clinton's Welfare Reform," *Atlantic*, Feb. 5, 2018, www.theatlantic.com/politics/archive/2018/02/welfare-reform-tanf-medicaid-food-stamps/552299.

302 *Conservatives in the 1990s*: Darling-Hammond, "Unequal Opportunity"; Brad Knickerbocker, "Gay Rights May Be Social Issue of 1990s," *Christian Science Monitor*, Feb. 11, 1993, www.csmonitor.com/1993/0211/11011.html.

302 *The Defense of Marriage Act*: Matthew Yglesias, "Bill and Hillary Clinton and the Defense of Marriage Act, Explained," *Vox*, Oct. 30, 2015, www.vox.com/policy-and-politics/2015/10/30/9642602/clinton-doma-constitutional-amendment.

302 *a world of utterly transformed*: Cobble, Gordon, and Henry, *Feminism Unfinished*, 227–31; Evans, *Tidal Wave*, 232–38; Stansell, *Feminist Promise*, 348–51.

304 *Today feminism is diffuse*: See, for example, Cobble, Gordon, and Henry, *Feminism Unfinished*, 185–220.

304 *Meanwhile, conservative women*: See, for example, Concerned Women for America, accessed Feb. 18, 2022, concernedwomen.org; Network of Enlightened Women, accessed Feb. 18, 2022, enlightenedwomen.org; and Women for America First, accessed Feb. 18, 2022, wfaf.org.

304 *In the wake*: On the Women's March and its aftermath, see Levenstein, *They Didn't See Us Coming*, esp. 2; Anemona Hartocollis and Yamiche Alcindor, "Women's March Highlights as Huge Crowds Protest Trump: 'We're Not Going Away,'" *New York Times*, Jan. 21, 2017, www.nytimes.com/2017/01/21/us/womens-march.html; and Keeanga-Yamahtta Taylor, "Turning the Women's March into a Mass Movement Was Never Going to Be Simple," *Nation*,

Jan. 18, 2019, www.thenation.com/article/archive/turning-the-womens-march-into-a-mass -movement-was-never-going-to-be-simple.

304 *The Me Too movement*: Tarana Burke, *Unbound: My Story of Liberation and the Birth of the Me Too Movement* (New York: Flatiron Books, 2021); "Inception," me too, accessed Feb. 18, 2022, metoomvmt.org/get-to-know-us/history-inception/see; Michael R. Sisak and Tom Hays, "Harvey Weinstein Found Guilty in Landmark #MeToo Moment," AP News, Feb. 24, 2020, apnews.com/article/ap-top-news-harvey-weinstein-sexual-assault-ca-state -wire-us-news-67057b46fcd3f1183cf6a699a399c886; Rachel Vogelstein and Meighan Stone, "#MeToo Helped Put Cosby in Prison. His Release Doesn't Diminish the Movement's Global Triumphs," *Washington Post*, July 31, 2021, www.washingtonpost.com/opinions/2021 /07/01/bill-cosby-released-metoo-movement.

304 *Women and queer people*: See, for example, Alicia Garza, "A Herstory of the #Black-LivesMatter Movement," *Feminist Wire*, Oct. 7, 2014, thefeministwire.com/2014/10 /blacklivesmatter-2.

304 *There are also women-led*: See, for example, the work of Moms Demand Action, accessed Feb. 18, 2022, momsdemandaction.org; National Women's Health Network, accessed Feb. 18, 2022, nwhn.org; and WomenOne, accessed Feb. 18, 2022, www.womenone.org.

304 *A reenergized coalition*: Patrick J. Lyons, Maggie Astor, and Maya Salem, "Why the Equal Rights Amendment Is Back," *New York Times*, Jan. 15, 2020, www.nytimes.com/2020 /01/15/us/what-is-equal-rights-amendment.html.

305 *"the largest organization"*: "About," National Organization for Women, accessed Feb. 17, 2022, now.org/about.

305 *NOW's website describes*: "Core Issues," National Organization for Women, accessed Feb. 17, 2022, now.org/issues; "Our Issues," National Organization for Women, accessed Feb. 17, 2022, now.org/about/our-issues.

305 *"the largest mass action"*: "Who We Are," National Organization for Women, accessed Feb. 17, 2022, now.org/about/who-we-are.

305 *More recently, the organization*: Emily Shugerman, "'Don't Forget the White Women!': Members Say Racism Ran Rampant at NOW," *Daily Beast*, June 6, 2020, www.thedailybeast .com/national-organization-for-women-members-say-racism-ran-rampant; Caroline Kitch-ener, "'How Many Women of Color Have to Cry?': Top Feminist Organizations Are Plagued by Racism, 20 Former Staffers Say," *Lily*, July 13, 2020, www.thelily.com/how-many-women -of-color-have-to-cry-top-feminist-organizations-are-plagued-by-racism-20-former-staffers -say; Scott Neuman, "NOW President Resigns amid Allegations of Creating Toxic Work Environment," WBUR, Aug. 18, 2020, www.wbur.org/npr/903254443/now-president-resigns -amid-allegations-of-creating-toxic-work-environment.

305 *No one from that office*: I contacted NOW's national office via its website on November 6, 2020, February 15, 2021, and April 22, 2021.

305 *Both discovered the group's*: Goodfriend, interview by author, Nov. 11, 2020; Porteous, interview by author, Nov. 17, 2020.

305 *"a great old house"*: Porteous, interview by author, 5.

306 *"a lot of opportunity"*: Goodfriend, interview by author, 3.

306 *"Standing up for"*: Porteous, interview by author, 7.

AFTERWORD: WHAT IT TAKES TO BEGIN AGAIN

307 *Some states immediately*: Caroline Kitchener et al., "Abortion Is Not Banned in These States. See Where Laws Have Changed," *Washington Post*, June 24, 2022, updated Aug. 6, 2022, www .washingtonpost.com/politics/2022/06/24/abortion-state-laws-criminalization-roe.

307 *The majority opinion*: Shefali Luthra, "From Marriage Equality to Interracial Marriage,

Supreme Court Conservatives Appear Divided on Handling Civil Rights After Roe Decision," The 19th, June 24, 2022, 19thnews.org/2022/06/supreme-court-conservatives-divided-civil-rights-after-abortion-decision.

307 Dobbs v. Jackson Women's Health Organization: *Dobbs v. Jackson Women's Health Organization*, No. 19–1392, 597 U.S. ___.

307 *"not deeply rooted"*: Brian Lyman, "Transgender Youth, Families: Alabama Ban on Transgender Medicine Violates Parental Rights," *Montgomery Advertiser*, Aug. 11, 2022, www.montgomeryadvertiser.com/story/news/2022/08/11/transgender-youth-families-alabama-ban-transgender-medicine-violates-parental-rights/10295613002.

307 *Alabama's provision builds upon*: Elizabeth Sharrow and Isaac Sederbaum, "Texas Isn't the Only State Denying Essential Medical Care to Trans Youths. Here's What's Going On," *Washington Post*, March 10, 2022, www.washingtonpost.com/politics/2022/03/10/texas-trans-kids-abortion-lgbtq-gender-ideology; "Anti-transgender Medical Care Bans," *Equality Tracker*, accessed Aug. 11, 2022, www.equalityfederation.org/tracker/anti-transgender-medical-care-bans; Dustin Jones, "Not Just Florida: More Than a Dozen States Propose So-Called 'Don't Say Gay' Bills," NPR, April 10, 2022, www.npr.org/2022/04/10/1091543359/15-states-dont-say-gay-anti-transgender-bills.

307 *"I'm just reeling"*: "Dobbs Decision: Reactions to the End of Roe v. Wade," *Chicago Sun-Times*, June 24, 2022, chicago.suntimes.com/2022/6/24/23181663/dobbs-decision-roe-v-wade-reaction-supreme-court-2022.

308 *"People won't ever stop"*: Amelia Winger, "Fear, Numbness, Tears of Joy and Rage Are Just the Beginning of Mental Health Effects of Abortion Shifts," *Public Source*, July 28, 2022, www.publicsource.org/roe-wade-dobbs-abortion-rights-mental-health-pittsburgh-pennsylvania.

308 *"second wave feminist"*: Elayne Clift, "Roe Ruling: Feminism Isn't Dead, but It's Exhausted," *Morrisville (Vt.) News & Citizen*, June 30, 2022, www.vtcng.com/news_and_citizen/opinion/opinion_columns/roe-ruling-feminism-isn-t-dead-but-it-s-exhausted/article_e6481f04-f89e-11ec-a806-db1e5b92f008.html.

308 *"pop feminism's . . . faith"*: Faludi, "Feminism Made a Faustian Bargain with Celebrity Culture."

308 *"The failure of folks"*: Charlotte Alter, "The Failure of the Feminist Industrial Complex," *Time*, June 24, 2022, time.com/6190225/feminist-industrial-complex-roe-v-wade.

308 *"the power of"*: Andrea Grimes, "Where Is the Post-Roe Leadership?," *Dame*, July 26, 2022, www.damemagazine.com/2022/07/26/where-is-the-post-roe-leadership.

308 *"I have been out here"*: Lexi Solomon and Rachael Riley, "'We Are Outraged and Heartbroken and Ready to Fight': Fayetteville Residents React to Roe v. Wade Ruling," *Fayetteville Observer*, June 24, 2022, www.fayobserver.com/story/news/2022/06/24/roe-v-wade-supreme-court-abortion-ruling-fayetteville-residents/7658603001.

308 *In West Virginia*: Madeline Edwards, "Morgantown National Organization for Women Encourage Residents to Attend Abortion Ban Public Hearing," WDTV, July 26, 2022, www.wdtv.com/2022/07/27/morgantown-national-organization-women-encourage-residents-attend-abortion-ban-public-hearing.

308 *"to continue to work"*: Melissa B. Froemming, "Letter to the Editor," *Cape Gazette* (Rehoboth Beach, Del.), June 28, 2022, www.capegazette.com/article/delaware-now-will-work-women%E2%80%99s-rights/242181.

309 *"gain the tools needed"*: Tanya Christian, "Women's Convention Seeks to Build Political Power in Aftermath of Roe Decision," *Ebony*, Aug. 10, 2022, www.ebony.com/news/womens-convention-seeks-to-build-political-power-in-aftermath-of-roe-decision.

INDEX

ACKNOWLEDGMENTS

This book began in 2003 as my Northwestern University undergraduate honors thesis, which was advised by Nancy MacLean and developed in a seminar led by Peter Hayes. I could not have written it without excellent child-care workers: Madeleine Fraley, Michaela Gibson, Krystal Glass, Amanda Horne, Sara Lind, Tyler Litke, Krista Powell, Victoria Sacks, and Katema Stewart. Nor could this book exist without the women who made this history. NOW's records are housed in archives all over the country, many of which I was able to visit. I thank the people whose lives and labors made this research possible, including the three dozen women who shared their stories with me, the activists who donated their materials, and the archivists who keep and open these records to scholars.

This project received support from the American Bar Foundation, the Arthur and Elizabeth Schlesinger Library on the History of Women in America, the Institute for the Arts and Humanities at UNC–Chapel Hill, the National Endowment for the Humanities, and the Department of History and College of Arts and Sciences at UNC–Chapel Hill. A fellowship at the Harvard Radcliffe Institute in 2018–19 allowed me to build community with Tomiko Brown-Nagin, Katie Bugyis, Stephanie DeGooyer, Lauren Groff, Sam Klug, Durba Mitra, Meredith Quinn, and my treasured writing group of Robin Bernstein, Corinne Field, Tanisha Ford, Malick Ghachem, and Dana Sajdi.

My current and former UNC Department of History colleagues have offered many kinds of assistance for this project. Thanks especially to Karen Auerbach,

Fitzhugh Brundage, Emily Burrill, Kathleen DuVal, William Reynolds Ferris, Joe Glatthaar, Jerma Jackson, Lauren Jarvis, Michelle King, Miguel La Serna, Lisa Lindsay, Aaron Pattillo-Lunt, Susan Dabney Pennybacker, Melanie Sheehan, Ana Maria Silva Campo, William Sturkey, John Wood Sweet, Benjamin Waterhouse, and Molly Worthen.

For their encouragement, aid, and insights, thanks to Felice Batlan, Eileen Boris, Margot Canaday, Mary Anne Case, Nancy Cott, Caley Horan, Dan Horowitz, Ajay Mehrotra, Susan Ware, and Leandra Zarnow. Four generous scholars read and offered comments on an early manuscript draft: Jacquelyn Dowd Hall, Nancy MacLean, Serena Mayeri, and James Sparrow. Thanks also to the research assistants Clara Bates, Teddy Brokaw, Lauren Fadiman, Julia Fine, Frances Hisgen, Emma Rothberg, Hooper Schultz, Jordan Villegas, and Marama Whyte. I am indebted to Marisa Chappell, who sent key materials cross-country, and especially to Rebecca Davison, who shared her interviews and unpublished manuscript.

Audiences helpfully engaged with this project in presentations at Agnes Scott College, Coastal Carolina University, Columbia University, the Harvard Radcliffe Institute, the Massachusetts Historical Society, Monmouth College, the National Parks Service, the University of Chicago Law School, the University of Mississippi, the University of North Carolina at Chapel Hill, Princeton University, the University of Rochester, and Wofford College.

My literary agent, Lucy Cleland, has been essential, as have the editors and assistants at Farrar, Straus and Giroux: Colin Dickerman, Jenna Johnson, Katharine Liptak, and Lydia Zoells.

I am grateful to friends and family. Thanks especially to Anthony Cotton and Vinesh Winodan, who hosted me in Washington; Betty Luther Hillman, who trekked to Cambridge for conversations about this book and everything else; and my parents, Mary Lee Jontz Turk and Charles Turk, who support me and my work in many ways.

Erik Gellman is my first, last, and best reader. He convinced me that my curiosity about NOW should grow into a book. I thank Erik and our daughter, Vivian Jontz Gellman, for filling every day with love and joy.

A NOTE ABOUT THE AUTHOR

Katherine Turk is the author of *Equality on Trial: Gender and Rights in the Modern American Workplace*, which was awarded the Mary Nickliss Prize in U.S. Women's and/or Gender History from the Organization of American Historians. She is an associate professor of history and an adjunct associate professor of women's and gender studies at the University of North Carolina at Chapel Hill.